BARBECUES 400

BARBECUES 400

BURGERS, KEBABS, FISH-STEAKS, VEGETARIAN DISHES AND TEMPTING SALADS, DESSERTS AND ACCOMPANIMENTS, DEMONSTRATED STEP BY STEP WITH MORE THAN 1500 VIBRANT PHOTOGRAPHS

ALL YOU NEED FOR THE PERFECT BARBECUE, FROM HELPFUL TIPS ON CHOOSING AND PREPARING YOUR GRILL TO INSPIRATIONAL RECIPES FROM ALL AROUND THE WORLD

BEVERLEY JOLLANDS

LORENZ BOOKS

This edition is published by Lorenz Books, an imprint of
Anness Publishing Ltd, Hermes House, 88–89 Blackfriars Road,
London SE1 8HA; tel. 020 7401 2077; fax 020 7633 9499
www.lorenzbooks.com; www.annesspublishing.com

If you like the images in this book and would like to investigate using
them for publishing, promotions or advertising, please visit our website
www.practicalpictures.com for more information.

© Anness Publishing Ltd 2008

ETHICAL TRADING POLICY
At Anness Publishing we believe that business should be conducted in
an ethical and ecologically sustainable way, with respect for the environ-
ment and a proper regard to the replacement of the natural resources
we employ.

As a publisher, we use a lot of wood pulp to make high-quality paper
for printing, and that wood commonly comes from spruce trees. We
are therefore currently growing more than 500,000 trees in two
Scottish forest plantations near Aberdeen – Berrymoss (130 hectares/
320 acres) and West Touxhill (125 hectares/305 acres). The forests
we manage contain twice the number of trees employed each year in
paper-making for our books.

Because of this ongoing ecological investment programme, you, as
our customer, can have the pleasure and reassurance of knowing that a
tree is being cultivated on your behalf to naturally replace the materials
used to make the book you are holding.

Our forestry programme is run in accordance with the UK
Woodland Assurance Scheme (UKWAS) and will be certified by the
internationally recognized Forest Stewardship Council (FSC). The
FSC is a non-government organization dedicated to promoting responsible management of the world's forests. Certification ensures forests
are managed in an environmentally sustainable and socially responsible
way. For further information about this scheme, go to
www.annesspublishing.com/trees

A CIP catalogue record for this book is available from the British
Library.

Parts of this edition previously appeared in *180 Barbecues* and
The Barbecue Book

Publisher: Joanna Lorenz
Editorial Director: Helen Sudell
Contributing Editor: Beverley Jollands
Project Editor: Rosie Gordon
Cover Design: Jonathan Davison
Page Design: Adelle Morris and Diane Pullen
Production Controller: Steve Lang

Recipes: Linda Tubby, Carla Capalbo, Jaqueline Clark, Carole
Clements, Roz Denny, Nicola Diggins, Tessa Evelegh, Joanna Farrow,
Christine France, Silvana Franco. Soheila Kimberley, Ruby Le Bois,
Sue Maggs, Katherine Richmond, Steven Wheeler and Elizabeth
Wolf-Cohen
Photography and Food Styling: Martin Brigdale, Helen Trent, Karl
Adamson, William Lingwood, Edward Allwright, Steve Baxter, James
Duncan, John Freeman, Michelle Garrett, Amanda Heywood, Don
Last, Michael Michaels, Patrick McLeavey, Debbie Patterson and Juliet
Piddington

NOTES
Bracketed terms are intended for American readers.
For all recipes, quantities are given in both metric and imperial measures and, where appropriate, in standard cups and spoons. Follow one
set, but not a mixture, because they are not interchangeable.
Standard spoon and cup measures are level. 1 tsp = 5ml, 1 tbsp =
15ml, 1 cup = 250ml/8fl oz.
Australian standard tablespoons are 20ml. Australian readers should
use 3 tsp in place of 1 tbsp for measuring small quantities of gelatine,
flour, salt, etc.
American pints are 16fl oz/2 cups. American readers should use 20fl
oz/2.5 cups in place of 1 pint when measuring liquids.
Electric oven temperatures in this book are for conventional ovens.
When using a fan oven, the temperature will probably need to be
reduced by about 10–20°C/20–40°F. Since ovens vary, you should
check with your manufacturer's instruction book for guidance.
The nutritional analysis given for each recipe is calculated per portion
(i.e. serving or item), unless otherwise stated. If the recipe gives a range,
such as Serves 4–6, then the nutritional analysis will be for the smaller
portion size, i.e. 6 servings. Measurements for sodium do not include
salt added to taste.
Medium (US large) eggs are used unless otherwise stated.

Main front cover image shows Rosemary-scented Lamb – for recipe,
see page 217.

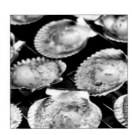

CONTENTS

INTRODUCTION 6

BARBECUE WITH SUCCESS 8

    CHOOSING YOUR BARBECUE 10

    SETTING UP YOUR BARBECUE 12

    INGREDIENTS AND FLAVOURINGS 14

    BARBECUE TECHNIQUES 18

APPETIZERS AND LIGHT BITES 22

FISH AND SHELLFISH 86

POULTRY 154

MEAT 208

THE VEGETARIAN BARBECUE 262

SIDE DISHES AND SALADS 308

MARINADES AND ACCOMPANIMENTS 382

DESSERTS AND DRINKS 448

INDEX 508

INTRODUCTION

It's one of the greatest pleasures of the summer – *al fresco* eating and relaxing in the garden or on the beach around a sizzling barbecue. When food is cooked over an open fire the smells, smoky flavours and convivial atmosphere are hard to beat. A barbecue is a sociable affair, loved by children and adults alike, perhaps because it's the best way to celebrate the joy of relaxed, sunny days and balmy evenings.

A LONG TRADITION

Although the origins of the word "barbecue" are uncertain, it probably derived from the Spanish word *barbacoa* in the mid-17th century, which originally meant "a wooden frame on posts". This might have been equipment for smoking meat, and it is believed that the Caribbean Arawak Indians taught the Spanish sailors the art of smoking meat in this way.

Barbecuing has certainly been popular in America for a long time. Even before the Civil War, people in the South were roasting pigs outdoors at social gatherings. In the 1800s cowboys on the cattle ranches would roast tougher cuts of meat for several hours over an open fire, and churches, political rallies and parties were using the barbecue as a great way to get people together.

Above: An impromptu barbecue on the beach is the perfect way to celebrate the warm summer evenings.

Over the years, even in cooler climes, the barbecue has become one of the exciting things about summer – eating outside in the warm air, and getting together with other people in a uniquely convivial atmosphere. This is a time when everyone feels relaxed, especially if the kids are playing and running outside while the adults cook and enjoy a long, cool drink.

Because barbecues come in all sizes and to suit all pockets, there's one for every situation, so you can cook outside even if you have a fairly small space, as long as you are careful not to site the barbecue unsafely, such as under a garage door or a carport, or within 3m/10ft of the house.

Of course, cooking over an open fire goes back to our ancestors' distant past and is still an essential part of the culinary traditions of countries all over the world. In hotter climes daily cooking takes place outdoors for a variety of reasons, especially because the heat (as well as the smoke) makes it unbearable to cook inside. Once cooking is transferred outside it takes on a completely different appeal; it becomes informal and that's probably

the most important aspect of the barbecue today: chatting over drinks while the food cooks, perhaps nibbling appetizers or helping to prepare a salad. And because the juices of barbecued food drip on to the coals and form aromatic smoke, it has that special, taste-bud-tingling smell. Indeed, the smell is so delicious and outdoor eating so enjoyable that it really stimulates the appetite, so when catering for a barbecue, cook plenty!

BARBECUING TODAY

Modern barbecues have made cooking more efficient. The kettle barbecue, for example, has a lid and this helps to create an even temperature for cooking small items of food as well as whole joints. Some barbecues have spits, and these days if you don't want to get messy with the charcoal you can use a gas or electric barbecue, which are available in a variety of sizes.

RECIPES FOR SUCCESS

A barbecue can be a wonderfully spontaneous affair with food quickly prepared and cooked. Choose good quality ingredients and a few simple recipes, perhaps using the griddle, for that fast, fun and no-fuss barbecue.

Below: Use aromatic wood to add a smoky flavour to barbecued foods.

Griddles are an ideal accessory for the spontaneous barbecue, and for cooking little appetizers, so that the main course can be cooked when the heat is less fierce. Tips and techniques like these are explained in the book.

If you are catering for larger numbers of people, careful planning will ensure a relaxed event. Have all the preparation completed in advance, and if you are cooking away from home everything will need to be easily transportable to the picnic site. Make sure you have plenty of equipment for carrying raw food (as well as keeping it cool) and clean equipment for the food once cooked. You can make life easy by preparing certain foods the day before – breads, pasta salads, marinades, sauces and desserts will all be much appreciated and are easy to do in advance.

BE ADVENTUROUS

Once you learn how versatile your barbecue can be, you can enjoy a world of different flavours and textures. Not only can you cook up your favourite burgers and other quick, simple but nevertheless delicious meals, but you can also create tasty kebabs, steaks, parcels of fish wrapped in leaves or foil, whole chickens and also griddled main

Above: Fresh summer corn is at its best when simply grilled in the husk.

courses or side dishes of meat, fish and vegetables – flavoured in all kinds of different ways! And if you want to stay healthy and keep trim for the summer, barbecued food can be made healthy and low in fat simply by replacing oily marinades with low-fat ones and misting

with oil, and by using lean meat or fish.

The other great thing about all the barbecue recipes in this book is that they can be cooked indoors under a grill (broiler), in the oven, or over the hob, so you can try some of the hearty barbecued dishes in the winter too. Of course, you must never cook with a barbecue indoors unless it is specially designed for this purpose, as are some electric barbecues.

Use this book to help you choose the right recipe for the right occasion, and to understand the basics of setting up and cooking. By trying out the many techniques given in the following pages, you will become a truly versatile cook, able to experiment with new flavours and to present the food beautifully. Recipes from all over the world are included, and many have helpful hints to ensure that you have all the information you need for enjoyable and successful barbecues all summer long.

Below: Sprigs of herbs can be smoked over coals to add extra flavour.

BARBECUE WITH SUCCESS

Barbecue cooking should always be a relaxed affair if possible — in fact, one of its advantages is that you can use the simplest type of equipment to achieve a tasty meal in the garden or on outings to the beach or the country. Even a disposable barbecue or an old grill rack over coals on the beach will do the trick, but if you want to barbecue more often or cook larger cuts of meat or whole birds, it's worth finding out about all the different kinds of barbecue available. This section introduces gas, electric and charcoal barbecues with tips on how best to use them, as well as the additional equipment you will need for easy and safe cooking outdoors. Hints on what food to buy and how to prepare it are also included, as well as techniques and recipes for giving food extra flavour by marinating or adding savoury butters, and how to cut down on fat while keeping food flavoursome. With a useful Basic Timing Guide to help you judge the correct cooking time, you will be ready to try your hand at the fabulous selection of recipes in this book.

CHOOSING YOUR BARBECUE

Barbecuing food gives it a delicious smoky taste, but it is not the charcoal that flavours the food. When the food cooks, melted fat is released and drips on to the heat source. This then gives off smoke, which permeates the food. If you marinate the food first in herbs, or in spice-and-oil combinations, they will contribute to the taste, as will aromatic wood chips or herbs strewn over the charcoals or used in a smoking box in a gas barbecue. So, whether you choose a charcoal or a gas barbecue, you will still achieve fantastic flavours.

The main thing to consider when choosing your barbecue is how often you intend to use it. If you enjoy regular family meals al fresco or party barbecues in the garden, a larger one might be the best for you. If, however, you like to act spontaneously and light up a barbecue on the beach or in the countryside you will need something portable – and this smaller kind of barbecue would also be perfect if you plan to use a barbecue at home only occasionally. Remember that the larger barbecues will need to be stored somewhere dry when not in use, so you will most likely need a shed or a corner of the garage to tuck them away into.

CHARCOAL BARBECUES

Among the plethora of barbecues you will find in any showroom are the three basic types of charcoal barbecue. In the first category is the original small and compact Japanese hibachi, which is basically a firebox on short legs with a tray in the base to hold the coals. There are several rungs for the grill rack so that the height can be adjusted over the heat source. On some models, the lid opens to create a windshield at the back; and when closed the unit is easily transported.

Above: You can use an old grill rack to improvise a beach-style barbecue.

Also in this category are small disposable barbecues that contain their own coals set beneath a grill rack. The heat cannot be controlled so you must keep the food moving all the time, and it's best to choose food that cooks quickly for these easily portable all-in-one barbecues that are used just once.

The second category is the brazier type, which normally has an open firebox on a stand with a windshield at the back. The pedestal barbecue, made from stainless steel, comes into this category. It comprises a pillar that is packed with newspaper beneath a rounded bowl containing the coals and grill rack. When the paper is lit the coals soon ignite. Although pedestal barbecues look stylish, beware that the pillar gets very hot indeed and needs to be positioned on a stable and level flameproof surface.

The pot-bellied or barrel type of barbecue also comes into this second category. It is made from cast iron and has air vents to speed up the

Left: The Japanese-style hibachi barbecue is small, inexpensive and ideal for impromptu meals at home, or when planning an outing in the country.

burning process. The coals will be ready to use in 30 minutes. The grill rack can be adjusted to several heights.

The third category of barbecue is the kettle barbecue, which is made from steel and is usually round. It has a lid that can be lifted off and there are air vents in the firebox and the lid. Kettle barbecues come in a range of sizes and the smaller ones are portable. Because this has a lid it is probably the most efficient barbecue, as it enables you to cook either directly over the coals or indirectly (when the coals are pushed to either side of a drip tray) so that larger cuts of meat, such as whole chickens, can be cooked. With the lid on, the food cooks evenly in the all-round heat and this is beneficial for indirect and direct cooking.

GAS AND ELECTRIC BARBECUES

If you are not keen on the hands-on, getting-mucky-with-the-coals type of barbecuing, a gas or electric one will probably be a wise choice, as they are easy to use and efficient. You will still achieve the authentic barbecue aroma and taste with a gas barbecue because

Above: Brazier barbecues are popular with those seeking portable, fold-away barbecues, and their tall legs make them very accessible to the cook.

the juices from the food will drop on to the ceramic rocks, hot lava rocks, or vitreous enamelled steel bars, and once connected up to the gas bottle it is lit by the flick of a switch. You will find small portable ones as well as table-height versions that are easily moved around on their trolley units.

The heat from an electric barbecue comes from heated elements beneath the grill rack. Electric barbecues are probably the easiest to use and heat up almost immediately. The lack of smoke means that they are the only kind of barbecue viable for use inside. Quick and clean, they are, however, usually smaller than gas grills. If you decide on one, you will probably need to use an extension lead for cooking outside.

EQUIPMENT

For ease of cooking and safety, always use long-handled tools. Here are some of the most useful items of equipment.

Brushes

As well as using a long-handled basting brush, you can make herb brushes by tying together twigs of thyme, bay, rosemary or sage to give flavour to foods when basting. Soak them in oil for a few hours beforehand to flavour the oil.

Dishes

Use shallow, non-corrosive dishes and bowls for marinating that are large enough to hold the food in a single layer (do not use aluminium or metal).

Drip trays

When cooking by indirect heat, place a metal drip tray beneath the food to catch the juices. You can use disposable foil trays or make your own from heavy-duty foil.

Foil

Heavy-duty foil is useful for making a lid if your barbecue does not have one. Use regular foil for wrapping food in parcels for cooking. Tented parcels can be used to gently steam many meat, fish and vegetable dishes – and are particularly useful for holding fragile foods, such as those with a filling.

Above: Make tented foil parcels to cook delicate foods such as stuffed vegetables.

Fork

Use a long-handled fork for lifting large pieces of meat from the barbecue.

Gloves or mitts

For the best protection choose oven gloves or mitts with a long sleeve.

Griddle

A cast-iron ridged griddle makes cooking small items of food on the barbecue easier. As it needs high heat, it is best to use it when the coals are first alight (or you can increase the heat if using a gas or electric barbecue).

Grills

Hinged wire grills are available to hold burgers, fish and small items. They come in a range of shapes, make turning easy and keep foods intact that might otherwise easily disintegrate.

Skewers

Keep a range of skewers in different thicknesses and lengths. Choose flat

Below: A large spatula made of wood or metal will help when turning hot foods.

Above: Metal skewers can be used to hold food in place during cooking.

metal skewers, as they will stop food from spinning round as you turn them. Try cocktail sticks (toothpicks) and wooden and bamboo skewers as well, but always soak them in water for 30 minutes before use.

Spatula

A wide spatula or pizza server with a long handle will make turning flat foods, such as steaks, easier.

Tongs

Use one pair of tongs for the coals, another pair for handling raw food and another for cooked food.

Trays

Metal trays are ideal for carrying raw food to the barbecue; keep others handy to hold the cooked food.

Wire brush

Use a stiff wire brush to clean the grill rack after cooking. Scrub clean with lots of hot soapy water.

Below: Use long-handled tongs for arranging hot coals.

SETTING UP YOUR BARBECUE

Have everything ready to hand before you set up the barbecue, including anything you need in case of accidents – see the Safety Tips opposite.

GETTING STARTED

Whichever type of barbecue you are using, always ensure it is stable before lighting it. For a gas barbecue check that you have enough fuel in the gas bottle before lighting up and follow the manufacturer's instructions carefully. Once switched on, the barbecue will be ready to use within about 15 minutes. Ensure that an electric barbecue is safely connected away from any patches of water before switching it on.

Charcoal barbecues are a little more involved to get started; understanding the properties of different types of fuel will help to ensure success. Lumpwood charcoal and charcoal briquettes are the most frequently used types of fuel and are ideal for all uses; wood, however, is less easy to use.

Lumpwood charcoal is usually made from softwood and comes in lumps of varying sizes, although the larger sizes are best. It is easier to ignite than briquettes but tends to burn up faster.

Charcoal briquettes will burn for a long time with the minimum of smell and smoke, although they can take a

Below: If using a fire chimney to light a barbecue, fill it with newspaper first.

little while to ignite. Use charcoal from sustainable managed forests; these will carry the FSC (Forest Stewardship Council) logo.

Self-igniting charcoal is simply lumpwood or briquettes that have been treated with a flammable substance. Always wait until the ignition agent has burnt off before cooking, or the smell may taint the food.

Wood

Hardwoods such as oak, apple, olive and cherry are best for barbecues, as they burn slowly with a pleasant aroma – which should keep everyone in the vicinity happy too. Softwoods, however, burn too fast and give off sparks and smoke. Wood can be used as kindling or to add aroma while cooking, but as it requires more care than charcoal it is best to use for impromptu beach barbecues than garden parties.

Firelighters

Use only odourless barbecue firelighters and push two between the pieces of fuel. Use a long match to light them. If using firelighter fluid or gel, spray or squeeze on to the cold fuel, leave for a few minutes, then light with a long match, following the manufacturer's instructions carefully.

Below: Light the newspaper using a long match and it will soon ignite the charcoal.

Above: Always use a long match or taper to light a barbecue.

Aromatics

Woodchips or herbs can be added to the coals to give a pleasant aroma to the food. Scatter them straight on to the coals during cooking, or place them in the drip tray under the grill rack. Try hickory or oak chips (soaked for 30 minutes before use), which are easily available from barbecue stockists, or scatter twigs of juniper, rosemary, thyme, sage or fennel over the fire. They can also be added to a smoke box for use with a gas barbecue. Put the aromatics into the smoke box and position it to one side on the grill rack.

LIGHTING A CHARCOAL BARBECUE

1 Spread a layer of wood, charcoal or briquettes on the fire grate, about 5cm/2in deep. Pile the fuel into a small pyramid in the centre of the grate. Use newspaper or kindling beneath the pile, if you wish, or push two firelighter sticks into the centre of the pyramid.

Alternatively, add barbecue firelighter liquid or gel over the fuel, according to the manufacturer's instructions, then leave for 1 minute.

2 Light with a long match or taper and leave until the coals are covered with a grey ash – this will take about 25 minutes. (While the coals glow red with a light dusting of white or grey ash, thin foods can be seared quickly, and it is ideal for cooking rare steaks, but most other foods require a grey ash.)

3 Use tongs to arrange the coals. For cooking by direct heat spread them evenly over the surface of the fire grate;

for indirect heat either push them all to one side or part them in the centre so that a drip tray will fit into the space.

4 Place the grill rack over the heated coals and leave for about 10 minutes to heat up before adding the food.

USING A FIRE CHIMNEY

A metal, tube-shaped fire chimney is an easy way to get the fire going. Place the chimney on the fire grate and fill with newspaper. Pile coals on to the paper. Light the paper with a long-handled match and leave it to ignite the coals. When the top coals are dusted with ash, lift off the fire chimney. The coals will then spread evenly over the fire grate.

CLEANING

Brush the grill rack with a wire brush after use while still hot – you can turn on a gas barbecue to reheat the rack if necessary. For charcoal barbecues brush the grill rack after use while the coals are still warm. Brush again thoroughly before use when heating up.

Make sure gas and electric barbecues are turned off at the gas tank or power switch. If your barbecue has a lid, close this and close the air vents. If on the beach, make sure that the coals are fully extinguished before leaving.

Below: You can cook whole poultry, fish and large joints of meat on a barbecue.

STORAGE

You can buy plastic covers to protect charcoal and gas barbecues for short periods when they are not in use. However, note that these covers will provide limited protection if a barbecue is left outside for several months. When storing for winter, make sure that the equipment is thoroughly cleaned and dried before putting away in a dry utility space, such as an attic or cellar.

Controlling the heat
All you need to control the heat on a gas or electric barbecue is to turn the control knob to high, medium-high, medium or low heat – so nothing could be simpler. For charcoal barbecues, however, there are three basic ways to control the heat during cooking:

1 Raise the grill rack for slow cooking; or use the lowest level for searing foods.

2 Push the burning coals apart for a lower heat; or pile them closer together to increase the heat.

3 Open the air vents to make the fire hotter; or close them to lower the temperature.

Safety Tips
• Ensure the barbecue is firmly sited on a level surface before lighting it. Never move a lit barbecue. Position the barbecue away from trees and shrubs, and shelter from the wind.
• Read the manufacturer's instructions for your barbecue, as there are some types that use only one type of fuel.
• Never pour flammable liquid, such as firelighter fluid, on to the lit barbecue.
• Extinguish a flare-up by closing the lid and all vents and turning off a gas barbecue. Use a fire extinguisher or bucket of sand if it gets out of control. Do not use water.
• Keep children and pets away from the fire.
• Keep a first-aid kit handy. Hold burnt skin under cold water immediately.
• Always use long-handled tools and oven gloves or mitts.
• If using a frying pan or griddle over the barbecue, opt for one with a metal handle if possible. If the handle is plastic, it may melt upon prolonged contact with the heat, so wrap it in thick foil before using and reserve it for quick cooking only.
• Keep raw foods cold until ready to cook. A cool bag is useful if you are barbecuing away from home. Keep raw and cooked foods apart.
• Make sure meats are thoroughly cooked with no traces of pink in the juices. Test by piercing the thickest part of the flesh; the juices should run clear.
• Wash your hands after handling raw meats and before touching other foods. Use different utensils for raw and cooked foods, and never return cooked food to a plate where raw has been.
• Trim excess fat from meat and avoid using too much oil in marinades as fatty foods can cause dangerous flare-ups.

INGREDIENTS AND FLAVOURINGS

For the tastiest barbecues always buy the freshest ingredients. Most of the food will have to be freshly bought although there are several store cupboard (pantry) essentials and some items can also be frozen.

FRESH FOOD

Although supermarkets now stock most of the fresh foods you need for your main ingredients, remember that quality fishmongers and butchers can provide food of excellent quality. Fish from the fishmonger should be super-fresh and the fishmonger will clean, gut and fillet fish for you. Try to buy organic meat, poultry and vegetables if possible for the best flavour. You might be able to subscribe to a weekly organic vegetable box where you live, and some organic suppliers also provide fruit, dairy produce, meat and poultry.

Barbecued food is an adventure in flavour combinations and so fresh herbs are a must. Supermarkets now stock many different types and you can also

Below: Use pitta bread to serve tasty morsels of cooked food. Pittas can also be grilled over the barbecue.

Above: Choose the freshest ingredients for the best possible flavour.

buy large bunches from greengrocers and market stalls. You could also try growing your own; even a few plants in pots or a window box will be useful and always available to make a fresh and flavoursome difference to your cooking. Some of the more unusual flavours are also suitable for barbecuing. Lavender,

Try something new
Look round ethnic markets to source other rare flavourings such as Australian aniseed myrtle, Mexican oregano, ground sumac and dried pink rose petals. While you're at a market, look out for banana and pandanus leaves, as these make good parcels for cooking food and keeping it moist.

for example, is delightful with chicken and lamb, and combines wonderfully well with summer fruits such as berries.

Salads are ideal and refreshing accompaniments to barbecued food and can be made with a variety of leaves including mizuna and rocket. Look out for bags of mixed leaves from your local organic greengrocer or supermarket. Choose tomatoes ripened on the vine for the fullest flavour; summer is the best time to buy these sumptuous vegetable fruits. Cherry tomatoes are perfect in salads, and a combination of yellow and red will add a dash of colour. Experiment with flavour combinations and textures: crunchy radishes, red

Below: Pandanus and banana leaves make great packets for barbecuing, ensuring the food inside stays moist and succulent.

onions and bright (bell) peppers, crisp beansprouts, succulent cucumbers, peppery watercress, bitter chicory.

To accompany your barbecued food think about using flat breads, such as pitta bread. This book includes some useful bread recipes, but if you are short of time you can buy them fresh. You can warm them quickly on the grill rack and they make great pockets for holding food such as kebabs, and children love them. Corn and wheat tortilla wraps are also useful and can be stored in the freezer, as can ciabatta bread. You could serve a quick starter of slices of ciabatta bread toasted on the grill rack and then topped with warm chopped or cherry tomatoes and olives in oil – cooked using the griddle.

IN THE STORE CUPBOARD

Many barbecued foods are marinated before cooking and usually oil is one of the ingredients, so keep a good quality olive oil in the store cupboard. Chilli oil and other flavoured oils are also handy for flavouring foods and can be made at home: half-fill a jar with washed and dried fresh herbs such as rosemary or basil, or a chilli. Pour over olive oil to cover, then seal the jar and place in a cool, dark place for 3 days. Strain the oil into a clean jar or bottle and discard the herbs or chilli.

Stock a few different types of vinegar as well – wine, cider, balsamic, rice and raspberry are some of the most useful kinds – because these, too, are used in marinades as well as salad dressings. Strong flavourings such as tamari and shoyu are available from health food shops and ethnic stores, which will also sell spice mixes such as ras al hanout.

ADDING FLAVOUR

Herbs, spices and aromatics such as garlic and lemon grass transform food when it is barbecued. The flavourings can be used in stuffings, rubs or glazes during cooking, and there is a stunning variety of flavourful combinations. Unlike marinades, which foods are left to absorb, rubs are added just before cooking and glazes are brushed on towards the end.

Above: Combinations of crushed spices can be applied to meats as a dry rub.

FISH AND SHELLFISH

Whole fish are wonderful filled with flavourings. Try lemon and lime slices combined with one or more of the following – sprigs of parsley, dill or fennel, or bay leaves – packed inside the cleaned fish, as these flavourings will complement the delicate taste of the fish without overpowering it.

Once filled, the fish can be wrapped in foil before barbecuing. If you do this, you could add more flavourings inside the packet. The stronger flavour of basil is particularly suitable for oily fish such as trout or mackerel and goes very well with the lemon slices. Remember to season the cavity after filling it.

MEAT AND POULTRY

As with fish, small birds such as quail or poussins are excellent when stuffed and cooked over the barbecue. Spatchcocking will keep the stuffing in place, or you can wrap them in foil. Another popular method of giving a flavour boost to all meats is to add a dry rub or sticky glaze. The stronger flavours of the food go well with robust aromatics such as crushed cumin seeds or peppercorns, as well as more delicate flavourings. Try the following combinations for meaty main dishes:

Cajun spice rub for steaks and chicken

Mix together 5ml/1 tsp each dried thyme, oregano, finely crushed black peppercorns, salt, crushed cumin seeds and hot paprika. Rub the spice mix into the raw meat or poultry then barbecue until cooked.

Above: Apply the mixture to raw meats using your fingertips, then cook to taste.

Chilli rub for meat and poultry

Mix together 10ml/2 tsp each of chilli flakes, paprika, caster (superfine) sugar, soft light brown sugar, salt and ground black pepper. Add 5ml/1 tsp each of ground cumin and cayenne pepper. Mix well and rub in.

Mildly spiced sticky mustard glaze for chicken, pork and red meat

Mix 45ml/3 tbsp each of Dijon mustard, clear honey and demerara (raw) sugar with 2.5ml/1/2 tsp chilli powder and 1.5ml/1/4 tsp ground cloves. Add salt and ground black pepper. Brush the glaze over the meat about 10 minutes before the end of the cooking time.

Ginger and honey glaze for chicken and pork

Put 2.5cm/1in fresh root ginger (peeled and grated) into a pan with 90ml/6 tbsp clear honey, 30ml/2 tbsp dry sherry and the grated rind and juice of 1 lime. Season, bring to the boil and allow to simmer for 3 minutes. Apply as above.

Below: Herb and chilli oils are easily prepared at home.

MAGICAL MARINADES

Meat, poultry and fish are so often marinated before barbecuing as this gives them a beautiful flavour and succulent moistness. Generally, use oily marinades for dry foods, such as lean meat or white fish, and use wine- or vinegar-based marinades for rich foods with a higher fat content. Many of the lemon and herb combinations used for fish work equally well with chicken. For the best results, marinate overnight.

Fillets of fish can be marinated in olive oil with crushed garlic and the grated rind and juice of a lime. One of the quickest marinades for salmon fillets can be made from a little light olive oil and a split vanilla pod (bean).

How much will you need?
The amount of marinade you will need to prepare depends on the quantity and type of food, but, as a guide, use about 150ml/1/4 pint/ 2/3 cup for about 500g/11/4lb food.

Above: Wherever possible, marinate foods the night before to allow maximum time for flavour to permeate.

Herb marinade for salmon

Roughly chop the leaves of a large handful of fresh herb sprigs, such as chervil, thyme, parsley, sage, chives, rosemary and oregano. Combine with 45ml/3 tbsp olive oil and 30ml/2 tbsp tarragon vinegar. Add 1 crushed garlic clove, 2 chopped spring onions (scallions) or shallots and some ground black pepper. Mix well.

Red wine marinade for red meats

Mix 150ml/1/4 pint/2/3 cup red wine, 15ml/1 tbsp olive oil, 15ml/1 tbsp red wine vinegar, 2 crushed garlic cloves, 2 crumbled dried bay leaves and ground black pepper.

Lavender balsamic marinade for lamb

Mix 1 finely chopped shallot with 45ml/3 tbsp chopped fresh lavender and 15ml/1 tbsp balsamic vinegar. Add 30ml/2 tbsp olive oil and 15ml/1 tbsp lemon juice. Mix well. Scatter a few lavender sprigs over the grill rack before cooking the lamb.

How to marinate

Many barbecue recipes include a marinade so it is important to plan ahead to allow for the correct length of marinating time. Not only do marinades flavour foods in all kinds of different ways but they also tenderize meat and keep food moist during cooking. However, be careful of salting food that is marinating, as salt will draw out the natural juices if left to marinate for too long. If you are marinating for longer than 30 minutes, follow this guide:

Adding salt
Meat salt 30 minutes before cooking
Fish and vegetables salt 15 minutes before cooking

1 Place the food for marinating in a wide dish or bowl, preferably large enough to allow it to lie in a single layer. (Always use a non-corrosive dish if the marinade contains wine, vinegar or citrus juices.)

2 Mix together the ingredients for the marinade thoroughly.

3 Pour the marinade over the food and turn the food to coat it evenly.

4 Cover the dish and refrigerate for 30 minutes or up to several hours depending on the recipe. As a rough guide, marinate red meat, poultry and game for 2 hours at room temperature or 24 hours in the refrigerator. Fish, seafood and vegetables should be marinated for between 30 minutes and 2 hours in the refrigerator.

5 Turn the food over occasionally and spoon the marinade over it. If marinating for long periods, add salt as above.

6 Remove the food with a slotted spoon or lift it out using tongs, and drain off and reserve the marinade. Allow the food to come to room temperature before cooking.

7 If basting or brushing the food during cooking, make sure the last coat is added in time for it to be well cooked before the food is served.

Lemon grass and lime marinade for fish

Finely chop 1 lemon grass stalk. Whisk the grated rind and juice of 1 lime with 45ml/3 tbsp olive oil, black pepper and the lemon grass. This also works well with chicken.

Honey citrus marinade for chicken

Mix together the finely grated rind and juice of 1/2 lime, 1/2 lemon and a small orange. Add 45ml/3 tbsp sunflower oil, 30ml/2 tbsp clear honey, 15ml/1 tbsp soy sauce and 5ml/1 tsp Dijon mustard. Season with pepper. This marinade also works well with fish.

Lemon grass and ginger marinade for chicken or pork

Chop the bulb end of two lemon grass stalks and put them in the bowl of a food processor with 30ml/2 tbsp sliced fresh root ginger, 6 chopped garlic cloves and 4 chopped shallots. Add a bunch chopped coriander (cilantro) roots, 30ml/2 tbsp each Thai fish sauce and light soy sauce, 120ml/4fl oz/1/2 cup coconut milk and 15ml/1 tbsp palm sugar (jaggery). Process until smooth.

Using it as a sauce?

Remember: if a marinade is also intended as a sauce, you can either divide the mixture into two and retain one half to marinate or brush over the food while it cooks, or heat up the marinade in a pan until bubbling for at least 1 minute before serving with the cooked food.

Marinades, butters and more

Turn to page 382 for more recipes for marinades, butters, dips and other barbecue essentials.

Right: Herb butters make an excellent impromptu sauce for baked fish. Simply prepare and chill, and then slice as needed. They will keep for several days.

Above: Black olives combine very well with butter when finely chopped.

BUTTERS

Herb butters are easy to make and, because they are made in advance, are useful for entertaining. Add a knob (pat) of cold herb butter to top cooked fish, meat, poultry or vegetables; as it melts over the surface it creates a delicious sauce. Fresh aromatic herbs such as tarragon and chives combine well with the butter, but other ingredients can be used too – try chopping up a few pitted olives, or some anchovy fillets from the store-cupboard. Then transfer to a piece of clear film (plastic wrap) and form into a roll. Refrigerate until hard. Slice the chilled butter and use to top the hot food. The following combinations should be mixed with 115g/4oz softened butter.

Anchovy butter for white fish

Rinse 6 canned anchovy fillets in cold water and dry on kitchen paper. Rub through a sieve and mix with the butter.

Lemon butter for fish, chicken and vegetables

Mix the grated rind of 1 lemon, and salt and pepper with the butter.

Herb or garlic butter for fish, meat or vegetables

Finely chop 50g/2oz fresh herbs, such as chives, tarragon, parsley, chervil or thyme or crush 3 garlic cloves. Mix with the butter, adding salt and pepper.

Horseradish butter for beef

Pound 60ml/4 tbsp grated horseradish in a pestle and mortar and mix with the butter for a sharp-tasting melt-in-the-mouth sauce.

Mustard butter for meat and fish

Mix 15m/1 tbsp dry English mustard or made Dijon mustard (for a milder flavour) with the butter.

Olive butter

Finely chop 50g/2oz pitted black or green olives and mix with the butter and the grated rind of 1/2 lemon.

BARBECUE TECHNIQUES

A successful impromptu barbecued meal can be put together at the last minute with very little planning. If you are cooking for a crowd or planning something special, however, think through your menu carefully and organize yourself so that everything will run smoothly when you begin cooking. It's worth getting to know some basic preparation techniques and cooking procedures before you start.

GETTING READY

For smooth barbecuing, have everything prepared in advance so that as soon as the coals reach the correct temperature cooking can begin. This means that all chopping, marinating, stuffing and skewering should be done beforehand. Plan your menu thoughtfully; for example, if you are using a griddle it's

Above: By learning a few simple techniques, you can use the barbecue to prepare all kinds of dishes.

best to take advantage of the fierce early heat for this, so perhaps your first course could be griddled. During preparation, remember to trim all excess fat away from meat as this can drip on to the coals, causing flare-ups.

Remember to take any foods out of the freezer in good time, but if you are using frozen seafood try to cook it when it has just thawed and before the juices start to flow.

HOW TO GRILL

The key to successful grilling is to give the food just enough time to allow the heat to penetrate fully to the centre without overcooking the outside. To

Preparing whole fish for grilling
Small whole fish are ideal for barbecuing, especially oily fish such as mackerel or trout. You can ask your fishmonger to prepare them but it is also very easy to do yourself. A hinged wire basket is ideal for barbecuing fish.

1 Cut off the fins and strip out the gills with scissors.

2 Hold the fish firmly at the tail end and use the back of a small knife blade to remove the scales, scraping towards the head end. Rinse under cold water.

3 Cut a long slit under the fish, from just under the tail to just behind the gills, to open up the belly. Use the knife to push out the entrails and discard them. Rinse the fish in cold water.

4 Rub the inside cavity of the fish with salt and rinse again; then dry with kitchen paper.

achieve that lovely caramelized and smoky taste, sear the food for just a short period first, then continue to cook over a lower heat.

Cooking in foil parcels

Delicate foods or foods that are best cooked slowly in their own steam can be cooked in foil parcels and either placed directly into the coals or on the grill rack. You can wrap all kinds of flavourings in the foil parcels, too.

1 Use heavy-duty foil and cut two equal pieces to make a double thickness large enough to wrap each fish or portion of food. Lightly brush the centre of the foil with melted butter or oil.

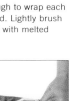

2 Place the food in the centre of the foil and add any flavourings and seasonings. Pull up the edges of the foil on opposite sides, over the food.

3 Make a double fold in the top of the foil so that food will cook gently in its own steam.

4 Fold over the ends of the foil or twist them together, making sure the parcel is sealed completely, so that the juices cannot escape.

will need a lid or tented foil for this method. Most small portions of food will be cooked directly over the coals (direct heat). If you are cooking a large joint of food as well as smaller foods, move the coals to one side so that the joint can be positioned in the cooler part and smaller foods can be cooked over the coals. Gas barbecues can be set to cook using indirect heat.

HOW LONG WILL FOOD TAKE TO COOK?

You might prefer beef or lamb to be slightly pink inside but poultry or pork must always be well done until all the juices run clear with no trace of pink. Most foods need to be turned only once but small items such as kebabs or sausages may need to be turned more frequently to ensure even cooking. Foods cooked in foil will take a little longer to cook.

If your barbecue allows you to adjust the height of the grill rack, this is the easiest way to adjust the heat of the coals during cooking. For a medium heat the grill rack should be about 10cm/4in from the coals. Raise the rack to obtain a lower heat or lower it for a higher heat. If you wish to sear food, such as steaks, over a very high heat,

Below: This ornamental barbecue has slats for grilling kebabs on skewers.

Be careful not to leave a large piece of meat over a high heat for too long or all the juices will bubble up to the surface and a thick crust will form and blacken, but the insides will be cold; or if the food is cooked over a longer period it will become tough. Once it is seared and golden, move the food frequently between the cooler and hotter areas of the barbecue for the remainder of the cooking time. A kettle barbecue is useful, as when you close the lid you will have an all-round heat.

Before serving, rest meat and fish away from the heat. They will continue to cook for a little while and meat needs to rest to allow the juices to settle.

Try to avoid turning food more often if the recipe tells you to turn only once. Also avoid the temptation to prod or cut meat while it is cooking to test if it is done, as this will allow the juices to escape. You can check for doneness by piercing cooked meat with a skewer – the juices should run clear if it is ready. Similarly, avoid pressing down with a spatula while food is cooking as this will also cause moisture to be lost.

COOKING FOOD WITH DIRECT AND INDIRECT HEAT

Although we usually associate barbecued food with individual portions of food such as steaks, burgers, small fish and chicken portions, larger cuts can also be cooked using a barbecue. Some barbecues have a spit attached, which is useful for cooking whole chickens and joints of meat directly over the coals at high heat; otherwise cook them over indirect heat. For charcoal, this is when the coals are moved either to one side of the fire grate or parted in the centre and a drip tray placed in the space. The meat is then positioned over the drip tray. You

Above: Meat can be cooked on a spit over a high heat and brushed regularly to keep it moist.

move the rack to 4–5cm/1¹/₂–2in from the coals and then finish cooking over a lower heat. If the barbecue has air vents you can also use these to control the heat.

The chart to the right gives you a rough guide to the lengths of time that different types of meat, poultry and fish take to cook.

HOW TO KNOW WHEN IT'S DONE

In addition to piercing the thickest part of the meat as advised, you can also test for doneness by pressing it with your finger:
• Rare meat will be soft to the touch.
• Medium meat will be springy.
• Well-cooked meat will be very firm to the touch.

For large joints of meat use a meat thermometer to check the temperature inside: chicken 85°C/185°F; beef 65°C/150°F; lamb 60°C/140°F; pork 75°C/170°F.

USING A GRIDDLE

A ridged, cast-iron griddle is a useful piece of equipment to use on a hot barbecue. It is important that it is searing hot and very dry when the food is first put on it. Test by splashing a few drops of water on to the surface; they should evaporate instantly. Oil the food rather than the pan and, to help reduce the amount of smoke, pat any excess

marinade off with kitchen paper. You need only a very small amount of oil. A good time to use the griddle is while the coals glow red with a light dusting of white or grey ash; this is just before they are ready. Use this time to sear thin foods, remembering to lower the heat when they are done.

LOW-FAT BARBECUES

Although barbecuing is often associated with rich foods – meats in particular – there are many ways to cook healthy foods over hot coals. You just need to give a little thought to preparation, and to substitute one or two of the more indulgent ingredients in a dish.

BASIC TIMING GUIDE

type of food	weight or thickness	heat	cooking time (total)
beef			
steaks	2.5cm/1in	hot	rare: 5 minutes; medium: 8 minutes; well done: 12 minutes
burgers	2cm/³/₄in	hot	6–8 minutes
kebabs	2.5cm/1in	hot	5–8 minutes
joints, such as rump or sirloin	1.6kg/3¹/₂lb	spit or indirect heat medium	2–3 hours
lamb			
leg steaks	2cm/³/₄in	medium	10–15 minutes
chops	2.5cm/1in	medium	10–15 minutes
kebabs	2.5cm/1in	medium	6–15 minutes
butterflied leg	7.5cm/3in	low	rare: 40–45 minutes well done: 1 hour
rolled shoulder	1.6kg/3¹/₂lb	spit or indirect heat medium	1¹/₄–1¹/₂ hours
pork			
chops	2.5cm/1in	medium	15–18 minutes
kebabs	2.5cm/1in	medium	12–15 minutes
spare ribs		medium	30–40 minutes
sausages	thick	medium	8–10 minutes
joints, such as shoulder or loin	1.6kg/3¹/₂lb	spit or indirect heat medium	2–3 hours
chicken			
whole	1.6kg/3¹/₂lb	spit or indirect heat medium	1–1¹/₄ hours
quarters, leg or breast		medium	30–35 minutes
breast fillets, boneless		medium	10–15 minutes
drumsticks		medium	25–30 minutes
kebabs		medium	6–10 minutes
poussin, whole	450kg/1lb	spit or indirect heat medium	25–30 minutes
poussin, spatchcocked	450kg/1lb	medium	25–30 minutes
duck			
whole	2.25kg/5lb	spit or indirect heat high	1–1¹/₂ hours
half		medium	35–45 minutes
breast fillets, boneless		medium	15–20 minutes
fish			
large, whole	2.25–4.5kg/5–10lb	low/medium	allow 10 minutes per 2.5cm/1in thickness
small, whole	500–900kg/1¹/₄–2lb	hot/medium	12–20 minutes
sardines		hot/medium	4–6 minutes
fish steaks or fillets	2.5cm/1in	medium	6–10 minutes
kebabs	2.5cm/1in	medium	5–8 minutes
large prawns, in shell		medium	6–8 minutes
scallops/mussels, in shell		medium	until open
large prawns, shelled		medium	4–6 minutes
scallops/mussels, shelled or skewered		medium	5–8 minutes
half lobster		low/medium	15–20 minutes

Above: An upside-down wok will fit snugly over a small grill rack as a lid, and helps to seal in moisture.

Which foods?

Red meats such as lamb and beef are particularly high in saturated fats and should either be avoided or kept to a minimum if you are following a low-fat diet or want to reduce the unhealthy fats (saturated fats) in your diet. Chicken and turkey, however, are good low-fat meats, although it is best to remove the skin. This can be done after cooking, if you like.

When choosing fish, look out for white fish such as cod or monkfish for a low-fat diet (although oily fish contains the healthy omega-3 fatty acids so can be included in most healthy diets). Be creative with the vegetable dishes that you barbecue – adding marinated tofu to vegetable kebabs, for example.

Avoiding too much fat

Keep oil to a minimum and use olive oil in preference during marinating and cooking. You can always adjust a recipe to use the minimum amount of olive oil supplemented with citrus juices or fat-free yogurt mixed with spices. Baste the food with the marinade to keep it moist but do this sparingly so that you are not replacing oil that has already dripped away. Brush once just before you turn the food during cooking, and if the food becomes dry, squeeze on a little citrus juice. You can also buy oil misters, which can be useful for adding a fine haze of oil before cooking.

Barbecue fish in its skin to keep it moist; it is easy to skin once cooked.

Above: Stuffing meat and fish with citrus is a great way of adding flavour without fat.

Cook small vegetables, baked potatoes or fish in foil parcels to seal in the moisture and avoid using too much oil.

Use wine, cider, vinegar, lemon or lime juice to provide liquid in place of large amounts of oil. Avoid using large amounts of wine, however, as the alcohol may not burn off sufficiently from quickly cooked foods.

Adding flavour without fat

It's not necessary to use lots of fat to add flavour into your food. Try rubbing herbs, spices and crushed garlic into

skinless chicken before cooking, or pierce the skin and tuck herbs and garlic underneath to trap in their flavour during cooking. Remove the skin before eating. Try prepared mustard marinades to spread over skinless chicken breasts to trap in moisture and add piquancy. Use finely chopped shallots, onions or spring onions for a pronounced flavour in marinades.

Brighten up the taste buds by accompanying your barbecued food with a refreshing salsa or relish made from finely chopped fruit or vegetables, spring onions and chopped fresh herbs. These are also delicious tucked into pitta bread kebabs. Salads with light dressings and fat-free dips also taste great with barbecued food, and a pile of wholemeal rolls or pitta breads make a healthy, substantial accompaniment, and are, of course, useful for soaking up juices. Remember to choose low-fat yogurt, fromage frais or crème fraîche for your marinades or dips – they will taste just as delicioius as their full-fat counterparts and are guilt-free!

Below: Use the timing guide opposite to cook lean cuts of meat according to your preference.

APPETIZERS AND LIGHT BITES

As soon as the barbecue is set alight, appetites awaken and everyone gets ready to enjoy some exceptionally flavourful food. Exciting and adventurous nibbles and appetizers will get your barbecue off to a great start. Many of the recipes in this chapter use the griddle, which can be placed over coals that are too hot for cooking direct on the grill rack, so you can take advantage of the first flush of heat from the barbecue. You will be surprised at the variety of foods that you can cook on the barbecue, from mini pizzas and griddled corn cakes to hot avocado halves and tender morsels of meat mounted on sticks, plus quickly cooked shellfish that needs hardly any preparation. And remember that many of these light bites can also be included on the side as part of a main course, or are simply perfect as finger food.

VEGETABLES <u>WITH</u> TAPENADE <u>AND</u> HERB AÏOLI

A BEAUTIFUL PLATTER OF CRISP, FLAVOURFUL SUMMER VEGETABLES, SERVED WITH ONE OR TWO INTERESTING SAUCES, MAKES A REALLY TEMPTING AND INFORMAL APPETIZER, PERFECT FOR NIBBLING WHILE THE BARBECUE HEATS UP. EVERYTHING CAN BE PREPARED IN ADVANCE.

SERVES SIX

INGREDIENTS
2 red (bell) peppers
30ml/2 tbsp olive oil
225g/8oz new potatoes
115g/4oz green beans
225g/8oz baby carrots
225g/8oz young asparagus
12 quails' eggs
fresh herbs, to garnish
coarse salt, for sprinkling
For the tapenade
175g/6oz/1½ cups pitted
  black olives
50g/2oz can anchovy fillets, drained
30ml/2 tbsp capers
120ml/4fl oz/½ cup olive oil
finely grated rind of 1 lemon
15ml/1 tbsp brandy (optional)
ground black pepper
For the herb aïoli
5 garlic cloves, crushed
2 egg yolks
5ml/1 tsp Dijon mustard
10ml/2 tsp white wine vinegar
250ml/8fl oz/1 cup light olive oil
45ml/3 tbsp chopped mixed fresh
  herbs, such as chervil, parsley
  and tarragon
30ml/2 tbsp chopped watercress
salt and ground black pepper

1 To make the tapenade, finely chop the olives, anchovies and capers and place them in a mixing bowl. Add the olive oil, lemon rind and brandy, if using, and beat together until thoroughly combined. (Alternatively, lightly process all the ingredients in a blender or food processor.)

2 Season the tapenade with pepper (it will not need salt) and blend in a little more oil if the mixture seems very dry. Transfer to a dish, cover with clear film (plastic wrap) and chill until you are ready to serve.

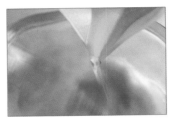

3 To make the aïoli, beat together the garlic, egg yolks, mustard and vinegar. Gradually blend in the olive oil, a drop at a time, whisking well until thick.

4 Stir in the mixed herbs and watercress. Season with salt and pepper to taste, adding a little more vinegar if necessary. Cover with clear film and chill until ready to serve.

5 Cut the peppers vertically into thick strips and brush them with oil. Grill the strips on a hot barbecue or under a hot grill (broiler), until they are just beginning to char in places. Set them aside until cool enough to handle.

6 Cook the potatoes in a large pan of boiling, salted water until tender. Add the beans and carrots and blanch for 1 minute. Add the asparagus and cook for a further 30 seconds. Drain the vegetables. Cook the quails' eggs in boiling water for 2 minutes.

7 When all the vegetables are cool enough to handle, arrange them on a serving platter with the eggs and the sauces. Garnish with fresh herbs and serve with coarse salt, for sprinkling.

COOK'S TIPS
• Any leftover tapenade is delicious tossed with pasta or spread on to toast.
• If you are preparing the vegetables in advance, allow them to cool before packing in an airtight container. Store the quails' eggs in their original box.
• If the aïoli splits while you are adding the oil, beat another egg yolk with a little water in a fresh bowl and slowly whisk the curdled mixture into it.

Energy 583kcal/2408kJ; Protein 10.7g; Carbohydrate 14.6g, of which sugars 8g; Fat 54g, of which saturates 8.6g; Cholesterol 199mg; Calcium 104mg; Fibre 4.3g; Sodium 1050mg.

ROASTED PEPPER ANTIPASTO

JARS OF ITALIAN MIXED PEPPERS PRESERVED IN OLIVE OIL ARE A COMMON SIGHT IN SUPERMARKETS, YET NONE CAN COMPETE WITH THIS FRESHLY MADE VERSION OF THE CLASSIC SALAD, WHICH IS PERFECT AS AN APPETIZER OR AS AN ACCOMPANIMENT TO GRILLED MEATS.

SERVES SIX

INGREDIENTS

3 red (bell) peppers
2 yellow or orange peppers
2 green peppers
50g/2oz/½ cup sun-dried tomatoes
  in oil, drained
1 garlic clove
30ml/2 tbsp balsamic vinegar
75ml/5 tbsp olive oil
few drops of chilli sauce
4 canned artichoke hearts, drained
  and sliced
salt and ground black pepper
fresh basil leaves, to garnish

COOK'S TIP
If you prefer your peppers to have a softer texture and sweeter flavour, let them cool in a plastic bag after grilling, then peel them with a sharp knife.

1 Cook all the whole peppers over medium-hot coals or under a hot grill (broiler), turning frequently, for about 10–15 minutes until the skins begin to char. Remove the peppers, cover them with a clean dish towel and leave to cool for 5 minutes.

2 While the peppers are cooling, use a sharp kitchen knife to slice the sun-dried tomatoes into thin strips. Thinly slice the garlic clove.

3 To make the dressing for the salad, beat together the balsamic vinegar, olive oil and chilli sauce in a small bowl, then season with a little salt and pepper.

4 Remove the stalks from the cooled peppers, scrape out the seeds and slice the flesh into thin strips. Put in a serving bowl and mix with the sliced artichokes, sun-dried tomatoes and garlic. Pour over the dressing and scatter with basil leaves.

Energy 163kcal/675kJ; Protein 2.1g; Carbohydrate 12.7g, of which sugars 12.1g; Fat 11.8g, of which saturates 1.8g; Cholesterol 0mg; Calcium 23mg; Fibre 3.3g; Sodium 18mg.

POTATO SKINS <u>WITH</u> CAJUN DIP

AS AN ALTERNATIVE TO DEEP-FRYING, COOKING POTATO SKINS ON THE BARBECUE CRISPS THEM UP IN NO TIME AND GIVES THEM A WONDERFUL CHARGRILLED FLAVOUR. A CREAMY YOGURT DIP SPICED WITH CHILLI MAKES THE PERFECT PARTNER FOR THESE APPETIZING NIBBLES.

SERVES FOUR

INGREDIENTS
 4 large baking potatoes
 olive oil for brushing
 250ml/8fl oz/1 cup natural (plain)
  yogurt
 2 garlic cloves, crushed
 10ml/2 tsp tomato purée (paste)
 5ml/1 tsp green chilli paste or
  1 small green chilli, chopped
 2.5ml/½ tsp celery salt
 salt and freshly ground black pepper

1 Pierce the skins of the potatoes in one or two places and bake or microwave them until tender. Holding the hot potatoes in a cloth to protect your hands, cut them in half and scoop out the flesh with a large spoon, leaving a thin layer of potato on the skins.

VARIATION
If you don't have any chilli paste or fresh chillies, you can add one or two drops of hot pepper sauce to the dip instead, adjusting the flavour to taste.

COOK'S TIP
The scooped out potato can be reserved for another meal, such as a meat or fish pie topped with mashed potato, or fish cakes. Store it in the fridge or freeze it for future use.

2 Cut each potato shell in half again and lightly brush the skins with olive oil. Cook on a medium-hot barbecue for 4–5 minutes, or until crisp.

3 Mix together the remaining ingredients in a bowl to make the dip. Serve the potato skins with the Cajun dip on the side.

Energy 210kcal/873kJ; Protein 2.7g; Carbohydrate 12.5g, of which sugars 3.3g; Fat 17g, of which saturates 2.2g; Cholesterol 0mg; Calcium 61mg; Fibre 0.7g; Sodium 35mg.

SMOKED AUBERGINE AND YOGURT PURÉE

THIS DELICIOUS GARLIC-FLAVOURED PURÉE COMES FROM TURKEY, WHERE IT IS ONE OF THE MOST POPULAR ELEMENTS OF A MEZE, THE SELECTION OF SMALL, APPETIZING DISHES THAT IS USUALLY EATEN AS A SNACK WITH DRINKS. IN TURKEY THE RECIPE VARIES FROM HOUSE TO HOUSE AND FROM REGION TO REGION: SOMETIMES IT IS MADE WITH A HEAVY HAND OF GARLIC OR A KICK OF CHILLI, OR WITH THE FRESH TASTE OF DILL, MINT OR PARSLEY. IT IS HEAVENLY WHEN FRESHLY MADE WITH BARBECUED AUBERGINES, SERVED WITH CHUNKS OF CRUSTY BREAD FOR SCOOPING IT UP.

SERVES FOUR

INGREDIENTS
2 large, plump aubergines
   (eggplants)
30ml/2 tbsp olive oil, plus extra
   for drizzling
juice of 1 lemon
2–3 garlic cloves, crushed
225g/8oz/1 cup thick and creamy
   natural (plain) yogurt
salt and ground black pepper
a few fresh dill fronds, to garnish
lemon wedges, to serve

1 The aubergines need to be cooked over direct heat to char the skin in order to produce the distinctive smoky flavour of this purée. Place them on a barbecue rack over hot coals, or over a gas flame on the hob (see Cook's Tip) and cook for 15–20 minutes, turning them from time to time until they are soft – the skin will blacken and remain firm, but the flesh will cook and soften.

VARIATION
Smoked aubergines prepared as above can also be used to make a salad. Once the skin has been removed, cut the flesh into dice and toss with the olive oil and lemon juice. Add some sliced spring onions (scallions), a few tomatoes, skinned, seeded and chopped, and some fresh parsley and dill.

2 Lift the aubergines off the barbecue rack, place them on a chopping board and slit open lengthways with a sharp knife. Scoop the flesh off the charred skin. Alternatively, hold each aubergine by the stalk under cold running water and gently peel off the charred skin until you are left with just the smooth bulbous flesh.

3 Squeeze the flesh with your fingers to get rid of any excess water and juices and place it on a chopping board.

4 Chop the flesh to a pulp. Put it in a bowl with 30ml/2 tbsp oil, the lemon juice and garlic.

5 Beat well to mix, then beat in the yogurt and season with salt and pepper. Alternatively, put the aubergine flesh in a food processor with the garlic. Whizz to a pulp, then blend in the lemon juice and oil and stir in the yogurt and seasoning, adjusting to taste.

6 Transfer to a bowl, drizzle with olive oil and garnish with dill. Serve at room temperature, with lemon wedges on the side for squeezing.

COOK'S TIP
If you are not making this dish as part of a barbecue, the aubergines can be prepared on the stove. Put them directly over the gas flame on top of the stove, or under a conventional grill (broiler), and turn them from time to time until the skin is charred on all sides and the flesh feels soft. Place the aubergines in a plastic bag and leave for a few minutes until the steam has loosened the skin and they are cool enough to handle, then skin as above.

Energy 103kcal/431kJ; Protein 4.4g; Carbohydrate 7.7g, of which sugars 6.4g; Fat 6.5g, of which saturates 1.2g; Cholesterol 1mg; Calcium 118mg; Fibre 2.3g; Sodium 49mg.

FALAFEL

THESE DEEP-FRIED CHICKPEA FRITTERS ARE CLASSIC MIDDLE-EASTERN SNACK FOOD. THE SECRET TO GOOD FALAFEL IS USING WELL-SOAKED, BUT NOT COOKED, CHICKPEAS. DO NOT USE CANNED CHICKPEAS AS THEY WILL BE MUSHY AND THE FALAFEL WILL FALL APART WHEN THEY ARE FRIED.

SERVES SIX

INGREDIENTS
   250g/9oz/generous 1⅓ cups
      dried chickpeas
   1 litre/1¾ pints/4 cups water
   45–60ml/3–4 tbsp bulgur wheat
   1 large or 2 small onions,
      finely chopped
   5 garlic cloves, crushed
   75ml/5 tbsp chopped fresh parsley
   75ml/5 tbsp chopped fresh coriander
      (cilantro) leaves
   45ml/3 tbsp ground cumin
   15ml/1 tbsp ground coriander
   5ml/1 tsp baking powder
   5m/1 tsp salt
   small pinch to 1.5ml/¼ tsp ground
      black pepper
   small pinch to 1.5ml/¼ tsp
      cayenne pepper
   5ml/1 tsp curry powder with a pinch
      of cardamom seeds added (optional)
   45–60ml/3–4 tbsp gram flour
   crumbled wholemeal (whole-wheat)
      bread or flour, if necessary
   vegetable oil, for deep-frying
   6 pitta breads, hummus, crunchy
      salad, tahini, Tabasco or other hot
      pepper sauce, pickles and olives,
      to serve

1 Place the chickpeas in a large bowl and pour over the water. Leave to soak for at least 4 hours to soften them, then drain the chickpeas and grind them in a food processor.

2 Put the ground chickpeas in a mixing bowl and stir in the bulgur wheat, onion, garlic, parsley, fresh coriander, ground cumin and coriander, baking powder, salt, black pepper and cayenne pepper, and curry powder, if using. Stir in 45ml/3 tbsp water and leave to stand for about 45 minutes.

3 Stir the gram flour into the falafel batter, adding a little water if it is too thick or a little crumbled wholemeal bread or flour if it is too thin.

4 Using a wet tablespoon and wet hands, shape heaped tablespoons of the falafel mixture into 12–18 balls.

5 Heat the oil for deep-frying in a pan until it is hot enough to brown a cube of bread in 30 seconds. Lower the heat.

6 Add the falafel to the hot oil in batches and cook for 3–4 minutes until golden brown. Remove the cooked falafel with a slotted spoon and drain on kitchen paper before adding more to the oil.

7 Serve the freshly cooked falafel tucked into grilled pitta bread with a spoonful of hummus, a little crunchy salad and a drizzle of tahini. Accompany with hot pepper sauce, pickles and olives.

COOK'S TIP
Prepare the falafel in advance, frying them lightly. Thread them on skewers, alternating them with cherry tomatoes and onion slices, and grill until browned.

Energy 303kcal/1282kJ; Protein 18.5g; Carbohydrate 44.7g, of which sugars 5.2g; Fat 6.9g, of which saturates 1.2g; Cholesterol 0mg; Calcium 88mg; Fibre 7.2g; Sodium 16mg.

GRILLED VEGETABLE STICKS

FOR THIS JAPANESE KEBAB-STYLE DISH, MADE WITH TOFU, KONNYAKU — THE PROCESSED CORM OF THE KONJAC PLANT — AND AUBERGINE, YOU WILL NEED 40 BAMBOO SKEWERS, SOAKED IN WATER OVERNIGHT. THREADING EACH KEBAB ON TWO STICKS MAKES THEM EASY TO TURN OVER ON THE GRILL RACK.

SERVES FOUR

INGREDIENTS
  300g/11oz firm tofu
  250g/9oz packet konnyaku
  2 small aubergines (eggplants)
  25ml/1½ tbsp toasted sesame oil
For the yellow and green sauces
  45ml/3 tbsp shiro-miso
  15ml/1 tbsp caster (superfine) sugar
  5 young spinach leaves
  2.5ml/½ tsp sansho
  salt
For the red sauce
  15ml/1 tbsp aka-miso
  5ml/1 tsp caster (superfine) sugar
  5ml/1 tsp mirin
To garnish
  pinch of white poppy seeds
  15ml/1 tbsp toasted sesame seeds

1 Drain the liquid from the packet of tofu and wrap the tofu in three or four layers of kitchen paper. Set a chopping board on top to press out the remaining liquid. Leave for 30 minutes, until the excess liquid has been absorbed by the kitchen paper. Unwrap the block of tofu and cut it into eight 7.5 × 2 × 1cm/ 3 × ¾ × ½in slices.

2 Drain the liquid from the konnyaku. Cut the block in half and put the pieces in a small pan with enough water to cover. Bring to the boil and cook for about 5 minutes. Drain the konnyaku well and cut it into eight 6 × 2 × 1cm/ 2½ × ¾ × ½in slices.

3 Cut the aubergines in half lengthways, then halve the thickness to make four flat slices. Place in a dish, add cold water to cover and leave to soak for 15 minutes. Drain well and pat thoroughly dry on kitchen paper.

4 To make the yellow sauce, mix the shiro-miso and sugar in a pan, then cook over a low heat, stirring to dissolve the sugar. Remove from the heat. Place half the sauce in a small bowl.

5 Blanch the spinach leaves in rapidly boiling water with a pinch of salt for 30 seconds until just beginning to wilt. Drain the spinach, then cool under cold running water. Squeeze out the water and chop finely.

6 Transfer the chopped spinach to a mortar and pound to a paste using a pestle. Mix the spinach paste and the sansho pepper into the bowl containing half the yellow sauce to make the green sauce.

7 Put all the red sauce ingredients in a small pan and cook over a low heat, stirring constantly, until the sugar has dissolved. Remove from the heat.

8 Prepare the barbecue. Thread each slice of tofu, konnyaku and aubergine on to two bamboo skewers. Brush the aubergine with sesame oil and grill over hot coals for 7–8 minutes on each side, turning several times.

9 Grill the konnyaku and tofu for 3–5 minutes each side, until golden.

10 Spread the red miso sauce on the aubergine slices. Spread one side of the tofu slices with green sauce and one side of the konnyaku with the yellow miso sauce. Grill the slices for 1–2 minutes. Sprinkle the aubergines with poppy seeds. Sprinkle the konnyaku with sesame seeds. Serve together.

Energy 178kcal/742kJ; Protein 12.9g; Carbohydrate 9.3g, of which sugars 8.6g; Fat 10.2g, of which saturates 1.4g; Cholesterol 0mg; Calcium 761mg; Fibre 1.9g; Sodium 17mg.

CORN TOSTADITAS WITH SALSA

THIS IS JUST THE RIGHT SNACK OR APPETIZER TO COOK WHEN THE COALS ARE VERY HOT, AS IT USES A GRIDDLE. THE SALSA AND GUACAMOLE ARE QUICK TO PREPARE AND TASTE WONDERFUL WITH THE STRIPY TOSTADITAS. MAKE SURE THE GRIDDLE HAS HEATED UP WELL BEFORE YOU ADD THE TOSTADITAS.

SERVES SIX

INGREDIENTS
30ml/2 tbsp chipotle or
    other chilli oil
15ml/1 tbsp sunflower oil
8 yellow corn tortillas, about
    300g/11oz total weight
For the salsa
4 tomatoes
30ml/2 tbsp chopped fresh basil
juice of ½ lime
20ml/4 tsp good quality sweet
    chilli sauce
1 small red onion, finely chopped
    (optional)
salt and ground black pepper
For the guacamole
4 avocados
juice of ½ lime
1 fresh fat mild chilli, seeded and
    finely chopped
salt and ground black pepper

1 Make the salsa 1 or 2 hours ahead if possible, to allow the flavours to blend. Cut the tomatoes in half, remove the cores and scoop out most of the seeds. Dice the flesh. Add the chopped basil, lime juice and sweet chilli sauce. Stir in the onion, if using, then add salt and pepper to taste.

2 To make the guacamole, cut the avocados in half, prize out the stones (pits), then scoop the flesh into a bowl. Add the lime juice, chopped chilli and seasoning. Mash with a fork to a fairly rough texture. Prepare the barbecue.

3 Mix the chilli and sunflower oils together. Stack the tortillas on a board. Lift the first tortilla off the stack and brush it lightly with the oil mixture. Turn it over and place it on the board, then brush the top with oil. Repeat with the other tortillas to produce a new stack.

4 Slice this stack of tortillas diagonally to produce six fat triangles. Heat the griddle on the grill rack over hot coals. Peel off a few tostaditas to griddle for 30 seconds on each side, pressing each one down lightly into the ridges.

5 Transfer the tostaditas to a bowl, so that they are supported by its sides. As they cool, they will shape themselves to the curve of the bowl. Serve with the salsa and guacamole.

Energy 334kcal/1396kJ; Protein 5.6g; Carbohydrate 36.8g, of which sugars 6.3g; Fat 19.1g, of which saturates 3.6g; Cholesterol 0mg; Calcium 71mg; Fibre 4.4g; Sodium 313mg.

CROSTINI

THIS IS A GREAT WAY TO KEEP HUNGER PANGS AT BAY WHILE YOU WAIT FOR THE MAIN COURSE. AS SOON AS THE BARBECUE IS READY, SIMPLY GRILL THE SLICED BREAD, HEAP ON THE SAUCE AND DRIZZLE OVER PLENTY OF GOOD EXTRA VIRGIN OLIVE OIL.

SERVES SIX

INGREDIENTS

2 sfilatino (Italian bread sticks), sliced lengthways into 3 pieces
1 garlic clove, cut in half
leaves from 4 fresh oregano sprigs
18 Kalamata olives, slivered
extra virgin olive oil, for drizzling
ground black pepper
For the aromatic tomatoes
800g/1¾lb ripe plum tomatoes
30ml/2 tbsp extra virgin olive oil
2 garlic cloves, crushed to a paste with a pinch of salt
1 small piece of dried chilli, seeds removed, finely chopped

VARIATION

Baguettes or ciabatta bread, cut diagonally to give long slices, will work just as well as sfilatino.

1 Prepare the barbecue. To make the aromatic tomatoes, plunge the tomatoes into boiling water for 30 seconds, then refresh in cold water. Peel away the skins, remove the seeds and core and roughly chop the flesh. Mix the oil and crushed garlic in a large frying pan.

2 Place on the stove over a high heat. Once the garlic starts to sizzle, add the tomatoes and the chilli; do not let the garlic burn. Cook for 2 minutes. The aim is to evaporate the liquid rather than pulp the tomatoes, which should keep their shape.

3 Toast the bread on both sides either by laying it on the grill rack or by using a griddle. If you use the griddle, press the bread down with a spatula to produce the attractive stripes. Generously rub each slice with the cut side of a piece of garlic.

4 Roughly chop all but a few of the oregano leaves and mix them into the tomato sauce. Pile the mixture on to the toasted sfilatino. Scatter over the whole oregano leaves and the olive slivers. Sprinkle with plenty of pepper, drizzle with lots of olive oil and serve at once.

Energy 261kcal/1103kJ; Protein 7.8g; Carbohydrate 38.8g, of which sugars 6.2g; Fat 9.4g, of which saturates 1.4g; Cholesterol 0mg; Calcium 95mg; Fibre 3.1g; Sodium 558mg.

CORN GRIDDLE CAKES

KNOWN AS AREPAS, THESE GRIDDLE CAKES ARE A STAPLE BREAD IN SEVERAL LATIN AMERICAN COUNTRIES. THEY ARE DELICIOUS FILLED WITH SOFT WHITE CHEESE, AS IN THIS RECIPE, OR SIMPLY EATEN PLAIN AS AN ACCOMPANIMENT. WITH THEIR CRISP CRUST AND CHEWY INTERIOR, AREPAS MAKE AN UNUSUAL AND TASTY SNACK OR ACCOMPANIMENT TO A BARBECUE MEAL.

MAKES FIFTEEN

INGREDIENTS
200g/7oz/1¾ cups *masarepa*
  or *masa harina* (see Cook's Tip)
2.5ml/½ tsp salt
300ml/½ pint/1¼ cups cold
  water
15ml/1 tbsp oil
200g/7oz fresh white cheese, such
  as queso fresco or mozzarella,
  roughly chopped

1 Combine the *masarepa* or *masa harina* and salt in a mixing bowl. Gradually stir in the measured water to make a soft dough, then set aside for about 20 minutes to rest.

2 Divide the dough into 15 equal-sized balls, then, using your fingers, flatten each ball into a small circle, approximately 1cm/½ in thick. Leave the *arepas* in a cool place while you prepare the barbecue. When the coals are hot, place a large, heavy frying pan or flat griddle over them to heat to medium-hot.

3 Add 5ml/1 tsp oil to the frying pan or griddle. Using a piece of kitchen paper, gently wipe the surface of the pan, leaving it just lightly greased.

4 Place five of the *arepas* in the frying pan or on the griddle. Cook for about 4 minutes, then flip over and cook for a further 4 minutes. The *arepas* should be blistered on both sides and beginning to char lightly.

5 Open the *arepas* and fill each with a few small pieces of fresh white cheese. Return to the pan to cook until the cheese begins to melt. Remove from the heat and keep warm.

6 Cook the remaining ten *arepas* in the same way, oiling the pan and wiping with kitchen paper in between batches, to ensure it is always lightly greased. Serve the *arepas* while still warm so that the melted cheese is soft and runny.

COOK'S TIP
Masarepa is a flour made with the white corn grown in the Andes. Look for it in Latin American food stores. If it is not available, replace it with *masa harina*, the flour used to make tamales. The result will not be quite as delicate, but the *arepas* will be equally delicious.

VARIATION
Instead of cheese, try a delicious beef filling. Simply fry some minced (ground) beef in oil in a frying pan with ½ chopped onion, 1 small red chilli, finely chopped, 1 crushed garlic clove, ground black pepper and fresh thyme. When thoroughly cooked, stuff the mixture inside the *arepas*.

Energy 86kcal/363kJ; Protein 3.7g; Carbohydrate 10.4g, of which sugars 0.2g; Fat 3.6g, of which saturates 2g; Cholesterol 8mg; Calcium 67mg; Fibre 0.4g; Sodium 53mg.

CIABATTA WITH MOZZARELLA AND ONIONS

*CIABATTA BREAD IS READILY AVAILABLE AND IS EVEN MORE DELICIOUS WHEN MADE WITH SPINACH,
SUN-DRIED TOMATOES OR OLIVES: YOU CAN FIND THESE VARIATIONS IN MOST SUPERMARKETS.*

MAKES FOUR

INGREDIENTS
    1 ciabatta loaf
    60ml/4 tbsp red pesto
    2 small onions
    olive oil, for brushing
    225g/8oz mozzarella cheese, sliced
    8 large black olives, halved
      and pitted

1 Prepare the barbecue. Cut the ciabatta in half horizontally and toast the cut sides lightly on the barbecue. Spread the toasted sides evenly with the red pesto.

2 Peel the onions and cut them horizontally into thin slices. Brush with oil and cook on a hot barbecue for 4–5 minutes until the edges of the rings are caramelized.

3 Arrange the slices of mozzarella on the bread. Add the onion slices and scatter some olives over. Cut each piece in half. Return to the barbecue or grill (broiler) to melt the cheese.

Energy 828kcal/3484kJ; Protein 34.8g; Carbohydrate 109.9g, of which sugars 10.4g; Fat 30.7g, of which saturates 11.7g; Cholesterol 40mg; Calcium 562mg; Fibre 6g; Sodium 1664mg.

CROSTINI WITH TOMATO AND ANCHOVY

FOR THESE SMALL CROSTINI, ROUNDS OF BREAD CUT FROM A BAGUETTE ARE CRISPLY TOASTED THEN COVERED WITH A SAVOURY MIXTURE OF TOMATO AND ANCHOVY.

MAKES EIGHT

INGREDIENTS

60ml/4 tbsp olive oil
2 garlic cloves
4 tomatoes, peeled, deseeded and
  roughly chopped
15ml/1 tbsp chopped fresh basil
15ml/1 tbsp tomato purée (paste)
1 small baguette (large enough to
  give 8 slices)
8 canned anchovy fillets, drained
12 black olives, halved and
  pitted
salt and ground black pepper
fresh basil, to garnish

1 Heat half the olive oil in a frying pan and fry the whole garlic cloves with the chopped tomatoes for about 4 minutes.

2 Stir in the chopped basil, tomato purée and season with plenty of salt and ground black pepper.

3 Cut the bread diagonally into 8 slices about 1cm/½in thick and brush the cut sides with the remaining olive oil. Toast the slices on the barbecue until golden, turning once.

4 Spoon a little tomato mixture on to each slice of bread. Place an anchovy fillet on each one and dot with the halved olives. Serve the crostini garnished with a sprig of fresh basil.

VARIATION

As an alternative topping for the crostini, make this onion and olive mixture, which has a classic Provençal flavour. Gently fry 2 large onions, thinly sliced, in 30ml/ 2 tbsp olive oil until golden and very soft, stirring occasionally to prevent them browning. Stir in 8 chopped anchovy fillets, 12 halved, pitted black olives and 5ml/1 tsp dried thyme. Season to taste with a little salt and plenty of ground black pepper. Spread the toasted slices of bread with 15ml/1 tbsp tapenade and cover with the warm onion and olive mixture.

Energy 116kcal/488kJ; Protein 4.8g; Carbohydrate 15.9g, of which sugars 3.2g; Fat 4.1g, of which saturates 1g; Cholesterol 5mg; Calcium 60mg; Fibre 1.3g; Sodium 301mg.

STUFFED <u>AND</u> GRILLED THIN TOFU

THIN SLICES OF DEEP-FRIED FIRM TOFU, CALLED ABURA-AGE IN JAPANESE, ARE AVAILABLE FROM ASIAN MARKETS AND CAN BE USED AS POCKETS LIKE PITTA BREADS. HERE, A GENEROUS AMOUNT OF CHOPPED SPRING ONION AND OTHER AROMATIC INGREDIENTS FILL THE POCKETS.

SERVES FOUR

INGREDIENTS
1 packet thin deep-fried tofu
   (abura-age)
4 spring onions (scallions), trimmed
   and very finely chopped
about 15ml/1 tbsp shoyu
1 garlic clove, grated or crushed
30ml/2 tbsp lightly toasted
   sesame seeds

COOK'S TIP
If the thin slices of deep-fried tofu prove
difficult to open horizontally, insert the
blade of a round-bladed knife in the side
at the cut edge, moving it gently from
side to side to open out the pocket.

1 Put the thin deep-fried tofu in a sieve
(strainer) and pour hot water from a
kettle over it to wash off any excess oil.
Leave to drain for a few minutes and
gently dry on kitchen paper.

2 Put one piece of thin deep-fried tofu
on a chopping board and roll over it
several times with a rolling pin. Cut the
thin deep-fried tofu in half and carefully
open at the cut edge to make two
pockets. Repeat with the remaining
piece of tofu.

3 Mix together the spring onions, shoyu,
garlic and sesame seeds in a small
bowl. Check the seasoning and add
more shoyu, if required. Prepare the
barbecue or preheat the grill (broiler).

4 Divide the filling equally among the
four pockets. Grill over hot coals or
under the grill for 3–4 minutes on each
side, until crisp and lightly browned.

5 With a sharp knife, cut each tofu bag
into four triangles and arrange them on
four small plates. Serve hot.

GRIDDLED CHEESE WITH ROCKET SALAD

CYPRIOT HALLOUMI IS IDEAL FOR COOKING ON THE GRIDDLE. IN GREEK TAVERNAS THE CHEESE IS OFTEN BROUGHT TO THE TABLE STILL SIZZLING IN A HOT IRON PAN. HALLOUMI HAS A REALLY DELICIOUS, SMOKY FLAVOUR, AND SHOULD BE EATEN QUICKLY WHILE IT'S TENDER AND PIPING HOT.

SERVES FOUR

INGREDIENTS
　30ml/2 tbsp olive oil
　8 slices Kefalotyri or Halloumi
　　cheese, each about
　　1cm/½in thick
　ground black pepper
　lemon wedges, to serve
For the salad
　15ml/1 tbsp red wine vinegar
　60ml/4 tbsp extra virgin
　　olive oil
　a large handful of rocket
　　(arugula) leaves

1 Start by making the salad. Whisk the vinegar and extra virgin olive oil in a bowl and dress the rocket leaves. Spread them out on a platter.

2 Heat a large griddle and oil the surface with the olive oil. Lay the slices of cheese, side by side, on the griddle. Do not allow the slices to touch as they may stick together as they cook. Let them sizzle for a couple of minutes, turning each one over using tongs or a metal spatula as it starts to get crisp at the sides.

3 Sprinkle the cheese slices with pepper. As soon as the bases turn golden, remove them from the pan and arrange them on the dressed rocket. Serve immediately, with the lemon wedges to squeeze over the top.

Energy 289kcal/1195kJ; Protein 10.7g; Carbohydrate 0.8g, of which sugars 0.8g; Fat 27g, of which saturates 9.3g; Cholesterol 29mg; Calcium 266mg; Fibre 1.1g; Sodium 268mg.

HAM PIZZETTAS WITH MANGO

THESE INDIVIDUAL LITTLE PIZZAS ARE TOPPED WITH AN UNUSUAL BUT VERY SUCCESSFUL COMBINATION OF SMOKED HAM, BRIE AND JUICY CHUNKS OF FRESH MANGO.

SERVES SIX

INGREDIENTS
225g/8oz/2 cups strong white
    bread flour
10g/¼oz sachet easy-blend
    (rapid-rise) dried yeast
150ml/¼ pint/⅔ cup warm water
60ml/4 tbsp olive oil
For the topping
1 ripe mango
150g/5oz smoked ham, sliced
    wafer-thin
150g/5oz Brie, diced
12 yellow cherry tomatoes, halved
salt and ground black pepper

1 In a large bowl, stir together the flour and yeast, with a pinch of salt. Make a well in the centre and stir in the water and 45ml/3 tbsp of the olive oil. Stir until thoroughly mixed.

2 Turn the dough out on to a floured surface and knead it for about 5 minutes, or until smooth. (Alternatively, put all the ingredients for the dough in a food processor and blend until smooth.)

3 Return the dough to the mixing bowl and cover it with a damp cloth or oiled clear film (plastic wrap). Leave the dough to rise in a warm place for about 30 minutes, or until it has doubled in size and is springy to the touch.

4 Prepare the barbecue. Divide the dough into six and roll each piece into a ball. Flatten each piece of dough out with your hand and use your knuckles to press it into a round of about 15cm/6in diameter. Leave the dough a little thicker at the edge to create a raised lip that will contain the filling.

5 Halve, stone (pit) and peel the mango and cut it into small dice. Arrange with the ham on top of the pizzettas. Top with cheese and tomatoes and sprinkle with salt and ground black pepper.

6 Drizzle the remaining oil over the pizzettas. Place them on the oiled grill rack of a medium-hot barbecue and cook for 8 minutes, or until golden brown and crisp underneath.

COOK'S TIP
These small rounds of dough are thin enough to cook through when placed directly on the barbecue rack, and the delicate topping needs no cooking. The coals should not be too hot or the bases will burn before they are done. If you have a kettle barbecue you can cook pizzas with the lid in place to create all-round heat like that of an oven.

Energy 326kcal/1369kJ; Protein 13.6g; Carbohydrate 34g, of which sugars 5.3g; Fat 15.5g, of which saturates 6g; Cholesterol 38mg; Calcium 124mg; Fibre 2.2g; Sodium 444mg.

SMOKY AUBERGINE ON CIABATTA

Cooking the aubergines whole, over an open flame, gives them a distinctive smoky flavour and aroma, as well as tender, creamy flesh. Cook them when the heat is fierce. They then need to cool for about 20 minutes before they are chopped and served.

SERVES FOUR TO SIX

INGREDIENTS
2 aubergines (eggplants)
2 red (bell) peppers
3–5 garlic cloves, chopped, or more
  to taste
2.5ml/½ tsp ground cumin
juice of ½–1 lemon, to taste
2.5ml/½ tsp sherry or wine vinegar
45–60ml/3–4 tbsp extra virgin
  olive oil
1–2 shakes of cayenne pepper,
  Tabasco or other hot pepper sauce
coarse sea salt
chopped fresh coriander (cilantro),
  to garnish
pitta bread wedges or thinly sliced
  French bread or ciabatta bread,
  sesame seed crackers and cucumber
  slices, to serve

1 Prepare the barbecue. Place the aubergines and peppers over a medium-low heat on the grill rack. Turn the vegetables frequently until they appear deflated and the skins are evenly charred.

2 Put the aubergines and peppers in a plastic bag and seal tightly. Leave for 20 minutes for the skins to loosen.

3 Peel the vegetables, reserving the juices, and roughly chop the flesh. Put the flesh in a bowl and add the juices, garlic, cumin, lemon juice, vinegar, olive oil, hot pepper seasoning and salt. Mix well to combine. Turn the mixture into a serving bowl and garnish with coriander. Serve with bread, toasted on the barbecue, sesame seed crackers and cucumber slices.

Energy 95kcal/391kJ; Protein 1.3g; Carbohydrate 5g, of which sugars 4.7g; Fat 7.9g, of which saturates 1.2g; Cholesterol 0mg; Calcium 12mg; Fibre 2.5g; Sodium 4mg.

WALNUT BREAD WITH MASHED AUBERGINE

THIS TURKISH DISH OF GRILLED MASHED AUBERGINE WITH CHEESE IS SERVED WITH OLIVES AND TOASTED BREAD. YOU CAN BUY MARINATED OLIVES INSTEAD OF MAKING YOUR OWN, BUT IT'S FUN TO DO IT YOURSELF, BY STEEPING THE OLIVES WITH VARIOUS FLAVOURINGS IN A GOOD QUALITY OIL.

SERVES EIGHT

INGREDIENTS

3 aubergines (eggplants), about
   675g/1½lb total weight, cut
   widthways into 5mm/¼in slices
60ml/4 tbsp finely grated Kefalotiri
   or Kasseri cheese
juice of ½ lemon
1 loaf walnut bread, sliced as thinly
   as possible
extra virgin olive oil, for brushing
salt and ground black pepper

For the marinated olives
175g/6oz/1 cup olives of
   various colours
fennel seeds or dried fennel
   seed heads and ground black
   pepper
fresh hot chillies and rosemary sprigs
lemon slices and fresh thyme sprigs
120ml/4fl oz/½ cup extra virgin
   olive oil

1 To make the marinated olives, divide them among three bowls and add a different flavouring combination to each: try the fennel seeds and pepper with mixed olives, the chillies and rosemary with black olives, and the lemon and thyme with green olives. Divide the oil among the bowls and leave to stand for several hours.

2 Prepare the barbecue. Heat the griddle on the grill rack over hot coals. Brush the aubergine slices with some of the oil from the olives and griddle for 5 minutes, or until soft and branded with griddle marks on both sides. Tip the slices into a small bowl and mash to a rough pulp.

3 While the mixture is still hot, add the finely grated cheese and lemon juice, and stir well to mix these ingredients in thoroughly. Add salt and pepper to taste. Drain most of the oil from the olives and mix it into the pulp. Cover the aubergine mixture and put in a cool place until needed.

4 Brush the bread slices sparingly with oil on one side and toast on the griddle or on an oiled grill rack over the barbecue. Keep an eye on the toast because it just needs to become crisp, not blacken, and the coals are hot at this stage.

5 Serve the toast with small bowls of the aubergine and cheese mixture and the marinated olives.

COOK'S TIP
This dish can also be cooked next to a slow-cooking main course. Get the main course going, then cook the aubergines beside it directly on the grill rack.

Energy 240kcal/1004kJ; Protein 7.5g; Carbohydrate 23.2g, of which sugars 2.5g; Fat 13.5g, of which saturates 3.1g; Cholesterol 7mg; Calcium 94mg; Fibre 5.2g; Sodium 823mg.

CHARGRILLED VEGETABLES WITH PECORINO

AUBERGINES, COURGETTES, PEPPERS AND TOMATOES MAKE A MARVELLOUS MEDLEY WHEN BARBECUED UNTIL THEY ARE SMOKY AND SWEET, THEN DRIZZLED WITH FRAGRANT OLIVE OIL. SHAVINGS OF SHEEP'S MILK PECORINO ADD THE PERFECT FINISHING TOUCH.

SERVES FOUR TO SIX

INGREDIENTS
1 aubergine (eggplant), sliced
2 courgettes (zucchini),
   sliced diagonally
2 (bell) peppers (red or yellow or one
   of each), cored and quartered
1 large onion, thickly sliced
2 large carrots, cut in sticks
4 firm plum tomatoes, halved
extra virgin olive oil
45ml/3 tbsp chopped fresh parsley
45ml/3 tbsp pine nuts,
   lightly toasted
125g/4oz piece of Pecorino cheese
salt and ground black pepper
crusty bread, to serve (optional)

1 Layer the aubergine slices in a colander, sprinkling each layer with a little salt. Leave over a sink or plate for about 20 minutes for any bitter juices to drain away, then rinse thoroughly, drain well and pat dry with kitchen paper. Prepare the barbecue.

2 Spread out the prepared vegetable slices and brush them lightly with olive oil. Lay them on the grill rack of a medium-hot barbecue and cook, turning frequently, until they are lightly browned and the skins on the peppers have begun to blister.

3 Transfer the vegetables to a large serving platter. If you like, remove the skin from the peppers. Season with salt and ground black pepper. As the vegetables cool, sprinkle them with more oil (preferably extra virgin olive oil). When they are cool, mix in the parsley and pine nuts.

4 Using a vegetable peeler, cut thin shavings of Pecorino and scatter the shavings over the vegetables. Serve with crusty bread as an appetizer or as an accompaniment to barbecued meat or fish dishes.

VARIATION
Any hard sheep's milk cheese can be used for the topping. Try Spanish Manchego or British Malvern.

Energy 225kcal/936kJ; Protein 11.7g; Carbohydrate 13.2g, of which sugars 11.9g; Fat 14.3g, of which saturates 4.8g; Cholesterol 19mg; Calcium 288mg; Fibre 4.5g; Sodium 230mg.

CLASSIC QUESADILLAS

THESE CHEESE-FILLED TORTILLAS ARE THE MEXICAN EQUIVALENT OF TOASTED SANDWICHES. SERVE THEM HOT OR THEY WILL BECOME CHEWY. IF YOU ARE MAKING THEM FOR A CROWD, YOU COULD FILL AND FOLD THE TORTILLAS IN ADVANCE THEN ADD THE CHILLI AND COOK THEM TO ORDER.

SERVES EIGHT

INGREDIENTS

400g/14oz mozzarella, Monterey Jack
  or mild Cheddar cheese
2 fresh Fresno chillies (optional)
16 wheat flour tortillas, about
  15cm/6in across
onion relish or tomato salsa, to serve

1 If using mozzarella cheese, drain it thoroughly then pat it dry and slice into thin strips. Monterey Jack and Cheddar cheese should both be coarsely grated, as finely grated cheese will melt and ooze away during cooking. Set the cheese aside in a bowl.

2 Prepare the barbecue. If using fresh chillies, spear them on a long-handled metal skewer and roast them over high heat or directly over a flame until the skin blisters and darkens. Do not let the flesh burn. Place the roasted chillies in a plastic bag and seal tightly or cover them with an upturned bowl. Set aside for 20 minutes for the skins to loosen.

VARIATIONS

Try spreading some salsa on the tortillas before adding the cheese, or add some cooked chicken or prawns (shrimp) before folding the tortillas.

COOK'S TIP

It is best to wear gloves to peel the roasted chillies. It is the membrane attached to the seeds, rather than the flesh, that emits the stinging toxins.

3 Remove the roasted chillies from the bag and carefully peel off the skin. Cut off the stalk, then slit the chillies and scrape out all the seeds. Cut the flesh into 16 even-sized thin strips.

4 Heat the griddle or a frying pan on the grill rack over hot coals. Place one tortilla on the griddle or pan at a time, sprinkle about one sixteenth of the cheese on to one half and add a strip of chilli, if using. Fold the tortilla over the cheese and press the edges together gently to seal. Cook the filled tortilla for 1 minute, then turn over and cook the other side for 1 minute.

5 Remove the filled tortilla from the griddle or pan, cut it into three triangles or four strips and serve immediately while it is still hot, with the onion relish or tomato salsa.

Energy 392kcal/1645kJ; Protein 18.2g; Carbohydrate 44.8g, of which sugars 0.8g; Fat 16.8g, of which saturates 10.4g; Cholesterol 53mg; Calcium 428mg; Fibre 1.8g; Sodium 545mg.

GRIDDLED CHEESE BITES

THESE GRIDDLED CHEESE CUBES WRAPPED IN AROMATIC LEAVES ARE DELICIOUS WITH A COLD RESINOUS WINE, PLENTY OF EXCELLENT OLIVES, FRUITY OLIVE OIL AND RUSTIC BREAD. THEY TAKE ONLY MINUTES TO COOK AND MAKE THE PERFECT PRE-DINNER SNACK FOR A CROWD.

SERVES SIX

INGREDIENTS
18 large bay leaves or mixed bay and
   lemon leaves
275g/10oz Kefalotiri or Kasseri
   cheese, cut into 18 cubes
20ml/4 tsp extra virgin olive oil
ground black pepper

COOK'S TIP
Kefalotiri is a mature ewe's milk cheese with a sharp nutty flavour. It originates from the island of Crete.

1 Soak 18 short wooden skewers in cold water for 30 minutes. Add the bay and/or lemon leaves to the water to prevent them from burning when cooked in the griddle.

2 Put the cheese cubes in a dish large enough to hold the skewers. Pour over the olive oil. Sprinkle over a little pepper and toss well. Drain the skewers, then thread them with the cheese and drained bay leaves and/or lemon leaves. Put the skewers of cheese back in the oil until ready to cook.

3 Prepare the barbecue. Heat the griddle on the grill rack over hot coals. When the griddle is hot, lower the heat a little or move it away from the coals and place the skewers on the griddle, spacing them evenly.

4 Leave the cheese to cook for only about 5 seconds on each side. The cubes of cheese should be hot through and marked with golden-brown lines from the griddle, and should just be starting to melt. Serve immediately on the skewers.

Energy 213kcal/880kJ; Protein 11.8g; Carbohydrate 0g, of which sugars 0g; Fat 18.4g, of which saturates 10.6g; Cholesterol 48mg; Calcium 316mg; Fibre 0g; Sodium 307mg.

CHEESE AND CHILLI POLENTA

POLENTA HAS BECOME AS WIDELY ACCEPTED AS MASHED POTATO AND CAN CONFIDENTLY BE CLASSED AS COMFORT FOOD. HERE IT IS FLAVOURED WITH PASILLA CHILLIES, WHICH HAVE A DRIED FRUIT AND SLIGHT LIQUORICE HINT TO THEM. SERVE IT WITH A TANGY SALSA CALLED PEBRE.

SERVES SIX TO TWELVE

INGREDIENTS
- 10ml/2 tsp crushed dried pasilla chilli flakes
- 1.3 litres/2¼ pints/5⅔ cups water
- 250g/9oz/2¼ cups quick-cook polenta
- 50g/2oz/¼ cup butter
- 75g/3oz Parmesan cheese, finely grated
- 30ml/2 tbsp chopped fresh dill
- 30ml/2 tbsp chopped fresh coriander (cilantro)
- 30ml/2 tbsp olive oil
- salt

For the salsa
- ½ pink onion, finely chopped
- 4 drained bottled sweet cherry peppers, finely chopped
- 1 fresh medium hot red chilli, seeded and finely chopped
- 1 small red (bell) pepper, quartered and seeded
- 10ml/2 tsp raspberry vinegar
- 30ml/2 tbsp olive oil
- 4 tomatoes, halved, cored, seeded and roughly chopped
- 45ml/3 tbsp chopped fresh coriander (cilantro)

1 Chop the chilli flakes finely. Put them in a pan with the water. Bring to the boil and add salt to taste. Pour the polenta into the water in a continuous stream, whisking all the time. Reduce the heat and continue to whisk for a few minutes. When the polenta is thick and bubbling like a volcano, whisk in the butter, Parmesan and herbs.

2 Pour into a greased 33 x 23cm/ 13 x 9in baking tray and leave to cool. Leave uncovered so that the surface firms up, and chill overnight.

3 About an hour before you plan to serve the meal, make the salsa. Place the onion, sweet cherry peppers and chilli in a mortar. Slice the skin from the red pepper quarters. Dice the flesh finely and add it to the mortar with the raspberry vinegar and olive oil.

4 Pound with a pestle for 1 minute, then tip into a serving dish. Stir in the tomatoes and coriander. Cover and chill.

5 Remove the polenta from the refrigerator and leave for about 30 minutes. Cut into 12 even triangles and brush the top with oil.

6 Prepare the barbecue. Heat a griddle on a grill rack over hot coals. Lower the heat to medium and grill the polenta triangles in batches, oiled-side down, for about 2 minutes, then turn through 180 degrees and cook for 1 minute more, to get a striking chequered effect. (Alternatively, you can sear them directly on the oiled grill rack.) Serve the polenta at once, with the chilled salsa.

Energy 181kcal/751kJ; Protein 5g; Carbohydrate 17.3g, of which sugars 2g; Fat 10g, of which saturates 4g; Cholesterol 15mg; Calcium 88mg; Fibre 1.2g; Sodium 98mg.

HERB POLENTA

*GOLDEN POLENTA WITH FRESH SUMMER HERBS MAKES A DELICIOUS
APPETIZER, STARTER OR LIGHT SNACK, ESPECIALLY WHEN SERVED
WITH SWEET, JUICY BARBECUED TOMATOES.*

SERVES FOUR

INGREDIENTS
750ml/1¼ pints/3 cups stock
   or water
5ml/1 tsp salt
175g/6oz/1 cup quick-cook polenta
25g/1oz/2 tbsp butter
75ml/5 tbsp mixed chopped fresh
   parsley, chives and basil, plus extra
   to garnish
olive oil for brushing
4 large plum or beef
   tomatoes, halved
salt and ground black pepper

4 Lightly oil a wide tin or dish and tip
the polenta into it, spreading it out into
an even layer. Leave for several hours,
preferably overnight, until cold and set.
Leave the dish uncovered so that the
surface of the polenta firms up.

1 Prepare the polenta in advance:
place the stock or water in a pan, with
the salt, and bring to the boil. Reduce
the heat and stir in the polenta.

2 Stir constantly over a moderate heat
for 5 minutes, until the polenta begins
to thicken and come away from the
sides of the pan.

5 Turn out the polenta on to a board
and cut it into squares or stamp out
rounds with a large biscuit (cookie)
cutter. Prepare the barbecue.

6 Brush both sides of the polenta with
olive oil. Lightly brush the tomato halves
with olive oil and sprinkle with salt and
black pepper.

7 Cook the tomatoes and polenta on the
grill rack over medium-hot coals for
about 5 minutes, turning once. Serve
garnished with fresh herbs.

3 Remove the pan from the heat and
stir in the butter, chopped herbs and
black pepper.

COOK'S TIPS
• Try using fresh basil or fresh chives
alone, to give the polenta a more
distinctive flavour.
• Polenta makes a great accompaniment
for grilled meat and fish.

*Energy 147kcal/612kJ; Protein 3.2g; Carbohydrate 23.4g, of which sugars 2.1g; Fat 4.2g, of which saturates 1.5g;
Cholesterol 5mg; Calcium 6mg; Fibre 1.3g; Sodium 349mg.*

BRIE PARCELS <u>WITH</u> ALMONDS

MILD FRENCH BRIE WRAPPED IN FRAGRANT VINE LEAVES MELTS TO A SOFT CREAMINESS WHEN COOKED BRIEFLY ON THE BARBECUE. SERVED HOT WITH PLENTY OF CRUSTY FRENCH BREAD TO MOP IT UP, IT MAKES A SOPHISTICATED APPETIZER OR A LIGHT MEAL.

2 Cut the Brie into four evenly-sized chunks and place each chunk in the centre of a vine leaf.

3 Mix together the chopped chives, ground almonds, peppercorns and olive oil, and place a spoonful of the mixture on top of each piece of cheese. Sprinkle with flaked almonds.

4 Fold the vine leaves over tightly to enclose the cheese completely. Brush the parcels with olive oil.

5 Cook the parcels on a grill rack over hot coals for about 3–4 minutes, turning carefully, until the cheese is hot and melting. Serve immediately.

SERVES FOUR

INGREDIENTS
    4 large vine leaves, preserved
      in brine
    200g/7oz piece ripe Brie cheese,
      rind trimmed
    30ml/2 tbsp chopped fresh chives
    30ml/2 tbsp ground almonds
    5ml/1 tsp coarsely crushed
      black peppercorns
    15ml/1 tbsp olive oil
    small handful of flaked
      almonds

1 Rinse the vine leaves thoroughly and dry well. Spread the leaves out on a clean work surface or chopping board.

Energy 275kcal/1139kJ; Protein 13.2g; Carbohydrate 2.2g, of which sugars 1.9g; Fat 22.7g, of which saturates 10g; Cholesterol 47mg; Calcium 187mg; Fibre 1.8g; Sodium 285mg.

SWEET ROMANOS STUFFED
WITH TWO CHEESES AND CHERRY PEPPERS

ROMANOS ARE WONDERFUL MEDITERRANEAN PEPPERS. THEIR SWEETNESS IS NICELY BALANCED BY THE
RICOTTA SALATA, A MATURE DRIED AND SLIGHTLY SALTY VERSION OF THE POPULAR CHEESE.

SERVES FOUR

INGREDIENTS
   4 sweet romano peppers, preferably
     in mixed colours, total weight about
     350g/12oz
   90ml/6 tbsp extra virgin olive oil
   200g/7oz mozzarella cheese
   10 bottled sweet cherry
     peppers, drained and finely
     chopped
   115g/4oz ricotta salata
   30ml/2 tbsp chopped fresh
     oregano leaves
   24 black olives
   2 garlic cloves, crushed
   salt and ground black pepper
   dressed mixed salad leaves and
     bread, to serve

1 Prepare the barbecue. Split the peppers lengthways and remove the seeds and membrane, leaving the stalks in place.

2 Rub 15ml/1 tbsp of the oil all over the peppers. Place them on a flat tray, hollow sides uppermost.

COOK'S TIP
Romano peppers, long, pointed and slighty gnarled, look a little like large poblano chillies. They are exceptionally sweet and well flavoured. However, if they are not available this dish can be made with ordinary bell peppers. Choose red, orange or yellow peppers: green peppers are underripe and less sweet.

3 Slice the mozzarella and divide equally among the pepper halves. Scatter over the chopped cherry peppers, season lightly and crumble the ricotta salata over the top, followed by the oregano leaves and olives. Mix the garlic with the remaining oil and add a little salt and pepper. Spoon about half the mixture over the peppers.

4 Once the flames have died down, rake the coals to one side of the barbecue. Position a lightly oiled grill rack over the coals to heat.

5 When the coals are medium-hot, or with a moderate coating of ash, place the filled peppers on the section of grill rack that is not over the coals. Cover with a lid, wok lid or tented foil.

6 Grill the peppers for about 6 minutes, then spoon the remaining oil mixture over the filling, replace the lid and continue to grill for 6–8 minutes more, or until the peppers are lightly charred and the cheese has melted.

7 Serve the piping hot peppers with a dressed green leafy salad, perhaps of spinach and rocket, and crusty bread.

Energy 95kcal/399kJ; Protein 5.6g; Carbohydrate 12.8g, of which sugars 12g; Fat 2.8g, of which saturates 0.7g; Cholesterol 48mg; Calcium 53mg; Fibre 4.5g; Sodium 301mg.

HERB-STUFFED MINI VEGETABLES

THESE LITTLE HORS D'OEUVRES ARE IDEAL FOR PARTIES AS THEY CAN BE PREPARED IN ADVANCE, AND SIMPLY ASSEMBLED AND COOKED AT THE LAST MINUTE.

MAKES THIRTY

INGREDIENTS
   30 mini vegetables: courgettes
      (zucchini), patty pan squash and
      large button (white) mushrooms
   30ml/2 tbsp olive oil
   fresh basil or parsley, to garnish
For the stuffing
   30ml/2 tbsp olive oil
   1 onion, finely chopped
   1 garlic clove, finely chopped
   115g/4oz button mushrooms,
      finely chopped
   1 courgette, finely chopped
   1 red (bell) pepper, finely chopped
   65g/2½oz/⅓ cup orzo pasta or
      long grain rice
   90ml/6 tbsp/⅓ cup passata
   2.5ml/½ tsp dried thyme
   120ml/4fl oz/½ cup chicken stock
   5–10ml/1–2 tsp chopped fresh basil
      or parsley
   50g/2oz mozzarella or fontina
      cheese, coarsely grated
   salt and ground black pepper

1 To make the stuffing, heat the oil over a medium heat in a frying pan. Add the chopped onion and cook for 2 minutes until tender. Stir in the garlic, mushrooms, courgette and red pepper. Season and cook for 2 minutes until the vegetables soften.

2 Stir in the pasta or rice, the passata, thyme and stock and bring to the boil, stirring. Reduce the heat and simmer for 10–12 minutes until reduced and thickened. Remove from the heat and cool slightly. Stir in the basil or parsley and the cheese.

3 Drop the courgettes and squash into boiling water and cook for 3 minutes. Drain and refresh under cold water. Trim the bottoms so they lie flat, slice off the tops and scoop out the centres with a spoon or melon baller. Remove the stems from the mushrooms. Brush all the vegetables with olive oil.

4 Fill the vegetables with the stuffing and arrange on a rack. Grill over medium-hot coals for 10–15 minutes until the filling is hot and bubbling. Garnish with fresh basil or parsley and serve warm or cool.

Energy 38kcal/158kJ; Protein 2.2g; Carbohydrate 4.1g, of which sugars 2.1g; Fat 1.5g, of which saturates 0.4g; Cholesterol 1mg; Calcium 29mg; Fibre 1g; Sodium 30mg.

TOFU STEAKS

VEGETARIANS AND MEAT-EATERS ALIKE WILL ENJOY THIS BARBECUED TOFU. THE COMBINATION OF INGREDIENTS IN THE SIMPLE MARINADE GIVES THE TENDER STEAKS A DISTINCTLY JAPANESE FLAVOUR.

SERVES FOUR

INGREDIENTS
1 packet fresh firm tofu (10 x 8 x 3cm/4 x 3¼ x 1¼in), 300g/11oz drained weight
2 spring onions (scallions), thinly sliced, to garnish
dressed mixed salad leaves, to serve
For the marinade
45ml/3 tbsp sake
30ml/2 tbsp soy sauce
5ml/1 tsp sesame oil
1 garlic clove, crushed
15ml/1 tbsp grated fresh root ginger
1 spring onion (scallion), chopped

1 Wrap the block of tofu in a clean dish towel or several layers of kitchen paper and place it on a chopping board. Put a large plate or another board on top and leave the tofu for 30 minutes to remove any excess water.

2 Slice the tofu horizontally into three pieces, then cut the slices into quarters. Set aside.

3 Mix the ingredients for the marinade in a large bowl. Add the pieces of tofu to the bowl in a single layer and leave to marinate for 30 minutes while you prepare the barbecue.

4 Drain the tofu steaks and reserve the marinade to use for basting.

5 Grill the steaks for 3 minutes on each side, basting with the marinade, or fry them for 3 minutes in a large pan.

6 Arrange three tofu steaks on each plate. Any remaining marinade can be heated in a pan and then poured over the steaks. Sprinkle with the spring onions and serve immediately with mixed salad leaves.

COOK'S TIP
Firm tofu, from supermarkets and health food stores, is an ideal alternative to meat, particularly for barbecues as it readily absorbs the flavours of marinades and the smokiness of the coals.

Energy 65kcal/270kJ; Protein 6.4g; Carbohydrate 1.1g, of which sugars 0.7g; Fat 3.9g, of which saturates 0.5g; Cholesterol 0mg; Calcium 386mg; Fibre 0.1g; Sodium 271mg.

LITTLE COURGETTE WRAPS

THIS IS A TASTY FIRST COURSE OR VEGETABLE SIDE DISH USING MINI MOZZARELLA BALLS WRAPPED IN SUCCULENT STRIPS OF COURGETTE. SERVE IT WITH STRONGLY FLAVOURED SALAD LEAVES.

SERVES SIX

INGREDIENTS
    2 large yellow courgettes (zucchini),
       about 675g/1½lb total weight
    45ml/3 tbsp olive oil
    250g/9oz baby leaf spinach
    250g/9oz mini mozzarella balls
    salad burnet, rocket (arugula) and
       mizuna leaves, to garnish (optional)
For the dressing
    2 whole, unpeeled garlic cloves
    30ml/2 tbsp white wine vinegar
    30ml/2 tbsp olive oil
    15ml/1 tbsp extra virgin olive oil
    45ml/3 tbsp walnut oil
    salt and ground black pepper

COOK'S TIP
Sweeter than the popular green variety,
yellow courgettes are quite easy to find.

1 To make the dressing, place the garlic in a small pan with water to cover. Bring to the boil, lower the heat and simmer for 5 minutes. Drain. When cool enough to handle, pop the garlic cloves out of their skins and crush to a smooth paste with a little salt. Scrape into a bowl and add the vinegar. Whisk in the oils and season to taste.

2 Slice each courgette lengthways into six or more broad strips, about 3mm/⅛in wide. Lay them on a tray a little apart from each other. Set aside 5ml/1 tsp of the oil and brush the rest over the strips, making sure each one is evenly coated in the oil.

3 Place a wok over a high heat. When it starts to smoke, add the reserved oil and stir-fry the spinach for 30 seconds.

4 When the spinach is just beginning to wilt over the heat, tip it into a sieve (strainer) and drain well, then pat the leaves dry with kitchen paper. Tear or slice the mozzarella balls in half and place on kitchen paper to drain.

5 Prepare the barbecue. Position a lightly oiled grill rack over medium-hot coals. Grill the courgettes on one side only for 2–3 minutes, or until striped golden. As each strip cooks, return it to the tray, grilled-side up.

6 Place small heaps of spinach towards one end of each courgette strip. Lay two pieces of mozzarella on each pile of spinach. Season well.

7 Using a metal spatula, carefully transfer the topped strips, a few at a time, back to the barbecue rack and grill for about 2 minutes, or until the underside of each is striped with golden-brown grill marks.

8 When the cheese starts to melt, fold the plain section of each courgette over the filling to make a wrap. Lift off carefully and drain on kitchen paper. Serve with the garnish of salad leaves, if you like, and drizzle the dressing over.

COOK'S TIP
You need large courgettes measuring about 19cm/7½in, to create good-sized wraps when cut into strips.

Energy 237kcal/977kJ; Protein 11g; Carbohydrate 2.7g, of which sugars 2.5g; Fat 20.2g, of which saturates 7.4g; Cholesterol 24mg; Calcium 250mg; Fibre 1.9g; Sodium 224mg.

GRILLED BABY ARTICHOKES

THIS IS AN ENJOYABLE WAY TO EAT ARTICHOKES. JUST HOLD THE SKEWER WITH THE ARTICHOKE IN
ONE HAND, TEAR OFF A LEAF WITH THE OTHER AND DIP THAT INTO THE HOT MELTED BUTTER.

SERVES SIX

INGREDIENTS
    12 baby artichokes with stalks,
      about 1.3kg/3lb total weight
    1 lemon, halved
    200g/7oz/scant 1 cup butter
    2 garlic cloves, crushed with a pinch
      of salt
    15ml/1 tbsp chopped fresh flat
      leaf parsley
    salt and ground black pepper

1 Soak 12 wooden skewers in cold
water for 30 minutes. Drain, then
skewer a baby artichoke on to each
one. Bring a large pan of salted water
to the boil. Squeeze the juice of one
lemon half, and add it, with the lemon
shell, to the pan.

2 Place the artichokes head first into
the pan and boil for 5–8 minutes, or
until just tender. Drain well. Set aside
for up to 1 hour or use at once.

3 Prepare the barbecue. Put the butter,
garlic and parsley into a small pan and
squeeze in the juice of the remaining
half-lemon.

4 Position a lightly oiled grill rack over
medium hot coals. If the artichokes
have been allowed to cool, wrap the
heads in foil and place them on the grill
for 3 minutes, then unwrap and grill for
1 minute, turning frequently. If they
are still hot, grill without the foil for
4 minutes, turning often.

5 When the artichokes are almost ready,
melt the butter sauce in the pan on the
barbecue. Either transfer the sauce to
six small serving bowls or pour a little
on to each plate. Serve it with the
artichokes on their skewers.

COOK'S TIP
Have plenty of napkins on hand to catch
any stray drops of butter sauce!

Energy 263kcal/1084kJ; Protein 1.4g; Carbohydrate 2.5g, of which sugars 1.2g; Fat 27.7g, of which saturates 17.4g; Cholesterol 71mg; Calcium 49mg; Fibre 1.4g; Sodium 262mg.

HOT AVOCADO HALVES

IF YOU MAKE THE BASIL OIL IN ADVANCE, OR BUY A READY PREPARED BASIL OIL, THIS IS AN ULTRA-SIMPLE DISH THAT CAN BE READY IN A FLASH. IT MAKES AN EYE-CATCHING FIRST COURSE AND IS AN EXCELLENT APPETITE TEASER TO SERVE WHILE THE REST OF THE MEAL IS BARBECUING.

SERVES SIX

INGREDIENTS
3 ready-to-eat avocados, preferably
    Hass for flavour
105ml/7 tbsp balsamic vinegar
For the basil oil
40g/1½oz/1½ cups fresh basil
    leaves, stalks removed
200ml/7fl oz/scant 1 cup olive oil

COOK'S TIPS
• When choosing Hass avocados, watch out for any with marked indentations in their bumpy skin – this indicates that the flesh underneath may be bruised.
• The griddle is ready to use when a few drops of water sprinkled on to the surface evaporate instantly.

1 To make the basil oil, place the leaves in a bowl and pour boiling water over. Leave for 30 seconds. Drain, refresh under cold water and drain again. Squeeze dry and pat with kitchen paper to remove as much moisture as possible.

2 Place in a food processor with the oil and process to a purée. Put into a bowl, cover and chill overnight.

3 Next day, line a sieve (strainer) with muslin (cheesecloth), set it over a deep bowl and pour in the basil purée. Leave undisturbed for 1 hour, or until all the oil has filtered into the bowl. Discard the solids and pour into a bottle, then chill until ready to cook.

4 Prepare the barbecue. Cut each avocado in half and prize out the stone (pit). Brush with a little of the basil oil.

5 Heat the balsamic vinegar gently in a pan, on the stove or on the barbecue. When it starts to boil, simmer for 1 minute, or until it is just beginning to turn slightly syrupy.

6 Heat the griddle on the grill rack over hot coals. Lower the heat a little and place the avocado halves cut-side down on the griddle. Cook for 30–60 seconds until branded with grill marks. (Move the avocados around carefully with tongs to create a chequered effect.) Serve hot with the vinegar and extra oil drizzled over.

Energy 222kcal/916kJ; Protein 1g; Carbohydrate 1g, of which sugars 0.3g; Fat 23.8g, of which saturates 4.1g; Cholesterol 0mg; Calcium 6mg; Fibre 1.7g; Sodium 3mg.

MUSHROOMS WITH GARLIC AND CHILLI SAUCE

WHEN YOU ARE PLANNING A BARBECUE FOR FRIENDS AND FAMILY, IT CAN BE TRICKY FINDING SOMETHING REALLY SPECIAL FOR THE VEGETARIANS IN THE PARTY. THESE TASTY MUSHROOM KEBABS ARE IDEAL BECAUSE THEY LOOK, SMELL AND TASTE WONDERFUL.

SERVES FOUR

INGREDIENTS

   12 large field (portabello), chestnut
   or oyster mushrooms or a mixture,
   cut in half
   4 garlic cloves, coarsely
   chopped
   6 coriander (cilantro) roots,
   coarsely chopped
   15ml/1 tbsp sugar
   30ml/2 tbsp light soy sauce
   ground black pepper
For the dipping sauce
   15ml/1 tbsp sugar
   90ml/6 tbsp rice vinegar
   5ml/1 tsp salt
   1 garlic clove, crushed
   1 small fresh red chilli, seeded
   and finely chopped

1 If using wooden skewers, soak eight of them in cold water for at least 30 minutes to prevent them burning. Prepare the barbecue.

2 Make the dipping sauce by heating the sugar, rice vinegar and salt in a small pan, stirring occasionally until the sugar and salt have dissolved. Add the garlic and chilli, pour into a serving dish and keep warm.

3 Thread three mushroom halves on to each skewer. Lay the filled skewers side by side in a shallow dish.

4 In a mortar or spice grinder pound or blend the garlic and coriander roots. Scrape into a bowl and mix with the sugar, soy sauce and a little pepper.

5 Brush the soy sauce mixture over the mushrooms and leave to marinate for 15 minutes. Cook the mushrooms over medium heat for 5–6 minutes on each side. Serve with the dipping sauce.

BUTTERFLY PRAWNS

THE SUCCESS OF THIS DISH STEMS FROM THE QUALITY OF THE PRAWNS, SO IT IS WORTH GETTING REALLY GOOD ONES, SUCH AS KING PRAWNS, WITH GREAT FLAVOUR AND TEXTURE. A FRUITY, SLIGHTLY SPICY DIP IS A VERY EASY BUT FABULOUS ACCOMPANIMENT.

4 Stir the chilli into the raspberry purée. When the dip is cool, cover and leave in a cool place until ready to serve with the prawns.

5 Butterfly each prawn by making an incision down the curved back, just as you would when deveining. Use a piece of kitchen paper to wipe away the dark spinal vein.

6 Mix the oil with a little sea salt in a bowl. Add the prawns and toss to coat, then thread them on to the drained skewers, spearing them head first.

7 Position a lightly oiled grill rack over the coals to heat. Grill the prawns over high heat for about 5 minutes, depending on size, turning them over once. Serve hot, with the chilli and raspberry dip.

SERVES SIX

INGREDIENTS
    30 raw king prawns (jumbo shrimp), peeled, with heads removed but tails left on
    15ml/1 tbsp sunflower oil
    coarse sea salt
For the chilli and raspberry dip
    30ml/2 tbsp raspberry vinegar
    15ml/1 tbsp sugar
    115g/4oz/⅔ cup raspberries
    1 large fresh red chilli, seeded and finely chopped

1 Prepare the barbecue. Soak 30 wooden skewers in cold water for 30 minutes.

2 Make the dip by mixing the vinegar and sugar in a small pan. Heat gently until the sugar has dissolved, stirring, then add the raspberries.

3 When the raspberry juices start to flow, tip the mixture into a sieve (strainer) set over a bowl. Push the raspberries through the sieve using the back of a ladle. Discard the seeds.

VARIATION
These prawn dippers also taste delicious when served with a vibrant chilli and mango dip. Use one large, ripe mango in place of the raspberries and slice the flesh thinly.

Energy 44kcal/185kJ; Protein 5.6g; Carbohydrate 0.9g, of which sugars 0.9g; Fat 2.1g, of which saturates 0.3g; Cholesterol 59mg; Calcium 29mg; Fibre 0.5g; Sodium 58mg.

FETA-STUFFED SQUID

HERE IS A FABULOUS RECIPE FROM GREECE THAT COMBINES TWO OF THE MOST POPULAR INGREDIENTS FROM THAT COUNTRY: SQUID AND FETA CHEESE. SCENTED WITH MARJORAM AND GARLIC, THE SQUID CONTAINS A CREAMY MARINATED FETA CHEESE FILLING. IT IS SIMPLE TO PREPARE AND QUICK TO COOK.

SERVES FOUR

INGREDIENTS
  4 medium-sized squid, about
    900g/2lb total weight, prepared
  4–8 finger-length slices of
    feta cheese
  lemon wedges, to serve
For the marinade
  90ml/6 tbsp olive oil
  2 garlic cloves, crushed
  3–4 fresh marjoram sprigs, leaves
    removed and chopped
  salt and ground black pepper

COOK'S TIP
Ask your fishmonger to prepare the squid for you, keeping the bodies intact for stuffing. The tentacles and the two side fins will be severed, and you can cook these separately.

1 Rinse the squid thoroughly, inside and out, and drain well. Lay the squid bodies and tentacles in a shallow dish that will hold them in a single layer. Tuck the pieces of cheese between the squid.

2 To make the marinade, pour the oil into a jug (pitcher) or bowl and whisk in the garlic and marjoram. Season to taste with salt and pepper. Pour the marinade over the squid and the cheese, then cover and leave in a cool place to marinate for 2–3 hours, turning once. Soak four wooden skewers in water for 30 minutes.

3 Insert 1 or 2 pieces of cheese and a few pieces of marjoram from the marinade into each squid and thread the tentacles on skewers by piercing at the centre to hold them in place.

4 Prepare the barbecue. Position a lightly oiled grill rack over the hot coals. Grill the stuffed squid over medium heat for about 6 minutes, then turn them over carefully. Grill them for 1–2 minutes more, then add the skewered tentacles. Grill them for 2 minutes on each side, until they start to scorch. Serve the stuffed squid with the tentacles. Add a few lemon wedges, for squeezing over the seafood.

Energy 357kcal/1496kJ; Protein 42.5g; Carbohydrate 3.5g, of which sugars 0.8g; Fat 19.4g, of which saturates 8.5g; Cholesterol 541mg; Calcium 209mg; Fibre 0g; Sodium 968mg.

ICED OYSTERS WITH MERGUEZ SAUSAGES

CHILLI-SPICED MERGUEZ SAUSAGE COMES FROM NORTH AFRICA AND IS POPULAR THROUGHOUT EUROPE. QUELL THE SPICY HEAT WITH THE CLEAN, COOL TEXTURE OF AN ICE-COLD OYSTER. THESE TWO INGREDIENTS MAY SOUND AN UNLIKELY COMBINATION BUT COMPLEMENT EACH OTHER PERFECTLY.

SERVES SIX

INGREDIENTS
675g/1½lb Merguez sausages
crushed ice for serving
24 oysters
2 lemons, cut into wedges

1 Prepare the barbecue. Position a lightly oiled grill rack over the coals to heat. Place the sausages on the grill rack over medium-high heat. Grill them for 8 minutes, or until cooked through and golden, turning often.

2 Meanwhile, spread out the crushed ice on a platter and keep it chilled while you prepare the oysters. Scrub the oyster shells with a stiff brush to remove any sand. Make sure all the oysters are tightly closed, and discard any that aren't.

3 Place them on the grill rack, a few at a time, with the deep-side down, so that as they open the juices will be retained in the lower shell. They will begin to ease open after 3–5 minutes and must be removed from the heat immediately, so that they don't start to cook.

4 Lay the oysters on the ice. When they have all eased open, get to work with a sharp knife, opening them fully if need be. Remove the oysters from the flat side of the shell and place them with the juices on the deep half shells. Discard any oysters that fail to open. Serve with the hot, cooked sausages, and lemon wedges for squeezing.

SIZZLING CHILLI SCALLOPS

SCALLOPS HAVE A BEAUTIFUL RICH FLAVOUR AND TASTE WONDERFUL BARBECUED WITH A SUBTLE CHILLI AND HONEY GLAZE. IF YOU ARE ABLE TO BUY QUEEN SCALLOPS IN THE HALF-SHELL THEY WILL BE READY TO GO ON THE BARBECUE — NOTHING COULD BE SIMPLER FOR A QUICK AND TASTY DISH.

SERVES FOUR TO SIX

INGREDIENTS
  1 fresh fat mild green chilli, seeded
    and finely chopped
  ½–1 fresh Scotch bonnet or
    habañero chilli, seeded and
    finely chopped
  1 small shallot, finely chopped
  15ml/1 tbsp clear honey
  60ml/4 tbsp olive oil
  24 queen scallops on the half shell
  2 lemons, cut into thin wedges
  salt and ground black pepper

1 Prepare the barbecue. While it is heating, mix the chillies, shallot, honey and oil in a bowl.

2 Set out the scallops on a tray. Sprinkle each one with a pinch of salt, then top with a little of the chilli mixture. Position a grill rack over the coals to heat. Place the scallops, on their half shells, on the grill rack over medium-high heat.

3 Cook the scallops for 1½–2 minutes only. If your barbecue has enough space, cook as many as possible at once, moving them from the edge to the centre of the grill rack as necessary. Take care not to overcook them, or they will toughen. Place them on a serving platter, with the lemon wedges for squeezing. Serve immediately.

Energy 133kcal/554kJ; Protein 11.7g; Carbohydrate 3.6g, of which sugars 1.9g; Fat 8g, of which saturates 1.3g; Cholesterol 24mg; Calcium 15mg; Fibre 0g; Sodium 90mg.

GRILLED PRAWNS <u>WITH</u> ROMESCO SAUCE

THIS SAUCE COMES FROM THE CATALAN REGION OF SPAIN AND IS OFTEN SERVED WITH FISH AND SEAFOOD. ITS MAIN INGREDIENTS ARE SWEET PEPPER, TOMATOES, GARLIC AND ALMONDS.

SERVES FOUR

INGREDIENTS
    24 raw king prawns
        (jumbo shrimp)
    30–45ml/2–3 tbsp olive oil
    flat leaf parsley, to garnish
    lemon wedges, to serve
For the sauce
    2 well-flavoured tomatoes
    60ml/4 tbsp olive oil
    1 onion, chopped
    4 garlic cloves, chopped
    1 canned pimiento, chopped
    2.5ml/½ tsp dried chilli flakes
        or powder
    75ml/5 tbsp fish stock
    30ml/2 tbsp white wine
    10 blanched almonds
    15ml/1 tbsp red wine vinegar
    salt

COOK'S TIP
Some versions of this classic sauce include ground toasted hazelnuts as well as almonds. It can also be served with vegetables, meat or pasta.

1 To make the sauce, immerse the tomatoes in boiling water for about 30 seconds, then refresh them under cold running water. Peel away the skins and roughly chop the flesh.

2 Heat 30ml/2 tbsp of the oil. Add the onion and three of the garlic cloves and cook until soft. Add the pimiento, tomatoes, chilli, fish stock and wine. Cover and simmer for 30 minutes.

3 Toast the almonds under the grill until golden. Transfer to a blender or food processor and grind coarsely. Add the remaining 30ml/2 tbsp of oil, the vinegar and the last garlic clove and process until evenly combined. Add the tomato and pimiento sauce and process until smooth. Season with salt.

4 Prepare the barbecue. Remove the heads from the prawns, leaving the rest of the shells in place. With a sharp knife, slit each prawn down the back and wipe away the dark vein with kitchen paper. Rinse the prawns and pat dry on kitchen paper.

5 Toss the prawns in olive oil, then spread them out on the barbecue and cook over a medium heat for about 2–3 minutes on each side, until pink. Serve immediately, garnished with parsley and accompanied by lemon wedges and the romesco sauce.

Energy 265kcal/1097kJ; Protein 12.9g; Carbohydrate 4.7g, of which sugars 3.6g; Fat 21.2g, of which saturates 2.8g; Cholesterol 117mg; Calcium 78mg; Fibre 1.5g; Sodium 120mg.

GRILLED PARSLEY AND PARMESAN MUSSELS

THESE MUSSELS LOOK AS DELICIOUS AS THEY TASTE, AND RELEASE AN IRRESISTIBLE AROMA AS THEY COOK ON THE BARBECUE, SO DON'T BE SURPRISED IF THEY ARE DEVOURED THE MOMENT THEY ARE READY. FRESHLY BAKED BREAD AND A SQUEEZE OF LEMON MAKE IDEAL ACCOMPANIMENTS.

4 Snap the top shell off each mussel, leaving the flesh still attached to the bottom shell.

5 In a large bowl, mix together the melted butter, olive oil, grated Parmesan cheese, chopped parsley, garlic and ground black pepper.

SERVES FOUR

INGREDIENTS
    450g/1lb fresh mussels
    45ml/3 tbsp water
    15ml/1 tbsp melted butter
    15ml/1 tbsp olive oil
    45ml/3 tbsp freshly grated
    Parmesan cheese
    30ml/2 tbsp chopped fresh parsley
    2 garlic cloves, finely chopped
    2.5ml/½ tsp coarsely ground
    black pepper

1 Scrub the mussels, scraping off any barnacles and pulling out the beards. Tap any closed mussels sharply with a knife and discard any that fail to open.

2 Place the mussels with the water in a large pan. Cover with the lid and steam for 5 minutes, or until all of the mussels have opened.

3 Drain the mussels, discarding any that remain closed. (Reserve the stock to give flavour to another fish dish.)

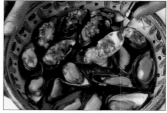

6 Using a spoon, place a small amount of the cheese and herb mixture on top of each mussel.

7 Arrange the mussels in a single layer in a large pan and cook over medium-hot coals for 2–3 minutes or until they are sizzling hot. Serve immediately, with crusty French bread.

Energy 114kcal/477kJ; Protein 10.9g; Carbohydrate 0.7g, of which sugars 0.3g; Fat 7.6g, of which saturates 4.4g; Cholesterol 33mg; Calcium 225mg; Fibre 0.7g; Sodium 220mg.

QUICK SEAFOOD PIZZA

MINI PIZZAS ARE GREAT FOR INFORMAL BARBECUE MEALS IN THE GARDEN, BUT IF YOU PREFER YOU CAN USE THE SAME QUANTITIES OF INGREDIENTS TO MAKE ONE LARGE PIZZA. THE BASES ARE PART-COOKED OVER THE HOT COALS BEFORE THE TOPPING IS ADDED.

SERVES FOUR

INGREDIENTS
For the pizza base
    5ml/1 tsp easy-blend (rapid-rise)
       yeast
    450g/1lb/4 cups strong bread flour
    15ml/1 tbsp sugar
    5ml/1 tsp sea salt
    300ml/½ pint/1¼ cups
       lukewarm water
    30ml/2 tbsp extra virgin olive oil
For the seafood topping
    15ml/1 tbsp olive oil
    1 onion, finely chopped
    800g/1¾lb canned or fresh plum
       tomatoes, chopped
    salt and ground black pepper
    15ml/1 tbsp chopped fresh thyme
    100g/4oz cherry tomatoes
    12 fresh anchovy fillets, or 1 can
       anchovy fillets, drained
    8 fresh, peeled prawns (shrimp)
    a few sprigs of fresh thyme,
       to garnish

3 Knock back the dough and knead for 5 minutes, then cut the dough into four. Shape each of the four pieces of dough into 13cm/5in circles.

4 Fry the onions until soft. Add the canned tomatoes, seasoning and thyme and simmer for 15 minutes.

5 Prepare the barbecue. Brush the pizza bases with oil and cook over medium-hot coals, oiled side down, for 6–8 minutes, until firm and golden.

6 Cut the cherry tomatoes in half. Oil the uncooked side of the pizza bases and turn them over. Assemble each of the pizzas with a spoonful of the sauce, a couple of anchovy fillets and prawns and the cherry tomatoes.

7 Return the pizzas to the barbecue and cook for a further 8–10 minutes until the bases are golden and crispy underneath. Scatter a few fresh sprigs of thyme on top of the pizzas and serve immediately.

1 Stir the easy-blend yeast into the flour in a large bowl. Add the sugar and sea salt and mix together well. Add the water and olive oil to the bowl, and stir to make a firm dough.

2 Knead the dough for about 10 minutes until smooth and elastic. Cover and leave in a warm place until it has doubled in size.

VARIATION
Add your favourite seafood, such as fresh mussels or clams, to the topping.

Energy 538kcal/2275kJ; Protein 19g; Carbohydrate 95.6g, of which sugars 9.5g; Fat 11.5g, of which saturates 1.8g; Cholesterol 54mg; Calcium 224mg; Fibre 6g; Sodium 425mg.

CHARGRILLED SARDINES in VINE LEAVES

THERE IS NOTHING TO BEAT THE AROMA AND TASTE OF SMALL SARDINES WHEN THEY ARE COOKED OVER A CHARCOAL BARBECUE IN THE OPEN AIR, ESPECIALLY IF THEY ARE FRESHLY PLUCKED FROM THE SEA. THE TANGY, CHARRED VINE LEAVES AND TOMATOES MAKE PERFECT PARTNERS FOR THE OILY FLESH OF THE FISH. FRESH MACKEREL AND RED MULLET CAN ALSO BE PREPARED AND COOKED THIS WAY.

SERVES THREE TO FOUR

INGREDIENTS

12 fresh sardines, scaled and gutted,
   heads left on
30ml/2 tbsp olive oil, plus extra
   for brushing
juice of ½ lemon
12 fresh or preserved vine leaves
   (see Cook's Tip)
4–6 vine tomatoes, halved
   or quartered
salt and ground black pepper
lemon wedges, to serve
For the dressing
   60ml/4 tbsp olive oil
   juice of 1 lemon
   15ml/1 tbsp balsamic or
     white wine vinegar
   5–10ml/1–2 tsp clear honey
   5ml/1 tsp hot paprika or 1 fresh red
     chilli, finely chopped
   a few fresh dill fronds and flat leaf
     parsley sprigs, finely chopped

1 Put all the dressing ingredients in a bowl, season with salt and pepper and mix well.

2 Wash the sardines thoroughly inside and out under cold running water. Pat them dry with kitchen paper.

COOK'S TIP
Fresh vine leaves are sold in Middle Eastern and Mediterranean stores when they are in season in the autumn. Plunged into boiling water for a minute, the bright green leaves soften and turn a deep olive colour, and are ready for use. If you can't get fresh vine leaves, you can use packaged leaves preserved in brine. They require soaking in water before use to remove the salt. Place them in a bowl, pour boiling water over them and leave to soak for about an hour. Drain and rinse under cold running water, then pat dry.

3 Get the barbecue ready for cooking. Meanwhile, lay the sardines in a flat dish. Mix 30ml/2 tbsp oil with the lemon juice and brush over the sardines.

4 Spread the vine leaves out on a flat surface and place a sardine on each leaf. Sprinkle each one with a little salt and wrap loosely in the leaf like a cigar, with the tail and head poking out.

5 Brush each leaf with a little oil and place the parcels on a grill rack seam side down to keep them from unravelling. Thread the pieces of tomato on skewers and sprinkle them with a little salt.

6 Cook the sardines and tomatoes on the barbecue for 2–3 minutes on each side, until the vine leaves are charred and the tomatoes are soft.

7 Transfer the sardines and tomatoes to a serving dish and drizzle the vine leaf parcels with the dressing. Serve immediately, with lemon wedges for squeezing over.

Energy 214kcal/893kJ; Protein 23.4g; Carbohydrate 0.2g, of which sugars 0.2g; Fat 13.2g, of which saturates 3.2g; Cholesterol 0mg; Calcium 131mg; Fibre 0.4g; Sodium 130mg.

CHARGRILLED TUNA SLICES

For this Japanese dish use sashimi-quality tuna from a Japanese food store or first-rate fishmonger, and ask for the piece of fish to be trimmed to a neat rectangular shape. Serve it with aromatic Japanese shiso leaves, chewy arame and crunchy mooli, which offer interesting contrasts of flavour, texture and colour.

SERVES FOUR

INGREDIENTS

- 15g/½oz dried arame seaweed, soaked in water
- 60ml/4 tbsp tamari
- 30ml/2 tbsp mirin
- 120ml/4fl oz/½ cup water
- 5ml/1 tsp white sesame seeds
- 15ml/1 tbsp black sesame seeds
- 10ml/2 tsp dried pink peppercorns
- 2.5ml/½ tsp sunflower oil
- 250g/9oz sashimi tuna
- 16 fresh shiso leaves
- 7.5ml/1½ tsp wasabi paste
- 50g/2oz mooli (daikon), finely grated

1 Drain the arame, then soak it in a bowl with the tamari, mirin and water for 1 hour. Pour the liquid from the arame into a small pan and put the arame in a serving bowl.

2 Bring the liquid to a simmer. Cook for 3–5 minutes, or until syrupy, cool for 2 minutes and pour over the arame. Scatter with the white sesame seeds and cover until needed.

3 Prepare the barbecue. Lightly grind the black sesame seeds and pink peppercorns in a spice mill. Brush the oil over the tuna, then roll the tuna into the spice mixture to coat it evenly.

4 Heat a griddle on a grill rack over hot coals. Sear the tuna for 30 seconds on each of the four sides. Using a very sharp knife, slice it into 5mm/¼in wide pieces and arrange on plates with the shiso leaves, a blob of wasabi and a mound each of arame and grated mooli.

Energy 96kcal/404kJ; Protein 15.3g; Carbohydrate 1.3g, of which sugars 1.2g; Fat 3.3g, of which saturates 0.8g; Cholesterol 18mg; Calcium 18mg; Fibre 0.2g; Sodium 743mg.

HOT TROUT WITH RED VEGETABLES

ROAST THE VEGETABLES IN ADVANCE FOR THIS FLAVOURSOME AND BRIGHTLY COLOURED MEDITERRANEAN-STYLE SANDWICH, AND THEN HAVE EVERYTHING READY TO ASSEMBLE WHEN THE TROUT IS COOKED.

SERVES FOUR

INGREDIENTS
  2 red (bell) peppers
  8 cherry tomatoes
  60ml/4 tbsp extra virgin olive oil
  30ml/2 tbsp lemon juice
  4 thin trout fillets, each about
    115g/4oz, skinned
  2 small ciabatta rolls
  15ml/1 tbsp red pesto
  30ml/2 tbsp mayonnaise
  115g/4oz rocket (arugula)
  salt and ground black pepper

1 Preheat the oven to 180°C/350°F/Gas 4. Place the whole peppers with the cherry tomatoes in a roasting pan and drizzle half the olive oil over.

2 Bake for 25–30 minutes or until the vegetables are soft and the pepper skins are blackened. Set aside to cool.

3 In a small bowl or jug (pitcher), whisk the remaining olive oil with the lemon juice and a little salt and ground black pepper. Place the trout in a shallow, non-metallic dish and pour over the oil and lemon juice. Turn the fish to make sure the fillets are thoroughly coated.

4 Peel the skin off the cooked peppers and discard the core and seeds. Cut the pepper flesh into strips.

5 Slice each ciabatta bread in half vertically, then cut each half in half horizontally. Mix the pesto and mayonnaise together.

6 Prepare the barbecue. Heat a griddle on the grill rack over hot coals. Lift the trout fillets carefully out of the marinade and grill them for 1–2 minutes, without adding any additional oil, until the fish is just cooked.

7 Spread the pesto and mayonnaise mixture over the bread. Divide the rocket among four halves of the bread and top with the trout, pepper strips and roasted tomatoes. Place the remaining bread on top and serve immediately.

COOK'S TIPS
• You can use any bread you like for the sandwiches, but make sure you slice it thickly.
• Small loaves of olive-oil bread, such as ciabatta and focaccia, are ideal for these sandwiches. Try the sun-dried tomato and black olive versions, to add extra flavour.
• This recipe would be delicious using smoked fish fillets as a filling for the sandwiches. Try smoking trout or salmon fillets over the barbecue using aromatic wood chips – you can follow the technique for hot smoked salmon that appears in the Fish and Shellfish chapter.
• If you can't find any red pesto, use 30ml/2 tbsp chopped fresh basil mixed with 15ml/1 tbsp sun-dried tomato paste.

Energy 538kcal/2253kJ; Protein 32.6g; Carbohydrate 46.7g, of which sugars 9.8g; Fat 25.7g, of which saturates 3.8g; Cholesterol 9mg; Calcium 206mg; Fibre 4.2g; Sodium 588mg.

SALMON WITH SPICY PESTO

THIS IS A GREAT WAY TO BONE SALMON STEAKS TO GIVE A SOLID PIECE OF FISH. THE PESTO USES SUNFLOWER KERNELS AND CHILLI AS ITS FLAVOURING, RATHER THAN THE CLASSIC BASIL AND PINE NUTS.

SERVES FOUR

INGREDIENTS
    4 salmon steaks, about
        225g/8oz each
    30ml/2 tbsp sunflower oil
    finely grated rind and juice of
        1 lime
    salt and ground black pepper
For the pesto
    6 mild fresh red chillies
    2 garlic cloves
    30ml/2 tbsp sunflower or
        pumpkin seeds
    juice and finely grated rind of
        1 lime
    75ml/5 tbsp olive oil

1 Insert a very sharp knife close to the top of the central bone in the salmon steak. Working close to the bone, cut your way to the end of the steak to release one side. Repeat with the other side. Pull out any additional visible bones with a pair of tweezers.

2 Sprinkle a little salt on the work surface and take hold of the end of the salmon piece, skin-side down. Insert the knife between the skin and the flesh and, working away from you, remove the skin, keeping the knife as close to it as possible. Repeat the process for each piece of fish.

COOK'S TIP
Sprinkling salt on the work surface helps to stop pieces of fish slipping when you are skinning them. Wipe off any salt that adheres to the flesh before cooking.

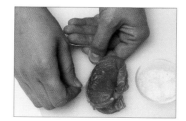

3 Curl each piece of fish into a round, with the thinner end wrapped around the fatter end. Secure the shape tightly with a length of string.

4 Rub the sunflower oil into the boneless fish rounds. Put the salmon into a large bowl or dish and add the lime juice and rind and the salt and pepper. Allow the salmon to marinate in the fridge for up to 2 hours.

5 For the pesto, de-seed the chillies and place with the garlic cloves, sunflower or pumpkin seeds, lime juice, rind and seasoning in a food processor. Process until well mixed. Pour the olive oil gradually over the moving blades until the sauce has thickened and emulsified. Drain the salmon from its marinade. Cook the fish steaks on a medium barbecue for 5 minutes each side and serve with the spicy pesto.

Energy 653kcal/2719kJ; Protein 50.5g; Carbohydrate 1.4g, of which sugars 0.1g; Fat 49.6g, of which saturates 7.5g; Cholesterol 122mg; Calcium 60mg; Fibre 0.5g; Sodium 111mg.

GRILLED CHICKEN BALLS

THESE TASTY JAPANESE CHICKEN BALLS, KNOWN AS TSUKUNE, ARE POPULAR WITH CHILDREN AS WELL AS ADULTS. YOU CAN MAKE THE BALLS IN ADVANCE UP TO THE END OF STEP 2, AND THEY FREEZE WELL. THEY MAKE AN UNUSUAL AND DELICIOUS ADDITION TO A BARBECUED MEAL.

SERVES FOUR

INGREDIENTS
  300g/11oz skinless chicken,
    minced (ground)
  2 eggs
  2.5ml/½ tsp salt
  10ml/2 tsp plain (all-purpose) flour
  10ml/2 tsp cornflour (cornstarch)
  90ml/6 tbsp dried breadcrumbs
  2.5cm/1in piece of fresh root
    ginger, grated
For the yakitori sauce
  60ml/4 tbsp sake
  75ml/5 tbsp shoyu
  15ml/1 tbsp mirin
  15ml/1 tbsp caster (superfine) sugar
  2.5ml/½ tsp cornflour (cornstarch)
    blended with 5ml/1 tsp water
  shichimi togarashi or sansho
    (optional), to serve

1 Soak eight bamboo skewers for 30 minutes in water. Put all the ingredients for the chicken balls, except the ginger, in a food processor and blend well.

2 Wet your hands and scoop about a tablespoonful of the mixture into your palm. Shape it into a small ball about half the size of a golf ball. Make a further 30–32 balls in the same way.

3 Squeeze the juice from the grated ginger into a small mixing bowl. Discard the pulp.

4 Add the ginger juice to a small pan of boiling water. Add the chicken balls, and boil for about 7 minutes, or until the colour of the meat changes and the balls float to the surface. Scoop out using a slotted spoon and drain on a plate covered with kitchen paper.

5 In a small pan, mix all the ingredients for the yakitori sauce, except for the cornflour liquid. Bring to the boil, then reduce the heat and simmer for about 10 minutes, or until the sauce has slightly reduced. Add the cornflour liquid and stir until the sauce is thick. Transfer to a small bowl.

6 Prepare the barbecue. Position a lightly oiled grill rack over the hot coals. Thread three to four balls on each skewer and turn over the heat for a few minutes until the balls start to brown. Brush with sauce and return to the heat. Repeat the process twice. Serve, sprinkled with shichimi togarashi or sansho, if you like.

COOK'S TIP
Sansho is a Japanese spice made by grinding the black seeds of pricky ash berries. It is an important ingredient in the seven-spice blend shichimi togarashi, which may also contain ground chilli, sesame seeds, seaweed and citrus peel. Shichimi togarashi can be made at home but is also available ready-made.

Energy 263kcal/1111kJ; Protein 24.1g; Carbohydrate 25.9g, of which sugars 4.8g; Fat 4.1g, of which saturates 1g; Cholesterol 148mg; Calcium 54mg; Fibre 0.6g; Sodium 520mg.

MINI CHICKEN FILLETS

THIS DISH IS SERVED WITH AJI AMARILLO, A YELLOWY ORANGE PERUVIAN CHILLI, WHICH IS VERY FRUITY AND QUITE HOT. IT IS A GOOD IDEA TO PREPARE THE MARMALADE THE DAY BEFORE SO THAT THE FLAVOURS CAN MELLOW AND BLEND. IT IS PERFECT WITH THESE GARLICKY CHICKEN FILLETS.

SERVES FOUR

INGREDIENTS
    500g/1¼lb mini chicken breast
    fillets or skinless chicken breast
    fillets, each cut into 4 long strips
    2 garlic cloves, crushed to a paste
    with 2.5ml/½ tsp salt
    30ml/2 tbsp olive oil
    ground black pepper
For the aji amarillo marmalade
    50g/2oz dried aji
    amarillo chillies
    120ml/4fl oz/½ cup water
    20ml/4 tsp olive oil
    2 onions, finely chopped
    3 garlic cloves, crushed
    5ml/1 tsp ground cumin
    10ml/2 tsp Mexican oregano
    130g/4½oz/scant ¾ cup sugar
    200ml/7fl oz/scant 1 cup cider or
    white wine vinegar
    2 small orange (bell) peppers,
    quartered and seeded

1 To make the aji amarillo marmalade, heat a heavy frying pan, add the dried chillies and roast them by stirring them continuously over the heat for about 1½ minutes without letting them scorch.

2 Put them in a bowl with just enough almost-boiling water to cover. Use a saucer to keep them submerged and leave to rehydrate for about 2 hours, or longer if you prefer.

3 Slit the chillies, remove the seeds and chop the flesh into small dice. Place in a blender, add the water and process to a purée.

4 Heat the oil in a heavy pan, add the onions and garlic and cook over a gentle heat for 5 minutes. Add the cumin, Mexican oregano and the chilli purée. Add the sugar and stir until turning syrupy, then add the vinegar and stir well. Bring the mixture to the boil, then lower the heat and simmer for 30 minutes.

5 Meanwhile, heat a griddle on the stove. Roast the peppers, skin-side down, until the skins char, then put the peppers under an upturned bowl. When they are cool enough to handle, rub off the skin and finely dice the flesh. Add to the chilli mixture and continue to simmer for about 25 minutes, or until the marmalade thickens. Transfer to a bowl. When cool, cover and chill for 30 minutes before serving.

COOK'S TIP
The aji amarillo marmalade will keep, chilled, for a week. It is also good eaten with hot smoked salmon.

6 Spread out the chicken pieces in a shallow dish and add the garlic, oil and pepper. Turn the fillets in the mixture, cover and set aside in a cool place for 30–45 minutes, turning occasionally.

7 Prepare the barbecue and position a lightly oiled grill rack over the coals to heat. Grill the chicken pieces over medium-high heat for 2½–3 minutes on each side, or until cooked through and branded with grill marks. Using tongs, carefully move the food about while cooking to avoid over-charring. Transfer to a platter, cover and leave in a warm place for 5 minutes before serving with the marmalade.

Energy 401kcal/1689kJ; Protein 32.2g; Carbohydrate 47.5g, of which sugars 44.9g; Fat 10.4g, of which saturates 1.7g; Cholesterol 88mg; Calcium 56mg; Fibre 2.8g; Sodium 84mg.

TANDOORI CHICKEN STICKS

THESE TENDER CHICKEN PIECES ARE TRADITIONALLY BAKED IN THE SPECIAL CLAY OVEN KNOWN AS A TANDOOR BUT COOK BEAUTIFULLY OVER HOT COALS, PERFUMING THE AIR WITH GLORIOUS SPICY AROMAS. THEY ARE EQUALLY DELICIOUS HOT OR COLD, AND MAKE IRRESISTIBLE APPETIZERS.

MAKES ABOUT TWENTY-FIVE

INGREDIENTS
   450g/1lb skinless
     chicken breast fillets
For the coriander yogurt
   250ml/8fl oz/1 cup natural
     (plain) yogurt
   30ml/2 tbsp whipping cream
   ½ cucumber, peeled, seeded and
     finely chopped
   15–30ml/1–2 tbsp fresh chopped
     coriander (cilantro) or mint
   salt and ground black pepper
For the marinade
   175ml/6fl oz/¾ cup natural yogurt
   5ml/1 tsp garam masala or
     curry powder
   1.5ml/¼ tsp ground cumin
   1.5ml/¼ tsp ground coriander
   1.5ml/¼ tsp cayenne pepper
     (or to taste)
   5ml/1 tsp tomato purée (paste)
   1–2 garlic cloves, finely chopped
   2.5cm/1in piece fresh root ginger,
     finely chopped
   grated zest and juice of ½ lemon
   15–30ml/1–2 tbsp fresh chopped
     coriander or mint

1 For the coriander yogurt, combine all the ingredients in a bowl. Season, cover and chill until ready to serve.

2 To prepare the marinade, place all the ingredients in a food processor and process until smooth. Pour into a shallow dish.

3 Freeze the chicken breast fillets for 5 minutes to firm them and make them easier to cut, then slice in half horizontally. Cut the slices into 2cm/¾in strips and add to the marinade. Toss to coat well. Cover with clear film (plastic wrap) and leave for 6–8 hours or overnight in the refrigerator.

4 Drain the chicken pieces and arrange on a rack, scrunching up the chicken slightly to make wavy shapes. Cook on a hot barbecue for 4–5 minutes until brown and cooked through, turning once. Alternatively, arrange on a foil-lined baking sheet and cook under a hot grill (broiler). Serve hot, threaded on cocktail sticks (toothpicks) or short skewers, with the yogurt dip.

COOK'S TIP
This chicken is also very good eaten cold, and makes great picnic food. Cool it after cooking and pack in a box.

Energy 32kcal/134kJ; Protein 5g; Carbohydrate 1.1g, of which sugars 0.8g; Fat 0.9g, of which saturates 0.4g; Cholesterol 14mg; Calcium 29mg; Fibre 0.2g; Sodium 23mg.

CHICKEN SATAY STICKS

PANDANUS LEAVES ARE COMMON TO THAI AND SOUTH-EAST ASIAN COOKING, AND ARE SOMETIMES ALSO KNOWN AS SCREWPINE OR BANDAN LEAVES. THEY ARE ENORMOUSLY VERSATILE, AND ARE USED HERE FOR THE DELICATE FLAVOUR THEY BRING TO THE CHICKEN, AS WELL AS THEIR VISUAL APPEAL.

SERVES SIX

INGREDIENTS
    about 1kg/2¼lb skinless chicken
      breast fillets
    30ml/2 tbsp olive oil
    5ml/1 tsp ground coriander
    2.5ml/½ tsp ground cumin
    2.5cm/1in piece of fresh root ginger,
      finely grated
    2 garlic cloves, crushed
    5ml/1 tsp caster (superfine) sugar
    2.5ml/½ tsp salt
    18 long pandanus leaves, each
      halved to give 21cm/8½in lengths
For the hot cashew nut sambal
    2 garlic cloves, roughly chopped
    4 small fresh hot green chillies
      (not tiny birdseye chillies), seeded
      and sliced
    50g/2oz/⅓ cup cashew nuts
    10ml/2 tsp sugar, preferably
      palm sugar
    75ml/5 tbsp light soy sauce
    juice of ½ lime
    30ml/2 tbsp coconut cream

1 To make the sambal, place the garlic and chillies in a mortar and grind them quite finely with a pestle. Add the nuts and continue to grind until the mixture is almost smooth, with just a bit of texture. Pound in the remaining ingredients, cover and leave in a cool place until needed.

2 Soak 36 long bamboo or wooden skewers in water for 30 minutes. Slice the chicken horizontally into thin pieces and then into strips about 2.5cm/1in wide. Toss in the oil. Mix the coriander, cumin, ginger, garlic, sugar and salt together. Rub this mixture into the strips of chicken. Leave to marinate while you prepare the barbecue.

3 Thread a strip of pandanus leaf and a piece of chicken lengthways on to each skewer. Once the flames have died down, rake the coals to one side. Position a lightly oiled grill rack over the coals to heat.

4 Place the satays meat-side down over the coals and cover with a lid or some tented heavy-duty foil and cook for 5–7 minutes. Once the meat has seared, move the satays around so that they are not cooking directly over the coals. This will avoid the leaves becoming scorched. Serve hot with the sambal.

COOK'S TIP
The easiest way to make the sambal is to use a deep Thai mortar. The resulting mixture will have a satisfying crunch rather than being a smooth purée.

Energy 280kcal/1178kJ; Protein 42.3g; Carbohydrate 5.9g, of which sugars 4.6g; Fat 9.8g, of which saturates 1.9g; Cholesterol 117mg; Calcium 19mg; Fibre 0.5g; Sodium 1026mg.

SPICY CHICKEN WINGS

THESE DELICIOUSLY STICKY BITES WILL APPEAL TO ADULTS AND CHILDREN ALIKE, ALTHOUGH YOUNGER EATERS MIGHT PREFER A LITTLE LESS CHILLI.

SERVES FOUR

INGREDIENTS
    8 plump chicken wings
    2 large garlic cloves, cut into slivers
    15ml/1 tbsp olive oil
    15ml/1 tbsp paprika
    5ml/1 tsp chilli powder
    5ml/1 tsp dried oregano
    salt and ground black pepper
    lime wedges, to serve

COOK'S TIP
This spice mixture can also be used to flavour strips of skinless, chicken breast, fillet brushed with oil.

1 Using a small sharp kitchen knife, make one or two cuts in the skin of each chicken wing and slide a sliver of garlic under the skin. Brush the wings generously with the olive oil.

2 In a large bowl, stir together the paprika, chilli powder and oregano and season with plenty of salt and pepper. Add the chicken wings and toss together until very lightly coated in the mixture. Leave in a cool place for the flavours to infuse while you prepare the barbecue.

3 Once the flames have died down, position a lightly oiled grill rack over the coals to heat. Cook the chicken wings over medium heat for 15 minutes until they are cooked through, with a blackened, crispy skin. Serve with fresh lime wedges to squeeze over.

Energy 350kcal/1455kJ; Protein 30.7g; Carbohydrate 2.6g, of which sugars 2.6g; Fat 24.1g, of which saturates 5.9g; Cholesterol 134mg; Calcium 11mg; Fibre 0.1g; Sodium 99mg.

CHICKEN WINGS TERIYAKI STYLE

THIS ORIENTAL GLAZE IS VERY SIMPLE TO PREPARE AND ADDS A UNIQUE FLAVOUR TO THE MEAT.
THE GLAZE CAN BE USED WITH ANY CUT OF CHICKEN OR WITH FISH.

SERVES FOUR

INGREDIENTS
  1 garlic clove, crushed
  45ml/3 tbsp soy sauce
  30ml/2 tbsp dry sherry
  10ml/2 tsp clear honey
  10ml/2 tsp grated fresh root ginger
  5ml/1 tsp sesame oil
  12 chicken wings
  15ml/1 tbsp sesame seeds, toasted

3 Cook the chicken wings on a fairly hot barbecue for about 20–25 minutes, turning occasionally and basting with the remaining marinade.

4 Sprinkle the chicken wings with sesame seeds. Serve the wings on their own or as a side dish, or with a crisp green salad.

1 Place the garlic, soy sauce, sherry, honey, grated ginger and sesame oil in a bowl large enough to hold all the chicken and beat with a fork, to mix the ingredients together evenly.

2 Add the chicken wings and toss them in the marinade, turning them carefully so they are thoroughly coated. Cover the bowl with clear film (plastic wrap) and chill for about 30 minutes, or longer. Meanwhile, prepare the barbecue.

COOK'S TIP
Teriyaki-style cooking involves the use of sweet marinades that give the finished dish a glossy, caramelized coating.

Energy 393kcal/1641kJ; Protein 30.5g; Carbohydrate 14.4g, of which sugars 14.4g; Fat 24.1g, of which saturates 6.3g; Cholesterol 134mg; Calcium 16mg; Fibre 0g; Sodium 91mg.

GRILLED FOIE GRAS

THE RICH FLAVOUR AND LUXURIOUS TEXTURE OF THE FOIE GRAS, SPEEDILY SEARED ON A HOT GRIDDLE, IS TEAMED HERE WITH A SHARP, TANGY JAPANESE SAUCE, PONZU JOYU. THE CARAMELIZED FLAVOUR OF THE ASIAN PEAR BALANCES THE DISH PERFECTLY.

SERVES FOUR

INGREDIENTS
  2 Asian (nashi) pears, each cut into
    eight wedges
  15ml/1 tbsp clear honey mixed
    with 45ml/3 tbsp water
  225g/8oz duck or goose foie gras,
    chilled and cut into eight
    1cm/½in slices
For the ponzu joyu
  45ml/3 tbsp mirin
  120ml/4fl oz/½ cup tamari
  75ml/5 tbsp dried bonito flakes
  45ml/3 tbsp rice vinegar
  juice of 1 large lemon
  4 strips dried kombu seaweed

1 To make the ponzu joyu, place the mirin in a small pan, bring to the boil and cook for about 30 seconds.

2 Pour into a small bowl and add all the remaining ingredients. Cool, then cover and chill for 24 hours. Strain into a screw-topped jar and chill until needed.

COOK'S TIP
You will find the ingredients for the ponzu joyu sauce in a Japanese supermarket. Bonito flakes are the dried shavings or flakes of Pacific bonito (a kind of small tuna). They are used to add flavour and are always strained out once their flavour has been absorbed. They are often used to season Japanese-style salads and vegetable dishes.

3 Toss the pear wedges in the honey mixture. Heat a griddle on the grill rack over hot coals. Griddle the pear wedges for about 30 seconds on each cut side. Wipe the pan with kitchen paper and heat again. When it is searing hot, grill the foie gras for 30 seconds on each side. Serve immediately with the ponzu joyu and pear wedges.

ASPARAGUS <u>WITH</u> CRISPY PROSCIUTTO

A MARVELLOUS COMBINATION OF INTENSELY FLAVOURED ASPARAGUS SPEARS AND CRISPLY COOKED ITALIAN HAM, THIS DISH MAKES A SIMPLE YET DELICIOUS APPETIZER. SERVE IT WITH CHUNKS OF ITALIAN BREAD, SUCH AS CIABATTA OR FOCACCIA.

SERVES FOUR

INGREDIENTS
    350g/12oz fine asparagus
      spears, trimmed
    30ml/2 tbsp olive oil
    1 small handful fresh basil leaves
    4 prosciutto slices
    salt and ground black pepper

COOK'S TIPS
• Choose tender, fine asparagus for this recipe, as it cooks through quickly without losing its flavour or texture.
• For the best flavour, get the prosciutto sliced for you at a delicatessen or at the cold meat counter of a supermarket. The ham needs to be cut thinly. If you buy more than you need, remember that it will dry out quite quickly – only keep for a few days in the refrigerator.

1 Put the asparagus in a shallow dish and drizzle with olive oil.

2 Sprinkle over the basil leaves and season with salt and ground black pepper. Gently stir to coat the asparagus in the seasoned oil.

3 Prepare the barbecue and when the flames die down heat a griddle on the grill rack over hot coals.

4 Lay the slices of prosciutto on top of the asparagus and barbecue for about 5 minutes, or until the prosciutto is crisp and the asparagus is just tender.

VARIATION
Instead of barbecuing, steam the asparagus, drizzle with an olive oil and balsamic dressing and serve warm with cold prosciutto.

Energy 82kcal/339kJ; Protein 4.4g; Carbohydrate 1.9g, of which sugars 1.8g; Fat 6.4g, of which saturates 1g; Cholesterol 6mg; Calcium 24mg; Fibre 1.5g; Sodium 121mg.

PORK ON LEMON GRASS STICKS

THIS SIMPLE RECIPE MAKES A SUBSTANTIAL APPETIZER, AND THE LEMON GRASS STICKS NOT ONLY ADD
A SUBTLE FLAVOUR BUT ALSO LOOK MOST ATTRACTIVE. YOU'LL FIND IT IS USUALLY MORE ECONOMICAL
TO BUY LEMON GRASS FROM ASIAN MARKETS OR STORES THAN FROM YOUR LOCAL SUPERMARKET.

SERVES FOUR

INGREDIENTS
    300g/11oz minced (ground) pork
    4 garlic cloves, crushed
    4 fresh coriander (cilantro) roots,
      finely chopped
    2.5ml/½ tsp sugar
    15ml/1 tbsp soy sauce
    8 x 10cm/4in lengths of lemon
      grass stalk
    salt and ground black pepper
    sweet chilli sauce, to serve

VARIATION
Slimmer versions of these pork sticks are
perfect for parties. The mixture will be
enough for 12 lemon grass sticks if you
use it sparingly.

1 Place the minced pork, crushed garlic,
chopped coriander root, sugar and soy
sauce in a large bowl. Season with salt
and pepper to taste, and mix well.

2 Divide into eight portions and mould
each one into a ball. It may help to
dampen your hands before shaping the
mixture to prevent it from sticking.

3 Stick a length of lemon grass halfway
into each ball, then press the meat
mixture around it.

4 Prepare the barbecue. Position a lightly
oiled grill rack over the hot coals. Cook
the pork sticks for 3–4 minutes on each
side, until golden and cooked through.
Serve with the chilli sauce for dipping.

Energy 97kcal/409kJ; Protein 16.6g; Carbohydrate 0.7g, of which sugars 0.6g; Fat 3.2g, of which saturates 1.1g; Cholesterol 47mg; Calcium 31mg; Fibre 0.6g; Sodium 324mg.

SKEWERED WILD BOAR ᵂᴵᵀᴴ GINGER SAUCE

MEAT THAT IS PARTICULARLY POPULAR IN ITALY, BREAD FROM GREECE AND A DIPPING SAUCE FROM CHINA COME TOGETHER IN THIS DISH. IT IS A GOOD EXAMPLE OF FUSION COOKING, BRINGING TOGETHER CHARACTERISTIC FLAVOURS AND METHODS FROM THREE COUNTRIES.

<u>SERVES FOUR</u>

INGREDIENTS
    450g/1lb lean wild boar
    15ml/1 tbsp clear honey
    50g/2oz/¼ cup butter
    15ml/1 tbsp dark soy sauce
For the dipping sauce
    2.5cm/1in piece fresh
      root ginger, peeled and
      finely chopped
    30ml/2 tbsp sesame oil
    60ml/4 tbsp hoisin sauce
To serve
    4 pitta breads
    shredded iceberg lettuce

1 Soak four bamboo skewers in warm water for about 30 minutes to help prevent them burning. Cut the wild boar into small, even-size cubes and thread the cubes on to the drained skewers. Prepare the barbecue.

2 Melt the honey and butter with the soy sauce in a small pan, and brush liberally over the skewered meat. Cook on a lightly oiled rack over medium-hot coals for about 12 minutes, turning frequently and brushing with glaze.

3 Meanwhile, cook the ginger in the sesame oil in a small pan for a few minutes. Stir in the hoisin sauce. Remove from the heat.

4 Warm the pitta breads. Split them, then smear a little of the sauce over the inside of each pitta and add some lettuce. Serve with the wild boar skewers and the remaining sauce.

Energy 259kcal/1079kJ; Protein 24.5g; Carbohydrate 6.5g, of which sugars 6.3g; Fat 15.1g, of which saturates 5.6g; Cholesterol 84mg; Calcium 12mg; Fibre 0.1g; Sodium 540mg.

SKEWERED LAMB WITH RED ONION SALSA

A SIMPLE SALSA MAKES A REFRESHING ACCOMPANIMENT TO THIS SUMMERY DISH — USE A MILD-FLAVOURED RED ONION THAT IS FRESH AND CRISP, AND A TOMATO THAT IS RIPE AND JUICY.

SERVES FOUR

INGREDIENTS

225g/8oz lean lamb, cubed
2.5ml/½ tsp ground cumin
5ml/1 tsp ground paprika
15ml/1 tbsp olive oil
salt and ground black pepper
For the salsa
1 red onion, very thinly sliced
1 large tomato, seeded and chopped
15ml/1 tbsp red wine vinegar
3–4 fresh basil or mint leaves,
  roughly torn
small mint leaves, to garnish

1 Place the lamb in a large bowl with the cumin, paprika and olive oil and season with plenty of salt and ground black pepper. Toss well. Cover the bowl with clear film (plastic wrap) and leave in a cool place for several hours, or in the refrigerator overnight, so that the lamb absorbs the flavours.

COOK'S TIP
Cubed lean lamb is widely available from supermarkets. Otherwise buy a piece of lamb fillet or leg steak and trim off any fat before cutting it up.

2 Spear the lamb cubes on four small skewers. If using wooden skewers, soak them first in cold water for at least 30 minutes to prevent them burning when placed on the barbecue.

3 To make the salsa, put the sliced onion, tomato, red wine vinegar and torn fresh basil or mint leaves in a small bowl and stir together until thoroughly blended. Season to taste with salt and garnish with mint.

4 Cook the skewered lamb on a hot barbecue, or under a hot grill (broiler), for about 5–10 minutes, turning the skewers frequently, until the lamb is well browned but still slightly pink in the centre. Serve hot, with the salsa.

Energy 294kcal/1224kJ; Protein 25.4g; Carbohydrate 3.3g, of which sugars 1.6g; Fat 20.1g, of which saturates 7.4g; Cholesterol 95mg; Calcium 22mg; Fibre 0.5g; Sodium 112mg.

STUFFED KIBBEH

KIBBEH IS A TASTY MIDDLE EASTERN SPECIALITY OF MINCED LAMB AND BULGUR WHEAT, WHICH CAN BE EATEN RAW OR SHAPED INTO PATTIES AND BARBECUED OR FRIED.

SERVES FOUR TO SIX

INGREDIENTS
    450g/1lb lean lamb
    45ml/3 tbsp olive oil
    avocado slices and fresh coriander
        (cilantro) sprigs, to serve
For the kibbeh
    225g/8oz/1⅓ cups bulgur wheat
    1 red chilli, seeded and
        roughly chopped
    1 onion, roughly chopped
    salt and ground black pepper
For the stuffing
    1 onion, finely chopped
    50g/2oz/⅔ cup pine nuts
    30ml/2 tbsp olive oil
    7.5ml/1½ tsp ground allspice
    60ml/4 tbsp chopped fresh coriander

1 Roughly cut the lamb into chunks, using a heavy kitchen knife. Process the chunks in a blender or food processor until finely minced (ground). Divide the minced meat into two equal portions and set aside until needed.

2 To make the kibbeh, soak the bulgur wheat for 15 minutes in cold water. Drain well, then process in the blender or food processor with the chopped chilli and onion, half the meat and plenty of salt and pepper.

3 To make the stuffing, fry the onion and pine nuts in the olive oil for 5 minutes. Add the allspice and remaining minced meat and fry gently, breaking up the meat with a wooden spoon, until browned. Stir in the coriander and a little seasoning.

4 Turn the kibbeh mixture out on to a clean work surface and use your hands to shape the mixture into a cake. Divide the cake into 12 wedges.

5 Flatten one wedge in the palm of your hand and spoon a little stuffing into the centre. Bring the edges of the kibbeh over the stuffing to enclose it. Mould into a firm egg-shaped cake between the palms of your hands, ensuring that the filling is completely encased. Repeat with the other kibbeh.

6 To barbecue the kibbeh, lightly brush with olive oil and cook on a medium barbecue for 10–15 minutes, turning carefully, until evenly browned and cooked through. To fry the kibbeh, heat oil to a depth of 5cm/2in in a large pan until a few kibbeh crumbs sizzle on the surface. Lower half the kibbeh into the oil and fry for about 5 minutes until golden. Drain on kitchen paper and keep hot while frying the remainder. Serve hot with avocado slices and fresh coriander sprigs.

Energy 452kcal/1883kJ; Protein 29.7g; Carbohydrate 22.8g, of which sugars 11.5g; Fat 27.7g, of which saturates 9.7g; Cholesterol 93mg; Calcium 230mg; Fibre 1.1g; Sodium 178mg.

SPICY MEATBALLS

THESE MEATBALLS ARE FIERY AND DELICIOUS. HOT SAUCE ON THE SIDE MEANS GUESTS CAN ADD AS MUCH HEAT AS THEY LIKE.

SERVES SIX

INGREDIENTS
115g/4oz fresh spicy sausages
115g/4oz minced (ground) beef
2 shallots, finely chopped
2 garlic cloves, finely chopped
75g/3oz/1½ cups fresh
  white breadcrumbs
1 egg, beaten
30ml/2 tbsp chopped fresh parsley,
  plus extra to garnish
15ml/1 tbsp olive oil
salt and ground black pepper
Tabasco or other hot chilli sauce,
  to serve

3 Prepare the barbecue and once the flames have died down place a lightly oiled rack over the coals. Brush the meatballs with olive oil and cook over medium heat for about 10–15 minutes, turning regularly until evenly browned and cooked through. Alternatively, fry the meatballs in a large pan.

1 Remove the skins from the spicy sausages, then place the sausagemeat in a mixing bowl and break it up gently with a fork.

4 Transfer the meatballs to a warm dish and sprinkle with chopped fresh parsley. Serve with chilli sauce.

2 Add the minced beef, shallots, garlic, breadcrumbs, beaten egg and parsley to the bowl, and season with plenty of salt and black pepper. Stir well with a wooden spoon until everything is well blended, then wet your hands and use them to shape the mixture into 18 small balls.

VARIATION
Use minced (ground) pork instead of the beef, flavoured with fresh sage.

Energy 213kcal/881kJ; Protein 13.2g; Carbohydrate 3.4g, of which sugars 2.6g; Fat 16.3g, of which saturates 5.1g; Cholesterol 41mg; Calcium 23mg; Fibre 0.5g; Sodium 180mg.

MINI BURGERS WITH MOZZARELLA

THESE ITALIAN-STYLE PATTIES ARE MADE WITH BEEF AND TOPPED WITH CREAMY MELTED MOZZARELLA AND SAVOURY ANCHOVIES. THEY MAKE A SUBSTANTIAL AND UNUSUAL APPETIZER.

SERVES SIX

INGREDIENTS
  ½ slice white bread, crusts removed
  45ml/3 tbsp milk
  675g/1½lb minced (ground) beef
  1 egg, beaten
  50g/2oz/⅔ cup dry breadcrumbs
  olive oil, for brushing
  2 beefsteak or other large tomatoes,
    sliced
  15ml/1 tbsp chopped fresh oregano
  1 mozzarella, cut into 6 slices
  6 drained, canned anchovy fillets,
    cut in half lengthways
  salt and ground black pepper

1 Put the bread and milk into a small pan and heat gently, until the bread absorbs all the milk. Mash and leave to cool.

2 Put the minced beef into a bowl and add the cooled bread mix. Stir in the beaten egg and season with plenty of salt and ground black pepper. Stir the mixture well.

3 Shape the mixture into six patties, using your hands. Sprinkle the dry breadcrumbs on to a plate and dredge the patties, coating them thoroughly all over.

4 Prepare the barbecue. Position a lightly oiled grill rack over the hot coals. Brush the patties with olive oil and cook them on the hot barbecue for 2–3 minutes on one side, or until brown. Turn them over.

5 Without removing the patties from the barbecue, lay a slice of tomato on the top, cooked side of each patty. Sprinkle the tomato slices with chopped oregano and season with salt and pepper. Place a slice of mozzarella on top of each one and arrange two strips of anchovy in a cross over the cheese.

6 Continue to cook for a further 4–5 minutes, or until the patties are cooked through and the mozzarella has melted. Serve immediately.

Energy 360kcal/1499kJ; Protein 28.6g; Carbohydrate 9.6g, of which sugars 2.2g; Fat 23.2g, of which saturates 10.9g; Cholesterol 82mg; Calcium 121mg; Fibre 0.7g; Sodium 374mg.

SIRLOIN STEAK BITES

INSTEAD OF A COMPLEX MARINADE, THIS KOREAN RECIPE RELIES ON THE TASTE OF HIGH QUALITY SIRLOIN STEAK. KNEADING THE MEAT WITH SALT MAKES IT DELICIOUSLY TENDER.

SERVES FOUR

INGREDIENTS
    450g/1lb beef sirloin
    2 round (butterhead) lettuces
For the marinade
    8 garlic cloves, chopped
    75g/3oz oyster mushrooms, sliced
    3 spring onions (scallions),
      finely chopped
    20ml/4 tsp mirin or rice wine
    10ml/2 tsp salt
    ground black pepper
For the spring onion mixture
    8 shredded spring onions
    20ml/4 tsp rice vinegar
    20ml/4 tsp Korean chilli powder
    10ml/2 tsp sugar
    10ml/2 tsp sesame oil

1 Slice the beef into bitesize strips and place in a bowl. Add the garlic, mushrooms and spring onions. Pour in the mirin or rice wine and add the salt and several twists of black pepper.

2 Mix together, evenly coating the beef. Knead the meat well to tenderize it. Chill, and leave for at least 2 hours.

3 Mix the spring onion ingredients together. Remove the outer leaves from the lettuce and rinse well. Prepare the barbecue.

COOK'S TIP
In Korea this dish would be accompanied by a bowl of thin *doenjang* soup, based on fermented soya bean paste.

4 Place a griddle on the barbecue over medium heat, and add the marinated beef. Cook gently until the meat has darkened, and then remove.

5 Serve by wrapping the meat in a lettuce leaf, and to garnish and complete, add a pinch of the seasoned shredded spring onion mixture.

Energy 188kcal/786kJ; Protein 27.6g; Carbohydrate 4g, of which sugars 3.9g; Fat 6.9g, of which saturates 2.6g; Cholesterol 57mg; Calcium 26mg; Fibre 0.9g; Sodium 83mg.

FISH AND SHELLFISH

Fresh seafood tastes great when it is barbecued, and there are
so many ways that fish and shellfish can be prepared. Wrap
them in leaves or steam inside foil parcels, cut them into
chunks and skewer, stuff them or simply brush with oil or a
fresh marinade and cook straight on the barbecue. Some of the
fastest foods to cook over coals are shellfish, so they are perfect
for an impromptu meal. Small whole fish are also an ideal
choice for a quick bite to eat, but if you have a little more
time, try some of the rewarding recipes that include sauces or
relishes. Many dishes require marinating a little way in
advance, and such simple preparations and techniques will
transform barbecued seafood. The delicious cooking aromas
wafting from the grill will tempt the tastebuds of any
party guest. If you are planning to eat on the beach, there
is even a Seafood Bake where you can cook locally caught
shellfish without using a conventional barbecue.

CLAMS AND MUSSELS IN BANANA LEAVES

THESE PRETTY RAFFIA-TIED PARCELS CAN EITHER BE COOKED AS SOON AS THEY ARE READY OR CHILLED FOR UP TO 30 MINUTES, OFFERING A MOMENT'S RESPITE BEFORE THE COOKING BEGINS. BANANA LEAVES MAKE NEAT LITTLE PARCELS BUT YOU COULD ALSO USE DOUBLE FOIL.

3 Top a sheet of foil with a piece of banana leaf, placing it smooth-side up. Place another piece of leaf on top, at right angles, so that the leaves form a cross. Don't worry if the leaves are slightly wet – it's more important to work quickly with the leaves at this stage, while they remain soft and pliable.

4 Pile one-sixth of the seafood mixture into the centre, then bring up the leaves and tie them into a money-bag shape, using the raffia. Do the same with the foil, scrunching slightly to seal the top. Make the remaining parcels in the same way, then chill the parcels until needed.

5 Prepare the barbecue. Position a lightly oiled grill rack over the coals to heat. Cook the parcels over medium-high heat for about 15 minutes. Carefully remove the outer layer of foil from each and put the parcels back on the grill rack for 1 minute.

6 Transfer to individual plates. The parcels retain heat for a while, so can be left to stand for up to 5 minutes. Untie the raffia and eat from the leaves. Serve with bread sticks, if you wish.

COOK'S TIP
Have a quick peek into all of the bags to make sure the shells have opened before serving. Discard any shellfish that haven't opened.

SERVES SIX

INGREDIENTS
15ml/1 tbsp olive oil
1 large onion, finely chopped
2 garlic cloves, crushed
1.5ml/¼ tsp saffron threads
60ml/4 tbsp Noilly Prat or other
   dry vermouth
30ml/2 tbsp water
30ml/2 tbsp chopped fresh flat
   leaf parsley
500g/1¼lb clams, scrubbed
900g/2lb mussels, cleaned
6 banana leaves
salt and ground black pepper
raffia, for tying
bread sticks, for serving

1 Heat the oil in a pan and add the chopped onion and garlic with the saffron threads. Cook over a gentle heat for 4 minutes. Add the vermouth and water, increase the heat and simmer for 2 minutes. Stir in the parsley, with salt and pepper to taste. Transfer to a bowl and leave to cool completely.

2 Tap the clam and mussel shells and discard any that stay open. Stir them into the bowl containing the onion mixture. Trim the hard edge from each banana leaf. Cut the leaves in half lengthways. Soak them in hot water for 10 minutes, then drain. Wipe any white residue from the leaves. Rinse, then pour over boiling water to soften.

Energy 116kcal/488kJ; Protein 14g; Carbohydrate 6.2g, of which sugars 4g; Fat 3.1g, of which saturates 0.5g; Cholesterol 40mg; Calcium 131mg; Fibre 0.9g; Sodium 498mg.

GIANT PRAWNS WRAPPED IN LIME LEAVES

THESE HUGE PRAWNS CAN GROW UP TO 33CM/13IN IN LENGTH, AND ARE PERFECT FOR GRILLING ON A BARBECUE. THIS DISH IS FAST AND EASY, YET IMPRESSIVE; IDEAL FOR A RELAXED POOLSIDE LUNCH WITH SALAD OR FOR SERVING AS AN APPETIZER WHILE THE MAIN COURSE IS COOKING.

SERVES SIX

INGREDIENTS
6 giant Mediterranean prawns
  (extra large jumbo shrimp),
  total weight about 900g/2lb
juice of 2 limes
60ml/4 tbsp olive oil
12 large kaffir lime leaves
12 pandanus leaves
2 limes cut into wedges, to serve

VARIATION
Serve these with an easy dip made by mixing 150ml/¼ pint/⅔ cup mayonnaise and 20ml/4 tsp Thai sweet chilli sauce.

1 Soak six wooden cocktail sticks (toothpicks) in water for 30 minutes. Make a shallow cut down the curved back of each prawn.

2 Put the giant prawns into a shallow dish, large enough to avoid cramming them on top of each other. In a separate bowl, mix the lime juice and oil together and pour over the prawns. Set aside for 15 minutes to allow the flavour to soak in.

3 Take each marinated prawn, lay two kaffir lime leaves on top, wrap two pandanus leaves around it and skewer with a cocktail stick.

4 Prepare the barbecue. Position a lightly oiled grill rack over the coals to heat. When the coals are medium-hot, grill the wrapped prawns for 3 minutes on each side. Serve with lime wedges. Unwrap the prawns, peel off the shell and remove the black vein with your fingers before eating.

COOK'S TIP
Many barbecue meals are hands-on affairs, so a few finger bowls are often useful. You can scent the water with citrus slices, herbs and flower essences, such as rose. Float fresh petals on top for a decorative touch, if you like.

Energy 122kcal/512kJ; Protein 12.9g; Carbohydrate 0.1g, of which sugars 0.1g; Fat 7.8g, of which saturates 1.2g; Cholesterol 158mg; Calcium 65mg; Fibre 0g; Sodium 900mg.

Seafood on Sugar Cane

Tolee molee is a Burmese term for the bits and pieces that go with a dish, such as herbs, crispy fried onions and the chilli and prawn paste called balachaung. If you prefer, spike the prawns on skewers rather than sugar cane.

MAKES TWELVE

INGREDIENTS

400g/14oz king prawns (jumbo shrimp), peeled
225g/8oz skinned cod or halibut fillet, roughly cut into pieces
pinch of ground turmeric
1.5ml/¼ tsp ground white pepper
1.5ml/¼ tsp salt
60ml/4 tbsp chopped fresh coriander (cilantro)
1 fresh long red chilli, seeded and finely chopped
a piece of sugar cane cut into 12 spikes (see Cook's Tip) or 12 wooden skewers
30ml/2 tbsp sunflower oil
For the tolee molee
25g/1oz/1 cup coriander (cilantro) leaves
45ml/3 tbsp olive oil
300g/11oz sweet onions, halved and finely sliced
90ml/6 tbsp balachaung
15ml/1 tbsp sugar
juice of ½ lime
30ml/2 tbsp water

1 Soak the sugar cane spikes or skewers in water for 30 minutes. Make a shallow cut down the centre of the curved back of the prawns. Pull out the black veins with a cocktail stick (toothpick). Slice the prawns roughly and place in a food processor with the fish, turmeric, pepper and salt.

2 Pulse until the mixture forms a paste. Add the coriander and chilli, and pulse lightly to combine with the other ingredients. Spoon into a bowl and chill for 30 minutes.

3 To make the tolee molee, place the coriander leaves in a small serving bowl filled with cold water. Chill. Heat the olive oil in a large frying pan and fry the sliced onions over a medium heat for 10 minutes, stirring occasionally and increasing the heat for the last few minutes so that the onions become golden and crisp.

4 Pile the cooked onions into a serving bowl. Place the balachaung in another serving bowl, and mix in the sugar, lime juice and measured water. Stir the mixture thoroughly and set aside.

5 Using damp hands, mould the seafood mixture around the drained sugarcane spikes or wooden skewers, so that it forms an oval sausage shape.

6 Prepare the barbecue. Position a lightly oiled grill rack over the hot coals. Brush the seafood with the sunflower oil and grill over medium-high heat for about 3 minutes on each side until just cooked through. Serve with the tolee molee.

COOK'S TIP
To make sugar cane spikes, chop through the length using a cook's knife and split into 1cm/½in shards. The sugar cane can be bought from ethnic grocers.

Energy 98kcal/410kJ; Protein 9.9g; Carbohydrate 3.5g, of which sugars 2.9g; Fat 5.1g, of which saturates 0.7g; Cholesterol 74mg; Calcium 52mg; Fibre 0.8g; Sodium 78mg.

SPICED PRAWNS <u>WITH</u> VEGETABLES

*THIS IS A LIGHT AND NUTRITIOUS INDIAN DISH, EXCELLENT SERVED EITHER ON A BED OF LETTUCE
LEAVES, OR WITH PLAIN BOILED RICE OR CHAPPATIS.*

SERVES FOUR

INGREDIENTS

    20 cooked king prawns (jumbo
      shrimp), peeled
    1 medium courgette (zucchini)
    1 medium onion
    8 cherry tomatoes
    8 baby corn cobs
    mixed salad leaves, to serve
For the marinade
    30ml/2 tbsp chopped fresh
      coriander (cilantro)
    5ml/1 tsp salt
    2 fresh green chillies
    45ml/3 tbsp lemon juice
    30ml/2 tbsp vegetable oil

1 To make the marinade, blend the
coriander, salt, chillies, lemon juice and
oil together in a food processor.
(Remove the seeds from the chillies
before processing if you prefer a milder
flavour for the marinade.)

2 Empty the contents from the
processor and transfer to a bowl.

3 Add the peeled king prawns to the
mixture in the bowl and stir to make
sure that all the prawns are well coated.
Cover the bowl with clear film (plastic
wrap) and set aside, in a cool place, to
marinate for about 30 minutes.

4 Prepare the barbecue. Thickly slice
the courgette and cut the onion into
eight chunks. Arrange the vegetables
and prawns alternately on four long
skewers. Cook over medium-hot coals
for 5 minutes, turning frequently, until
the ingredients are cooked and
browned. Serve immediately, on a
bed of mixed salad leaves.

Energy 121kcal/502kJ; Protein 12.9g; Carbohydrate 3.1g, of which sugars 2.6g; Fat 6.4g, of which saturates 0.8g; Cholesterol 122mg; Calcium 93mg; Fibre 1.6g; Sodium 759mg.

CALAMARI WITH TWO-TOMATO STUFFING

CALAMARI, OR BABY SQUID, ARE QUICK TO COOK, BUT DO TURN AND BASTE THESE LITTLE DELICACIES OFTEN TO AVOID OVERCOOKING THEM, WHICH MAY SPOIL THE DELICATE FLAVOUR.

SERVES FOUR

INGREDIENTS

500g/1¼ lb baby squid, prepared
   and cleaned
1 garlic clove, crushed
3 plum tomatoes, skinned
   and chopped
8 sun-dried tomatoes in oil, drained
   and chopped
60ml/4 tbsp chopped fresh basil,
   plus extra, to serve
60ml/4 tbsp fresh white breadcrumbs
45ml/3 tbsp olive oil
15ml/1 tbsp red wine vinegar
salt and ground black pepper
lemon juice, to serve

1 Remove the tentacles from the squid and roughly chop them; leave the main part of the squid whole.

2 Mix together the crushed garlic, plum tomatoes, sun-dried tomatoes, chopped fresh basil and breadcrumbs. Stir in 15ml/1 tbsp of the olive oil and the vinegar. Season well with plenty of salt and ground black pepper.

3 Soak some wooden cocktail sticks (toothpicks) in water for 10 minutes before use, to prevent them burning on the barbecue.

COOK'S TIP
Baby squid are widely available ready prepared, but it is advisable to feel inside each sac before stuffing to make sure that the transparent quill has been completely removed.

4 Using a teaspoon, fill the squid with the stuffing mixture. Secure the open end of each sac by pinning the layers with a cocktail stick to hold the stuffing mixture in place.

5 Brush the squid with the remaining olive oil and cook over a medium-hot barbecue for 4–5 minutes, turning often. Sprinkle with lemon juice and extra chopped fresh basil to serve.

Energy 335kcal/1414kJ; Protein 39.1g; Carbohydrate 15.9g, of which sugars 3.8g; Fat 11.5g, of which saturates 2.2g; Cholesterol 555mg; Calcium 87mg; Fibre 1.8g; Sodium 432mg.

SEAFOOD BAKE

A BEACH BAKE IS GREAT FUN AND A SEMI-PRECISE SCIENCE, WHICH REQUIRES COMMITMENT BY AT LEAST TWO HIGHLY MOTIVATED PARTIES WITH A PENCHANT FOR DIGGING HOLES. BASE YOUR CATCH ON THE INGREDIENTS BELOW, MULTIPLIED AS REQUIRED.

FOR EACH PERSON

INGREDIENTS
    2 freshwater crayfish
    4 langoustines
    2 large clams, about 6cm/2½in
      across
    6 small clams
    3 whelks
    12 cockles
    lemons, bread and good quality
      olive oil
Other things you will need
    sand or earth
    shovels and buckets
    dry pebbles
    newspaper and dry twigs
      for kindling
    plenty of dry firewood
    matches or a lighter
    long-handled rake
    seaweed, well washed and soaked
      in water
    a large piece of canvas, soaked
      in water
    12 heavy stones
    heatproof gloves
    cocktail sticks (toothpicks)

1 Dig a pit at least 90cm/3ft square x 30cm/1ft deep; you will need to make it larger if you are catering for a crowd. Line the pit with large, dry pebbles, taking them right across the base and part of the way up the sides. Build a pyramid-shaped mound of kindling in the middle of the square, placing some scrunched-up newspaper at the base with which to light the fire.

2 Start the fire. When the wood is burning well, add larger pieces to the fire so that it eventually covers the entire surface area of the pit. Keep the fire well stoked up for about 45–60 minutes, then let it burn down to a stage where small glowing embers remain. Using a long-handled rake, pull as many of the dying embers as possible from the pit without dislodging the pebbles.

3 At this point it is important to retain the oven-like temperature of the pebbles so, working quickly, spread half the seaweed evenly over the pebbles. Arrange the seafood over the seaweed, with the smallest items towards the edges for easy access, as these will cook first. Cover with the rest of the seaweed, then cover the lot with the wet canvas. This should extend beyond the perimeter of the pit and should be weighted down with 12 heavy stones, placed well away from the pit.

4 Leave the seafood to bake undisturbed for 1–2 hours. The hotter the pebbles, the faster the food will cook, so after 1 hour, have a sneaky peek to see if the cockles and small clams are cooked. These can be taken out at this stage and eaten, and the rest of the seafood enjoyed when it is ready.

COOK'S TIP
Before leaving the site, take care to douse any discarded embers with water to ensure they are not left hot.

Energy 175kcal/742kJ; Protein 38.9g; Carbohydrate 0.9g, of which sugars 0g; Fat 1.8g, of which saturates 0.4g; Cholesterol 268mg; Calcium 164mg; Fibre 0g; Sodium 1139mg.

MARINATED OCTOPUS ᴼⁿ STICKS

OCTOPUS THAT IS FROZEN AND THEN THAWED BECOMES TENDER IN THE PROCESS, AND SO IT COOKS QUICKLY. CHECK WITH THE FISHMONGER BEFORE BUYING, BECAUSE FRESH OCTOPUS WILL NEED CONSIDERABLY MORE SIMMERING TIME. SERVE WITH RED PIPIAN FOR A SPICY PUNCH.

SERVES EIGHT

INGREDIENTS
1kg/2¼lb whole octopus
1 onion, quartered
2 bay leaves
30ml/2 tbsp olive oil
grated rind and juice of 1 lemon
15ml/1 tbsp chopped fresh coriander
   (cilantro)
For the red pipian
1 ancho chilli (dried poblano)
4 whole garlic cloves, peeled
1 small pink onion, chopped
500g/1¼lb plum tomatoes, cored
   and seeded
30ml/2 tbsp olive oil
5ml/1 tsp sugar
30ml/2 tbsp pine nuts
30ml/2 tbsp pumpkin seeds
pinch of ground cinnamon
15ml/1 tbsp chipotles in adobo
   or other sweet and smoky
   chilli sauce
45ml/3 tbsp vegetable stock
leaves from 4 large fresh thyme
   sprigs, finely chopped
salt
fresh coriander (cilantro) sprigs,
   to garnish

1 Make the red pipian. Preheat the oven to 200°C/400°F/Gas 6. Put the ancho chilli in a bowl and cover with hot water. Leave to soak for about 20 minutes.

2 Place the garlic, onion and tomatoes in a roasting pan and drizzle with the olive oil, then sprinkle the sugar and a little salt over the top. Roast for 15 minutes. Add the pine nuts, pumpkin seeds and cinnamon to the top of the mixture and roast for a further 5 minutes. Meanwhile, drain the ancho chilli, remove the seeds and chop the flesh.

3 Transfer the roasted mixture and the ancho chilli to a food processor with the chipotles or chilli sauce, vegetable stock and thyme. Pulse the mixture to a purée, then scrape into a serving bowl and leave to cool.

COOK'S TIP
Cook the skewered octopus on a griddle, if you prefer. The timing will be the same.

4 Trim the tentacles from the head of the octopus. Leave the skin on, but trim any large flaps with kitchen scissors. Discard the head. Place the tentacles in a large pan, cover with cold water and add the onion and bay leaves. Bring slowly to the boil, lower the heat and simmer for about 20 minutes if pre-frozen, and up to 2 hours if fresh.

5 Drain the tentacles and rinse under cold water, rubbing off any loose dark membrane. Thread the tentacles on to eight metal skewers and put in a plastic bag with the olive oil, lemon rind and juice, and chopped coriander. Tie shut and shake to mix. Leave to marinate in a cool place for at least 1 hour or up to 12 hours.

6 Prepare the barbecue. When the flames have died down, position a lightly oiled grill rack over the hot coals. Grill the octopus skewers on the rack over medium-high heat for 2–4 minutes each side, or until nicely golden. Serve the octopus accompanied by the red pipian and garnished with sprigs of fresh coriander.

SEAFOOD AND SPRING ONION SKEWERS

MONKFISH IS A FINE FISH FOR BARBECUING, AS ITS FIRM FLESH HOLDS ITS SHAPE WELL AND IS EASY TO SPEAR ON TO SKEWERS. IT HAS A LOVELY SWEET FLAVOUR, VERY SIMILAR TO SHELLFISH, AND HERE IT IS PARTNERED WITH SCALLOPS OR KING PRAWNS, MAKING AN ATTRACTIVE AND DELICIOUS COMBINATION.

MAKES NINE

INGREDIENTS
    675g/1½lb monkfish, filleted,
      skinned and membrane removed
    1 bunch thick spring onions
      (scallions), cut into 5cm/2in pieces
    75ml/5 tbsp olive oil
    1 garlic clove, finely chopped
    15ml/1 tbsp lemon juice
    5ml/1 tsp dried oregano
    30ml/2 tbsp chopped fresh flat
      leaf parsley
    12–18 small scallops or raw king
      prawns (jumbo shrimp)
    75g/3oz/1½ cups fine fresh
      breadcrumbs
  salt and ground black pepper
For the tartare sauce
    2 egg yolks
    300ml/½ pint/1¼ cups olive oil,
      or vegetable oil and olive oil mixed
    15–30ml/1–2 tbsp lemon juice
    5ml/1 tsp French mustard, preferably
      tarragon mustard
    15ml/1 tbsp chopped gherkin or
      pickled cucumber
    15ml/1 tbsp chopped capers
    30ml/2 tbsp chopped fresh flat
      leaf parsley
    30ml/2 tbsp chopped fresh chives
    5ml/1 tsp chopped fresh tarragon

1 Soak nine wooden skewers in water for 30 minutes to prevent them from scorching on the barbecue.

2 To make the tartare sauce, whisk the egg yolks and a pinch of salt. Whisk in the oil, adding just one drop at a time at first. When about half the oil has been incorporated, add the rest in a thin stream, whisking constantly. Stop when the mayonnaise is thick.

3 Whisk in 15ml/1 tbsp lemon juice, then a little more oil. Stir in the mustard, chopped gherkin or cucumber, capers, parsley, chives and tarragon. Add more lemon juice and seasoning to taste.

4 Cut the monkfish into 18 pieces. In a bowl, mix the oil, garlic, lemon juice, oregano and half the parsley with seasoning. Add the seafood and spring onions. Leave to marinate for 15 minutes.

5 Mix the breadcrumbs and remaining parsley together. Toss the seafood and spring onions in the mixture to coat.

6 Prepare the barbecue. Position a lightly oiled grill rack over the hot coals. Drain the wooden skewers and thread the monkfish, scallops or prawns and spring onions on to them. Drizzle with a little marinade then cook over medium heat for 7–8 minutes in total, turning once and drizzling with the marinade, until the fish is just cooked. Serve immediately with the tartare sauce.

Energy 352kcal/1462kJ; Protein 16.6g; Carbohydrate 6.9g, of which sugars 0.6g; Fat 28.9g, of which saturates 4.3g; Cholesterol 88mg; Calcium 41mg; Fibre 0.4g; Sodium 111mg.

WHOLE STUFFED SQUID

Fresh squid tastes wonderful when it is barbecued, and the squid body is perfect for a rich walnut stuffing. The tentacles are particularly tasty, so be sure to skewer them and cook them as well.

SERVES SIX

INGREDIENTS

- 12 whole small squid, total weight about 675g/1½lb
- 45ml/3 tbsp extra virgin olive oil, plus extra for coating
- 2 onions, finely chopped
- 3 garlic cloves, crushed
- 25g/1oz/2 tbsp walnuts, finely chopped
- 7.5ml/1½ tsp ground sumac or a squeeze of lemon juice
- 1.5ml/¼ tsp chilli flakes, finely chopped
- 75–90g/3–3½oz rocket (arugula), any tough stalks removed
- 115g/4oz/1 cup cooked rice
- salt and ground black pepper
- lemon and lime wedges, to serve

1 To prepare the squid, hold the body firmly in one hand and grasp the tentacles at their base with the other. Pull the head away from the body, bringing the entrails with it. Cut the tentacles (and part of the head above the eyes) away from the entrails. Snip out the hard beak in the middle of the clump of tentacles and discard this, along with the entrails attached to the remainder of the head.

2 Peel the purplish membrane away from the body, then pull out the hard transparent quill and discard. Wash the clumps of tentacles and bodies well, inside and out, under cold running water.

3 Pull the side flaps or wings away from the body, chop them finely and set aside. Put the tentacles with the bodies on a plate, cover and chill.

COOK'S TIPS
- You can ask your fishmonger to prepare the squid for you, if you prefer.
- If you stuff the squid in advance and chill them, let them return to room temperature before cooking.

4 Heat a frying pan. Add the oil, onions and garlic and fry for 5 minutes, or until the onions are soft and golden. Add the chopped squid wings and fry for about 1 minute, then stir in the walnuts, sumac and chilli flakes. Add the rocket and continue to stir-fry until it has wilted. Stir in the cooked rice, season well and tip into a bowl to cool. Meanwhile, soak six wooden skewers in water for 30 minutes.

5 Prepare the barbecue. Stuff each squid with the cold mixture and thread two on to each skewer, with two clumps of tentacles. Toss in oil and salt. Position a lightly oiled grill rack over the coals to heat. Grill the squid over medium-high heat for about 1½ minutes on each side.

6 Once they are pale golden, move them to a cooler part of the grill to cook for 1½ minutes more on each side to ensure the filling is hot. Baste with any remaining oil and salt mixture as they are turned. Serve them with the lemon and lime wedges.

Energy 212kcal/887kJ; Protein 19.3g; Carbohydrate 10.3g, of which sugars 2.2g; Fat 10.7g, of which saturates 1.6g; Cholesterol 253mg; Calcium 56mg; Fibre 1g; Sodium 146mg.

TIGER PRAWN SKEWERS

LARGE PRAWNS ARE FULL OF FLAVOUR AND IDEAL FOR BARBECUING — AND THEY ARE SO QUICK TO COOK. IN THIS RECIPE THEY ARE MARINATED IN AN UNUSUAL WALNUT PESTO, WHICH IS SIMPLE TO PREPARE AND CAN BE MADE THE DAY BEFORE. MARINATE OVERNIGHT FOR THE BEST RESULTS.

SERVES FOUR

INGREDIENTS

12–16 large, raw, shell-on tiger
  prawns (jumbo shrimp)
50g/2oz/½ cup walnut pieces
60ml/4 tbsp chopped fresh flat
  leaf parsley
60ml/4 tbsp chopped fresh basil
2 garlic cloves, chopped
45ml/3 tbsp grated fresh
  Parmesan cheese
30ml/2 tbsp extra virgin olive oil
30ml/2 tbsp walnut oil
salt and ground black pepper

1 Peel the prawns, removing the head but leaving the tail on. Devein the prawns using a cocktail stick (toothpick) and then put them in a large bowl.

VARIATION

For garlic prawns, clean the prawns and thread on skewers. Brush with oil and grill as before. Melt 50g/2oz/¼ cup butter in a small pan on the barbecue. Add 2 crushed garlic cloves, 30ml/2 tbsp chopped fresh parsley, the grated rind of ¼ lemon and 15ml/1 tbsp lemon juice. Serve with the prawns.

2 To make the pesto, place the walnuts, parsley, basil, garlic, cheese and oils in a food processor and process until finely chopped. Season.

3 Add half the pesto to the prawns in the bowl, toss them well, then cover and chill for a minimum of 1 hour, or leave them overnight.

4 Soak four wooden skewers in water for 30 minutes. Prepare the barbecue. Position a lightly oiled grill rack over the hot coals. Thread the prawns on to the skewers and cook them over high heat for 3–4 minutes, turning once. Serve with the remaining pesto and a green salad, if you like.

Energy 256kcal/1062kJ; Protein 13.9g; Carbohydrate 0.9g, of which sugars 0.8g; Fat 21.9g, of which saturates 4.2g; Cholesterol 90mg; Calcium 209mg; Fibre 1.3g; Sodium 578mg.

MARINATED MONKFISH AND MUSSEL KEBABS

THIS RECIPE COMBINES SEAFOOD WITH TURKEY, GIVING THE KEBABS EXTRA RICHNESS. THE SIMPLE MARINADE TAKES NO TIME AT ALL TO PREPARE. THE MARINADE WILL MAKE THE MONKFISH BOTH DELICIOUSLY FLAVOURED AND QUICKER TO BARBECUE, SO OBSERVE THE COOKING TIME CLOSELY.

SERVES FOUR

INGREDIENTS

450g/1lb monkfish, skinned
  and boned
5ml/1 tsp olive oil
30ml/2 tbsp lemon juice
5ml/1 tsp paprika
1 garlic clove, crushed
4 turkey rashers
8 cooked mussels
8 large raw prawns (shrimp)
15ml/1 tbsp chopped fresh dill
salt and ground black pepper
lemon wedges, to garnish
salad and rice, to serve

1 Mix together the oil, lemon juice, paprika, and garlic in a bowl and season with pepper.

2 Cut the monkfish into 2.5cm/1in cubes and place in a shallow glass or earthenware dish.

3 Pour the marinade over the fish and toss to coat all the pieces evenly. Cover the dish and leave in a cool place for 30 minutes.

4 Cut the turkey rashers in half and wrap each strip around a mussel. Thread on to skewers alternating with the fish cubes and raw prawns.

COOK'S TIP
Threading the kebabs on to two parallel skewers makes them easier to turn over.

5 Prepare the barbecue. Position a lightly oiled grill rack over the hot coals. Cook the kebabs over high heat for 7–8 minutes, turning once and basting with the marinade during cooking. Sprinkle with chopped dill and salt. Garnish with the lemon wedges and serve immediately, accompanied with salad and rice.

Energy 126kcal/534kJ; Protein 26.5g; Carbohydrate 0.3g, of which sugars 0g; Fat 2.1g, of which saturates 0.5g; Cholesterol 67mg; Calcium 26mg; Fibre 0g; Sodium 103mg.

GRILLED LOBSTER

THIS IS A SMART YET UNPRETENTIOUS DISH AND WELL WORTH THE LITTLE BIT OF EXTRA EFFORT.
LOBSTER IS A FANTASTIC INGREDIENT TO COOK WITH BUT, IF YOU ARE A BIT SQUEAMISH, DISPATCHING
IT IS A VERY HARD THING TO DO, IN WHICH CASE IT IS A JOB PROBABLY BEST LEFT TO THE
FISHMONGER. INSTRUCTIONS FOR KILLING IT HUMANELY ARE GIVEN BELOW.

SERVES TWO TO FOUR

INGREDIENTS
15 fresh basil leaves, roughly
  chopped
60ml/4 tbsp olive oil
1 garlic clove, crushed
2 freshly killed lobsters, cut in
  half lengthways and cleaned
  (see Cook's Tip)
salt and ground black pepper
2 limes, halved, to serve
For the basil oil and mayonnaise
40g/1½oz/1½ cups basil leaves
  stripped from their stalks
175ml/6fl oz/¾ cup sunflower oil,
  plus extra if needed
45ml/3 tbsp olive oil
1 small garlic clove, crushed
2.5ml/½ tsp dry English (hot)
  mustard
10ml/2 tsp lemon juice
2 egg yolks
ground white pepper

1 To make the basil oil, place the basil leaves in a bowl and pour boiling water over them. Leave for about 30 seconds until the leaves turn a brighter green. Drain, refresh under cold running water, drain again, then squeeze dry in kitchen paper. Place the leaves in a food processor. Add both oils and process to a purée. Scrape into a bowl, cover and chill overnight.

2 Line a sieve (strainer) with muslin (cheesecloth) and set it over a deep bowl. Pour in the basil and oil purée and leave for about 1 hour, or until all the oil has filtered through into the bowl. Discard the solids left behind.

3 To make the mayonnaise, you will need 200ml/7fl oz/ scant 1 cup of the basil oil. If you do not have enough, make it up with more sunflower oil. Place the crushed garlic in a bowl. Add the mustard with 2.5ml/½ tsp of the lemon juice and a little salt and white pepper.

4 Whisk in the egg yolks, then start adding the basil oil, a drop at a time, whisking continuously until the mixture starts to thicken. At this stage it is usually safe to start adding the oil a little faster. When you have 45ml/3 tbsp oil left, whisk in the remaining lemon juice and then add the rest of the oil. Finally, whisk in 7.5ml/1½ tsp cold water. Cover the mayonnaise and chill.

5 Prepare the barbecue. Chop the basil and mix it with the oil and garlic in a bowl. Season lightly. Once the flames have died down, rake the coals to get more on one side than the other. Position a lightly oiled grill rack over the coals to heat.

6 Brush some of the oil mixture over the cut side of each lobster half. Place cut-side down on the grill rack on the side away from the bulk of the coals. Grill for 5 minutes. Turn the lobsters over, baste with more oil mixture and cook for 10–15 minutes more, basting and moving them about the rack.

7 Grill the lime halves at the same time, placing them cut-side down for 3 minutes to caramelize. Serve the lobster with the mayonnaise and the grilled lime halves.

COOK'S TIP
If you have to kill a lobster yourself, you can do so humanely. Either put the live lobster in a freezerproof dish or tray and cover with crushed ice to render it unconscious, or put it into the freezer for 2 hours. When the lobster is very cold and no longer moving, place it on a chopping board and drive the tip of a large, sharp and heavy knife or a very strong skewer through the centre of the cross on its head. According to experts, death is instantaneous.

To clean, split in half by laying the lobster on its back and stretching out the body. Use a sharp, heavy knife to cut the lobster neatly in half along the entire length. Discard the whitish sac and the feathery gills from the head and the grey-black intestinal sac that runs down the tail. The greenish tomalley (liver) and the coral (roe) are delicious, so retain these.

Energy 518kcal/2144kJ; Protein 21.8g; Carbohydrate 0.4g, of which sugars 0.3g; Fat 47.9g, of which saturates 6.5g; Cholesterol 201mg; Calcium 92mg; Fibre 0.6g; Sodium 309mg.

SCALLOPS WITH LIME BUTTER

CHARGRILLING FENNEL RELEASES ITS ANISEED FLAVOUR, WHICH TASTES GREAT WITH SWEET AND RICH SCALLOPS. THESE WONDERFUL SHELLFISH ARE IDEAL FOR THE BARBECUE BECAUSE THEY HAVE FIRM FLESH THAT COOKS QUICKLY — SIMPLY TOSS IN LIME JUICE BEFORE COOKING.

SERVES FOUR

INGREDIENTS
1 head fennel
2 limes
12 large scallops, cleaned
1 egg yolk
90ml/6 tbsp melted butter
olive oil for brushing
salt and ground black pepper

COOK'S TIP
When choosing fennel, look for bulbs that are white and firm.

1 Trim any feathery leaves from the fennel and reserve them. Slice the rest lengthways into thin wedges.

2 Cut one lime into wedges. Finely grate the rind and squeeze the juice of the other lime and toss half the juice and rind on to the scallops. Season well with salt and ground black pepper.

3 Place the egg yolk and remaining lime rind and juice in a small bowl and whisk until pale and smooth.

4 Gradually whisk in the melted butter and continue whisking until thick and smooth. Finely chop the reserved fennel leaves and stir them in, with seasoning.

5 Prepare the barbecue. Position a lightly oiled grill rack over the hot coals. Brush the fennel wedges with olive oil and cook them over high heat for 3–4 minutes, turning once.

6 Add the scallops and cook for a further 3–4 minutes, turning once. Serve with the lime and fennel butter and the lime wedges.

COOK'S TIP
Thread small scallops on to flat skewers to make turning them easier.

Energy 232kcal/961kJ; Protein 10g; Carbohydrate 2.2g, of which sugars 0.9g; Fat 20.5g, of which saturates 12.3g; Cholesterol 116mg; Calcium 31mg; Fibre 1.1g; Sodium 211mg.

GRILLED SALTED SARDINES

WHOLE GRILLED SARDINES ARE CLASSIC MEDITERRANEAN BEACH FOOD, EVOKING MEMORIES OF LAZY LUNCHES UNDER RUSTIC AWNINGS, JUST A STEP AWAY FROM THE SEA. HERE THEY ARE SERVED WITH SALMORIGLIO, AN ITALIAN HERB SALSA POUNDED WITH SEA SALT.

SERVES FOUR TO EIGHT

INGREDIENTS

8 sardines, total weight about
    800g/1¾lb, scaled and gutted
50g/2oz/¼ cup salt
oil, for brushing
focaccia, to serve
For the salmoriglio
    5ml/1 tsp sea salt flakes
    60ml/4 tbsp chopped fresh tarragon
    leaves
    40g/1½oz/generous 1 cup chopped
    flat leaf parsley
    1 small red onion, very finely
    chopped
    105ml/7 tbsp extra virgin olive oil
    60ml/4 tbsp lemon juice

1 Rub the sardines inside and out with salt. Cover and put in a cool place for 30–45 minutes. Make the salmoriglio by putting the salt in a mortar and pounding all the ingredients one at a time with a pestle.

2 Meanwhile, prepare the barbecue. Rinse the salt off the sardines. Pat them dry with kitchen paper, then leave to air-dry for 15 minutes. Position a lightly oiled grill rack over the hot coals.

3 Brush the sardines with a little oil and put them in a small, hinged, wire barbecue fish basket. Grill them over medium-high heat for about 3 minutes on one side and about 2½ minutes on the other. When ready, lift out of the basket and serve hot with the salmoriglio and focaccia.

COOK'S TIP

Hinged wire fish baskets come in various shapes and sizes, often oval to accommodate a whole fish, square to hold fillets and steaks, or more elaborate in design to hold a number of smaller fish (see left). The idea is that you turn the basket over the barbecue rather than the fish, which is ideal for delicate dishes. If you do not have one, you can of course grill the fish directly on the rack. Do make sure to oil it well first, and turn the fish only when the undersides are crisp.

Energy 210kcal/873kJ; Protein 15.7g; Carbohydrate 0.8g, of which sugars 0.6g; Fat 16g, of which saturates 3.2g; Cholesterol 0mg; Calcium 90mg; Fibre 0.4g; Sodium 87mg.

SARDINES WITH WARM HERB SALSA

PLAIN GRILLING IS THE VERY BEST WAY TO COOK FRESH SARDINES. SERVED WITH THIS LUSCIOUS HERB SALSA THE ONLY OTHER ESSENTIAL ITEM IS FRESH, CRUSTY BREAD, TO MOP UP THE TASTY JUICES.

2 While the barbecue heats up, make the salsa. Melt the butter in a small pan until foaming and gently sauté the spring onions and chopped garlic for about 2 minutes or until softened, shaking the pan occasionally to prevent them browning.

3 Add the lemon rind and remaining salsa ingredients to the onions and garlic in the pan and stir them together. Keep the pan warm on the edge of the barbecue, stirring occasionally. Do not allow to boil.

4 Brush the sardines lightly with oil and sprinkle evenly with lemon juice, salt and pepper. Cook for about 2 minutes on each side, over moderately hot coals. Serve at once with the warm salsa and crusty bread.

SERVES FOUR

INGREDIENTS
  12–16 fresh sardines
  oil for brushing
  juice of 1 lemon
For the salsa
  15ml/1 tbsp butter
  4 spring onions (scallions), chopped
  1 garlic clove, finely chopped
  rind of 1 lemon
  30ml/2 tbsp finely chopped
    fresh parsley
  30ml/2 tbsp finely chopped
    fresh chives
  30ml/2 tbsp finely chopped
    fresh basil
  30ml/2 tbsp green olive paste
  10ml/2 tsp balsamic vinegar
  salt and ground black pepper

1 To clean the sardines, use a pair of small kitchen scissors to slit the fish along the belly from the vent to the head and pull out the innards. Rinse the fish under cold running water, wipe them inside and out with kitchen paper and then arrange them on a lightly oiled grill rack. Use a hinged wire sardine basket if available.

COOK'S TIP
Sardines deteriorate very quickly and must be bought and eaten on the same day. Be careful when buying: the eyes and gills should not be too pink. If the fish "melts" like cheese when grilled, don't bother to eat it.

Energy 221kcal/919kJ; Protein 23.8g; Carbohydrate 0.7g, of which sugars 0.6g; Fat 13.6g, of which saturates 4.8g; Cholesterol 8mg; Calcium 148mg; Fibre 1g; Sodium 324mg.

STUFFED SARDINES

THIS MIDDLE EASTERN-INSPIRED DISH DOESN'T TAKE MUCH PREPARATION AND IS A MEAL IN ITSELF.
JUST SERVE WITH A CRISP GREEN SALAD TOSSED IN A FRESH LEMON VINAIGRETTE TO MAKE IT COMPLETE.

SERVES FOUR

INGREDIENTS
10g/¼oz fresh parsley
3–4 garlic cloves, crushed
8–12 fresh sardines, gutted
  and cleaned
30ml/2 tbsp lemon juice
50g/2oz plain (all-purpose) flour
2.5ml/½ tsp ground cumin
olive oil, for brushing
salt and ground black pepper
naan bread and green salad leaves,
  to serve

VARIATION

Add 5ml/1 tsp paprika to the flour with
the cumin, plus a pinch of cayenne
pepper if you wish.

1 Finely chop the parsley and mix in a small bowl with the garlic. Pat the parsley and garlic mixture all over the outsides and insides of the prepared sardines. Sprinkle the sardines with lemon juice, then place them in a dish, cover and set aside in a cool place for up to 2 hours, to absorb the flavours.

2 Place the flour on a large plate and season with the cumin, salt and pepper. Roll the sardines in the flour.

3 Brush the sardines with olive oil and cook on a medium-hot barbecue for about 3 minutes each side. Serve with naan bread and a green salad.

Energy 550kcal/2299kJ; Protein 42.8g; Carbohydrate 28.7g, of which sugars 13.2g; Fat 30g, of which saturates 5.6g; Cholesterol 8mg; Calcium 258mg; Fibre 1.8g; Sodium 829mg.

JAPANESE ROLLED SARDINES WITH PLUM PASTE

MAKE THIS SIMPLE AND DELIGHTFUL RECIPE WHEN SARDINES ARE IN SEASON. PERFECTLY FRESH SARDINES ARE ROLLED UP AROUND LAYERS OF SHISO LEAVES AND UMEBOSHI, A SOUR JAPANESE APRICOT (OFTEN CALLED "JAPANESE PLUM") THAT IS PICKLED IN SALT.

SERVES FOUR

INGREDIENTS

    8 fresh sardines, cleaned
     and filleted
    5ml/1 tsp salt
    4 umeboshi, about 30g/1¼oz total
     weight (choose the soft type)
    5ml/1 tsp sake
    5ml/1 tsp toasted sesame seeds
    16 shiso leaves, cut in
     half lengthways
    1 lime, thinly sliced, the centre
     hollowed out to make rings,
     to garnish

COOK'S TIP

Umeboshi (literally "dried ume") are a popular ingredient in Japanese lunch boxes, often placed in the centre of a dish of rice. They are credited with various health-giving properties.

1 Carefully cut the sardine fillets in half lengthways and place them side by side in a large, shallow container. Sprinkle with salt on both sides.

2 Remove the stones (pits) from the umeboshi and put the fruit in a small mixing bowl with the sake and toasted sesame seeds. With the back of a fork, mash the umeboshi, mixing well to form a smooth paste.

3 Wipe the sardine fillets with kitchen paper to dry them and remove the excess salt. With a butter knife, spread some umeboshi paste thinly on to one of the sardine fillets, then press some shiso leaves on top.

4 Roll up each sardine fillet, starting from the tail, and pierce with a wooden cocktail stick (toothpick). Repeat to make 16 rolls.

5 Prepare the barbecue. When the flames have died down position a lightly oiled grill rack over the hot coals. Grill the rolled sardines over medium-high heat for 4–6 minutes on each side, or until golden brown, turning once.

6 Lay a few lime rings on four individual plates and arrange the rolled sardines alongside. Serve hot.

Energy 248kcal/1037kJ; Protein 31.1g; Carbohydrate 0.7g, of which sugars 0.7g; Fat 13.3g, of which saturates 3.7g; Cholesterol 0mg; Calcium 161mg; Fibre 0.2g; Sodium 171mg.

SPICED SARDINES WITH GRAPEFRUIT AND FENNEL SALAD

SARDINES SPICED WITH CUMIN AND CORIANDER ARE POPULAR IN THE COASTAL REGIONS OF MOROCCO, BOTH IN RESTAURANTS AND AS STREET FOOD. THE SPICES ARE MIXED TO A PASTE WITH OIL AND RUBBED WELL INTO THE FISH SO THAT THEIR WARM FLAVOURS PERMEATE THE FLESH.

SERVES FOUR TO SIX

INGREDIENTS
12 fresh sardines, gutted
1 onion, grated
60–90ml/4–6 tbsp olive oil
5ml/1 tsp ground cinnamon
10ml/2 tsp cumin seeds, roasted
  and ground
10ml/2 tsp coriander seeds, roasted
  and ground
5ml/1 tsp paprika
5ml/1 tsp ground black pepper
small bunch of fresh coriander
  (cilantro), chopped
coarse salt
2 lemons, cut into wedges, to serve
For the salad
2 ruby grapefruits
5ml/1 tsp sea salt
1 fennel bulb
2–3 spring onions (scallions),
  finely sliced
2.5ml/½ tsp ground roasted cumin
30–45ml/2–3 tbsp olive oil
handful of black olives

3 Leave the sardines to stand for about 1 hour to allow the flavours of the spices to penetrate the flesh.

4 To prepare the salad, peel the grapefruits, removing all the pith and peel in neat strips down the outside of the fruit. Cut between the membranes to remove the segments of fruit intact. Cut each grapefruit segment in half, place in a bowl and sprinkle with salt.

5 Trim the fennel and slice finely. Toss it lightly with the grapefruit, spring onions, cumin, olives and olive oil.

6 Prepare the barbecue. When the flames have died down arrange a lightly oiled grill rack over the hot coals, or arrange the sardines in a hinged wire sardine basket.

7 Cook the sardines for 3–4 minutes on each side, basting with any leftover marinade.

8 Transfer the sardines to a warmed serving platter or individual plates. Sprinkle with fresh coriander and serve immediately, with lemon wedges for squeezing over and the refreshing grapefruit and fennel salad.

1 Rinse the sardines and pat them dry on kitchen paper, then rub inside and out with a little coarse salt.

2 In a bowl, mix the grated onion with the olive oil, cinnamon, ground roasted cumin and coriander, paprika and black pepper. Make a few slashes down each side of the sardines and smear the onion and spice mixture all over, inside and out, pushing it into the gashes.

Energy 177kcal/740kJ; Protein 20.9g; Carbohydrate 0.7g, of which sugars 0.7g; Fat 9.9g, of which saturates 2.8g; Cholesterol 0mg; Calcium 94mg; Fibre 0.2g; Sodium 121mg.

MACKEREL WITH TOMATOES, PESTO AND ONION

RICH OILY FISH LIKE MACKEREL NEEDS A SHARP, FRESH-TASTING SAUCE TO GO WITH IT, AND THIS AROMATIC PESTO IS EXCELLENT DRIZZLED OVER THE TOP. HOMEMADE PESTO IS SO MUCH BETTER THAN THE SHOP-BOUGHT VERSION AND THIS RECIPE MAKES THE MOST OF THE WONDERFUL FLAVOUR.

SERVES FOUR

INGREDIENTS
4 mackerel, gutted and cleaned
30ml/2 tbsp olive oil
115g/4oz onion, roughly chopped
450g/1lb tomatoes, skinned and
   roughly chopped
salt and ground black pepper
For the pesto
50g/2oz pine nuts
30ml/2 tbsp fresh basil leaves
2 garlic cloves, crushed
30ml/2 tbsp freshly grated
   Parmesan cheese
150ml/¼ pint/⅔ cup extra virgin
   olive oil

COOK'S TIP
The fish can be cooked under a hot grill (broiler) instead of using the barbecue.

1 To make the pesto, place the pine nuts, fresh basil leaves and garlic in a food processor and blend to a rough paste. Add the Parmesan and, with the blades running, gradually add the oil.

2 Season the mackerel well with plenty of salt and ground black pepper and cook on a medium-hot barbecue for about 12–15 minutes, turning once.

3 Meanwhile, heat the olive oil in a large, heavy-based saucepan and sauté the chopped onions until soft and golden brown.

4 Stir the chopped tomatoes into the contents of the saucepan and cook for 5 minutes. Serve the fish on top of the tomato mixture and top with a generous spoonful of the pesto.

Energy 668kcal/2765kJ; Protein 25.4g; Carbohydrate 11.7g, of which sugars 9.4g; Fat 58.1g, of which saturates 9.9g; Cholesterol 62mg; Calcium 135mg; Fibre 2.7g; Sodium 158mg.

MACKEREL WITH NUTTY BACON STUFFING

THIS DISH IS INSPIRED BY A POPULAR TURKISH RECIPE FOR MACKEREL COOKED WITH NUTS AND SPICES. THE FISH ARE STUFFED, TIED WITH RAFFIA AND THEN GRILLED. THEY TASTE JUST AS GOOD COLD, SO MAKE EXTRA FOR LUNCH NEXT DAY AND SERVE WITH HORSERADISH MAYONNAISE.

SERVES SIX

INGREDIENTS

    45ml/3 tbsp olive oil
    2 onions, finely chopped
    2 garlic cloves, crushed
    6 rindless smoked bacon rashers
    (strips), diced
    50g/2oz/½ cup pine nuts
    45ml/3 tbsp chopped fresh
    sweet marjoram
    6 mackerel, about 300g/11oz each,
    gutted and cleaned but with heads
    left on
    salt and ground black pepper
    raffia, soaked in water
    lemon wedges, to serve

1 Heat the oil in a large frying pan and sweat the chopped onions and garlic over a medium heat for 5 minutes.

2 Increase the heat and add the bacon and pine nuts. Fry the mixture for a further 5–7 minutes, stirring occasionally, until golden. Tip into a bowl to cool. Gently fold in the sweet marjoram, season lightly, cover and chill until needed.

3 To prepare each fish, snip the backbone at the head end. Extend the cavity opening at the tail end so that you can reach the backbone more easily. Turn the fish over and, with the heel of your hand, press firmly along the entire length of the backbone to loosen it. Snip the bone at the tail end and it will lift out surprisingly easily. Season the insides lightly.

COOK'S TIPS
• If you are cooking these mackerel on a charcoal kettle barbecue and the heat becomes too intense, you can reduce it a little by half-closing the air vents.
• If your barbecue has a lid, it is especially useful for this recipe. This will help you achieve an even golden skin without needing to move the fish about.

4 Stuff the cavity in each mackerel with some of the chilled onion mixture, then tie the mackerel along its entire length with raffia to hold in the stuffing. Chill the fish for at least 15 minutes. They can be chilled for up to 2 hours, but if so, allow them to come to room temperature for about 15 minutes before grilling.

5 Prepare the barbecue. Position a lightly oiled grill rack over the hot coals. Transfer the mackerel to the grill rack and cook for about 8 minutes on each side over medium-high heat, or until cooked and golden.

6 Transfer the cooked fish to warmed serving plates, and snip the raffia in several places, but otherwise leave it wrapped around the fish to add visual appeal. Serve the mackerel with lemon wedges and black pepper.

COOK'S TIP
Raffia is a strong, pliable and water-resistant natural fibre, obtained from the raffia palm, native to Madagascar. Use undyed raffia for culinary purposes.

Energy 858kcal/3561kJ; Protein 64.5g; Carbohydrate 5.8g, of which sugars 4.3g; Fat 64.1g, of which saturates 12.9g; Cholesterol 175mg; Calcium 69mg; Fibre 1.5g; Sodium 641mg.

MACKEREL KEBABS WITH SWEET PEPPER SALAD

MACKEREL IS DELICIOUS WHEN VERY FRESH AND IS AN EXCELLENT FISH FOR BARBECUING BECAUSE ITS NATURAL OILS KEEP IT MOIST AND TASTY. THIS RECIPE COMBINES MACKEREL WITH COLOURFUL GRILLED PEPPERS AND TOMATOES IN A FLAVOURSOME SUMMER SALAD.

SERVES FOUR

INGREDIENTS
   4 medium mackerel, about 225g/8oz
     each, filleted
   2 small red onions, cut in wedges
   30ml/2 tbsp chopped fresh marjoram
   60ml/4 tbsp dry white wine
   45ml/3 tbsp olive oil
   juice of 1 lime
For the salad
   1 red (bell) pepper
   1 yellow (bell) pepper
   1 small red onion
   2 large plum tomatoes
   15ml/1 tbsp chopped fresh marjoram
   10ml/2 tsp balsamic vinegar
   salt and ground black pepper

1 Soak eight wooden skewers in water for 30 minutes to prevent them from scorching on the barbecue.

2 Drain the skewers and thread one through the centre of each mackerel fillet, piercing the fish several times to support it. Stick an onion wedge on each end of each skewer. Arrange the prepared fish in a dish.

3 Mix together the marjoram, wine, oil and lime juice and spoon over the mackerel. Cover and chill for at least 30 minutes, turning once so the fish is well coated in the marinade.

4 Prepare the barbecue. To make the salad, quarter and seed both the peppers and halve the onion. Place the peppers and onion, skin-side down, with the whole tomatoes, on a hot barbecue and leave until the skins are blackened and charred.

5 Remove the vegetables from the barbecue and leave until they are cool enough to handle. Use a sharp knife to peel off and discard the skins.

6 Chop the vegetables roughly and put them in a bowl. Stir in the marjoram and balsamic vinegar and season to taste. Toss thoroughly.

7 Remove the kebabs from the refrigerator and cook over the hot coals for about 10–12 minutes, turning occasionally and basting with the marinade. Serve with the pepper salad.

COOK'S TIP
The best way to obtain mackerel for barbecuing is to catch it yourself. It is still abundant in many areas, and is ideal for a beach barbecue, as it is essential to eat the fish very fresh – within hours if possible. At the fishmonger, look for stiff fish with skin that is brightly coloured with silver, green and purple. Mackerel is very nutritious, being an excellent source of omega 3 and vitamin B12.

VARIATION
Other oily fish can be used for this dish: try fillets or cubes of herring, rainbow trout or salmon instead.

Energy 704kcal/2923kJ; Protein 50.3g; Carbohydrate 13.6g, of which sugars 12.4g; Fat 49g, of which saturates 9.6g; Cholesterol 133mg; Calcium 76mg; Fibre 3.9g; Sodium 161mg.

SMOKED MACKEREL <u>WITH</u> BLUEBERRIES

FRESH BLUEBERRIES BURST WITH FLAVOUR WHEN COOKED, AND THEIR SHARPNESS COMPLEMENTS THE RICH FLESH OF MACKEREL VERY WELL. ACCOMPANY THE DISH WITH CRUSTY BREAD AND A FRESH GREEN SALAD TO BALANCE THE INTENSITY OF THE FISH AND FRUIT.

SERVES FOUR

INGREDIENTS
- 15g/½oz plain (all-purpose) flour
- 4 hot-smoked mackerel fillets
- 50g/2oz/4 tbsp unsalted (sweet) butter
- juice of ½ lemon
- salt and ground black pepper

For the blueberry sauce
- 450g/1lb blueberries
- 25g/1oz caster (superfine) sugar
- 15g/½oz/1 tbsp unsalted butter
- salt and ground black pepper

COOK'S TIP
The mackerel fillets can be eaten without further cooking, so are grilled just to heat them and give them a crisp finish.

1 Season the flour with salt and ground black pepper. Coat each fish fillet in the flour, covering it well.

2 Brush the fillets with butter and cook on a medium barbecue for a few minutes until heated through with a crisp coating.

3 To make the sauce, place the blueberries, sugar, butter and salt and pepper in a small roasting pan and cook on the barbecue, stirring occasionally, for about 10 minutes. Serve immediately, drizzling the lemon juice over the mackerel and with the blueberries on the side.

Energy 395kcal/1641kJ; Protein 15.7g; Carbohydrate 25.2g, of which sugars 17.9g; Fat 26.3g, of which saturates 6.7g; Cholesterol 87mg; Calcium 24mg; Fibre 2.4g; Sodium 586mg.

HOT SMOKED SALMON

HICKORY CHIPS ADDED TO THE COALS WHILE THE FOOD COOKS GIVE IT AN AUTHENTIC SMOKY FLAVOUR, WHICH IS PERFECT FOR THIS QUICKLY SMOKED SALMON DISH THAT IS SERVED WITH A FRUITY MOJO. IT'S A GREAT DISH FOR A SPECIAL OCCASION — RICH AND FULL OF COLOUR AND FLAVOUR.

SERVES SIX

INGREDIENTS
  6 salmon fillets, each about
    175g/6oz, with skin
  15ml/1 tbsp sunflower oil
  salt and ground black pepper
  2 handfuls hickory wood chips,
    soaked in cold water for as much
    time as you have available,
    preferably 30 minutes
For the mojo
  1 ripe mango, diced
  4 drained canned pineapple
    slices, diced
  1 small red onion, finely chopped
  1 fresh long mild red chilli, seeded
    and finely chopped
  15ml/1 tbsp good quality sweet
    chilli sauce
  grated rind and juice of 1 lime
  leaves from 1 small lemon basil
    plant or 45ml/3 tbsp fresh
    coriander (cilantro) leaves,
    shredded or chopped

1 First, make the mojo by putting the mango, pineapple, onion, and chilli together in a bowl.

2 Add the chilli sauce, lime rind and juice, and the herb leaves. Stir to mix well. Cover tightly and leave in a cool place until needed.

3 Prepare the barbecue. When the flames have died down, position a lightly oiled grill rack over the hot coals. Rinse the salmon fillets and pat dry with kitchen paper, then brush each with oil.

4 Place the fillets skin side down on the grill rack over medium-high heat. Cover the barbecue with a lid or tented heavy-duty foil and cook the fish for 3–5 minutes.

COOK'S TIPS
• When sweet pineapples are in season, you may prefer to use a fresh one in the mojo. You will need about half a medium pineapple. Slice off the skin, remove the core and cut the flesh into chunks.
• To dice a mango, slice alongside the stone (pit) on both sides. Cut the flesh in a criss-cross pattern, then turn it inside out and slice off the cubes.

5 Drain the hickory chips into a colander and sprinkle about a third of them as evenly as possible over the coals. Carefully drop them through the slats in the grill rack, taking care not to scatter the ash as you do so.

6 Replace the barbecue cover and continue cooking the salmon for a further 8 minutes, adding a small handful of hickory chips to the coals twice more during this time to intensify the flavour.

7 Serve the salmon hot or cold, accompanied by the mojo.

Energy 365kcal/1522kJ; Protein 36g; Carbohydrate 7.8g, of which sugars 7.5g; Fat 21.3g, of which saturates 3.6g; Cholesterol 88mg; Calcium 61mg; Fibre 1.3g; Sodium 83mg.

MEXICAN BARBECUE SALMON

THESE SALMON FILLETS COOK QUICKLY ON THE BARBECUE, AND BECAUSE THEY'VE BEEN MARINATED IN
THE TOMATO SAUCE, THEY REMAIN BEAUTIFULLY MOIST AND SUCCULENT.

SERVES FOUR

INGREDIENTS
  25g/1oz/2 tbsp butter
  1 small red onion, finely chopped
  1 garlic clove, crushed
  6 plum tomatoes, diced
  45ml/3 tbsp tomato ketchup
  30ml/2 tbsp Dijon mustard
  30ml/2 tbsp soft dark brown sugar
  15ml/1 tbsp clear honey
  5ml/1 tsp ground cayenne pepper
  15ml/1 tbsp ancho chilli powder
  15ml/1 tbsp paprika
  15ml/1 tbsp Worcestershire sauce
  4 salmon fillets, about 175g/6oz each
  fresh flat leaf parsley sprigs,
    to garnish

1 Melt the butter in a large, heavy pan and cook the onion and garlic gently for about 5 minutes until softened and translucent. Stir occasionally to ensure that the onion does not brown. Add the diced tomatoes, bring to the boil and reduce the heat.

2 Simmer the tomato mixture for 15 minutes, stirring occasionally with a wooden spoon so that the tomatoes do not catch on the base of the pan.

3 Add the ketchup, mustard, sugar, honey, cayenne pepper, chilli powder, paprika and Worcestershire sauce. Stir well, then simmer for a further 20 minutes. Pour into a food processor and process until smooth. Leave to cool.

4 Put the salmon in a shallow dish, brush with the sauce and chill for 2 hours. Prepare the barbecue. Position a lightly oiled grill rack over the hot coals. Cook the salmon over medium-high heat for 2–3 minutes on each side, brushing with the sauce. Garnish and serve.

Energy 437kcal/1827kJ; Protein 36.9g; Carbohydrate 17.5g, of which sugars 17g; Fat 24.9g, of which saturates 6.7g; Cholesterol 101mg; Calcium 65mg; Fibre 1.8g; Sodium 360mg.

SALMON STEAKS WITH OREGANO SALSA

THIS COMBINATION OF SALMON WITH PIQUANT TOMATO WORKS INCREDIBLY WELL, AND COOKING ON THE BARBECUE GIVES THE SALMON AN EXQUISITE FLAVOUR, SERVED HOT OR COLD.

SERVES FOUR

INGREDIENTS

15ml/1 tbsp butter
4 salmon steaks, about
    225g/8oz each
120ml/4fl oz/½ cup dry white wine
ground black pepper
For the salsa
    10ml/2 tsp chopped fresh oregano,
    plus sprigs to garnish
    4 spring onions (scallions), trimmed
    and roughly sliced
    225g/8oz ripe tomatoes, peeled,
    cored and seeded
    30ml/2 tbsp extra virgin olive oil
    2.5ml/½ tsp caster (superfine)
    sugar
    15ml/1 tbsp tomato purée (paste)

1 Butter four squares of double-thickness foil. Put a salmon steak on each and add a little wine and a grinding of ground black pepper. Wrap the salmon steaks loosely in the squares, sealing the edges securely. Cook on a medium-hot barbecue for 10 minutes, until just cooked. If serving the steaks hot, keep them warm.

2 Put the chopped fresh oregano in a food processor and chop it very finely. Add the spring onions, tomatoes and remaining salsa ingredients. Pulse until chopped but not a smooth purée.

3 Serve the salmon hot or cold with the salsa, garnished with a sprig of fresh oregano.

VARIATION

Brown trout is a good alternative to salmon in this recipe and many others. The flesh is just as pink and succulent but slightly more delicate, so cook for less time.

Energy 569kcal/2367kJ; Protein 51.7g; Carbohydrate 3.8g, of which sugars 3.7g; Fat 36.5g, of which saturates 7.6g; Cholesterol 133mg; Calcium 90mg; Fibre 1.5g; Sodium 155mg.

TANGY GRILLED SALMON <u>WITH</u> PINEAPPLE

FRESH PINEAPPLE REALLY BRINGS OUT THE FLAVOUR OF SALMON. HERE, IT IS COMBINED WITH LIME JUICE TO MAKE A LIGHT AND REFRESHING DISH, WHICH TASTES GREAT WITH WILD RICE AND A SIMPLE GREEN SALAD TOSSED WITH A GRAPEFRUIT VINAIGRETTE DRESSING.

SERVES FOUR

INGREDIENTS
    4 salmon fillets, each about
      200g/7oz
    1 small pineapple
    30ml/2 tbsp sesame seeds
    fresh chives, to garnish
    wild rice and a green salad,
      to serve
For the marinade
    grated rind and juice of 2 limes
    15ml/1 tbsp olive oil
    1cm/½in piece of fresh root ginger,
      peeled and grated
    1 garlic clove, crushed
    30ml/2 tbsp clear honey
    15ml/1 tbsp soy sauce
    ground black pepper

1 To make the marinade, put the lime rind in a jug (pitcher) and stir in the lime juice, olive oil, ginger, garlic, honey and soy sauce. Taste and add a little ground black pepper. The inclusion of soy sauce in the marinade means that salt will probably not be needed.

2 Place the salmon fillets in a single layer in a shallow, non-metallic dish. Pour the marinade over the salmon. Cover and chill for at least 1 hour, turning the salmon halfway through.

3 Carefully cut the skin off the pineapple, removing as many of the small black "eyes" as possible. Cut the pineapple into four thick rings. Use an apple corer to remove the tough central core from each slice and cut away any remaining eyes with a small knife.

COOK'S TIPS
• To cook wild rice, put it in a pan of cold salted water. Bring to the boil, then simmer for 30–40 minutes, or as directed on the packet, until tender. This would make a perfect salad lightly dressed with oil and vinegar and flavoured with chopped fresh herbs.
• Serve the grilled salmon with a mixed leaf salad. For the dressing, mix 45ml/3 tbsp grapefruit juice with 10ml/2 tsp balsamic vinegar and a pinch each of salt, ground black pepper and sugar, then whisk in 120ml/4fl oz/ ½ cup mild olive oil.

4 Preheat the grill (broiler) to high. Sprinkle the sesame seeds over a piece of foil and place under the grill for a minute or two until they turn golden brown. Set aside.

5 If using the barbecue, position a lightly oiled grill rack over the hot coals. Remove the salmon fillets from the marinade and put them on the grill rack with the pineapple rings, or on a foil-covered rack under the grill (broiler).

6 Grill the fish and pineapple for 10 minutes over medium-high heat, brushing occasionally with the marinade and turning everything over once, until the fish is cooked through and the pineapple rings are golden brown. Brush over the final layer of marinade no less than 2 minutes before the end of cooking to ensure it cooks thoroughly.

7 Transfer the fish to serving plates, placing each fillet on a bed of wild rice. Top with the pineapple slices. Sprinkle the sesame seeds over the top and garnish with the chives. Serve with a green salad.

Energy 487kcal/2036kJ; Protein 42.4g; Carbohydrate 17.1g, of which sugars 17.1g; Fat 28.2g, of which saturates 4.6g; Cholesterol 100mg; Calcium 120mg; Fibre 2.4g; Sodium 95mg.

SALMON WITH TROPICAL FRUIT SALSA

FRESH BARBECUED SALMON REALLY NEEDS LITTLE ADORNMENT, BUT NOW THAT FARMED SALMON IS SO ABUNDANT, DIFFERENT TREATMENTS HELP TO RING THE CHANGES. THE FISH COMBINES VERY WELL WITH THE EXOTIC FRUITS IN THIS COLOURFUL SALSA.

SERVES FOUR

INGREDIENTS
    4 salmon steaks, about 175g/6oz each
    finely grated rind and juice of 1 lime
    1 small, ripe mango
    1 small, ripe paw-paw
    1 red chilli
    45ml/3 tbsp chopped fresh coriander
      (cilantro)
    salt and ground black pepper

1 Place the salmon in a wide dish and sprinkle over half the lime rind and juice. Season with salt and pepper.

2 Cut the mango in half, cutting either side of the stone (pit), and remove the stone. Cut off the peel, chop the mango flesh into small dice and place the pieces in a mixing bowl.

3 Halve the paw-paw, scoop out the seeds with a spoon and remove the peel. Cut the flesh into small dice and add it to the mango in the bowl.

COOK'S TIP
If you use salmon fillets instead of steaks they may need less cooking time.

4 Cut the chilli in half lengthways. Leave the seeds in if you want to make the salsa hot and spicy, or remove them for a milder flavour. Finely chop the chilli. (Wash your hands after handling the chilli.)

5 Combine the mango, paw-paw, chilli and coriander in a bowl and stir in the remaining lime rind and juice. Season to taste with plenty of salt and ground black pepper.

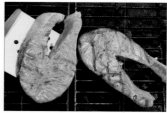

6 Prepare the barbecue. Place a lightly oiled grill rack over the hot coals and cook the salmon over medium heat for about 5–8 minutes, turning once. Serve with the fruit salsa.

Energy 374kcal/1563kJ; Protein 36.2g; Carbohydrate 14.2g, of which sugars 14.1g; Fat 19.5g, of which saturates 3.4g; Cholesterol 88mg; Calcium 72mg; Fibre 3.4g; Sodium 86mg.

SALMON WITH RED ONION MARMALADE

SALMON BARBECUES WELL BUT IS MOST SUCCESSFUL WHEN THE PIECES ARE QUITE THICK, SO THAT THE FLESH REMAINS MOIST IN THE CENTRE. THE RED ONION MARMALADE IS RICH AND DELICIOUS, AND YOU CAN USE PURÉED BLACKCURRANTS INSTEAD OF CRÈME DE CASSIS IF YOU PREFER.

SERVES FOUR

INGREDIENTS
    4 salmon steaks, about
        175g/6oz each
    30ml/2 tbsp olive oil
    salt and ground black pepper
For the red onion marmalade
    5 medium red onions, peeled and
        finely sliced
    50g/2oz/4 tbsp butter
    175ml/6floz/¾ cup red wine vinegar
    50ml/2fl oz/¼ cup crème de cassis
    50ml/2fl oz/¼ cup grenadine
    50ml/2fl oz/¼ cup red wine

COOK'S TIP
Buy authentic, good-quality grenadine to
add flavour as well as colour.

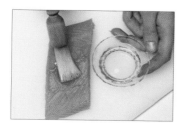

1 Use your hands to rub the olive oil
into the salmon flesh and season well
with plenty of salt and freshly ground
black pepper.

2 Melt the butter in a large heavy pan
and add the sliced onions. Sauté the
onions for 5 minutes until they are
golden brown.

3 Stir in the vinegar, crème de cassis,
grenadine and wine and continue to
cook for about 10 minutes until the
liquid has almost entirely evaporated
and the onions are glazed. Season well.

4 Brush the fish with a little more oil,
and cook on a medium barbecue for
about 6–8 minutes, turning once.

Energy 585kcal/2430kJ; Protein 38.4g; Carbohydrate 19.9g, of which sugars 14.1g; Fat 32.8g, of which saturates 10.2g; Cholesterol 114mg; Calcium 102mg; Fibre 3.5g; Sodium 163mg.

SALMON KEBABS WITH COCONUT

KEBABS MAKE EXCITING BARBECUE FOOD, BECAUSE YOU CAN COOK A VARIETY OF FLAVOURS TOGETHER WITHOUT LOSING THEIR INDIVIDUAL IDENTITIES. INSPIRED BY FLAVOURS FROM THE WEST INDIES, THIS RECIPE COMBINES COCONUT AND LIME TO COMPLEMENT THE SUBTLE TASTE OF THE SEAFOOD.

3 Cut each lime into six slices. Thread the coconut, salmon, scallops and pieces of lime alternately on to the skewers.

4 Add the lime juice, soy sauce, honey and sugar to the coconut liquor to make the marinade. Season with pepper.

5 Place the prepared kebabs in a single layer in a shallow non-metallic dish. Pour the marinade over. Cover and chill for at least 3 hours.

SERVES SIX

INGREDIENTS
    450g/1lb salmon fillet, skinned
    1 small fresh coconut
    2 limes
    12 scallops
    45ml/3 tbsp freshly squeezed
        lime juice
    30ml/2 tbsp soy sauce
    30ml/2 tbsp clear honey
    15ml/1 tbsp soft light brown sugar
    ground black pepper

COOK'S TIP
The easiest way to open a coconut is to hold it in the palm of one hand, with the "eyes" just above your thumb. The fault line lies between the eyes. Hold the coconut over a bowl to catch the liquid, then carefully hit the line with the blunt side of a cleaver or hammer so that it splits into two halves.

1 Soak six wooden skewers in water for 30 minutes. Using a sharp knife, cut the salmon into bite-size chunks and place these in a shallow bowl.

2 Halve the coconut (see Cook's Tip) and pour the liquor into a jug (pitcher). Using a small, sharp knife, remove the coconut flesh from the inside of the shell and cut it into chunks, making them about the same size as the pieces of salmon.

6 Preheat the barbecue. Position a lightly oiled grill rack over the hot coals. Transfer the kebabs to the barbecue and cook for 4 minutes on each side, basting with the marinade.

Energy 265kcal/1102kJ; Protein 20.8g; Carbohydrate 3.2g, of which sugars 2.5g; Fat 18.9g, of which saturates 10.4g; Cholesterol 47mg; Calcium 26mg; Fibre 2.3g; Sodium 193mg.

HERBY WRAPPED SALMON

THIS PARSI DISH, WITH ITS ORIGINS IN PERSIAN COOKING, USES A TOPPING FOR SALMON THAT IS BURSTING WITH THE FLAVOURS OF COCONUT, GARLIC, CHILLI, FRESH HERBS AND FENUGREEK. IT IS WRAPPED IN MOIST BANANA LEAVES TO SEAL IN THE FLAVOUR AND COOK THE FISH PERFECTLY.

SERVES SIX

INGREDIENTS

50g/2oz fresh coconut, skinned and finely grated, or 65g/2½oz/scant 1 cup desiccated (dry unsweetened shredded) coconut, soaked in 30ml/2 tbsp water
1 large lemon, skin, pith and seeds removed, roughly chopped
4 large garlic cloves, crushed
3 large fresh mild green chillies, seeded and chopped
50g/2oz/2 cups fresh coriander (cilantro), roughly chopped
25g/1oz/1 cup fresh mint leaves, roughly chopped
5ml/1 tsp ground cumin
5ml/1 tsp sugar
2.5ml/½ tsp fenugreek seeds, finely ground
5ml/1 tsp salt
2 large, whole banana leaves
6 salmon fillets, about 1.2kg/2½lb total weight, skinned

1 Place all the ingredients except the banana leaves and salmon in a food processor. Pulse to a fine paste. Scrape the mixture into a bowl, cover and chill for 30 minutes.

2 Prepare the barbecue. To make the parcels, cut each banana leaf widthways into three and cut off the hard outside edge from each piece. Put the pieces of leaf and the edge strips in a bowl of hot water. Leave for about 10 minutes. Drain, gently wipe off any white residue, rinse the leaves and strips, and pour over boiling water to soften. Drain, then place the leaves, smooth-side up, on a clean board.

3 Smear the top and bottom of each fillet with the coconut paste, then place one on each leaf. Bring the trimmed edge of the leaf over the salmon, then fold in the sides. Bring up the remaining edge to cover the salmon and make a neat parcel. Tie securely with a leaf strip.

4 Lay each parcel on a sheet of heavy-duty foil, bring up the edges and scrunch the tops together to seal. Position a lightly oiled grill rack over the hot coals. Place the salmon parcels on the grill rack and cook over medium-high heat for about 10 minutes, turning them over once.

5 Place the foil-wrapped parcels on individual plates and leave to stand for 2–3 minutes – the salmon will continue to cook for a while in the residual heat of the parcel. Remove the foil, then carefully unwrap so that the fish is resting on the opened leaves, then eat straight out of the banana leaf parcel.

COOK'S TIP
Serve little rice parcels with the fish. Fill six more banana leaf packages with cooked basmati rice coloured with ground turmeric, secure each one with a skewer and reheat on the barbecue.

Energy 430kcal/1789kJ; Protein 41.4g; Carbohydrate 1.1g, of which sugars 0.9g; Fat 28.9g, of which saturates 9.6g; Cholesterol 100mg; Calcium 70mg; Fibre 1.9g; Sodium 96mg.

TROUT <u>WITH</u> BACON

THE SMOKY, SAVOURY FLAVOUR OF GRILLED BACON PERFECTLY COMPLEMENTS THE DELICATE FLESH OF THE TROUT IN THIS SIMPLE DISH. WRAPPING THE BACON ROUND THE FISH HELPS TO KEEP IT INTACT, WHILE THE BACON ITSELF BECOMES DELICIOUSLY CRISP DURING COOKING.

SERVES FOUR

INGREDIENTS
   4 trout, cleaned and gutted
   25g/1oz/1 tbsp plain (all-purpose)
     flour
   4 rashers (strips) smoked streaky
     (fatty) bacon
   30ml/2 tbsp olive oil
   juice of ½ lemon
   salt and ground black pepper

COOK'S TIP
Either brown or rainbow trout can be used for this dish, but buy the freshest fish you can find.

1 Place the trout on a chopping board and pat dry with kitchen paper. Season the flour with a moderate pinch of salt and ground black pepper. Stretch the bacon rashers out thinly with the back of a heavy kitchen knife.

2 Roll the fish in the seasoned flour mixture and wrap tightly in the bacon. Brush with olive oil and cook on a medium-hot barbecue for 10–15 minutes, turning once. Squeeze lemon juice over and serve immediately.

Energy 324kcal/1357kJ; Protein 44.4g; Carbohydrate 0.4g, of which sugars 0.3g; Fat 16.1g, of which saturates 5.1g; Cholesterol 174mg; Calcium 60mg; Fibre 0.3g; Sodium 997mg.

MARINATED SEA TROUT

SEA TROUT HAS A SUPERB TEXTURE AND A FLAVOUR LIKE THAT OF WILD SALMON. IT'S BEST SERVED WITH STRONG BUT COMPLEMENTARY FLAVOURS SUCH AS CHILLIES AND LIME THAT CUT THE RICHNESS OF THE FLESH. USE HINGED WIRE BASKETS TO MAKE COOKING AND TURNING EASIER.

SERVES SIX

INGREDIENTS

  6 sea trout cutlets, about 115g/4oz
    each, or wild or farmed salmon
  2 garlic cloves, chopped
  1 fresh long red chilli, seeded
    and chopped
  45ml/3 tbsp chopped Thai basil
  15ml/1 tbsp palm sugar (jaggery) or
    granulated sugar
  3 limes
  400ml/14fl oz/1⅔ cups coconut milk
  15ml/1 tbsp Thai fish sauce

1 Place the sea trout cutlets in a shallow dish. Using a pestle, pound the garlic and chilli in a large mortar to break it up roughly. Add 30ml/2 tbsp of the Thai basil with the sugar and continue to pound to a rough paste.

2 Grate the rind from 1 lime and squeeze it. Mix the rind and juice into the chilli paste, with the coconut milk. Pour the mixture over the cutlets, cover and chill the mixture for about 1 hour. Cut the remaining limes into wedges.

COOK'S TIP
This recipe uses the marinade as a sauce to accompany the fish. You can do this with most marinades as long as you boil them first. Boil up the marinade in a small pan on the barbecue then move it to the side to simmer for 5 minutes. Never use a marinade to brush over food just before serving or as a sauce unless it has been thoroughly cooked first.

3 Remove the fish from the refrigerator so that it can return to room temperature before you cook it on the barbecue. Prepare the barbecue. Position a lightly oiled grill rack over the hot coals. Remove the cutlets from the marinade and reserve the marinade. Place them in an oiled hinged wire fish basket or directly on the grill rack. Cook the fish over medium-high heat for 4 minutes on each side, trying not to move them. They may stick to the grill rack if not seared first.

4 Strain the remaining marinade into a pan, reserving the contents of the sieve (strainer). Bring the marinade to the boil, simmer gently for 5 minutes at the side of the barbecue, then stir in the contents of the sieve and continue to simmer for 1 minute more.

5 Add the Thai fish sauce and the remaining Thai basil to the pan. When the fish is cooked lift each cutlet on to a plate, pour over the sauce and serve with the lime wedges.

Energy 157kcal/662kJ; Protein 23.1g; Carbohydrate 5.9g, of which sugars 5.9g; Fat 4.7g, of which saturates 0.1g; Cholesterol 0mg; Calcium 46mg; Fibre 0.4g; Sodium 141mg.

HAM-WRAPPED TROUT

SERRANO HAM IS USED TO STUFF AND WRAP TROUT FOR THIS UNUSUAL RECIPE FROM SPAIN, ENSURING A WONDERFUL FLAVOUR. ONE OF THE BEAUTIES OF THIS METHOD IS THAT THE SKINS COME OFF IN ONE PIECE, LEAVING THE SUCCULENT, MOIST FLESH TO BE EATEN WITH THE CRISPED, SALT HAM.

SERVES FOUR

INGREDIENTS
    4 brown or rainbow trout, about
        250g/9oz each, cleaned
    16 thin slices Serrano ham, about
        200g/7oz
    50g/2oz/¼ cup melted butter, plus
        extra for greasing
    salt and ground black pepper
    buttered potatoes, to
        serve (optional)

1 Extend the belly cavity of each trout, cutting up one side of the backbone. Slip a knife behind the rib bones to loosen them (sometimes just flexing the fish makes them pop up). Snip these off from both sides with scissors, and season the fish well inside.

2 Fold a piece of ham into each belly. Use smaller or broken bits of ham for this, and reserve the eight best slices.

COOK'S TIP
Serrano ham is less fatty than prosciutto, which should help to avoid flare-ups.

3 Prepare the barbecue. Position a lightly oiled grill rack over the hot coals. Brush each trout with a little butter, seasoning the outside lightly with salt and pepper. Wrap two ham slices round each one, crossways, tucking the ends into the belly.

4 Put the fish into oiled hinged wire fish baskets or directly on to the grill rack. The combined grilling time should be 4 minutes on each side, though it is wise to turn the fish every 2 minutes to ensure that the ham does not become charred.

5 Serve the trout hot, with the butter spooned over the top. Diners should open the trout on their plates, and eat them from the inside, pushing the flesh off the skin.

Energy 369kcal/1546kJ; Protein 48g; Carbohydrate 0.6g, of which sugars 0.6g; Fat 19.4g, of which saturates 8.8g; Cholesterol 216mg; Calcium 66mg; Fibre 0g; Sodium 821mg.

SWORDFISH WITH ROASTED TOMATOES

SUN-RIPENED TOMATOES ARE NATURALLY FULL OF FLAVOUR AND SWEETNESS, AND IN THIS MOROCCAN RECIPE THEY ARE ROASTED WITH SUGAR AND SPICES SO THAT THEY SIMPLY MELT IN THE MOUTH. AS AN ACCOMPANIMENT TO CHARGRILLED FISH OR POULTRY, THEY ARE SENSATIONAL.

SERVES FOUR

INGREDIENTS

1kg/2¼lb large vine or plum
  tomatoes, peeled, halved and seeded
5–10ml/1–2 tsp ground cinnamon
pinch of saffron threads
15ml/1 tbsp orange flower water
60ml/4 tbsp olive oil
45–60ml/3–4 tbsp sugar
4 swordfish steaks, about
  225g/8oz each
rind of ½ preserved lemon,
  finely chopped
small bunch of fresh coriander
  (cilantro), finely chopped
handful of blanched almonds
knob (pat) of butter
salt and ground black pepper

1 Preheat the oven to 110°C/225°F/
Gas ¼. Place the tomatoes on a baking
sheet. Sprinkle with the cinnamon,
saffron and orange flower water. Trickle
half the oil over, being sure to moisten
every tomato half, and sprinkle with
sugar. Place the tray in the bottom of
the oven and cook the tomatoes for
about 3 hours, then turn the oven off
and leave them to cool.

2 Prepare the barbecue. Heat a griddle
on a grill rack over hot coals. Brush the
remaining olive oil over the swordfish
steaks and season with salt and pepper.
Cook the steaks for 3–4 minutes on
each side. Sprinkle the chopped
preserved lemon rind and coriander
over the steaks towards the end of the
cooking time.

3 In a separate pan, fry the almonds in
the butter until golden and sprinkle
them over the tomatoes. Then serve the
steaks immediately with the tomatoes.

VARIATION
If swordfish steaks are not available, use
tuna or shark steaks. Or, if you prefer, try
the recipe with a piece of lean sirloin or
thinly cut fillet steak (beef tenderloin).
The lemon and coriander flavours lift the
meat beautifully.

Energy 463kcal/1941kJ; Protein 47.2g; Carbohydrate 19.9g, of which sugars 19.8g; Fat 22.2g, of which saturates 4.1g; Cholesterol 103mg; Calcium 59mg; Fibre 3.1g; Sodium 352mg.

GRILLED SWORDFISH SKEWERS

FOR A HINT OF THE GREEK ISLANDS, TRY THESE TANTALIZING SWORDFISH SKEWERS. BARBECUED WITH PEPPERS AND ONIONS, THEY ALSO HAVE A HINT OF OREGANO. TRY THROWING SOME OREGANO SPRIGS OVER THE COALS AS YOU COOK, FOR ADDED FLAVOUR.

SERVES FOUR

INGREDIENTS

2 red onions, quartered
2 red (bell) peppers, quartered and
  seeded
20–24 thick cubes of swordfish,
  prepared weight
  675–800g/1½–1¾lb
75ml/5 tbsp extra virgin olive oil
1 garlic clove, crushed
large pinch of dried oregano
salt and ground black pepper

1 Carefully separate the onion quarters into pieces each composed of two or three layers. Slice each pepper quarter in half widthways to make 16 even-sized pieces.

2 Make the kebabs by threading five or six pieces of swordfish on to each of four long metal skewers, alternating with pieces of the pepper and onion. Lay the assembled kebabs across a grill pan or roasting tray and set aside while you make the basting sauce.

3 Whisk the olive oil, crushed garlic and oregano in a bowl. Add salt and pepper, and whisk again. Brush the kebabs generously on all sides with the basting sauce.

4 Prepare the barbecue. When the flames have died down position a lightly oiled grill rack over the hot coals. Transfer the kebabs to the barbecue. Cook for 8–10 minutes over medium heat, turning the skewers several times, until the fish is cooked and the peppers and onions have begun to scorch around the edges. Every time you turn the skewers, brush them with more of the basting sauce.

5 Serve the kebabs immediately, with a cucumber, onion and olive salad.

COOK'S TIP
The fishmonger will be happy to prepare the cubes of swordfish for you, but if you prefer to do this yourself you will need to buy about 800g/1¾lb swordfish. The cubes should be fairly big – about 5cm/2in square.

Energy 322kcal/1345kJ; Protein 32.5g; Carbohydrate 13.5g, of which sugars 11g; Fat 15.7g, of which saturates 2.8g; Cholesterol 69mg; Calcium 39mg; Fibre 2.8g; Sodium 226mg.

SWORDFISH KEBABS

SWORDFISH HAS A FIRM MEATY TEXTURE THAT MAKES IT IDEAL FOR COOKING ON A BARBECUE.
MARINATING THE FISH FIRST HELPS TO KEEP IT MOIST, BUT AS WITH ALL FISH IT IS IMPORTANT TO
WATCH IT CONSTANTLY AND NOT ALLOW IT TO OVERCOOK.

SERVES FOUR TO SIX

INGREDIENTS
900g/2lb thick swordfish steaks
45ml/3 tbsp olive oil
juice of ½ lemon
1 garlic clove, crushed
5ml/1 tsp paprika
4–6 cherry or small vine tomatoes
2 green (bell) peppers, cut into
  chunks
2 white onions, cut into wedges
salt and ground black pepper
lettuce and pitta bread, to serve

1 Cut the swordfish into large cubes. Arrange the cubes in a single layer in a large shallow dish.

2 Blend together the olive oil, lemon juice, garlic, paprika and seasoning in a bowl, and pour over the fish. Cover the dish loosely with clear film (plastic wrap) and leave to marinate in a cool place for up to 2 hours.

3 Thread the fish cubes on to metal skewers, alternating them with the vegetable chunks.

4 Barbecue the kebabs for 5–10 minutes, basting frequently with the marinade and turning occasionally. Serve with salad and pitta bread.

Energy 322kcal/1345kJ; Protein 32.5g; Carbohydrate 13.5g, of which sugars 10.9g; Fat 15.7g, of which saturates 2.8g; Cholesterol 69mg; Calcium 39mg; Fibre 2.8g; Sodium 226mg.

RED MULLET WITH BASIL AND CITRUS

THIS ITALIAN RECIPE IS FULL OF THE WARM, DISTINCTIVE FLAVOURS OF THE MEDITERRANEAN. SERVE THE DISH WITH PLAIN BOILED RICE AND A GREEN SALAD, OR WITH LOTS OF FRESH CRUSTY BREAD.

SERVES FOUR

INGREDIENTS

4 red mullet, about 225g/8oz
  each, filleted
60ml/4 tbsp olive oil
10 peppercorns, crushed
2 oranges, one peeled and thinly
  sliced and one squeezed
1 lemon
15g/½oz/1 tbsp butter
2 canned anchovies, drained
  and chopped
60ml/4 tbsp shredded fresh basil
salt and ground black pepper

1 Place the red mullet fillets in a shallow dish into which they will just fit in a single layer. Pour the olive oil over the fish and sprinkle with the crushed peppercorns. Lay the slices of orange on top of the fish. Cover the dish with clear film (plastic wrap), and leave to marinate in the refrigerator for at least 4 hours, turning the fish once if possible.

COOK'S TIP

You could serve the fish without the sauce if you dislike the strong flavour of anchovy. Alternatively, make the sauce in advance and simply reheat it on the barbecue in a suitable dish.

2 Cut the lemon in half. Remove the skin and all the white pith from one half using a small, sharp knife, and slice the flesh thinly, removing any pips. Squeeze the juice from the other half and reserve with the orange juice.

3 Drain the fish, reserving the marinade and orange slices, and cook on a medium-hot barbecue for about 10–12 minutes, turning once and basting with the marinade.

4 Melt the butter in a pan with any remaining marinade. Add the chopped anchovies and cook until completely soft. Stir in the orange and lemon juice and allow to simmer on the edge of the barbecue until slightly reduced. Stir in the basil and check the seasoning. Pour over the fish and garnish with the reserved orange slices and the lemon slices. Serve immediately.

Energy 355kcal/1480kJ; Protein 23.4g; Carbohydrate 11g, of which sugars 5.2g; Fat 24.6g, of which saturates 4.4g; Cholesterol 9mg; Calcium 125mg; Fibre 1.3g; Sodium 198mg.

RED MULLET <u>WITH</u> LAVENDER

ADDING LAVENDER TO RED MULLET GIVES A WONDERFUL FLAVOUR. SPRINKLE SOME LAVENDER FLOWERS ON THE COALS TOO, WHILE THE FISH IS COOKING, TO GIVE A PERFUMED AMBIENCE.

SERVES FOUR

INGREDIENTS

4 red mullet, scaled, gutted
    and cleaned
30ml/2 tbsp olive oil
For the marinade
    45ml/3 tbsp fresh lavender flowers or
    15ml/1 tbsp dried lavender leaves,
    roughly chopped
    roughly chopped rind of 1 lemon
    4 spring onions (scallions), roughly
    chopped
    salt and ground black pepper

1 Place the fish in a shallow dish. Mix the ingredients for the marinade and pour over the fish. Cover with clear film (plastic wrap) and leave in the fridge to marinate for at least 3 hours.

2 Remove the fish from the marinade and brush it with olive oil. Cook the fish on a hot barbecue for about 10–15 minutes, turning once and basting with olive oil as it cooks.

Energy 219kcal/918kJ; Protein 28.6g; Carbohydrate 0.6g, of which sugars 0.6g; Fat 11.4g, of which saturates 0.8g; Cholesterol 0mg; Calcium 126mg; Fibre 0.7g; Sodium 141mg.

SEA BASS WRAPPED IN VINE LEAVES

THIS DISH IS EFFORTLESS BUT MUST BE STARTED IN ADVANCE BECAUSE THE RICE NEEDS TO BE COLD BEFORE IT IS USED IN THE LITTLE PARCELS. ONCE THE FISH HAVE BEEN WRAPPED, ALL YOU HAVE TO DO IS KEEP THEM CHILLED, READY TO POP ON TO THE BARBECUE.

3 Season the sea bass fillets. Wash the vine leaves in water, then pat dry with kitchen paper. Lay each leaf in the centre of a double layer of foil. Top with a sea bass fillet. Divide the rice mixture among the fillets, spooning it towards one end. Fold the fillet over the rice, trickle over the remaining oil, lay the second vine leaf on top and bring the foil up around the fish and scrunch it together to seal. Chill the packages for up to 3 hours, or until needed.

4 Take the fish out of the refrigerator and prepare the barbecue. Position a lightly oiled grill rack over the hot coals. Place the parcels on the edge of the rack. Cook for 5 minutes over high heat, turning them around by 90 degrees halfway through. Open up the top of the foil a little and cook for 2 minutes more. Gently remove from the foil and transfer the vine parcels to plates to serve.

COOK'S TIP
For a quick salsa, chop half a seeded cucumber and half a pink onion. Place in a bowl and add 30ml/2 tbsp seasoned sushi vinegar and mix well. Add a little chilli to put a bit of a kick in it.

MAKES EIGHT

INGREDIENTS
90g/3½oz/½ cup Chinese
    black rice
400ml/14fl oz/1⅔ cups boiling water
45ml/3 tbsp extra virgin olive oil
1 small onion, chopped
1 fresh mild chilli, seeded and
    finely chopped
8 sea bass fillets, about 75g/3oz
    each, with skin
16 large fresh vine leaves
salt and ground black pepper

1 Place the Chinese black rice in a large pan. Add the measured boiling water and simmer for 15 minutes. Add a little salt to taste and simmer for a further 10 minutes, or until tender. Drain well and tip into a bowl.

2 Meanwhile, heat half the oil in a frying pan. Fry the onion gently for 5 minutes until softened but not browned. Add the chilli. Stir into the rice mixture and season with salt and pepper according to taste. Cool the rice completely and cover and chill until needed.

Energy 157kcal/656kJ; Protein 15.5g; Carbohydrate 9.9g, of which sugars 0.7g; Fat 6.1g, of which saturates 0.9g; Cholesterol 60mg; Calcium 105mg; Fibre 0.2g; Sodium 52mg.

SEA BASS <u>WITH</u> FENNEL

THE CLASSIC COMBINATION OF SEA BASS AND FENNEL WORKS PARTICULARLY WELL WHEN THE FISH IS COOKED OVER CHARCOAL. FENNEL TWIGS ARE TRADITIONALLY USED INSIDE THE FISH BUT THIS VERSION OF THE RECIPE USES FENNEL SEEDS, WHICH FLAVOUR THE FISH BEAUTIFULLY.

SERVES SIX

INGREDIENTS
 1 sea bass, about 1.3–1.6kg/
  3–3½lb, cleaned and scaled
 60ml/4 tbsp olive oil
 10ml/2 tsp fennel seeds
 2 large fennel bulbs
 60ml/4 tbsp Pernod
 salt and ground black pepper

1 Make four deep slashes in each side of the fish. Brush the fish with olive oil and season well with salt and freshly ground black pepper. Sprinkle the fennel seeds in the cavity and slashes of the fish.

2 Trim and slice the fennel bulbs thinly, reserving any leafy fronds to use as a garnish for the dish.

3 Prepare the barbecue. When the flames have died down part the coals in the centre and position a drip tray. Position a lightly oiled grill rack over the hot coals. Put the fish inside a hinged wire basket or straight on to the grill rack over the drip tray. Cook over indirect medium heat using a lid or tented foil, for 20 minutes, basting occasionally and turning once.

4 Meanwhile, brush the slices of fennel with olive oil and cook on the barbecue for about 8–10 minutes, turning the fennel occasionally, until tender. Remove the fish and fennel from the heat.

5 Scatter the fennel slices on a serving plate. Lay the fish on top and garnish with the reserved fennel fronds.

6 When ready for eating, heat the Pernod in a small pan on the side of the barbecue, light it and pour it, flaming, over the fish. Serve immediately.

Energy 180kcal/750kJ; Protein 19.9g; Carbohydrate 1.2g, of which sugars 1.1g; Fat 8.1g, of which saturates 1.2g; Cholesterol 80mg; Calcium 146mg; Fibre 1.6g; Sodium 76mg.

GRILLED SEA BASS <u>WITH</u> CITRUS FRUIT

SEA BASS IS A BEAUTIFUL FISH WITH A SOFT, DENSE TEXTURE AND A DELICATE FLAVOUR. IN THIS RECIPE IT IS COMPLEMENTED BY CITRUS FRUITS AND FRUITY OLIVE OIL.

SERVES SIX

INGREDIENTS
1 small grapefruit
1 orange
1 lemon
1 sea bass, about 1.5kg/3–3½lb,
  gutted, cleaned and scaled
6 fresh basil sprigs
45ml/3 tbsp olive oil
4–6 shallots, halved
60ml/4 tbsp dry white wine
15g/½oz/1 tbsp butter
salt and ground black pepper
fresh dill, to garnish

1 Using a vegetable peeler, remove the rind from the grapefruit, orange and lemon, leaving the white pith behind. Cut the rind into thin julienne strips. Peel the pith from the fruits with a sharp knife and, working over a bowl to catch the juice, cut out the segments from the grapefruit and the orange and set aside for the garnish. Slice the lemon thickly.

2 Prepare the barbecue. Season the cavity of the fish with salt and ground black pepper and slash the skin and flesh three times on each side. Reserving a few basil sprigs for the garnish, fill the cavity with the remaining basil, the lemon slices and half the julienne strips of citrus rind. Brush the fish with olive oil.

3 Barbecue the fish in a hinged wire fish basket or cook on a lightly oiled grill rack over low–medium heat for about 20 minutes, basting occasionally and turning once.

4 Meanwhile, heat 15ml/1 tbsp olive oil in a pan and cook the shallots gently until soft. Add the wine and 30–45ml/2–3 tbsp of the fruit juice to the pan. Bring to the boil over a high heat, stirring. Stir in the remaining julienne strips of rind and boil for 2–3 minutes, then whisk in the butter.

5 When the fish is cooked, transfer it to a serving dish. Remove and discard the cavity stuffing. Spoon the shallots and sauce around the fish and garnish with fresh dill sprigs, the reserved basil and segments of grapefruit and orange.

Energy 258kcal/1081kJ; Protein 32.7g; Carbohydrate 3.9g, of which sugars 3.9g; Fat 11.8g, of which saturates 2.8g; Cholesterol 139mg; Calcium 241mg; Fibre 0.7g; Sodium 133mg.

GRILLED SNAPPER WITH HOT MANGO SALSA

A RIPE MANGO PROVIDES THE BASIS FOR A DELICIOUSLY RICH FRUITY SALSA. THE DRESSING NEEDS NO OIL AND FEATURES THE TROPICAL FLAVOURS OF CORIANDER, GINGER AND CHILLI.

SERVES FOUR

INGREDIENTS
  350g/12oz new potatoes
  3 eggs
  115g/4oz French beans, topped,
    tailed and halved
  4 red snapper, about 350g/12oz
    each, cleaned, scaled and gutted
  30ml/2 tbsp olive oil
  175g/6oz mixed lettuce leaves, such
    as frisée or Webb's
  2 cherry tomatoes
  salt and ground black pepper
For the salsa
  45ml/3 tbsp chopped fresh coriander
    (cilantro)
  1 medium-sized ripe mango, peeled,
    stoned (pitted) and diced
  ½ red chilli, seeded and chopped
  2.5cm/1in fresh root ginger, grated
  juice of 2 limes
  generous pinch of celery salt

1 Bring the potatoes to the boil in a large pan of salted water and simmer for 15–20 minutes. Drain.

2 Bring a second large pan of salted water to the boil. Boil the eggs for 4 minutes, then add the beans and cook for a further 6 minutes, so that the eggs have had a total of 10 minutes. Remove the eggs and cool under cold running water. Drain and refresh the beans. Shell the eggs and cut into quarters.

VARIATION
If fresh mangoes are unavailable, use canned, draining well. Sea bream are also good served with this hot mango salsa.

3 Prepare the barbecue. Slash each snapper three times on either side. Brush with olive oil and cook over medium-hot coals for 12 minutes, basting occasionally and turning once.

4 To make the salsa, place the chopped fresh coriander in a food processor. Add the mango chunks, chilli, grated ginger, lime juice and celery salt and process until smooth.

5 Dress the lettuce leaves with olive oil and distribute them evenly between four large plates.

6 Arrange the snapper on the lettuce and season to taste. Halve the new potatoes and distribute them among the places, arranging them with the beans, tomatoes and quartered hard-boiled eggs over the salad. Serve immediately, with the salsa.

Energy 381kcal/1612kJ; Protein 51.6g; Carbohydrate 21.8g, of which sugars 8.4g; Fat 10.7g, of which saturates 2.4g; Cholesterol 223mg; Calcium 174mg; Fibre 3.6g; Sodium 276mg.

BARBECUED RED SNAPPER

THE RED SNAPPER IS A LINE-CAUGHT REEF FISH FROM THE INDIAN OCEAN AND THE CARIBBEAN.
ALTHOUGH BEAUTIFUL TO LOOK AT, IT HAS VICIOUS SPINES AND A FAIRLY IMPENETRABLE ARMOUR OF
SCALES, SO IT IS PROBABLY BEST TO ASK THE FISHMONGER TO SCALE IT. LEAVE THE FINS ON,
HOWEVER, SO THAT IT RETAINS ITS LOVELY NATURAL QUALITY.

SERVES FOUR

INGREDIENTS

2 red snapper, about 900g/2lb each,
cleaned and scaled, or tilapia
15ml/1 tbsp olive oil
5cm/2in piece of fresh root ginger,
thinly sliced
4 banana shallots, total weight about
150g/5oz, thinly sliced
3 garlic cloves, thinly sliced
30ml/2 tbsp sugar
3 lemon grass stalks, 1 thinly sliced
grated rind and juice of 1 lime
5ml/1 tsp salt
4 small fresh green or red chillies,
thinly sliced
2 whole banana leaves
30ml/2 tbsp chopped fresh coriander
(cilantro)
For the dipping sauce
1 large fresh red chilli, seeded and
finely chopped
juice of 2 limes
30ml/2 tbsp Thai fish sauce
5ml/1 tsp sugar
60ml/4 tbsp water

1 Soak six wooden skewers in cold
water for 30 minutes to prevent them
burning on the barbecue. Make four
slashes in the flesh on either side of
each fish and rub the skin with oil.

2 Make the dipping sauce by mixing
together all the ingredients in a bowl.
Cover and chill until needed.

3 Place half the ginger and shallots and
the garlic in a mortar. Add half the
sugar, the thinly sliced lemon grass, a
little of the lime juice, the salt and the
chillies and pound to break up and
bruise. Mix in the remaining sugar and
lime juice, with the lime rind. Rub a
little of the mixture into the slashes and
the bulk of it into the cavity of each fish.

4 Trim the hard edge from each banana
leaf and discard it. Soak the banana
leaves in hot water for 10 minutes, then
drain. Wipe any white residue from the
leaves. Rinse, then pour over boiling
water to soften. Drain again.

5 Lay a fish on each leaf and scatter the
remaining ginger and shallots over
them. Split the lemon grass stalks
lengthways and lay the pieces over each
fish. Bring the sides of the leaves up
over the fish and secure using three
wooden skewers for each envelope.
Wrap in clear film (plastic wrap) to keep
the skewers moist, and chill for at least
30 minutes, but no more than 6 hours.

6 Prepare the barbecue. Bring the
dipping sauce to room temperature.
Remove the clear film from each
banana leaf envelope and place each
on a sheet of foil. Bring the sides of the
foil up around each envelope to enclose
it loosely. This will protect the base of
each banana leaf wrapper.

7 Position a lightly oiled grill rack over
the hot coals. Lay the envelopes on the
grill rack and cook for 15 minutes over
medium-high heat. Turn the envelopes
around 180 degrees and cook for about
10 minutes more, opening up the foil
for the last 5 minutes.

8 Remove from the barbecue and leave
to stand for a further 5 minutes, then
check to see if the fish is cooked by
inserting a skewer – it should flake
easily when the skewer is removed.

9 Place the envelopes on a large,
warmed dish, open them and sprinkle
the fish with the chopped coriander.
Serve the fish immediately in individual
serving bowls, with smaller bowls for
the dipping sauce.

COOK'S TIPS

• Serve leaf-wrapped rice parcels with
the fish. Heat them up in foil next to the
fish for the last 5 minutes. They can be
found in larger Asian food stores.
• Banana shallots have longer bulbs than
most shallots or onions, and varieties
include Long Red Florence and Longor.

Energy 305kcal/1293kJ; Protein 57.3g; Carbohydrate 2.9g, of which sugars 2.9g; Fat 7.5g, of which saturates 1.4g; Cholesterol 104mg; Calcium 157mg; Fibre 1.2g; Sodium 541mg.

INDONESIAN CHARGRILLED FISH WITH SAMBAL BADJAK

*IN THE COASTAL REGIONS OF INDONESIA, GRILLING FISH OVER CHARCOAL IS A COMMON SIGHT IN THE
TOURIST RESORTS, IN THE VILLAGES, ON THE BEACH AND BY THE ROADSIDE. THIS IS A PLEASINGLY
SPICY AND WELL FLAVOURED DISH THAT LOOKS GOOD AND IS SURE TO BE POPULAR WITH GUESTS.*

2 Meanwhile, prepare the *sambal*. Put
the tamarind paste in a bowl, pour over
the boiling water and leave to soak for
30 minutes. Strain into a separate bowl,
pressing the paste through a sieve
(strainer). Discard the solids and put
the tamarind juice aside.

3 Using a mortar and pestle, pound the
shallots, garlic, chillies, galangal and
lime leaves to a coarse paste. Add the
terasi and sugar and beat together until
combined.

4 Heat the oil in a small wok, stir in the
paste and fry for 2–3 minutes. Stir in
the tamarind juice and boil until it
reduces to a thick paste. Turn into a
serving bowl.

SERVES FOUR

INGREDIENTS
    30ml/2 tbsp coconut oil
    60ml/4 tbsp dark soy sauce
    2 garlic cloves, crushed
    juice of 1 lime
    1 whole large sea fish, such as
        grouper, red snapper, sea bass,
        large piece of sword fish, or 4
        whole smaller fish, such as
        sardines, gutted and cleaned
    cooked rice, to serve
For the *sambal badjak*
    50g/2oz tamarind paste
    150ml/¼ pint/⅔ cup boiling water
    4 shallots, chopped
    4 garlic cloves, chopped
    4–6 red chillies, seeded and
        chopped
    25g/1oz galangal, chopped
    2 kaffir lime leaves, crumbled
    10ml/2 tsp *terasi* (Indonesian
        shrimp paste)
    10ml/2 tsp palm sugar
    30ml/2 tbsp coconut or palm oil

1 In a small bowl, mix the coconut oil,
soy sauce, garlic and lime juice
together. Put the fish in a shallow dish
and slash the flesh at intervals with a
sharp knife. Spoon the marinade over
the fish and rub it into the skin and
slashes. Leave for about 1 hour.

5 Prepare the barbecue. Place the fish
on the grill (broiler) and cook for 5
minutes each side, depending on the
size of fish, basting it with any leftover
marinade.

6 Transfer the fish to a serving plate
and serve with the *sambal* and rice.

COOK'S TIP
If you can't find some of these
ingredients, try using the following:
• fresh ginger root mixed with a little
    lemon juice instead of galangal
• lime zest with a bay leaf, or lemon
    thyme instead of kaffir lime leaves
• Worcestershire sauce or lime juice
    instead of tamarind.

Energy 359kcal/1507kJ; Protein 42.3g; Carbohydrate 11.8g, of which sugars 9.3g; Fat 16.4g, of which saturates 2.3g; Cholesterol 75mg; Calcium 117mg; Fibre 1.4g; Sodium 1263mg.

CHARGRILLED TUNA WITH FIERY PEPPER PURÉE

TUNA IS AN OILY FISH THAT BARBECUES WELL AND IS MEATY ENOUGH TO COMBINE SUCCESSFULLY WITH OTHER STRONG FLAVOURS — EVEN HOT CHILLI, WHICH IS USED TO SPICE THIS RED PEPPER PURÉE. THE DISH IS EXCELLENT SERVED WITH CRUSTY BREAD.

SERVES FOUR

INGREDIENTS

4 tuna steaks, about 175g/6oz each
finely grated rind and juice of 1 lime
30ml/2 tbsp olive oil
salt and ground black pepper
lime wedges, to serve

For the pepper purée
2 red (bell) peppers, halved
45ml/3 tbsp olive oil, plus extra
for brushing
1 small onion
2 garlic cloves, crushed
2 red chillies
1 slice white bread without
crusts, diced
salt

1 Trim any skin from the tuna and place the steaks in a single layer in a wide glass or ceramic dish. Sprinkle over the lime rind and juice and the olive oil, and season on both sides with salt and black pepper. Cover the dish with clear film (plastic wrap) and chill the tuna until required.

2 Prepare the barbecue and when the flames have died down arrange a rack over the coals. To make the pepper purée, brush the pepper halves with a little olive oil and cook them, skin-side down, over hot coals, until the skin is charred and blackened. Place the onion, still in its skin, on the barbecue and cook until browned on all sides, turning it occasionally.

3 Place the peppers in a plastic bag or leave them under an upturned bowl so that the steam loosens the skin. When the peppers and the onion are cool enough to handle, remove the skins using a sharp kitchen knife.

4 Cut the cooked peppers and onion into chunks and place them in a food processor with the garlic, chillies, bread and olive oil. Process until smooth. Add salt to taste.

5 Drain the tuna steaks from the marinade and cook them on a hot barbecue for 4–5 minutes, turning once, until browned but still a little pink inside. Serve the steaks with the pepper purée and lime wedges.

COOK'S TIP

The pepper purée can be made in advance, cooking the peppers and onion under a hot grill (broiler); keep it in the refrigerator until you cook the fish.

Energy 411kcal/1718kJ; Protein 43.1g; Carbohydrate 10.1g, of which sugars 6.4g; Fat 22.3g, of which saturates 4.2g; Cholesterol 49mg; Calcium 46mg; Fibre 1.7g; Sodium 121mg.

SEARED TUNA WITH GINGER

THIS NORTH AFRICAN RECIPE IS UNBEATABLE FAST, NUTRITIOUS FARE FOR THE BARBECUE. TUNA STEAKS ARE RUBBED WITH HARISSA AND THEN GRIDDLED QUICKLY OVER HIGH HEAT AND SERVED WITH A DELICIOUS WARM SALAD SPICED WITH GINGER AND CHILLIES. NO MARINATING TIME IS NEEDED.

SERVES FOUR

INGREDIENTS
30ml/2 tbsp olive oil
5ml/1 tsp harissa
5ml/1 tsp clear honey
4 tuna steaks, about 200g/7oz each
salt and ground black pepper
lemon wedges, to serve
For the salad
30ml/2 tbsp olive oil
a little butter
25g/1oz fresh root ginger, peeled and
  finely sliced
2 garlic cloves, finely sliced
2 green chillies, seeded and
  finely sliced
6 spring onions (scallions), cut into
  bite-size pieces
2 large handfuls of watercress or
  rocket (arugula)
juice of ½ lemon

1 Prepare the barbecue. While the coals are heating up, combine the olive oil, harissa, honey and salt in a bowl, and rub the mixture over the tuna steaks using your fingers.

2 Heat a griddle on the grill rack over hot coals. Sear the tuna steaks for about 2 minutes on each side. They should still be pink on the inside when pierced with a skewer.

3 Keep the tuna warm while you quickly prepare the salad: heat the olive oil and butter in a heavy pan on the side of the barbecue. Add the ginger, garlic, chillies and spring onions. Cook until the mixture begins to colour, then add the watercress or rocket. When it begins to wilt, toss in the lemon juice and season well.

4 Tip the warm salad on to a serving dish or individual plates. Slice the tuna steaks and arrange on top of the salad. Serve immediately with lemon wedges for squeezing over.

VARIATION
Prawns (shrimp) and scallops can be cooked in the same way. The shellfish will just need to be cooked briefly – too long and they will become rubbery.

Energy 176kcal/731kJ; Protein 12.3g; Carbohydrate 1.6g, of which sugars 1.6g; Fat 13.4g, of which saturates 2.2g; Cholesterol 14mg; Calcium 18mg; Fibre 0.4g; Sodium 25mg.

GRILLED STINGRAY <u>WITH</u> CHILLI SAMBAL

CHARGRILLED STINGRAY HAS A BEAUTIFUL FLAVOUR AND FIRM TEXTURE, AND HERE IS SERVED ON A BANANA LEAF WITH A GENEROUS DOLLOP OF CHILLI SAMBAL. BANANA LEAVES ARE AVAILABLE IN CHINESE AND ASIAN MARKETS, BUT OF COURSE YOU CAN OMIT THEM AND SERVE ON PLATES.

SERVES FOUR

INGREDIENTS

4 medium-sized stingray wings,
 about 200g/7oz each, rinsed and
 patted dry
salt
4 banana leaves, about
 30cm/12in square
2 fresh limes, halved
For the chilli *sambal*
6–8 red chillies, seeded and chopped
4 garlic cloves, chopped
5ml/1 tsp shrimp paste
15ml/1 tbsp tomato purée (paste)
15ml/1 tbsp palm sugar (jaggery)
juice of 2 limes
30ml/2 tbsp vegetable or groundnut
 (peanut) oil

1 First make the chilli *sambal*. Using a mortar and pestle, grind the chillies with the garlic to form a paste. Beat in the shrimp paste, tomato purée and sugar. Add the lime juice and bind with the oil. Alternatively put all the ingredients into a food processor and process to a smooth purée.

2 Prepare the barbecue and place a lightly oiled rack over the hot coals. Rub each stingray wing with a little chilli *sambal* and place them on the rack. Cook for 3–4 minutes on each side, until tender. Sprinkle with salt and serve on banana leaves with the remaining chilli sambal and the limes.

Energy 195Kcal/823kJ; Protein 30.4g; Carbohydrate 4.5g, of which sugars 4.5g; Fat 6.3g, of which saturates 0.7g; Cholesterol 0mg; Calcium 83mg; Fibre 0.1g; Sodium 249mg.

MONKFISH <u>WITH</u> PEPPERED CITRUS MARINADE

MONKFISH IS A FIRM, MEATY FISH THAT COOKS BEAUTIFULLY ON THE BARBECUE AND KEEPS ITS SHAPE WELL. IT IS IDEAL FOR KEBABS, BUT IN THIS RECIPE THE TAILS ARE FILLETED AND COOKED WHOLE, SPIKED WITH REFRESHING CITRUS FLAVOURS, TO MAKE A SPECTACULAR PARTY DISH. SERVE THE FISH IN CHUNKY SLICES, ACCOMPANIED BY A GREEN SALAD.

SERVES FOUR

INGREDIENTS
 2 monkfish tails, about
  350g/12oz each
 1 lime
 1 lemon
 2 oranges
 handful of fresh thyme sprigs
 30ml/2 tbsp olive oil
 15ml/1 tbsp mixed peppercorns,
  roughly crushed
 salt and ground black pepper

1 Using a sharp kitchen knife, remove any skin from the monkfish tails. Cut carefully down one side of the backbone, sliding the knife between the bone and flesh, to remove the fillet on one side.

2 Turn the fish and repeat on the other side, to remove the second fillet. Repeat on the second tail. (If you prefer, you can ask your fishmonger to do this for you.) Lay the four fillets out flat on a chopping board.

3 Cut two slices from each of the citrus fruits and arrange them over two of the fillets. Add a few sprigs of fresh thyme and sprinkle with plenty of salt and ground black pepper. Finely grate the rind from the remaining fruit and sprinkle it over the fish.

4 Lay the other two fillets on top and tie them firmly at intervals with thread.

5 Lay the two pieces of fish in a glass or ceramic dish. Squeeze the juice from the citrus fruits and mix it with the olive oil and more salt and pepper. Spoon over the fish. Cover with clear film (plastic wrap) and leave to marinate in the refrigerator for about 1 hour, turning occasionally and spooning the marinade over the fish.

6 Prepare the barbecue and lay a lightly oiled rack over the hot coals. Drain the monkfish, reserving the marinade, and sprinkle with the crushed peppercorns. Cook over medium-hot coals for 15–20 minutes, basting with the marinade and turning occasionally.

COOK'S TIP
Try to find plump, juicy lemons and limes for this recipe. The small, hard ones that are often available impart a slightly bitter taste.

Energy 202kcal/851kJ; Protein 31.4g; Carbohydrate 5.6g, of which sugars 5.6g; Fat 6.4g, of which saturates 1g; Cholesterol 28mg; Calcium 37mg; Fibre 0g; Sodium 38mg.

COD FILLET WITH FRESH MIXED-HERB CRUST

USE FRESH HERBS AND WHOLEMEAL BREADCRUMBS TO MAKE A DELICIOUS CRISP CRUST FOR THE FISH, WHICH HOLDS ITS SHAPE BEAUTIFULLY WHEN CHARGRILLED. SEASON THE FISH WELL AND BARBECUE UNTIL JUST OPAQUE IN THE CENTRE. SERVE WITH LARGE LEMON WEDGES.

SERVES FOUR

INGREDIENTS
25g/1oz/2 tbsp butter
15ml/1 tbsp fresh chervil
15ml/1 tbsp fresh flat leaf
  parsley, plus a few extra sprigs
  to garnish
15ml/1 tbsp fresh chives
175g/6oz/3 cups fresh wholemeal
  (whole-wheat) breadcrumbs
4 thick pieces of cod fillet, about
  225g/8oz each, skinned
15ml/1 tbsp olive oil
salt and ground black pepper
lemon wedges, to garnish

1 Melt the butter and chop all the herbs finely, using a sharp knife. Brush the cod fillets with melted butter and mix any remaining butter with the breadcrumbs, fresh herbs and plenty of salt and ground black pepper.

2 Press a quarter of the mixture on to each fillet, spreading evenly, and lightly sprinkle with olive oil. Cook on a medium barbecue for 8–10 minutes, turning once. Serve garnished with lemon wedges and fresh parsley.

Energy 410kcal/1725kJ; Protein 46.6g; Carbohydrate 34.2g, of which sugars 1.4g; Fat 10.4g, of which saturates 3.9g; Cholesterol 117mg; Calcium 98mg; Fibre 1.5g; Sodium 509mg.

GRIDDLED HALIBUT

ANY THICK WHITE FISH FILLETS CAN BE COOKED IN THIS VERSATILE DISH; TURBOT AND BRILL ARE ESPECIALLY DELICIOUS, BUT THE FLAVOURSOME SAUCE OF TOMATOES, CAPERS, ANCHOVIES AND HERBS ALSO GIVES HUMBLER FISH SUCH AS COD, HADDOCK OR HAKE A REAL LIFT.

SERVES FOUR

INGREDIENTS
  2.5ml/½ tsp fennel seeds
  2.5ml/½ tsp celery seeds
  5ml/1 tsp mixed peppercorns
  105ml/7 tbsp olive oil
  5ml/1 tsp chopped fresh
    thyme leaves
  5ml/1 tsp chopped fresh
    rosemary leaves
  5ml/1 tsp chopped fresh oregano or
    marjoram leaves
  675–800g/1½–1¾lb middle cut of
    halibut, about 3cm/1¼in thick, cut
    into 4 pieces
  coarse sea salt
For the sauce
  105ml/7 tbsp extra virgin olive oil
  juice of 1 lemon
  1 garlic clove, finely chopped
  2 tomatoes, peeled, seeded
    and diced
  5ml/1 tsp small capers
  2 drained canned anchovy
    fillets, chopped
  5ml/1 tsp chopped fresh chives
  15ml/1 tbsp chopped fresh
    basil leaves
  15ml/1 tbsp chopped fresh chervil

1 Prepare the barbecue. Heat a griddle on the grill rack over the hot coals. Mix the fennel and celery seeds with the peppercorns in a mortar. Crush with a pestle, and then stir in coarse sea salt to taste. Spoon the mixture into a shallow dish large enough to hold the fish in one layer and stir in the herbs and the olive oil.

2 Add the pieces of halibut to the olive oil mixture in the dish and turn them to coat them thoroughly on both sides, then arrange them on the griddle. Cook for about 3–4 minutes then turn carefully and continue to cook for another 3–4 minutes, or until the fish is cooked all the way through and the skin has browned.

3 Combine all the sauce ingredients except the fresh herbs in a pan and heat gently on the grill rack until warm but not hot. Stir in the chives, basil and chervil.

4 Place the halibut on four warmed plates. Spoon the sauce around and over the fish and serve immediately.

Energy 363kcal/1513kJ; Protein 37.4g; Carbohydrate 1.9g, of which sugars 1.8g; Fat 22.9g, of which saturates 3.3g; Cholesterol 60mg; Calcium 82mg; Fibre 1.1g; Sodium 169mg.

HALIBUT WITH TOMATO AND BASIL SALSA

HANDLE THE FISH CAREFULLY WHEN COOKING THIS DISH AS HALIBUT HAS A TENDENCY TO BREAK EASILY, ESPECIALLY WHEN THE SKIN HAS BEEN REMOVED. SEASON WELL TO BRING OUT THE FLAVOUR OF THE FISH AND THE TASTE OF THE SAUCE.

SERVES FOUR

INGREDIENTS

    4 halibut fillets, about
       175g/6oz each
    45ml/3 tbsp olive oil
For the salsa
    1 medium tomato, roughly chopped
    1 small jalapeño pepper, finely
      chopped
    30ml/2 tbsp balsamic vinegar
    ¼ red onion, finely sliced
    10 large fresh basil leaves
    15ml/1 tbsp olive oil
    salt and ground black pepper

1 To make the salsa, mix together the chopped tomato, jalapeño pepper and balsamic vinegar in a bowl. Break up the red onion slices into slivers and stir them in. Slice the fresh basil leaves finely, using a sharp kitchen knife, or tear them into shreds, and add.

2 Stir in the oil and season to taste. Cover with clear film (plastic wrap) and leave to marinate for at least 3 hours.

3 Rub the halibut with oil and season. Barbecue for 3–4 minutes each side. Serve with the salsa.

Energy 265kcal/1112kJ; Protein 38.1g; Carbohydrate 2g, of which sugars 1.7g; Fat 11.7g, of which saturates 1.7g; Cholesterol 61mg; Calcium 61mg; Fibre 0.6g; Sodium 109mg.

Mid-Continent Public Library

Checked Out Items 6/6/2018 15:00
XXXXXXXXXX8421

m Title	Due Date
003017992072	7/5/2018
e _smoke : a pitmaster's secrets	
003010366969	7/5/2018
even Raichlen's Planet Barbecue! : an	
ectrifying journey around the world's	
rbecue trail	
003004723464	7/5/2018
rbecues 400 : burgers, kebabs, fish	
eaks, vegetarian dishes, and tempting	
lads, desserts and accompaniments,	
monstrated step-by-step with more	
an 1500 vibrant photographs	

ve a great day!

PAPRIKA-CRUSTED MONKFISH

*SUCH A CHUNKY FISH AS MONKFISH IS JUST PERFECT FOR SKEWERING, AS IT IS NOT LIKELY TO
DISINTEGRATE BEFORE YOUR EYES AND FALL BETWEEN THE GRILL BARS AS YOU COOK. MONKFISH CAN
ALSO TAKE SOME STRONG FLAVOURS, SUCH AS THIS SMOKY PAPRIKA CRUST WITH CHORIZO.*

SERVES FOUR

INGREDIENTS

   1 monkfish tail, about 1kg/2¼lb,
      trimmed and filleted
   10ml/2 tsp smoked red paprika
   2 red (bell) peppers, halved
      and seeded
   15ml/1 tbsp extra virgin olive oil
   16 thin slices of chorizo
   salt and ground black pepper
For the cucumber and mint sauce
   150ml/¼ pint/⅔ cup Greek
      (US strained plain) yogurt
   ½ cucumber, halved lengthways
      and seeded
   30ml/2 tbsp chopped fresh
      mint leaves

1 Place the fish in a flat dish. Rub all
over with 5ml/1 tsp salt, then cover and
leave in a cool place for 20 minutes. To
make the sauce, pour the yogurt into a
food processor. Cut the cucumber into
it, season with a little salt and pulse to a
pale green purée. Transfer to a serving
bowl and stir in the mint.

2 Prepare the barbecue. Rinse the salt
off the fish and lightly pat dry with
kitchen paper. Mix the smoked red
paprika with a pinch of salt and rub the
mixture evenly over the fish. Slice each
pepper into 12 long strips and cut each
monkfish fillet into ten equal pieces.
Thread six pieces of pepper and five
pieces of fish on to each of four long
skewers and brush one side with a little
extra virgin olive oil.

3 Position a lightly oiled grill rack over
the hot coals. Grill the skewered food,
oiled-side down over medium-high heat,
for about 3½ minutes. Lightly brush the
top side with oil, turn over and cook for
3–4 minutes more. Remove the skewers
from the heat and keep warm.

4 Grill the chorizo slices for a second or
two until just warm. Thread one piece
of chorizo on to the end of each skewer
and serve the rest alongside on
individual plates. Serve with the
prepared cucumber and mint sauce.

COOK'S TIP
If it is easier, fry the chorizo on a
hot griddle set on the grill rack for
30 seconds on each side.

Energy 375kcal/1572kJ; Protein 51.7g; Carbohydrate 7.1g, of which sugars 6.8g; Fat 15.9g, of which saturates 5.6g; Cholesterol 57mg; Calcium 115mg; Fibre 2.1g; Sodium 445mg.

GRILLED FISH IN VINE LEAVES

ALMOST ANY KIND OF FIRM, WHITE FISH WILL DO FOR THESE KEBABS. THE FISH IS FIRST MARINATED IN CHERMOULA AND THEN WRAPPED IN VINE LEAVES TO SEAL IN THE FLAVOURS. THE VINE-LEAF PARCEL BECOMES CRISP WHEN COOKED TO CONTRAST WITH ITS SUCCULENT, AROMATIC CONTENTS.

3 Meanwhile, prepare the dipping sauce. Heat the vinegar or lemon juice with the sugar and water until the sugar has dissolved. Bring to the boil and boil for about 1 minute, then leave to cool. Add the remaining ingredients and mix well to combine. Spoon the sauce into small individual bowls and set aside.

4 Drain the vine leaves and pat dry on kitchen paper. Lay a vine leaf flat on the work surface and place a piece of marinated fish in the centre. Fold the edges of the leaf over the fish, then wrap up the fish and leaf into a small parcel. Repeat with the remaining pieces of fish and vine leaves. Thread the parcels on to kebab skewers and brush with any leftover marinade.

5 Heat the grill (broiler) on the hottest setting and cook the kebabs for 2–3 minutes on each side. Serve immediately, with the sweet and sour chilli sauce for dipping.

SERVES FOUR

INGREDIENTS
   about 30 preserved vine leaves
   4–5 large white fish fillets, skinned,
     such as haddock, ling or monkfish
For the chermoula
   small bunch of fresh coriander
     (cilantro), finely chopped
   2–3 garlic cloves, chopped
   5–10ml/1–2 tsp ground cumin
   60ml/4 tbsp olive oil
   juice of 1 lemon
   salt
For the dipping sauce
   50ml/2fl oz/¼ cup white wine vinegar
     or lemon juice
   115g/4oz/½ cup caster
     (superfine) sugar
   15–30ml/1–2 tbsp water
   pinch of saffron threads
   1 onion, finely chopped
   2 garlic cloves, finely chopped
   2–3 spring onions (scallions),
     finely sliced
   25g/1oz fresh root ginger, peeled
     and grated
   2 hot red or green chillies, seeded
     and finely sliced
   small bunch fresh coriander
     (cilantro), finely chopped
   small bunch of mint, finely chopped

1 To make the chermoula, pound the ingredients together in a mortar with a pestle, or put them in a food processor and process to a fairly smooth paste, then set aside.

2 Rinse the vine leaves in a bowl, then soak them in cold water. Remove any bones from the fish and cut each fillet into about eight bite-size pieces. Coat the pieces of fish in the chermoula, cover and chill for 1 hour.

VARIATION
The dipping sauce in this recipe will also taste good with prawns (jumbo shrimp). Marinate king prawns in the chermoula, but omit the vine leaves and simply grill them with half shells or threaded on to wetted cocktail sticks (toothpicks) or wooden kebab skewers.

COOK'S TIP
Chermoula is a marinade used widely in Moroccan and North African cooking. It is usually based on a blend of coriander (cilantro), lemon and garlic, and often includes saffron and paprika. It is especially popular with fish, but can also be used with poultry and meat.

Energy 295kcal/1232kJ; Protein 40.7g; Carbohydrate 3.8g, of which sugars 2.3g; Fat 13g, of which saturates 1.8g; Cholesterol 98mg; Calcium 111mg; Fibre 1.6g; Sodium 139mg.

FISH BROCHETTES WITH PEPERONATA

IN THIS DISH, THE PEPPERS FOR THE PEPERONATA ARE ROASTED AND SKINNED, GIVING IT A LOVELY SMOKY FLAVOUR AND SMOOTH TEXTURE, WHILE THE VERJUICE, AN UNFERMENTED GRAPE JUICE, ADDS AN UNDERLYING TARTNESS. IT IS EXCELLENT SERVED WITH THE FISH BROCHETTES.

SERVES FOUR

INGREDIENTS

   8 fresh sprigs of bay leaves
   675g/1½lb mahi-mahi, swordfish or
     marlin fillet, skinned
   1 lime, halved
   1 lemon, halved
   60ml/4 tbsp olive oil
   1 small garlic clove, crushed
   salt and ground black pepper
For the peperonata
   2 large red (bell) peppers, quartered
     and seeded
   2 yellow (bell) peppers,
     quartered and seeded
   90ml/6 tbsp extra virgin olive oil
   2 sweet onions, thinly sliced
   1 garlic clove, thinly sliced
   5ml/1 tsp sugar
   4 tomatoes, peeled, seeded and
     roughly chopped
   2 bay leaves
   1 large fresh thyme sprig
   15ml/1 tbsp red verjuice or red wine

1 To make the peperonata, spread out the peppers on a board and brush the skin side with oil. Heat the remaining oil in a pan and add the onions and garlic. Fry over a medium-high heat for 6–8 minutes, or until lightly golden.

2 Prepare the barbecue. Heat a griddle on a grill rack over hot coals. Add the peppers, skin-side down. Lower the heat a little and grill them for 5 minutes until the skins are charred. Remove from the heat and put them under an upturned bowl. When cool enough to handle, rub off the skins and slice each piece into six or seven strips.

3 Add the pepper strips to the onion mixture, stir in the sugar and cook over a medium heat for about 2 minutes. Add the tomatoes and herbs and bring to the boil. Transfer the pan to the barbecue. Stir in the verjuice or wine, and simmer, uncovered, for about 30 minutes. Remove from the heat and cover to keep warm.

4 Meanwhile, soak eight wooden skewers with the bay leaf sprigs in a bowl of cold water for 30 minutes so that they do not char during cooking.

5 Cut the fish into 12 large cubes and place in a bowl. Squeeze the juice from half a lime and half a lemon into a small bowl. Whisk in 45ml/3 tbsp of the oil. Cream the garlic and plenty of seasoning to a paste, add to the oil mixture and pour over the fish. Cover the bowl with clear film (plastic wrap) and leave to marinate for 30 minutes.

COOK'S TIPS
• The fish suggested for this dish all have a firm meaty texture, ideal for chargrilling. Take care not to overcook.
• The brochettes can also be cooked on an oiled grill rack over a medium to high heat. Cook for 8–10 minutes, turning the skewers several times, until the fish is cooked through and the rind of the citrus fruits has begun to scorch.
• You may prefer to quickly re-heat the peperonata while keeping the kebabs warm.

6 Cut the remaining lime and lemon halves into four wedges each. Using two skewers placed side by side instead of the usual one, thread alternately with three pieces of fish, one lime and one lemon wedge and two sprigs of bay leaves. Make three more brochettes in the same way.

7 Replace the griddle over a high heat and test that it is hot. Brush the brochettes with the remaining oil and grill for 3–4 minutes on each side, or until the fish is cooked through and nicely branded. Cover the kebabs and keep them warm for up to 5 minutes before serving with the peperonata in a little bowl on the side.

Energy 426kcal/1777kJ; Protein 34g; Carbohydrate 22.2g, of which sugars 19.4g; Fat 22.6g, of which saturates 3.9g; Cholesterol 69mg; Calcium 53mg; Fibre 5.2g; Sodium 239mg.

SPICED FISH BAKED THAI STYLE

BANANA LEAVES MAKE A PERFECT, NATURAL WRAPPING FOR BARBECUED FOODS, PROTECTING THE DELICATE FLESH FROM THE HEAT, BUT IF THEY ARE NOT AVAILABLE YOU CAN USE FOIL INSTEAD.

SERVES FOUR

INGREDIENTS

4 red snapper or mullet, about
   350g/12oz each
banana leaves
1 lime
1 garlic clove, thinly sliced
2 spring onions (scallions),
   thinly sliced
30ml/2 tbsp Thai red
   curry paste
60ml/4 tbsp coconut milk

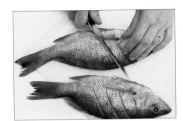

1 Clean and scale the fish, and make several deep slashes in the side of each with a sharp knife. Place each fish on a layer of banana leaves.

2 Thinly slice half the lime and tuck the slices into the slashes in the fish, with the slivers of garlic. Scatter the sliced spring onions over the fish.

3 Grate the rind and squeeze the juice from the remaining half-lime and mix with the curry paste and the coconut milk. Spoon some of this mixture over each fish.

4 Wrap the leaves over the fish, folding in the sides, to enclose them completely. Tie firmly with string and cook on a medium-hot barbecue for 15–20 minutes, turning occasionally. To serve, open up the parcels by cutting along the top edge with a knife and fanning out the leaves.

Energy 240kcal/1017kJ; Protein 44.4g; Carbohydrate 2.2g, of which sugars 0.9g; Fat 6.2g, of which saturates 1.1g; Cholesterol 81mg; Calcium 133mg; Fibre 1.2g; Sodium 246mg.

SEA BREAM <u>WITH</u> ORANGE BUTTER SAUCE

SEA BREAM IS A REVELATION TO ANYONE UNFAMILIAR WITH ITS CREAMY RICH FLAVOUR. THE FISH HAS A FIRM WHITE FLESH THAT GOES WELL WITH THIS RICH BUTTER SAUCE, SHARPENED WITH ORANGE.

SERVES TWO

INGREDIENTS

   2 sea bream, about 350g/12oz each,
     scaled and gutted
   10ml/2 tsp Dijon mustard
   5ml/1 tsp fennel seeds
   30ml/2 tbsp olive oil
   50g/2oz watercress
   175g/6oz mixed lettuce leaves, such
     as curly endive or frisée
For the orange butter sauce
   30ml/2 tbsp frozen orange
     juice concentrate
   175g/6oz/¾ cup unsalted
     butter, diced
   salt and cayenne pepper

1 Prepare the barbecue and place a grill rack over the hot coals. Slash into the flesh of the sea bream four times on either side. Combine the mustard and fennel seeds, then spread over both sides of the fish.

2 Brush the fish with a little olive oil and cook over medium-hot coals for 10–12 minutes, turning once, until the flesh is cooked through and the skin is crisp and brown.

COOK'S TIPS
• This recipe works as well on the barbecue as it does using a regular grill (broiler), so it's a safe bet when you are unsure what the weather holds in store!
• Always choose firm, glossy fish with bright eyes, as freshness makes all the difference to the flavour.

3 Place the orange juice concentrate in a bowl and heat over a pan of simmering water. Remove the pan from the heat and gradually whisk in the butter until creamy. Season well.

4 Dress the watercress and lettuce leaves with the remaining olive oil, and arrange with the fish on two plates. Spoon the sauce over the fish and serve with baked potatoes, if liked.

Energy 978kcal/4043kJ; Protein 37.5g; Carbohydrate 5.3g, of which sugars 5.2g; Fat 89.9g, of which saturates 47.4g; Cholesterol 263mg; Calcium 169mg; Fibre 1.2g; Sodium 916mg.

FISH PARCELS

DELICATELY FLAVOURED SEA BASS IS ESPECIALLY GOOD FOR THIS RECIPE, BUT YOU COULD ALSO USE SMALL WHOLE TROUT OR A WHITE FISH FILLET SUCH AS COD OR HADDOCK.

SERVES FOUR

INGREDIENTS
    4 pieces sea bass fillet, or 4 small
        sea bass, about 450g/1lb each
    olive oil for brushing
    2 shallots, thinly sliced
    1 garlic clove, chopped
    15ml/1 tbsp capers
    6 sun-dried tomatoes, finely chopped
    4 black olives, stoned (pitted) and
        thinly sliced
    grated rind and juice of 1 lemon
    5ml/1 tsp paprika
    salt and ground black pepper

1 Clean the fish if whole. Cut four squares of double-thickness foil, large enough to enclose the fish; brush lightly with a little olive oil.

2 Place a piece of fish in the centre of each piece of oiled foil and season well with plenty of salt and ground black pepper.

3 Scatter over the shallots, chopped garlic, capers, tomatoes, sliced olives and grated lemon rind. Sprinkle with the lemon juice and paprika.

COOK'S TIP
These parcels can also be baked in the oven: place them on a baking sheet and cook at 200°C/400°F/Gas 6 for about 15–20 minutes.

VARIATION
Try different flavourings in the parcels, such as chervil, parsley or other fresh herbs, and replace the lemon juice with a splash of dry white wine.

4 Fold over the baking foil to enclose the fish loosely, sealing the edges firmly so that none of the juices can escape during cooking.

5 Prepare a barbecue and place a rack over the hot coals. Lay the parcels on the rack and cook over moderately hot coals for about 8–10 minutes until the fish is just cooked through (open one of the parcels to check). To serve, place each of the parcels on a plate and loosen the tops to open. This will also release some steam and help prevent over-cooking.

Energy 343kcal/1441kJ; Protein 63.2g; Carbohydrate 2g, of which sugars 1.6g; Fat 9.1g, of which saturates 1.5g; Cholesterol 260mg; Calcium 433mg; Fibre 0.7g; Sodium 396mg.

POULTRY

*Chicken is one of the most popular barbecue meats, and the
reason is perhaps that it can be transformed in so many ways
by using different marinades, stuffings or quick glazes.
The pages that follow contain a host of different ways to
prepare and present poultry, whether as breast fillets,
drumsticks or as bite-sized pieces threaded on to skewers;
all achieve exceptionally flavourful results. If you're planning
to feed a gathering of family and friends, and have a little
time to spare, you can also roast a whole chicken — even
without the aid of a rotisserie. You do need a lid, but a
home-made one will do nicely. This chapter includes a turkey
recipe as well as ways to barbecue the ever-popular duck,
which achieves fantastically crispy skin while retaining moist
flesh. Small birds are also great for grilling either whole or
spatchcocked: try the recipes for poussins and delicate quail.*

SPICY INDONESIAN CHICKEN SATAY

CHILLIES, GARLIC AND SOY SAUCE GIVE THESE INDONESIAN CHICKEN SATAYS PIQUANCY, AND THE
REMAINING MARINADE IS COOKED TO MAKE A TASTY ACCOMPANYING DIP.

SERVES FOUR

INGREDIENTS
  ½ onion, sliced
  oil, for deep-frying
  4 chicken breast fillets, about
    175g/6oz each, skinned and cut
    into 2.5cm/1in cubes
For the sambal kecap
  1 fresh red chilli, seeded and
    finely chopped
  2 garlic cloves, crushed
  60ml/4 tbsp dark soy sauce
  20ml/4 tsp lemon juice or 15–25ml/
    1–1½ tbsp tamarind juice
  30ml/2 tbsp hot water

1 Deep-fry the onion until golden.
Set aside.

2 To make the sambal kecap, mix all
the ingredients in a bowl. Leave to
stand for 30 minutes to give the flavours
time to blend.

3 Place the chicken breast cubes in a
bowl with the sambal kecap and mix
thoroughly. Cover the bowl with clear
film (plastic wrap) and leave in a cool
place to marinate for 1 hour.

4 Meanwhile, soak eight wooden
skewers in water for 30 minutes.

5 Tip the chicken and marinade into a
sieve (strainer) placed over a pan and
leave to drain for a few minutes. Set the
sieve with the chicken aside.

6 Add 30ml/2 tbsp hot water to the
marinade and bring to the boil. Lower
the heat and simmer for 2 minutes,
then pour into a bowl and leave to cool.
When cool, add the deep-fried onion.

7 Prepare the barbecue. Position a
lightly oiled grill rack over the hot coals.
Thread the skewers with the chicken
and cook over medium heat for about
10 minutes, turning regularly, until
golden brown and cooked through.
Serve with the sambal kecap as a dip.

Energy 197kcal/835kJ; Protein 42.5g; Carbohydrate 2.5g, of which sugars 2g; Fat 2g, of which saturates 0.5g; Cholesterol 123mg; Calcium 15mg; Fibre 0.4g; Sodium 640mg.

FIERY CHICKEN WINGS WITH BLOOD ORANGES

THIS IS A GREAT RECIPE FOR THE BARBECUE — IT IS QUICK AND EASY, AND BEST EATEN WITH THE FINGERS. THE ORANGES PROVIDE AN INTENSE BURST OF JUICE TO COUNTERACT THE FIERY SPICES.

SERVES FOUR

INGREDIENTS
    60ml/4 tbsp fiery harissa
    30ml/2 tbsp olive oil
    16–20 chicken wings
    4 blood oranges, quartered
    icing (confectioners') sugar
    small bunch of fresh coriander
        (cilantro), chopped
    salt

COOK'S TIP
The oranges can be cooked separately or threaded alternately with the chicken wings on skewers. Cherry tomatoes can be used as well, as it is the burst of juice that makes this dish so delicious.

1 Put the harissa in a small bowl with the olive oil and mix to form a loose paste. Add a little salt and stir to combine. Brush this mixture over the chicken wings so that they are well coated. Cook the wings on a hot barbecue or under a hot grill (broiler), for 5 minutes on each side.

2 Once the wings begin to cook, dip the orange quarters lightly in icing sugar and grill them for a few minutes, until they are slightly burnt but not black and charred. Serve the chicken wings immediately with the oranges, sprinkled with a little chopped fresh coriander.

Energy 537kcal/2235kJ; Protein 45.9g; Carbohydrate 8.5g, of which sugars 8.5g; Fat 35.7g, of which saturates 8.9g; Cholesterol 196mg; Calcium 61mg; Fibre 1.7g; Sodium 137mg.

THAI GRILLED CHICKEN

THIS RECIPE FOR SPICE-INFUSED THAI CHICKEN IS ESPECIALLY DELICIOUS WHEN COOKED ON THE BARBECUE. SERVE IT ON A BED OF CRISP SALAD WITH LIME WEDGES TO OFFSET ITS RICHNESS.

SERVES FOUR TO SIX

INGREDIENTS
    900g/2lb chicken drumsticks
      or thighs
    crisp lettuce leaves, to serve
    ½ cucumber, cut into strips,
      to garnish
    4 spring onions (scallions), trimmed,
      to garnish
    salt and ground black pepper
    2 limes, quartered, to garnish
For the marinade
    5ml/1 tsp black peppercorns
    2.5ml/½ tsp caraway or cumin seeds
    20ml/4 tsp sugar
    10ml/2 tsp paprika
    2cm/¾in piece fresh root
      ginger, chopped
    3 garlic cloves, crushed
    15g/½oz coriander (cilantro), white
      root or stem, finely chopped
    45ml/3 tbsp vegetable oil

1 Chop through the narrow end of each drumstick, if using, with a heavy knife. Score the chicken pieces deeply to allow the marinade to penetrate and arrange in a shallow bowl.

COOK'S TIP
It is generally cheaper to buy Asian cooking ingredients from a specialist store rather than the local supermarket.

2 Grind the peppercorns, caraway or cumin seeds and sugar in a pestle and mortar or a food processor. Add the paprika, ginger, garlic, coriander and oil and grind to a paste.

3 Spread the marinade over the chicken, working it well into the flesh. Cover the bowl with clear film (plastic wrap) and leave to marinate in the refrigerator for 6 hours or overnight.

4 Prepare the barbecue. Lift the chicken out of the marinade and cook over medium-hot coats for about 20 minutes, basting with the marinade and turning once. Season, arrange on a bed of lettuce and garnish with cucumber strips, spring onions and lime quarters.

Energy 205kcal/861kJ; Protein 24.6g; Carbohydrate 7.6g, of which sugars 7g; Fat 8.8g, of which saturates 2.3g; Cholesterol 129mg; Calcium 20mg; Fibre 0g; Sodium 121mg.

CHICKEN WITH PINEAPPLE

THE PINEAPPLE JUICE IN THIS INDIAN RECIPE IS USED TO TENDERIZE THE MEAT, BUT IT ALSO GIVES THE CHICKEN A DELICIOUSLY TANGY SWEETNESS. USE PORK INSTEAD OF CHICKEN IF YOU WISH.

SERVES SIX

INGREDIENTS
225g/8oz can pineapple chunks
   in juice
5ml/1 tsp ground cumin
5ml/1 tsp ground coriander
1 garlic clove, crushed
5ml/1 tsp chilli powder
5ml/1 tsp salt
30ml/2 tbsp natural (plain) low-fat
   yogurt
15ml/1 tbsp chopped fresh coriander
   (cilantro)
few drops orange food colouring
   (optional)
275g/10oz/2 cups chicken breast and
   thigh meat, skinned and boned
½ red (bell) pepper
½ yellow or green (bell) pepper
1 large onion
6 cherry tomatoes
15ml/1 tbsp vegetable oil

1 Drain the canned pineapple into a bowl. Reserve 12 large chunks. Squeeze the juice from the remaining chunks into the bowl, then discard the chunks. You should be left with about 120ml/4fl oz/½ cup pineapple juice.

2 In a large bowl, blend together the cumin, ground coriander, garlic, chilli powder, salt, yogurt, fresh coriander and food colouring, if using. Pour in the pineapple juice and mix together.

3 Cut the chicken into cubes, add to the yogurt and spice mixture and leave to marinate for about 1–1½ hours. Cut the peppers and onion into chunks.

4 Arrange the chicken pieces, vegetables and reserved pineapple chunks alternately on six skewers.

5 Brush the kebabs with oil and cook on a medium barbecue for about 10 minutes, turning regularly and basting the chicken pieces with the marinade, until cooked through. Serve with salad or plain boiled rice.

Energy 124kcal/522kJ; Protein 12.6g; Carbohydrate 12.8g, of which sugars 10.9g; Fat 2.9g, of which saturates 0.4g; Cholesterol 32mg; Calcium 26mg; Fibre 1.8g; Sodium 32mg.

CITRUS KEBABS

*SERVE THESE SUCCULENT BARBECUED CHICKEN KEBABS ON A BED OF LETTUCE LEAVES, GARNISHED
WITH SPRIGS OF FRESH MINT AND ORANGE AND LEMON SLICES.*

2 Mix the marinade ingredients together in a large mixing bowl, add the chicken and cover with clear film (plastic wrap). Leave to marinate for at least 2 hours, or overnight in the refrigerator.

3 Thread the chicken on to metal skewers and cook on a medium barbecue or under a hot grill (broiler) for 10 minutes, basting with the marinade and turning frequently. Garnish with mint and citrus slices.

SERVES FOUR

INGREDIENTS
  4 chicken breast fillets, skinned
  fresh mint sprigs, to garnish
  orange, lemon or lime slices,
    to garnish
For the marinade
  finely grated rind and juice
    of ½ orange
  finely grated rind and juice of
    ½ lemon or lime
  30ml/2 tbsp olive oil
  30ml/2 tbsp clear honey
  30ml/2 tbsp chopped fresh mint
  1.5ml/¼ tsp ground cumin
  salt and ground black pepper

1 Trim any visible fat from the chicken fillets and use a heavy knife to cut the meat into 2.5cm/1in cubes.

Energy 221kcal/928kJ; Protein 36.1g; Carbohydrate 3g, of which sugars 3g; Fat 7.2g, of which saturates 1.2g; Cholesterol 105mg; Calcium 15mg; Fibre 0.2g; Sodium 92mg.

SWEET AND SOUR KEBABS

THE MARINADE FOR THIS DISH CONTAINS SUGAR AND WILL BURN VERY EASILY, SO COOK THE KEBABS SLOWLY AND TURN THEM OFTEN. SERVE THE KEBABS WITH HARLEQUIN RICE.

SERVES FOUR

INGREDIENTS
  2 chicken breast fillets, skinned
  8 pickling onions or
  2 medium onions
  4 rindless streaky (fatty) bacon
    rashers (strips)
  3 firm bananas
  1 red (bell) pepper, diced
For the marinade
  30ml/2 tbsp soft brown sugar
  15ml/1 tbsp Worcestershire sauce
  30ml/2 tbsp lemon juice
  salt and ground black pepper
For the harlequin rice
  30ml/2 tbsp olive oil
  1 small red (bell) pepper, diced
  225g/8oz/generous 1 cup cooked
    long-grain rice
  115g/4oz/1 cup cooked peas

1 Mix together the marinade ingredients in a bowl. Cut each chicken fillet into four pieces and add to the marinade. Cover with clear film (plastic wrap) and leave for at least 4 hours, or preferably overnight, in the refrigerator.

2 Peel the onions. Bring a pan of water to the boil and blanch the onions in boiling water for 5 minutes. Drain. If using medium onions, quarter them after blanching.

3 Cut each rasher of bacon in half with a sharp knife. Peel the bananas and cut each one into three pieces. Wrap half a bacon rasher around each of the banana pieces.

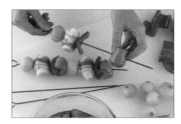

4 Thread the bacon and bananas on to metal skewers with the chicken pieces, onions and pepper pieces. Brush generously with the marinade.

5 Cook on a low barbecue for about 15 minutes, turning and basting frequently with the marinade.

6 While the chicken is cooking, heat the oil in a frying pan and stir-fry the diced pepper briefly until beginning to soften and brown. Add the rice and the cooked peas and stir until heated through. Serve the harlequin rice with the kebabs.

CHICKEN COOKED IN SPICES AND COCONUT

THIS CHICKEN DISH CAN BE PREPARED IN ADVANCE AND LEFT TO MARINATE UNTIL YOU ARE READY TO LIGHT THE BARBECUE. SERVE THE CHICKEN WITH NAAN BREAD.

SERVES FOUR

INGREDIENTS

200g/7oz block creamed coconut
300ml/½ pint/1¼ cups boiling water
3 garlic cloves, chopped
2 spring onions (scallions), chopped
1 fresh green chilli, chopped
5cm/2in piece fresh root
  ginger, chopped
5ml/1 tsp fennel seeds
2.5ml/½ tsp black peppercorns
seeds from 4 cardamom pods
30ml/2 tbsp ground coriander
5ml/1 tsp ground cumin
5ml/1 tsp ground star anise
5ml/1 tsp ground nutmeg
2.5ml/½ tsp ground cloves
2.5ml/½ tsp ground turmeric
4 large chicken breast fillets, skinned
onion rings and fresh coriander
  (cilantro) sprigs, to garnish

1 Break up the block of creamed coconut and put it in a jug (pitcher). Pour the boiling water over and leave until the coconut has dissolved, stirring occasionally.

2 Place the chopped garlic, spring onions, chilli, ginger and all of the spices in the goblet of a blender or food processor. Pour in the dissolved coconut mixture and blend to a smooth paste.

3 Make several diagonal cuts across the chicken fillets, cutting about halfway through. Arrange in a layer in a shallow dish. Spoon over half the coconut mixture and toss well to coat the chicken fillets evenly.

4 Cover the dish with clear film (plastic wrap) and leave to marinate for at least 30 minutes. If convenient, chill the chicken and leave to marinate overnight in the refrigerator.

5 Prepare the barbecue and arrange a lightly oiled rack over the hot coals. Lift the chicken out of the marinade and cook it over medium-hot coals for about 12–15 minutes, turning once and basting with the marinade, until well browned and thoroughly cooked.

6 Pour the remaining coconut mixture into a small pan and heat it gently on the barbecue until it is boiling. Leave it to bubble for a few minutes until it has thickened slightly.

7 Serve the chicken with the coconut sauce, garnished with onion rings and sprigs of coriander.

Energy 357kcal/1483kJ; Protein 24.3g; Carbohydrate 8g, of which sugars 7.9g; Fat 25.5g, of which saturates 6.5g; Cholesterol 121mg; Calcium 46mg; Fibre 0.8g; Sodium 154mg.

GRILLED CASHEW NUT CHICKEN

THIS DISH COMES FROM THE BEAUTIFUL INDONESIAN ISLAND OF BALI, WHERE NUTS ARE WIDELY USED AS A BASE FOR SAUCES AND MARINADES. SERVE IT WITH A GREEN SALAD AND A HOT CHILLI DIPPING SAUCE.

SERVES FOUR

INGREDIENTS
4 chicken legs
radishes, sliced, to garnish
½ cucumber, sliced, to garnish
Chinese leaves, to serve
For the marinade
50g/2oz raw cashew or
  macadamia nuts
2 shallots, or 1 small onion,
  finely chopped
2 garlic cloves, crushed
2 small red chillies, chopped
5cm/2in piece lemon grass
15ml/1 tbsp tamarind sauce
30ml/2 tbsp dark soy sauce
15ml/1 tbsp Thai fish sauce
10ml/2 tsp sugar
2.5ml/½ tsp salt
15ml/1 tbsp rice or
  white wine vinegar

1 Using a sharp kitchen knife, slash the chicken legs several times through to the bone. Chop off the knuckle end and discard.

2 To make the marinade, place the cashew or macadamia nuts in a food processor or pestle and mortar and grind until fine.

COOK'S TIP
Macadamias are native to the tropical rainforests of Australia and are sometimes described as the world's most delicious nut. They are very rich in mono-unsaturated fat, but are about twice the price of cashew nuts.

3 Add the chopped shallots or onion, garlic, chillies and lemon grass to the ground nuts and blend in the mortar or food processor. Add the remaining marinade ingredients and blend again.

4 Spread the marinade over the chicken and chill for up to 8 hours. Cook the chicken on a medium barbecue for about 25 minutes, basting with the marinade and turning occasionally. Garnish with radishes and cucumber and serve on a bed of Chinese leaves.

Energy 297kcal/1244kJ; Protein 32g; Carbohydrate 12.5g, of which sugars 9g; Fat 13.6g, of which saturates 2.5g; Cholesterol 79mg; Calcium 51mg; Fibre 2.4g; Sodium 131mg.

CARIBBEAN CHICKEN KEBABS

RUM, LIME JUICE AND CINNAMON MAKE A ROBUST MARINADE FOR CHICKEN, WHICH IS THEN BARBECUED WITH MANGOES TO MAKE AN UNUSUAL AND FRESH-TASTING DISH. YOU CAN SERVE THE KEBABS WITH RICE, OR SLIDE THEM OFF THE SKEWERS STRAIGHT INTO PITTA BREAD FOR AN INFORMAL BARBECUE MEAL.

2 Soak four wooden skewers in water for 30 minutes. Cut the mangoes into cubes by cutting slices, scoring into cubes and slicing away from the skin.

3 Prepare the barbecue. Position a lightly oiled grill rack over the hot coals. Drain the chicken, saving the juices, and thread on to the wooden skewers, alternating with the mango cubes.

SERVES FOUR

INGREDIENTS
   500g/1¼lb skinless chicken
     breast fillets
   finely grated rind of 1 lime
   30ml/2 tbsp fresh lime juice
   15ml/1 tbsp rum or sherry
   15ml/1 tbsp light muscovado
     (brown) sugar
   5ml/1 tsp ground cinnamon
   2 mangoes
   rice and salad, to serve

1 Cut the chicken into bite-size chunks, and place in a bowl with the lime rind and juice, rum or sherry, sugar and cinnamon. Toss well, cover and leave to stand for 1 hour in a cool place.

4 Grill the skewers over high heat for 8–10 minutes, turning occasionally and basting with the reserved juices, until the chicken is tender and golden brown and the mango is slightly caramelized at the edges. Serve the kebabs immediately with rice and a salad.

Energy 195kcal/826kJ; Protein 30.6g; Carbohydrate 14.6g, of which sugars 14.3g; Fat 1.5g, of which saturates 0.5g; Cholesterol 88mg; Calcium 18mg; Fibre 2g; Sodium 77mg.

SPICY MASALA CHICKEN

SPICES, HERBS AND HONEY MAKE A LOVELY SWEET-AND-SOUR MARINADE FOR CHICKEN PIECES, WHICH TASTE GREAT WHEN COOKED OVER THE COALS. SERVE WITH SALADS AND CRUSTY BREAD OR RICE. REMEMBER YOU CAN ALWAYS ADD SOME HERB SPRIGS TO THE COALS TO ADD TO THE SMOKY FLAVOUR.

SERVES SIX

INGREDIENTS
    12 chicken thighs
    90ml/6 tbsp lemon juice
    5ml/1 tsp chopped fresh root ginger
    5ml/1 tsp chopped garlic
    5ml/1 tsp crushed dried red chillies
    5ml/1 tsp salt
    5ml/1 tsp soft light brown sugar
    30ml/2 tbsp clear honey
    30ml/2 tbsp chopped fresh
        coriander (cilantro)
    1 green chilli, finely chopped
    30ml/2 tbsp vegetable oil
    fresh coriander sprigs, to garnish

1 Prick the chicken thighs with a fork, rinse, pat dry and set aside.

2 In a large mixing bowl, make the marinade by mixing together the lemon juice, ginger, garlic, crushed dried red chillies, salt, sugar and honey.

3 Transfer the chicken thighs to the spice mixture and coat well. Set aside for about 45 minutes, or chill and leave in the fridge until ready to cook.

4 Prepare the barbecue. Position a lightly oiled grill rack over the hot coals. Add the coriander and green chilli to the chicken thighs and place them in a flameproof dish.

5 Pour any remaining marinade over the chicken and baste lightly with the oil, taking care not to remove the marinade. Transfer to the grill rack.

6 Grill the chicken thighs over medium heat for 15–20 minutes, turning and basting with the marinade occasionally, until they are cooked. Add the final basting no less than 5 minutes before the end of the cooking time to ensure the marinade is fully cooked.

7 Serve the chicken garnished with a few sprigs of fresh coriander and accompanied with rice or barbecued potatoes and a salad.

COOK'S TIP
If you are cooking by gas and don't have a smoke box but want to add some aromatics, you can use a foil container and cover it with a piece of foil. Make some holes in the top for the smoke to escape.

Energy 165kcal/694kJ; Protein 18.9g; Carbohydrate 9.1g, of which sugars 9.1g; Fat 6.2g, of which saturates 1.2g; Cholesterol 95mg; Calcium 9mg; Fibre 0g; Sodium 409mg.

JERK CHICKEN

TRADITIONALLY "JERK" REFERS TO THE BLEND OF HERB AND SPICE SEASONING RUBBED INTO MEAT BEFORE IT IS ROASTED OVER CHARCOAL SPRINKLED WITH PIMIENTO BERRIES. IN JAMAICA, JERK SEASONING WAS ORIGINALLY USED ONLY FOR PORK, BUT JERK CHICKEN IS EQUALLY GOOD.

SERVES FOUR

INGREDIENTS
  8 chicken pieces
  salad leaves, to serve
For the marinade
  5ml/1 tsp ground allspice
  5ml/1 tsp ground cinnamon
  5ml/1 tsp dried thyme
  1.5ml/¼ tsp freshly grated nutmeg
  10ml/2 tsp demerara (raw) sugar
  2 garlic cloves, crushed
  15ml/1 tbsp finely chopped onion
  15ml/1 tbsp chopped spring onion
    (scallion)
  15ml/1 tbsp vinegar
  30ml/2 tbsp oil, plus extra for
    brushing
  15ml/1 tbsp lime juice
  1 hot chilli, chopped
  salt and ground black pepper

1 Combine all the ingredients for the marinade in a small bowl. Using a fork, mash them together thoroughly to form a thick paste.

2 Lay the chicken pieces on a plate or board and make several lengthways slits in the flesh. Rub the marinade all over the chicken, working it into the slits so that the flavours permeate the flesh.

3 Place the chicken in a dish, cover with clear film (plastic wrap) and leave to marinate in the refrigerator for 2 hours or overnight.

4 Prepare the barbecue. Position a lightly oiled grill rack over the hot coals. Shake off any excess marinade from the chicken and brush with oil. Place on the grill rack.

5 Cook over medium heat for 30 minutes, turning often until done. Serve hot with salad leaves.

COOK'S TIP
Always use tongs to turn meat over rather than using a fork, as the tines can easily pierce the meat and so allow the juices to escape.

Energy 298kcal/1257kJ; Protein 54.2g; Carbohydrate 2.5g, of which sugars 2.2g; Fat 8g, of which saturates 1.5g; Cholesterol 158mg; Calcium 16mg; Fibre 0.2g; Sodium 136mg.

CHICKEN WITH LEMON GRASS AND GINGER

CHICKEN COOKED ON A BARBECUE IS SERVED AS STREET FOOD IN COMMUNITIES ALL OVER THE WORLD, FROM ROADSIDE STALLS TO SPORTS STADIA. THIS DISH USES TYPICAL THAI FLAVOURINGS THAT ARE NOT TOO SPICY FOR KIDS. THE CHICKEN PIECES ARE PERFECT TO NIBBLE ON AT PARTIES.

SERVES FOUR TO SIX

INGREDIENTS
1 chicken, about 1.3–1.6kg/3–3½lb,
  cut into 8–10 pieces
lime wedges and fresh red chillies,
  to garnish
For the marinade
2 lemon grass stalks, roots trimmed
2.5cm/1in piece fresh root ginger,
  peeled and thinly sliced
6 garlic cloves, coarsely chopped
4 shallots, coarsely chopped
½ bunch coriander (cilantro)
  roots, chopped
15ml/1 tbsp palm sugar or light
  muscovado (brown) sugar
120ml/4fl oz/½ cup coconut milk
30ml/2 tbsp Thai fish sauce
30ml/2 tbsp light soy sauce

1 To make the marinade, cut off the lower 5cm/2in of the lemon grass stalks and chop them coarsely. Put into a food processor with the ginger, garlic, shallots, coriander, sugar, coconut milk and sauces, and process until smooth.

2 Place the chicken pieces in a dish, pour over the marinade and stir to coat the pieces thoroughly. Cover the dish and leave in a cool place to marinate for at least 4 hours, or leave in the refrigerator overnight.

3 Prepare the barbecue. Position a lightly oiled grill rack over the hot coals. Drain the chicken, reserving the marinade, and transfer the pieces to the grill rack.

4 Cook the chicken over medium heat for 20–30 minutes. Turn the pieces frequently and brush with the reserved marinade once or twice, but add the final basting no less than 5 minutes before the end of the cooking time to ensure the marinade is fully cooked.

5 As soon as the chicken pieces are golden brown and cooked through, transfer them to a serving platter, garnish with the lime wedges and red chillies and serve immediately.

COOK'S TIPS
• Coconut milk is available fresh or in cans or cartons from Asian food stores and most supermarkets and you may also find it in powdered form. Alternatively, use 50g/2oz creamed coconut from a packet and add warm water, stirring all the time, until it has completely dissolved.
• Coriander roots are more intensely flavoured than the leaves, but the herb is not always available with the roots intact.

Energy 361kcal/1502kJ; Protein 28.8g; Carbohydrate 8.3g, of which sugars 6.7g; Fat 23.9g, of which saturates 18.4g; Cholesterol 140mg; Calcium 28mg; Fibre 0.9g; Sodium 478mg.

SPICY COATED BARBECUED CHICKEN

THIS AROMATIC SPICED CHICKEN DEVELOPS A DELIGHTFULLY CRISPY SKIN WHEN BARBECUED THANKS TO A SIMPLE YET INSPIRED MARINADE, STRONGLY SCENTED WITH CUMIN AND CINNAMON. DO LEAVE TO MARINATE OVERNIGHT IF YOU CAN — THE RESULTING FLAVOUR WILL BE SECOND TO NONE.

SERVES FOUR

INGREDIENTS

    5 garlic cloves, chopped
    30ml/2 tbsp ground cumin
    7.5ml/1½ tsp ground cinnamon
    5ml/1 tsp paprika
    juice of 1 lemon
    30ml/2 tbsp olive oil
    1.3kg/3lb chicken, cut into
      8 portions
    salt and ground black pepper
    fresh coriander (cilantro) leaves,
      to garnish
    warmed pitta bread, salad and
      lemon wedges, to serve

VARIATION
Use 7.5ml/1½ tsp turmeric and a
pinch of ground cardamom in place
of the cinnamon.

1 In a bowl, combine the garlic, cumin, cinnamon, paprika, lemon juice, oil, salt and pepper. Add the chicken portions and turn in the spice mixture to coat thoroughly. Leave to marinate for at least 1 hour or cover and place in the refrigerator overnight.

2 Prepare the barbecue. Position a lightly oiled grill rack over the hot coals.

3 Arrange the dark meat on the grill rack and cook for 10 minutes, turning once.

4 Place the remaining chicken on the grill rack and cook for 7–10 minutes, turning occasionally, until the chicken is golden brown and the juices run clear when it is pricked with a skewer. Serve immediately with pitta bread, salad and lemon wedges.

Energy 250kcal/1051kJ; Protein 43.2g; Carbohydrate 2.5g, of which sugars 0.3g; Fat 7.5g, of which saturates 1.3g; Cholesterol 123mg; Calcium 12mg; Fibre 0.6g; Sodium 106mg.

GRIDDLED CHICKEN <u>WITH</u> SALSA

*THINLY POUNDED CHICKEN BREAST FILLETS COOK IN THE MINIMUM OF TIME WHEN USING THE GRIDDLE.
MARINATE THEM FIRST TO MAKE THEM EXTRA DELICIOUS AND MOIST, AND THEN SERVE WITH A SALSA OF
FRESH SUMMER INGREDIENTS WITH ROASTED CHILLI TO MAKE A SIMPLE DISH THAT IS FULL OF FLAVOUR.*

SERVES FOUR

INGREDIENTS
   4 skinless chicken breast fillets,
     about 175g/6oz each
   30ml/2 tbsp fresh lemon juice
   30ml/2 tbsp olive oil
   10ml/2 tsp ground cumin
   10ml/2 tsp dried oregano
   15ml/1 tbsp coarse black pepper
For the salsa
   1 green chilli
   450g/1lb plum tomatoes, seeded
     and chopped
   3 spring onions (scallions), chopped
   15ml/1 tbsp chopped fresh parsley
   30ml/2 tbsp chopped fresh coriander
     (cilantro)
   30ml/2 tbsp fresh lemon juice
   45ml/3 tbsp olive oil

1 With a meat mallet, pound the
chicken fillets between two sheets of
clear film (plastic wrap) until thin.

2 In a shallow dish, combine the lemon
juice, oil, cumin, oregano and pepper.
Add the chicken and turn to coat. Cover
and leave to marinate for 2 hours, or in
the refrigerator overnight.

3 To make the salsa, char the chilli skin
either over a gas flame or under the grill
(broiler). Leave to cool for 5 minutes.
Carefully rub off the charred skin,
taking care to wash your hands
afterwards. For a less hot flavour,
discard the seeds.

4 Chop the chilli very finely and
place in a bowl. Add the tomatoes, the
spring onions, parsley and coriander,
lemon juice and olive oil, and mix to
blend thoroughly.

5 Prepare the barbecue. Heat a griddle
on the grill rack over hot coals. Remove
the chicken from the marinade.
Griddle the chicken on one side until
browned, for about 3 minutes. Turn over
and cook for a further 4 minutes. Serve
with the chilli salsa.

Energy 312kcal/1309kJ; Protein 43.4g; Carbohydrate 4.5g, of which sugars 4.4g; Fat 13.5g, of which saturates 2.2g; Cholesterol 123mg; Calcium 46mg; Fibre 2g; Sodium 121mg.

CHARGRILLED CHICKEN
WITH PEPPERS

CHICKEN IS TRANSFORMED BY CHARGRILLING, AND HERE FRENCH MUSTARD, GARLIC AND CHILLIES MAKE A SIMPLE BUT PIQUANT MARINADE THAT TASTES FANTASTIC WITH THE SWEET VEGETABLES.

SERVES FOUR TO SIX

INGREDIENTS

1½ chickens, total weight about
    2.25kg/5lb, jointed, or
    12 chicken pieces
2–3 red or green (bell) peppers,
    quartered and seeded
4–5 tomatoes, halved horizontally
lemon wedges, to serve

For the marinade
90ml/6 tbsp extra virgin olive oil
juice of 1 large lemon
5ml/1 tsp French mustard
4 garlic cloves, crushed
2 fresh red or green chillies, seeded
    and chopped
5ml/1 tsp dried oregano
salt and ground black pepper

1 If you are jointing the chicken yourself, divide the legs into thigh and drumstick joints. Make a couple of slits in the skin and into the deepest part of the flesh of each piece of chicken, using a small sharp knife. This will help the marinade to be absorbed more efficiently and allow the chicken to cook thoroughly.

2 Beat together all the marinade ingredients in a bowl large enough to hold all the chicken. Add the chicken pieces and turn them over to coat them thoroughly in the marinade.

3 Cover the bowl with clear film (plastic wrap) and place in the refrigerator for 4–8 hours or overnight if possible, turning the chicken pieces over in the marinade a couple of times.

4 Prepare the barbecue. Position a lightly oiled grill rack over the hot coals. Transfer the chicken pieces to the grill. Add the pepper pieces and the tomatoes to the marinade and set it aside for 15 minutes.

5 Cook the chicken pieces over medium-hot coals for 20–25 minutes. Watch them closely and move the pieces away from the area where the heat is most fierce if they start to burn before the flesh is cooked through.

6 Turn the chicken pieces over and barbecue them for 20–25 minutes more, until thoroughly cooked.

7 Meanwhile, thread the peppers on two long metal skewers. Add them to the barbecue grill, with the tomatoes, for the last 15 minutes of cooking. Remember to keep an eye on them and turn them over at least once. Serve the chicken with the peppers and tomatoes, accompanied by lemon wedges.

COOK'S TIP
You can cook these chicken pieces under the grill (broiler). Allow about 15 minutes each side on a high heat.

Energy 337kcal/1419kJ; Protein 57.6g; Carbohydrate 7.2g, of which sugars 6.9g; Fat 8.7g, of which saturates 1.6g; Cholesterol 163mg; Calcium 48mg; Fibre 2.5g; Sodium 154mg.

CHARGRILLED CAJUN DRUMMERS

THIS IS A CLASSIC AMERICAN DEEP-SOUTH METHOD OF COOKING IN A SPICY COATING, WHICH CAN BE USED FOR POULTRY, MEAT OR FISH AS WELL AS DELICIOUS CORN ON THE COB. THE COATING SHOULD BEGIN TO CHAR AND BLACKEN SLIGHTLY AT THE EDGES DURING GRILLING.

2 Pull the husks and silks off the corn cobs, then rinse them under cold running water and pat them dry with kitchen paper. Cut the cobs into thick slices, using a heavy kitchen knife.

3 Mix together all the spices. Brush the chicken and corn with the melted butter and sprinkle the spices over. Toss well to coat evenly. Prepare the barbecue.

4 Prepare a lightly oiled grill rack over the hot coals. Cook the chicken pieces over medium-high heat for about 25 minutes, turning occasionally. Add the corn after 15 minutes, and grill, turning often, until golden brown. Serve garnished with chopped parsley.

SERVES FOUR

INGREDIENTS
- 8 chicken joints (drumsticks, thighs or wings)
- 2 whole ears of corn on the cob
- 10ml/2 tsp garlic salt
- 10ml/2 tsp ground black pepper
- 7.5ml/1½ tsp ground cumin
- 7.5ml/1½ tsp paprika
- 5ml/1 tsp cayenne pepper
- 45ml/3 tbsp melted butter
- chopped fresh parsley, to garnish

1 Trim any excess fat from the chicken, but leave the skin in place. Slash the thickest parts with a knife to allow the flavours to penetrate the meat as much as possible.

Energy 266kcal/1108kJ; Protein 22g; Carbohydrate 5.9g, of which sugars 0.8g; Fat 17.3g, of which saturates 8g; Cholesterol 132mg; Calcium 20mg; Fibre 0.8g; Sodium 174mg.

BARBECUED CHICKEN TIKKA

MARINATED IN LOW-FAT YOGURT AND SPICES, THE CHICKEN HAS ALL THE FLAVOUR YOU WOULD EXPECT FROM A BARBECUED DISH AND YET IT IS A HEALTHY LOW-FAT MEAL. LEAVE IT OVERNIGHT TO MARINATE, IF YOU CAN, FOR THE BEST FLAVOUR. RED FOOD COLOURING ADDS A DASH OF TRADITIONAL COLOUR.

SERVES FOUR

INGREDIENTS

    4 skinless chicken breast fillets
    lemon wedges and mixed salad
       leaves, such as frisée and oakleaf
       lettuce or radicchio, to serve
For the marinade
    150ml/1/4 pint/2/3 cup low-fat natural
      (plain) yogurt
    5ml/1 tsp paprika
    10ml/2 tsp grated fresh root ginger
    1 garlic clove, crushed
    10ml/2 tsp garam masala
    2.5ml/1/2 tsp salt
    few drops of red food
      colouring (optional)
    juice of 1 lemon

3 Remove the chicken pieces from the marinade and cook over high heat for 30–40 minutes, or until tender, turning occasionally and basting with a little of the marinade.

4 Arrange the cooked chicken pieces on a bed of salad leaves and add lemon wedges for squeezing over. Serve immediately. Alternatively, the chicken can be served cold.

1 Mix all the marinade ingredients in a large dish. Add the chicken pieces and turn to coat them thoroughly. Cover the dish and leave for at least 4 hours or overnight in the refrigerator to allow the flavours to penetrate the flesh.

2 Prepare the barbecue. Position a lightly oiled grill rack over the hot coals.

COOK'S TIP

This is an example of a dish that is usually very high in fat, but with a few basic changes its fat level can be dramatically reduced. This can also be achieved with other similar dishes, by substituting low-fat yogurt for full-fat versions and creams, and by removing the skin from the chicken, as well as by reducing the amount of oil used.

Energy 169kcal/716kJ; Protein 36.8g; Carbohydrate 1.3g, of which sugars 1.3g; Fat 1.9g, of which saturates 0.5g; Cholesterol 105mg; Calcium 38mg; Fibre 0.2g; Sodium 199mg.

SMOKED CHICKEN WITH BUTTERNUT PESTO

WHOLE CHICKEN SMOKED OVER HICKORY WOOD CHIPS ACQUIRES A PERFECTLY TANNED SKIN AND SUCCULENT PINKISH FLESH. THE BUTTERNUT SQUASH ROASTS ALONGSIDE IT, WRAPPED IN FOIL, AND IS LATER TRANSFORMED INTO A DELICIOUS PESTO. THE CHICKEN ALSO TASTES GREAT COLD.

SERVES FOUR TO SIX

INGREDIENTS
1.3kg/3lb roasting chicken
1 lemon, quartered
8–10 fresh bay leaves
3 branches fresh rosemary
15ml/1 tbsp olive oil
salt and ground black pepper
4 handfuls hickory wood chips
   soaked in cold water for at least
   30 minutes
For the pesto
1 butternut squash, about
   675g/1½lb, halved and seeded
2 garlic cloves, sliced
2 fresh thyme sprigs
45ml/3 tbsp olive oil
25g/1oz/⅓ cup freshly grated
   Parmesan cheese

1 Prepare the barbecue. Cut away any excess fat from the opening to the chicken cavity, season the inside and stuff with lemon quarters, bay leaves and the sprigs from one branch of rosemary. Tie the legs together with kitchen string (twine) and rub the bird all over with the oil. Season the skin of the chicken lightly.

2 To prepare the butternut squash for the pesto, cut it into eight pieces and lay them on a piece of double foil. Season well and scatter with the slices of garlic and the thyme leaves. Drizzle over 15ml/1 tbsp of the olive oil and a sprinkling of water. Bring the sides of the foil up to completely enclose the squash and fold them together tightly to secure the parcel.

3 Once the flames have died down, rake the hot coals to one side and insert a drip tray beside them. Fill the drip tray with water. Position a lightly oiled grill rack over the hot coals. Place the chicken on the grill rack above the drip tray, with the squash next to it, over the coals. Cover with a lid or tented heavy-duty foil. Cook the squash for 35 minutes, or until tender.

4 Drain the hickory chips and carefully add a handful to the coals, then replace the lid. Cook the chicken for 1–1¼ hours more, adding a handful of hickory chips every 15 minutes. Add the remaining rosemary to the coals with the last batch of hickory chips. When the chicken is done, transfer it to a plate, cover with tented foil and leave to stand for 10 minutes.

5 Unwrap the butternut squash. Leaving the thyme stalk behind, scoop the flesh and the garlic into a food processor. Pulse until the mixture forms a thick purée. Add the Parmesan, then the remaining oil, pulsing to ensure it is well combined. Spoon into a bowl and serve with the hot chicken. If the chicken is to be eaten cold, cover it once cool.

COOK'S TIP
With small barbecues, the coals may need to be replenished during cooking: do this before the heat gets too low. The coals will take about 10 minutes to heat sufficiently: allow for this when timing.

Energy 257kcal/1078kJ; Protein 34.4g; Carbohydrate 2.5g, of which sugars 1.9g; Fat 12.2g, of which saturates 2.7g; Cholesterol 98mg; Calcium 89mg; Fibre 1.1g; Sodium 126mg.

TANDOORI DRUMSTICKS

NO SELF-RESPECTING BOOK ON BARBECUING COULD LEAVE OUT A TANDOORI DISH — IN THIS CASE, SERVED WITH A CHILLI ONION SALAD. WHEN MAKING KACHUMBAR, USE THE PINK ONIONS AVAILABLE IN WEST INDIAN MARKETS IF YOU CAN, BUT WHITE SWEET ITALIAN ONES WOULD DO.

SERVES SIX

INGREDIENTS

12 small chicken drumsticks, skinned

3 garlic cloves, crushed to a paste with a pinch of salt

150ml/¼ pint/⅔ cup Greek (US strained plain) yogurt

10ml/2 tsp ground coriander

5ml/1 tsp ground cumin

5ml/1 tsp ground turmeric

1.5ml/¼ tsp cayenne pepper

2.5ml/½ tsp garam masala

15ml/1 tbsp curry paste

juice of ½ lemon

salt

warmed naan breads, to serve

For the kachumbar

2 pink onions, halved and thinly sliced

10ml/2 tsp salt

4cm/1½in piece of fresh root ginger, finely shredded

2 fresh long green chillies, seeded and finely chopped

20ml/4 tsp sugar, preferably palm sugar

juice of ½ lemon

60ml/4 tbsp chopped fresh coriander (cilantro)

1 Cut each drumstick around the flesh that attaches itself to the tip of the bone. Place the drumsticks in a bowl. Put the garlic, yogurt, spices, curry paste and lemon juice in a food processor and whizz until smooth. Pour the mixture over the drumsticks to coat, then cover and chill overnight.

2 Two hours before serving, make the kachumbar. Put the onion slices in a bowl, sprinkle them with the salt, cover and leave to stand for 1 hour. Tip into a sieve (strainer), rinse well under cold running water, then drain and pat dry. Roughly chop the slices and put them in a serving bowl. Add the remaining ingredients and mix well.

3 About an hour before cooking, drain the drumsticks in a sieve set over a bowl. Remove the wobbly knuckle bone at the end of each drumstick with a sharp knife and scrape the flesh down a little to make the bone look clean. Return the drumsticks to the marinade.

4 Prepare the barbecue. About 30 minutes before you are ready to cook, salt the drumsticks. Once the flames have died down, part the coals in the centre and insert a drip tray. Position a lightly oiled grill rack over the hot coals. Carefully lift the drumsticks out of the marinade. Wrap the tips with strips of foil to prevent them from burning, then place on the grill rack so that they are not directly over the coals.

5 Cover with a lid or tented heavy-duty foil and cook for 5 minutes, turning frequently. Brush the drumsticks with a little of the marinade and cook for 5–7 minutes more, or until cooked. Serve hot with the kachumbar and naan breads.

Energy 155kcal/654kJ; Protein 23g; Carbohydrate 6.4g, of which sugars 6.1g; Fat 4.5g of which saturates 1.3g; Cholesterol 108mg; Calcium 81mg; Fibre 0.6g; Sodium 160mg.

STUFFED CORN-FED CHICKEN

THIS IS ONE OF THOSE DISHES THAT IS IDEAL TO COOK FOR FRIENDS. IT REQUIRES HARDLY ANY EFFORT BUT LOOKS AND TASTES AS IF YOU HAVE GONE TO HUGE AMOUNTS OF TROUBLE. SERVE GRILLED MEDITERRANEAN VEGETABLES, OR USE SIMPLY DRESSED SALAD LEAVES WITH THE CHICKEN.

SERVES FOUR TO SIX

INGREDIENTS

4–6 chicken breast fillets,
  preferably from a corn-fed bird
115g/4oz firm goats' cheese,
  crumbled
60ml/4 tbsp chopped fresh oregano
20ml/4 tsp maple syrup
juice of 1 lemon
oil, for brushing
salt and ground black pepper

1 Slash a pocket horizontally in each piece of chicken. Mix the goats' cheese, chopped oregano and 10ml/2 tsp of the maple syrup in a small bowl. Stuff the pockets in the chicken with the mixture. Don't overfill.

2 Put the remaining maple syrup into a shallow dish large enough to hold the chicken fillets in a single layer. Stir in the lemon juice. Add the chicken fillets and rub them all over with the maple syrup mixture, then cover the dish and leave in a cool place for about 20 minutes, turning the chicken pieces occasionally. Season with salt and pepper and marinate for a further 10 minutes.

3 Prepare the barbecue. Once the flames have died down, rake the hot coals to one side and insert a drip tray flat beside them. Position a lightly oiled grill rack over the hot coals. Lay the chicken fillets, skin-side up, on the grill rack over the drip tray. Cover with a lid or tented heavy-duty foil.

4 Grill the chicken over high heat for about 15 minutes in total, turning and moving the pieces around the grill rack so that they cook evenly without getting too charred. Baste with any remaining marinade 5 minutes before the end of cooking.

5 When the chicken is cooked through, transfer the pieces to a dish to rest and keep warm at the side of the barbecue for about 5 minutes before serving.

COOK'S TIP
You can cook these on a griddle. They take about 20 minutes. Sear on a high heat then lower the heat. Turn often.

VARIATION
If you don't like goats' cheese, replace it with crumbled feta or a mixture of ricotta and grated Parmesan.

Energy 180kcal/756kJ; Protein 28.3g; Carbohydrate 3g, of which sugars 3g; Fat 6.1g, of which saturates 3.7g; Cholesterol 88mg; Calcium 44mg; Fibre 0.3g; Sodium 186mg.

CHICKEN <u>WITH</u> HERB <u>AND</u> RICOTTA STUFFING

THESE LITTLE CHICKEN DRUMSTICKS ARE FULL OF FLAVOUR. THE SOFT CHEESE STUFFING AND A WRAPPING OF BACON HELP TO KEEP THE MEAT MOIST AND TENDER.

2 Loosen the skin on each drumstick, being careful not to tear it. Using a small spoon, insert a little of the herb stuffing under the skin of each one, then smooth the skin back over it firmly to hold the stuffing in place.

3 Wrap a bacon rasher tightly around the wide end of each drumstick. This will help to baste the flesh as well as holding the skin in place over the stuffing during cooking.

SERVES FOUR

INGREDIENTS
  60ml/4 tbsp ricotta cheese
  1 garlic clove, crushed
  45ml/3 tbsp mixed chopped fresh
    herbs, such as chives, flat-leaf
    parsley and mint
  30ml/2 tbsp fresh brown
    breadcrumbs
  8 chicken drumsticks
  8 smoked streaky (fatty) bacon
    rashers (strips)
  5ml/1 tsp wholegrain mustard
  15ml/1 tbsp sunflower oil
  salt and ground black pepper

1 To make the stuffing, break up the ricotta in a mixing bowl and add the crushed garlic, herbs and brown breadcrumbs. Season well with plenty of salt and pepper.

4 Prepare the barbecue. Mix together the mustard and oil and brush the mixture over the bacon-wrapped chicken. Cook the drumsticks over medium-hot coals for about 25 minutes, turning occasionally.

Energy 431kcal/1799kJ; Protein 52.6g; Carbohydrate 0.9g, of which sugars 0.8g; Fat 24.1g, of which saturates 7.9g; Cholesterol 253mg; Calcium 44mg; Fibre 0.7g; Sodium 913mg.

CHICKEN WITH FRESH HERBS AND GARLIC

A WHOLE CHICKEN CAN BE ROASTED ON A SPIT ON THE BARBECUE. THIS MARINADE KEEPS THE FLESH MOIST AND DELICIOUS AND THE FRESH HERBS ADD SUMMERY FLAVOURS.

SERVES FOUR

INGREDIENTS
1.75kg/4½lb chicken, preferably
    free-range
finely grated rind and juice
    of 1 lemon
1 garlic clove, crushed
30ml/2 tbsp olive oil
2 fresh thyme sprigs
2 fresh sage sprigs
90ml/6 tbsp unsalted (sweet)
    butter, softened
salt and ground black pepper

COOK'S TIP
If roasting the chicken in the oven, preheat the oven to 230°C/450°F/ Gas 8 and reduce the heat to 190°C/375°F/ Gas 5 after 10 minutes. If you are roasting a chicken to serve cold, cooking it in foil helps to keep it succulent – open the foil for the last 20 minutes to brown the skin, then close it as the chicken cools.

1 Season the chicken well inside and out with freshly ground black pepper and put it in a non-metallic container. Mix the lemon rind and juice, crushed garlic and olive oil together and pour the mixture over the chicken. Cover the dish and leave the chicken in the refrigerator to marinate for at least 2 hours.

2 Prepare the barbecue. When the flames have died down move the coals aside and arrange a drip tray under the spit-roasting attachment.

3 Place the herbs in the cavity of the bird and smear the butter over the skin. Season well. Spear the chicken on the spit and cook for 1½–1¾ hours, basting with the marinade, until the juices run clear when the thigh is pierced with a skewer. Leave the bird to rest for 15 minutes before carving.

VARIATION
Tarragon is great with chicken. Chop the leaves from 3 good sprigs and use them instead of the thyme and sage.

Energy 498kcal/2062kJ; Protein 38.5g; Carbohydrate 0.4g, of which sugars 0.3g; Fat 37.9g, of which saturates 10.2g; Cholesterol 200mg; Calcium 41mg; Fibre 0.6g; Sodium 161mg.

BARBECUED CHICKEN SALAD

THIS DISH IS REMARKABLY SIMPLE BUT TASTES WONDERFUL. SIMPLY BARBECUED CHICKEN IS TOSSED IN A CRISP SALAD OF BABY SPINACH AND CHERRY TOMATOES WITH A HERBY, NUTTY DRESSING. THIS WOULD MAKE A SUPER FILLING TO POP INTO WARMED SPLIT PITTA BREADS FOR OUTDOOR EATING.

SERVES FOUR

INGREDIENTS

30ml/2 tbsp olive oil, plus extra
  for brushing
30ml/2 tbsp hazelnut oil
15ml/1 tbsp white wine vinegar
1 garlic clove, crushed
15ml/1 tbsp chopped fresh
  mixed herbs
225g/8oz baby spinach leaves
250g/9oz cherry tomatoes, halved
1 bunch spring onions
  (scallions), chopped
2 skinless chicken breast fillets
salt and ground black pepper

1 First make the dressing. Place 30ml/ 2 tbsp of the olive oil, the hazelnut oil, vinegar, garlic and herbs in a small bowl or jug (pitcher) and whisk together until thoroughly mixed. Set the dressing aside.

2 Trim any long stalks from the spinach leaves and discard, then place the leaves in a large serving bowl with the tomatoes and spring onions, and toss together to mix.

3 Prepare the barbecue. Position a lightly oiled grill rack over the hot coals. Brush the chicken breasts all over with oil and then grill them over medium heat for 15–20 minutes, turning regularly, until cooked through and golden brown. Brush the pieces with oil if necessary during cooking to keep them moist. When cooked through, cut the chicken into thin slices.

4 Scatter the chicken pieces over the salad, give the dressing a quick whisk to blend, then drizzle it over the salad and gently toss all the ingredients together to mix. Season to taste and serve immediately.

COOK'S TIP
Remember to cut up your cooked chicken on a different plate to that which held the raw chicken, as it is essential to avoid cross-contamination when cooking meat or poultry.

VARIATION
You can try out different dressings for this salad. For example, try a piquant combination of 20ml/4 tsp olive oil, 15ml/1 tbsp balsamic vinegar, 10ml/ 2 tsp honey and 30ml/2 tbsp mustard.

Energy 436kcal/1830kJ; Protein 37.3g; Carbohydrate 34.6g, of which sugars 12.8g; Fat 17.5g, of which saturates 4.6g; Cholesterol 105mg; Calcium 96mg; Fibre 3.9g; Sodium 194mg.

HOT AND SOUR CHICKEN SALAD

THIS SALAD FROM VIETNAM IS A GREAT DISH FOR A LARGE BARBECUE PARTY, ESPECIALLY GOOD FOR THOSE WHO PREFER A HEALTHIER OPTION. THE CHICKEN HAS A SWEET, FIERY FLAVOUR.

SERVES FOUR TO SIX

INGREDIENTS
2 skinless chicken breast fillets
115g/4oz bean sprouts
1 head Chinese leaves, shredded
2 medium carrots, cut
   into matchsticks
1 red onion, thinly sliced
2 large gherkins, sliced
For the marinade
1 small red chilli, seeded and
   finely chopped
1cm/½in piece fresh ginger, chopped
1 garlic clove, crushed
15ml/1 tbsp crunchy peanut butter
30ml/2 tbsp chopped fresh
   coriander (cilantro)
5ml/1 tsp sugar
2.5ml/½ tsp salt
15ml/1 tbsp rice or white
   wine vinegar
60ml/4 tbsp vegetable oil
10ml/2 tsp Thai fish sauce

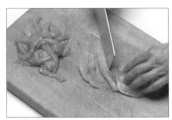

1 Slice the chicken fillets thinly and place in a shallow bowl.

2 Grind the chilli, ginger and garlic in a food processor or pestle and mortar, then add the peanut butter, chopped fresh coriander, sugar and salt.

3 Add the rice or white wine vinegar, 30ml/2 tbsp of the oil and the fish sauce to the ingredients in the food processor or mixing bowl. Combine well.

4 Cover the chicken with the spice mixture and leave to marinate for at least 2–3 hours.

5 When you are nearly ready to serve, wash, dry and arrange all the salad ingredients on a serving dish.

6 Prepare the barbecue, if you plan to use it to cook the chicken.

7 Clear an area on your medium hot barbecue and stir-fry the chicken in a wok over the coals or on the hob for about 5 minutes, until cooked and lightly browned. Arrange on top of the salad and serve immediately.

COOK'S TIP
Chicken can be extremely inexpensive, but when you are buying only a small amount, as for this recipe, it is worth looking for quality, free-range meat.

VARIATION
This salad is equally delicious made with prawns (shrimp). Allow 450g/1lb large raw king prawns (jumbo shrimp) to serve four people.

Energy 148kcal/615kJ; Protein 10g; Carbohydrate 6g, of which sugars 5.1g; Fat 9.5g, of which saturates 1.4g; Cholesterol 23mg; Calcium 44mg; Fibre 2.1g; Sodium 42mg.

CHICKEN SALAD <u>WITH</u> LAVENDER <u>AND</u> HERBS

THE DELIGHTFUL SCENT OF LAVENDER HAS A NATURAL AFFINITY WITH GARLIC, ORANGE AND WILD HERBS. THE ADDITION OF FRIED POLENTA MAKES THIS SALAD BOTH FILLING AND DELICIOUS.

SERVES FOUR

INGREDIENTS
    4 chicken breast fillets
    900ml/1½ pints/3¾ cups light
      chicken stock
    175g/6oz/1 cup fine polenta
      or cornmeal
    50g/2oz butter, plus extra
      for greasing
    450g/1lb young spinach
    175g/6oz lamb's lettuce
    8 sprigs fresh lavender
    8 small tomatoes, halved
    salt and ground black pepper
For the marinade
    6 fresh lavender flowers
    10ml/2 tsp finely grated orange rind
    2 garlic cloves, crushed
    10ml/2 tsp clear honey
    30ml/2 tbsp olive oil
    10ml/2 tsp chopped fresh thyme
    10ml/2 tsp chopped fresh marjoram
    salt

1 To make the marinade, strip the lavender flowers from the stems and combine with the grated orange rind, garlic, honey and salt. Add the oil and herbs. Make several deep slashes into the chicken fillets and put them in a non-metallic bowl. Spread the marinade over the meat, cover the bowl and leave to marinate for about 20 minutes.

2 To make the polenta or cornmeal, bring the chicken stock to the boil in a heavy pan. Add the grain in a steady stream, stirring all the time until thick. Turn the cooked polenta out on to a shallow buttered tray and leave to cool.

3 Cook the chicken on a medium barbecue or under the grill (broiler) for about 15 minutes, basting with the marinade and turning once. Keep warm.

4 Cut the polenta into 2.5cm/1in cubes using a wet knife. Heat the butter in a large frying pan and fry the polenta until golden. Alternatively, cut the cold polenta into wedges and grill them on an oiled rack over hot coals for about 3 minutes on each side.

5 Divide the salad leaves between four dinner plates. Slice each chicken fillet and arrange over the salad. Arrange the polenta on the salad, decorate with sprigs of lavender and tomato halves, season with salt and ground black pepper and serve.

VARIATION
If you think that lavender might not be to your taste, then sprigs of thyme can happily be substituted. You could then use chopped fresh tarragon instead of fresh thyme in the marinade.

Energy 555kcal/2318kJ; Protein 56.6g; Carbohydrate 34.6g, of which sugars 2.4g; Fat 20.7g, of which saturates 8.1g; Cholesterol 167mg; Calcium 279mg; Fibre 4.3g; Sodium 415mg.

CHICKEN SALAD WITH CORIANDER DRESSING

SERVE THIS SALAD WARM TO MAKE THE MOST OF THE WONDERFUL FLAVOUR OF BARBECUED CHICKEN BASTED WITH A MARINADE OF CORIANDER, SESAME AND MUSTARD.

SERVES SIX

INGREDIENTS
    4 skinless chicken breast fillets
    225g/8oz mangetout (snow peas)
    2 heads decorative lettuce such as
       lollo rosso or feuille de chêne, or
       mixed salad leaves
    3 medium carrots, cut into
       matchsticks
    175g/6oz button (white) mushrooms,
       sliced
    6 bacon rashers (slices), fried until
       crisp and chopped
    15ml/1 tbsp chopped fresh coriander
       (cilantro), to garnish
For the coriander dressing
    120ml/4fl oz/½ cup lemon juice
    30ml/2 tbsp wholegrain mustard
    250ml/8fl oz/1 cup olive oil
    65ml/2½fl oz/⅓ cup sesame oil
    5ml/1 tsp coriander seeds,
       crushed

1 Mix all the dressing ingredients in a bowl. Place the chicken fillets in a dish and pour over half the dressing. Cover the dish and leave to marinate in the refrigerator for several hours or overnight. Chill the remaining dressing.

2 Cook the mangetout for 2 minutes in boiling water, then refresh in cold water. Tear the lettuces into small pieces and mix all the other salad ingredients and the bacon together.

3 Prepare the barbecue. Cook the chicken fillets over medium-hot coals for 10–15 minutes, basting with the marinade and turning once, until cooked through. Slice them on the diagonal into thin pieces.

4 Arrange the salad in individual bowls and divide the chicken among them. Pour over the remaining dressing, toss gently and scatter some fresh coriander over each bowl.

Energy 251kcal/1045kJ; Protein 21.6g; Carbohydrate 3g, of which sugars 2.7g; Fat 17g, of which saturates 3.2g; Cholesterol 56mg; Calcium 47mg; Fibre 2g; Sodium 382mg.

MARYLAND SALAD

BARBECUE-GRILLED CHICKEN, CORN, BACON, BANANA AND WATERCRESS COMBINE HERE IN A SENSATIONAL MAIN COURSE SALAD. SERVE WITH BUTTERED BAKED POTATOES.

SERVES FOUR

INGREDIENTS
    4 chicken breast fillets
    olive oil, for brushing
    225g/8oz rindless unsmoked bacon
      rashers (strips)
    4 whole ears corn on the cob,
      husks stripped back and silk
      removed
    45ml/3 tbsp melted butter
    4 ripe bananas, peeled and
      halved
    4 tomatoes, halved
    1 escarole or butterhead lettuce
    1 bunch watercress
    salt and ground black pepper
For the dressing
    75ml/5 tbsp groundnut oil
    15ml/1 tbsp white wine vinegar
    10ml/2 tsp maple syrup
    10ml/2 tsp mild mustard

4 Combine the dressing ingredients with 15ml/1 tbsp water in a screw-top jar and shake well to mix. Wash and spin the lettuce leaves, then toss the salad in the dressing.

5 Distribute the dressed leaves between four large plates. Slice the chicken and arrange over the leaves with the bacon, banana, sweetcorn and tomatoes. Season well and serve.

1 Prepare the barbecue and arrange a grill rack over the coals. Season the chicken fillets with salt and pepper, brush with oil and cook over medium-hot coals for 15–20 minutes, turning once. Add the bacon to the rack and barbecue for 8–10 minutes, or until crisp and browned.

2 Bring a large pan of water to the boil and cook the corn cobs for about 10 minutes, until tender. For extra flavour, brush with the cobs with butter and brown on the barbecue.

3 Barbecue the sliced bananas and tomatoes for 6–8 minutes: brush these with butter too if you wish.

Energy 613kcal/2562kJ; Protein 48.9g; Carbohydrate 29.3g, of which sugars 26.8g; Fat 34.1g, of which saturates 12.2g; Cholesterol 156mg; Calcium 102mg; Fibre 3.3g; Sodium 1193mg.

CHICKEN FAJITAS

FAJITAS, TORTILLA WRAPS STUFFED WITH FRESHLY GRILLED MEAT, MAKE PERFECT BARBECUE FOOD.
BURSTING WITH TENDER CHICKEN AND A WONDERFUL BLEND OF VEGETABLES AND SALSA, THEY ARE
ALWAYS A GREAT HIT, AND ARE PERFECT FOR PARTIES BECAUSE YOU CAN EAT THEM WITH YOUR FINGERS
WITHOUT GETTING MESSY. KIDS JUST LOVE THEM.

SERVES SIX

INGREDIENTS
   finely grated rind of 1 lime and the
      juice of 2 limes
   105ml/7 tbsp olive oil, plus extra
      for brushing
   1 garlic clove, finely chopped
   2.5ml/½ tsp dried oregano
   good pinch of dried red chilli flakes
   5ml/1 tsp coriander seeds, crushed
   6 chicken breast fillets
   3 Spanish onions, thickly sliced
   2 large red, yellow or orange (bell)
      peppers, seeded and cut lengthwise
      into strips
   30ml/2 tbsp chopped fresh
      coriander (cilantro)
   salt and ground black pepper
For the tomato salsa
   450g/1lb tomatoes, peeled, seeded
      and chopped
   2 garlic cloves, finely chopped
   1 small red onion, finely chopped
   1–2 green chillies, seeded
      and chopped
   finely grated rind of ½ lime
   30ml/2 tbsp chopped fresh
      coriander (cilantro)
   pinch of caster (superfine) sugar
   2.5–5ml/½–1 tsp ground roasted
      cumin seeds
To serve
   12–18 soft flour tortillas
   guacamole
   120ml/4fl oz/½ cup sour cream
   crisp lettuce leaves
   coriander (cilantro) sprigs
   lime wedges

1 In an ovenproof dish, combine the lime rind and juice, 75ml/5 tbsp of the oil, the garlic, oregano, chilli flakes and coriander seeds. Season with salt and pepper. Slash the skin on the chicken breast fillets several times and put them into the garlic mixture. Turn them in the mixture, then cover and set aside to marinate for several hours.

2 To make the tomato salsa, combine the tomatoes, garlic, onion, chillies, lime rind and chopped coriander. Season to taste with salt, pepper, caster sugar and cumin seeds. Set aside for 30 minutes to allow the flavours to blend, then taste and adjust the seasoning, adding more cumin and sugar, if necessary. Put the salsa in a serving bowl.

3 Prepare the barbecue. When the flames have died down, position a lightly oiled grill rack over the hot coals. Thread the onion slices on to a metal skewer. Brush them with the remaining oil and season. Grill until softened and slightly charred in places, then set aside.

4 Grill the chicken breast fillets over medium heat for 15–20 minutes, turning regularly, until they are cooked through and golden brown. Baste the chicken with the marinade during cooking, but add the final basting no less than 5 minutes before the end of the cooking time to ensure the marinade is fully cooked.

5 Heat a griddle on the grill rack over hot coals.

6 Brush the pepper strips with oil and cook on the griddle for 8–10 minutes, or until they are softened and browned in places.

7 Add the grilled onions to the griddle and mix with the peppers for 2 minutes. Stir in the chopped coriander. Put in a bowl.

8 Heat the tortillas in batches by putting them on to the grill rack very briefly, for about 30 seconds on each side. As they are done, stack the hot tortillas on a serving plate and cover them with a clean dish towel to keep them warm.

9 Using a sharp knife, cut the grilled chicken into strips and transfer to a serving dish.

10 Set out the dishes of chicken, onions and peppers, and salsa with the stack of tortillas and serve them with bowls of guacamole, sour cream, lettuce and coriander so that everyone can assemble their own fajitas. Add a bowl of lime wedges for squeezing over the chicken.

COOK'S TIP
If avocados are in season, make your own guacamole. Roughly mash the flesh of three large avocados with a good squeeze of lime juice, a tablespoon of olive oil, a pinch of salt and finely chopped red chilli and garlic, to taste.

Per Fajita: Energy 174kcal/732kJ; Protein 14.9g; Carbohydrate 13.9g, of which sugars 5.1g; Fat 7g, of which saturates 1.8g; Cholesterol 42mg; Calcium 38mg; Fibre 1.6g; Sodium 78mg.

TURKEY SOSATIES <u>WITH</u> APRICOT SAUCE

TURKEY IS A LARGE BIRD, IDEAL FOR CATERING FOR LARGE NUMBERS AND VERY ECONOMICAL. IT IS ALSO ONE OF THE HEALTHIEST MEATS. HERE, TENDER CHUNKS ARE MARINATED IN A FABULOUS SWEET-AND-SOUR SPICED SAUCE IN THIS RECIPE FROM SOUTH AFRICA. MOP UP THE SPARE SAUCE WITH SOME CRUSTY BREAD OR PLAIN BOILED RICE, OR SERVE A NUTTY COUSCOUS SALAD ON THE SIDE.

SERVES FOUR

INGREDIENTS
  5ml/1 tsp vegetable oil
  1 onion, finely chopped
  1 garlic clove, crushed
  2 bay leaves
  juice of 1 lemon
  30ml/2 tbsp curry powder
  60ml/4 tbsp apricot jam
  60ml/4 tbsp apple juice
  675g/1½lb turkey fillet
  30ml/2 tbsp low-fat crème fraîche
  salt

VARIATION
Chicken fillets could be substituted for the turkey.

COOK'S TIP
Serve with couscous and grilled mixed vegetables.

1 Heat the oil in a pan. Add the onion, garlic and bay leaves and cook gently for 10 minutes. Add the lemon juice, curry powder, apricot jam and apple juice, with salt to taste. Cook for 5 minutes. Transfer to a bowl and cool.

2 Cut the turkey into 2cm/¾in cubes and add to the bowl. Mix well, cover and leave to marinate for at least 2 hours or overnight in the refrigerator.

3 Prepare the barbecue. Position a lightly oiled grill rack over the hot coals. Thread the turkey on to four metal skewers and cook for 6–8 minutes over medium heat, turning several times.

4 Meanwhile, transfer the marinade to a pan and simmer on the grill rack for 2 minutes. Stir in the crème fraîche, allow to heat through gently, and serve the sauce with the sosaties.

Energy 325kcal/1381kJ; Protein 59.4g; Carbohydrate 12.2g, of which sugars 12.1g; Fat 4.8g, of which saturates 1.9g; Cholesterol 125mg; Calcium 18mg; Fibre 0g; Sodium 162mg.

TURKEY PATTIES

MINCED TURKEY MAKES DELICIOUSLY LIGHT PATTIES, WHICH ARE IDEAL FOR SUMMER MEALS. THE RECIPE IS A FLAVOURFUL VARIATION ON A CLASSIC BURGER. SERVE THE PATTIES IN SPLIT AND TOASTED BUNS OR IN CHUNKS OF CRUSTY BREAD, WITH CHUTNEY, SALAD LEAVES AND CHUNKY FRIES. A REAL TREAT IS A TOPPING OF MELTED BRIE AND CRANBERRY JELLY.

<u>SERVES SIX</u>

INGREDIENTS
    675g/1½lb minced (ground) turkey
    1 small red onion, finely chopped
    grated rind and juice of 1 lime
    small handful of fresh thyme leaves
    15–30ml/1–2 tbsp olive oil
    salt and ground black pepper

VARIATIONS
Minced (ground) chicken or pork could be used instead of turkey in these burgers. You could also try chopped oregano, parsley or basil in place of the thyme, and lemon rind instead of lime.

1 Mix together the turkey, onion, lime rind and juice, thyme and seasoning. Cover and chill for up to 4 hours to allow the flavours to infuse, then divide the mixture into six equal portions and shape into round patties.

2 Preheat a griddle. Brush the patties with oil, then place them on the griddle and cook for 10–12 minutes. Turn the patties over, brush with more oil and cook for 10–12 minutes on the second side, or until cooked through.

Energy 141kcal/596kJ; Protein 24.8g; Carbohydrate 0.8g, of which sugars 0.6g; Fat 4.4g, of which saturates 1.1g; Cholesterol 69mg; Calcium 15mg; Fibre 0.2g; Sodium 62mg.

MEDITERRANEAN TURKEY SKEWERS

THESE ATTRACTIVE KEBABS CAN BE ASSEMBLED IN ADVANCE AND LEFT TO MARINATE UNTIL YOU ARE READY TO COOK THEM. BARBECUING INTENSIFIES THE MEDITERRANEAN FLAVOURS OF THE VEGETABLES.

SERVES FOUR

INGREDIENTS

    2 medium courgettes (zucchini)
    1 long thin aubergine (eggplant)
    300g/11oz boneless turkey, cut into
      5cm/2in cubes
    12–16 pickling onions
    1 red or yellow (bell) pepper, cut into
      5cm/2in squares
For the marinade
    90ml/6 tbsp olive oil
    45ml/3 tbsp fresh lemon juice
    1 garlic clove, finely chopped
    30ml/2 tbsp chopped fresh basil
    salt and ground black pepper

1 To make the marinade, pour the olive oil and lemon juice into a small bowl and add the garlic and chopped fresh basil. Season well with plenty of salt and black pepper.

2 Slice the courgettes and aubergine lengthways into strips 5mm/¼in thick. Cut them crossways about two-thirds down their length. Discard the shorter lengths. Wrap half the turkey pieces with the courgette slices and the other half with the aubergine slices.

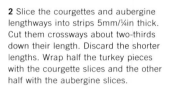

3 Prepare the skewers by alternating the turkey pieces in their two vegetable wrappings, interspersing them with the onions and pepper pieces. Lay the prepared skewers on a platter and pour the flavoured oil over them. Leave to marinate for at least 30 minutes, turning them in the marinade so that they are well coated.

4 Cook on a medium barbecue or under a grill (broiler) for 10–15 minutes, turning the skewers occasionally, until the turkey is cooked and the vegetables are tender and browned.

COOK'S TIP
Buy skinless turkey breast fillets for this dish and look for thick slices so that you can cut them into neat, large cubes of even size.

Energy 198kcal/829kJ; Protein 21.7g; Carbohydrate 13g, of which sugars 10.4g; Fat 7g, of which saturates 1.2g; Cholesterol 43mg; Calcium 55mg; Fibre 3.7g; Sodium 44mg.

TURKEY ROLLS WITH GAZPACHO SAUCE

THIS SPANISH-STYLE RECIPE USES QUICK-COOKING TURKEY STEAKS, BUT YOU COULD ALSO COOK VEAL ESCALOPES IN THE SAME WAY. THE SAUCE IS BASED ON A CLASSIC SPANISH SOUP.

SERVES FOUR

INGREDIENTS
    4 turkey breast steaks
    15ml/1 tbsp red pesto
    4 chorizo sausages
    15ml/1 tbsp olive oil
    salt and ground black pepper
For the gazpacho sauce
    1 green (bell) pepper, chopped
    1 red (bell) pepper, chopped
    7.5cm/3in piece cucumber
    1 medium tomato
    1 garlic clove
    45ml/3 tbsp olive oil
    15ml/1 tbsp red wine vinegar

1 To make the gazpacho sauce, place the peppers, cucumber, tomato, garlic, 30ml/2 tbsp of the olive oil and the vinegar in a food processor and process until almost smooth. Season to taste with salt and ground black pepper.

2 Prepare the barbecue and arrange a lightly oiled grill rack over the coals.

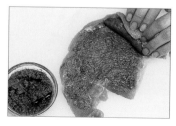

3 Lay the turkey breasts out flat on a board. Spread a layer of red pesto over each piece of turkey, place a chorizo sausage on each piece and roll the meat up firmly.

4 Slice the rolls thickly and thread them on to metal skewers. Brush with oil and cook over medium-hot coals for about 10–12 minutes, turning once. Serve with the gazpacho sauce.

Energy 421kcal/1762kJ; Protein 39g; Carbohydrate 13.1g, of which sugars 7.9g; Fat 24.1g, of which saturates 7.4g; Cholesterol 112mg; Calcium 47mg; Fibre 2.1g; Sodium 502mg.

PHEASANTS <u>WITH</u> SAGE <u>AND</u> LEMON

PHEASANT IS QUICK TO COOK AND MAKES A REALLY SPECIAL MEAL. WHEN PHEASANT IS NOT IN SEASON, THIS RECIPE CAN ALSO BE USED FOR GUINEA FOWL.

SERVES FOUR

INGREDIENTS
   2 pheasants, about 450g/1lb each
   1 lemon
   60ml/4 tbsp chopped fresh sage
   3 shallots
   5ml/1 tsp Dijon mustard
   15ml/1 tbsp brandy or dry sherry
   150ml/5fl oz/⅔ cup crème fraîche
   salt and ground black pepper
   lemon wedges and sage sprigs,
     to garnish

1 Place the pheasants, breast-side upwards, on a chopping board and cut them in half lengthways, using poultry shears or a sharp kitchen knife.

2 Finely grate the rind from half the lemon and slice the rest thinly. Mix together the grated lemon rind and half the chopped sage in a small bowl.

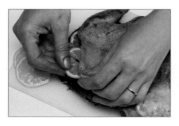

3 Loosen the skin on the breasts and legs of the pheasants, being careful not to tear it, and push a little of the sage and lemon mixture under each flap of skin. Tuck the lemon slices under the skin, smoothing the skin back firmly.

4 Prepare the barbecue. When the flames have died down place a lightly oiled grill rack over the coals. Arrange the half-pheasants on the rack over medium-hot coals and cook for about 25–30 minutes, turning once, until cooked through and well browned.

5 While the pheasants are cooking, cook the shallots alongside them on the barbecue for about 10–12 minutes, turning occasionally, until the skin is blackened and the inside very soft. Peel off the skins, chop the flesh roughly and mash it with the Dijon mustard and brandy or sherry.

6 Stir in the crème fraîche and add the reserved chopped sage. Season with plenty of salt and ground black pepper.

7 Place the pheasant halves on a warm plate or on individual serving plates, with wedges of lemon and the creamy sauce on the side. Decorate with sprigs of young sage.

COOK'S TIPS
• Although not an obvious choice for a barbecue, pheasant comes into season in autumn when the weather is still mild enough for outdoor cooking.
• Try to choose pheasants with undamaged skins, so that the flavourings stay in place during cooking.
• Guinea fowl are available year-round and are similar in size or a little larger than pheasants. Although reared as poultry, they have a texture and flavour more like those of game birds.

Energy 476kcal/1985kJ; Protein 47.6g; Carbohydrate 5.3g, of which sugars 4g; Fat 28.7g, of which saturates 14.7g; Cholesterol 42mg; Calcium 130mg; Fibre 1.3g; Sodium 199mg.

DUCK SAUSAGES WITH SPICY PLUM SAUCE

THE RICH FLAVOUR OF DUCK SAUSAGES GOES EXTREMELY WELL WITH SWEET POTATO MASH AND A PLUM SAUCE. THE RECIPE WOULD ALSO WORK WELL WITH PORK OR GAME SAUSAGES — OR A LUXURIOUS HICKORY-SMOKED SAUSAGE FOR A REAL BOOST TO FLAVOUR.

SERVES FOUR

INGREDIENTS
8–12 duck sausages
For the sweet potato mash
   1.5kg/3¼lb sweet potatoes, cut
     into chunks
   25g/1oz/2 tbsp butter or 30ml/2 tbsp
     olive oil
   60ml/4 tbsp milk
   sea salt and ground black pepper
For the plum sauce
   30ml/2 tbsp olive oil
   1 small onion, chopped
   1 small red chilli, seeded
     and chopped
   450g/1lb plums, stoned (pitted)
     and chopped
   30ml/2 tbsp red wine vinegar
   45ml/3 tbsp clear honey

1 Put the sweet potatoes in a pan and add water to cover. Bring to the boil, then reduce the heat and simmer for 20 minutes, or until tender.

2 To make the plum sauce, heat the oil in a small pan and fry the onion and chilli gently for 5 minutes. Stir in the plums, vinegar and honey, then simmer gently for 10 minutes.

3 Drain and mash the potatoes and leave them in the pan.

VARIATION
If you'd rather not go to the bother of cooking the sweet potato mash, try a quick and easy polenta mash, perhaps combined with steamed spinach.

4 Prepare the barbecue and place a lightly oiled grill rack over the hot coals. Arrange the duck sausages on the rack and cook over medium heat for 25–30 minutes, turning the sausages two or three times during cooking to ensure that they brown and cook evenly.

5 When the sausages are nearly cooked place the pan containing the sweet potato mash on the grill rack and reheat for about 5 minutes. Stir the mashed potato frequently to dry it out and prevent it catching on the bottom of the pan. Beat in the butter or oil and milk, and season to taste.

6 Serve the freshly cooked sausages accompanied by the sweet potato mash and plum sauce.

Energy 894kcal/3755kJ; Protein 17.8g; Carbohydrate 110.8g, of which sugars 42.9g; Fat 45.5g, of which saturates 17.9g; Cholesterol 67mg; Calcium 170mg; Fibre 11.6g; Sodium 1052mg.

RARE GINGERED DUCK

THIS IS JAPANESE AND CHINESE FUSION FOOD: THE TARE IS JAPANESE BUT THE PANCAKES ARE CHINESE.
YOU CAN COOK THE DUCK USING A GRIDDLE OR DIRECTLY ON THE GRILL RACK OF THE BARBECUE. BOTH
METHODS USE HIGH HEAT TO SEAR THE FLESH AND REMOVE THE FAT FOR SUCCULENT AND TASTY MEAT.

SERVES FOUR

INGREDIENTS
   4 large duck breast fillets, total
      weight about 675g/1½lb
   5cm/2in piece of fresh root ginger,
      finely grated
   ½ large cucumber
   12 Chinese pancakes
   6 spring onions (scallions),
      finely shredded
For the tare
   105ml/7 tbsp tamari
   105ml/7 tbsp mirin
   25g/1oz/2 tbsp sugar
   salt and ground black pepper

1 Make four slashes in the skin of each duck breast fillet, then lay them skin-side up on a plate. Squeeze the grated ginger over the duck to extract every drop of juice; discard the pulp. Generously rub the juice all over the duck, especially into the slashes. Using a vegetable peeler, peel the cucumber in strips, then cut it in half, scoop out the seeds and chop the flesh. Set aside in a bowl.

2 To make the tare, mix the tamari, mirin and sugar in a heavy pan and heat gently together until the sugar has dissolved. Increase the heat and simmer for 4–5 minutes, or until the syrup has reduced by about one-third.

3 Prepare the barbecue. Heat a griddle on the grill rack over hot coals. Sear the duck breasts in batches, placing them skin-side down.

4 When the fat has been rendered, and the skin is nicely browned, remove the duck from the pan. Drain off the fat and wipe the pan clean with kitchen paper. Reheat it, return the duck, flesh-side down and cook over a medium heat for about 3 minutes.

5 Brush on a little of the tare, turn the duck over, then, using a clean brush, brush the other side with tare and turn again. This should take about 1 minute, by which time the duck should be cooked rare. You can test for this by pressing the meat lightly: there should be some give in the flesh.

6 Remove from the pan and let the duck rest for a few minutes before slicing each breast across at an angle.

7 Warm the pancakes in a steamer for about 3 minutes. Serve with the duck, tare, spring onions and cucumber.

COOK'S TIP
To cook straight on the grill rack, part the coals and insert a drip tray. Position a lightly oiled grill rack over the hot coals. Sear the duck breasts directly over the coals, then move them over the drip tray. Cover with a lid or tented heavy-duty foil and cook as above, from step 4.

Energy 558kcal/2332kJ; Protein 36.4g; Carbohydrate 29.6g, of which sugars 7.6g; Fat 36.4g, of which saturates 6.1g; Cholesterol 186mg; Calcium 73mg; Fibre 1.2g; Sodium 293mg.

APRICOT DUCK WITH BEANSPROUTS

DUCK IS A RICHLY FLAVOURED BIRD AND IT GOES EXTREMELY WELL WHEN COOKED WITH FRUIT. HERE APRICOTS ARE USED TO STUFF DUCK BREASTS, WHICH ARE THEN BARBECUED WITH A HONEY GLAZE, MAKING DELICIOUSLY CRISPY SKIN ENCLOSING BEAUTIFULLY MOIST MEAT.

SERVES FOUR

INGREDIENTS

4 plump duck breast fillets
1 small red onion, thinly sliced
115g/4oz/½ cup ready-to-eat
   dried apricots
15ml/1 tbsp clear honey
5ml/1 tsp sesame oil
10ml/2 tsp ground star anise
salt and ground black pepper

For the salad
½ head Chinese leaves,
   finely shredded
150g/5oz/2 cups beansprouts
2 spring onions (scallions), shredded
15ml/1 tbsp light soy sauce
15ml/1 tbsp groundnut (peanut) oil
5ml/1 tsp sesame oil
5ml/1 tsp clear honey

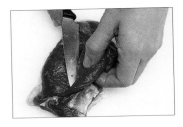

1 Place the duck breast fillets, skin side down, on a chopping board or clean work surface and cut a long slit down one side of each breast with a sharp kitchen knife, cutting not quite through the meat. This will form a large pocket.

2 Tuck the slices of onion and the apricots inside the pocket and press the breast firmly back into shape. Secure with metal skewers.

3 Prepare the barbecue. Position a lightly oiled grill rack over the hot coals. Mix together the clear honey and sesame oil, and brush the mixture generously over the duck, paying particular attention to the skin. Sprinkle over the star anise and season with plenty of salt and black pepper.

4 Cook the duck over medium-high heat for 12–15 minutes, turning once, until golden brown. The duck should be slightly pink in the centre.

5 Meanwhile, make the salad. Mix together the Chinese leaves, beansprouts and spring onions in a large bowl. Shake together the soy sauce, groundnut oil, sesame oil and honey in a screw-topped jar. Season to taste with salt and pepper.

6 Toss the salad with the dressing and serve with the duck.

Energy 338kcal/1420kJ; Protein 36.5g; Carbohydrate 19.7g, of which sugars 18.6g; Fat 16g, of which saturates 2.9g; Cholesterol 186mg; Calcium 79mg; Fibre 3.7g; Sodium 197mg.

GLAZED DUCK BREASTS

In this Cajun recipe, sliced and barbecued sweet potatoes go particularly well with duck breasts that have been brushed with a sweet glaze. The dish is quick to prepare and cook, making it ideal for a fuss-free barbecue.

SERVES TWO

INGREDIENTS
2 duck breast fillets
1 sweet potato, about 400g/14oz
30ml/2 tbsp red pepper jelly
15ml/1 tbsp sherry vinegar
50g/2oz/4 tbsp butter, melted
coarse sea salt and ground
   black pepper

COOK'S TIP
Choose cylindrical sweet potatoes for the neatest slices.

1 Prepare the barbecue. Position a lightly oiled grill rack over the hot coals. Slash the skin of the duck breast fillets diagonally at 2.5cm/1in intervals and rub plenty of salt and pepper over the skin and into the cuts.

2 Scrub the sweet potato and cut into 1cm/½in slices, discarding the ends.

3 Cook the duck breast fillets over medium heat, skin side down, for 5 minutes. Turn and cook for a further 8–10 minutes, according to preference.

4 Meanwhile, brush the sweet potato slices with melted butter and sprinkle with coarse sea salt. Cook on the hottest part of the barbecue for 8–10 minutes until soft, brushing regularly with more butter and sprinkling liberally with salt and pepper every time you turn them. Keep an eye on them so that they do not char.

5 Warm the red pepper jelly and sherry vinegar together in a bowl set over a pan of hot water, stirring to mix them as the jelly melts. Brush the skin of the duck with the jelly and return to the barbecue, skin side down, for 2–3 minutes to caramelize it. Slice and serve with the sweet potatoes.

Energy 643kcal/2702kJ; Protein 42.1g; Carbohydrate 53.1g, of which sugars 21.9g; Fat 34.2g, of which saturates 15.8g; Cholesterol 273mg; Calcium 79mg; Fibre 4.8g; Sodium 456mg.

SPICED DUCK WITH PEARS

THIS DELICIOUS CASSEROLE CAN BE COOKED ON THE BARBECUE OR STOVE. THE BROWNED PEARS ARE ADDED TOWARDS THE END OF COOKING, ALONG WITH A PINE NUT AND GARLIC PASTE, WHICH NOT ONLY ADDS FLAVOUR BUT ALSO HELPS TO THICKEN THE SAUCE.

SERVES SIX

INGREDIENTS
  6 duck portions, either breast or
    leg pieces
  15ml/1 tbsp olive oil
  1 large onion, thinly sliced
  1 cinnamon stick, halved
  2 thyme sprigs
  475ml/16fl oz/2 cups duck or
    chicken stock
To finish
  3 firm ripe pears, peeled and cored
  30ml/2 tbsp olive oil
  2 garlic cloves, sliced
  25g/1oz/⅓ cup pine nuts
  2.5ml/½ tsp saffron strands
  25g/1oz/2 tbsp raisins
  salt and ground black pepper
  thyme sprigs or parsley, to garnish

1 Prepare the barbecue and position a lightly oiled rack over the coals. Brush the duck portions with oil and cook them over hot coals for 8–10 minutes, until golden. Alternatively, fry the duck portions in olive oil for 5 minutes, until golden. Transfer the duck to a large flameproof dish. If frying, drain off all but 15ml/1 tbsp of fat left in the pan.

2 Fry the onion in the frying pan for 5 minutes until golden. Add the cinnamon stick, thyme and stock and bring to the boil. Pour over the duck in the dish and cook slowly on a low barbecue for about 1¼ hours.

3 Halve the pears, brush with oil and barbecue until brown, or fry the pears in the oil in the pan. Pound the garlic, pine nuts and saffron with a pestle and mortar, to make a thick, smooth paste.

4 Add the paste, raisins and pears to the dish. Continue to cook for 15 minutes until the pears are tender.

5 Season to taste and garnish with the fresh herbs. Serve with mashed potatoes and a green vegetable, if liked.

COOK'S TIP
A good stock is essential for this dish. Buy a large duck (plus two extra duck breasts if you want portions to be generous) and joint it yourself, using the giblets and carcass to make the stock. If you buy duck portions, use a well-flavoured chicken stock.

Energy 296kcal/1235kJ; Protein 21.5g; Carbohydrate 14.7g, of which sugars 11.3g; Fat 18.8g, of which saturates 2.8g; Cholesterol 110mg; Calcium 40mg; Fibre 2.3g; Sodium 147mg.

DUCK WITH PINEAPPLE AND CORIANDER

THIS RECIPE COMES FROM SOUTH-EAST ASIA AND REFLECTS THE ABUNDANCE OF PINEAPPLES GROWN IN THE REGION. SERVE IT WITH STEAMED RICE AND A CRUNCHY SALAD FOR A DELICIOUS MEAL. REMEMBER TO ALLOW PLENTY OF TIME FOR THE DUCK TO MARINATE.

SERVES FOUR TO SIX

INGREDIENTS

1 small duck, skinned, trimmed
  and jointed
1 pineapple, skinned, cored and
  cut in half crossways
45ml/3 tbsp sesame or vegetable oil
4cm/1½ in fresh root ginger, peeled
  and finely sliced
1 onion, sliced
salt and ground black pepper
1 bunch fresh coriander (cilantro),
  stalks removed, to garnish

For the marinade

3 shallots
45ml/3 tbsp soy sauce
30ml/2 tbsp Thai fish sauce
10ml/2 tsp five-spice powder
15ml/1 tbsp sugar
3 garlic cloves, crushed
1 bunch fresh basil, stalks removed,
  leaves finely chopped

1 To make the marinade, grate the shallots into a bowl, then add the remaining marinade ingredients and beat together until the sugar has dissolved. Place the duck in a wide dish and rub with the marinade. Cover and chill for 6 hours or overnight.

2 Take one of the pineapple halves and cut it into 4–6 slices, and then again into half-moons, and set aside. Take the other pineapple half and chop it to a pulp. Using your hands, squeeze all the juice from the pulp into a bowl. Discard the pulp and reserve the juice.

3 Heat 30ml/2 tbsp of the oil in a wide pan. Stir in the ginger and onion. When they begin to soften, add the duck to the pan and brown on both sides. Pour in the pineapple juice and any remaining marinade, then add water so that the duck is just covered. Bring to the boil, reduce the heat and simmer for about 25 minutes.

4 Meanwhile, heat the remaining oil in a heavy pan and sear the pineapple slices on both sides – you may have to do this in two batches. Add the seared pineapple to the duck, season to taste with salt and pepper and cook for a further 5 minutes, or until the duck is tender. Arrange on a warm dish, garnish with the coriander leaves and serve.

COOK'S TIP

This is quite a fancy dish and a little more time-consuming than some to prepare, so it might be one reserved for celebrations. You can find this dish in Vietnamese and Cambodian restaurants listed as *duck à l'ananas*, demonstrating the French influence on the cuisines of those countries.

Energy 356Kcal/1489kJ; Protein 28g; Carbohydrate 19g, of which sugars 13g; Fat 20g, of which saturates 4g; Cholesterol 131mg; Calcium 122mg; Fibre 2g; Sodium 150mg

DUCK BREASTS WITH RED PLUMS

THE RICH SAUCE FOR THIS DISH IS FRUITY AND INTENSELY FLAVOURED, COMBINING BRANDY AND RED PLUMS WITH DOUBLE CREAM AND CORIANDER. THE SAUCE CAN BE MADE IN A PAN ON THE BARBECUE WHILE THE DUCK IS COOKING. SERVE WITH CRUSTY BREAD AND A SALAD.

SERVES FOUR

INGREDIENTS

4 duck breast fillets, about 175g/6oz
  each, skinned
10ml/2 tsp crushed cinnamon stick
50g/2oz/¼ cup butter
15ml/1 tbsp plum brandy or
  Cognac
250ml/8fl oz/1 cup chicken stock
250ml/8fl oz/1 cup double
  (heavy) cream
6 fresh red plums, stoned (pitted)
  and sliced
6 sprigs fresh coriander (cilantro)
  leaves, plus extra to garnish
salt and ground black pepper

1 Score the duck fillets and sprinkle with salt. Press the crushed cinnamon on to both sides of the duck fillets. Brush with butter and cook on a medium barbecue for 15–20 minutes, turning once, until the duck is tender.

2 To make the sauce, melt half the remaining butter in a saucepan. Add the plum brandy or Cognac and set it alight. When the flames have died down, add the stock and cream and allow to simmer gently until the sauce is reduced and thick. Add salt and ground black pepper to taste.

3 In a pan, melt the other half of the butter and fry the plums and coriander just enough to soften the fruit.

4 Place the duck fillets on warm serving plates and pour some sauce around each one, then garnish with the plum slices and the chopped fresh coriander.

Energy 608kcal/2515kJ; Protein 15.1g; Carbohydrate 17.4g, of which sugars 17g; Fat 53.5g, of which saturates 14.5g; Cholesterol 0mg; Calcium 35mg; Fibre 2.2g; Sodium 102mg.

BAKED POUSSINS WITH YOGURT AND SAFFRON

IN MIDDLE EASTERN MARKETS, CHICKENS ARE OFTEN ON THE SMALL SIDE, AND ARE OFTEN SPLIT OR SPATCHCOCKED BEFORE BEING COOKED OVER HOT COALS. POUSSINS CAN BE TREATED IN THE SAME WAY, AND TASTE PARTICULARLY GOOD WHEN MARINATED IN YOGURT, SAFFRON AND OTHER SPICES.

SERVES FOUR

INGREDIENTS
    475ml/16fl oz/2 cups natural
      (plain) yogurt
    60ml/4 tbsp olive oil
    1 large onion, grated
    2 garlic cloves, crushed
    2.5ml/½ tsp paprika
    2–3 saffron threads, dissolved in
      15ml/1 tbsp boiling water
    juice of 1 lemon
    4 poussins, halved
    salt and ground black pepper
    cos or romaine lettuce salad, to serve

COOK'S TIP
The oil in the marinade will help to stop the poussins drying out.

1 Blend together the yogurt, oil, onion, garlic, paprika, saffron liquid and lemon juice, and season with salt and pepper.

2 Place the poussin halves in a shallow, non-metallic dish, pour over the marinade and then cover and allow to marinate for at least 4 hours in a cool place or overnight in the refrigerator.

3 Prepare the barbecue and position a lightly oiled grill rack over the coals. Arrange the poussin halves on the rack and cook over medium heat for about 30 minutes, turning occasionally and basting frequently with the marinade. Alternatively, bake them in a preheated oven at 180°C/350°F/Gas 4 for 30–45 minutes. Serve with a lettuce salad.

Energy 326Kcal/1358kJ; Protein 24.8g; Carbohydrate 7.6g, of which sugars 6.2g; Fat 22.2g, of which saturates 5.4g; Cholesterol 116mg; Calcium 94mg; Fibre 0.9g; Sodium 113mg.

SKEWERED POUSSINS <u>WITH</u> LIME <u>AND</u> CHILLI

*THE POUSSINS IN THIS RECIPE ARE FLATTENED OUT — SPATCHCOCKED — SO THAT THEY WILL COOK
EVENLY AND QUICKLY. THE BREAST IS STUFFED WITH CHILLI AND SUN-DRIED TOMATO BUTTER, WHICH
KEEPS THE MEAT MOIST AND MAKES IT TASTE WONDERFUL.*

SERVES FOUR

INGREDIENTS

    4 poussins, about 450g/1lb each
    40g/1½oz/3 tbsp butter
    30ml/2 tbsp sun-dried tomato paste
    finely grated rind of 1 lime
    10ml/2 tsp chilli sauce
    juice of ½ lime
    flat leaf parsley sprigs, to garnish
    lime wedges, to serve

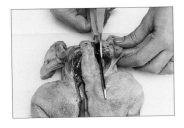

1 Place each poussin on a board,
breast side up, and press down firmly
with the palm of your hand, to break
the breastbone.

2 Turn the poussin over and, with
poultry shears or strong kitchen
scissors, cut down either side of the
backbone and remove it.

COOK'S TIP
If you wish to serve half a poussin per
portion, use poultry shears or a large
sharp knife to cut through the
breastbone and then the backbone.

3 Turn the poussin over again, so that it
is breast side up, and flatten it neatly.
Lift the breast skin carefully and gently
ease your fingertips underneath, to
loosen it from the flesh.

4 Mix together the butter, sun-dried
tomato paste, lime rind and chilli sauce.
Spread about three-quarters of the
mixture under the skin of the poussins,
smoothing it evenly.

VARIATION
If you don't particularly like hot, spicy
flavours then omit the chili sauce from
the paste. You could add 2 teaspoons of
mild barbecue spices and a teaspoon of
olive oil instead.

5 To hold the poussins flat during
cooking, thread two skewers through
each bird, crossing at the centre. Each
skewer should pass through a wing and
then out through a drumstick on the
other side.

6 Prepare the barbecue. Position a
lightly oiled grill rack over the hot coals.
Mix the remaining tomato and butter
mixture with the lime juice and brush it
over the skin of the skewered poussins.
Cook them over a medium-high heat,
turning occasionally, for 25–30 minutes,
or until the juices run clear when the
thickest part of the leg is pierced.
Garnish with flat leaf parsley and serve
with lime wedges.

COOK'S TIP
Poussins are available ready
spatchcocked and skewered from some
supermarkets, or you can ask your
butcher to prepare the birds for you in
this way.

Energy 607kcal/2526kJ; Protein 50.4g; Carbohydrate 1.1g, of which sugars 1.1g; Fat 44.7g, of which saturates 15.1g; Cholesterol 282mg; Calcium 23mg; Fibre 0.2g; Sodium 259mg.

QUAIL WITH A FIVE-SPICE MARINADE

BLENDING AND GRINDING YOUR OWN FIVE-SPICE POWDER WILL GIVE THE FRESHEST-TASTING RESULTS FOR THIS VIETNAMESE-STYLE DISH OF SPATCHCOCKED QUAIL. IF YOU ARE SHORT OF TIME, BUY A GOOD-QUALITY READY-MIXED FIVE-SPICE BLEND FROM THE SUPERMARKET.

SERVES FOUR TO SIX

INGREDIENTS
6 quails, cleaned
To garnish
    1 mandarin orange or satsuma
    2 spring onions (scallions),
        roughly chopped
    banana leaves, to serve
For the marinade
    2 pieces star anise
    10ml/2 tsp ground cinnamon
    10ml/2 tsp fennel seeds
    10ml/2 tsp Sichuan pepper
    a pinch ground cloves
    1 small onion, finely chopped
    1 garlic clove, crushed
    60ml/4 tbsp clear honey
    30ml/2 tbsp dark soy sauce

COOK'S TIP
If you prefer, or if quails are not available, you could use other small poultry such as poussins. Poussins will take around 25–30 minutes to cook using the method given in this recipe.

1 Soak 12 wooden skewers in water for 30 minutes. Remove the backbones from the quails by cutting down either side with a pair of strong kitchen scissors.

2 Flatten the birds with the palm of your hand and secure each bird using two bamboo skewers. Each skewer should pass through a wing and then out through a drumstick on the other side.

3 To make the marinade, place the whole spices in a mortar or spice mill and grind into a fine powder. Add the onion, garlic, clear honey and soy sauce, and combine until the ingredients are thoroughly mixed.

4 Arrange the quails on a flat dish and pour over the marinade. Cover with clear film (plastic wrap) and leave in the refrigerator for 8 hours or overnight for the flavours to mingle.

5 Preheat the barbecue. Position a lightly oiled grill rack over the hot coals. Cook the quails over medium-high heat for 5 minutes then cover with a lid or tented heavy-duty foil and cook for 10 minutes more until golden brown. Baste occasionally with the marinade during cooking.

6 To make the garnish, remove the outer zest from the mandarin orange or satsuma, using a vegetable peeler. Shred the zest finely and combine with the chopped spring onions. Arrange the quails on a bed of banana leaves and garnish with the orange zest and spring onions.

COOK'S TIP
Banana leaves are available from Asian markets, and add an exotic appearance and a subtle aroma to the dish.

Energy 159kcal/664kJ; Protein 13.2g; Carbohydrate 5.6g, of which sugars 5.6g; Fat 9.5g, of which saturates 2.6g; Cholesterol 68mg; Calcium 7mg; Fibre 0.1g; Sodium 404mg.

SPATCHCOCKED QUAIL <u>WITH</u> COUSCOUS

These delicate baby birds can be cooked very efficiently on a kettle barbecue with a lid. If your barbecue doesn't have its own lid, improvise with a large upturned wok with a wooden handle or use tented foil. Serve with a herby cherry tomato salad.

SERVES EIGHT

INGREDIENTS
8 quail
400ml/14fl oz/1²⁄₃ cups water
2 lemons
60ml/4 tbsp extra virgin olive oil
45ml/3 tbsp chopped fresh
  tarragon leaves
125g/4¼oz/¾ cup couscous
15g/½oz dried (bell) peppers,
  finely chopped
8 black olives, stoned (pitted)
  and chopped
salt and ground black pepper
16 wooden or metal skewers

1 Cut the backbones away from each quail and place the bones in a pan. Add the measured water and bring to the boil, then simmer gently to reduce by half. While the stock is cooking, wipe the insides of each bird with kitchen paper. If you find a heart inside, add it to the stock pot. Place each quail in turn, breast uppermost, on a board, and flatten it by pressing firmly on the breastbone. Carefully loosen the quail skin over the breasts with your fingers, creating a pocket for stuffing later.

COOK'S TIP
A lid is important for these fragile quail as it is best not to turn them. When enclosed, the heat circulates around the food, cooking it on all sides.

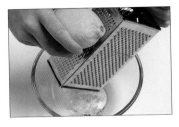

2 Grate the rind from the lemons. Set half the rind aside and put the rest in a flat dish. Squeeze both lemons and add the juice to the dish with 30ml/2 tbsp of the oil and 15ml/1 tbsp of the tarragon. Add the quail, turn to coat them well, cover and leave to marinate while you prepare the couscous stuffing for the birds.

3 Place the couscous in a medium bowl and add the dried peppers and salt and pepper. The stock should have reduced considerably by now. Strain 200ml/7fl oz/scant 1 cup over the couscous, cover with a dry cloth and leave to stand for 10 minutes.

4 Mix the reserved lemon rind into the couscous with the olives and the remaining tarragon and oil. Spread the mixture on a plate to cool, then cover and chill. When cold, ease a little stuffing into the breast pocket of each quail. If using wooden skewers, soak them in cold water for 30 minutes.

5 Prepare the barbecue. Pin the legs and wings of each quail to the body by driving a long skewer right through from either side to form a cross. If you want, wrap the leg tips with foil to prevent them from getting too charred.

6 Once the flames have died down, position a lightly oiled grill rack over the hot coals. Place the spatchcocked quail on the grill rack and cook over medium-high heat for about 5 minutes, moving the birds around occasionally. Cover with a lid or tented heavy-duty foil and cook for 10 minutes. Check if they are cooked; if they are plump and nicely browned they will almost certainly be done. If not, allow them to cook for a further 5 minutes. Let them stand for a few minutes to cool a little before serving, as they are best eaten with the fingers.

Energy 314kcal/1308kJ; Protein 23.2g; Carbohydrate 8.3g, of which sugars 0.2g; Fat 21.2g, of which saturates 5.1g; Cholesterol 116mg; Calcium 15mg; Fibre 0.2g; Sodium 221mg.

MEAT

It is surprising how many types and cuts of meat are appropriate for successful barbecuing. Meat can be minced and formed into koftas or burgers, or cut into chunks for kebabs. Finely ground meat can be made into wonderfully spiced home-made sausages, while whole joints of meat can be cooked on the barbecue - try the Barbecue Roast Beef, which is "mopped" with a horseradish and beer sauce during cooking to keep it beautifully succulent and moist. As well as steaks, chops of all kinds are great favourites for barbecuing, and are made even more mouthwatering by the addition of fragrant marinades or a herb butter. This chapter includes recipes for lamb, bacon, pork, beef and venison that are a step away from the ordinary. Even old faithfuls have a new slant, such as beef burgers with a melted Stilton centre or the richly flavoured Indonesian Beef Burgers, which contain coconut. These classic meaty barbecue recipes have never tasted so good.

LAMB KEBABS <u>WITH</u> MINT CHUTNEY

THESE LITTLE ROUND LAMB KEBABS OWE THEIR EXOTIC FLAVOUR TO RAS EL HANOUT, A NORTH AFRICAN SPICE WHOSE HEDONISTIC QUALITIES ARE ACHIEVED BY ADDING HIGHLY PERFUMED DRIED DAMASK ROSE PETALS TO OVER TEN DIFFERENT SPICES. THE RESULT IS SUBLIME.

SERVES FOUR TO SIX

INGREDIENTS
  30ml/2 tbsp extra virgin
    olive oil
  1 onion, finely chopped
  2 garlic cloves, crushed
  35g/1¼oz/5 tbsp pine nuts
  500g/1¼lb/2½ cups minced
    (ground) lamb
  10ml/2 tsp ras el hanout spice mix
  10ml/2 tsp dried pink rose petals
    (optional)
  salt and ground black pepper
For the fresh mint chutney
  40g/1½oz/1½ cups fresh
    mint leaves
  10ml/2 tsp sugar
  juice of 2 lemons
  2 eating apples, peeled and
    finely grated
To serve (optional)
  150ml/¼ pint/⅔ cup Greek
    (US strained plain) yogurt
  7.5ml/1½ tsp rose harissa

1 If using wooden skewers, soak 18 in cold water for 30 minutes. Heat the oil in a frying pan on the stove. Add the onion and garlic, and fry gently for 7 minutes. Stir in the pine nuts. Fry for about 5 minutes more, or until the mixture is slightly golden, then set aside to cool.

2 Make the fresh mint chutney. Chop the mint finely by hand or in a food processor, then add the sugar, lemon juice and grated apple. Stir or pulse to mix.

3 Prepare the barbecue. Place the minced lamb in a large bowl and add the ras el hanout and rose petals, if using. Tip in the cooled onion mixture and add salt and pepper. Using your hands, mix well, then form into 18 balls. Drain the skewers and mould a ball on to each one. Once the flames have died down, rake a few hot coals to one side. Position a lightly oiled grill rack over the hot coals.

4 Place the kebabs on the grill over the part with the most coals to cook over medium heat. If it is easier, cover the barbecue with a lid or tented heavy-duty foil so that the heat will circulate and they will cook evenly all over. Otherwise, you will need to stay with them, turning them frequently for about 10 minutes. This prevents the kebabs from forming a hard crust before the meat is cooked right through to the centre.

5 Serve with yogurt mixed with rose harissa, if you like. The kebabs can also be wrapped in Middle Eastern flat bread such as lavash with a green salad and cucumber slices piled in with them.

COOK'S TIPS
• You can also cook these kebabs on a hot griddle. They will take about 10 minutes. Sear on a high heat then lower the heat and turn frequently.
• The dried pink rose petals can be bought at Middle Eastern food stores.

Energy 257kcal/1070kJ; Protein 17.2g; Carbohydrate 5.1g, of which sugars 4.5g; Fat 18.8g, of which saturates 6g; Cholesterol 64mg; Calcium 33mg; Fibre 0.6g; Sodium 59mg.

SHISH KEBABS

SUMAC IS A SPICE, GROUND FROM A DRIED PURPLE BERRY WITH A SOUR, FRUITY FLAVOUR. IN THIS RECIPE IT BLISSFULLY COMPLEMENTS THE RICHNESS OF THE LAMB AND YOGURT. THESE KEBABS ARE EXCELLENT SERVED WITH LITTLE BOWLS OF INDIVIDUAL HERBS DRESSED AT THE LAST MINUTE.

MAKES EIGHT

INGREDIENTS

675g/1½lb lamb neck (US shoulder or breast) fillet, trimmed and cut into 2.5cm/1in pieces
5ml/1 tsp each fennel, cumin and coriander seeds, roasted and crushed
1.5ml/¼ tsp cayenne pepper
5cm/2in piece of fresh root ginger
150ml/¼ pint/⅔ cup Greek (US strained plain) yogurt
2 small red (bell) peppers
2 small yellow (bell) peppers
300g/11oz small or baby (pearl) onions
30ml/2 tbsp olive oil
15ml/1 tbsp ground sumac
salt and ground black pepper

To serve
8 Lebanese flat breads
150ml/¼ pint/⅔ cup Greek (US strained plain) yogurt
5ml/1 tsp ground sumac
1 bunch rocket (arugula), about 50g/2oz
50g/2oz/2 cups fresh flat leaf parsley
10ml/2 tsp olive oil
juice of ½ lemon

COOK'S TIP
If you want to use a griddle on the barbecue, cook the kebabs over a high heat to begin with, then lower the heat, and turn them frequently.

1 Place the lamb pieces in a bowl and sprinkle over the crushed seeds and the cayenne pepper. Grate the ginger and squeeze it over the lamb. When all the juices have been extracted, discard the pulp. Pour over the yogurt. Mix well, then cover and marinate overnight in the refrigerator.

2 Prepare the barbecue. Stand a large sieve (strainer) over a bowl and pour in the lamb mixture. Leave to drain well. Cut the peppers in half, remove the cores and seeds, then cut the flesh into rough chunks. Place in a bowl. Add the onions and the olive oil.

3 Pat the drained lamb with kitchen paper to remove excess marinade. Add the lamb to the bowl, season and toss well. Divide the lamb, peppers and onions into eight equal portions and thread on to eight long metal skewers.

4 Position a lightly oiled grill rack over the coals to heat. Grill the kebabs for about 10 minutes over medium-high heat, turning every 2 minutes to prevent the meat and vegetables from getting too charred. When cooked, transfer the kebabs to a platter, lightly sprinkle with the sumac, cover loosely with foil, and leave to rest for a few minutes.

5 Wrap the breads in foil and put them on the barbecue to warm. Place the yogurt in a small serving bowl and sprinkle the surface with sumac. Arrange the rocket and parsley in separate bowls and pour over the oil and lemon juice. Serve with the kebabs and the warmed flat bread.

COOK'S TIP
Take care not to pack the lamb pieces too tightly on the skewers because they will not brown properly.

Energy 361kcal/1515kJ; Protein 22.5g; Carbohydrate 38.4g, of which sugars 8.1g; Fat 14.1g, of which saturates 5.1g; Cholesterol 64mg; Calcium 133mg; Fibre 3g; Sodium 249mg.

IRANIAN KEBABS

THESE KEBABS ARE SO POPULAR IN THEIR NATIVE IRAN THAT MANY RESTAURANTS SERVE NOTHING ELSE. THE MEAT IS NOT CUBED, AS ELSEWHERE, BUT CUT INTO STRIPS BEFORE BEING MARINATED AND THREADED ON TO SKEWERS. TOMATOES ARE GRILLED ON SEPARATE SKEWERS.

SERVES FOUR

INGREDIENTS
    450g/1lb lean lamb or beef fillet
    2–3 saffron threads
    1 large onion, grated
    4–6 tomatoes, halved
    15ml/1 tbsp butter, melted
    salt and ground black pepper
    45ml/3 tbsp sumac, to garnish
        (optional)
    cooked rice, to serve

1 Using a sharp knife remove and discard any excess fat from the meat and cut the meat into strips, 1cm/½in thick and 4cm/1½in long.

COOK'S TIP
The kebabs can also be cooked under a very hot grill (broiler).

2 Soak the saffron in 15ml/1 tbsp boiling water, pour into a small bowl and mix with the grated onion. Add to the meat and stir a few times so that the meat is thoroughly coated.

3 Cover the bowl loosely with clear film (plastic wrap) and leave to marinate for at least 3–4 hours or preferably overnight, in the refrigerator.

4 Season the meat with salt and pepper and then thread it on to flat skewers, aligning the strips in neat rows. Thread the tomatoes on to two separate skewers.

5 Grill the kebabs and tomatoes over hot charcoal for 10–12 minutes, basting with butter and turning occasionally. Serve with cooked rice, sprinkled with sumac, if you like.

Energy 268Kcal/1119kJ; Protein 23.5g; Carbohydrate 7.9g, of which sugars 6.5g; Fat 16.1g, of which saturates 7.9g; Cholesterol 94mg; Calcium 32mg; Fibre 1.9g; Sodium 130mg.

SKEWERED LAMB WITH CORIANDER YOGURT

THESE TURKISH KEBABS ARE TRADITIONALLY MADE WITH LAMB, BUT LEAN BEEF OR PORK WORK EQUALLY WELL. YOU CAN ALTERNATE PIECES OF PEPPER, LEMON OR ONIONS WITH THE MEAT FOR EXTRA FLAVOUR AND COLOUR. THE CORIANDER YOGURT IS A DELICIOUS, CREAMY ACCOMPANIMENT.

SERVES FOUR

INGREDIENTS
- 900g/2lb lean boneless lamb
- 1 large onion, grated
- 3 bay leaves
- 5 thyme or rosemary sprigs
- grated rind and juice of 1 lemon
- 2.5ml/½ tsp caster (superfine) sugar
- 75ml/3fl oz/⅓ cup olive oil
- salt and ground black pepper
- sprigs of fresh rosemary, to garnish
- barbecued lemon wedges, to serve
For the coriander yogurt
- 150ml/¼ pint/⅔ cup thick natural (plain) yogurt
- 15ml/1 tbsp chopped fresh mint
- 15ml/1 tbsp chopped fresh coriander (cilantro)
- 10ml/2 tsp grated onion

1 To make the coriander yogurt, mix together the natural yogurt, chopped fresh mint, chopped fresh coriander and grated onion. Transfer the yogurt to a serving bowl.

2 To make the kebabs, cut the lamb into 2.5cm/1in cubes and put in a bowl. Mix together the onion, herbs, lemon rind and juice, sugar and oil, then season to taste.

COOK'S TIP
Choose lean lamb such as leg or neck (US shoulder) fillet, but there should be a small amount of fat on the meat. This will melt during cooking, keeping the meat moist and adding flavour.

3 Pour the marinade over the meat in the bowl and stir to ensure the meat is thoroughly coated. Cover with clear film (plastic wrap) and leave to marinate in the fridge for several hours or overnight.

4 Drain the meat and thread on to metal skewers. Cook on a hot barbecue for about 10 minutes. Garnish with rosemary and barbecued lemon wedges and serve with the coriander yogurt.

Energy 548kcal/2282kJ; Protein 46.6g; Carbohydrate 4.9g, of which sugars 4.5g; Fat 38.3g, of which saturates 13.7g; Cholesterol 172mg; Calcium 118mg; Fibre 0.8g; Sodium 229mg.

GRILLED SKEWERED LAMB

IN GREECE, THIS SKEWERED LAMB DISH IS KNOWN AS SOUVLAKIA. TENDER LAMB IS MARINATED IN HERBS, OLIVE OIL AND LEMON JUICE AND THEN BARBECUED WITH SWEET PEPPERS AND RED ONIONS. THE SOUVLAKIA ARE AT THEIR BEST SERVED WITH TZATZIKI, A LARGE TOMATO SALAD AND BARBECUED BREAD.

SERVES FOUR

INGREDIENTS
1 small shoulder of lamb, boned and
  with most of the fat removed
2–3 onions, preferably red onions,
  quartered
2 red or green (bell) peppers,
  quartered and seeded
75ml/5 tbsp extra virgin olive oil
juice of 1 lemon
2 garlic cloves, crushed
5ml/1 tsp dried oregano
2.5ml/½ tsp dried thyme or some
  sprigs of fresh thyme, chopped
salt and ground black pepper

1 Ask your butcher to trim the meat and cut it into 4cm/1½in cubes. (A little fat is desirable with souvlakia, because it keeps them moist and succulent during cooking.) Separate the onion quarters into pieces, each composed of two or three layers, and slice each pepper quarter in half widthways.

2 Put the oil, lemon juice, garlic and herbs in a large bowl. Season with salt and pepper, and whisk well to combine. Add the meat cubes, stirring to coat them in the mixture.

3 Cover the bowl tightly and leave to marinate for 4–8 hours in the refrigerator, stirring several times.

VARIATION
If you prefer, you can use 4–5 lamb neck fillets instead of shoulder.

4 Lift out the meat cubes, reserving the marinade, and thread them on to long metal skewers, alternating each piece of meat with a piece of pepper and a piece of onion. Lay them across a grill pan or baking tray and brush them with the reserved marinade.

5 Prepare the barbecue. Position a lightly oiled grill rack over the hot coals. Cook the souvlakia over medium-high heat for 10 minutes, or until they start to get scorched. Turn the skewers over, brush them again with the marinade (or a little olive oil) and cook them for 10–15 minutes more. Serve the souvlakia immediately.

COOK'S TIP
Although these souvlakia cook best with a little fat left on the meat, always be sure to trim excess fat from meats that are to be barbecued, as the fat will drip on to the coals and can cause flare-ups.

Energy 419kcal/1743kJ; Protein 32.3g; Carbohydrate 16.3g, of which sugars 13.1g; Fat 25.4g, of which saturates 8.4g; Cholesterol 138mg; Calcium 51mg; Fibre 3.4g; Sodium 89mg.

MOROCCAN SPICED LAMB

THIS MOROCCAN SPECIALITY OFTEN CONSISTS OF A WHOLE LAMB GRILLED SLOWLY OVER A CHARCOAL FIRE FOR MANY HOURS. THIS VERSION IS FOR A LARGE SHOULDER, RUBBED WITH SPICES AND CHARGRILLED. WHEN COOKED, THE MEAT IS HACKED OFF AND DIPPED IN ROASTED SALT AND CUMIN.

SERVES FOUR TO SIX

INGREDIENTS
1 whole shoulder of lamb, about
    1.8kg/4lb
4 garlic cloves, crushed
15ml/1 tbsp paprika
15ml/1 tbsp freshly ground
    cumin seeds
105ml/7 tbsp extra virgin olive oil
45–60ml/3–4 tbsp finely chopped
    mint leaves
a few sturdy thyme sprigs,
    for basting
salt and ground black pepper
To serve
45ml/3 tbsp cumin seeds
25ml/1½ tbsp coarse sea salt

1 Open up the natural pockets in the flesh at each end of the shoulder, and stuff with the garlic. Mix the paprika, ground cumin and seasoning, and rub all over the shoulder. Cover and leave the lamb for about 1 hour. Mix the oil and mint in a bowl for basting the meat during roasting.

2 Prepare a barbecue. Once the flames have died down, rake the hot coals to one side and insert a drip tray flat beside them. Position a lightly oiled grill rack over the hot coals.

3 Place the lamb shoulder on the grill rack over medium-high heat and directly over the drip tray. Cover with a lid or tented heavy-duty foil. For the initial 30 minutes turn the meat frequently, basting using the thyme branches and mint oil. Then roast the joint for a further 2 hours, turning and basting every 15 minutes so that it remains moist.

4 If you need to replenish the coals, do so before the heat is too low. It will take about 10 minutes to heat sufficiently to continue the cooking.

5 Dry-roast the cumin seeds and coarse salt for 2 minutes in a heavy frying pan. Do not let them burn. Tip them into a mortar and pound with the pestle until roughly ground.

6 When the meat is cooked, remove it from the barbecue, wrap in double foil and leave to rest for 15 minutes. Serve sliced with the roasted cumin seeds and salt for dipping.

Energy 618kcal/2564kJ; Protein 42.7g; Carbohydrate 0.8g, of which sugars 0.1g; Fat 49.3g, of which saturates 21.2g; Cholesterol 183mg; Calcium 16mg; Fibre 0.2g; Sodium 150mg.

LAMB STEAKS WITH MINT AND SHERRY

THE UNUSUAL MARINADE IN THIS RECIPE IS EXTREMELY QUICK TO PREPARE, AND IS THE KEY TO ITS SUCCESS: THE SHERRY IMPARTS A WONDERFUL TANG TO THE STEAKS. THEY ARE BEST SERVED WITH A FRESH RATATOUILLE OR CHERRY TOMATO, ONION AND PEPPER KEBABS, WITH BUTTERED NEW POTATOES.

SERVES SIX

INGREDIENTS
  6 large lamb steaks or
    12 smaller chops
For the marinade
  30ml/2 tbsp chopped fresh
    mint leaves
  15ml/1 tbsp black peppercorns
  1 medium onion, chopped
  120ml/4fl oz/½ cup sherry
  60ml/4 tbsp extra virgin olive oil
  2 garlic cloves

COOK'S TIP
Use a medium-dry Amontillado sherry for the marinade if available.

1 Blend the mint leaves and peppercorns in a food processor until finely chopped. Add the onion and process until smooth. Add the rest of the marinade ingredients and process until completely mixed. The marinade should have a thick consistency.

2 Add the marinade to the steaks or chops. Cover and leave in the refrigerator to marinate overnight.

3 Cook the steaks on a medium barbecue for 10–15 minutes, basting occasionally with the marinade.

Energy 314kcal/1311kJ; Protein 29.7g; Carbohydrate 0.7g, of which sugars 0.2g; Fat 20.5g, of which saturates 8.3g; Cholesterol 114mg; Calcium 13mg; Fibre 0.1g; Sodium 130mg.

ROSEMARY-SCENTED LAMB

THE BEST THING ABOUT THIS RECIPE IS THAT ALL THE WORK IS DONE THE NIGHT BEFORE. YOU CAN ASK YOUR BUTCHER TO FRENCH TRIM THE LAMB RACKS IF YOU WANT TO MAKE YOUR PREPARATION TIME QUICKER. ALLOW PLENTY OF TIME FOR MARINATING, ALTHOUGH THE COOKING TIME IS QUICK.

SERVES FOUR TO EIGHT

INGREDIENTS

2 x 8-chop racks of lamb, chined
8 large fresh rosemary sprigs
2 garlic cloves, thinly sliced
90ml/6 tbsp extra virgin olive oil
30ml/2 tbsp verjuice or red wine
salt and ground black pepper

1 Cut the fat off the ribs down the top 5cm/2in from the bone ends. Turn the joint over and score between the bones. Cut and scrape away the meat between the bones. Cut the racks into eight portions, each of two linked chops, and tie a rosemary sprig to each one.

2 Lay the lamb in a single layer in a wide dish. Mix the garlic, oil and verjuice or wine, and pour over the lamb. Cover and chill overnight, turning them as often as possible.

COOK'S TIP
Verjuice, the sour juice of unripe grapes, is ideal for adding sharpness to dishes that will be eaten with wine.

3 Bring the marinating chops to room temperature 1 hour before cooking. Prepare the barbecue. Remove the lamb from the marinade, and discard the marinade. Season the meat 15 minutes before cooking.

4 Position a lightly oiled grill rack over the hot coals. Stand the lamb chops upright on the rack over medium-high heat, propping them against each other. Cover with a lid or tented heavy-duty foil and grill for 2 minutes.

5 Carefully turn the chops on to one side, and grill for a further 4 minutes each side for rare meat or 5 minutes if you prefer lamb medium cooked. Remove the chops from the grill, transfer to serving plates, cover and rest for 5–10 minutes before serving.

COOK'S TIP
Allowing the hot chops to stand before serving will give the juices time to gather on the plate and create a light sauce.

Energy 433kcal/1788kJ; Protein 23.4g; Carbohydrate 0g, of which sugars 0g; Fat 37.6g, of which saturates 16.4g; Cholesterol 101mg; Calcium 17mg; Fibre 0g; Sodium 83mg.

LAMB CUTLETS <u>WITH</u> LAVENDER

LAVENDER IS AN UNUSUAL FLAVOUR TO USE WITH MEAT, BUT ITS HEADY, SUMMERY SCENT WORKS WELL WITH BARBECUED LAMB. AS WELL AS ADDING LAVENDER TO THE MARINADE, YOU CAN SCATTER SPRIGS ON THE COALS OR GRILL RACK TO SMOKE. IF YOU PREFER, ROSEMARY CAN TAKE ITS PLACE.

SERVES FOUR

INGREDIENTS
    4 racks of lamb, with 3–4 cutlets each
    1 shallot, finely chopped
    45ml/3 tbsp chopped fresh lavender
    15ml/1 tbsp balsamic vinegar
    30ml/2 tbsp olive oil
    15ml/1 tbsp lemon juice
    salt and ground black pepper
    handful of lavender sprigs

COOK'S TIP
Ask your butcher to prepare the cutlets or see the instructions in Rosemary Scented Lamb on page 217.

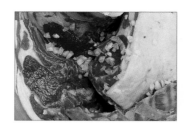

1 Prepare the barbecue. Position a lightly oiled grill rack over the hot coals. Place the trimmed racks of lamb in a wide dish and sprinkle the chopped shallot over them ensuring that each one is covered.

2 Sprinkle the chopped fresh lavender over the lamb racks.

3 Beat together the vinegar, olive oil and lemon juice, and pour them over the lamb. Season well with salt and pepper and then turn to coat evenly.

4 When you are ready to cook the lamb, scatter lavender sprigs over the grill rack or on the hot coals. Cook the lamb over medium-high heat for 15–20 minutes, turning once and basting with the marinade, until the meat is golden brown on the outside and slightly pink in the centre. Remove the meat from the barbecue and leave it to rest for 5–10 minutes before serving.

Energy 565kcal/2333kJ; Protein 31.4g; Carbohydrate 1.2g, of which sugars 0.9g; Fat 48.3g, of which saturates 21.5g; Cholesterol 135mg; Calcium 26mg; Fibre 0.2g; Sodium 111mg.

LAMB BURGERS <u>WITH</u> REDCURRANT SAUCE

THESE RATHER SPECIAL BURGERS TAKE A LITTLE EXTRA TIME TO PREPARE BUT ARE WELL WORTH IT,
BECAUSE EACH CONTAINS SOME MELTINGLY SOFT MOZZARELLA CHEESE. THE REDCURRANT CHUTNEY IS
THE PERFECT COMPLEMENT TO THE MINTY LAMB TASTE OF THE BURGERS.

<u>SERVES FOUR</u>

INGREDIENTS
   500g/1¼lb/2½ cups minced
     (ground) lean lamb
   1 small onion, finely chopped
   30ml/2 tbsp finely chopped fresh mint
   30ml/2 tbsp finely chopped
     fresh parsley
   115g/4oz mozzarella cheese
   30ml/2 tbsp oil, for basting
   salt and ground black pepper
For the redcurrant chutney
   115g/4oz/1½ cups fresh or
     frozen redcurrants
   10ml/2 tsp clear honey
   5ml/1 tsp balsamic vinegar
   30ml/2 tbsp finely chopped mint

1 In a large bowl, mix together the
lamb, onion, mint and parsley until
evenly combined. Season well with
plenty of salt and pepper.

2 Roughly divide the minced meat
mixture into eight equal pieces and use
your hands to press each of the pieces
into flat rounds.

3 Cut the mozzarella cheese into four
chunks. Place one chunk of cheese on
half the lamb rounds. Top each with
another round of meat mixture.

4 Press the two rounds of meat together
firmly around the cheese, making a
flattish burger shape. Use your fingers
to blend the edges and seal in the
cheese completely. Repeat with the
remaining three burgers.

5 Prepare the barbecue. Position a
lightly oiled grill rack over the hot coals.
Place all the ingredients for the chutney
in a bowl and mash them together with
a fork. Season well with salt and ground
black pepper.

6 Brush the lamb burgers with olive oil
and cook them over a medium-high
heat for about 15 minutes, turning
once, until they are golden brown and
cooked through. Serve with the
redcurrant chutney.

Energy 344kcal/1432kJ; Protein 30.1g; Carbohydrate 5g, of which sugars 4.6g; Fat 22.8g, of which saturates 11.7g; Cholesterol 113mg; Calcium 171mg; Fibre 1.9g; Sodium 206mg.

HERB-FLAVOURED LAMB

This boned leg of lamb is butterflied so that it cooks quickly on the barbecue, remaining tender and rare inside. The native Australian herb, aniseed myrtle, adds a subtle flavour to the meat. You can bone and butterfly the lamb yourself or ask the butcher to do it for you.

2 Cover and marinate in the refrigerator overnight. Remove it from the refrigerator 1½ hours before you start cooking. After 30 minutes, rub some salt all over the lamb.

3 Prepare the barbecue. Lift the lamb out of the marinade, and reserve the marinade. Pat the lamb dry with kitchen paper to remove all the excess marinade, then skewer the lamb in three places using long metal skewers to keep it flat.

4 Once the flames have died down, rake the hot coals to one side and insert a drip tray beside them. Position a lightly oiled grill rack over the hot coals. Lay the lamb on the grill rack over high heat directly above the coals for 3–5 minutes to lightly char one side.

5 Turn the lamb over and put it back on the grill rack, this time over the drip tray. Cover with a lid or tented heavy-duty foil. Grill the lamb for 20 minutes, basting the charred side occasionally with the marinade to keep it moist.

6 Move the lamb so that it is over the coals, replace the lid and grill it for 5–8 minutes more so that it chars slightly. Lift it on to a tray and let it rest under tented foil for 10–15 minutes. Cut into thick slices and serve with the juices from the drip tray.

SERVES SIX

INGREDIENTS
- 1 leg of lamb, about 1.8kg/4lb, boned and butterflied
- juice of 1 lemon
- 15ml/1 tbsp ground Australian aniseed myrtle or 5ml/1 tsp fennel seeds ground with 10ml/2 tsp dried thyme
- 90ml/6 tbsp extra virgin olive oil
- salt and ground black pepper

COOK'S TIP
Australian aniseed myrtle, available from specialist suppliers, has a subtle Pernod-like flavour with a sweet aftertaste. It can be used with meat, seafood or in baking.

1 Cut down the length of the leg of lamb down to the bone and remove the bones. Cut into the thickest parts of the meat to flatten it. Lay the lamb in a flat dish. Squeeze the lemon juice over both sides then season with ground black pepper. Rub the myrtle or fennel and thyme, and the oil, all over the meat.

Energy 302kcal/1260kJ; Protein 29.7g; Carbohydrate 0g, of which sugars 0g; Fat 20.4g, of which saturates 5.4g; Cholesterol 100mg; Calcium 7mg; Fibre 0g; Sodium 63mg.

BARBECUED LAMB STEAKS WITH SALSA

VIBRANT RED PEPPER SALSA BRINGS OUT THE BEST IN SUCCULENT LAMB STEAKS TO MAKE A DISH THAT LOOKS AS GOOD AS IT TASTES. SERVE A SELECTION OF SALADS AND CRUSTY BREAD WITH THE LAMB. BARBECUE THE PEPPERS INSTEAD OF ROASTING THEM FOR A SMOKIER FLAVOUR.

SERVES SIX

INGREDIENTS
  6 lamb steaks
  about 15g/½oz fresh rosemary leaves
  2 garlic cloves, sliced
  60ml/4 tbsp olive oil
  30ml/2 tbsp maple syrup
  salt and ground black pepper
  fresh flat leaf parsley sprigs,
    to garnish
For the salsa
  200g/7oz red (bell) peppers,
    roasted, peeled, seeded
    and chopped
  1 plump garlic clove, finely chopped
  15ml/1 tbsp chopped chives
  30ml/2 tbsp extra virgin olive oil

1 Place the lamb steaks in a dish and season with salt and pepper. Scatter the rosemary leaves all over the meat. Add the slices of garlic, then drizzle the oil and maple syrup over the top. Cover and chill until ready to cook. The lamb can be left to marinate in the refrigerator for up to 24 hours.

2 Prepare the barbecue. Make sure the steaks are liberally coated with the marinating ingredients, then grill them over hot coals for 2–5 minutes on each side. The cooking time depends on the heat of the barbecue and the thickness of the steaks as well as the result required by your guests – rare, medium or well cooked.

3 While the lamb steaks are cooking, mix together all the ingredients for the salsa. Serve the barbecued lamb steaks freshly cooked, and offer the salsa separately or spoon it on to the plates with the meat. Garnish with sprigs of flat leaf parsley.

Energy 390kcal/1627kJ; Protein 44.1g; Carbohydrate 2.1g, of which sugars 2g; Fat 22.8g, of which saturates 6.8g; Cholesterol 158mg; Calcium 33mg; Fibre 0.5g; Sodium 106mg.

BARBECUED LAMB ^{WITH} POTATO SLICES

A TRADITIONAL MIXTURE OF FRESH HERBS ADDS A SUMMERY FLAVOUR TO THIS SIMPLE LAMB DISH. A LEG OF LAMB MAKES A LOVELY CENTREPIECE FOR A BARBECUE MEAL, BUT THE MEAT IS EASIER TO COOK EVENLY AND TAKES FAR LESS TIME TO GRILL IF IT'S BONED OUT, OR "BUTTERFLIED" FIRST. CHARGRILLED SLICED POTATOES MAKE AN EASY BUT DELICIOUS ACCOMPANIMENT.

SERVES FOUR

INGREDIENTS

1 leg of lamb, about 1.75kg/4½lb
1 garlic clove, thinly sliced
handful of fresh flat-leaf parsley
handful of fresh sage
handful of fresh rosemary
handful of fresh thyme
90ml/6 tbsp dry sherry
60ml/4 tbsp walnut oil
500g/1¼lb medium-size potatoes
salt and ground black pepper

1 Place the lamb on a board, smooth side downwards, so that you can see where the bone lies. Using a sharp heavy knife, make a long cut through the flesh down to the bone.

2 Use a sharp kitchen knife to scrape away the meat from the bone on both sides, until the bone is completely exposed. Carefully remove the bone and cut away any sinews and excess fat from the meat.

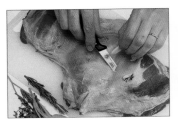

3 Cut through the thickest part of the meat so that you can open it out as flat as possible. Turn the meat skin side up and make several cuts into the flesh with a sharp kitchen knife. Push slivers of garlic and sprigs of fresh herbs into the cuts. Place the meat in a bowl that holds it snugly.

COOK'S TIP
If you have a spit-roasting attachment, the boned leg of lamb can be rolled and tied with the fresh herbs inside, and spit roasted for 1–1½ hours. A spit makes it much easier to cook larger pieces of lamb, as well as other meat and poultry, on the barbecue.

4 Pour over the sherry and walnut oil. Chop half the remaining herbs and scatter over the meat. Cover the bowl with a clean dish towel, refrigerate and leave to marinate for 30 minutes.

5 Remove the lamb from the marinade and season. Cook on a medium-hot barbecue for 30–35 minutes, turning occasionally and basting with the reserved marinade.

6 Scrub the potatoes, then cut them in thick slices. Brush with the marinade and place around the lamb. Cook for about 15 minutes, until golden brown.

Energy 544kcal/2277kJ; Protein 46.6g; Carbohydrate 20.5g, of which sugars 1.9g; Fat 31.2g, of which saturates 12.3g; Cholesterol 171mg; Calcium 51mg; Fibre 1.9g; Sodium 212mg.

STUFFED AUBERGINES WITH LAMB

LAMB AND AUBERGINES GO TOGETHER BEAUTIFULLY. THIS IS AN ATTRACTIVE DISH, USING DIFFERENT COLOURED PEPPERS IN THE LIGHTLY SPICED STUFFING MIXTURE. SERVE IT WITH RICE.

SERVES FOUR

INGREDIENTS
    2 medium aubergines (eggplants)
    30ml/2 tbsp vegetable oil
    1 medium onion, sliced
    5ml/1 tsp grated fresh root ginger
    5ml/1 tsp chilli powder
    1 garlic clove, crushed
    1.5ml/¼ tsp turmeric
    5ml/1 tsp salt
    5ml/1 tsp ground coriander
    1 medium tomato, chopped
    350g/12oz lean minced (ground) lamb
    1 medium green (bell) pepper,
       roughly chopped
    1 medium orange (bell) pepper,
       roughly chopped
    30ml/2 tbsp chopped fresh coriander
       (cilantro)
For the garnish
    ½ onion, sliced
    2 cherry tomatoes, quartered
    fresh coriander (cilantro) sprigs

1 Cut the aubergines in half lengthways with a heavy knife. Scoop out most of the flesh and reserve it for another dish. Brush the shells with a little vegetable oil.

2 In a medium pan, heat 15ml/1 tbsp oil and fry the sliced onion until golden brown. Stir in the grated ginger, chilli powder, garlic, turmeric, salt and ground coriander. Add the chopped tomato, lower the heat and cook for about 5 minutes, stirring continuously.

3 Add the minced lamb to the pan and continue to cook over medium heat for about 7–10 minutes. Stir in the chopped fresh peppers and the fresh coriander. Prepare the barbecue.

4 Spoon the lamb mixture into the aubergine shells and brush the edges of the shells with the remaining oil. Cook on a medium barbecue for 15–20 minutes until cooked through and browned. Garnish with sliced onion, cherry tomatoes and coriander.

Energy 291kcal/1211kJ; Protein 19.5g; Carbohydrate 13.3g, of which sugars 11.7g; Fat 18.1g, of which saturates 6.5g; Cholesterol 67mg; Calcium 48mg; Fibre 4.6g; Sodium 563mg.

MIXED GRILL SKEWERS

THIS SELECTION OF MEATS, COOKED ON SKEWERS AND DRIZZLED WITH HORSERADISH SAUCE, MAKES A HEARTY MAIN COURSE. KEEP ALL THE PIECES ABOUT THE SAME THICKNESS SO THEY COOK EVENLY.

SERVES FOUR

INGREDIENTS

- 4 small lamb noisettes, each about 2.5cm/1in thick
- 4 lambs' kidneys
- 4 streaky (fatty) bacon rashers (strips)
- 8 cherry tomatoes
- 8 chipolata sausages
- 12–16 bay leaves
- salt and ground black pepper
- For the horseradish sauce
- 30ml/2 tbsp horseradish relish
- 45ml/3 tbsp melted butter

1 Trim any excess fat from the lamb noisettes with a sharp knife. Halve the kidneys and remove the cores, using kitchen scissors.

2 Cut each bacon rasher in half and wrap each piece around a cherry tomato or a piece of kidney.

3 Thread the lamb noisettes, bacon-wrapped kidneys and cherry tomatoes, chipolatas and bay leaves on to four long metal skewers. Set aside while you prepare the sauce.

4 Mix the horseradish relish with the melted butter and stir until thoroughly blended. Put half the sauce into a serving bowl.

5 Brush a little of the horseradish sauce from the pan over the meat and sprinkle with salt and pepper.

6 Prepare the barbecue. Position a lightly oiled grill rack over the hot coals. Cook the skewers over medium heat for 12 minutes, turning occasionally, until the meat is golden brown and thoroughly cooked. Serve hot, drizzled with the horseradish sauce from the serving bowl.

COOK'S TIP

Throw some bay leaves on to the hot coals during cooking if you like, to add extra smoky flavour to the meat.

VARIATION

If you are cooking for anyone who detests kidneys, they could be replaced by firm, well-flavoured mushrooms.

Energy 422kcal/1756kJ; Protein 27.2g; Carbohydrate 7g, of which sugars 3.4g; Fat 31.9g, of which saturates 14.2g; Cholesterol 323mg; Calcium 68mg; Fibre 1g; Sodium 955mg.

BACON KOFTAS

KOFTA KEBABS CAN BE MADE WITH ANY TYPE OF MINCED MEAT, BUT BACON IS VERY SUCCESSFUL. YOU WILL NEED A FOOD PROCESSOR FOR THE BEST RESULT AS THE INGREDIENTS NEED TO BE CHOPPED FINELY. THEY GO VERY NICELY WITH A BULGUR WHEAT SALAD, WHICH IS SUBSTANTIAL AND QUICK TO MAKE.

3 To make the salad, place the bulgur wheat in a bowl and pour over boiling water to cover. Leave the bulgur to stand for 30 minutes, until the grains have absorbed the water and are tender. Meanwhile, prepare the barbecue. Position a lightly oiled grill rack over the hot coals.

4 Drain the bulgur wheat well, then stir in the sunflower seeds, olive oil, salt and pepper. Stir in the celery leaves.

SERVES FOUR

INGREDIENTS
  250g/9oz lean streaky (fatty)
    bacon rashers (strips), roughly
    chopped
  1 small onion, roughly chopped
  1 celery stick, roughly chopped
  75ml/5 tbsp fresh wholemeal
    (whole-wheat) breadcrumbs
  45ml/3 tbsp chopped fresh thyme
  30ml/2 tbsp Worcestershire sauce
  1 egg, beaten
  salt and ground black pepper
  olive oil, for brushing
For the salad
  115g/4oz/¾ cup bulgur wheat
  60ml/4 tbsp toasted sunflower seeds
  15ml/1 tbsp olive oil
  salt and ground black pepper
  handful of celery leaves,
    roughly chopped

1 Soak eight bamboo skewers in water for 30 minutes. Place the bacon, onion, celery and breadcrumbs in a food processor and process until chopped. Add the thyme, Worcestershire sauce and seasoning. Bind to a firm mixture with the egg.

2 Divide the mixture into eight equal portions and use your hands to shape them around eight bamboo skewers.

5 Cook the kofta skewers over medium-high heat for 8–10 minutes, turning occasionally, until golden brown. Serve with the salad.

Energy 340kcal/1417kJ; Protein 14g; Carbohydrate 31.7g, of which sugars 2.5g; Fat 18.2g, of which saturates 5.5g; Cholesterol 41mg; Calcium 55mg; Fibre 0.7g; Sodium 1025mg.

SAUSAGES WITH PRUNES AND BACON

SAUSAGES ARE A PERENNIAL BARBECUE FAVOURITE AND ARE GREAT JUST AS THEY ARE, BUT THIS METHOD OF STUFFING THEM WITH TANGY PRUNES AND MUSTARD IS A DELICIOUS WAY TO RING THE CHANGES. SERVE THEM WITH CRUSTY FRENCH BREAD OR WARMED CIABATTA.

SERVES FOUR

INGREDIENTS
  8 large, meaty sausages, such as
    Toulouse or other good-quality
    pork sausages
  30ml/2 tbsp Dijon mustard, plus
    extra to serve
  24 ready-to-eat stoned (pitted)
    prunes
  8 smoked streaky (fatty) bacon
    rashers (strips)

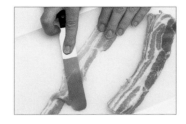

3 Cut the rind off the bacon if there is any, then lay each rasher on a board and stretch it out, using the back of a palette knife or metal spatula.

4 Wrap one bacon rasher tightly around each sausage to hold it in shape. Cook over hot coals for 15–18 minutes, turning occasionally, until evenly browned and cooked. Serve with lots of fresh crusty bread and mustard.

1 Prepare the barbecue. Position a lightly oiled grill rack over the hot coals. Use a sharp knife to cut a long slit down the length of each sausage, about three-quarters of the way through.

2 Open out the sausages carefully and spread the cut surfaces generously with mustard. Then place three prunes inside each sausage, pressing them in firmly.

VARIATION
Use ready-to-eat dried apricots in place of the prunes.

Energy 492kcal/2058kJ; Protein 17.4g; Carbohydrate 49.1g, of which sugars 44g; Fat 26.5g, of which saturates 9.7g; Cholesterol 57mg; Calcium 75mg; Fibre 7.4g; Sodium 1349mg.

OYSTER AND BACON BROCHETTES

SIX OYSTERS PER PERSON MAKE A GENEROUSLY SIZED APPETIZER, SERVED WITH THE SEASONED OYSTER LIQUOR TO TRICKLE OVER THE SKEWERS. ALTERNATIVELY, SERVE NINE PER PERSON AND EAT THEM AS A MAIN COURSE, ACCOMPANIED BY A COOL SALAD.

SERVES FOUR TO SIX

INGREDIENTS
36 oysters
18 thin-cut rashers (strips) streaky
   (fatty) bacon
15ml/1 tbsp paprika
5ml/1 tsp cayenne pepper
ground black pepper
celery leaves and red chillies,
   to garnish
For the sauce
   ½ red chilli pepper, seeded and
      very finely chopped
   1 garlic clove, crushed
   2 spring onions (scallions), very
      finely chopped
   30ml/2 tbsp finely chopped
      fresh parsley
   liquor from the oysters
   juice of ¼–½ lemon, to taste
   salt and ground black pepper

1 Open the oysters over a bowl to catch their liquor for the sauce. Wrap your left hand (if you are right-handed) in a clean, folded dish towel and cup the deep shell of each oyster in your wrapped hand. Work the point of a strong, short-bladed knife into the hinge between the two shells, or into the side if you find that easier, and twist the knife firmly. Try not to push any broken shell into the oyster.

2 Push the knife in and cut the muscle, holding the shell closed. Tip the liquor into the bowl. Cut the oyster free and drop it into another bowl. Discard the drained shells and reserve the liquor from the oysters.

3 Prepare the barbecue. Make the sauce as the coals heat up; mix the chilli, garlic, spring onions and parsley into the oyster liquid and sharpen to taste with lemon juice. Season with salt and pepper and transfer to a dish.

4 Cut each bacon rasher across the middle. Season the oysters lightly with paprika, cayenne and freshly ground black pepper and wrap each one in half a bacon rasher, then thread them on to wetted skewers. Leave a little space between the oysters so that the bacon cooks and crisps evenly.

5 Cook the brochettes over hot coals for about 5 minutes, turning frequently, until the bacon is crisp and brown. Garnish with celery leaves and red chillies and serve with the reserved liquor from the oysters poured over.

Energy 355kcal/1481kJ; Protein 21.9g; Carbohydrate 19.7g, of which sugars 0.6g; Fat 21.6g, of which saturates 4.7g; Cholesterol 84mg; Calcium 196mg; Fibre 1.1g; Sodium 1613mg.

PORK AND PINEAPPLE SATAY

SATAY, WHICH MAY BE MADE WITH DICED LAMB, BEEF OR CHICKEN AS WELL AS PORK, IS A POPULAR CHARGRILLED SNACK THROUGHOUT SOUTH-EAST ASIA. THIS VARIATION ON THE CLASSIC SATAY HAS ADDED PINEAPPLE, BUT KEEPS THE TRADITIONAL COCONUT AND PEANUT SAUCE.

SERVES FOUR

INGREDIENTS
    500g/1¼lb pork fillet (tenderloin)
    1 small onion, chopped
    1 garlic clove, chopped
    60ml/4 tbsp soy sauce
    finely grated rind of ½ lemon
    5ml/1 tsp ground cumin
    5ml/1 tsp ground coriander
    5ml/1 tsp ground turmeric
    5ml/1 tsp dark muscovado
        (brown) sugar
    1 small fresh pineapple, peeled and
        diced, or 225g/8oz can pineapple
        chunks in juice, drained
    salt and ground black pepper
For the satay sauce
    175ml/6fl oz/¾ cup coconut milk
    115g/4oz/6 tbsp crunchy
        peanut butter
    1 garlic clove, crushed
    10ml/2 tsp soy sauce
    5ml/1 tsp dark muscovado
        (brown) sugar

1 Using a sharp kitchen knife, trim any excess fat from the pork fillet and cut the meat into 2.5cm/1in cubes. Place the pieces in a large mixing bowl and set aside.

2 Prepare the barbecue. When the flames have died down arrange a lightly oiled rack over the hot coals. Place the chopped onion, garlic, soy sauce, lemon rind, spices and sugar in a blender or food processor. Add two pieces of pineapple and process until the mixture is almost smooth.

3 Add the paste to the pork, tossing well to coat evenly. Thread the pieces of pork on to bamboo skewers, with the remaining pineapple pieces.

4 To make the sauce, pour the coconut milk into a pan and stir in the peanut butter and the remaining sauce ingredients. Heat gently, stirring until smooth and hot. Cover and keep warm on the edge of the barbecue.

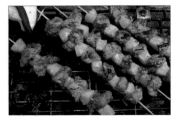

5 Cook the satay over medium-hot coals for 10–12 minutes, turning occasionally, until golden brown and thoroughly cooked. Serve with the satay sauce.

COOK'S TIP
If you cannot buy coconut milk, use creamed coconut in a block. Dissolve a 50g/2oz piece in 150ml/½ pint/⅔ cup boiling water and use as above.

Energy 373kcal/1560kJ; Protein 33.8g; Carbohydrate 15.2g, of which sugars 13g; Fat 20.1g, of which saturates 5.5g; Cholesterol 79mg; Calcium 41mg; Fibre 2.1g; Sodium 415mg.

BASIL AND PECORINO STUFFED PORK

THIS IS A VERY EASY DISH TO MAKE AND LOOKS EXTREMELY IMPRESSIVE. IT IS GOOD FOR A BIG PARTY, BECAUSE YOU CAN GET SEVERAL FILLETS ON A BARBECUE GRILL, AND EACH ONE YIELDS ABOUT EIGHT CHUNKY SLICES. SERVE WITH A CHICKPEA AND ONION SALAD.

1 Make a 1cm/½in slit down the length of one of the fillets. Continue to slice, cutting along the fold of the meat, until you can open it out flat. Lay it between two sheets of baking parchment and pound with a rolling pin to an even thickness of about 1cm/½in. Lift off the top sheet of parchment and brush the meat with a little oil. Press half the basil leaves on to the surface, then scatter over half the Pecorino cheese and chilli flakes. Add a little black pepper.

2 Roll up lengthways to form a sausage and tie with kitchen string (twine). Repeat with the second fillet. Put them in a shallow bowl with the remaining oil, cover and put in a cool place until ready to cook.

3 Prepare the barbecue. Twenty minutes before you are ready to cook, season the meat with salt. Wipe any excess oil off the meat. Once the flames have died down, rake the hot coals to one side and insert a drip tray beside them. Position a lightly oiled grill rack over the hot coals.

4 Put the tenderloins on to the grill rack over high heat, directly over the coals. Grill for 5 minutes over the coals, turning to sear on all sides, then move them over the drip tray and grill for 15 minutes more. Cover with a lid or tented heavy-duty foil, and turn them over from time to time. When done, remove and wrap in foil. Leave to rest for 10 minutes before slicing into rounds and serving.

SERVES SIX TO EIGHT

INGREDIENTS
2 pork fillets (tenderloins), each about 350g/12oz
45ml/3 tbsp olive oil
40g/1½oz/1½ cups fresh basil leaves, chopped
50g/2oz Pecorino cheese, grated
2.5ml/½ tsp chilli flakes
salt and ground black pepper

COOK'S TIP
• If you don't use a lid and drip tray, move the coals so there are less on one side than the other. Move the pork during cooking to prevent burning.
• Pork fillets are incredibly versatile and perfect for the barbecue. Not only can they be exquisitely stuffed, but the large surface area, and the fact that they are cooked on all sides, makes for exceptionally flavourful meat dishes.

Energy 174kcal/725kJ; Protein 21.3g; Carbohydrate 0.1g, of which sugars 0.1g; Fat 9.7g, of which saturates 3.1g; Cholesterol 61mg; Calcium 91mg; Fibre 0.3g; Sodium 131mg.

PORK RIBS <u>WITH</u> GINGER RELISH

THIS DISH WORKS BEST WHEN THE PORK RIBS ARE GRILLED IN WHOLE, LARGE SLABS, THEN SLICED TO SERVE. NOT ONLY DOES THIS KEEP THE MEAT SUCCULENT, BUT IT ALSO CREATES PERFECT-SIZED PORTIONS FOR GUESTS TO GRAB! MAKE THE GINGER RELISH THE DAY BEFORE IF POSSIBLE.

SERVES FOUR

INGREDIENTS

4 pork rib slabs, each with 6 ribs,
    total weight about 2kg/4½lb
40g/1½oz/3 tbsp light muscovado
    (brown) sugar
3 garlic cloves, crushed
5cm/2in piece of fresh root ginger,
    finely grated
10ml/2 tsp Sichuan peppercorns,
    finely crushed
2.5ml/½ tsp ground black pepper
5ml/1 tsp finely ground star anise
5ml/1 tsp Chinese five-spice powder
90ml/6 tbsp dark soy sauce
45ml/3 tbsp sunflower oil
15ml/1 tbsp sesame oil
For the relish
60ml/4 tbsp sunflower oil
300g/11oz banana shallots,
    finely chopped
9 garlic cloves, crushed
7.5cm/3in piece of fresh root ginger,
    finely grated
60ml/4 tbsp seasoned rice
    wine vinegar
45ml/3 tbsp sweet chilli sauce
105ml/7 tbsp tomato ketchup
90ml/6 tbsp water
60ml/4 tbsp chopped fresh coriander
    (cilantro) leaves
salt

1 Lay the slabs of pork ribs in a large shallow dish. Mix the remaining ingredients in a bowl and pour the marinade over the ribs, making sure they are evenly coated. Cover and chill the ribs overnight.

2 To make the relish, heat the oil in a heavy pan, add the shallots and cook them gently for 5 minutes. Add the garlic and ginger and cook for about 4 minutes more. Increase the heat and add all the remaining ingredients except the coriander. Cover and simmer gently for 10 minutes until thickened. Tip into a bowl and stir in the coriander. When completely cold, chill until needed.

3 Remove the ribs from the refrigerator 1 hour before cooking. Prepare the barbecue. Remove the ribs from the marinade and pat them dry with kitchen paper. Pour the marinade into a pan. Bring it to the boil on the stove, then simmer for 3 minutes.

4 Once the flames have died down, rake the hot coals to one side and insert a large drip tray beside them. Position a lightly oiled grill rack over the hot coals. Lay the ribs over high heat directly over the coals and cook them for 3 minutes on each side, then move over the drip tray. Cover with a lid or tented heavy-duty foil and cook for a further 30–35 minutes, turning and basting occasionally with the marinade.

5 The meat should be ready when it is golden-brown in appearance. If, towards the end of the cooking time, the ribs need crisping up a bit, move them quickly back over the coals. Stop basting with the marinade 5 minutes before cooking time. Cut into single ribs to serve, with the relish.

Energy 665kcal/2761kJ; Protein 46.6g; Carbohydrate 17g, of which sugars 14.8g; Fat 45.9g, of which saturates 14.2g; Cholesterol 155mg; Calcium 59mg; Fibre 1.4g; Sodium 1111mg.

PORK SATAY KEBABS

MACADAMIA NUTS HAVE AN UNMISTAKABLY RICH FLAVOUR AND ARE USED HERE WITH ASIAN FLAVOURINGS AND CHILLIES TO MAKE A HOT AND SPICY MARINADE FOR BITE-SIZE PIECES OF TENDER PORK.

MAKES EIGHT TO TWELVE

INGREDIENTS
450g/1lb pork fillet (tenderloin)
15ml/1 tbsp light muscovado (brown) sugar
1cm/½in cube shrimp paste
30ml/2 tbsp coriander seeds
1–2 lemon grass stalks
6 macadamia nuts or blanched almonds
2 onions, roughly chopped
3–6 fresh red chillies, seeded and roughly chopped
2.5ml/½ tsp ground turmeric
300ml/½ pint/1¼ cups canned coconut milk
30ml/2 tbsp groundnut (peanut) oil or sunflower oil
salt

1 Soak 8–12 bamboo skewers in water for 30 minutes to prevent them scorching on the barbecue.

2 Cut the pork into small, bite-size chunks, then spread it out in a single layer in a shallow dish. Sprinkle with the sugar, to help release the juices, and then set aside.

3 Wrap the cube of shrimp paste in foil and fry the parcel briefly in a dry frying pan to heat it. Alternatively, warm the foil parcel on a skewer held over the gas flame. Dry fry the coriander seeds in the frying pan.

4 Cut off the lower 5cm/2in of the lemon grass stalks and chop finely. Process the dry-fried coriander seeds to a powder in a food processor.

5 Add the macadamia nuts or almonds and the chopped lemon grass to the food processor, process briefly, then add the onions, chillies, shrimp paste, turmeric and a little salt; process to a fine paste.

6 Pour in the coconut milk and oil. Switch the machine on very briefly to mix the ingredients. Pour the mixture over the pork and leave to marinate for 1–2 hours.

7 Prepare the barbecue. Position a lightly oiled grill rack over the hot coals. Thread three or four pieces of marinated pork on to each bamboo skewer and grill over medium heat for 8–10 minutes, or until tender, basting frequently with the remaining marinade up until the final 5 minutes. Serve the skewers immediately while hot.

COOK'S TIP
Shrimp paste, known as belacan in Malaysia and terasi in Indonesia, is available from Asian markets or from large supermarkets. Heating it before use releases its unique aroma. It varies in colour and flavour, some varieties being less pungent than others.

Energy 103kcal/432kJ; Protein 13.1g; Carbohydrate 5.2g, of which sugars 4.4g; Fat 3.5g, of which saturates 0.8g; Cholesterol 33mg; Calcium 20mg; Fibre 0.5g; Sodium 54mg.

PORK CHOPS <u>WITH</u> FIELD MUSHROOMS

LEMON GRASS AND TYPICAL AROMATIC THAI FLAVOURINGS MAKE A SUPERB MARINADE FOR PORK CHOPS, WHICH ARE ACCOMPANIED BY A FIERY SAUCE THAT IS SIMPLY PUT TOGETHER IN A PAN ON THE BARBECUE GRILL RACK. SERVE THESE CHOPS WITH THE MUSHROOMS, A SALAD AND CRUSTY BREAD.

3 Lift the chops out of the marinade and place them on the grill rack. Cook over high heat for 5–7 minutes on each side. Brush with the marinade during cooking up until the final 5 minutes of cooking. Meanwhile, brush both sides of the mushrooms with 15ml/1 tbsp of the oil and cook them for about 2 minutes without turning.

4 Heat the remaining oil in a wok or small frying pan on the grill rack, then remove the pan from the heat and stir in the chillies, fish sauce, lime juice, shallots, ground rice and chopped spring onions.

SERVES FOUR

INGREDIENTS
    4 pork chops
    4 large field (portabello) mushrooms
    45ml/3 tbsp vegetable oil
    4 fresh red chillies, seeded and
        thinly sliced
    45ml/3 tbsp Thai fish sauce
    90ml/6 tbsp fresh lime juice
    4 shallots, chopped
    5ml/1 tsp roasted ground rice
    30ml/2 tbsp spring onions
        (scallions), chopped, plus shredded
        spring onions to garnish
    coriander (cilantro) leaves, to garnish
For the marinade
    2 garlic cloves, chopped
    15ml/1 tbsp sugar
    15ml/1 tbsp Thai fish sauce
    30ml/2 tbsp soy sauce
    15ml/1 tbsp sesame oil
    15ml/1 tbsp whisky or dry sherry
    2 lemon grass stalks, finely chopped
    2 spring onions (scallions), chopped

1 To make the marinade, combine the garlic, sugar, sauces, oil and whisky or sherry in a large, shallow dish. Stir in the lemon grass and spring onions.

2 Add the pork chops, turning to coat them in the marinade. Cover and leave to marinate for 1–2 hours. Prepare the barbecue. Position a lightly oiled grill rack over the hot coals.

5 Put the pork chops and mushrooms on a large serving plate and spoon over the sauce. Garnish with the coriander leaves and shredded spring onion.

COOK'S TIP
Look for outdoor-reared, free-range pork for the best flavour. Pork loin chops are very lean and tender, and are ideal for the barbecue. Spare rib chops include a little more fat, but this helps to adds flavour to the meat.

Energy 408kcal/1705kJ; Protein 49.7g; Carbohydrate 9.8g, of which sugars 8.3g; Fat 19.1g, of which saturates 4.9g; Cholesterol 123mg; Calcium 62mg; Fibre 2g; Sodium 1176mg.

CHA SHAO BARBECUE PORK

THIS ATTRACTIVE WAY OF COOKING PORK IS VERY POPULAR IN SOUTHERN CHINA AND MALAYSIA AND SINGAPORE. IT IS AN IDEAL DISH FOR A BARBECUE FOR A LARGE NUMBER OF PEOPLE, AS YOU CAN SLICE AND SERVE THE MEAT WHILE OTHER ITEMS ARE STILL COOKING.

<u>SERVES SIX</u>

INGREDIENTS
　　900g/2lb pork fillet (tenderloin)
　　15ml/1 tbsp clear honey
　　45ml/3 tbsp rice wine or
　　　medium-dry sherry
　　spring onion (scallion) curls,
　　　to garnish
For the marinade
　　150ml/1/4 pint/2/3 cup dark
　　　soy sauce
　　90ml/6 tbsp rice wine or
　　　medium-dry sherry
　　150ml/1/4 pint/2/3 cup well-flavoured
　　　chicken stock
　　15ml/1 tbsp soft brown sugar
　　1cm/1/2in piece fresh root ginger,
　　　peeled and finely sliced
　　40ml/21/2 tbsp chopped onion

1 Mix all the marinade ingredients in a pan and stir over a medium heat until the mixture boils. Lower the heat and simmer gently for 15 minutes, stirring from time to time. Leave to cool.

2 Put the fillets in a dish that is large enough to hold them side by side. Pour over 250ml/8fl oz/1 cup of the marinade, cover and chill for at least 8 hours, turning the meat several times, before barbecuing for 10 minutes.

COOK'S TIP
You will have extra marinade when making this dish. Chill or freeze this and use to baste other grilled (broiled) dishes or meats, such as spare ribs.

3 If using an oven, preheat to 200°C/ 400°F/Gas 6. Drain the pork, reserving the marinade in the dish. Place the meat on a rack over a roasting pan and pour water into the pan to a depth of 1cm/1/2in. Place the pan in the oven and roast for 20 minutes.

4 Stir the honey and rice wine or sherry into the marinade. Remove the meat from the barbecue or oven and place in the marinade, turning to coat. Put back on the rack and roast for 20–30 minutes or until cooked. Serve in slices, garnished with spring onion curls.

Energy 350kcal/14656kJ; Protein 46.5g; Carbohydrate 20g, of which sugars 12.6g; Fat 8g, of which saturates 2.5g; Cholesterol 146mg; Calcium 46mg; Fibre 1g; Sodium 459mg.

FARMHOUSE PIZZA

PIZZA IS NOT A DISH USUALLY ASSOCIATED WITH BARBECUE COOKING, BUT IN FACT THE OPEN FIRE GIVES A FRESHLY MADE PIZZA BASE A WONDERFULLY CRISP TEXTURE. YOU CAN SHAPE THE DOUGH TO FIT THE GRILL RACK OF YOUR BARBECUE.

SERVES EIGHT

INGREDIENTS

90ml/6 tbsp olive oil
225g/8oz button (white) mushrooms
300g/11oz packet pizza-base mix
300ml/½ pint/1¼ cups tomato sauce
300g/11oz mozzarella cheese,
   thinly sliced
115g/4oz wafer-thin smoked
   ham slices
6 bottled artichoke hearts in oil,
   drained and sliced
50g/2oz can anchovy fillets, drained
   and halved lengthways
10 stoned (pitted) black olives,
   halved
30ml/2 tbsp chopped fresh oregano
45ml/3 tbsp freshly grated
   Parmesan cheese
ground black pepper

1 Heat 30ml/2 tbsp oil in a pan, add the mushrooms and fry over medium heat until all the juices have evaporated. Remove from the heat and leave to cool. Meanwhile, prepare the barbecue and arrange a lightly oiled grill rack over the coals.

2 Make up the pizza dough according to the directions on the packet. Roll it out on a floured surface to a 30 x 25cm/ 12 x 10in rectangle, or to a size that fits your barbecue grill rack. Brush with oil and place, oiled side down, over medium-hot coals. Cook for 6 minutes until the dough is firm.

3 Brush the uncooked side of the dough with oil and turn it over on to a baking sheet. Spread the tomato sauce over the pizza and arrange the sliced mozzarella on top. Scrunch up the smoked ham and arrange on top with the artichoke hearts, anchovies and cooked mushrooms.

4 Dot with the halved olives, then sprinkle over the fresh oregano and Parmesan cheese. Drizzle over the remaining olive oil and season with black pepper.

5 Slide the pizza back on to the barbecue and cook for a further 8–10 minutes, or until the dough is golden brown and crisp and the topping is bubbling. Serve immediately.

Energy 412kcal/1725kJ; Protein 17.2g; Carbohydrate 36.4g, of which sugars 2g; Fat 23g, of which saturates 8g; Cholesterol 38mg; Calcium 259mg; Fibre 2.4g; Sodium 822mg.

PORK SCHNITZEL

THIN PORK ESCALOPES ARE IDEAL FOR ROLLING AROUND A RICHLY FLAVOURED STUFFING AND THEN BARBECUING IN THIS VARIATION OF A CROATIAN RECIPE. SERVE THEM WITH A CREAMY SAUCE FLAVOURED WITH MUSHROOMS AND BACON, AND SOME COUNTRY-STYLE CRUSTY BREAD.

SERVES FOUR

INGREDIENTS
    4 pork leg steaks or escalopes (US
      pork scallop), about 200g/7oz each
    60ml/4 tbsp olive oil
    115g/4oz chicken livers, chopped
    1 garlic clove, crushed
    salt and ground black pepper
    15ml/1 tbsp chopped fresh parsley,
      to garnish
For the sauce
    1 onion, thinly sliced
    115g/4oz streaky (fatty) bacon,
      thinly sliced
    175g/6oz/2 cups sliced mixed
      wild mushrooms
    120ml/4fl oz/½ cup olive oil
    5ml/1 tsp ready-made mustard
    150ml/¼ pint/⅔ cup white wine
    120ml/4fl oz/½ cup sour cream
    250ml/8fl oz/1 cup double
      (heavy) cream

1 Soak eight cocktail sticks (toothpicks) in water for 30 minutes. Place each pork steak between two sheets of damp clear film (plastic wrap) and flatten with a meat mallet or rolling pin until about 15 x 10cm/6 x 4in. Season well.

2 Heat half the oil in a frying pan and cook the chicken livers and garlic for 1–2 minutes. Remove, drain on kitchen paper and leave to cool.

COOK'S TIP
Veal or chicken breast fillet would also work well with this recipe.

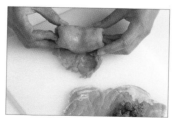

3 Divide the chicken livers evenly between the four prepared pork steaks and roll up into neat parcels. Secure with cocktail sticks. Alternatively, tie up each roll with string.

4 To make the sauce, fry the onion, bacon and mushrooms in the oil for 2–3 minutes, then add the mustard, white wine and sour cream. Stir to simmering point, then add the double cream and season.

5 Prepare the barbecue. Position a lightly oiled grill rack over the hot coals. Brush the pork rolls with oil and cook over medium heat for 8–10 minutes on each side, brushing with oil as necessary, until golden brown.

6 Reheat the sauce over the barbecue. Remove the cocktail sticks or string from the rolls. Serve the schnitzels with the sauce and garnish with a little parsley.

Energy 969kcal/4009kJ; Protein 50.2g; Carbohydrate 3.8g, of which sugars 3.3g; Fat 81.6g, of which saturates 33.7g; Cholesterol 248mg; Calcium 83mg; Fibre 0.7g; Sodium 532mg.

FIVE-SPICED PORK RIBS

BARBECUED PORK SPARE RIBS MARINATED WITH CHINESE FLAVOURINGS HAVE GOT TO BE ONE OF THE ALL-TIME FAVOURITES. CHOOSE THE MEATIEST SPARE RIBS YOU CAN FIND TO MAKE THE DISH A REAL SUCCESS AND HAVE PLENTY OF NAPKINS HANDY.

SERVES FOUR

INGREDIENTS

    1kg/2¼lb Chinese-style pork
      spare ribs
    10ml/2 tsp Chinese five-spice
      powder
    2 garlic cloves, crushed
    15ml/1 tbsp grated fresh
      root ginger
    2.5ml/½ tsp chilli sauce
    60ml/4 tbsp dark soy sauce
    45ml/3 tbsp muscovado
      (brown) sugar
    15ml/1 tbsp sunflower oil
    4 spring onions (scallions)

1 If the spare ribs are still attached to each other, cut between them to separate them into single ribs (or you could ask your butcher to do this when you buy them). Place the spare ribs in a large bowl.

2 Mix together all the remaining ingredients, except the spring onions, and pour over the ribs. Toss well to coat evenly. Cover the bowl and leave to marinate in the refrigerator overnight.

3 Prepare the barbecue. Position a lightly oiled grill rack over the hot coals. Cook the spare ribs over medium-high heat, turning frequently, for about 30–40 minutes. Brush occasionally with the remaining marinade up until the final 5 minutes.

4 While the ribs are cooking, trim the spring onions and slice them finely on the diagonal. Scatter them over the ribs and serve immediately.

BELMONT SAUSAGE WITH MUSHROOM RELISH

NOTHING QUITE BEATS GOOD QUALITY SAUSAGE, AND THIS RECIPE ENSURES YOU GET JUST THAT. YOU CAN CHANGE THE COMBINATION OF HERBS AND SPICES OR TWIST THE SAUSAGE INTO SMALL LENGTHS. IT REALLY IS A VERY ADAPTABLE RECIPE, AND THE MUSHROOM RELISH IS PERFECT TO GO WITH IT.

SERVES SIX TO EIGHT

INGREDIENTS

450g/1lb skinless and boneless belly
   pork, cut into large pieces
450g/1lb pork shoulder, cut into
   large pieces
300–400g/11–14oz back fat, cut into
   large pieces
50g/2oz/1 cup freshly made
   breadcrumbs
2 garlic cloves, crushed
10ml/2 tsp salt
10ml/2 tsp ground coriander
5ml/1 tsp ground black pepper
5ml/1 tsp ground cumin
1.5ml/¼ tsp cayenne pepper
1.5ml/¼ tsp ground cinnamon
45ml/3 tbsp chopped fresh basil
60ml/4 tbsp chopped fresh marjoram
60ml/4 tbsp chopped fresh flat
   leaf parsley
enough cleaned sausage casing for
   just over 900g/2lb sausage: about
   50g/2oz or 2.7m/9ft
30ml/2 tbsp olive oil for brushing
6 metal skewers
For the relish
45ml/3 tbsp extra virgin olive oil
2 onions, finely chopped
2 garlic cloves, finely chopped
150g/5oz/2 cups finely chopped
   chestnut mushrooms
25g/1oz/3 tbsp drained sun-dried
   tomatoes in oil, finely chopped
90ml/6 tbsp water
20ml/4 tsp sugar
30ml/2 tbsp chopped fresh flat
   leaf parsley
30ml/2 tbsp sherry vinegar
salt and ground black pepper

1 Pass both meats through the mincer (grinder) once and the back fat twice, using the plate with the widest holes. Place in a large bowl and add the breadcrumbs. Add the garlic with a pinch of the salt, and the remaining sausage ingredients except the remaining salt, the casings and the oil. Mix thoroughly. Cover and chill overnight.

2 Rinse the casing by running cold water through it. Fit the casing on to the sausage-making attachment of the mincer, or use a piping bag with a wide nozzle. Add the remaining salt to the mixture and mix well. Fill the casing in one continuous length, leaving a gap of 13cm/5in of empty casing halfway. Separate into two sausages, securing by tying the ends. Curl each sausage into a round, cover and chill.

3 To make the relish, heat the oil in a pan and fry the onions and garlic for about 10 minutes. Add the mushrooms and tomatoes and fry for 1 minute. Stir in the measured water and boil until it has evaporated. Stir in the sugar, parsley and vinegar. Season, cover and cool.

4 Prepare the barbecue. Once the flames have died down, rake the hot coals to one side and insert a drip tray beside them. Position a lightly oiled grill rack over the hot coals.

5 Skewer the sausages to maintain the round shape. Brush them with a little oil and place them on the grill rack over the drip tray. Cover with a lid or tented heavy-duty foil, and cook for about 5–7 minutes on each side, until cooked and golden. Serve with the relish.

Energy 765kcal/3159kJ; Protein 21.9g; Carbohydrate 6.1g, of which sugars 4.9g; Fat 72.7g, of which saturates 26.8g; Cholesterol 117mg; Calcium 38mg; Fibre 1.4g; Sodium 87mg.

VEAL CHOPS WITH BASIL BUTTER

SUCCULENT VEAL CHOPS FROM THE LOIN ARE AN EXPENSIVE CUT AND ARE BEST COOKED QUICKLY AND SIMPLY. THE FLAVOUR OF BASIL GOES PARTICULARLY WELL WITH VEAL, BUT OTHER HERBS CAN BE USED INSTEAD IF YOU PREFER. SERVE WITH BARBECUED VEGETABLES OR A SALAD.

SERVES TWO

INGREDIENTS
    25g/1oz/2 tbsp butter, softened
    15ml/1 tbsp Dijon mustard
    15ml/1 tbsp chopped fresh basil
    olive oil, for brushing
    2 veal loin chops, 2.5cm/1in thick,
      about 225g/8oz each
    salt and ground black pepper
    fresh basil sprigs, to garnish

COOK'S TIP
Chilled herb butters make perfect impromptu sauces for cooked meats and fish. Basil butter is a firm favourite, but other fresh herbs such as chives, tarragon and parsley also work well.

1 To make the basil butter, cream the softened butter with the Dijon mustard and chopped fresh basil in a large mixing bowl, then season with plenty of ground black pepper.

2 Prepare the barbecue. Position a lightly oiled griddle over the hot coals.

3 Brush both sides of each chop with olive oil and season with a little salt. Cook the chops over high heat for 7–10 minutes, basting with oil and turning once, until done to your liking.

4 Top each chop with basil butter and serve immediately, garnished with basil.

Energy 718kcal/3017kJ; Protein 113.8g; Carbohydrate 0.3g, of which sugars 0.0g; Fat 29.13g, of which saturates 16.0g; Cholesterol 3135mg; Calcium 35mg; Fibre 0.3g; Sodium 448mg.

HOME-MADE BURGERS WITH RELISH

MAKING YOUR OWN BURGERS MEANS YOU CONTROL WHAT GOES INTO THEM. THESE ARE FULL OF FLAVOUR AND ALWAYS PROVE POPULAR. SERVE IN BUNS WITH LETTUCE AND THE TANGY RATATOUILLE RELISH, WHICH IS VERY EASY TO MAKE.

SERVES FOUR

INGREDIENTS

2 shallots, unpeeled
450g/1lb/2 cups fresh lean minced (ground) beef
30ml/2 tbsp chopped parsley
30ml/2 tbsp tomato ketchup
1 garlic clove, crushed
1 fresh green chilli, seeded and finely chopped
15ml/1 tbsp olive oil
400g/14oz can ratatouille
4 burger buns
lettuce leaves
salt and ground black pepper

VARIATION

These burgers also taste great with spicy corn relish on the side. To make the relish, heat 30ml/2 tbsp oil in a pan and fry 1 onion, 2 crushed garlic cloves and 1 seeded and finely chopped red chilli until soft. Add 10ml/2 tsp garam masala and cook for 2 minutes, then mix in a 320g/11¼oz can of corn and the grated rind and juice of 1 lime.

1 Prepare the barbecue. Put the shallots in a bowl with boiling water to cover. Leave for 1–2 minutes, then slip off the skins and chop the shallots finely.

2 Mix 1 shallot with the beef in a bowl. Add the parsley and tomato ketchup, with salt and pepper to taste. Mix well with clean hands. Divide the mixture into four. Knead each portion into a ball, then flatten it into a burger.

3 Make a spicy relish by cooking the remaining shallot with the garlic and green chilli in the olive oil for 2–3 minutes, or until softened.

4 Add the canned ratatouille to the pan containing the vegetables. Bring to the boil, then simmer for 5 minutes. Position a lightly oiled grill rack over the hot coals.

5 Transfer the pan to the edge of the barbecue. Cook the burgers over high heat for about 5 minutes on each side, until they are well browned and throroughly cooked.

6 Split the burger buns. Arrange the lettuce leaves on the bun bases, add the burgers and top with the warm relish and the tops of the buns. Serve immediately.

Energy 487kcal/2037kJ; Protein 27.9g; Carbohydrate 31.7g, of which sugars 7.8g; Fat 28.6g, of which saturates 9g; Cholesterol 68mg; Calcium 92mg; Fibre 2g; Sodium 492mg.

STILTON BURGERS

A VARIATION ON THE TRADITIONAL BURGER, THIS TASTY RECIPE CONTAINS A DELICIOUS SURPRISE: A CREAMY FILLING OF LIGHTLY MELTED STILTON CHEESE. HOME-MADE BURGERS ARE QUITE QUICK TO MAKE AND TASTE SUPERIOR TO BOUGHT ONES. CHOOSE GOOD QUALITY BEEF FOR THE BEST FLAVOUR.

SERVES FOUR

INGREDIENTS

450g/1lb/2 cups minced
  (ground) beef
1 onion, chopped
1 celery stick, chopped
5ml/1 tsp dried mixed herbs
5ml/1 tsp prepared mustard
50g/2oz/½ cup crumbled
  Stilton cheese
4 burger buns
salt and ground black pepper

1 Prepare the barbecue. Position a lightly oiled grill rack over the coals. Mix the minced beef with the onion, celery, mixed herbs and mustard. Season well with salt and pepper, and bring together with your hands to form a firm mixture.

2 Divide the beef mixture into eight equal portions. Shape four of the portions into rounds and flatten each one slightly. Place a little of the crumbled cheese in the centre of each round.

3 Shape and flatten the remaining four portions and place on top. Use your hands to mould the rounds together, encasing the crumbled cheese, and shaping them into four burgers.

4 Cook over medium-high heat for about 5 minutes on each side. Split the burger buns and place a burger inside each. Serve with salad and mustard pickle, if you like.

Energy 428kcal/1789kJ; Protein 29.6g; Carbohydrate 25.9g, of which sugars 2.2g; Fat 23.5g, of which saturates 10.7g; Cholesterol 79mg; Calcium 113mg; Fibre 1.1g; Sodium 454mg.

PEPPERED STEAKS IN BEER AND GARLIC

STEAKS GO VERY WELL WITH A ROBUST MARINADE OF GARLIC, WORCESTERSHIRE SAUCE AND BEER.
MARINADES HAVE A DUAL PURPOSE OF FLAVOURING AS WELL AS TENDERIZING MEAT AND SO WILL
IMPROVE THE TEXTURE AS WELL AS THE TASTE. SERVE WITH A BAKED POTATO AND CRISP MIXED SALAD.

SERVES FOUR

INGREDIENTS

    4 beef sirloin or rump steaks, about
      175g/6oz each
    2 garlic cloves, crushed
    120ml/4fl oz/½ cup brown ale
      or stout
    30ml/2 tbsp dark muscovado
      (molasses) sugar
    30ml/2 tbsp Worcestershire
      sauce
    15ml/1 tbsp corn oil
    15ml/1 tbsp crushed
      black peppercorns

1 Place the steaks in a dish and add the garlic, ale or stout, Worcestershire sauce, sugar and oil. Turn to coat evenly, then leave to marinate in the refrigerator for 2–3 hours or overnight.

2 Prepare the barbecue. Position a lightly oiled grill rack over the hot coals. Remove the steaks from the marinade, reserving the marinade. Sprinkle the crushed black peppercorns over both sides of the steaks and press them into the surface.

3 Cook the steaks over high heat, basting them occasionally with the reserved marinade during cooking. (Take care when basting, as the alcohol will tend to flare up: spoon or brush on just a small amount at a time and allow the final basting to cook through.)

4 Turn the steaks once during cooking, and cook them for about 3–6 minutes on each side, depending on how rare you like them.

Energy 355kcal/1480kJ; Protein 39.8g; Carbohydrate 4.7g, of which sugars 4.7g; Fat 19g, of which saturates 7.1g; Cholesterol 102mg; Calcium 13mg; Fibre 0g; Sodium 114mg.

STEAK CIABATTA

THIS ALL-TIME FAVOURITE TASTES ALL THE BETTER WHEN ENJOYED ON A BEACH AFTER AN AFTERNOON SPENT BATTLING THE SURF.

SERVES FOUR

INGREDIENTS
2 romaine or cos lettuces
3 garlic cloves, crushed to a paste
   with enough salt to season
   the steaks
30ml/2 tbsp extra virgin olive oil
4 sirloin steaks, 2.5cm/1in thick,
   total weight about 900g/2lb
4 small ciabatta rolls
salt and ground black pepper
For the dressing
10ml/2 tsp Dijon mustard
5ml/1 tsp cider or white wine vinegar
15ml/1 tbsp olive oil

2 Mix the garlic and oil together in a shallow dish. Add the steaks and rub the mixture into both surfaces. Cover and leave in a cool place until ready to cook.

3 Prepare the barbecue. Position a lightly oiled grill rack over the hot coals. Transfer the steaks to the grill rack. For rare meat, cook the steaks for 2 minutes on one side, without moving, then turn over and grill the other side for 3 minutes. For medium steaks, cook for 4 minutes on each side. Transfer to a plate, cover loosely and leave to rest for 2 minutes.

1 Separate the lettuce leaves and clean them. Put into an airtight container until ready to use. Make a dressing for the salad by mixing the mustard and vinegar in a small jar. Gradually whisk in the oil, then season to taste.

4 Dress the lettuce leaves. Split each ciabatta. Place the ciabatta cut-side down on the grill rack for a minute to heat. Slice the steaks and arrange on top of the ciabatta, with some of the leaves. Replace the lids and cut each filled ciabatta in half to serve.

COOK'S TIP
A steak sandwich is also delicious spread with hummus. Follow the hummus recipe given in the Accompaniments chapter.

Energy 665kcal/2796kJ; Protein 64g; Carbohydrate 53.5g, of which sugars 4.4g; Fat 23.2g, of which saturates 6.4g; Cholesterol 115mg; Calcium 158mg; Fibre 3g; Sodium 698mg

SIRLOIN STEAKS <u>WITH</u> BLOODY MARY SAUCE

THIS COCKTAIL OF INGREDIENTS IS JUST AS DELICIOUS AS THE DRINK THAT INSPIRED IT, AND AS THE ALCOHOL EVAPORATES IN COOKING YOU NEED NOT WORRY ABOUT A HANGOVER.

3 Put the tomatoes in a bowl and pour over boiling water. Leave for 30 seconds then drain and refresh under cold water. Peel and quarter the tomatoes, remove the seeds and chop the flesh.

4 Place the chopped tomatoes, with the rest of the sauce ingredients in a food processor and blend to a fairly smooth texture. If the tomatoes were not quite ripe, add a little tomato purée. Prepare the barbecue. Position a lightly oiled grill rack over the hot coals.

5 Pour the sauce into a pan, bring to the boil and simmer for about 5 minutes. Keep the sauce warm at the side of the barbecue.

6 Remove the steaks from the dish and discard the marinade. Cook the steaks over medium-hot coals for about 3–6 minutes each side, depending on how rare you like them, turning once during cooking. Serve the steaks with the Bloody Mary sauce.

SERVES FOUR

INGREDIENTS
  4 sirloin steaks, about 225g/8oz each
For the marinade
  30ml/2 tbsp dark soy sauce
  60ml/4 tbsp balsamic vinegar
  30ml/2 tbsp olive oil
For the Bloody Mary sauce
  1kg/2¼lb very ripe tomatoes
  tomato purée (paste), if required
  50g/2oz/½ cup chopped onions
  2 spring onions (scallions)
  5ml/1 tsp chopped fresh coriander
    (cilantro)
  5ml/1 tsp ground cumin
  5ml/1 tsp salt
  15ml/1 tbsp fresh lime juice
  120ml/4fl oz/½ cup beef consommé
  60ml/4 tbsp vodka
  15ml/1 tbsp Worcestershire sauce

1 Lay the steaks in a shallow dish in which they will just fit in a single layer. Mix together all the ingredients for the marinade and pour the mixture over the steaks, ensuring they are all coated.

2 Cover the dish with clear film (plastic wrap) and leave to marinate in the refrigerator for at least 2 hours, turning the steaks once or twice.

Energy 366kcal/1538kJ; Protein 51.1g; Carbohydrate 7.3g, of which sugars 7.3g; Fat 11.2g, of which saturates 4.6g; Cholesterol 136mg; Calcium 30mg; Fibre 2.4g; Sodium 159mg.

BEEF RIB WITH ONION SAUCE

RIB OF BEEF CAN BE A LARGE JOINT, BUT JUST ONE RIB, BARBECUED ON THE BONE THEN CARVED INTO SUCCULENT SLICES, MAKES A PERFECT DISH FOR TWO. SERVE WITH A MELLOW RED ONION SAUCE.

SERVES TWO

INGREDIENTS

1 beef rib on the bone, about
   1kg/2¼lb and about 4cm/1½in
   thick, well trimmed of fat
5ml/1 tsp "steak pepper" or lightly
   crushed black peppercorns
15ml/1 tbsp coarse sea salt,
   crushed
30–45ml/2–3 tbsp olive oil
For the red onion sauce
   40g/1½oz butter
   1 large red onion or
      8–10 shallots, sliced
   250ml/8fl oz/1 cup fruity red wine
   250ml/8fl oz/1 cup beef or
      chicken stock
   15–30ml/1–2 tbsp redcurrant jelly or
      seedless raspberry preserve
   1.5ml/¼ tsp dried thyme
   salt and ground black pepper

COOK'S TIP
Cooking the meat on the bone helps to keep it moist and succulent, and adds flavour. Ask the butcher to remove the "chine" bone from the joint to make carving easier but leave the rib bone in place until the meat is cooked.

1 Wipe the piece of beef with damp kitchen paper. Mix the steak pepper or crushed peppercorns with the crushed salt and press on to both sides of the meat. Leave the meat to stand, loosely covered, for 30 minutes. Meanwhile, prepare the barbecue. When the flames have died down, arrange a lightly oiled grill rack over the coals.

2 To make the sauce, melt the butter over a medium heat. Add the onion or shallots and cook for 3 minutes until softened. Add the wine, stock, jelly or preserve and thyme and bring to the boil. Reduce the heat and simmer for 30–35 minutes until the liquid has evaporated and the sauce has thickened. Season and keep warm.

3 Brush the meat with olive oil and cook on a hot barbecue, or in a pan over a high heat, for 5–8 minutes each side, depending on how rare you like it. Transfer the beef to a board, cover loosely and leave to stand for about 10 minutes. Using a knife, loosen the meat from the rib bone, then carve into thick slices. Serve with the red onion sauce.

Energy 238kcal/990kJ; Protein 13.1g; Carbohydrate 9.1g, of which sugars 7.9g; Fat 12.2g, of which saturates 6.9g; Cholesterol 53mg; Calcium 28mg; Fibre 0.8g; Sodium 281mg.

THAI BEEF SALAD

THIS HEARTY SALAD OF BEEF AND CRUNCHY VEGETABLES IS LACED WITH A TANGY CHILLI AND LIME DRESSING AND INFUSED BY CHARACTERISTIC THAI FLAVOURINGS. BARBECUING THE MEAT GIVES A TRULY DELICIOUS FLAVOUR TO THE SALAD.

SERVES FOUR

INGREDIENTS

2 sirloin steaks, about 225g/8oz
  each
1 red onion, finely sliced
½ cucumber, finely sliced
  into matchsticks
1 stalk lemon grass, finely chopped
30ml/2 tbsp chopped spring onions
  (scallions)
juice of 2 limes
15–30ml/1–2 tbsp Thai fish sauce
2–4 red chillies, finely sliced,
  to garnish
fresh coriander (cilantro), Chinese
  mustard cress and mint leaves,
  to garnish

1 Barbecue or pan-fry the beef steaks until they are medium-rare. Allow the steaks to rest for 10–15 minutes.

2 When the steaks have cooled slightly, slice them thinly, using a heavy knife, and put the slices into a large bowl.

3 Add the sliced onion, cucumber matchsticks, lemon grass and spring onions. Toss and season with lime juice and Thai fish sauce. Serve at room temperature or chilled, garnished with the chillies, coriander, mustard cress and mint.

Energy 381kcal/1591kJ; Protein 39.8g; Carbohydrate 4.1g, of which sugars 3.8g; Fat 23g, of which saturates 6.6g; Cholesterol 103mg; Calcium 105mg; Fibre 2.5g; Sodium 352mg.

SPICY BEEF KOFTAS <u>WITH</u> CHICKPEA PURÉE

WHEREVER YOU GO IN THE MIDDLE EAST YOU WILL ENCOUNTER THESE TASTY KEBABS, AS STREET FOOD, ON BARBECUES, AT BEACH BARS AND AT FAMILY MEALS. CHICKPEA PURÉE IS THE TRADITIONAL ACCOMPANIMENT, AND A MIXED SALAD WILL ALSO GO WELL WITH THE RICH FLAVOURS.

<u>SERVES SIX</u>

INGREDIENTS
    500g/1¼lb/2½ cups finely minced
      (ground) beef
    1 onion, grated
    10ml/2 tsp ground cumin
    10ml/2 tsp ground coriander
    10ml/2 tsp paprika
    4ml/¾ tsp cayenne pepper
    5ml/1 tsp salt
    small bunch of fresh flat leaf parsley,
      finely chopped
    small bunch of fresh coriander
      (cilantro), finely chopped
For the chickpea purée
    225g/8oz/1¼ cups dried chickpeas,
      soaked overnight, drained and
      cooked until soft
    50ml/2fl oz/¼ cup olive oil
    juice of 1 lemon
    2 garlic cloves, crushed
    5ml/1 tsp cumin seeds
    30ml/2 tbsp light tahini paste
    60ml/4 tbsp thick Greek (US strained
      plain) yogurt
    40g/1½oz/3 tbsp butter, melted
    salt and ground black pepper
    salad and bread, to serve

1 Mix the minced beef with the onion, cumin, ground coriander, paprika, cayenne, salt, parsley and fresh coriander. Knead the mixture well, then pound it until smooth in a mortar with a pestle or in a blender or food processor. Place the minced beef mixture in a dish then cover and leave to stand in a cool place for 1 hour.

2 Meanwhile, make the chickpea purée. Preheat the oven to 200°C/400°F/Gas 6. In a blender or food processor, process the chickpeas with the olive oil, lemon juice, garlic, cumin seeds, tahini and yogurt until well mixed. Season with salt and pepper, tip the purée into an ovenproof dish, cover with foil and heat through in the oven for 20 minutes. Prepare the barbecue. Position a lightly oiled grill rack over the hot coals.

3 Divide the meat mixture into six portions. Gently squeeze and pat the meat mixture into shape along each of six skewers so that it is quite thick and resembles a fat sausage. Cook the koftas over high heat for 4–5 minutes on each side.

4 Melt the butter in a small pan on the barbecue and pour it over the hot chickpea purée. Serve the koftas with the hot chickpea purée, a mixed salad and bread.

Energy 449kcal/1870kJ; Protein 26.3g; Carbohydrate 20.5g, of which sugars 2.5g; Fat 29.7g, of which saturates 10.7g; Cholesterol 64mg; Calcium 141mg; Fibre 5g, Sodium 134mg.

INDONESIAN BEEF BURGERS

THIS UNUSUAL INDONESIAN RECIPE CONTAINS COCONUT, WHICH GIVES THE BURGERS A RICH AND SUCCULENT FLAVOUR. THEY TASTE GREAT WITH A SHARP YET SWEET MANGO CHUTNEY AND CAN BE EATEN IN MINI NAAN OR PITTA BREADS. VINE LEAVES MAKE AN ATTRACTIVE GARNISH.

MAKES EIGHT

INGREDIENTS

 500g/1¼lb/2½ cups minced
  (ground) beef
 5ml/1 tsp anchovy paste
 10ml/2 tsp tomato purée (paste)
 10ml/2 tsp ground coriander
 5ml/1 tsp ground cumin
 7.5ml/1½ tsp finely grated fresh
  root ginger
 2 garlic cloves, crushed
 1 egg white
 75g/3oz solid creamed coconut,
  grated or 40g/1½oz desiccated (dry
  unsweetened shredded) coconut
 45ml/3 tbsp chopped fresh
  coriander (cilantro)
 salt and ground black pepper
 8 fresh vine leaves (optional),
  to serve

1 Mix the minced beef, anchovy paste, tomato purée, coriander, cumin, ginger and garlic in a bowl. Add the egg white, with salt and pepper to taste. Mix well using your hands. Add the grated creamed coconut and work it into the meat mixture, handling it gently so that it doesn't melt, or stir the desiccated coconut into the meat. Stir in the chopped fresh coriander.

2 Divide the mixture into eight equal sized pieces and form chunky burgers, about 7.5cm/3in in diameter. Chill for 30 minutes.

3 Prepare the barbecue. Once the flames have died down, rake the hot coals to one side and insert a drip tray beside them. Position a lightly oiled grill rack over the hot coals. Cook the chilled burgers over medium-high heat directly over the drip tray for 10–15 minutes, turning them over once or twice. Check they are cooked by breaking off a piece of one of the burgers.

4 If you are using the vine leaves, wash them and pat dry with kitchen paper. Wrap one around each burger. Serve with mango chutney and mini naan or pitta breads.

Energy 177kcal/734kJ; Protein 13.4g; Carbohydrate 0.8g, of which sugars 0.7g; Fat 13.4g, of which saturates 7g; Cholesterol 38mg; Calcium 22mg; Fibre 1.1g; Sodium 90mg.

BARBECUED MARINATED BEEF

THIS DISH OF THINLY SLICED BEEF MARINATED WITH SUGAR, SOY SAUCE AND GARLIC IS IDEAL FOR FLASH-FRYING ON A GRIDDLE OR FOR GRILLING OVER A CLOSE-MESHED BARBECUE. SERVE IT WITH A QUICK VERSION OF THE KOREAN FERMENTED-CABBAGE DISH, KIMCHI, AND A SPINACH SALAD.

SERVES FOUR

INGREDIENTS
   500g/1¼lb beef fillet (tenderloin)
   15ml/1 tbsp sugar
   30ml/2 tbsp light soy sauce
   30ml/2 tbsp sesame oil
   2 garlic cloves, mashed to a paste
      with a further 5ml/1 tsp sugar
   2.5ml/½ tsp finely ground
      black pepper
For the kimchi
   500g/1¼lb Chinese leaves (Chinese
      cabbage), sliced across into
      2.5cm/1in pieces
   60ml/4 tbsp sunflower oil
   15ml/1 tbsp sesame oil
   50g/2oz/¼ cup sugar
   105ml/7 tbsp white rice vinegar
   2.5cm/1in piece of fresh root ginger,
      finely chopped
   3 garlic cloves, finely chopped
   1 fresh fat medium-hot red chilli
   2 spring onions (scallions),
      thinly sliced
For the sigumchi namul
   350g/12oz baby spinach leaves
   10ml/2 tsp sesame oil
   30ml/2 tbsp light soy sauce
   15ml/1 tbsp mirin
   10ml/2 tsp sesame seeds, finely
      toasted

1 Freeze the beef for 1 hour to make it easier to slice. Remove it from the freezer and slice it as thinly as possible. Layer in a shallow dish, sprinkling each layer with sugar. Cover and chill for 30 minutes. Mix the soy sauce, sesame oil, garlic paste and pepper together in a bowl and pour over the beef, ensuring all the pieces are thoroughly coated in the mixture. Cover and chill overnight.

COOK'S TIP
This meat dish will cook very successfully on a close-meshed disposable barbecue but the meat may fall through the gaps in grill racks of other barbecues, so a griddle may be preferable.

2 To make the kimchi, blanch the Chinese leaves in plenty of boiling water for 5 seconds, drain and refresh under cold running water. Drain again and pat with kitchen paper to remove excess water. Put the Chinese leaves in a bowl. Mix the remaining ingredients together and add to the leaves. Toss to mix, cover and chill. The mixture can be made up to 2 days ahead, but tastes best if eaten within 2 hours.

3 To make the sigumchi namul, blanch the spinach in boiling water for 1 minute, drain it and refresh under cold water. Drain again, pat with kitchen paper to remove any excess water and put into a serving bowl. Mix the oil, soy sauce and mirin together. Fold into the spinach with the sesame seeds. Cover and keep in a cool place (not the refrigerator). Serve within 2 hours.

4 Prepare the barbecue. Heat a griddle on the grill rack over hot coals. Flash-fry the meat in batches for 15–20 seconds on each side. Serve immediately with the sigumchi namul and the kimchi.

THE GAUCHO BARBECUE

*THIS TRADITIONAL SOUTH AMERICAN BEEF DISH CONSISTS OF
SHORT RIBS AND RUMP STEAK ACCOMPANIED BY PORK SAUSAGES. IT
INVOLVES NO MARINATING, BUT THE MEAT IS BRUSHED WITH BRINE
DURING COOKING TO KEEP IT MOIST. SERVE EACH MEAT AS IT IS
COOKED, ACCOMPANIED BY A SELECTION OF SALADS AND SALSAS.*

SERVES SIX

INGREDIENTS
    50g/2oz/¼ cup coarse sea salt
    200ml/7fl oz/scant 1 cup
      warm water
    6 pork sausages
    1kg/2¼lb beef short ribs
    1kg/2¼lb rump (round) steak, in
      one piece
    salads, salsas and breads, to serve

1 Dissolve the sea salt in the measured
water in a bowl. Leave to cool.

2 Prepare the barbecue. Position a
lightly oiled grill rack over the hot coals.

3 Start by cooking the sausages, which
should take 15–20 minutes over
medium heat, depending on their size.
Once cooked on all sides, slice the
sausages thickly and arrange them on a
plate. Let guests help themselves while
you cook the remaining meats.

4 Place the short ribs bony side down
on the grill rack. Cook for 15 minutes,
turn, brush the cooked side of each rib
with brine and grill for a further
25–30 minutes and continue basting.
Slice the meat and transfer to a plate
for guests to help themselves.

5 Place the whole rump steak on the
grill rack and cook for 5 minutes, then
turn over and baste the browned side
with brine.

6 Continue turning and basting in this
way for 20–25 minutes in total, until the
meat is cooked to your liking. Allow the
meat to rest for 5 minutes under tented
heavy-duty foil, then slice thinly and
serve with salads, salsa and bread.

COOK'S TIPS
• This dish is quite quick to cook over
the barbecue: don't be tempted to
partially precook any meat and then to
finish it off on the barbecue, as this will
encourage bacteria to grow.
• Remember that if you are not cooking
at home you will need to transport meat
in a cooler bag or box and take out what
you need as and when you need it to
avoid it becoming warm before it
is cooked.
• Always pack the cooler with the foods
you are going to cook first on the top and
close the cooler completely each time
you take an item of food out.

VARIATION
A selection of meat cuts can be used,
from sirloin to flank steak or chuck
steak. Sweetbreads, skewered chicken
hearts and kidneys are popular additions
to the Gaucho barbecue, as well as
chicken, lamb and pork. The star of the
show, however, will always be the beef.

*Energy 873kcal/3637kJ; Protein 84.4g; Carbohydrate 6.3g, of which sugars 0.9g; Fat 56.7g, of which saturates 23.8g;
Cholesterol 246mg; Calcium 46mg; Fibre 0.3g; Sodium 1333mg.*

SPICED BEEF SATAY

TENDER STRIPS OF STEAK THREADED ON SKEWERS AND SPICED WITH THE CHARACTERISTIC FLAVOURS OF INDONESIA ARE POPULAR WITH EVERYONE. SERVE THEM WITH A LIVELY DIPPING SAUCE.

3 Pour the marinade over the meat and spices in the bowl and toss well together. Cover the bowl with clear film (plastic wrap) and leave to marinate for at least 1 hour.

4 Meanwhile, soak some bamboo skewers in water to prevent them from burning while cooking. Prepare the barbecue. Thread five or six pieces of meat on to each skewer and sprinkle with salt. Cook over medium-hot coals, turning the skewers frequently and basting with the marinade, until the meat is tender.

5 Serve with cucumber chunks and wedges of lemon or lime for squeezing over the meat. Sambal kecap makes a traditional accompaniment.

MAKES SIX–EIGHT SKEWERS

INGREDIENTS
450g/1lb rump (round) steak, cut in
  1cm/½in strips
5ml/1 tsp coriander seeds, dry-fried
  and ground
2.5ml/½ tsp cumin seeds, dry-fried
  and ground
5ml/1 tsp tamarind pulp
1 small onion
2 garlic cloves
15ml/1 tbsp brown sugar
15ml/1 tbsp dark soy sauce
salt
To serve
  cucumber chunks
  lemon or lime wedges
  sambal kecap (see Cook's Tip)

1 Mix the meat and spices in a large non-metallic bowl. Soak the tamarind pulp in 75ml/3fl oz/⅓ cup water.

2 Strain the tamarind and reserve the juice. Put the onion, garlic, tamarind juice, sugar and soy sauce in a food processor and blend well.

COOK'S TIP
To make the *sambal kecap*, mix 1 fresh red chilli, seeded and finely chopped, 2 crushed garlic cloves and 60ml/4 tbsp dark soy sauce with 20ml/4 tsp lemon juice and 30ml/2 tbsp hot water in a bowl. Leave to stand for 30 minutes before serving.

Energy 117kcal/486kJ; Protein 17.1g; Carbohydrate 4.5g, of which sugars 3.3g; Fat 3.3g, of which saturates 1.2g; Cholesterol 45mg; Calcium 12mg; Fibre 0g; Sodium 225mg.

VEGETABLE-STUFFED BEEF ROLLS

THESE JAPANESE-STYLE BEEF ROLLS ARE VERY POPULAR FOR AL FRESCO MEALS. YOU COULD ROLL UP MANY OTHER VEGETABLES IN THE SLICED BEEF. PORK IS ALSO VERY GOOD COOKED THIS WAY.

SERVES FOUR

INGREDIENTS
  50g/2oz carrot
  50g/2oz green (bell) pepper
  bunch of spring onions (scallions)
  400g/14oz beef topside (pot roast),
    thinly sliced
  plain (all-purpose) flour, for dusting
  15ml/1 tbsp olive oil
  fresh parsley sprigs, to garnish
For the sauce
  30ml/2 tbsp sugar
  45ml/3 tbsp soy sauce
  45ml/3 tbsp mirin

1 Use a sharp knife to shred the carrot and green pepper into 4–5cm/1½–2in lengths. Wash and peel the outer skins from the spring onions, then halve them lengthways. Shred the spring onions diagonally into 4–5cm/1½–2in lengths.

2 The beef slices should be no more than 2mm/½in thick, and about 15cm/6in square. Top a slice of beef with strips of the carrot, green pepper and spring onion. Roll up quite tightly and dust lightly with flour. Repeat with the remaining beef and vegetables.

3 Secure the beef rolls with cocktail sticks (toothpicks), soaked in water to prevent them from burning, and cook on a medium barbecue or in a pan over a medium heat, for 10–15 minutes, turning frequently, until golden brown and thoroughly cooked.

4 Blend the ingredients for the sauce in a small pan and cook to dissolve the sugar and form a glaze. Halve the cooked rolls, cutting at a slant, and stand them on a plate with the sloping cut ends facing upwards. Dress with the sauce and garnish with fresh parsley.

Energy 258kcal/1079kJ; Protein 28.7g; Carbohydrate 9.8g, of which sugars 9.8g; Fat 11.7g, of which saturates 4.8g; Cholesterol 73mg; Calcium 20mg; Fibre 0.3g; Sodium 82mg.

BARBECUE ROAST BEEF

"MOPPING" IS BIG IN THE SOUTHWESTERN STATES OF THE USA, WHERE THE TECHNIQUE IS OFTEN USED TO KEEP LARGE PIECES OF MEAT MOIST AND SUCCULENT DURING LONG, SLOW COOKING. THE TECHNIQUE HAS BEEN ADAPTED FOR THIS RECIPE. ONCE SEARED, MOP THE MEAT CONSTANTLY.

ERVES FOUR

REDIENTS

Og/1¾lb beef fillet (tenderloin)
ml/2 tbsp bottled grated
eradish
2 tbsp olive oil
4fl oz/½ cup Chimay (see
Tip)
round black pepper

dry with kitchen paper
dish. Rub it all over
the horseradish and
the dish and leave
for about 2 hours

the meat with
barbecue. Mix
with the beer

3 Season the meat well. Position a lightly oiled grill rack over the coals to heat. Cook the beef over high heat for about 2 minutes on each side, so that the outside sears and acquires a good colour.

4 Set the spit turning over the coals. Dip a large basting brush in the horseradish and beer mixture and generously mop the meat all over with it. Continue to mop, as the meat turns, for a total grilling time of 11 minutes. Use all of the basting mixture.

COOK'S TIP
Chimay is a naturally brewed beer from Belgium, which could be substituted with any other good-quality beer you fancy. Non-alcoholic beers are also fine, or even soda water, if you want.

5 Rest the meat in a warm place under tented foil for about 10 minutes before slicing thickly. This dish is great served hot, with roasted vegetables, or left to go cold and eaten with thick slices of country-style bread and horseradish-flavoured mayonnaise.

Carbohydrate 0.8g, of which sugars 0.8g; Fat 24.1g, of which saturates 8.4g; Cholesterol 116mg; Calcium 12mg; Fibre 0g; Sodium 130mg.

NEW ORLEANS STEAK SALAD

THE NEW ORLEANS "POOR BOY" STARTED LIFE IN THE ITALIAN CREOLE COMMUNITY, AND WAS ORIGINALLY A SANDWICH FILLED WITH LEFTOVER SCRAPS OF BEEF. THIS SALAD, MADE WITH TENDER BEEF STEAK, IS A REALLY APPETIZING VARIATION ON THE SANDWICH.

SERVES FOUR

INGREDIENTS

4 sirloin or rump (round) steaks,
    about 175g/6oz each
1 escarole lettuce
1 bunch watercress
4 tomatoes, quartered
4 large gherkins, sliced
4 spring onions (scallions), sliced
4 canned artichoke hearts, halved
175g/6oz button (white) mushrooms,
    sliced
12 green olives
120ml/4fl oz French dressing
salt and ground black pepper

1 Season the steaks with plenty of black pepper and cook on a hot barbecue, or under a hot grill (broiler), for 4–6 minutes, turning once, until medium-rare. Cover and leave the steaks to rest in a warm place.

2 Combine the salad leaves with the remaining ingredients, and toss with the French dressing. Divide the salad among four plates. Slice each steak diagonally and arrange over the salad. Season with salt and pepper and serve.

Energy 573kcal/2379kJ; Protein 43.2g; Carbohydrate 6g, of which sugars 5.8g; Fat 35.1g, of which saturates 10.4g; Cholesterol 102mg; Calcium 105mg; Fibre 3.9g; Sodium 990mg.

VENISON CHOPS WITH ROMESCO SAUCE

ROMESCO IS THE CATALAN WORD FOR THE LOCAL ÑORA CHILLI, A MILD, DRIED CHILLI THAT LENDS A SPICY ROUNDNESS TO ONE OF SPAIN'S GREATEST SAUCES, FROM TARRAGONA. THE SAUCE ALSO CONTAINS GROUND TOASTED NUTS AND OFTEN ANOTHER FIERCER CHILLI.

SERVES FOUR

INGREDIENTS

    4 venison chops, cut 2cm/¾ in thick
      and about 175–200g/6–7oz each
    30ml/2 tbsp olive oil
    50g/2oz/¼ cup butter
For the romesco sauce
    3 ñora chillies
    1 hot dried chilli
    25g/1oz/¼ cup almonds
    150ml/¼ pint/⅔ cup olive oil
    1 slice stale bread, crusts removed
    3 garlic cloves, chopped
    3 tomatoes, peeled, seeded and
      roughly chopped
    60ml/4 tbsp sherry vinegar
    60ml/4 tbsp red wine vinegar
    salt and ground black pepper

COOK'S TIP
The juice of chillies can irritate cuts or the eyes if it touches them. Wear rubber gloves or rub olive oil over the fingers before handling them and scrub your hands thoroughly afterwards.

1 To make the romesco sauce, slit both types of chilli and remove the seeds, then leave the chillies to soak in warm water for about 30 minutes until soft. Drain the chillies, dry them on kitchen paper and chop finely.

2 Dry-fry the almonds in a frying pan over a medium heat, shaking the pan occasionally, until the nuts are toasted evenly. Transfer the nuts to a food processor or blender.

3 Add 45ml/3 tbsp of the oil to the frying pan and fry the bread slice until golden on both sides. Lift it out with a slotted spoon and drain on kitchen paper. Tear the bread and add to the food processor or blender. Fry the chopped garlic in the oil remaining in the pan.

COOK'S TIP
This classic sauce can be served hot, as here, with grilled meat or fish, or with pasta, or cold as a dip for vegetables.

4 Add the soaked chillies and tomatoes to the processor or blender. Tip in the garlic, with the flavoured olive oil from the pan, and blend the mixture to form a smooth paste.

5 With the motor running, gradually add the remaining olive oil and then the vinegars. When the sauce is smooth and well blended, scrape it into a bowl and season with salt and ground black pepper to taste. Cover with clear film (plastic wrap) and chill for 2 hours. Transfer to a small pan.

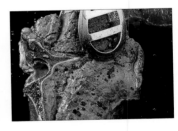

6 Prepare the barbecue. Position a lightly oiled grill rack over the hot coals. Melt the butter with the oil in a small pan on the grill rack and use this mixture to brush over the chops. Cook the chops for 5–6 minutes on each side until golden brown and cooked to your liking.

7 Meanwhile, heat the romesco sauce gently. If it is too thick, stir in a little boiling water. Serve the sauce with the chops, accompanied by vegetables or salad.

Energy 531kcal/2206kJ; Protein 30.3g; Carbohydrate 6g, of which sugars 2.9g; Fat 43.9g, of which saturates 11.8g; Cholesterol 89mg; Calcium 43mg; Fibre 1.5g; Sodium 185mg.

JUNIPER-SPICED VENISON CHOPS

THIS IS A DISH THAT WILL GO DOWN VERY WELL AT A SMALL BARBECUE SUPPER WITH SOME GOOD, FRUITY RED WINE. DEPENDING ON THE TYPE OF VENISON YOUR BUTCHER HAS AVAILABLE, THE CHOPS WILL VARY IN SIZE, SO YOU WILL NEED EITHER ONE OR TWO PER PERSON.

SERVES FOUR

INGREDIENTS
    4–8 venison chops
    250ml/8 fl oz/1 cup red wine
    2 medium red onions
    6 juniper berries, crushed
    1 cinnamon stick, crumbled
    1 dried bay leaf, crumbled
    thinly pared strip of orange rind
    olive oil, for brushing
    salt and ground black pepper

1 Place the venison chops in a large bowl and pour over the red wine. Using a sharp knife, cut the red onions in half crossways and add them to the bowl.

2 Add the juniper berries, cinnamon, bay leaf and orange rind. Toss well to coat evenly and then cover the bowl and leave to marinate for at least an hour, or overnight in the refrigerator.

COOK'S TIP
Tender farmed venison is widely available from supermarkets and good butchers, but if venison is difficult to find, beef steaks could be used instead.

3 Prepare the barbecue and arrange a lightly oiled grill rack over the coals. Drain the venison and onions and reserve the marinade. Brush the venison and onions generously with the olive oil and sprinkle with plenty of salt and ground black pepper.

4 Cook the venison and onions over medium-hot coals for 8–10 minutes on each side, turning once and basting regularly with the marinade. The venison should still be slightly pink inside, even when fully cooked, and the onions softened and browned.

Energy 248kcal/1047kJ; Protein 44.4g; Carbohydrate 0.1g, of which sugars 0.1g; Fat 7.2g, of which saturates 2g; Cholesterol 100mg; Calcium 12mg; Fibre 0g; Sodium 112mg.

HOME-MADE VENISON SAUSAGES

VENISON SAUSAGES HAVE AN EXCELLENT FLAVOUR, A MUCH LOWER FAT CONTENT THAN MOST SAUSAGES AND THEY'RE EASY TO MAKE IF YOU FORGET ABOUT SAUSAGE SKINS AND JUST SHAPE THE MIXTURE. GRIDDLED ONIONS AND TOMATOES AND BARBECUED MUSHROOMS GO VERY NICELY WITH THE SAUSAGES.

SERVES EIGHT

INGREDIENTS

900g/2lb/4 cups finely minced (ground) venison
450g/1lb/2 cups finely minced (ground) belly of pork
15ml/1 tbsp salt
10ml/2 tsp ground black pepper
1 garlic clove, crushed
5ml/1 tsp dried thyme
1 egg, beaten
plain (all-purpose) flour, for dusting
oil, for brushing
griddled onions and tomatoes, and barbecued field (portabello) mushrooms, to serve

1 Combine all the sausage ingredients, except the flour and oil, in a bowl. Take a small piece of the mixture and fry it in a little oil in a heavy frying pan, then taste to check the seasoning for the batch. Adjust if necessary.

2 Form the mixture into chipolata-size sausages using floured hands.

3 Prepare the barbecue. Position a lightly oiled grill rack over the hot coals. Brush the sausages with oil and cook over high heat for 10 minutes or until they are golden brown and cooked right through.

4 If you use a large pan, you'll be able to fry some onion rings alongside the sausages. At the same time, cook some mushrooms and halved tomatoes on a griddle to serve on the side.

COOK'S TIP
As these sausages are made without casings you may find them rather awkward to turn on the grill rack. A hinged wire basket is useful for cooking delicate items over the barbecue.

Per Sausage: Energy 156kcal/652kJ; Protein 15.3g; Carbohydrate 0g, of which sugars 0g; Fat 10.9g, of which saturates 3.9g; Cholesterol 54mg; Calcium 6mg; Fibre 0g; Sodium 377mg

KANGAROO WITH TAMARIND CHILLI SAUCE

SIMILAR TO VENISON IN FLAVOUR, KANGAROO MEAT IS AVAILABLE INTERNATIONALLY FROM SPECIALIST PRODUCERS. BUTTERED NOODLES AND A LIGHTLY DRESSED MIXED GREEN LEAF SALAD ARE GOOD ACCOMPANIMENTS FOR RICH, DENSE KANGAROO STEAKS IN A SIMPLE SPICY SAUCE.

SERVES FOUR

INGREDIENTS

    4 kangaroo steaks, each about
      175g/6oz
    parsley, to garnish
    buttered noodles and salad, to serve
For the sauce
    15ml/1 tbsp chilli sauce
    45ml/3 tbsp tamarind paste
    15ml/1 tbsp clear honey
    50g/2oz/¼ cup butter

COOK'S TIP

Tamarind paste is available from South-east Asian food stores, and you may also find it in some large supermarkets.

1 Prepare the barbecue. To make the sauce, mix together the chilli sauce, tamarind paste and clear honey in a small bowl. Melt the butter in a small pan over a low heat, then pour the butter into the bowl and blend into the sauce until it is smooth.

2 Brush the sauce liberally over the kangaroo steaks. Grill the steaks over hot coals for 3–5 minutes, then brush with the remaining sauce and turn them. Cook the steaks for a further 3–5 minutes, then serve with noodles and salad. Garnish with parsley.

Energy 301kcal/1263kJ; Protein 42.3g; Carbohydrate 5.8g, of which sugars 5.7g; Fat 12.2g, of which saturates 7g; Cholesterol 149mg; Calcium 13mg; Fibre 0.1g; Sodium 344mg.

THE VEGETARIAN
BARBECUE

Barbecuing vegetables gives them a delicious flavour and they can be combined with cheese, nuts, beans and tofu to make some exciting main courses that will appeal to everyone. The smoky flavours created by chargrilling really enhance vegetables, fruits and roots such as aubergines, squashes, peppers and asparagus, which can then be served with dips and sauces, such as a peanut satay sauce or a yogurt pesto. Halloumi cheese is a super ingredient for the vegetarian barbecue because it has a firm texture that does not melt in the same way as other cheeses and so is useful to cook as an accompaniment to a mélange of grilled vegetables. You can also make rolls or parcels from vegetables, such as sliced aubergines, and cook these on the barbecue, as well as filling vegetables with aromatic stuffings and then cooking them over the coals or inside foil packets.

With so many fantastic, flavourful combinations, it's easy to plan a vegetarian barbecue feast.

THAI VEGETABLE CAKES

*HERE, NUTTY-TASTING TEMPEH, WHICH IS MADE FROM SOYBEANS,
IS COMBINED WITH A FRAGRANT BLEND OF LEMON GRASS, FRESH
CORIANDER AND GINGER, AND FORMED INTO SMALL PATTIES
BEFORE BEING GRILLED. SERVE WITH THE DIPPING SAUCE,
ACCOMPANIED BY A SWEET SAKE OR RICE WINE.*

MAKES EIGHT

INGREDIENTS
    1 lemon grass stalk, outer leaves
      removed and inside chopped
    2 garlic cloves, chopped
    2 spring onions (scallions), chopped
    2 shallots, chopped
    2 chillies, seeded and chopped
    2.5cm/1in piece fresh root
      ginger, chopped
    60ml/4 tbsp chopped fresh coriander
      (cilantro), plus extra to garnish
    250g/9oz tempeh, thawed if
      frozen, sliced
    15ml/1 tbsp lime juice
    5ml/1 tsp sugar
    45ml/3 tbsp plain (all-purpose) flour
    1 egg, lightly beaten
    vegetable oil, for frying
    salt and ground black pepper
For the dipping sauce
    45ml/3 tbsp mirin
    45ml/3 tbsp white wine vinegar
    2 spring onions (scallions),
      thinly sliced
    15ml/1 tbsp sugar
    2 chillies, finely chopped
    30ml/2 tbsp chopped fresh
      coriander (cilantro)
    large pinch of salt

1 Prepare the barbecue. To make the
dipping sauce, mix all the ingredients
together in a small bowl and set aside.

2 Place the lemon grass, garlic, spring
onions, shallots, chillies, ginger and
coriander in a food processor or
blender and process to a coarse paste.
Add the tempeh, lime juice and sugar,
then process to combine.

3 Add the salt and pepper, flour and
egg. Process again until the mixture
forms a coarse, sticky paste. Position a
lightly oiled grill rack over the hot
coals, or heat an oiled frying pan.

4 Take one-eighth of the tempeh
mixture at a time and form into balls
with your hands – the mixture will be
quite sticky, so it may help to dampen
your palms. Gently flatten the balls.

5 Brush the tempeh cakes with oil.
Cook over high heat for 5–6 minutes,
turning once, until golden. Drain on
kitchen paper. Garnish and serve warm
with the dipping sauce.

COOK'S TIP
These make a good appetizer for a
dinner party and can be shared by
guests, perhaps with tempura
vegetables or Thai fish cakes, and a
variety of dips. Frying produces good
results, so they can be eaten at any
time, not just in barbecue season.

*Energy 119kcal/494kJ; Protein 4.5g; Carbohydrate 8.2g, of which sugars 3.6g; Fat 7.8g, of which saturates 1g; Cholesterol
24mg; Calcium 202mg; Fibre 1g; Sodium 15mg.*

RED BEAN AND MUSHROOM BURGERS

VEGETARIANS AND MEAT-EATERS ALIKE WILL ENJOY THESE HEALTHY, LOW-FAT VEGGIE BURGERS.
WITH SALAD, PITTA BREAD AND GREEK-STYLE YOGURT, THEY MAKE A SUBSTANTIAL MEAL. YOU MAY
FIND A HINGED WIRE BASKET USEFUL FOR COOKING THE BURGERS TO KEEP THEM IN SHAPE.

SERVES FOUR

INGREDIENTS

15ml/1 tbsp olive oil
1 small onion, finely chopped
1 garlic clove, crushed
5ml/1 tsp ground cumin
5ml/1 tsp ground coriander
2.5ml/½ tsp ground turmeric
115g/4oz/1½ cups finely
   chopped mushrooms
400g/14oz can red kidney beans
30ml/2 tbsp chopped fresh
   coriander (cilantro)
wholemeal (whole-wheat)
   flour (optional)
olive oil, for brushing
salt and ground black pepper
Greek (US strained plain) yogurt,
   to serve

1 Heat the olive oil in a frying pan and fry the onion and garlic over a medium heat, stirring, until softened. Add the spices and cook for a further minute, stirring continuously.

2 Add the mushrooms and cook, stirring, until softened and dry. Remove the pan from the heat and empty the contents into a large bowl.

3 Drain the red kidney beans thoroughly, place them in a bowl and mash them roughly with a fork.

4 Stir the kidney beans into the frying pan, with the fresh coriander, and mix thoroughly. Season the mixture well with plenty of salt and pepper. Prepare the barbecue. Position a lightly oiled grill rack over the hot coals.

5 Using floured hands, form the mixture into four flat burger shapes. If the mixture is too sticky to handle, mix a little wholemeal flour into it before shaping the burgers.

6 Lightly brush the burgers with olive oil and cook on a hot barbecue for 8–10 minutes, turning once, until golden brown. Serve with a spoonful of yogurt and a mixed salad, if you like.

COOK'S TIP
Bean burgers are not quite as firm as meat burgers, and will need careful handling on the barbecue to prevent them breaking up.

Energy 159kcal/666kJ; Protein 7.6g; Carbohydrate 19.1g, of which sugars 4.5g; Fat 6.3g, of which saturates 0.9g; Cholesterol 0mg; Calcium 77mg; Fibre 6.7g; Sodium 392mg.

VEGETABLE KEBABS WITH PEPPERCORN SAUCE

VEGETABLES INVARIABLY TASTE GOOD WHEN COOKED ON THE BARBECUE, AS THIS METHOD OF COOKING INTENSIFIES THEIR FLAVOUR. YOU CAN INCLUDE OTHER VEGETABLES IN THESE KEBABS, DEPENDING ON WHAT IS AVAILABLE AT THE TIME.

SERVES FOUR

INGREDIENTS
24 mushrooms
16 cherry tomatoes
16 large fresh basil leaves
2 courgettes (zucchini), cut into
   16 thick slices
16 large fresh mint leaves
1 large red (bell) pepper, cut into
   16 squares
To baste
120ml/4fl oz/½ cup melted butter
1 garlic clove, crushed
15ml/1 tbsp green peppercorns,
   crushed
salt
For the green peppercorn sauce
50g/2oz/¼ cup butter
45ml/3 tbsp brandy
250ml/8fl oz/1 cup double (heavy)
   cream
5ml/1 tsp green peppercorns,
   crushed

1 Soak eight wooden skewers in water to prevent them burning when placed on the barbecue. Thread a mixture of vegetables on to each skewer, placing the fresh basil leaves immediately next to the tomatoes, and wrapping the mint leaves around the courgette slices. Prepare the barbecue.

2 Mix the basting ingredients in a bowl and baste the kebabs thoroughly. Cook the skewers over medium-hot coals, turning and basting regularly until the vegetables are just cooked – this should take about 5–7 minutes.

3 While the kebabs are cooking, heat the butter for the green peppercorn sauce in a frying pan, then add the brandy and set light to it. When the flames have died down, stir in the cream and the crushed green peppercorns. Cook for 2 minutes at the side of the barbecue, stirring all the time. Serve the sauce with the barbecued kebabs.

Energy 580kcal/2391kJ; Protein 6.1g; Carbohydrate 8.3g, of which sugars 7.8g; Fat 55.5g, of which saturates 34.2g; Cholesterol 139mg; Calcium 76mg; Fibre 3.6g; Sodium 180mg.

CASSAVA AND VEGETABLE KEBABS

SO MANY VEGETABLES ARE SUITABLE FOR COOKING ON THE BARBECUE: THIS RECIPE INCLUDES AN ATTRACTIVE AND DELICIOUS ASSORTMENT OF AFRICAN VEGETABLES, MARINATED IN A SPICY GARLIC SAUCE. SERVE THE VEGETABLES ACCOMPANIED BY A CREAMY BEAN DIP, SUCH AS HUMMUS.

SERVES FOUR

INGREDIENTS
175g/6oz cassava
1 onion, cut into wedges
1 aubergine (eggplant), cut into bite-size pieces
1 courgette (zucchini), sliced
1 ripe plantain, sliced
½ red (bell) pepper and ½ green (bell) pepper, cut into squares
16 cherry tomatoes
rice or couscous, to serve
For the marinade
60ml/4 tbsp lemon juice
60ml/4 tbsp olive oil
45–60ml/3–4 tbsp soy sauce
15ml/1 tbsp tomato purée (paste)
1 green chilli, seeded and finely chopped
½ onion, grated
2 garlic cloves, crushed
5ml/1 tsp mixed (apple pie) spice
pinch of dried thyme

1 Soak eight wooden skewers in water for 30 minutes to stop them burning on the barbecue. Peel the cassava and cut the flesh into bite-size pieces. Place the pieces in a large bowl, cover with boiling water and leave to blanch for about 5 minutes. Drain well.

2 Place all the prepared vegetables, including the cassava, in a large mixing bowl and turn the mixture with your hands so that all the vegetables are evenly distributed.

3 Blend the marinade ingredients in a jug (pitcher) and pour over the vegetables. Cover the bowl with clear film (plastic wrap) and leave to marinate for 1–2 hours.

4 Prepare the barbecue. Position a lightly oiled grill rack over the hot coals. Thread the vegetables, with the cherry tomatoes, on to the skewers, making sure the different kinds are evenly distributed, and cook over high heat for about 15 minutes until tender and browned. Turn the skewers frequently and baste the vegetables occasionally with the marinade.

5 Meanwhile, pour the remaining marinade into a small pan and simmer on the grill rack for about 10 minutes to reduce. Strain the reduced marinade into a jug. Serve the kebabs on a bed of rice or couscous, with the sauce on the side.

Energy 167kcal/702kJ; Protein 3g; Carbohydrate 26.1g, of which sugars 7.6g; Fat 6.3g, of which saturates 1g; Cholesterol 0mg; Calcium 34mg; Fibre 3.3g; Sodium 7mg.

SWEET AND SOUR VEGETABLES WITH PANEER

THE FRESH INDIAN CHEESE USED IN THIS RECIPE, CALLED PANEER, IS OFTEN MADE AT HOME BUT CAN BE BOUGHT FROM ASIAN STORES, OR YOU CAN USE TOFU IN ITS PLACE. PANEER HAS A GOOD FIRM TEXTURE AND COOKS VERY WELL ON THE BARBECUE.

<u>SERVES FOUR</u>

INGREDIENTS
    1 green (bell) pepper, cut into
      squares
    1 yellow (bell) pepper, cut into
      squares
    8 cherry, or 4 medium, tomatoes
    8 cauliflower florets
    8 pineapple chunks, fresh or canned
      in juice
    8 cubes paneer
    plain boiled rice, to serve
For the seasoned oil
    15ml/1 tbsp soya oil
    30ml/2 tbsp lemon juice
    5ml/1 tsp salt
    5ml/1 tsp ground black pepper
    15ml/1 tbsp clear honey
    30ml/2 tbsp chilli sauce

1 Thread the prepared vegetables, pineapple and paneer cubes on to four skewers, alternating the ingredients. Prepare the barbecue. Arrange a lightly oiled grill rack over the hot coals.

2 Pour all the ingredients for the seasoned oil into a mixing bowl and whisk together. If the mixture seems a little too thick for brushing, add a small amount of water to loosen it.

3 Brush the vegetables with the seasoned oil and cook over hot coals for 10 minutes, turning the skewers often and basting with the seasoned oil. Serve on a bed of plain boiled rice.

Energy 137kcal/576kJ; Protein 6g; Carbohydrate 18.7g, of which sugars 18.2g; Fat 4.7g, of which saturates 1.1g; Cholesterol 3mg; Calcium 58mg; Fibre 3.9g; Sodium 75mg.

SUMMER VEGETABLE KEBABS

THERE'S NOTHING NEW ABOUT THREADING VEGETABLE CHUNKS ON SKEWERS, BUT THIS METHOD OF TOSSING THEM IN A SPICY OIL AND LEMON JUICE MARINADE MAKES ALL THE DIFFERENCE. SERVE THEM WITH THE HOT AND CREAMY DIP AND YOU'LL HAVE VEGETARIAN GUESTS ASKING FOR MORE.

SERVES FOUR

INGREDIENTS

   2 aubergines (eggplants), part peeled
     and cut into chunks
   2 courgettes (zucchini), cut
     into chunks
   2–3 red or green (bell) peppers,
     cut into chunks
   12–16 cherry tomatoes
   4 small red onions, quartered
   60ml/4 tbsp olive oil
   juice of ½ lemon
   1 garlic clove, crushed
   5ml/1 tsp ground coriander
   5ml/1 tsp ground cinnamon
   10ml/2 tsp clear honey
   5ml/1 tsp salt
For the harissa and yogurt dip
   450g/1lb/2 cups Greek (US strained
     plain) yogurt
   30–60ml/2–4 tbsp harissa
   small bunch of fresh coriander
     (cilantro), finely chopped
   small bunch of mint, finely chopped
   salt and ground black pepper

1 Prepare the barbecue. Position a lightly oiled grill rack over the hot coals. Put all the vegetables in a bowl. Mix together the olive oil, lemon juice, garlic, ground coriander, cinnamon, honey and salt, and pour over the vegetables.

2 Using your hands, turn the vegetables gently in the marinade, then thread them on to metal skewers. Cook the kebabs over high heat, turning them occasionally, until the vegetables are nicely browned all over.

3 Meanwhile, make the dip. Put the yogurt in a bowl and beat in the harissa, making it as fiery in taste as you like by adding more harissa. Add most of the chopped coriander and mint, reserving a little to garnish, and season well with salt and pepper.

4 While they are still hot, slide the vegetables off the skewers and dip them into the yogurt dip before eating. Garnish with the reserved herbs.

COOK'S TIP
Make sure you cut the aubergines, courgettes and peppers into fairly even-size chunks, so that they will all cook at the same rate.

TOFU AND PEPPER KEBABS

A CRUNCHY COATING OF GROUND, DRY-ROASTED PEANUTS PRESSED ON TO CUBED TOFU PROVIDES PLENTY OF ADDITIONAL TEXTURE AND COLOUR. ALONG WITH THE CHARGRILLED, SUCCULENT CHUNKS OF RED AND GREEN PEPPERS, THESE SIMPLE ADDITIONS GIVE THE KEBABS A SUBTLE FLAVOUR.

SERVES TWO

INGREDIENTS
    250g/9oz firm tofu
    50g/2oz/½ cup dry-roasted peanuts
    45ml/3 tbsp olive oil
    2 red and 2 green (bell) peppers
    60ml/4 tbsp sweet chilli
       dipping sauce
    salt and ground black pepper

1 Soak four long wooden skewers in water for 30 minutes. Pat the tofu dry on kitchen paper and then cut it into small cubes.

2 Grind the peanuts coarsely in a blender or food processor and transfer them to a plate. Put the oil in a bowl and add the tofu cubes. Toss in the oil until well coated. Lift the tofu cubes out of the oil and turn them in the ground nuts to coat.

3 Prepare the barbecue. When the flames have died down position a lightly oiled grill rack over the hot coals. Halve and seed the peppers, and cut them into large chunks.

4 Brush the chunks of pepper with the oil remaining in the bowl and thread them on to the skewers, alternating with the coated tofu cubes. Season with salt and pepper. Place the skewers on the grill rack.

5 Cook the kebabs over medium heat, turning frequently, for 10–12 minutes, or until the peppers and peanuts are beginning to brown. Serve the kebabs immediately with the dipping sauce.

COOK'S TIP
Chilli sauces vary from fairly mild to searingly hot, while some are quite sweet. The hot ones go particularly well with these kebabs.

Energy 516kcal/2143kJ; Protein 20.3g; Carbohydrate 30.2g, of which sugars 26.8g; Fat 35.6g, of which saturates 5.6g; Cholesterol 0mg; Calcium 681mg; Fibre 7.4g; Sodium 461mg.

TOFU SATAY

SMOKED MARINATED TOFU IS GRILLED WITH PEPPERS AND SERVED WITH A PEANUT SAUCE. TOFU READILY TAKES ON FLAVOURS, SO YOU COULD ALSO SPREAD SOME MOISTENED HERBS OVER THE COALS.

SERVES FOUR TO SIX

INGREDIENTS
   2 x 200g/7oz packs smoked tofu
   45ml/3 tbsp light soy sauce
   10ml/2 tsp sesame oil
   1 garlic clove, crushed
   1 yellow and 1 red (bell) pepper,
     cut into squares
   8–12 fresh bay leaves
   sunflower oil, for brushing
For the peanut sauce
   2 spring onions (scallions),
     finely chopped
   2 garlic cloves, crushed
   good pinch of chilli powder, or a few
     drops of hot chilli sauce
   5ml/1 tsp sugar
   15ml/1 tbsp white wine vinegar
   30ml/2 tbsp light soy sauce
   45ml/3 tbsp crunchy peanut butter

1 Soak 8–12 satay sticks in water for 30 minutes to prevent them burning on the barbecue. Cut the tofu into bite-size cubes and place them in a large bowl.

2 Add the soy sauce, sesame oil and crushed garlic to the tofu and mix well. Cover the bowl with clear film (plastic wrap) and leave the tofu to marinate for at least 20 minutes.

3 Beat all the peanut sauce ingredients together in a large bowl, using a wooden spoon, until well blended. Avoid using a food processor for this, as the texture should be slightly chunky. Prepare the barbecue. Position a lightly oiled grill rack over the hot coals.

4 Drain the tofu and thread the cubes on to the satay sticks, alternating the tofu with the pepper squares and bay leaves. (Larger bay leaves may need to be halved before threading.)

5 Brush the tofu and peppers with sunflower oil and cook over high heat, turning the sticks occasionally, until the tofu and peppers are browned and crisp. Serve hot with the peanut sauce.

COOK'S TIP
If you can only find plain tofu, leave it to marinate for 30 minutes to 1 hour for the best flavour.

VARIATION
Add mushrooms, cherry tomatoes and onion segments to the skewers if you like.

Energy 143kcal/593kJ; Protein 7.8g; Carbohydrate 6.2g, of which sugars 5.2g; Fat 9.8g, of which saturates 1.7g; Cholesterol 0mg; Calcium 350mg; Fibre 1.4g; Sodium 210mg.

PEANUT AND TOFU CUTLETS

THESE DELICIOUS PATTIES MAKE A FILLING AND SATISFYING MIDWEEK MEAL SERVED WITH LIGHTLY STEAMED GREEN VEGETABLES OR A CRISP SALAD, AND A TANGY SALSA OR KETCHUP.

SERVES FOUR

INGREDIENTS

90g/3½oz/½ cup brown rice
15ml/1 tbsp vegetable oil
1 onion, finely chopped
1 garlic clove, crushed
200g/7oz/1¾ cups peanuts
small bunch of fresh coriander
  (cilantro) or parsley, chopped
  (optional)
250g/9oz firm tofu, drained
  and crumbled
30ml/2 tbsp soy sauce

VARIATIONS
The herbs and nuts in this mixture can be varied if you like. Try the following combinations:
• Walnuts with rosemary or sage
• Cashew nuts with coriander (cilantro) or parsley
• Hazelnuts with parsley, thyme or sage.

1 Cook the rice according to the instructions on the packet until tender, then drain. Heat the vegetable oil in a large, heavy frying pan and cook the onion and garlic over a low heat, stirring occasionally, for about 5 minutes, until softened and golden.

2 Meanwhile, spread out the peanuts on a baking sheet and toast under a hot grill (broiler) for a few minutes, until browned. Place the peanuts, chopped onion, garlic, rice, tofu, coriander or parsley, if using, and soy sauce in a blender or food processor and process until the mixture comes together in a thick paste.

3 Divide the paste into eight equal-size mounds and form each mound into a cutlet shape or square. Prepare the barbecue. When the flames have died down position a lightly oiled grill rack over the hot coals.

4 Grill the cutlets over medium-hot coals for 5–10 minutes on each side, until golden brown and heated through. Serve immediately.

5 Alternatively, heat 30ml/2tbsp olive oil in a frying pan and shallow fry the cutlets, in two batches if necessary. Remove the cutlets from the pan with a metal spatula and drain on kitchen paper. Keep the first batch warm while you cook the remaining cutlets, then serve immediately.

Energy 495kcal/2059kJ; Protein 20.2g; Carbohydrate 27.1g, of which sugars 5.3g; Fat 34.7g, of which saturates 5.9g; Cholesterol 0mg; Calcium 381mg; Fibre 4.4g; Sodium 543mg.

VEGETABLE TOFU BURGERS

THESE SOFT GOLDEN PATTIES ARE STUFFED FULL OF DELICIOUS VEGETABLES. THEY ARE QUICK AND EASY TO MAKE AND POPULAR WITH CHILDREN. SERVE IN SESAME SEED BAPS WITH SALAD AND KETCHUP.

SERVES FOUR

INGREDIENTS
    4 potatoes, peeled and cubed
    250g/9oz frozen mixed vegetables,
        such as corn, green beans,
        (bell) peppers
    45ml/3 tbsp vegetable oil
    2 leeks, coarsely chopped
    1 garlic clove, crushed
    250g/9oz firm tofu, drained
        and crumbled
    30ml/2 tbsp soy sauce
    15ml/1 tbsp tomato purée (paste)
    115g/4oz/2 cups fresh
        breadcrumbs
    small bunch of fresh coriander
        (cilantro) or parsley (optional)
    sea salt and ground black pepper

1 Cook the potatoes in salted, boiling water for 10–12 minutes, until tender, then drain. Cook the frozen vegetables in a separate pan of salted, boiling water for 5 minutes, or until tender, then drain well.

2 Meanwhile, heat 15ml/1 tbsp of the oil in a large frying pan. Add the leeks and garlic and cook over a low heat, stirring occasionally, for about 5 minutes, until softened and golden.

3 Prepare the barbecue. Mash the potatoes, then add the vegetables and all the other ingredients except the oil but including the leeks and garlic. Season to taste, then mix well and divide into eight equal-size mounds.

4 Shape each mound into a burger and grill over a low heat for 4–5 minutes on each side, until golden brown.

COOK'S TIP
To preserve their vitamins, cook the potatoes whole for 20 minutes, then peel.

MARRAKESH PIZZA

IN MOROCCO, COOKS TEND TO PLACE FLAVOURINGS INSIDE RATHER THAN ON TOP OF THE DOUGH, SO THAT THE FLAVOURS PERMEATE RIGHT THROUGH. THE RESULT IS SURPRISING — AND QUITE DELICIOUS.

MAKES FOUR

INGREDIENTS
  5ml/1 tsp sugar
  10ml/2 tsp dried yeast
  450g/1lb/4 cups strong white
    bread flour
  10ml/2 tsp salt
  melted butter, for brushing
  rocket (arugula) salad and olives,
    to serve
For the filling
  1 small onion, very finely chopped
  2 tomatoes, skinned, seeded
    and chopped
  25ml/1½ tbsp chopped fresh
    parsley
  25ml/1½ tbsp chopped fresh
    coriander (cilantro)
  5ml/1 tsp paprika
  5ml/1 tsp ground cumin
  50g/2oz/⅓ cup shredded vegetable
    suet (chilled, grated shortening)
  40g/1½oz Cheddar cheese, grated

1 First prepare the yeast. Place 150ml/¼ pint/⅔ cup warm water in a small bowl, stir in the sugar and then sprinkle with the yeast. Stir once or twice, then set the bowl aside in a warm place for about 10 minutes until the yeast mixture is frothy.

2 Meanwhile, make the filling for the pizza. Mix together the onion, tomatoes, chopped parsley, chopped coriander, paprika, cumin, suet and cheese, then season with salt and set aside.

3 In a large bowl, mix together the flour and 10ml/2 tsp salt. Add the yeast mixture and enough warm water to make a fairly soft dough (about 250ml/8fl oz/1 cup). Knead the mixture into a ball and then knead on a floured work surface for 10–12 minutes until the dough is firm and elastic.

4 Divide the dough into four pieces and roll each into a rectangle, measuring 20 x 30cm/8 x 12in. Spread the filling down the centre of each rectangle, then fold into three, to make a rectangle measuring 20 x 10cm/8 x 4in.

COOK'S TIP
The pizzas can be cooked on a lightly oiled grill rack over medium coals if you prefer.

5 Roll out the dough again, until it is the same size as before and again fold into three to make a smaller rectangle. (The filling will be squeezed out in places, but don't worry – just push it back inside the dough.)

6 Place the pizzas on a buttered baking sheet, cover with oiled clear film (plastic wrap) and leave in a warm place for about 1 hour until slightly risen. Prepare the barbecue.

7 Heat a griddle and brush with butter. Prick the pizzas with a fork five or six times on both sides and then fry for about 8 minutes on each side, until the dough is crisp and golden. Serve the pizzas immediately, with a little melted butter if you like, and accompanied by rocket salad and black olives.

Energy 548Kcal/2313kJ; Protein 14.2g; Carbohydrate 92.7g, of which sugars 5.3g; Fat 16g, of which saturates 8g; Cholesterol 11mg; Calcium 259mg; Fibre 4.8g; Sodium 1063mg.

ROASTED VEGETABLE QUESADILLAS

THIS RECIPE IS A WONDERFUL EXAMPLE OF HOW THE GRIDDLE AND GRILL RACK ON A BARBECUE CAN BE USED SIMULTANEOUSLY TO COPE WITH A RANGE OF INGREDIENTS. PLACE A LONG GRIDDLE ON ONE SIDE OF THE GRILL RACK ON WHICH TO COOK THE ONIONS AND PEPPERS, AND THEN THE TORTILLAS; MEANWHILE, THE AUBERGINES CAN BE COOKED ON THE GRILL RACK ITSELF.

SERVES SIX TO EIGHT

INGREDIENTS
1 yellow and 1 orange (bell) pepper,
  each quartered and seeded
2 red (bell) peppers, quartered
  and seeded
2 red onions, cut into wedges with
  root intact
8 long baby aubergines (eggplants),
  total weight about 175g/6oz,
  halved lengthways
30ml/2 tbsp olive oil
400g/14oz mozzarella
2 fresh green chillies, seeded and
  sliced into rounds
15ml/1 tbsp Mexican tomato sauce
8 corn or wheat flour tortillas
handful of fresh basil leaves
salt and ground black pepper

1 Prepare the barbecue. Position a lightly oiled grill rack over the hot coals. Heat a griddle on the grill rack.

COOK'S TIPS
• The quesadillas can be cut into wedges and eaten as soon as they come off the griddle, or the batches can be wrapped in foil to keep warm while the rest are cooked.
• When cooking for vegetarians as well as non-vegetarians, always remember to keep one side of the barbecue for cooking the vegetarian dishes only so that they do not come in contact with meat.

2 Toss the peppers, onions and aubergines in the oil on a large baking tray. Place the peppers, skin-side down, on the griddle or directly on the grill rack over medium-high heat and cook until seared and browned underneath. If the food starts to char, remove the griddle until the coals cool down. Put the peppers under an upturned bowl and set aside to cool slightly so that the skins will loosen.

3 Grill the onions and aubergines until they have softened slightly and are branded with brown grill marks, then set them aside. Rub the skins off the peppers with your fingers, cut each piece of pepper in half and add to the other vegetables.

4 Cut the mozzarella into 20 slices. Place them, along with the roasted vegetables, in a large bowl and add the chillies and tomato sauce. Stir well to mix, and season with salt and pepper to taste. Place the griddle over a medium heat and cook all the tortillas on one side only.

5 Lay a tortilla on the griddle, cooked-side up, and pile about a quarter of the vegetable mixture into the centre of the tortilla. Scatter over some basil leaves. When the tortilla browns underneath, put another tortilla on top, cooked side down. Carefully turn the quesadilla over using a wide pizza server with a tubular handle and continue to cook until the underside has browned and the cheese just starts to melt. Remove from the pan with the pizza server and either serve immediately or wrap in foil to keep warm while you cook the remaining three quesadillas.

VARIATION
Thinly sliced courgettes (zucchini) are also delicious when griddled and can be added to the mixture here or used instead of the aubergines.

GRILLED GOATS' CHEESE PIZZA

A PIZZA WITH A THIN CRUST CAN BE COOKED ON THE BARBECUE, AND THIS METHOD PRODUCES A DELICIOUS, CRISPY AND GOLDEN BASE. A FINE WIRE MESH RACK IS USEFUL TO KEEP THE BASE FLAT — ROLL OUT THE DOUGH TO SUIT THE SIZE OF THE RACK.

SERVES FOUR

INGREDIENTS

150g/5oz packet pizza-base mix
    or home-made pizza dough (see
    Cook's Tip)
olive oil, for brushing
150ml/¼ pint/⅔ cup passata
30ml/2 tbsp red pesto
1 small red onion, thinly sliced
8 cherry tomatoes, halved
115g/4oz firm goats' cheese,
    thinly sliced
1 handful shredded fresh
    basil leaves
salt and ground black pepper

1 Prepare the barbecue. Position a lightly oiled grill rack over the hot coals. Make up the dough according to the directions on the packet, and roll out a 25cm/10in round on a floured surface.

2 Brush the dough with olive oil and place, oiled side down, on the rack over medium heat. Cook for 6–8 minutes until firm and golden underneath. Brush the top with oil and turn the pizza over.

3 Mix together the passata and red pesto, and quickly spread over the cooked side of the pizza, to within about 1cm/½in of the edge. Arrange the onion, tomatoes and cheese on top, and sprinkle with salt and pepper. Cook the pizza for 10 minutes more, until golden brown and crisp. Sprinkle with fresh basil and serve.

COOK'S TIP
For home-made pizza dough, sift 175g/6oz/1½ cups strong white bread flour and 1.5ml/¼ tsp salt in a bowl. Stir in 5ml/1 tsp easy-blend (rapid-rise) dried yeast. Pour in about 120ml/4fl oz/½ cup lukewarm water and 15ml/1 tbsp olive oil. Mix to form a dough. Knead until smooth. Place in a greased bowl, cover and leave to rise for 1 hour. Knock back (punch down) the dough and use as required.

Energy 338kcal/1420kJ; Protein 11g; Carbohydrate 46g, of which sugars 5g; Fat 13.5g, of which saturates 3.5g; Cholesterol 13mg; Calcium 218mg; Fibre 1.9g; Sodium 327mg.

POTATO AND CHEESE POLPETTES

THESE LITTLE MORSELS OF POTATO AND GREEK FETA CHEESE, FLAVOURED WITH DILL AND LEMON JUICE, ARE EXCELLENT WHEN GRILLED ON THE BARBECUE. THEY CAN BE ACCOMPANIED WITH A TOMATO SAUCE, IF YOU LIKE, OR A NICELY DRESSED SALAD OF TOMATOES, SALAD LEAVES AND ONIONS.

SERVES FOUR

INGREDIENTS
    500g/1¼lb potatoes
    115g/4oz feta cheese
    4 spring onions (scallions),
        chopped
    45ml/3 tbsp chopped fresh dill
    1 egg, beaten
    15ml/1 tbsp lemon juice
    15ml/1 tbsp olive oil
    salt and ground black pepper

1 Boil the potatoes in their skins in salted water until soft. Drain, then peel while still warm. Place the cooked potatotes in a bowl and mash them.

2 Crumble the feta cheese into the mashed potatoes and add the spring onions, dill, egg and lemon juice. Season the mixture with pepper and a little salt. Stir well, then cover and chill until firm. Prepare the barbecue.

3 Divide the mixture into walnut-size balls, then flatten them slightly. Brush lightly with olive oil. Position a lightly oiled grill rack over the hot coals. Cook the polpettes over medium heat, turning once, until golden. Serve immediately.

Energy 230kcal/960kJ; Protein 8.4g; Carbohydrate 20.9g, of which sugars 2.3g; Fat 13.1g, of which saturates 5.3g; Cholesterol 68mg; Calcium 122mg; Fibre 1.4g; Sodium 446mg.

ROASTED RED PEPPERS WITH COUSCOUS

COUSCOUS MAKES A GOOD BASIS FOR A STUFFING, AND IN THIS RECIPE IT IS STUDDED WITH RAISINS AND FLAVOURED WITH FRESH MINT. CHARRED PEPPERS MAKE THE COMBINATION OF FLAVOURS TRULY SPECIAL AND THE PEPPERS ARE SIMPLE TO COOK IN THEIR FOIL PARCELS.

SERVES FOUR

INGREDIENTS
  6 (bell) peppers
  25g/1oz/2 tbsp butter
  1 onion, finely chopped
  5ml/1 tsp olive oil
  2.5ml/½ tsp salt
  175g/6oz/1 cup couscous
  25g/1oz/2 tbsp raisins
  30ml/2 tbsp chopped fresh mint
  1 egg yolk
  salt and ground black pepper
  mint leaves, to garnish

1 Carefully slit each pepper with a sharp knife and remove the core and seeds. Melt the butter in a small pan and add the chopped onion. Cook until soft but not browned.

2 To cook the couscous, bring 250ml/8fl oz/1 cup water to the boil. Add the oil and salt, then remove from the heat and add the couscous. Stir and leave to stand, covered, for 5 minutes. Stir in the onion, raisins and mint. Season well and stir in the egg yolk. Prepare the barbecue. Position a grill rack over the hot coals.

3 Use a teaspoon to fill the peppers with the couscous mixture to about three-quarters full (the couscous will swell while cooking). Wrap each pepper in a piece of oiled baking foil.

4 Cook over medium heat for 20 minutes, or until tender. Serve hot or cold, garnished with fresh mint leaves.

Energy 262kcal/1094kJ; Protein 5.8g; Carbohydrate 42.4g, of which sugars 18.9g; Fat 8.7g, of which saturates 4g; Cholesterol 64mg; Calcium 40mg; Fibre 3.9g; Sodium 53mg.

MOROCCAN-STYLE CHARGRILLED VEGETABLES

CHARGRILLED VEGETABLES ARE GIVEN EXTRA FLAVOUR BY ADDING GARLIC, GINGER, ROSEMARY AND HONEY, AND TASTE DELICIOUS WITH COUSCOUS. YOGURT AND HARISSA GO VERY WELL WITH THE DISH. SERVE WITH A SALAD OF MOZZARELLA TOSSED WITH DRESSED SALAD LEAVES.

SERVES SIX

INGREDIENTS
75ml/5 tbsp olive oil
6 garlic cloves, crushed
25g/1oz fresh root ginger, grated
a few large fresh rosemary sprigs
10ml/2 tsp clear honey
3 red onions, peeled and quartered
2–3 courgettes (zucchini), halved
  lengthways and cut into 2–3 pieces
2–3 red, green or yellow (bell)
  peppers, seeded and quartered
2 aubergines (eggplants), cut into
  6–8 long segments
2–3 leeks, cut into long strips
2–3 sweet potatoes, peeled,
  halved lengthways and cut
  into long strips
4–6 tomatoes, quartered
salt and ground black pepper
natural (plain) yogurt and harissa,
  to serve
For the couscous
500g/1¼lb/2¾ cups couscous
5ml/1 tsp salt
600ml/1 pint/2½ cups warm water
45ml/3 tbsp sunflower oil
about 25g/1oz/2 tbsp butter, diced

1 Preheat the oven to 200°C/400°F/
Gas 6. Put the couscous in a bowl. Stir
the salt into the water, then pour it over
the couscous, stirring to make sure it is
absorbed evenly. Leave to stand for 10
minutes for the couscous to plump up
then, using your fingers, rub the
sunflower oil into the grains to air them
and break up any lumps. Tip the
couscous into an ovenproof dish,
arrange the butter over the top, cover
with foil and heat in the oven for about
20 minutes.

2 Meanwhile, prepare the barbecue.
Position a lightly oiled grill rack over
the hot coals and heat a griddle on the
grill rack.

3 Pour the oil into a large baking tray
and add the garlic, ginger, rosemary
and honey. Season with salt and
pepper. Toss the vegetables in the
flavoured oil to coat evenly.

4 Cook the larger pieces of vegetables
directly on the grill rack and the smaller
pieces, such as the tomatoes and
onions, on the griddle, brushing with oil
as required. As the vegetables cook,
transfer them to a dish and keep warm.

5 To serve, use your fingers to work the
melted butter into the grains of
couscous and fluff it up, then pile it on
a large dish and shape into a mound
with a little pit at the top. Spoon some
vegetables into the pit and arrange the
rest around the dish. Serve immediately
with yogurt and harissa.

COOK'S TIP
Harissa, the fiery red paste used in the
cuisines of Tunisia, Algeria and Morocco,
is made from chillies, olive oil and garlic.
The chillies are often smoked, and other
flavourings include coriander and cumin.

Energy 337kcal/1416kJ; Protein 11.5g; Carbohydrate 43.5g, of which sugars 7.1g; Fat 14.2g, of which saturates 5.9g; Cholesterol 23mg; Calcium 206mg; Fibre 5.3g; Sodium 613mg.

STUFFED TOMATOES
AND PEPPERS

*COLOURFUL PEPPERS AND TOMATOES MAKE PERFECT CONTAINERS
FOR MEAT AND VEGETABLE STUFFINGS. THE BARBECUED FLAVOURS
IN THIS DISH ARE SIMPLY SUPERB.*

SERVES FOUR

INGREDIENTS

2 large ripe tomatoes
1 green (bell) pepper
1 yellow or orange (bell) pepper
60ml/4 tbsp olive oil, plus extra
　for sprinkling
2 onions, chopped
2 garlic cloves, crushed
50g/2oz/½ cup blanched
　almonds, chopped
75g/3oz/scant ½ cup long grain rice,
　boiled and drained
30ml/2 tbsp fresh mint,
　roughly chopped
30ml/2 tbsp fresh parsley,
　roughly chopped
25g/1oz/2 tbsp sultanas
　(golden raisins)
45ml/3 tbsp ground almonds
salt and ground black pepper
chopped mixed fresh herbs,
　to garnish

2 Prepare the barbecue. Position a
lightly oiled grill rack over the hot coals.
Halve the peppers, leaving the stalks
intact. Scoop out the seeds. Brush the
peppers with 15ml/1 tbsp olive oil and
cook over medium coals for 10 minutes,
cut side down. Place the peppers and
tomatoes on a rack, cut sides up, and
season well with salt and pepper.

3 Fry the onions in the remaining olive
oil for 5 minutes. Add the crushed
garlic and chopped almonds to the pan
and fry for a further minute.

1 Cut the tomatoes in half and scoop
out the pulp and seeds, using a
teaspoon. Leave the tomatoes to drain
on kitchen paper, with the cut sides
facing down. Roughly chop the tomato
pulp and set it aside.

COOK'S TIP
When buying the vegetables for this dish,
look for even-sized peppers of rounded,
regular shape, so that they will be easy
to divide neatly in half.

4 Remove the pan from the heat and
stir in the cooked rice, chopped tomato
flesh, mint, parsley and sultanas.
Season well with salt and pepper and
spoon the mixture into the tomatoes
and peppers.

5 Scatter the ground almonds over the
top and sprinkle with a little extra olive
oil. Cook on a medium barbecue for
about 15 minutes. Garnish with fresh
herbs and serve immediately.

*Energy 234kcal/981kJ; Protein 5.7g; Carbohydrate 32.5g, of which sugars 14.5g; Fat 9.9g, of which saturates 1.2g;
Cholesterol 0mg; Calcium 71mg; Fibre 3.6g; Sodium 14mg.*

LOOFAH AND AUBERGINE RATATOUILLE

LOOFAHS ARE GOURDS WITH SPONGY, CREAMY-WHITE FLESH. THE FRUITS BECOME FIBROUS AS THEY MATURE BUT ARE EDIBLE WHEN YOUNG. LIKE AUBERGINE, THEIR FLAVOUR IS INTENSIFIED BY ROASTING. COOKING THE VEGETABLES IN A PAN OVER THE BARBECUE WILL RETAIN THEIR JUICES.

SERVES FOUR

INGREDIENTS

1 large or 2 medium aubergines
  (eggplants)
450g/1lb young loofahs
  (sponge gourds)
1 large red (bell) pepper, cut into
  large chunks
225g/8oz cherry tomatoes
225g/8oz shallots
10ml/2 tsp ground coriander
60ml/4 tbsp olive oil
2 garlic cloves, finely chopped
a few fresh coriander (cilantro) sprigs
salt and ground black pepper

1 Cut the aubergines into thick chunks and sprinkle the pieces with salt to draw out the bitter juices. Leave to drain for about 45 minutes, then rinse under cold running water and pat dry with kitchen paper. Prepare the barbecue.

2 Slice the loofahs into 2cm/¾in pieces. Place them with the aubergines, pepper pieces, cherry tomatoes and shallots, in a roasting pan large enough to take all the vegetables in a single layer.

COOK'S TIP
Edible loofahs are harvested while immature and resemble courgettes (zucchini). Buy them in Asian markets.

3 Sprinkle the vegetables with the ground coriander and olive oil. Scatter the chopped garlic and fresh coriander leaves on top and season to taste.

4 Cook on the barbecue for about 25 minutes, stirring the vegetables occasionally, until the loofah is golden and the peppers are beginning to char. As an alternative, you could thread the vegetables on skewers and cook them under a hot grill (broiler).

COOK'S TIP
This is a great recipe to adapt if you have a late-summer glut of homegrown vegetables such as marrows and onions.

Energy 194kcal/806kJ; Protein 3.9g; Carbohydrate 14.6g, of which sugars 13.2g; Fat 13.7g, of which saturates 2.1g; Cholesterol 0mg; Calcium 49mg; Fibre 4.7g; Sodium 19mg.

BAKED STUFFED COURGETTES

THE TANGY GOATS' CHEESE STUFFING CONTRASTS WELL WITH THE VERY DELICATE FLAVOUR OF THE COURGETTES IN THIS RECIPE. WRAP THE COURGETTES AND BAKE THEM IN THE EMBERS OF THE FIRE. TRY TO USE SMALL, YOUNG AND FIRM COURGETTES.

SERVES FOUR

INGREDIENTS

   8 small courgettes (zucchini), about
     450g/1lb total weight
   15ml/1 tbsp olive oil, plus extra
     for brushing
   75–115g/3–4oz goats' cheese,
     cut into thin strips
   a few sprigs of fresh mint, finely
     chopped, plus extra to garnish
   ground black pepper

1 Cut eight pieces of heavy-duty foil, each large enough to encase one courgette, and lightly brush each piece with olive oil. Trim the courgettes and cut a thin slit along the length of each.

2 Insert thin slices of goats' cheese in the slits to fill the courgettes. Add a little chopped mint and sprinkle over the oil and black pepper.

COOK'S TIP

No salt is included in this recipe as the goats' cheese will provide a salty tang, but add a sprinkling of salt if you are using a very young, bland cheese.

3 Wrap each courgette in foil, place in the embers of the fire and bake for about 25 minutes, until tender.

VARIATIONS

• While almost any cheese can be used in this way, mild cheeses such as Emmental or mozzarella will best allow the flavour of the courgettes to be appreciated.

• Once the courgettes are cooked, either serve them in foil or slice them and toss the soft chunks of cheesy courgette into a mixed leaf salad, dressed with lemon juice, olive oil and salt and pepper. Adding sweet chargrilled slices of red pepper makes this into a really delicious side salad that goes well with grilled meat, particularly lamb.

Energy 105kcal/434kJ; Protein 6g; Carbohydrate 2.2g, of which sugars 2.1g; Fat 8g, of which saturates 3.9g; Cholesterol 17mg; Calcium 53mg; Fibre 1g; Sodium 114mg.

SQUASH STUFFED <u>WITH</u> GOATS' CHEESE

GEM SQUASH HAS A SWEET, SUBTLE FLAVOUR THAT CONTRASTS WELL WITH OLIVES AND SUN-DRIED TOMATOES IN THIS RECIPE. THE RICE ADDS SUBSTANCE WITHOUT CHANGING ANY OF THE FLAVOURS.

2 To make the stuffing, mix together the rice, tomatoes, olives, goats' cheese, olive oil and basil in a bowl.

3 Divide the rice mixture evenly between the squashes and place them individually on pieces of oiled, double thickness heavy-duty foil. Wrap the foil around each squash and gather securely at the top to make a parcel. Place the squash parcels in among the coals of a medium-hot barbecue.

4 Bake for 45 minutes–1 hour, or until the squashes are tender when pierced with a skewer. Unwrap the parcels and garnish with basil sprigs. Serve with a green salad, if you like.

COOK'S TIP
The amount of time required to cook these vegetable parcels depends on the size of the squashes, and the heat of the coals. To maintain a medium-to-high temperature throughout the cooking time, keep rearranging the coals so that the hotter ones are nearest to the vegetable parcels. You can gauge the heat by the layer of ash that gathers on the coals.

SERVES TWO

INGREDIENTS
4 whole gem squashes
225g/8oz/2 cups cooked white
  long grain rice
75g/3oz/1½ cups sun-dried
  tomatoes, chopped
40g/1½ oz/⅓ cup stoned (pitted)
  black olives, chopped
50g/2oz/¼ cup soft goats' cheese
10ml/2 tsp olive oil
15ml/1 tbsp chopped fresh basil,
  plus basil sprigs to serve
green salad, to serve (optional)

1 Prepare the barbecue. Trim away the base of each squash so that it will stand up, slice off the top and scoop out and discard the seeds.

Energy 337kcal/1416kJ; Protein 11.5g; Carbohydrate 43.5g, of which sugars 7.1g; Fat 14.2g, of which saturates 5.9g; Cholesterol 23mg; Calcium 206mg; Fibre 5.3g; Sodium 613mg.

BAKED SQUASH WITH PARMESAN

ALMOST ALL TYPES OF SQUASH ARE SUITABLE FOR BARBECUE COOKING: SIMPLY WRAP THEM IN BAKING FOIL AND PLACE THEM IN THE HOT EMBERS UNTIL THEY SOFTEN TO A SWEET, MELLOW TREAT.

SERVES FOUR

INGREDIENTS

2 acorn or butternut squashes, about
   450g/1lb each
15ml/1 tbsp olive oil
50g/2oz/4 tbsp butter, melted
75g/3oz/1 cup grated
   Parmesan cheese
60ml/4 tbsp pine nuts, toasted
salt and ground black pepper
2.5ml/½ tsp freshly grated nutmeg,
   to serve

4 Leave the parcels until cool enough to handle. Unwrap the squashes from the foil parcels and scoop out the flesh, leaving the skins intact.

5 Dice the flesh, then stir in the melted butter. Add the Parmesan, pine nuts, salt and pepper. Toss well to mix.

6 Spoon the mixture back into the shells. Sprinkle with nutmeg to serve.

COOK'S TIP
Spaghetti squash can also be cooked in this way. Scoop out the strands and toss with butter and Parmesan cheese.

1 Prepare the barbecue. Cut the squashes in half and scoop out the seeds with a spoon.

2 Brush the cut surfaces and cavities of the squash with oil and sprinkle with salt and black pepper.

3 Sandwich each squash together again. Wrap in baking foil and place in the embers of the fire. Cook for 25–30 minutes, until tender. Turn the parcels round occasionally so that the squashes cook evenly.

Energy 597kcal/2467kJ; Protein 13g; Carbohydrate 10.4g, of which sugars 8g; Fat 56.2g, of which saturates 35.4g; Cholesterol 148mg; Calcium 419mg; Fibre 3.9g; Sodium 622mg.

VEGETABLE PARCELS WITH FLOWERY BUTTER

NASTURTIUM LEAVES AND FLOWERS ARE EDIBLE AND BOTH HAVE A DISTINCTIVE PEPPERY FLAVOUR.
THE FLOWERS MAKE A PRETTY GARNISH FOR SUMMER BARBECUE DISHES AND IN THIS RECIPE THE
LEAVES ARE CHOPPED AND USED TO MAKE AN UNUSUAL HERB BUTTER.

SERVES FOUR

INGREDIENTS
    200g/7oz baby carrots
    250g/9oz yellow patty-pan squashes
      or yellow courgettes (zucchini)
    115g/4oz baby corn
    1 onion, thinly sliced
    50g/2oz/4 tbsp butter, plus extra
      for greasing
    finely grated rind of ½ lemon
    6 young nasturtium leaves
    4–8 nasturtium flowers
    salt and ground black pepper

1 Prepare the barbecue. Trim the vegetables and leave them whole or, if large, cut them into even-size pieces.

2 Divide the vegetables between four double-thickness squares of buttered baking foil and season well.

3 Mix the butter with the lemon rind in a small bowl. Roughly chop the nasturtium leaves and add them to the butter. Place a generous spoonful of the butter on each pile of vegetables in the squares of baking foil.

4 Fold over the foil and seal the edges to make four neat parcels. Cook on a medium-hot barbecue for 30 minutes, or until all the vegetables are tender. Open the foil parcels and top each one with one or two nasturtium flowers. Serve immediately.

Energy 142kcal/584kJ; Protein 3.5g; Carbohydrate 7.6g, of which sugars 6.6g; Fat 11g, of which saturates 6.6g; Cholesterol 27mg; Calcium 39mg; Fibre 2.9g; Sodium 802mg

GRILLED VEGETABLES WITH YOGURT PESTO

CHARGRILLED SUMMER VEGETABLES MAKE A MEAL ON THEIR OWN, OR ARE DELICIOUS SERVED AS A MEDITERRANEAN-STYLE SIDE DISH WITH GRILLED MEATS AND FISH. THE YOGURT PESTO MAKES A CREAMY ACCOMPANIMENT TO THE RICH FLAVOURS OF THE GRILLED VEGETABLES.

SERVES EIGHT

INGREDIENTS

4 small aubergines (eggplants)
4 large courgettes (zucchini)
2 red and 2 yellow (bell) peppers
2 fennel bulbs
2 red onions
300ml½ pint/1¼ cups Greek
  (US strained plain) yogurt
90ml/6 tbsp pesto
olive oil, for brushing
salt and ground black pepper

1 Cut the aubergines into 1cm/½in slices. Sprinkle with salt and leave to drain for about 30 minutes to draw out any bitter juices. Rinse the slices well in cold running water and pat dry.

2 Use a sharp kitchen knife to trim the courgettes and cut them in half lengthways. Cut the peppers in half, cutting through the stalks and cores. Remove the seeds but leave the stalks in place.

3 Slice the fennel bulbs and the red onions into thick wedges, using a sharp kitchen knife.

COOK'S TIP

Baby vegetables are excellent for grilling whole on the barbecue, so look out for baby aubergines and peppers, in particular. There's no need to salt the aubergines if they are small as any bitterness develops only as the fruits mature.

4 Prepare the barbecue. When the flames die down position a lightly oiled grill rack over the hot coals. Stir the yogurt and pesto lightly together in a bowl, to make a marbled sauce. Spoon into a serving bowl and set aside.

VARIATION

Barbecue some halloumi cheese, sliced and brushed with oi,l to serve with the vegetables, if you like.

5 Arrange the vegetables on the grill rack over high heat. Brush generously with olive oil and sprinkle with plenty of salt and ground black pepper.

6 Cook the vegetables until golden brown and tender, turning occasionally. The aubergines and peppers will take 6–8 minutes to cook, the courgettes, onion and fennel 4–5 minutes. Serve the vegetables as soon as they are cooked, with the yogurt pesto.

Energy 146kcal/606kJ; Protein 6.9g; Carbohydrate 12.3g, of which sugars 11.8g; Fat 8g, of which saturates 1.9g; Cholesterol 4mg; Calcium 163mg; Fibre 5.1g; Sodium 86mg.

GRILLED VEGETABLES WITH SAFFRON DIP

HERE A DELICATELY FLAVOURED SAFFRON DIP IS SERVED WITH SLICED ROOT VEGETABLES AND ASPARAGUS SPEARS. THIS IS AN ATTRACTIVE DISH THAT IS QUICK TO COOK.

SERVES FOUR TO SIX

INGREDIENTS
4 small sweet potatoes, total weight
    about 675g/1½lb
4 carrots, total weight about
    375g/13oz
4 parsnips, total weight about
    400g/14oz
4 raw beetroot (beets), total weight
    about 400g/14oz
450g/1lb asparagus, trimmed
60ml/4 tbsp extra virgin olive oil
salt and ground black pepper
For the saffron dip
    15ml/1 tbsp boiling water
    small pinch of saffron threads
    200ml/7fl oz/scant 1 cup fromage
       frais or crème fraîche
    10 fresh chives, chopped
    10 fresh basil leaves, torn

1 To make the saffron dip, pour the measured boiling water into a small bowl and add the saffron strands. Leave for 3 minutes for the colour and flavour to infuse.

2 Beat the fromage frais or crème fraîche until smooth, then stir in the infused saffron liquid.

3 Add the chopped chives and basil leaves. Season and stir to combine. Transfer to a serving bowl.

4 Prepare the barbecue. Cutting lengthways, slice each sweet potato and carrot into eight pieces, each parsnip into seven and each beetroot into ten. Toss all the vegetables except the beetroot in most of the oil in a large flameproof tray.

5 Put the beetroot on a separate tray, because it might otherwise bleed over all the other vegetables. Gently toss the beetroot in the remaining oil and season all the vegetables well.

6 Position a lightly oiled grill rack over the hot coals. Arrange the vegetables on the grill rack over medium heat.

7 Lightly grill the vegetables for 3 minutes on each side, or until tender and branded with grill lines. Remove them as they cook and serve hot or warm with the saffron dip.

VARIATION
You can cut potato chips, parboiling them slightly before you oil and grill them, which may be more popular with children than the root vegetables. Alternatively, do a mixture of potatoes and root vegetables.

COOK'S TIP
Saffron has a unique flavour, which is often likened to hay or grass with a bitter edge. It also adds a beautiful golden yellow colour to food. Though its production is labour intensive and it is therefore the most expensive of spices, it is an indispensable ingredient in many of the world's traditional dishes, from India to Cornwall.

Energy 397kcal/1660kJ; Protein 7g; Carbohydrate 44.6g, of which sugars 21.6g; Fat 22.4g, of which saturates 10.5g; Cholesterol 38mg; Calcium 123mg; Fibre 9.8g; Sodium 119mg.

STUFFED VEGETABLE CUPS

THE SPICY, TOMATO-RED FILLING OF THESE VEGETABLES CARRIES AN IRRESISTIBLY TART CITRUS TANG.
THESE VERSATILE VEGETARIAN TREATS ARE EQUALLY DELICIOUS HOT OR COLD AND ARE IDEAL SERVED
AS AN APPETIZER OR AS A LIGHT MAIN COURSE.

SERVES FOUR

INGREDIENTS

4 potatoes, peeled
4 onions, skinned
4 courgettes (zucchini),
  halved widthways
2–4 garlic cloves, chopped
45–60ml/3–4 tbsp olive oil
45–60ml/3–4 tbsp tomato
  purée (paste)
1.5ml/¼ tsp ras al hanout or
  curry powder
large pinch of ground allspice
seeds of 2–3 cardamom pods
juice of ½ lemon
30–45ml/2–3 tbsp chopped
  fresh parsley
90–120ml/6–8 tbsp vegetable stock
salt and ground black pepper
salad, to serve (optional)

1 Bring a large pan of salted water to the boil. Starting with the potatoes, then the onions and finally the courgettes, add to the boiling water and cook until they become almost tender but not cooked through. Allow about 10 minutes for the potatoes, 8 minutes for the onions and 4–6 minutes for the courgettes. Remove the vegetables from the pan, drain and leave to cool.

2 When the vegetables are cool enough to handle, hollow them out carefully, leaving walls about 5mm/¼in thick to support the filling. Reserve the scooped-out flesh.

3 Prepare the barbecue. When the flames have died down position a grill rack over the hot coals.

4 Finely chop the scooped-out vegetable flesh and put it in a mixing bowl. Add the garlic, half the olive oil, the tomato purée, ras al hanout or curry powder, allspice, cardamom seeds, lemon juice, parsley and salt and pepper, and mix well together. Use the stuffing mixture to fill the hollowed out vegetables.

5 Place each stuffed vegetable on a double-thickness square of foil and drizzle with the stock and the remaining oil. Wrap the foil tightly around the vegetables. Cook over medium-high heat for 35–40 minutes or until tender. Serve warm with a salad, if you like.

COOK'S TIPS
• Ras al hanout is a Moroccan spice blend whose name literally means "top of the shop" – the best the merchant can provide. It may include as many as 30 different spices.
• If you have one, use a small melon baller or apple corer to hollow out the vegetables. It will be much easier and quicker, and will make a neater job than a teaspoon.

Energy 225kcal/937kJ; Protein 6.4g; Carbohydrate 30.2g, of which sugars 12.3g; Fat 9.5g, of which saturates 1.4g; Cholesterol 0mg; Calcium 98mg; Fibre 4.8g; Sodium 47mg.

PERUVIAN SALAD

THIS REALLY IS A SPECTACULAR-LOOKING SALAD. IT COULD BE SERVED AS A SIDE DISH OR WOULD MAKE A DELICIOUS LIGHT LUNCH. IN PERU, WHITE RICE WOULD BE USED, BUT BROWN RICE ADDS AN INTERESTING TEXTURE AND FLAVOUR.

SERVES FOUR

INGREDIENTS
- 225g/8oz/2 cups cooked long grain brown or white rice
- 15ml/1 tbsp chopped fresh parsley
- 1 red (bell) pepper
- 1 small onion, sliced
- olive oil, for sprinkling
- 115g/4oz green beans, halved
- 50g/2oz/½ cup baby corn
- 4 quails' eggs, hard-boiled
- 25–50g/1–2oz Spanish ham, cut into thin slices (optional)
- 1 small avocado
- lemon juice, for sprinkling
- 75g/3oz mixed salad
- 15ml/1 tbsp capers
- about 10 stuffed olives, halved

For the dressing
- 1 garlic clove, crushed
- 60ml/4 tbsp olive oil
- 45ml/3 tbsp sunflower oil
- 30ml/2 tbsp lemon juice
- 45ml/3 tbsp natural (plain) yogurt
- 2.5ml/½ tsp mustard
- 2.5ml/½ tsp sugar
- salt and ground black pepper

1 Make the dressing for the salad by placing all the dressing ingredients in a bowl and whisking with a fork until smooth. Alternatively, shake the ingredients together in a jam jar.

2 Put the cooked rice into a large, glass salad bowl and spoon in half the dressing. Add the chopped parsley, stir well and set aside.

3 Prepare the barbecue. Position a lightly oiled grill rack over the hot coals. Cut the pepper in half, remove the seeds and pith, then place the halves, skin side down, over medium-hot coals. Sprinkle the onion rings with a little olive oil and add them to the rack. Grill for 5–6 minutes until the pepper blackens and blisters and the onion is golden. You may need to stir the onion once or twice so that it grills evenly.

4 Stir the onion in with the rice. Put the pepper in a plastic bag and knot the bag. When the steam has loosened the skin on the pepper halves and they are cool enough to handle, peel them and cut the flesh into thin strips.

5 Cook the green beans in boiling water for 2 minutes, then add the corn and cook for 1–2 minutes more, until tender. Drain both vegetables, refresh them under cold water, then drain again. Place in a large mixing bowl and add the red pepper strips, quails' eggs and ham, if using.

6 Peel the avocado, remove the stone (pit), and cut the flesh into slices or chunks. Sprinkle with the lemon juice. Put the salad in a separate mixing bowl, add the avocado and mix lightly. Arrange the salad on top of the rice.

7 Stir about 45ml/3 tbsp of the remaining dressing into the green bean and pepper mixture. Pile this on top of the salad.

8 Scatter the capers and stuffed olives on top and serve the salad with the remaining dressing.

Energy 415kcal/1726kJ; Protein 9.1g; Carbohydrate 52.8g, of which sugars 6.6g; Fat 18.5g, of which saturates 3.2g; Cholesterol 48mg; Calcium 77mg; Fibre 3.3g; Sodium 417mg.

GRIDDLED HALLOUMI AND BEAN SALAD

HALLOUMI IS THE HARD, WHITE, SALTY CHEESE FROM CYPRUS THAT SQUEAKS WHEN YOU BITE IT. IT GRILLS REALLY WELL AND IS THE PERFECT COMPLEMENT TO THE LOVELY FRESH FLAVOURS OF YOUNG VEGETABLES. THIS SALAD CAN BE GRILLED DIRECTLY ON THE GRILL RACK OVER MEDIUM HEAT.

SERVES FOUR

INGREDIENTS

20 baby new potatoes, total weight
   about 300g/11oz
200g/7oz extra-fine green
   beans, trimmed
675g/1½lb broad (fava) beans,
   shelled (shelled weight about
   225g/8oz)
200g/7oz halloumi cheese, cut into
   5mm/¼in slices
1 garlic clove, crushed to a paste
   with a large pinch of salt
90ml/6 tbsp olive oil
5ml/1 tsp cider vinegar or white
   wine vinegar
15g/½oz/½ cup fresh basil
   leaves, shredded
45ml/3 tbsp chopped fresh savory
2 spring onions (scallions),
   finely sliced
salt and ground black pepper

1 Thread five potatoes on to each of four skewers, and cook in a large pan of salted boiling water for about 7 minutes, or until almost tender. Add the green beans and cook for 3 minutes more. Tip in the broad beans and cook for just 2 minutes. Drain all the vegetables in a large colander.

2 Remove the potatoes, still on their skewers, from the colander, then refresh the beans under cold running water. Pop each broad bean out of its skin to reveal the bright green inner bean. Place in a bowl, cover and set aside.

3 Place the halloumi slices and the potato skewers in a wide dish. Whisk the garlic and oil together with a generous grinding of black pepper. Add to the dish and toss the halloumi and potato skewers until they are coated in the mixture.

4 Prepare the barbecue and rake the hot coals to one side. Place the cheese and potato skewers on a griddle and cook over the coals for about 2 minutes on each side. If they over-char, move the griddle to the cooler side of the grill rack.

5 Add the vinegar to the oil and garlic in the dish and whisk. Toss in the broad beans, herbs and spring onions, with the cooked halloumi. Serve with the potato skewers laid alongside.

Energy 238kcal/996kJ; Protein 14.7g; Carbohydrate 21.3g, of which sugars 3.9g; Fat 11g, of which saturates 7g; Cholesterol 35mg; Calcium 244mg; Fibre 5.8g; Sodium 735mg.

GRILLED FENNEL SALAD

THIS IS SO TYPICALLY ITALIAN THAT IF YOU CLOSE YOUR EYES YOU COULD BE ON A TUSCAN HILLSIDE, SITTING UNDER A SHADY TREE AND ENJOYING AN ELEGANT LUNCH. FENNEL HAS MANY FANS, BUT IS OFTEN USED RAW OR LIGHTLY BRAISED, MAKING THIS GRIDDLE RECIPE A DELIGHTFUL DISCOVERY.

SERVES SIX

INGREDIENTS
    3 sweet baby orange (bell) peppers
    5 fennel bulbs with green tops, total
      weight about 900g/2lb
    30ml/2 tbsp olive oil
    15ml/1 tbsp cider or white wine
      vinegar
    45ml/3 tbsp extra virgin olive oil
    24 small niçoise olives
    2 long sprigs of fresh savory
    salt and ground black pepper

COOK'S TIP
If cooking directly on the barbecue, char
the peppers when the coals are hot, then
cool them ready for peeling. Grill the
fennel over medium-hot coals and turn
frequently once stripes have formed.

1 Prepare the barbecue. Heat a griddle
on the grill rack over hot coals. Roast
the baby peppers, turning them every
few minutes until charred all over.
Remove the pan from the heat, place
the peppers under an upturned bowl
and leave to cool a little and for the
skins to loosen.

2 Remove the green fronds from the
fennel and reserve. Slice the fennel
lengthways into five roughly equal
pieces. If the root looks a little tough,
cut it out.

3 Place the fennel pieces in a flat dish,
coat with the olive oil and season. Rub
off the charred skin from the grilled
peppers – it should come away easily –
remove the seeds and cut the flesh
into small dice.

4 Re-heat the griddle and test the
temperature again, then lower the heat
slightly and grill the fennel slices in
batches for about 8–10 minutes, turning
frequently, until they are branded with
golden grill marks. Monitor the heat so
they cook through without over-charring.
As each batch cooks, transfer it to a flat
serving dish.

5 Whisk the vinegar and olive oil
together until they are thoroughly
combined, then pour the dressing
over the fennel. Gently fold in the
diced baby orange peppers and the
niçoise olives.

6 Remove the savory leaves from the
sprigs. Tear them and the fennel fronds
roughly and scatter both over the salad.
Serve either warm or cold.

Energy 96kcal/397kJ; Protein 2.5g; Carbohydrate 9.1g, of which sugars 8.7g; Fat 5.7g, of which saturates 0.8g; Cholesterol 0mg; Calcium 52mg; Fibre 5.6g; Sodium 302mg.

PASTA SALAD <u>WITH</u> CHARGRILLED PEPPERS

ONE OF THE MANY WONDERFUL THINGS ABOUT SUMMER IS THE ABUNDANCE OF FRESH HERBS. LOTS OF BASIL AND CORIANDER MAKE THIS SALAD ESPECIALLY TASTY. LEAVE THE PASTA TO SOAK UP THE DRESSING AND THEN ADD THE HERBS JUST BEFORE YOU ARE READY TO BARBECUE THE PEPPERS.

SERVES FOUR

INGREDIENTS

    250g/9oz/2¼ cups dried
      fusilli tricolore
    1 handful fresh basil leaves, chopped
    1 handful fresh coriander (cilantro)
      leaves, chopped
    1 garlic clove, chopped
    1 large red and 1 large green
      (bell) pepper
    salt and ground black pepper
For the dressing
    30ml/2 tbsp pesto
    juice of ½ lemon
    60ml/4 tbsp extra virgin olive oil

VARIATION

Dry-roast some pine nuts over the barbecue to add crunch to the salad.

1 Bring a large pan of salted water to the boil. Add the pasta and cook for 10–12 minutes or according to the instructions on the packet.

2 Whisk the dressing ingredients together in a large mixing bowl. Drain the cooked pasta and tip it into the bowl of dressing. Toss well to mix and set aside to cool. Add the basil, coriander and garlic to the pasta and toss well to mix.

3 Prepare the barbecue. Position a lightly oiled grill rack over the hot coals. Put the peppers on the grill rack over high heat for about 10 minutes, turning frequently until they are charred on all sides. Put the hot peppers under an upturned bowl and leave to cool a little and for the skins to loosen.

4 Peel off the skins of the peppers with your fingers, split the peppers open and pull out the cores. Remove all the seeds.

5 Chop the peppers and add them to the dressed pasta. Toss the salad, taste and adjust the seasoning, if necessary, and serve.

Energy 402kcal/1688kJ; Protein 10.1g; Carbohydrate 51.6g, of which sugars 7.1g; Fat 18.7g, of which saturates 2.9g; Cholesterol 3mg; Calcium 75mg; Fibre 3.7g; Sodium 36mg.

AUBERGINE AND BUTTERNUT SALAD

BEAUTIFULLY GOLDEN BUTTERNUT SQUASH MAKES A SUBSTANTIAL SALAD WITH GRIDDLED AUBERGINE AND FETA CHEESE. LIKE ALL RECIPES FOR GRIDDLED FOOD, THIS SALAD CAN BE COOKED INDOORS AT ANY TIME OF THE YEAR AND IS JUST AS DELICIOUS IN THE WINTER AS IN THE SUMMER.

SERVES FOUR

INGREDIENTS

2 aubergines (eggplants)
1 butternut squash, about 1kg/2¼lb, peeled
120ml/4fl oz/½ cup extra virgin olive oil
5ml/1 tsp paprika
150g/5oz feta cheese
50g/2oz/⅓ cup pistachio nuts, roughly chopped
salt and ground black pepper

1 Slice the aubergines widthways into 5mm/¼in rounds. Spread them out on a tray and sprinkle with a little salt. Leave for 30 minutes to draw out any bitter juices. Slice the squash in the same way, scooping out any seeds with a spoon. Place the butternut squash slices in a bowl, season lightly and toss with 30ml/2 tbsp of the oil.

2 Prepare the barbecue. Heat a griddle on the grill rack over hot coals. Lower the heat a little and grill the butternut squash slices in batches. Sear for about 3 minutes on each side, then put them on a tray. Continue until all the slices have been cooked, then dust with a little of the paprika.

3 Rinse the aubergine slices under cold water and pat them dry. Toss with the remaining oil and season lightly. Cook in the same way as the squash. When all the slices are cooked, mix the aubergine and squash together in a bowl. Crumble the feta cheese over the warm salad, scatter the pistachio nuts over the top and dust with the remaining paprika.

VARIATION
Instead of aubergines try (bell) peppers or thinly sliced courgettes (zucchini) or add a few small onions or quartered onions with the root attached. Add a few raisins as well, if you like.

Energy 393kcal/1626kJ; Protein 11.2g; Carbohydrate 10.4g, of which sugars 8.5g; Fat 34.3g, of which saturates 9.2g; Cholesterol 26mg; Calcium 236mg; Fibre 6.3g; Sodium 609mg.

AUBERGINE ROLLS IN TOMATO SAUCE

THIS IS A USEFUL AND TASTY VEGETARIAN DISH THAT CAN BE PREPARED IN ADVANCE AND SIMPLY FINISHED OVER THE BARBECUE. LITTLE AUBERGINE ROLLS CONTAIN A FILLING OF RICOTTA AND GOATS' CHEESE WITH RICE, FLAVOURED WITH BASIL AND MINT, AND THEY GO VERY WELL WITH A TOMATO SAUCE.

SERVES FOUR

INGREDIENTS

2 aubergines (eggplants)
olive oil, or sunflower oil for
    shallow frying
75g/3oz/scant ½ cup ricotta cheese
75g/3oz/scant ½ cup soft
    goats' cheese
225g/8oz/2 cups cooked long
    grain rice
15ml/1 tbsp chopped fresh basil
5ml/1 tsp chopped fresh mint, plus
    mint sprigs, to garnish
salt and ground black pepper
For the tomato sauce
15ml/1 tbsp olive oil
1 red onion, finely chopped
1 garlic clove, crushed
400g/14oz can chopped tomatoes
120ml/4fl oz/½ cup vegetable stock
    or white wine, or a mixture
15ml/1 tbsp chopped fresh parsley

1 To make the tomato sauce, heat the oil in a small pan and fry the onion and garlic for 3–4 minutes until softened. Add the tomatoes, vegetable stock and/or wine, and parsley. Season well. Bring the mixture to the boil, then lower the heat and simmer for 10–12 minutes, or until slightly thickened, stirring.

2 Cut each aubergine lengthways into 4–5 slices, discarding the two outer slices, which consist largely of skin.

3 Heat the oil in a large frying pan and fry the aubergine slices until they are golden brown on both sides. Drain on kitchen paper. Mix the ricotta cheese, goats' cheese, rice, chopped basil and mint in a bowl. Season well with salt and pepper.

4 Prepare the barbecue. Position a lightly oiled grill rack over the hot coals. Place a generous spoonful of the cheese and rice mixture at one end of each aubergine slice and roll up. Wrap the aubergine rolls in four foil parcels and place on the grill rack. Cook for 15 minutes over medium heat. Reheat the tomato sauce on the barbecue until thoroughly bubbling. Garnish with the mint sprigs and serve with the sauce.

COOK'S TIP
If you would prefer to use less oil for the aubergines, brush each slice with just a little oil, then barbecue until evenly browned.

Energy 233kcal/980kJ; Protein 8.9g; Carbohydrate 24.6g, of which sugars 6.7g; Fat 11.8g, of which saturates 5.8g; Cholesterol 25mg; Calcium 56mg; Fibre 3.3g; Sodium 125mg.

GRILLED AUBERGINE PARCELS

AUBERGINES ARE VERSATILE VEGETABLE FRUITS WITH SOFT FLESH THAT ABSORBS OTHER FLAVOURS. PREPARE THEM IN ADVANCE, BARBECUE THEM QUICKLY TO GET THAT LOVELY SMOKY FLAVOUR AND THEN ENJOY THEM WITH A BALSAMIC VINEGAR AND TOMATO DRESSING FOR A REAL TASTE OF ITALY.

SERVES FOUR

INGREDIENTS
2 large, long aubergines (eggplants)
225g/8oz mozzarella
2 plum tomatoes
16 large fresh basil leaves
30ml/2 tbsp olive oil
salt and ground black pepper
For the dressing
60ml/4 tbsp olive oil
5ml/1 tsp balsamic vinegar
15ml/1 tbsp sun-dried tomato paste
15ml/1 tbsp lemon juice
For the garnish
30ml/2 tbsp toasted pine nuts
torn fresh basil leaves

COOK'S TIP
The best cheese to use in these little parcels is undoubtedly mozzarella. Look for the authentic moist cheese, made from buffalo's milk, which is sold packed in whey. If you can find it, lightly smoked mozzarella would also work well, and would add additional flavour to the dish. It is labelled *mozzarella affumicata*. Alternatively, you could use a plain or smoked goats' cheese. Look for one with a similar texture to mozzarella.

1 Remove the stalks from the aubergines and cut the aubergines lengthways into thin slices – the aim is to get 16 slices in total, disregarding the outer two slices, which consist largely of skin. (If you have a mandolin, it will cut perfect, even slices for you – otherwise, use a sharp, long-bladed cook's knife.)

2 Bring a large pan of salted water to the boil and cook the aubergine slices for about 2 minutes. Drain the slices thoroughly, then dry on kitchen paper. Cut the mozzarella cheese into eight slices. Cut each tomato into eight slices, not counting the first and last slices.

3 Take two aubergine slices and place on a tray, in a cross. Place a slice of tomato in the centre, season with salt and pepper, then add a basil leaf, followed by a slice of mozzarella, another basil leaf, a slice of tomato and more seasoning.

4 Fold the ends of the aubergine slices around the mozzarella and tomato filling. Repeat to make eight parcels. Chill for about 20 minutes.

5 To make the tomato dressing, whisk together the oil, vinegar, tomato paste and lemon juice. Season to taste.

6 Prepare the barbecue. Position a lightly oiled grill rack over the hot coals. Brush the parcels with olive oil and cook over high heat for about 5 minutes on each side until golden. Garnish and serve hot, with the dressing.

Energy 350kcal/1449kJ; Protein 12.7g; Carbohydrate 5g, of which sugars 4.7g; Fat 31.2g, of which saturates 10.5g; Cholesterol 33mg; Calcium 223mg; Fibre 3.6g; Sodium 230mg.

GRILLED VEGETABLES WITH WILD RICE

THE MIXTURE OF WILD RICE AND LONG GRAIN RICE IN THIS DISH WORKS VERY WELL, AND MAKES AN
EXTREMELY TASTY VEGETARIAN MEAL. GRILLING THE VEGETABLES GIVES THEM AN INTENSE, SMOKY-
SWEET FLAVOUR, WHICH IS BEAUTIFULLY BALANCED BY THE TANGY DRESSING.

SERVES FOUR

INGREDIENTS

    225g/8oz/generous 1 cup mixed wild
      and long grain rice
    1 large aubergine (eggplant), sliced
    1 red (bell) pepper, cut into quarters
    1 yellow (bell) pepper, cut into
      quarters
    1 green (bell) pepper, cut into
      quarters
    2 red onions, sliced
    225g/8oz/3 cups brown cap or
      shiitake mushrooms
    2 small courgettes (zucchini), cut in
      half lengthways
    olive oil, for brushing
    30ml/2 tbsp chopped fresh thyme,
      plus whole sprigs to garnish
      (optional)
For the dressing
    90ml/6 tbsp extra virgin olive oil
    30ml/2 tbsp balsamic vinegar
    2 garlic cloves, crushed
    salt and ground black pepper

1 Put the wild and long grain rice in a
large pan of cold salted water. Bring to
the boil, then lower the heat, cover and
cook gently for 30–40 minutes until
tender.

2 Prepare the barbecue. Make the
dressing by whisking together the olive
oil, vinegar and garlic in a bowl, then
season to taste with salt and pepper.

3 Brush the vegetables with olive oil
and grill them over a medium barbecue
for about 5 minutes.

4 Brush the vegetables with more olive
oil, turn them over and grill for another
5–8 minutes, or until tender and
beginning to char in places.

5 Drain the rice, tip into a bowl and
toss in half the dressing. Spoon on to
individual plates and arrange the grilled
vegetables on top.

6 Pour over the remaining dressing,
scatter over the chopped thyme and
serve. Whole thyme sprigs can be used
as a garnish, if you like.

Energy 296kcal/1237kJ; Protein 7.8g; Carbohydrate 59.3g, of which sugars 13.5g; Fat 3g, of which saturates 0.5g; Cholesterol 0mg; Calcium 39mg; Fibre 4.7g; Sodium 460mg.

STUFFED ARTICHOKE HEARTS

THE DISTINCTIVE FLAVOUR OF GLOBE ARTICHOKES IS ACCENTUATED WHEN THEY ARE CHARGRILLED, AND IN THIS RECIPE THEY ARE TOPPED WITH AN INTENSELY SAVOURY STUFFING OF MUSHROOMS, GRUYÈRE CHEESE AND WALNUTS, MAKING THEM RICH AND FLAVOURSOME.

SERVES FOUR

INGREDIENTS

225g/8oz/3 cups mushrooms
15g/½oz/1 tbsp butter
2 shallots, finely chopped
50g/2oz/¼ cup full- or medium-fat
   soft cheese
30ml/2 tbsp chopped walnuts
45ml/3 tbsp grated Gruyère cheese
4 large or 6 small artichoke bottoms
   (from cooked artichokes, leaves and
   choke removed, or cooked frozen or
   canned artichoke hearts)
salt and ground black pepper
fresh parsley sprigs, to garnish

3 In a large bowl, combine the soft cheese and cooked mushrooms. Add the walnuts and half the Gruyère cheese, and stir well to combine the mixture.

4 Divide the mixture among the artichoke bottoms and sprinkle over the remaining cheese. Cook over medium heat for 12 minutes covered with a lid or tented foil. Garnish and serve.

1 To make the stuffing, put the mushrooms in a food processor or blender and pulse until finely chopped.

2 Melt the butter in a frying pan and cook the shallots over a medium heat for about 2–3 minutes, or until just softened. Add the mushrooms, raise the heat slightly, and cook for 5–7 minutes more, stirring frequently, until all the liquid from the mushrooms has been driven off and they are almost dry. Season with plenty of salt and ground black pepper. Prepare the barbecue. Position a lightly oiled grill rack over the hot coals.

COOK'S TIP

To cook fresh artichokes, trim the stalk and boil for 40–45 minutes. Trim away the leaves down to the base. Scrape away the hairy choke.

Energy 162kcal/672kJ; Protein 6.4g; Carbohydrate 2.2g, of which sugars 1.7g; Fat 14.1g, of which saturates 6g; Cholesterol 24mg; Calcium 103mg; Fibre 1.2g; Sodium 115mg.

ONIONS STUFFED WITH GOATS' CHEESE

CHARGRILLED ONIONS HAVE A SWEET TASTE AND GO VERY WELL WITH A GOATS' CHEESE, SUN-DRIED TOMATO AND PINE NUT FILLING. COOK THEM OVER INDIRECT HEAT TO ENSURE THEY COOK THROUGH WITHOUT BURNING. SERVE THEM WITH A SELECTION OF SALADS AND BREADS.

SERVES FOUR

INGREDIENTS

4 large onions
150g/5oz goats' cheese, crumbled
  or cubed
50g/2oz/1 cup fresh breadcrumbs
8 sun-dried tomatoes in olive oil,
  drained and chopped
1–2 garlic cloves, finely chopped
2.5ml/½ tsp chopped fresh
  thyme leaves
30ml/2 tbsp chopped fresh parsley
1 small egg, beaten
45ml/3 tbsp pine nuts, toasted
45ml/3 tbsp olive oil (from the jar of
  sun-dried tomatoes)
salt and ground black pepper

1 Bring a large pan of lightly salted water to the boil. Add the whole onions in their skins and boil them for about 10 minutes. Drain and cool, then cut each onion in half horizontally and slip off the skins, taking care to keep the onion halves from unravelling.

2 Using a teaspoon to scoop out the flesh, remove the centre of each onion, leaving a thick shell.

3 Chop the scooped-out onion flesh and place it in a bowl. Add the goat's cheese, breadcrumbs, sun-dried tomatoes, garlic, thyme, half the parsley and the egg. Mix well, then season to taste with salt and pepper, and add the toasted pine nuts.

4 Brush the outside of the onion shells with oil and divide the stuffing among the onions. Drizzle a little oil over the top.

5 Prepare the barbecue. Part the coals in the centre and insert a drip tray. Position a lightly oiled grill rack over the coals and drip tray. Cook over medium heat over the drip tray for 45 minutes– 1 hour, covered with a lid or tented heavy-duty foil. Brush with oil occasionally during cooking. When cooked, sprinkle with the remaining parsley to garnish.

VARIATIONS

• Omit the goat's cheese and add 115g/4oz finely chopped mushrooms and 1 grated carrot.
• Substitute feta cheese for the goat's cheese and raisins for the pine nuts.
• Substitute smoked mozzarella for the goat's cheese and substitute pistachio nuts for the pine nuts.
• Use red and yellow (bell) peppers preserved in olive oil instead of sun-dried tomatoes.

Energy 400kcal/1659kJ; Protein 14g; Carbohydrate 19g, of which sugars 7.3g; Fat 30.4g, of which saturates 9.2g; Cholesterol 82mg; Calcium 115mg; Fibre 2.4g; Sodium 345mg.

STUFFED PARSLEYED ONIONS

THESE STUFFED ONIONS ARE A POPULAR VEGETARIAN DISH SERVED WITH FRESH CRUSTY BREAD AND A CRISP SALAD, AND BARBECUING GIVES THEM AN UNBEATABLE FLAVOUR. THEY ALSO MAKE A VERY GOOD ACCOMPANIMENT TO MEAT DISHES FOR NON-VEGETARIANS.

SERVES FOUR

INGREDIENTS

4 large onions
60ml/4 tbsp cooked rice
20ml/4 tsp finely chopped fresh
  parsley, plus extra to garnish
60ml/4 tbsp strong Cheddar cheese,
  finely grated
30ml/2 tbsp olive oil
15ml/1 tbsp white wine
salt and ground black pepper

1 Cut a slice from the top of each onion and scoop out the centre to leave a fairly thick shell. Combine all the remaining ingredients in a large bowl and stir to mix, moistening with enough white wine to bind the ingredients together well.

2 Use a spoon to fill the onions, then wrap each one in a piece of oiled baking foil. Bake in the embers of the fire for 30–40 minutes, until tender, turning the parcels often so they cook evenly. Serve the onions garnished with chopped fresh parsley.

Energy 324kcal/1349kJ; Protein 12.5g; Carbohydrate 28.9g, of which sugars 11.8g; Fat 18.5g, of which saturates 5.4g; Cholesterol 49mg; Calcium 303mg; Fibre 3.6g; Sodium 338mg.

BEAN- AND LEMON-STUFFED MUSHROOMS

LARGE FIELD MUSHROOMS HAVE A RICH FLAVOUR AND A MEATY TEXTURE THAT GO WELL WITH THIS FRAGRANT HERB, BEAN AND LEMON STUFFING. THE GARLIC AND PINE NUT ACCOMPANIMENT IS A TRADITIONAL MIDDLE EASTERN DISH WITH A SMOOTH, CREAMY CONSISTENCY.

SERVES FOUR

INGREDIENTS

200g/7oz/1 cup dried or 400g/14oz/
    2 cups drained, canned aduki beans
45ml/3 tbsp olive oil, plus extra
    for brushing
1 onion, finely chopped
2 garlic cloves, crushed
8 large field (portabello) mushrooms
30ml/2 tbsp chopped fresh thyme
50g/2oz/1 cup fresh wholemeal
    (whole-wheat) breadcrumbs
juice of 1 lemon
185g/6½oz/generous ¾ cup
    crumbled goats' cheese
salt and ground black pepper
For the pine nut paste
50g/2oz/½ cup pine nuts
50g/2oz/1 cup cubed white bread
2 garlic cloves, chopped
about 200ml/7fl oz/scant 1 cup milk
45ml/3 tbsp olive oil
15ml/1 tbsp chopped fresh parsley,
    to garnish (optional)

1 If using dried beans, soak them overnight, then drain and rinse well. Place the soaked beans in a pan, add water to cover and bring to the boil. Boil rapidly for 10 minutes, then reduce the heat, cook for 30 minutes, or until tender, then drain. If using canned beans, rinse them under cold running water, then drain well and set aside.

2 Heat the oil in a large, heavy frying pan, add the onion and garlic and cook over a low heat, stirring frequently, for 5 minutes, or until softened.

3 Remove the stalks from the mushrooms and chop them finely. Add them to the pan with the thyme and cook for a further 3 minutes, stirring occasionally, until tender.

4 Stir in the drained aduki beans, breadcrumbs and lemon juice, season to taste then cook gently for 2–3 minutes, or until heated through.

5 Mash about two-thirds of the beans with a fork or potato masher, leaving the remaining beans whole to add some texture to the stuffing, then mix thoroughly together. Prepare the barbecue. Position a lightly oiled grill rack over the hot coals.

6 To make the pine nut paste, put the pine nuts in a pan on the barbecue and toss them until lightly toasted. Place them in a food processor or blender with all the other ingredients for the paste and process until smooth and creamy. Add a little more milk if the mixture appears too thick. Sprinkle with parsley, if using.

7 Brush the base and sides of the mushrooms with olive oil. Fill each mushroom cap with a spoonful of the bean mixture. Cook over medium heat for 20 minutes covered with a lid or tented heavy-duty foil.

8 Remove the foil, top each mushroom with cheese and grill for 5 minutes more, or until the cheese is melted. Serve with a green leaf salad, if you like, or wilted spinach.

VARIATIONS
• Omit the goat's cheese and add 115g/4oz finely chopped mushrooms and 1 grated carrot.
• Substitute feta cheese for the goat's cheese and raisins for the pine nuts.

Energy 604kcal/2520kJ; Protein 25.5g; Carbohydrate 38.8g, of which sugars 8.7g; Fat 39.7g, of which saturates 12g; Cholesterol 46mg; Calcium 237mg; Fibre 8.8g; Sodium 858mg.

GRILLED VEGETABLES WITH SALSA VERDE

FRESH HERBS ARE AT THE HEART OF THE CLASSIC ITALIAN SALSA VERDE (GREEN SAUCE). THE SHARP, TANGY SAUCE TASTES WONDERFUL WITH THIS SWEET, RICH VEGETABLE MIXTURE, WHICH MAY BE CHARGRILLED OR ROASTED. SERVE IT WITH RICE OR A MIXTURE OF RICE AND VERMICELLI.

SERVES 4

INGREDIENTS

   3 courgettes (zucchini), sliced
     lengthways
   1 large fennel bulb, cut into wedges
   450g/1lb butternut squash, cut into
     2cm/³/₄in chunks
   12 shallots
   2 red (bell) peppers, thickly sliced
   4 plum tomatoes, halved and seeded
   45ml/3 tbsp olive oil
   2 garlic cloves, crushed
   5ml/1 tsp balsamic vinegar
   salt and ground black pepper
For the salsa verde
   45ml/3 tbsp chopped fresh mint
   90ml/6 tbsp chopped fresh flat
     leaf parsley
   15ml/1 tbsp Dijon mustard
   juice of ¹/₂ lemon
   30ml/2 tbsp olive oil

1 Prepare the barbecue and position a grill rack over the hot coals, or, to roast the vegetables, preheat the oven to 220°C/425°F/Gas 7.

2 To make the salsa verde, place all the ingredients, except the olive oil, in a food processor or blender. Blend to a coarse paste, then add the oil, a little at a time, until the mixture forms a smooth purée. Season to taste.

COOK'S TIP
You could use whole cherry tomatoes instead of the seeded plum variety.

3 In a large bowl, toss the courgettes, fennel, squash, shallots, peppers and tomatoes in the olive oil, garlic and balsamic vinegar. Leave for 10 minutes to allow the flavours to mingle.

4 Set a griddle on the grill rack to heat, then lay the courgettes, fennel, shallots and peppers on it and grill for about 8 minutes. Alternatively, place the vegetables – apart from the squash and tomatoes – in a roasting pan. Brush with half the oil and vinegar mixture and season with plenty of salt and pepper. Roast for 25 minutes.

5 Add the squash and tomatoes to the vegetable mixture. Turn the vegetables over and brush with the rest of the oil and vinegar. Grill for another 8–10 minutes, or roast for 20–25 minutes, until all the vegetables are tender and lightly charred at the edges. Spoon the vegetables on to a serving platter and serve with the salsa verde.

Energy 556kcal/2314kJ; Protein 13.3g; Carbohydrate 83.5g, of which sugars 20.5g; Fat 18.9g, of which saturates 2.8g; Cholesterol 0mg; Calcium 173mg; Fibre 9.3g; Sodium 34mg.

ROASTED PUMPKIN
WITH SPICES

ROASTED PUMPKIN HAS A SWEET, RICH FLAVOUR ESPECIALLY WHEN CHARGRILLED WITH SPICES. EAT IT STRAIGHT FROM THE SKIN (EAT THE SKIN, TOO) OR SCOOP OUT THE COOKED FLESH, ADD SOME SALSA AND CRÈME FRAÎCHE, AND WRAP IT IN A WARM TORTILLA.

SERVES SIX

INGREDIENTS
 1kg/2¼lb pumpkin
 60ml/4 tbsp oil
 10ml/2 tsp hot chilli sauce
 2.5ml/½ tsp salt
 2.5ml/½ tsp ground allspice
 5ml/1 tsp ground cinnamon
 chopped fresh herbs, to garnish
 salsa and crème fraîche, to serve

1 Cut the pumpkin into wedges. Scoop out and discard the fibre and seeds. Score the flesh in several places.

2 Mix the oil and chilli sauce and drizzle most of the mixture evenly over the pumpkin pieces.

3 Put the salt in a small bowl and add the ground allspice and cinnamon. Sprinkle the mixture over the inner surface of the pumpkin. Prepare the barbecue. When the flames have died down, position a lightly oiled grill rack over the hot coals.

4 Cook the pumpkin over medium-high heat for 25 minutes, basting occasionally and turning regularly until the flesh is tender. Serve with the salsa and crème fraîche separately.

COOK'S TIP
Green-, grey- or orange-skinned pumpkins all roast well. The orange-fleshed varieties are the most colourful when cooked.

Energy 90kcal/371kJ; Protein 1.2g; Carbohydrate 4.2g, of which sugars 3.3g; Fat 7.7g, of which saturates 1.2g; Cholesterol 0mg; Calcium 49mg; Fibre 1.7g; Sodium 27mg.

SIDE DISHES AND SALADS

Many of the side dishes for barbecued main dishes can be cooked on (or even in) the barbecue itself. Vegetables can be simply roasted wrapped in foil nestling between the coals while you grill the main course on the grill rack above. Serve them with a smoky salsa or a richly flavoured butter and you will have vegetables that taste just as exciting as the main dish. You can also grill vegetables directly on the grill rack and they will have that wonderful smoky flavour — try buttery Husk-grilled Corn on the Cob or Grilled Potatoes with Chive Flowers. Probably the most useful side dishes are the salads that you can prepare in advance and bring out while everything is cooking. These salads that have been selected because they contrast well with barbecued meat, fish and poultry as well as grilled vegetarian feasts. You'll find dishes that are refreshing and crisp, deliciously creamy or rich and savoury — side orders to tempt every palate.

BARBECUED VEGETABLES WITH SMOKED TOMATO SALSA

USE A DOUBLE LAYER OF COALS TO START THE BARBECUE SO THAT THEY WILL BE DEEP ENOUGH TO MAKE A BED FOR THE FOIL-WRAPPED VEGETABLES, THEN GRILL THE TOMATOES ABOVE.

SERVES FOUR TO SIX

INGREDIENTS
   2 small whole heads of garlic
   2 butternut squash, about 450g/1lb
      each, halved lengthways and seeded
   4–6 onions, about 115g/4oz each,
      with a cross cut in the top of each
   4–6 baking potatoes, about
      175g/6oz each
   4–6 sweet potatoes, about
      175g/6oz each
   45ml/3 tbsp olive oil
   fresh thyme, bay leaf and
      rosemary sprigs
   salt and ground black pepper
   2 handfuls of hickory wood chips
      soaked in cold water for at least
      30 minutes
For the tomato salsa
   500g/1¼lb tomatoes, quartered
      and seeded
   2.5ml/½ tsp sugar
   a pinch of chilli flakes
   1.5ml/¼ tsp smoky sweet
      chilli powder
   30ml/2 tbsp good quality
      tomato chutney

1 Prepare a barbecue with plenty of coals. Wrap the garlic, squash and onions separately in a double layer of heavy-duty foil, leaving them open. Pair up the potatoes: one sweet, one ordinary. Drizzle a little oil over the contents of each packet, season well with salt and pepper and pop in a herb sprig. Spray with a little water and scrunch up the foil to secure the parcels.

2 Place the parcels on top of the coals heated to medium-high, noting what goes where, if possible. The garlic will take 20 minutes to cook, the squash 30 minutes, the onions 45 minutes and the potatoes 1 hour. As each vegetable cooks, remove the parcel and wrap it in an extra layer of foil to keep warm. Set aside. Shortly before serving, loosen the tops of all the parcels, except the garlic, and put them all back on the coals so that the vegetables dry out a little before being served.

3 Meanwhile, make the tomato salsa. Put a lightly oiled grill rack in place to heat. Sprinkle the tomatoes with sugar, chilli flakes and seasoning. Place them on the grill rack above the vegetables and cook, covered, for 5 minutes.

4 Drain the hickory chips and place a handful on the coals, replace the cover and leave to smoke for 5 minutes. Add some more wood chips and grill for 10 minutes more, or until the tomatoes have dried a little. Remove the tomatoes from the rack and spoon the flesh from the charred skins into a bowl, crush with a fork and mix in the other ingredients. Serve the salsa with the cooked vegetables.

COOK'S TIP
The vegetables taste wonderful with grilled marinated sirloin steaks, or with Parmesan cheese shaved on top.

Energy 244kcal/1029kJ; Protein 6.2g; Carbohydrate 42.4g, of which sugars 13g; Fat 6.7g, of which saturates 1.1g; Cholesterol 0mg; Calcium 65mg; Fibre 5.4g; Sodium 54mg.

VEGETABLES IN COCONUT AND GINGER PASTE

*SWEET POTATOES AND BEETROOT TAKE ON A WONDERFUL SWEETNESS WHEN CHARGRILLED, AND THEY
ARE DELICIOUS WITH THE SAVOURY ONIONS. ALL THE VEGETABLES ARE COATED IN AN AROMATIC
COCONUT, GINGER AND GARLIC PASTE. SERVE THEM TO ACCOMPANY SIMPLY GRILLED MEAT.*

SERVES FOUR

INGREDIENTS
  30ml/2 tbsp groundnut (peanut) oil
    or mild olive oil
  450g/1lb sweet potatoes, peeled and
    cut into thick strips or chunks
  4 beetroot (beets), cooked, peeled
    and cut into wedges
  450g/1lb small red or yellow
    onions, halved
  5ml/1 tsp coriander seeds
  3–4 small fresh red chillies, chopped
  salt and ground black pepper
  chopped fresh coriander (cilantro),
    to garnish
For the paste
  2 large garlic cloves, chopped
  1–2 green chillies, seeded
    and chopped
  15ml/1 tbsp chopped fresh
    root ginger
  45ml/3 tbsp chopped fresh
    coriander (cilantro)
  75ml/5 tbsp coconut milk
  30ml/2 tbsp groundnut (peanut) oil
    or mild olive oil
  grated rind of ½ lime
  2.5ml/½ tsp light muscovado
    (brown) sugar

1 First make the paste. Process the garlic, chillies, ginger, coriander and coconut milk in a food processor, blender or coffee grinder.

2 Turn the paste into a small bowl and beat in the oil, lime rind and muscovado sugar.

3 Prepare the barbecue. Position a lightly oiled grill rack over the hot coals and place a wire vegetable basket on the grill rack to heat.

COOK'S TIP
Orange-fleshed sweet potatoes look more attractive than white-fleshed ones in this dish – and they are more nutritious.

4 Put the oil in a large roasting pan and add the vegetables. Crush the coriander seeds lightly and sprinkle them over the vegetables. Toss to mix. Transfer to the wire basket and cook over medium-high heat for 15 minutes.

5 Return the vegetables to the roasting pan, add the coconut and ginger paste and toss to coat the vegetables thoroughly. Add the chillies and season well with salt and pepper.

6 Grill the vegetables for a further 25–35 minutes, or until the sweet potatoes and onions are fully cooked and tender. Shake the basket regularly. Serve immediately, sprinkled with a little chopped fresh coriander.

Energy 284kcal/1194kJ; Protein 4.8g; Carbohydrate 42.4g, of which sugars 21.6g; Fat 11.9g, of which saturates 1.7g; Cholesterol 0mg; Calcium 106mg; Fibre 6.8g; Sodium 139mg.

SMOKED AUBERGINE WITH CHILLI DRESSING

AUBERGINES CAN BE COOKED IN THE FLAMES OF A FIRE, OR OVER HOT CHARCOAL, OR DIRECTLY OVER THE GAS FLAME OF A STOVE, AND THEY ALWAYS TASTE GREAT. THIS DISH REALLY LENDS ITSELF TO EATING WITH GRILLED MEAT OR FISH, AND MAY BE PREPARED ON THE BARBECUE OR IN THE KITCHEN.

SERVES FOUR

INGREDIENTS

    2 large aubergines (eggplants)
    30ml/2 tbsp groundnut (peanut) or
      vegetable oil
    2 spring onions (scallions),
      finely sliced
    1–2 red Serrano chillies, seeded and
      finely sliced
    15ml/1 tbsp Thai fish sauce
    25g/1oz/½ cup fresh basil
      leaves, torn
    salt
    15ml/1 tbsp roasted peanuts,
      crushed
    nuoc cham (Vietnamese dipping
      sauce), to serve

1 Prepare the barbecue. When the flames have died down position a lightly oiled grill rack over the hot coals. Place the aubergines on the rack over hot coals and cook until the skin is charred and the flesh is soft when pressed. Carefully lift them by the stalk and put them into a plastic bag or under an upturned bowl to sweat.

2 As soon as the aubergines are cool enough to handle, pull off the tough, blackened skins, or slit the skin down one side and scoop out the flesh using a spoon. Pull the aubergine flesh apart in long strips. Place these strips in a serving dish.

3 Heat the oil in a small pan and quickly stir in the spring onions. Remove the pan from the heat and stir in the chillies, fish sauce, basil and a little salt to taste. Pour this dressing over the aubergines, toss gently and sprinkle the peanuts over the top.

4 Serve at room temperature and, for those who like a little extra fire, splash on some nuoc cham.

COOK'S TIP
The aubergines can be cooked under a hot grill (broiler) or directly over a gas flame, turning them until the skin is charred on all sides. Peel off the skin under cold running water and squeeze the excess water from the flesh.

Energy 215Kcal/890kJ; Protein 10g; Carbohydrate 6g, of which sugars 4g; Fat 17g, of which saturates 3g; Cholesterol 0mg; Calcium 425mg; Fibre 0.8g; Sodium 0.7g

BAKED SWEET POTATO SALAD

WHILE YOU ARE BARBECUING YOUR MAIN DISH, BAKE SWEET POTATOES IN FOIL PARCELS AMONG THE COALS OF THE BARBECUE AND THEN CUBE AND TOSS THE FLESH INTO A CHILLI-SPICED SALAD FOR A WARM SALAD WITH A DIFFERENCE. IT MAKES A FILLING PARTNER TO BARBECUED MEATS AND FISH.

SERVES FOUR TO SIX

INGREDIENTS
1kg/2¼lb sweet potatoes
For the dressing
45ml/3 tbsp chopped fresh
  coriander (cilantro)
juice of 1 lime
150ml/¼ pint/⅔ cup natural
  (plain) yogurt
For the salad
1 red (bell) pepper, seeded and
  finely diced
3 celery sticks, finely diced
¼ red-skinned onion, finely chopped
1 red chilli, finely chopped
salt and ground black pepper
coriander (cilantro) leaves, to garnish

1 Pierce the potatoes all over and rub the skins with plenty of salt and olive oil and then wrap each one tightly in a triple thickness of heavy-duty foil. Prepare the barbecue. Push the potatoes in between the coals heated to medium-high. Cook for 1 hour.

2 Combine the dressing ingredients in a bowl, season and chill.

3 In a large bowl mix the red pepper, celery, onion and chilli together. When the sweet potatoes are cooked, remove them from the foil packets and allow to cool for a few minutes. When just cool enough to handle, carefully remove the skin using a small, sharp knife.

4 Cut the peeled potatoes into cubes and add them to the bowl. Remove the dressing from the refrigerator, drizzle over the potato cubes and the rest of the salad and toss carefully. Season again to taste and serve, garnished with fresh coriander.

Energy 176kcal/749kJ; Protein 4g; Carbohydrate 40.4g, of which sugars 14g; Fat 1g, of which saturates 0.3g; Cholesterol 0mg; Calcium 115mg; Fibre 5.2g; Sodium 101mg.

PEPPERS WITH TOMATOES AND ANCHOVIES

THIS IS A SICILIAN-STYLE SALAD THAT IS FULL OF WARM MEDITERRANEAN FLAVOURS AND IS ALSO RICH WITH GLOWING COLOURS. THE SALAD IMPROVES IF IT IS MADE AND DRESSED AN HOUR OR TWO BEFORE SERVING. BARBECUING THE PEPPERS GIVES THEM A SMOKY INTENSITY.

SERVES FOUR

INGREDIENTS
    1 red (bell) pepper
    1 yellow (bell) pepper
    4 ripe plum tomatoes, sliced
    2 canned anchovies, drained
      and chopped
    4 sun-dried tomatoes in oil, drained
      and sliced
    15ml/1 tbsp capers, drained
    15ml/1 tbsp pine nuts
    1 garlic clove, very finely sliced
For the dressing
    75ml/5 tbsp extra virgin olive oil
    15ml/1 tbsp balsamic vinegar
    5ml/1 tsp lemon juice
    1 tbsp chopped fresh mixed herbs
    salt and ground black pepper

1 Prepare the barbecue. Cut the peppers in half and remove the seeds and stalks. Cut into quarters and cook, skin side down, on a lightly oiled grill rack over the hot coals until the skin has charred. Put them under an upturned bowl and leave until they are cool enough to handle. Peel the peppers and cut the flesh into strips.

2 Arrange the peppers and fresh tomatoes on a serving dish. Scatter over the anchovies, sun-dried tomatoes, capers, pine nuts and garlic.

3 To make the dressing, mix together the olive oil, vinegar, lemon juice and chopped fresh herbs and season with plenty of salt and pepper. Pour the dressing over the salad before serving.

Energy 235kcal/973kJ; Protein 3g; Carbohydrate 11.2g, of which sugars 10.9g; Fat 20.1g, of which saturates 2.8g; Cholesterol 1mg; Calcium 24mg; Fibre 3.2g; Sodium 78mg.

SEARED MIXED ONION SALAD

THIS IS A FINE MIX OF FLAVOURS. ON ITS OWN, IT MAKES A GOOD VEGETARIAN SALAD, BUT IT IS ALSO DELICIOUS SERVED WITH GRILLED MEAT SUCH AS BEEF. COMBINE AS MANY DIFFERENT ONIONS AS YOU WISH; LOOK IN ETHNIC MARKETS TO FIND A DIVERSE SELECTION.

SERVES FOUR TO SIX

INGREDIENTS
6 red spring onions (scallions), trimmed
6 green spring onions (scallions), trimmed and split lengthways
250g/9oz small or baby (pearl) onions, peeled and left whole
2 pink onions, sliced horizontally into 5mm/¼in rounds
2 red onions, sliced into wedges
2 small yellow onions, sliced into wedges
4 banana shallots, halved lengthways
200g/7oz shallots, preferably Thai
45ml/3 tbsp olive oil, plus extra for drizzling
juice of 1 lemon
45ml/3 tbsp chopped fresh flat leaf parsley
30ml/2 tbsp balsamic vinegar
salt and ground black pepper
kuchai flowers (optional), to garnish

1 Prepare the barbecue. Spread out the onions and shallots in a large flat dish. Whisk the oil and lemon juice together and pour over the onions. Turn the onions and shallots in the dressing so that they are all evenly coated. Season to taste.

2 Position a grill rack over the coals to heat. Place a griddle or perforated metal vegetable basket on the grill rack over medium-high heat, rather than cooking directly on the grill rack and risking losing onions through the gaps in the rack. Grill the onions in several batches, for 5–7 minutes, turning them occasionally.

3 As each batch of onions is cooked, lift them on to a platter and keep hot at the side of the barbecue. Just before serving, add the parsley and gently toss to mix, then drizzle over the balsamic vinegar and extra olive oil.

4 Garnish with a few kuchai flowers, if you like, and serve with warmed pitta bread and grilled halloumi as an appetizer or to accompany grilled meat or fish.

COOK'S TIP
When available, scatter the whole salad with a few kuchai flowers. These are the lovely blossoms of the Chinese chive. They are available all year round and are sold in Thai food stores.

ROASTED ONIONS WITH SUN-DRIED TOMATOES

ONIONS ROAST TO A WONDERFUL SWEET CREAMINESS WHEN COOKED IN THEIR SKINS. THEY NEED BUTTER, LOTS OF BLACK PEPPER AND SALTY FOOD TO SET OFF THEIR SWEETNESS. LET THEM COOK AWAY NEXT TO THE COALS WHILE YOU USE THE GRILL RACK TO COOK YOUR ACCOMPANYING DISH.

SERVES SIX

INGREDIENTS
  6 even-sized red onions, unpeeled
  olive oil, for drizzling
  175–225g/6–8oz crumbly cheese
    (such as Lancashire, Caerphilly or
    Cheshire), thinly sliced
  a few snipped chives
  salt and ground black pepper
For the sun-dried tomato butter
  115g/4oz/½ cup butter, softened
  65g/2½oz sun-dried tomatoes in
    olive oil, drained and finely chopped
  30ml/2 tbsp chopped fresh basil
    or parsley

COOK'S TIP
If you only have dry sun-dried tomatoes, you will need to soften them in boiling water beforehand.

1 To make the sun-dried tomato butter, cream the butter and then beat in the tomatoes and basil or parsley. Season to taste with salt and pepper and shape into a roll, then wrap in foil and chill.

2 Prepare the barbecue. Wrap the unpeeled onions separately in a double thickness of heavy-duty foil, leaving the top open. Drizzle in a little oil then close. Place the parcels among the coals heated to medium-high and cook for 1 hour, or until they are tender and feel soft when lightly squeezed.

VARIATIONS
• Use goats' cheese instead of Lancashire, Caerphilly or Cheshire.
• Fry fresh white breadcrumbs in butter with a little garlic until crisp and then mix with lots of chopped fresh parsley. Scatter over the onions before serving.

3 Slit the tops of the onions and open them up. Season them inside with plenty of black pepper and add a few chunks of the sun-dried tomato butter. Scatter the crumbled cheese and chives over the top and eat immediately, mashing the butter and cheese into the soft, sweet onion.

Energy 304kcal/1258kJ; Protein 9g; Carbohydrate 8.6g, of which sugars 6.3g; Fat 25.6g, of which saturates 16.3g; Cholesterol 69mg; Calcium 260mg; Fibre 1.9g; Sodium 334mg.

GRILLED LEEK AND PEPPER SALAD WITH GOATS' CHEESE

GRILL THE VEGETABLES FOR THIS SALAD OVER THE HOT COALS AS SOON AS THE BARBECUE HAS HEATED UP. YOU CAN THEN LEAVE THEM TO COOL WHILE YOU COOK THE REST OF THE MEAL.

3 Bring a pan of lightly salted water to the boil and cook the leeks for 3–4 minutes. Drain, cut into 10cm/4in lengths and place in a bowl. Add the olive oil, toss to coat, then season to taste. Place the leeks on the grill rack and grill for 3–4 minutes on each side.

4 Set the leeks aside. Place the peppers on the grill rack, skin side down, and grill until blackened and blistered. Place them in a plastic bag or under an upturned bowl and leave to steam for 10 minutes. Rub off the skin and cut the flesh into strips. Place in a bowl and add the grilled leeks, thyme and a little pepper.

5 Make the dressing by shaking all the ingredients together in a jar, adding seasoning to taste. Pour the dressing over the leek mixture, cover and chill for several hours.

6 Heat a little oil and fry the cheese until golden on both sides. Drain and cool, then cut into bite-size pieces. Toss the cheese and parsley into the salad and serve at room temperature.

SERVES SIX

INGREDIENTS
    4 x 1cm/¹/₂in slices goats' cheese
    75g/3oz/1 cup fine dry white
      breadcrumbs
    675g/1¹/₂lb young leeks
    15ml/1 tbsp olive oil
    2 large red (bell) peppers, halved
    few fresh thyme sprigs, chopped
    vegetable oil, for shallow frying
    45ml/3 tbsp chopped fresh flat
      leaf parsley
    salt and ground black pepper
For the dressing
    75ml/5 tbsp extra virgin olive oil
    1 small garlic clove, finely chopped
    5ml/1 tsp Dijon mustard
    15ml/1 tbsp red wine vinegar

1 Roll the cheese slices in the breadcrumbs, pressing them in so that the cheese is well coated. Chill the cheese for 1 hour.

2 Prepare the barbecue. When the flames have died down arrange a lightly oiled grill rack over the hot coals.

Energy 265kcal/1100kJ; Protein 5.7g; Carbohydrate 17g, of which sugars 6.5g; Fat 19.7g, of which saturates 3.9g; Cholesterol 8mg; Calcium 60mg; Fibre 3.7g; Sodium 174mg.

BARBECUED BEETROOT WITH GARLIC BREAD SAUCE

BEETROOT HAS A LOVELY SWEET AND EARTHY FLAVOUR THAT IS BRILLIANT WITH SMOKY BARBECUED FOOD. IN GREECE IT IS OFTEN SERVED WITH THIS GARLIC SAUCE CALLED SKORTHALIA.

SERVES FOUR

INGREDIENTS
675g/1½lb medium or small
  beetroot (beets)
75–90ml/5–6 tbsp extra virgin
  olive oil
salt
For the garlic sauce
  4 medium slices of bread, crusts
    removed, soaked in water for
    10 minutes
  2–3 garlic cloves, chopped
  15ml/1 tbsp white wine vinegar
  60ml/4 tbsp extra virgin olive oil

1 To make the garlic sauce, use your hands to squeeze most of the water out of the bread, but leave it quite moist. Place the bread in a blender or food processor. Add the garlic and vinegar, salt to taste, and blend until smooth.

2 While the blender or processor is running, drizzle in the olive oil through the lid or feeder tube. The sauce should be runny. Spoon it into a serving bowl and set it aside.

3 Prepare the barbecue. Rinse the beetroot under running water to remove any grit, but be careful not to pierce the skin or the colour will run.

4 Wrap the beetroot in groups of three or four in a double thickness of heavy-duty foil and leave the tops open. Drizzle over a little of the oil and sprinkle lightly with salt.

5 Close up the parcels and arrange them among the coals heated to medium-high. Bake for about 1½ hours until perfectly soft.

6 Remove the beetroot from the foil parcels. When they are just cool enough to handle, peel them. Slice them in thin round slices and serve with the remaining oil drizzled all over.

7 To serve, either spread a thin layer of garlic sauce on top, or hand it around separately. Serve with fresh bread, if you like.

Energy 344kcal/1435kJ; Protein 5.1g; Carbohydrate 25.7g, of which sugars 12.5g; Fat 25.4g, of which saturates 3.6g; Cholesterol 0mg; Calcium 62mg; Fibre 3.6g; Sodium 247mg.

BEETROOT WITH FRESH MINT

BARBECUED FOOD TASTES GOOD WITH SALADS, AND THIS BRIGHT AND DECORATIVE BEETROOT SALAD WITH A BALSAMIC DRESSING IS QUICK TO PREPARE AS WELL AS MAKING A GOOD ACCOMPANIMENT TO LEAFY SALADS. IT CAN BE PREPARED IN ADVANCE, WHICH IS ALWAYS USEFUL WHEN YOU ARE ENTERTAINING.

SERVES FOUR

INGREDIENTS

    4–6 cooked beetroot (beets)
    5–10ml/1–2 tsp sugar
    15–30ml/1–2 tbsp balsamic vinegar
    juice of ½ lemon
    30ml/2 tbsp extra virgin olive oil
    1 bunch fresh mint, leaves stripped
      and thinly sliced
    salt

VARIATION
To make spicy beetroot, add harissa to taste and substitute fresh coriander (cilantro) for the mint.

1 Slice the beetroot or cut into even-size dice with a sharp knife. Put the beetroot in a bowl. Add the sugar, balsamic vinegar, lemon juice, olive oil and a pinch of salt and toss together to combine.

2 Add half the thinly sliced fresh mint to the salad and toss lightly until well combined. Place the salad in the refrigerator and chill for about 1 hour. Serve garnished with the remaining mint leaves.

Energy 95kcal/399kJ; Protein 1.7g; Carbohydrate 10.2g, of which sugars 9.6g; Fat 5.6g, of which saturates 0.8g; Cholesterol 0mg; Calcium 21mg; Fibre 1.9g; Sodium 66mg.

SQUASH A LA GRECQUE

THIS SALAD MAKES A WONDERFUL SIDE DISH TO ALMOST ANY BARBECUED MEAL. COOK THE BABY SQUASHES UNTIL THEY ARE PERFECTLY TENDER AND ASSEMBLE THE SALAD IN ADVANCE SO THE VEGETABLES CAN FULLY ABSORB THE DELICIOUS FLAVOURS OF THE DRESSING.

SERVES FOUR

INGREDIENTS

175g/6oz patty-pan squashes
250ml/8fl oz/1 cup white wine
juice of 2 lemons
sprig of fresh thyme
1 bay leaf
handful of fresh chervil,
  roughly chopped
1.5ml/ ¼ tsp coriander seeds,
  crushed
75ml/5 tbsp olive oil
salt and ground black pepper

1 Blanch the patty-pan squashes in boiling water for 3 minutes, drain, then refresh under cold running water.

2 Place the remaining ingredients in a pan, add 150ml/¼ pint/⅔ cup water and bring to a simmer. Add the squashes and cook for 10 minutes, then remove.

3 Reduce the liquid by boiling hard for 10 minutes. Strain it and pour it over the squashes. Leave until cool for the flavours to be absorbed, and serve the dish cool, not chilled.

Energy 171kcal/704kJ; Protein 0.4g; Carbohydrate 1.4g, of which sugars 1.1g; Fat 13.8g, of which saturates 2g; Cholesterol 0mg; Calcium 18mg; Fibre 0.5g; Sodium 3mg

HUSK-GRILLED CORN
ON THE COB

Keeping the husks on the corn protects the kernels and encloses the butter, so the flavours are contained. Buy fresh corn with the husks intact if possible, but banana leaves or doubled foil can also be used as wrappings.

SERVES SIX

INGREDIENTS

3 dried chipotle chillies
250g/9oz/generous 1 cup butter,
   softened
7.5ml/1½ tsp lemon juice
45ml/3 tbsp chopped fresh flat
   leaf parsley
6 corn on the cob, with husks intact
salt and ground black pepper

1 Heat a heavy frying pan. Add the dried chillies and roast them by stirring them continuously for 1 minute without letting them scorch.

2 Put the chillies in a bowl with very hot, but not quite boiling water to cover. Use a saucer to keep them submerged, and leave them to rehydrate for up to 1 hour. Drain, remove the seeds and chop the chillies finely.

3 Place the butter in a bowl and add the chillies, lemon juice and parsley. Season and mix well.

4 Peel back the husks from each corn cob without tearing them. Remove the silk. Smear about 30ml/2 tbsp of the chilli butter over each cob. Pull the husks back over the cobs, ensuring that the butter is well hidden. Put the rest of the butter in a pot, smooth the top and chill to use later.

5 Place the cobs in a bowl of cold water and leave in a cool place for 1–3 hours; longer if that suits your work plan better.

6 Prepare the barbecue. Remove the corn cobs from the water and wrap in pairs in foil. When the flames have died down position a lightly oiled grill rack over the hot coals.

7 Grill the corn over medium-high heat for 15–20 minutes until softened.

8 Remove the foil wrappings and return the corn cobs to the rack. Cook them for about 5 minutes more, turning them frequently, to char the husks a little. Serve hot, accompanied by the rest of the chilli butter.

COOKS TIP
Turn the husks back when you serve the corn because the steam will need to escape for a few minutes. You can keep the leaves on to help you hold the cobs while you eat.

VARIATION
For a milder, but just as delicious result, omit the chillies and lemon juice from the butter and mix in a crushed clove of garlic and a pinch of freshly stripped thyme leaves instead.

Energy 435kcal/1805kJ; Protein 3.4g; Carbohydrate 27.1g, of which sugars 10.1g; Fat 35.6g, of which saturates 21.9g; Cholesterol 89mg; Calcium 28mg; Fibre 1.8g; Sodium 525mg.

BABY AUBERGINES <u>WITH</u> RAISINS <u>AND</u> PINE NUTS

THIS IS A RECIPE WITH AN ITALIAN INFLUENCE, MADE IN A STYLE THAT WOULD HAVE BEEN FAMILIAR IN RENAISSANCE TIMES. IT ACTUALLY TASTES BEST A DAY AFTER IT IS MADE, WHEN THE SWEET AND SOUR FLAVOURS HAVE HAD A CHANCE TO DEVELOP.

<u>SERVES FOUR</u>

INGREDIENTS

   12 baby aubergines (eggplant)
   250ml/8fl oz/1 cup olive oil
   juice of 1 lemon
   30ml/2 tbsp balsamic vinegar
   3 cloves
   25g/1oz/⅓ cup pine nuts
   25g/1oz/2 tbsp raisins
   15ml/1 tbsp sugar
   1 bay leaf
   large pinch of dried chilli flakes
   salt and ground black pepper

1 Halve the aubergines, brush with olive oil and grill over a hot barbecue for 10 minutes, until charred, turning once.

2 To make the dressing for the salad, combine the remaining olive oil with the lemon juice and vinegar in a jug (pitcher) and add the cloves, pine nuts, raisins, sugar and bay leaf. Add the chilli flakes and salt and pepper and mix well.

3 Place the hot aubergines in an earthenware or glass salad bowl, and pour the dressing over them. Leave to cool, turning the aubergines once or twice so that they absorb the flavours of the dressing evenly. Serve the salad cool but not chilled.

Energy 207kcal/857kJ; Protein 1.1g; Carbohydrate 6.8g, of which sugars 6.7g; Fat 19.7g, of which saturates 2.6g; Cholesterol 0mg; Calcium 9mg; Fibre 1.2g; Sodium 4mg.

RADICCHIO, ARTICHOKE <u>AND</u> WALNUT SALAD

THE DISTINCTIVE, EARTHY TASTE OF JERUSALEM ARTICHOKES MAKES A LOVELY CONTRAST TO THE BITTER EDGE OF RADICCHIO AND THE SHARP FRESHNESS OF LEMON IN THE DRESSING OF THIS SALAD. SERVE IT WARM OR COLD AS AN ACCOMPANIMENT TO BARBECUED MEATS.

SERVES FOUR

INGREDIENTS

1 large radicchio, trimmed and cut into 8–10 wedges, or 150g/5oz radicchio leaves, washed
40g/1½oz/6 tbsp walnut pieces
45ml/3 tbsp walnut oil
500g/1¼lb Jerusalem artichokes
grated rind and juice of 1 lemon
coarse sea salt and ground black pepper
flat leaf parsley, to garnish

1 Place the radicchio wedges or leaves in a flameproof dish. Scatter on the walnuts, drizzle with oil and season. Grill (broil) for 2–3 minutes.

2 Peel the artichokes and cut up any large ones so that the pieces are all roughly the same size. Bring a pan of salted water to the boil and add half the lemon juice. Add the artichokes to the pan and cook for 5–7 minutes until tender. Drain.

3 Toss the artichokes into the salad with the remaining lemon juice and the grated rind. Season with coarse sea salt and ground black pepper. Grill until just beginning to brown, then leave to cool. Serve garnished with fresh flat leaf parsley.

Energy 179kcal/739kJ; Protein 2.7g; Carbohydrate 7.3g, of which sugars 7.1g; Fat 15.7g, of which saturates 1.4g; Cholesterol 0mg; Calcium 87mg; Fibre 3.1g; Sodium 21mg

CHARGRILLED AUBERGINE AND LEMON SALAD

LEMON SUBTLY UNDERLINES THE FLAVOUR OF MELTINGLY SOFT AUBERGINE IN THIS CLASSIC SICILIAN DISH. IT IS DELICIOUS SERVED AS AN ACCOMPANIMENT TO A PLATTER OF COLD MEATS, WITH PASTA OR SIMPLY ON ITS OWN WITH SOME GOOD CRUSTY BREAD.

SERVES FOUR

INGREDIENTS
   1 large aubergine (eggplant),
     about 675g/1½lb
   60ml/4 tbsp olive oil
   grated rind and juice of
     1 lemon
   30ml/2 tbsp capers, rinsed
   12 stoned (pitted) green olives
   30ml/2 tbsp chopped fresh flat
     leaf parsley
   salt and ground black pepper

COOK'S TIP
This salad tastes even better if it is made the day before it is to be eaten. It will keep well, covered in the refrigerator, for up to 4 days. Return the salad to room temperature before serving.

1 Prepare the barbecue and heat a griddle over the coals. Cut the aubergine into 2.5cm/1in cubes. Place in a bowl, pour on the oil and toss well. Griddle the aubergine cubes in batches over medium heat for about 10 minutes, tossing frequently, until golden and softened. Remove with a slotted spoon, drain on kitchen paper and sprinkle with a little salt.

2 Place the aubergine cubes in a large serving bowl, toss with the lemon rind and juice, capers, olives and chopped parsley, and season well with salt and pepper. Serve at room temperature.

VARIATION
Add toasted pine nuts and shavings of Parmesan cheese for a main course dish.

SPICED AUBERGINE SALAD

SERVE THIS MIDDLE-EASTERN INFLUENCED SALAD WITH WARM PITTA BREAD AS A STARTER, OR AS AN ACCOMPANIMENT TO ANY NUMBER OF MAIN COURSE DISHES. IT IS BEST IF MADE IN ADVANCE SO THAT THE SPICY DRESSING HAS TIME TO PERMEATE THE AUBERGINES.

SERVES FOUR

INGREDIENTS
 2 small aubergines (eggplants),
  sliced
 75ml/5 tbsp olive oil
 50ml/2fl oz/¼ cup red wine
  vinegar
 2 garlic cloves, crushed
 15ml/1 tbsp lemon juice
 2.5ml/½ tsp ground cumin
 2.5ml/½ tsp ground coriander
 ½ cucumber, thinly sliced
 2 well-flavoured tomatoes,
  thinly sliced
 30ml/2 tbsp natural (plain) yogurt
 salt and ground black pepper
 chopped flat leaf parsley, to garnish

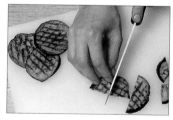

1 Prepare the barbecue or preheat a grill (broiler) or griddle. Brush the aubergine slices lightly with some of the olive oil and cook on a rack over the hot coals, under the hot grill or on the griddle until they are golden and tender, turning once. Leave the aubergine slices until cool enough to handle, then cut them into quarters.

2 Mix the remaining olive oil with the vinegar, garlic, lemon juice, cumin and ground coriander. Season with salt and pepper. Add the warm aubergines, stir well and chill for at least 2 hours. Add the cucumber and tomatoes. Transfer the salad to a serving dish and spoon the natural yogurt on top. Garnish with chopped parsley and serve.

Energy 161kcal/669kJ; Protein 2.3g; Carbohydrate 5.8g, of which sugars 5.5g; Fat 14.6g, of which saturates 2.2g; Cholesterol 0mg; Calcium 37mg; Fibre 3.7g; Sodium 15mg.

CHARGRILLED PEPPER SALAD <u>WITH</u> PESTO

THE INGREDIENTS OF THIS COLOURFUL SALAD ARE SIMPLE AND FEW, BUT THE OVERALL FLAVOUR IS QUITE INTENSE. SERVE IT LIGHTLY CHILLED OR AT ROOM TEMPERATURE.

SERVES FOUR

INGREDIENTS

1 large red (bell) pepper
1 large green (bell) pepper
250g/9oz/2¼ cups dried fusilli
   tricolore or other pasta shapes
1 handful fresh basil leaves
1 handful fresh coriander (cilantro)
   leaves
1 garlic clove
salt and ground black pepper
For the dressing
30ml/2 tbsp bottled pesto
juice of ½ lemon
60ml/4 tbsp extra virgin olive oil

1 Prepare the barbecue. When the flames have died down position a lightly oiled grill rack over the hot coals. Halve the red and green peppers and remove the seeds and cores.

2 Place the pepper halves, skin side down, on the rack and grill until the skins have blistered and are beginning to char. Transfer the peppers to a plastic bag or leave them under an unturned bowl until cool enough to handle, then rub off the skins.

3 Bring a large pan of lightly salted water to the boil and cook the pasta until it is al dente.

4 Whisk together the pesto, lemon juice and oil in a large bowl. Season to taste with salt and pepper. Drain the pasta well and tip it into the bowl of dressing. Toss thoroughly and set aside to cool.

5 Chop the pepper flesh and add it to the pasta. Chop most of the basil and coriander and the garlic and add to the pasta. Toss, season to taste, and serve, garnished with the reserved herbs.

SPICED COUSCOUS WITH HALLOUMI

DELICATE COURGETTE RIBBONS, APPETIZINGLY STRIPED FROM THE GRIDDLE, ADD COLOUR AND FLAVOUR TO THIS DELICIOUSLY SPICY VEGETARIAN DISH.

SERVES FOUR

INGREDIENTS
  275g/10oz/1²⁄₃ cups couscous
  500ml/17fl oz/generous 2 cups
    boiling water
  1 bay leaf
  1 cinnamon stick
  30ml/2 tbsp olive oil, plus extra
    for brushing
  1 large red onion, chopped
  2 garlic cloves, chopped
  5ml/1 tsp mild chilli powder
  5ml/1 tsp ground cumin
  5ml/1 tsp ground coriander
  5 cardamom pods, bruised
  50g/2oz/¹⁄₃ cup whole blanched
    almonds, toasted
  1 firm peach, peeled, stoned (pitted)
    and diced
  25g/1oz/2 tbsp butter
  3 courgettes (zucchini), thinly sliced
    lengthways into ribbons
  225g/8oz halloumi cheese, sliced
  salt and ground black pepper
  chopped fresh flat leaf parsley,
    to garnish

1 Place the couscous in a bowl and pour over the boiling water. Add the bay leaf and cinnamon stick and season with salt. Leave the couscous for 10 minutes. Prepare the barbecue.

2 Meanwhile, heat the oil in a large, heavy pan and sauté the onion and garlic until the onion has softened, stirring occasionally. Stir in the chilli powder, cumin, coriander and cardamom pods and cook for a further 3 minutes.

3 Fork the couscous to break up any lumps, then add it to the pan, with the almonds, diced peach and butter. Heat through for 2 minutes.

4 Brush a griddle with olive oil and heat on the barbecue until very hot. Place the courgettes on the griddle and cook over medium heat for 5 minutes, until tender and slightly charred. Turn them over, add the halloumi and continue cooking for 5 minutes more, turning the halloumi halfway through.

5 Remove the cinnamon stick, bay leaf and cardamom pods from the couscous mixture, then pile it on a plate and season to taste with salt and pepper. Top with the halloumi and courgettes. Sprinkle the parsley over the top and serve.

COOK'S TIP
Use a mandolin or vegetable peeler to cut the courgette into thin ribbons. Discard the first and last slices.

Energy 515kcal/2138kJ; Protein 19.9g; Carbohydrate 42.7g, of which sugars 6.1g; Fat 30.3g, of which saturates 12.5g; Cholesterol 46mg; Calcium 290mg; Fibre 2.9g; Sodium 264mg.

SWEET AND SOUR ONION SALAD

THIS RECIPE FOR TANGY, GLAZED ONIONS IN THE PROVENÇAL STYLE MAKES AN UNUSUAL AND
FLAVOURFUL ACCOMPANIMENT TO BARBECUED STEAKS. THE RAISINS PLUMP UP WHEN COOKED AND ADD
A LOVELY FRUITY NOTE TO THE CARAMELIZED SWEETNESS OF THE DISH.

SERVES SIX

INGREDIENTS
  450g/1lb baby onions, peeled
  50ml/2fl oz/¼ cup white wine
    vinegar
  45ml/3 tbsp olive oil
  40g/1½oz/3 tbsp caster (superfine)
    sugar
  45ml/3 tbsp tomato purée (paste)
  1 bay leaf
  2 parsley sprigs
  65g/2½oz/½ cup raisins
  salt and ground black pepper

1 Put all the ingredients in a pan with 300ml/½ pint/1¼ cups water. Bring to the boil and simmer gently, uncovered, for 45 minutes, or until the onions are tender and the liquid has evaporated.

2 Remove the bay leaf and parsley, from the pan and check the seasoning. Transfer the contents of the pan to a large serving dish. Serve the salad at room temperature.

Energy 138kcal/578kJ; Protein 1.5g; Carbohydrate 21.5g, of which sugars 19.7g; Fat 5.7g, of which saturates 0.8g; Cholesterol 0mg; Calcium 30mg; Fibre 1.5g; Sodium 27mg.

BEAN, MUSHROOM AND CHORIZO SALAD

THIS EARTHY, HEARTY SALAD CAN BE SERVED AS A FIRST COURSE WITH CHUNKS OF CRUSTY BREAD OR AS PART OF A BUFFET MENU. PREPARE IT A DAY IN ADVANCE TO ALLOW THE FLAVOURS TO MINGLE AND STORE IT IN THE REFRIGERATOR UNTIL ABOUT AN HOUR BEFORE SERVING.

SERVES FOUR

INGREDIENTS

675g/1½lb broad (fava) beans,
  shelled (shelled weight about
  225g/8oz)
175g/6oz chorizo sausage
60ml/4 tbsp extra virgin olive oil
225g/8oz brown cap (cremini)
  mushrooms, sliced
handful of fresh chives
salt and ground black pepper

1 Cook the broad beans in a large pan of boiling, salted water until just tender. Drain and refresh under cold running water. If the beans are large, peel away the tough outer skins.

2 Remove the skin from the chorizo sausage and cut it into small chunks. Heat the oil in a frying pan, add the chorizo and cook for 2 minutes. Empty into a bowl with the mushrooms, mix well and set aside to cool.

3 Chop half the chives and stir the beans and chopped chives into the mushroom mixture. Season to taste. Serve the salad at room temperature, garnished with the remaining chives.

COOK'S TIP
Although peeling the broad beans takes a little time it is well worth doing unless they are very young and tender, and the peeled beans are a lovely vivid green.

Energy 287kcal/1192kJ; Protein 10.7g; Carbohydrate 11g, of which sugars 2.1g; Fat 22.6g, of which saturates 5.7g; Cholesterol 26mg; Calcium 80mg; Fibre 4.7g; Sodium 384mg.

CANNELLINI BEAN SALAD

TENDER WHITE BEANS ARE DELICIOUS IN THIS SPICY DRESSING WITH THE BITE OF FRESH, CRUNCHY GREEN PEPPER IN THIS DISH FROM ISRAEL. IT IS PERFECT FOR PREPARING AHEAD OF TIME AND TASTES GREAT AS A FIRST COURSE WITH PITTA BREAD AS WELL AS ACCOMPANYING MAIN COURSE DISHES.

SERVES FOUR

INGREDIENTS

400g/14oz can cannellini beans
750g/1lb 10oz tomatoes, diced
1 onion, finely chopped
½–1 mild fresh chilli, finely chopped
1 green (bell) pepper, chopped
pinch of sugar
4 garlic cloves, chopped
45–60ml/3–4 tbsp olive oil
grated rind and juice of 1 lemon
15ml/1 tbsp cider vinegar or
  wine vinegar
salt and ground black pepper
chopped fresh parsley, to garnish

1 Rinse and drain the cannellini beans. Put them in a large bowl with the tomatoes, onion, chilli, green pepper, sugar, garlic, salt and plenty of ground black pepper and toss together.

2 Mix the olive oil with the lemon rind and juice and the vinegar. Pour the dressing over the salad and toss lightly to combine. Chill before serving, garnished with chopped parsley.

Energy 226kcal/947kJ; Protein 8.8g; Carbohydrate 27.6g, of which sugars 12.9g; Fat 9.6g, of which saturates 1.5g; Cholesterol 0mg; Calcium 92mg; Fibre 9g; Sodium 409mg.

WARM BROAD BEAN AND FETA SALAD

THIS RECIPE IS LOOSELY BASED ON A TYPICAL GREEK MEDLEY OF FRESH-TASTING SALAD INGREDIENTS
— BROAD BEANS, TOMATOES AND FETA CHEESE. IT'S LOVELY EITHER WARM OR COLD. TAKE CARE WHEN
SEASONING THE SALAD AS THE FETA WILL BE QUITE SALTY.

SERVES FOUR TO SIX

INGREDIENTS

900g/2lb fresh broad (fava) beans,
  shelled, or 350g/12oz frozen beans
60ml/4 tbsp olive oil
175g/6oz large plum tomatoes,
  quartered
4 garlic cloves, crushed
115g/4oz firm feta cheese, cut
  into chunks
45ml/3 tbsp chopped fresh dill,
  plus extra to garnish
12 black olives
salt and ground black pepper

1 Cook the broad beans in boiling,
salted water until they are just tender.
Drain and set aside until cool enough to
handle. Unless they are very young and
small, pop them out of their skins.

2 Heat the olive oil in a heavy-based
frying pan and add the quartered
tomatoes. Cook until the tomatoes are
beginning to colour, then add the garlic
and cook for a few minutes more.

3 Add the chunks of feta to the frying
pan and toss the ingredients together
for 1 minute to coat the cheese in the
garlicky oil. Mix with the drained beans
in a large bowl and add the dill, olives
and salt and pepper. Toss everything
together and serve garnished with the
extra chopped fresh dill.

Energy 175kcal/727kJ; Protein 8.3g; Carbohydrate 8.8g, of which sugars 2.2g; Fat 12g, of which saturates 3.8g; Cholesterol 13mg; Calcium 121mg; Fibre 4.7g; Sodium 342mg

CAESAR SALAD

THERE ARE FEW SALADS MORE FAMOUS THAN THIS COMBINATION OF CRISP LETTUCE LEAVES AND PARMESAN IN A FRESH EGG DRESSING. IT WAS INVENTED IN THE 1920s IN TIJUANA, MEXICO, BY THE ITALIAN RESTAURATEUR CAESAR CARDINI, AND REMAINS HUGELY POPULAR.

SERVES FOUR

INGREDIENTS

   2 large garlic cloves, halved
   45ml/3 tbsp extra virgin olive oil
   4 slices wholemeal (whole-wheat)
     bread
   1 small cos or 2 Little Gem lettuces
   50g/2oz piece of Parmesan cheese,
     shaved or coarsely grated
For the dressing
   1 egg
   10ml/2 tsp French mustard
   5ml/1 tsp Worcestershire sauce
   30ml/2 tbsp fresh lemon juice
   30ml/2 tbsp extra virgin olive oil
   salt and ground black pepper

1 Preheat the oven to 190°C/375°F/ Gas 5. Rub the inside of a salad bowl with one of the half cloves of garlic.

2 Heat the oil gently with the remaining garlic in a frying pan for 5 minutes, then remove and discard the garlic.

3 Remove the crusts from the bread and cut the crumb into small cubes. Toss these in the garlic-flavoured oil, making sure that they are well coated. Spread out the bread cubes on a baking sheet, and bake for about 10 minutes, until crisp. Remove from the oven, then leave to cool.

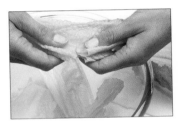

4 Separate the lettuce leaves, wash and dry them and arrange in a shallow salad bowl. Leave the bowl in the refrigerator until you are ready to assemble and serve the salad.

5 Bring a small pan of water to the boil, lower the egg into the water and boil for 1 minute. Crack it into a bowl. Scoop out and discard any softly set egg white. Using a balloon whisk, beat in the French mustard, Worcestershire sauce, lemon juice and olive oil, then season with salt and pepper to taste.

6 Sprinkle the Parmesan over the salad and then drizzle the dressing over. Scatter with the croûtons. Take the salad to the table, toss lightly and serve immediately.

Energy 261kcal/1083kJ; Protein 9.2g; Carbohydrate 11.5g, of which sugars 1.5g; Fat 20.1g, of which saturates 5g; Cholesterol 60mg; Calcium 190mg; Fibre 1.9g; Sodium 305mg

GRILLED HALLOUMI AND GRAPE SALAD

HALLOUMI CHEESE STAYS BEAUTIFULLY FIRM WHEN COOKED, AND IN THE EASTERN MEDITERRANEAN IT IS OFTEN SERVED GRILLED OR FRIED FOR BREAKFAST OR SUPPER. IN THIS RECIPE IT'S TOSSED WITH SWEET, JUICY GRAPES, WHICH COMPLEMENT ITS DISTINCTIVE FLAVOUR.

SERVES FOUR

INGREDIENTS

150g/5oz mixed green salad leaves
75g/3oz seedless green grapes
75g/3oz seedless black grapes
250g/9oz halloumi cheese
30ml/2 tbsp olive oil
fresh young thyme leaves or dill,
  to garnish
For the dressing
60ml/4 tbsp olive oil
15ml/1 tbsp lemon juice
2.5ml/½ tsp caster (superfine) sugar
15ml/1 tbsp chopped fresh thyme
  or dill
salt and ground black pepper

1 To make the dressing, mix the olive oil, lemon juice and sugar together in a bowl. Season well with plenty of salt and black pepper. Stir in the chopped fresh thyme or dill and set aside.

2 Prepare the barbecue. Toss together the mixed green salad leaves and the green and black grapes, then transfer to a large serving plate or salad bowl.

3 Slice the halloumi cheese. Brush the slices with olive oil and cook briefly over medium-hot coals, or pan-fry on the stove until golden, turning once.

4 Arrange the cooked cheese over the salad. Pour over the dressing and garnish with thyme or dill leaves.

5 Serve immediately while the cheese is hot and the salad fresh.

COOK'S TIP
The cheese will retain its tenderness for longer if you cut it into fairly thick slices, about 2cm/¾in. It can be eaten cold but in this case it is better chopped into smaller cubes after it cools.

Energy 365kcal/1513kJ; Protein 12.2g; Carbohydrate 7.2g, of which sugars 7.2g; Fat 32.2g, of which saturates 11.4g; Cholesterol 36mg; Calcium 250mg; Fibre 0.8g; Sodium 250mg.

CURLY ENDIVE SALAD <u>WITH</u> BACON

WHEN THEY ARE IN SEASON, YOUNG DANDELION LEAVES COULD BE INCLUDED IN THIS FRENCH SALAD. LIKE ENDIVE, THEY HAVE A SLIGHTLY ASTRINGENT FLAVOUR THAT GOES BEAUTIFULLY WITH THE ROBUST TASTE OF BACON. IF YOU WISH, SPRINKLE THE SALAD WITH CHOPPED HARD-BOILED EGG.

2 Heat 15ml/1 tbsp oil in a pan over a medium heat and add the bacon. Fry until browned. Remove the bacon and drain on kitchen paper.

3 Add another 30ml/2 tbsp oil to the pan and fry the bread cubes over a medium heat, turning frequently, until browned. Remove the bread cubes with a slotted spoon and drain on kitchen paper. Discard any remaining fat.

SERVES FOUR

INGREDIENTS
  225g/8oz/6 cups curly endive or
    escarole leaves
  75–90ml/5–6 tbsp extra virgin
    olive oil
  175g/6oz piece of smoked
    bacon, diced
  thick slice white bread, cubed
  1 small garlic clove, finely chopped
  15ml/1 tbsp red wine vinegar
  10ml/2 tsp Dijon mustard
  salt and ground black pepper

1 Tear the salad leaves into bite-size pieces and put them in a large salad bowl. Set the bowl aside.

4 Stir the chopped garlic, vinegar and mustard into the frying pan with the remaining oil and warm through. Season to taste. Pour the dressing over the salad and sprinkle with the fried bacon and croûtons.

Energy 226kcal/940kJ; Protein 10g; Carbohydrate 8.1g, of which sugars 1.5g; Fat 17.3g, of which saturates 3.2g; Cholesterol 14mg; Calcium 38mg; Fibre 0.8g; Sodium 721mg

CARROT AND ORANGE SALAD

THIS IS A WONDERFUL, FRESH-TASTING SALAD WITH SUCH A FABULOUS COMBINATION OF CITRUS FRUIT AND VEGETABLES THAT IT IS DIFFICULT TO KNOW WHETHER IT IS A SALAD OR A DESSERT. IT MAKES A REFRESHING ACCOMPANIMENT TO GRILLED MEAT, CHICKEN OR FISH.

SERVES FOUR

INGREDIENTS
    450g/1lb carrots
    2 large navel oranges
    15ml/1 tbsp extra virgin olive oil
    30ml/2 tbsp freshly squeezed
      lemon juice
    pinch of sugar (optional)
    30ml/2 tbsp chopped pistachio nuts
      or toasted pine nuts
    salt and ground black pepper

3 Blend the oil, lemon juice and orange juice in a small bowl to make a light dressing. Season with salt and ground black pepper, and a pinch of sugar, if you like.

4 Mix the oranges with the carrots and pour the dressing over. Toss to combine the ingredients and turn the salad into a serving bowl. Sprinkle over the pistachios or pine nuts and serve.

1 Peel the carrots and coarsely grate them into a large bowl.

2 Cut a thin slice of peel and pith from each end of the oranges. Place cut-side down on a plate and cut off the peel and pith in strips. Holding the oranges over a bowl and using a sharp knife, carefully cut out each segment, leaving the membrane behind. Squeeze the juice from the membrane into the bowl.

COOK'S TIP
Use large, mature carrots for this dish as they have most flavour and sweetness.

Energy 131kcal/547kJ; Protein 2.7g; Carbohydrate 14.6g, of which sugars 13.9g; Fat 7.3g, of which saturates 1.1g; Cholesterol 0mg; Calcium 65mg; Fibre 4.2g; Sodium 71mg.

CUCUMBER AND DILL SALAD

AROMATIC DILL IS A PARTICULARLY USEFUL HERB TO USE WITH SALADS. ITS ANISEED FLAVOUR IS A NATURAL PARTNER FOR COOL FRESH-TASTING CUCUMBER, AND HERE THE TWO ARE COMBINED IN A REFRESHING SOUR CREAM DRESSING. THIS IS AN IDEAL ACCOMPANIMENT FOR BARBECUED FISH.

2 Rinse well under cold running water, then pat dry with kitchen paper.

3 Finely chop about 45ml/3 tbsp fresh dill, setting aside one sprig for the garnish. Put the slices of cucumber in a bowl, add the chopped dill and combine the ingredients together, either mixing with your hands or with a fork.

SERVES FOUR

INGREDIENTS
2 cucumbers
5ml/1 tsp salt
5 sprigs fresh dill
15ml/1 tbsp white wine vinegar
150ml/¼ pint/⅔ cup sour cream
ground black pepper

4 In another bowl, stir the vinegar into the sour cream and season the mixture with pepper.

5 Pour the sour cream over the cucumber and chill for 1 hour before turning into a serving dish. Garnish with the sprig of dill, and serve.

COOK'S TIP
Salting the sliced cucumber draws out some of the moisture, thereby making it firmer and preventing the dressing from becoming watery. Make sure you rinse it thoroughly before using or the salad will be too salty.

1 Use a cannelle knife (zester) to peel away strips of rind from along the length of the cucumbers, creating a striped effect. Slice thinly. Put the slices in a sieve (strainer) or colander set over a bowl and sprinkle with the salt. Leave for 1 hour to drain.

Energy 91kcal/375kJ; Protein 2.2g; Carbohydrate 3.3g, of which sugars 3.1g; Fat 7.7g, of which saturates 4.7g; Cholesterol 23mg; Calcium 78mg; Fibre 1.2g; Sodium 23mg.

CUCUMBER AND SHALLOT SALAD

IN MALAYSIA THIS SALAD IS OFTEN SERVED WITH INDIAN FOOD AND WITH MANY OTHER SPICY FISH AND MEAT DISHES. IT CAN BE MADE AHEAD OF TIME AND KEPT IN THE REFRIGERATOR. SERVE IT CHILLED AS A SALAD OR AS A COOLING RELISH WITH GRILLED FOOD.

SERVES FOUR

INGREDIENTS

1 cucumber, peeled, halved
  lengthways and seeded
4 shallots, halved lengthways and
  sliced finely along the grain
1–2 green chillies, seeded and sliced
  finely lengthways
60ml/4 tbsp coconut milk
5–10ml/1–2 tsp cumin seeds,
  dry-roasted and ground to
  a powder
salt
1 lime, quartered, to serve

1 Slice the cucumber halves finely and sprinkle with salt. Set aside for about 15 minutes. Rinse well and drain off any excess water, then dry on kitchen paper. Put the cucumber in a bowl and add the shallots and chillies.

2 Pour in the coconut milk and toss well. Sprinkle most of the roasted cumin over the top. Just before serving, toss the salad again, season with salt and sprinkle the rest of the roasted cumin over the top. Serve with lime wedges.

Energy 17kcal/68kJ; Protein 0.7g; Carbohydrate 3.3g, of which sugars 2.7g; Fat 0.1g, of which saturates 0g; Cholesterol 0mg; Calcium 19mg; Fibre 0.7g; Sodium 15mg.

WILD GREEN SALAD

A MIXTURE OF SALAD LEAVES MAKES A REFRESHING ACCOMPANIMENT TO A MEAL, ESPECIALLY WHEN YOU CHOOSE THOSE THAT HAVE CONTRASTING FLAVOURS, LIKE THE ONES USED HERE.

SERVES FOUR

INGREDIENTS

1 large bunch wild rocket (arugula), about 115g/4oz
1 bag mixed salad leaves
¼ white cabbage, thinly sliced
1 cucumber, sliced
1 small red onion, chopped
2–3 garlic cloves, chopped
3–5 tomatoes, cut into wedges
1 green (bell) pepper, seeded and sliced
2–3 mint sprigs, sliced or torn
15–30ml/1–2 tbsp chopped fresh parsley and/or tarragon or dill
pinch of dried oregano or thyme
45ml/3 tbsp extra virgin olive oil
juice of ½ lemon
15ml/1 tbsp red wine vinegar
15–20 black olives
salt and ground black pepper

1 In a large salad bowl, put the rocket, mixed salad leaves, white cabbage, cucumber, onion and garlic. Toss gently to combine the leaves and vegetables.

COOK'S TIP
Accompany the salad with 50g/2oz crumbled feta cheese mixed into 115g/4oz natural (plain) yogurt and sprinkled with paprika.

2 Arrange the tomatoes, pepper, mint, fresh and dried herbs, salt and pepper on top of the greens and vegetables. Drizzle over the oil, lemon juice and vinegar, stud with the olives and serve.

VARIATION
Omit the cabbage, use fewer salad leaves and substitute 450g/1lb ripe cherry tomatoes for the tomatoes in the recipe.

Energy 146kcal/605kJ; Protein 3.1g; Carbohydrate 10g, of which sugars 9.4g; Fat 10.6g, of which saturates 1.6g; Cholesterol 0mg; Calcium 99mg; Fibre 3.9g; Sodium 337mg.

FENNEL, ORANGE AND ROCKET SALAD

AN UNUSUAL COMBINATION OF FENNEL, ROCKET, ORANGE AND OLIVES IS BROUGHT TOGETHER IN THIS REFRESHING SALAD, WHICH IS IDEAL SERVED WITH SPICY OR RICH FOOD.

SERVES FOUR

INGREDIENTS

 2 oranges
 1 fennel bulb
 115g/4oz rocket (arugula) leaves
 50g/2oz/⅓ cup black olives
For the dressing
 30ml/2 tbsp extra virgin olive oil
 15ml/1 tbsp balsamic vinegar
 1 small garlic clove, crushed
 salt and ground black pepper

1 With a vegetable peeler, cut strips of rind from the oranges, leaving the pith behind, and cut into thin julienne strips. Cook in boiling water for a few minutes. Drain. Peel the oranges, removing all the white pith. Slice them into thin rounds and discard any seeds.

2 Cut the fennel bulb in half lengthways with a sharp knife and slice across the bulb as thinly as possible, preferably in a food processor fitted with a slicing disc or using a mandolin.

3 Combine the oranges and fennel slices in a serving bowl and toss with the rocket leaves.

4 To make the dressing, mix together the olive oil, balsamic vinegar, crushed garlic and seasoning and pour over the salad in the bowl.

5 Toss the salad ingredients together well and leave to stand for a few minutes. Sprinkle with the black olives and julienne strips of orange rind.

Energy 123kcal/511kJ; Protein 2.1g; Carbohydrate 6.7g, of which sugars 6.6g; Fat 10g, of which saturates 1.4g; Cholesterol 0mg; Calcium 98mg; Fibre 3.2g; Sodium 330mg.

FATTOUSH

THIS IS A DELICIOUS LEBANESE DISH, FULL OF THE FLAVOUR OF FRESH HERBS AND LEMONS. IT MAKES A DELICIOUS SNACK OR AN EXCITING ADDITION TO A BUFFET TABLE.

SERVES FOUR

INGREDIENTS

1 yellow or red (bell) pepper
1 large cucumber
4–5 tomatoes
1 bunch spring onions (scallions)
30ml/2 tbsp finely chopped
   fresh parsley
30ml/2 tbsp finely chopped
   fresh mint
30ml/2 tbsp finely chopped fresh
   coriander (cilantro)
2 garlic cloves, crushed
75ml/5 tbsp olive oil
juice of 2 lemons
salt and ground black pepper
4 pitta breads

1 Slice the pepper, discarding the seeds and core, then slice or chop the flesh. Leaving the skin on the cucumber, roughly chop it. Dice the tomatoes. Place them in a large salad bowl.

2 Slice the spring onions. Add to the cucumber, tomatoes and pepper with the parsley, mint and coriander.

3 To make the dressing, mix the garlic with the olive oil and lemon juice. Whisk well, then season to taste.

4 Pour the dressing over the salad and toss lightly to mix.

5 Toast the pitta breads in a toaster or on the barbecue until crisp and serve them with the salad.

COOK'S TIP
Although the recipe calls for only 30ml/ 2 tbsp of each of the herbs, if you have plenty to hand, you can add as much as you like to this aromatic salad.

VARIATION
If you prefer, make this salad in the traditional way. After toasting the pitta breads until crisp, crush them in your hand and then sprinkle them all over the salad before serving.

Energy 120kcal/499kJ; Protein 2.4g; Carbohydrate 7.8g, of which sugars 7.5g; Fat 9.1g, of which saturates 1.4g; Cholesterol 0mg; Calcium 54mg; Fibre 3g; Sodium 18mg.

MANGO, TOMATO AND RED ONION SALAD

THIS SALAD MAKES AN APPETIZING SIDE DISH. THE MANGO HAS A SUBTLE SWEETNESS AND ITS FLAVOUR BLENDS WELL WITH THE TOMATO, ONION AND CUCUMBER.

SERVES FOUR

INGREDIENTS

1 firm mango
2 large tomatoes or 1 beefsteak
  tomato, sliced
½ red onion, sliced into rings
½ cucumber, peeled and thinly sliced
30ml/2 tbsp sunflower oil
15ml/1 tbsp lemon juice
1 garlic clove, crushed
2.5ml/½ tsp hot pepper sauce
salt and ground black pepper
sugar, to taste
chopped chives, to garnish

COOK'S TIP
Choose a mango that is slightly underripe: it should be firm but not hard.

1 Cut away two thick slices either side
of the mango stone (pit) and cut into
finer slices. Peel off the skin.

2 Arrange the mango, tomato, onion
and cucumber slices in circles on a
large serving plate.

3 Blend the oil, lemon juice, garlic, hot
pepper sauce, salt and pepper in a
blender or food processor, or place in
a small jar and shake vigorously. Add a
pinch of sugar to taste and mix again.

4 Using a teaspoon, drizzle the dressing
over the salad, taking care not to
disturb the slices of mango, tomato,
onion and cucumber. Sprinkle with the
chopped chives and serve.

Energy 89kcal/369kJ; Protein 1.1g; Carbohydrate 8.6g, of which sugars 7.9g; Fat 5.8g, of which saturates 0.8g; Cholesterol 0mg; Calcium 17mg; Fibre 1.9g; Sodium 7mg.

ASPARAGUS, TOMATO AND ORANGE SALAD

THIS SALAD COMES FROM SPAIN, WHERE COMPLICATED SALAD DRESSINGS ARE SELDOM USED. SPANISH COOKS SIMPLY RELY ON THE WONDERFUL TASTE OF A GOOD-QUALITY OLIVE OIL. USE EXTRA VIRGIN OIL FOR THE BEST FLAVOUR IN THIS RECIPE.

SERVES FOUR

INGREDIENTS

   225g/8oz asparagus, trimmed and
     cut into 5cm/2in pieces
   2 large oranges
   2 well-flavoured tomatoes, cut
     into eighths
   50g/2oz cos (romaine) lettuce
     leaves, shredded
   30ml/2 tbsp extra virgin olive oil
   2.5ml/½ tsp sherry vinegar
   salt and ground black pepper

VARIATIONS
• Little Gem (Bibb) lettuce can be used in place of cos lettuce.
• Grapefruit segments also work well in this salad. Use 1 ruby grapefruit instead of the oranges.

1 Cook the asparagus in a pan of boiling, salted water for 3–4 minutes, until just tender. Drain and refresh under cold water.

2 Grate the rind from half an orange and reserve. Peel both the oranges and cut into segments. Squeeze out the juice from the membrane and reserve it.

3 Put the asparagus, orange segments, tomatoes and lettuce into a salad bowl. Make the dressing by whisking together the oil and vinegar and adding 15ml/1 tbsp of the reserved orange juice and 5ml/1 tsp of the rind. Season with salt and pepper. Just before serving, pour the dressing over the salad and mix gently to coat.

Energy 92kcal/384kJ; Protein 2.6g; Carbohydrate 7.2g, of which sugars 7.1g; Fat 6.1g, of which saturates 0.9g; Cholesterol 0mg; Calcium 46mg; Fibre 2.4g; Sodium 8mg

AVOCADO, TOMATO AND ORANGE SALAD

This colourful salad has a feel of the Mediterranean with its warm, fruity flavours and textures, and goes very well with plainly grilled chicken or beef. Take care to choose avocados that are fully ripe, but not over-ripe.

SERVES FOUR

INGREDIENTS

2 oranges
4 well-flavoured tomatoes
2 small avocados
60ml/4 tbsp extra virgin olive oil
30ml/2 tbsp lemon juice
15ml/1 tbsp chopped fresh parsley
1 small onion, sliced into rings
salt and ground black pepper
25g/1oz/¼ cup flaked (sliced)
  almonds and olives, to garnish

COOK'S TIP
Use avocados that are just ripe. They should yield to gentle pressure. Avoid any with bruised areas, or that feel very soft. Unripe avocados will ripen in 4–7 days at room temperature; sooner if you put bananas in the same bowl.

1 Peel the oranges and slice into thick rounds. Plunge the tomatoes into boiling water for 30 seconds, then refresh in cold water. Peel off the skins, cut the tomatoes into quarters, remove the seeds and chop the flesh roughly.

2 Cut the avocados in half, remove the stones (pits) and carefully peel away the skin. Cut into chunks.

3 Whisk together the olive oil, lemon juice and parsley. Season with salt and pepper. Toss the avocados and tomatoes in half the dressing.

4 Arrange the sliced oranges on a plate and scatter over the onion rings. Drizzle with the rest of the dressing. Spoon the avocados, tomatoes, almonds and olives on top of the salad.

Energy 251kcal/1041kJ; Protein 2.7g; Carbohydrate 11.9g, of which sugars 10.9g; Fat 21.7g, of which saturates 3.8g; Cholesterol 0mg; Calcium 60mg; Fibre 4.3g; Sodium 155mg.

RED PEPPER <u>AND</u> TOMATO SALAD

THIS IS ONE OF THOSE LOVELY RECIPES THAT BRINGS TOGETHER PERFECTLY THE COLOURS, FLAVOURS AND TEXTURES OF SOUTHERN ITALIAN FOOD. SERVE IT AT ROOM TEMPERATURE.

SERVES FOUR

INGREDIENTS

3 red (bell) peppers
6 large plum tomatoes
2.5ml/½ tsp dried red chilli flakes
1 red onion, finely sliced
3 garlic cloves, finely chopped
grated rind and juice
  of 1 lemon
45ml/3 tbsp chopped fresh flat
  leaf parsley
30ml/2 tbsp extra virgin olive oil
salt
black and green olives and extra
  chopped flat leaf parsley, to garnish

COOK'S TIP
These peppers will keep for several weeks in a jar of olive oil, with a tight-fitting lid. Store in the refrigerator.

1 Grill the peppers and tomatoes over a hot barbecue, turning frequently, until the skins are charred, or preheat the oven to 220°C/425°F/Gas 7 and roast the peppers for 10 minutes. Add the tomatoes and bake for 5 minutes more.

2 Place the peppers in a plastic bag or under an upturned bowl and set them aside, with the tomatoes, to cool.

3 Skin and seed the peppers. Chop the peppers and tomatoes roughly and place them in a mixing bowl.

4 Add the chilli flakes, onion, garlic, lemon rind and juice. Sprinkle over the parsley. Mix well, then transfer to a serving dish. Season with salt, drizzle over the olive oil and sprinkle the olives and extra parsley over the top.

Energy 126kcal/527kJ; Protein 2.9g; Carbohydrate 14.6g, of which sugars 13.8g; Fat 6.6g, of which saturates 1.1g; Cholesterol 0mg; Calcium 49mg; Fibre 4.4g; Sodium 22mg.

GRILLED TOMATO AND MOZZARELLA SALAD

FRESH BASIL MAKES A VIVIDLY COLOURED OIL FOR SERVING WITH MOZZARELLA AND TOMATOES.
GRILLING THE TOMATOES BRINGS OUT THEIR FLAVOUR AND ADDS A NEW DIMENSION TO THIS SALAD.

SERVES FOUR

INGREDIENTS
    olive oil, for brushing
    6 large plum tomatoes
    2 balls fresh mozzarella cheese,
        cut into 8–12 slices
    salt and ground black pepper
    basil leaves, to garnish
For the basil oil
    25 basil leaves
    60ml/4 tbsp extra virgin olive oil
    1 garlic clove, crushed

COOK'S TIP
Make the basil oil just before serving to
retain its fresh flavour and bright colour.

1 Prepare the barbecue and position a
lightly oiled rack over the hot coals. Cut
the tomatoes in half lengthways and
remove the seeds. Brush with oil and
place skin-side down on the rack. Cook
for 4–6 minues, until the tomatoes are
tender but still retain their shape.

2 To make the basil oil, place the basil
leaves with the olive oil and the crushed
garlic in a food processor or blender
and process until smooth. Transfer the
oil to a bowl.

3 For each serving, place the tomato
halves on top of two or three slices of
mozzarella and drizzle over the oil.
Season well. Garnish with basil leaves
and serve immediately.

COOK'S TIP
The best mozzarella to use for this
salad is the traditional kind made
from buffalo's milk, which has the
greatest flavour.

Energy 525kcal/2174kJ; Protein 20.2g; Carbohydrate 7g, of which sugars 4.8g; Fat 46.4g, of which saturates 15.9g; Cholesterol 51mg; Calcium 371mg; Fibre 2.8g; Sodium 381mg.

SUN-RIPENED TOMATO AND FETA SALAD

THIS TASTY SALAD IS A VERSION OF A TRADITIONAL GREEK SALAD, WITH PLENTY OF PURSLANE ADDED TO THE TRADITIONAL COMBINATION OF TOMATO, PEPPER, ONION, CUCUMBER, FETA AND OLIVES. THIS RECIPE IS POPULAR IN RURAL COMMUNITIES IN GREECE, WHERE PURSLANE GROWS WILD.

SERVES FOUR

INGREDIENTS
  225g/8oz tomatoes, quartered
  1 red onion, thinly sliced
  1 green (bell) pepper, cored and
    sliced in thin ribbons
  1 piece of cucumber, about 15cm/
    6in in length, peeled and sliced
    in rounds
  150g/5oz feta cheese, cubed
  a large handful of fresh purslane,
    trimmed of thick stalks
  8–10 black olives
  90–105ml/6–7 tbsp extra virgin
    olive oil
  15ml/1 tbsp lemon juice
  1.5ml/¼ tsp dried oregano
  salt and ground black pepper

1 Put the tomatoes in a salad bowl. Add the onion, green pepper, cucumber, feta, purslane and olives.

COOK'S TP
If purslane is not available, you can use rocket (arugula) instead.

2 Sprinkle the extra virgin olive oil, lemon juice and oregano on top. Add salt and ground black pepper to taste, then toss to coat everything in the olive oil and lemon, and to amalgamate the flavours. If possible, let the salad stand for 10–15 minutes at room temperature before serving.

Energy 283kcal/1,168kJ; Protein 7.2g; Carbohydrate 6.8g, of which sugars 6.3g; Fat 25.4g, of which saturates 7.7g; Cholesterol 26mg; Calcium 158mg; Fibre 1.9g; Sodium 717mg.

WATERMELON AND FETA SALAD

THE COMBINATION OF SWEET AND JUICY WATERMELON WITH SALTY FETA CHEESE IS AN ISRAELI ORIGINAL AND WAS INSPIRED BY THE TURKISH TRADITION OF EATING WATERMELON WITH SALTY WHITE CHEESE IN THE HOT SUMMER MONTHS. IT'S GREAT WITH BARBECUED FOOD.

SERVES FOUR

INGREDIENTS
  30–45ml/2–3 tbsp extra virgin
    olive oil
  juice of ½ lemon
  5ml/1 tsp vinegar to taste
  sprinkling of fresh thyme
  pinch of ground cumin
  4 large slices of watermelon, chilled
  1 frisée lettuce, core removed
  130g/4½oz feta cheese,
    preferably sheeps' milk feta,
    cut into bite-size pieces
  handful of lightly toasted
    pumpkin seeds
  handful of sunflower seeds
  10–15 black olives

1 Pour the extra virgin olive oil, lemon juice and vinegar into a bowl or jug (pitcher). Add the fresh thyme and ground cumin, and whisk until well combined. Cover the dressing and set aside until you are ready to serve the salad, but do not chill.

2 Cut the rind off the watermelon and remove as many seeds as possible. Cut the flesh into triangular-shaped chunks.

3 Put the lettuce leaves in a bowl, pour over the dressing and toss together. Arrange the leaves on a serving dish or individual plates and add the watermelon, feta cheese, pumpkin and sunflower seeds, and the black olives. Serve the salad immediately.

COOK'S TIP
The best olives for this recipe are plump black Mediterranean olives such as Kalamata, and other shiny, brined varieties or dry-cured black olives.

Energy 242kcal/1006kJ; Protein 7.9g; Carbohydrate 11.4g, of which sugars 9.7g; Fat 18.6g, of which saturates 6g; Cholesterol 23mg; Calcium 147mg; Fibre 1.2g; Sodium 752mg.

GREEK SALAD

ANYONE WHO HAS SPENT A HOLIDAY IN GREECE WILL HAVE EATEN A VERSION OF THIS — THE GREEKS'
EQUIVALENT OF A MIXED SALAD. ITS SUCCESS RELIES ON USING ONLY THE FRESHEST INGREDIENTS,
INCLUDING SUN-RIPENED TOMATOES, AND A GOOD OLIVE OIL.

SERVES SIX

INGREDIENTS
  450g/1lb well-flavoured plum
    tomatoes, skinned
  1 small cos (romaine) lettuce,
    sliced
  1 cucumber, halved, seeded and
    sliced
  200g/7oz feta cheese, crumbled
  4 spring onions (scallions), sliced
  50g/2oz/½ cup stoned (pitted) black
    olives, halved
For the dressing
  90ml/6 tbsp extra virgin olive oil
  25ml/1½ tbsp lemon juice
  salt and ground black pepper

1 Place the tomatoes on a chopping board. Using a sharp cook's knife or a serrated knife, cut into quarters and then into eighths. Put them in a bowl and add the lettuce, cucumber, feta, spring onions and olives.

2 Make the dressing. In a bowl, whisk together the olive oil and lemon juice, then season with salt and ground black pepper, and whisk again. Pour the dressing over the salad. Mix well and serve immediately.

Energy 225kcal/935kJ; Protein 11.2g; Carbohydrate 11.8g, of which sugars 11.1g; Fat 15.1g, of which saturates 8.3g; Cholesterol 39mg; Calcium 249mg; Fibre 3.4g; Sodium 827mg.

SPICED TOMATO SALAD

SERVE THIS MIDDLE-EASTERN INFLUENCED SALAD WITH WARM PITTA BREAD AS AN APPETIZER OR TO
ACCOMPANY FLAME-GRILLED MEATS. IT IS ALSO GREAT WITH A MAIN-COURSE RICE PILAFF.

SERVES FOUR

INGREDIENTS
  2 small aubergines (eggplants),
    sliced
  75ml/5 tbsp olive oil
  60ml/4 tbsp red wine vinegar
  2 garlic cloves, crushed
  15ml/1 tbsp lemon juice
  2.5ml/½ tsp ground cumin
  2.5ml/½ tsp ground coriander
  7 well-flavoured tomatoes
  ½ cucumber
  30ml/2 tbsp natural (plain) yogurt
  salt and ground black pepper
  chopped flat leaf parsley, to garnish

VARIATION
Dice the aubergines, then fry them in olive oil with 1 chopped onion and 2 crushed garlic cloves. Stir in 5–10ml/1–2 tsp mild curry powder and 3 chopped tomatoes. Cook until soft. Serve with natural yogurt.

1 Prepare the barbecue. Brush the aubergine slices lightly with some of the oil and cook over the hot coals, turning once, until golden and tender. Cut each slice into quarters.

2 In a bowl, mix together the remaining oil, vinegar, garlic, lemon juice, cumin and coriander. Season with salt and pepper, and mix thoroughly. Add the warm aubergines, stir well and chill for at least 2 hours.

3 Using a sharp knife, slice, or if you prefer, cut the tomatoes into quarters. Slice the cucumber finely, leaving the seeds intact. Add both cucumber and tomato to the aubergine mixture.

4 Transfer the salad vegetables to a serving dish and arrange them decoratively. Spoon the natural yogurt over the aubergine mixture. Sprinkle with the freshly chopped flat leaf parsley and serve.

Energy 174kcal/722kJ; Protein 2.6g; Carbohydrate 8.1g, of which sugars 7.6g; Fat 14.8g, of which saturates 2.3g; Cholesterol 0mg; Calcium 47mg; Fibre 4g; Sodium 28mg.

ORANGE AND RED ONION SALAD WITH CUMIN

CUMIN AND MINT GIVE THIS REFRESHING, QUICK-TO-PREPARE SALAD A VERY MIDDLE-EASTERN FLAVOUR. SMALL, SEEDLESS ORANGES ARE MOST SUITABLE, IF AVAILABLE.

SERVES SIX

INGREDIENTS

6 oranges
2 red onions
15ml/1 tbsp cumin seeds
5ml/1 tsp coarsely ground
  black pepper
15ml/1 tbsp chopped fresh mint
90ml/6 tbsp olive oil
salt
fresh mint sprigs and black olives,
  to garnish

1 Slice the oranges thinly, catching any juices. Holding each orange slice in turn over a bowl, cut round with scissors to remove the peel and pith. Reserve the juice. Slice the onions thinly and separate into rings.

COOK'S TIP
Roasting the cumin seeds will give them a richer flavour.

2 Arrange the orange and onion slices in layers in a shallow dish, sprinkling each layer with cumin seeds, black pepper, chopped mint, olive oil and salt to taste. Pour over the reserved orange juice.

3 Leave the salad to marinate in a cool place for about 2 hours. Scatter over the mint sprigs and black olives, and serve.

Energy 199kcal/825kJ; Protein 1.6g; Carbohydrate 11.5g, of which sugars 11.3g; Fat 16.6g, of which saturates 2.4g; Cholesterol 0mg; Calcium 68mg; Fibre 2.3g; Sodium 7mg

ENSALADILLA

A SPANISH VERSION OF WHAT IS COMMONLY KNOWN AS RUSSIAN SALAD, THIS DISH IS ALMOST A MEAL IN ITSELF, BUT IS ALSO GREAT AS AN ACCOMPANIMENT TO CHARGRILLED MEAT AND FISH.

SERVES FOUR

INGREDIENTS

    8 new potatoes, scrubbed
      and quartered
    1 large carrot, diced
    115g/4oz fine green beans, cut into
      2cm/³⁄₄in lengths
    75g/3oz/³⁄₄ cup peas
    ½ Spanish onion, chopped
    4 cornichons or small
      gherkins, sliced
    1 small red (bell) pepper, seeded
      and diced
    50g/2oz/½ cup pitted black olives
    15ml/1 tbsp drained pickled capers
    15ml/1 tbsp freshly squeezed
      lemon juice
    30ml/2 tbsp chopped fresh fennel
      or parsley
    salt and ground black pepper
For the aïoli
    2 garlic cloves, finely chopped
    2.5ml/½ tsp salt
    150ml/¼ pint/⅔ cup mayonnaise

3 Add the onion, cornichons or gherkins, red pepper, olives and capers. Stir in the aïoli and season to taste with pepper and lemon juice.

4 Toss the vegetables and aïoli together, adjust the seasoning and chill well. Serve sprinkled with fennel or parsley.

VARIATION
This salad is delicious using any combination of chopped, cooked vegetables. Use whatever is available.

1 To make the aïoli, crush the garlic with the salt in a mortar with a pestle, or use the flat of a knife blade on a chopping board, then whisk or stir into the mayonnaise.

2 Cook the potatoes and diced carrot in a pan of boiling lightly salted water for 5–8 minutes until they are almost tender. Add the beans and peas to the pan and continue cooking for 2 minutes, or until all the vegetables are tender. Drain well and transfer the vegetables to a large bowl.

Energy 397kcal/1645kJ; Protein 4.9g; Carbohydrate 25.3g, of which sugars 7.8g; Fat 31.4g, of which saturates 4.9g; Cholesterol 28mg; Calcium 47mg; Fibre 4.4g; Sodium 609mg

SALAD OF FRESH CEPS WITH PARSLEY AND WALNUT DRESSING

THE DISTINCTIVE FLAVOUR OF WALNUTS IS A NATURAL PARTNER FOR MUSHROOMS. HERE, WILD MUSHROOMS AND WALNUTS MELD WITH FRENCH MUSTARD, LEMON, PARSLEY AND NUT OILS IN A RICHLY FLAVOURED SALAD. USE A CHARACTERFUL MIXTURE OF SALAD LEAVES.

3 Transfer the sliced mushrooms to a large bowl and combine with the dressing. Set aside for 10–15 minutes to allow the flavours to mingle.

4 Meanwhile, dry-fry the walnut pieces on a griddle for about a minute, shaking the pan to ensure they toast evenly. Alternatively, toast them under a grill (broiler) preheated to medium-hot.

5 Wash and spin the mixed salad leaves, then add to the mushrooms in the bowl and toss to combine.

6 To serve, spoon the salad on to four large plates, season well then scatter with the toasted walnuts and shavings of Parmesan cheese.

SERVES FOUR

INGREDIENTS
  350g/12oz/4¾ cups fresh small
    cep mushrooms
  50g/2oz/½ cup broken walnut pieces
  175g/6oz mixed salad leaves, to
    include Batavia, young spinach
    and frisée
  50g/2oz/⅔ cup freshly shaved
    Parmesan cheese
  salt and ground black pepper
For the dressing
  2 egg yolks
  2.5ml/½ tsp French mustard
  75ml/5 tbsp groundnut (peanut) oil
  45ml/3 tbsp walnut oil
  30ml/2 tbsp lemon juice
  30ml/2 tbsp chopped fresh parsley
  1 pinch caster (superfine) sugar

1 To make the dressing, place the egg yolks in a screw-top jar with the mustard, groundnut and walnut oils, lemon juice, parsley and sugar. Shake well to combine.

2 Slice the mushrooms thinly with a sharp knife, keeping the slices intact.

COOK'S TIP
If fresh ceps are unavailable, this salad can also be made with other fresh mushrooms. Chestnut mushrooms, fresh shiitake mushrooms and even button (white) mushrooms would all work well.

Energy 392kcal/1620kJ; Protein 10.2g; Carbohydrate 2.6g, of which sugars 2.3g; Fat 38g, of which saturates 7.5g; Cholesterol 113mg; Calcium 192mg; Fibre 1.8g; Sodium 148mg.

GRILLED LEEK AND FENNEL SALAD WITH SPICY TOMATO DRESSING

THIS IS AN EXCELLENT SALAD TO MAKE IN THE EARLY AUTUMN, WHEN YOUNG LEEKS ARE AT THEIR BEST AND RIPE TOMATOES ARE FULL OF FLAVOUR. SERVE WITH GOOD BREAD AS AN APPETIZER OR SERVE TO ACCOMPANY SIMPLY COOKED WHITE FISH FOR A MAIN COURSE.

SERVES SIX

INGREDIENTS
    675g/1½lb leeks
    2 large fennel bulbs
    120ml/4fl oz/½ cup extra virgin
        olive oil
    2 shallots, chopped
    150ml/¼ pint/⅔ cup dry white wine or
        white vermouth
    5ml/1 tsp fennel seeds, crushed
    6 fresh thyme sprigs
    2–3 bay leaves
    good pinch of dried red chilli
        flakes
    350g/12oz tomatoes, peeled, seeded
        and diced
    5ml/1 tsp sun-dried tomato
        paste (optional)
    good pinch of caster (superfine)
        sugar (optional)
    75g/3oz/¾ cup small black olives,
        stoned (pitted)
    salt and ground black pepper

1 Cook the leeks in boiling salted water for 4–5 minutes. Use a slotted spoon to remove the leeks and place them in a colander to drain thoroughly and cool. Reserve the cooking water in the pan. Squeeze out excess water and cut the leeks into 7.5cm/3in lengths.

2 Trim the fennel bulbs, reserving any feathery fronds for the garnish, if you like, and cut the bulbs either into thin slices or into thicker wedges, according to taste.

3 Cook the fennel pieces in the reserved cooking water for 5 minutes, then drain thoroughly and toss with 30ml/2 tbsp of the olive oil. Season to taste with black pepper.

4 Heat a ridged cast-iron griddle on the barbecue or hob. Cook the leeks and fennel on the griddle until tinged deep brown. Place the vegetables in a large shallow dish and set aside.

5 Place the remaining olive oil, the shallots, white wine or vermouth, crushed fennel seeds, thyme, bay leaves and chilli flakes in a large pan. Bring to the boil over medium heat, then lower the heat and simmer for about 10 minutes.

6 Add the diced tomatoes and cook briskly for 5–8 minutes, or until they have reduced and the consistency has thickened.

7 Add the tomato paste, if using, and adjust the seasoning, adding a good pinch of sugar if you think the dressing needs it.

8 Pour the dressing over the leeks and fennel, toss to mix and leave to cool. The salad may be made several hours in advance and kept in the refrigerator, but bring it back to room temperature before serving.

9 When ready to serve, stir the salad then sprinkle the black olives and the chopped fennel fronds, if using, over the top of the dish.

COOK'S TIP
When buying fennel, look for rounded bulbs; they have a better shape for this dish. The flesh should be crisp and white, with no signs of bruising. Avoid specimens with broken leaves or with brown or dried-out patches.

Energy 193kcal/801kJ; Protein 2.8g; Carbohydrate 6.7g, of which sugars 5.9g; Fat 14.7g, of which saturates 2.2g; Cholesterol 0mg; Calcium 53mg; Fibre 4.6g; Sodium 297mg.

TRADITIONAL COLESLAW

Every deli sells coleslaw but there is boring coleslaw and exciting coleslaw. The key to good coleslaw is a zesty dressing and an interesting selection of vegetables. Slicing the cabbage thinly is also essential and is best done using a mandolin, if you have one.

SERVES SIX TO EIGHT

INGREDIENTS
1 large white or green cabbage, very
   thinly sliced
3–4 carrots, coarsely grated
½ red and ½ green (bell) pepper,
   chopped
1–2 celery sticks, finely chopped or
   5–10ml/1–2 tsp celery seeds
1 onion, chopped
2–3 handfuls of raisins or sultanas
   (golden raisins)
45ml/3 tbsp white wine vinegar or
   cider vinegar
60–90ml/4–6 tbsp sugar, to taste
175–250ml/6–8fl oz/¾–1 cup
   mayonnaise, to bind
salt and ground black pepper

1 Put the cabbage, carrots, peppers, celery or celery seeds, onion, and raisins or sultanas in a salad bowl and mix to combine well. Add the vinegar, sugar, salt and ground black pepper and toss together well until thoroughly combined. Leave to stand for about 1 hour.

2 Stir enough mayonnaise into the salad to bind the ingredients together lightly. Taste the salad for seasoning and sweet-and-sour flavour, adding more sugar, salt and pepper if needed. Chill. Drain off any excess liquid from the salad and stir it again before serving.

Energy 222kcal/921kJ; Protein 2g; Carbohydrate 16.1g, of which sugars 15.4g; Fat 17g, of which saturates 2.6g; Cholesterol 16mg; Calcium 55mg; Fibre 3.4g; Sodium 120mg.

THE ULTIMATE DELI-STYLE SALAD

A potato salad, tossed in a light, creamy dressing and fresh with piquant flavours, is a must-have for any barbecue spread. It is tempting to pop along to your local deli for something ready-prepared, but you can make this one very easily at home.

SERVES SIX TO EIGHT

INGREDIENTS
1kg/2¼lb waxy salad
   potatoes, scrubbed
1 red or white onion, finely chopped
2–3 celery sticks, finely chopped
60–90ml/4–6 tbsp chopped
   fresh parsley
15–20 pimiento-stuffed olives, halved
3 hard-boiled eggs, chopped
60ml/4 tbsp extra virgin olive oil
60ml/4 tbsp white wine vinegar
15–30ml/1–2 tbsp mild or
   wholegrain mustard
celery seeds, to taste (optional)
175–250ml/6–8fl oz/
   ¾–1 cup mayonnaise
salt and ground black pepper
paprika, to garnish

1 Cook the potatoes in a pan of salted boiling water until tender. Drain, return to the pan and leave for 2–3 minutes to cool and dry a little.

2 When the potatoes are cool enough to handle but still very warm, cut them into chunks or slices and place in a salad bowl.

3 Sprinkle the potatoes with salt and pepper, then add the onion, celery, parsley, olives and the chopped eggs. In a jug (pitcher), combine the olive oil, vinegar, mustard and celery seeds, if using, pour over the salad and toss to combine. Add enough mayonnaise to bind the salad together. Chill before serving, sprinkled with a little paprika.

Energy 323kcal/1343kJ; Protein 5.2g; Carbohydrate 21.5g, of which sugars 2.7g; Fat 24.7g, of which saturates 4g; Cholesterol 88mg; Calcium 49mg; Fibre 2g; Sodium 149mg.

TANGY POTATO SALAD

IF YOU LIKE A GOOD KICK OF MUSTARD, YOU'LL LOVE THIS COMBINATION. IT'S ALSO WELL FLAVOURED WITH TARRAGON, WHICH IS USED IN THE DRESSING AND AS A GARNISH. WHEN THEY ARE AVAILABLE, YOU COULD USE SMALL RED OR EVEN BLUE POTATOES TO GIVE A NICE COLOUR TO THE SALAD.

<u>SERVES EIGHT</u>

INGREDIENTS

1.55kg/3lb small new or
   salad potatoes
75g/3oz/6 tbsp chopped red onion
30ml/2 tbsp white wine vinegar
15ml/1 tbsp Dijon mustard
45ml/3 tbsp vegetable or olive oil
125ml/4fl oz/½ cup mayonnaise
30ml/2 tbsp chopped fresh tarragon,
   or 7.5ml/1½ tsp dried tarragon
1 celery stick, thinly sliced
salt and ground black pepper
celery leaves, to garnish
tarragon leaves, to garnish

1 Cook the potatoes in their skins in salted water for 15–20 minutes.

2 Drain the potatoes well and when cool enough to handle, slice them into a bowl and add the chopped onion.

3 Mix together the vinegar and mustard, then slowly whisk in the oil. Season with salt and black pepper.

4 Pour the dressing over the salad and toss gently to combine. Leave to stand for at least 30 minutes. Mix the mayonnaise and tarragon and stir into the potatoes with the celery. Garnish with celery leaves and the fresh tarragon leaves.

Energy 283kcal/1182kJ; Protein 3.7g; Carbohydrate 32.4g, of which sugars 3.4g; Fat 16.2g, of which saturates 2.5g; Cholesterol 11mg; Calcium 18mg; Fibre 2.1g; Sodium 147mg.

POTATO AND FETA SALAD

A POTATO SALAD MAY SOUND MUNDANE BUT THIS ONE IS NOT, AS IT IS REDOLENT WITH THE AROMAS OF FRESH HERBS AND HAS LAYER UPON LAYER OF FLAVOURS. IT IS AN EASY DISH TO ASSEMBLE, SO IT MAKES A PERFECT SALAD FOR AN INFORMAL OUTDOOR PARTY.

SERVES FOUR

INGREDIENTS
    115g/4oz feta cheese
    500g/1¼lb small new or salad
      potatoes
    5 spring onions (scallions),
      green and white parts
      finely chopped
    15ml/1 tbsp bottled capers,
      rinsed
    8–10 black olives
    45ml/3 tbsp finely chopped fresh
      flat leaf parsley
    30ml/2 tbsp finely chopped
      fresh mint
    salt and ground black pepper
For the dressing
    90–120ml/6–8 tbsp extra virgin
      olive oil
    juice of 1 lemon, or to taste
    2 salted or preserved anchovies,
      rinsed and finely chopped
    45ml/3 tbsp Greek (US strained
      plain) yogurt
    45ml/3 tbsp finely chopped
      fresh dill, plus a few sprigs,
      to garnish
    5ml/1 tsp French mustard

1 Chop the feta cheese into small, even-sized cubes and crumble slightly.

2 Bring a pan of lightly salted water to the boil and cook the potatoes in their skins for 25–30 minutes, or until tender. Take care not to let them become soggy and disintegrate. Drain them thoroughly and let them cool a little.

3 When the potatoes are cool enough to handle, peel them with your fingers and place them in a large bowl. If they are very small, keep them whole; otherwise cut them into large cubes. Add the chopped spring onions, capers, olives, feta cheese and fresh herbs, and toss gently to mix.

4 To make the dressing, place the extra virgin olive oil in a bowl with the lemon juice and anchovies.

5 Whisk thoroughly for a few minutes until the dressing emulsifies and thickens; you may need to add a little more olive oil if it does not thicken. Whisk in the yogurt, dill and mustard, with salt and pepper to taste.

6 Dress the salad while the potatoes are still warm, tossing lightly.

COOK'S TIP
The salad tastes better if it is allowed to sit for an hour or so at room temperature for the flavours to blend.

Energy 138kcal/566kJ; Protein 1.3g; Carbohydrate 1.2g, of which sugars 1.1g; Fat 14.2g, of which saturates 2g; Cholesterol 0mg; Calcium 75mg; Fibre 1.4g; Sodium 40mg.

WARM POTATO SALAD <u>WITH</u> BACON

THIS TASTY SUMMER SALAD BECOMES A FAVOURITE WITH ALL WHO TRY IT. CHOOSE DRY-CURED BACON AND REAL NEW-SEASON POTATOES RATHER THAN ALL-YEAR "BABY" POTATOES, IF POSSIBLE. USING SUPERIOR INGREDIENTS MAKES THIS A SPECIAL DISH, AND IT'S IDEAL FOR A BARBECUE OR PARTY.

SERVES FOUR TO SIX

INGREDIENTS

900g/2lb small new potatoes
sprig of mint
15–30ml/1–2 tbsp olive oil
1 onion, thinly sliced
175g/6oz smoked bacon, cut into
  small strips
2 garlic cloves, crushed
30ml/2 tbsp chopped fresh parsley
1 small bunch of chives, chopped
15ml/1 tbsp wine vinegar or cider
  vinegar
15ml/1 tbsp wholegrain mustard
salt and ground black pepper

1 Scrape the new potatoes and cook in salted water with the mint for about 10 minutes, until just tender. Drain and cool a little, then tip into a salad bowl.

2 Heat the oil in a frying pan, add the onion and cook gently until just softening, stirring occasionally. Add the bacon and cook until it crisps.

3 Add the garlic and cook for another minute or so, then remove from the heat and add the chopped herbs, vinegar, mustard and seasoning to taste, remembering the bacon may be salty.

4 Pour the dressing over the potatoes. Toss gently to mix, and serve the salad while still warm.

Energy 206kcal/863kJ; Protein 2.8g; Carbohydrate 24.3g, of which sugars 2.1g; Fat 11.5g, of which saturates 1.7g; Cholesterol 0mg; Calcium 22mg; Fibre 1.8g; Sodium 19mg.

POTATO AND RADISH SALAD

RADISHES ADD A SPLASH OF CRUNCH AND PEPPERY FLAVOUR TO THIS HONEY-SCENTED SALAD. MOST POTATO SALADS ARE DRESSED IN A THICK, CREAMY SAUCE, BUT THIS ONE IS QUITE LIGHT AND COLOURFUL, WITH A TASTY YET DELICATE OIL AND VINEGAR DRESSING.

SERVES FOUR TO SIX

INGREDIENTS

    450g/1lb small new or salad
      potatoes
    45ml/3 tbsp olive oil
    15ml/1 tbsp walnut or hazelnut oil
      (optional)
    30ml/2 tbsp wine vinegar
    10ml/2 tsp coarse-grain mustard
    5ml/1 tsp honey
    about 6–8 radishes, thinly sliced
    30ml/2 tbsp chopped chives
    salt and ground black pepper

VARIATIONS

Sliced celery, diced red onion and/or chopped walnuts would make good alternatives to the radishes when they are not in season.

COOK'S TIP

For best effect, serve on a platter lined with frilly lettuce leaves.

1 Cook the potatoes in their skins in a large pan of boiling salted water until just tender. Drain the potatoes thoroughly and leave to cool slightly. When cool enough to handle, cut the larger potatoes in half, but leave any small ones whole. Return the potatoes to a large bowl.

2 To make the dressing, place the oils, vinegar, mustard, honey and seasoning in a bowl. Mix them together until thoroughly combined.

3 Pour the dressing over the potatoes in the bowl while they are still cooling. Toss and leave to stand for an hour or so to allow the flavours to penetrate.

4 Finally mix in the sliced radishes and chopped chives and chill the salad.

5 When ready to serve, toss the salad thoroughly again, as some of the dressing may have settled on the bottom. Taste again and adjust the seasoning if necessary.

Energy 108kcal/451kJ; Protein 1.5g; Carbohydrate 13g, of which sugars 1.9g; Fat 5.9g, of which saturates 0.9g; Cholesterol 0mg; Calcium 8mg; Fibre 0.9g; Sodium 36mg.

POTATO AND OLIVE SALAD

THIS DELICIOUS SALAD COMES FROM NORTH AFRICA. THE COMBINATION OF GARLIC, CUMIN AND LOTS OF FRESH CORIANDER MAKES IT PARTICULARLY TASTY AND YET IT IS QUICK AND SIMPLE TO PREPARE. IDEAL AS PART OF A SALAD SELECTION TO ACCOMPANY BARBECUED MEAT, FISH OR POULTRY.

SERVES FOUR

INGREDIENTS
  8 large new potatoes
  large pinch of salt
  large pinch of sugar
  3 garlic cloves, chopped
  15ml/1 tbsp vinegar of your choice,
    such as a fruit variety
  large pinch of ground cumin or whole
    cumin seeds
  pinch of cayenne pepper or hot
    paprika, to taste
  30–45ml/2–3 tbsp extra virgin
    olive oil
  30–45ml/2–3 tbsp chopped fresh
    coriander (cilantro) leaves
  10–15 dry-cured black
    Mediterranean olives

1 Peel the new potatoes and cut them into chunks. Put them in a pan, pour in water to cover and add the salt and sugar. Bring to the boil, then reduce the heat and boil gently for about 8–10 minutes, or until the potatoes are just tender. Drain well and leave in a colander to cool completely.

2 When cool enough to handle, cut the potatoes into thick slices and put them in a bowl.

3 Sprinkle the garlic, vinegar, cumin and cayenne or paprika over the salad. Drizzle with olive oil and sprinkle with coriander and olives. Chill before serving.

Energy 196kcal/822kJ; Protein 3g; Carbohydrate 24.5g, of which sugars 2.2g; Fat 10.2g, of which saturates 1.6g; Cholesterol 0mg; Calcium 42mg; Fibre 2.5g; Sodium 302mg.

GRILLED POTATOES WITH CHIVE FLOWERS

THERE IS SOMETHING VERY ENJOYABLE ABOUT USING EDIBLE FLOWERING PLANTS AND HERBS FROM THE GARDEN. GRABBING A HANDFUL OF THIS HERB OR THAT FLOWER IS ALL PART OF THE CREATIVITY OF COOKING AND EATING OUTDOORS, AND IT CAN PRODUCE REALLY EXCITING AND UNEXPECTED RESULTS.

SERVES FOUR TO SIX

INGREDIENTS

   900g/2lb salad potatoes, such as
     Charlotte, Jersey Royal or
     French ratte
   15ml/1 tbsp champagne or white
     wine vinegar
   105ml/7 tbsp olive oil
   45ml/3 tbsp chopped chives
   about 10 chive flowers
   4–6 small bunches yellow cherry
     tomatoes on the vine
   salt and ground black pepper

COOK'S TIP

If well established in the garden, chives will usually blossom in early spring.

1 Prepare the barbecue. Boil the potatoes in a large pan of lightly salted water for 10–15 minutes, or until just tender. Meanwhile, make the dressing by whisking the vinegar with 75ml/ 5 tbsp of the oil, then stirring in the chives and flowers. Drain the potatoes and cut them in half. Season to taste.

2 Position a lightly oiled grill rack over the hot coals. Toss the potatoes in the remaining oil and lay them on the grill rack over medium-high heat, cut-side down. Leave for about 5 minutes, then press the potatoes down a little so that they are imprinted with the marks of the grill rack.

3 Turn the potatoes over and cook the second side for about 3 minutes, pressing them on to the rack again. Place the potatoes in a bowl, pour over the dressing and toss lightly to mix.

4 Grill the tomatoes for 3 minutes, or until they are just beginning to blister. Serve with the potatoes, which can be hot, warm or cold.

Energy 232kcal/970kJ; Protein 3g; Carbohydrate 26.2g, of which sugars 4g; Fat 13.5g, of which saturates 2.1g; Cholesterol 0mg; Calcium 14mg; Fibre 2.2g; Sodium 23mg.

POTATO WEDGES WITH GARLIC AND ROSEMARY

Toss the potato wedges in fragrant, garlicky olive oil with chopped fresh rosemary before barbecuing them over the coals. They are irresistible eaten hot straight from the grill, with a dollop of salsa or crème fraîche to dip them into.

SERVES FOUR

INGREDIENTS

675g/1½lb medium-sized old
  potatoes
15ml/1 tbsp olive oil
2 garlic cloves, thinly sliced
60ml/4 tbsp chopped fresh
  rosemary
salt and ground black pepper

1 Cut each potato lengthways into four long wedges and par-boil in a large pan of salted water for about 5 minutes. Drain well.

2 Toss the potatoes in the olive oil with the garlic, rosemary and black pepper. Prepare the barbecue and position a lightly oiled grill rack over the coals.

3 Cook the potatoes over hot coals for about 15 minutes, turning occasionally, until the wedges are crisp and golden brown. Serve immediately.

Energy 150kcal/633kJ; Protein 3.5g; Carbohydrate 27.9g, of which sugars 2.5g; Fat 3.4g, of which saturates 0.6g; Cholesterol 0mg; Calcium 36mg; Fibre 2.4g; Sodium 23mg.

SPANISH POTATOES

THIS IS AN ADAPTATION OF A TRADITIONAL SPANISH RECIPE FOR PEPPERY FRIED POTATOES. COOK THE POTATOES IN A FLAMEPROOF DISH ON THE BARBECUE OR IN A PAN ON THE HOB, AND SERVE THEM WITH BARBECUED MEATS AND LEAFY SALADS.

SERVES FOUR

INGREDIENTS

 675g/1½lb small new or salad
  potatoes
 75ml/5 tbsp olive oil
 2 garlic cloves, sliced
 2.5ml/½ tsp crushed chillies
 2.5ml/½ tsp ground cumin
 10ml/2 tsp paprika
 30ml/2 tbsp red or white
  wine vinegar
 1 red or green (bell) pepper, sliced
 coarse sea salt, to serve (optional)

3 Meanwhile, crush together the garlic, chillies and cumin using a pestle and mortar. Add the paprika and wine vinegar to the mixture and stir to form a thick paste.

4 Add the garlic mixture to the potatoes with the sliced pepper and cook, stirring, for 2 minutes. Serve warm, or leave until cold. Scatter with coarse sea salt, if you wish, to serve.

1 Cook the potatoes in a pan of boiling salted water for 10–12 minutes until almost tender. Drain them well and cut into chunks.

2 Heat the olive oil in a large frying pan or sauté pan and fry the potatoes, turning them frequently, until they are tender and golden.

Energy 273kcal/1148kJ; Protein 4.6g; Carbohydrate 39.5g, of which sugars 5.9g; Fat 11.9g, of which saturates 1.9g; Cholesterol 0mg; Calcium 22mg; Fibre 3.1g; Sodium 39mg.

POTATO SKEWERS <u>WITH</u> MUSTARD DIP

POTATOES COOKED ON THE BARBECUE HAVE A TASTY FLAVOUR AND CRISP SKIN. THESE SKEWERS COMBINE THEM WITH SHALLOTS AND ARE SERVED WITH A THICK, GARLIC-RICH DIP.

2 With the motor running, add the oil, until the mixture forms a thick cream. Add the mustard and season.

3 Par-boil the potatoes in salted boiling water for about 5 minutes. Drain well and then thread them on to metal skewers with the shallots.

4 Brush with olive oil and sprinkle with sea salt. Cook for 10–12 minutes over a hot barbecue, turning often, until tender. Serve with the mustard dip.

SERVES FOUR

INGREDIENTS
   1kg/2¼lb small new potatoes
   200g/7oz/2 cups shallots, halved
   30ml/2 tbsp olive oil
   15ml/1 tbsp sea salt
For the mustard dip
   4 garlic cloves, crushed
   2 egg yolks
   30ml/2 tbsp lemon juice
   300ml/½ pint/1¼ cups extra virgin
   olive oil
   10ml/2 tsp whole-grain mustard
salt and ground black pepper

1 To make the mustard dip, place the garlic, egg yolks and lemon juice in a blender or food processor and process for a few seconds until smooth.

COOK'S TIP
Apart from supporting the ingredients, metal skewers will transmit heat to the potatoes so they cook more quickly.

Energy 488kcal/2024kJ; Protein 4.3g; Carbohydrate 29.5g, of which sugars 4.1g; Fat 40g, of which saturates 6.1g; Cholesterol 65mg; Calcium 28mg; Fibre 2.2g; Sodium 49mg.

SUMMER PASTA SALAD

RIPE RED TOMATOES, MOZZARELLA AND OLIVES MAKE A GOOD BASE FOR A FRESH AND TANGY SALAD THAT IS PERFECT AS PART OF A BUFFET TABLE FOR A SUMMER LUNCH.

SERVES FOUR

INGREDIENTS
350g/12oz/3 cups dried penne or
  other pasta shapes
150g/5oz packet mozzarella di
  bufala, drained and diced
3 ripe tomatoes, diced
10 black olives, sliced
10 green olives, sliced
1 spring onion (scallion), thinly
  sliced on the diagonal
1 handful fresh basil leaves
For the dressing
90ml/6 tbsp extra-virgin olive oil
15ml/1 tbsp balsamic vinegar or
  lemon juice
salt and ground black pepper

COOK'S TIP
Mozzarella made from buffalo milk has
the most flavour and is widely available.

1 Bring a large pan of salted water to
the boil, add the pasta and cook
according to the packet instructions,
until *al dente*. Drain and rinse under
cold running water, then drain
thoroughly again. Leave the pasta
to drain.

2 To make the dressing, whisk the
olive oil and balsamic vinegar or lemon
juice in a large bowl with a little salt
and pepper.

3 Add the pasta, mozzarella, tomatoes,
olives and spring onion to the dressing
and toss together well. Adjust the
seasoning and sprinkle with basil
before serving.

VARIATION
Make the salad more substantial by
adding other ingredients, such as sliced
peppers, toasted pine nuts, canned
artichoke hearts or baby corn cobs.

Energy 635kcal/2658kJ; Protein 18.7g; Carbohydrate 67.2g, of which sugars 5.3g; Fat 34.2g, of which saturates 9.1g; Cholesterol 22mg; Calcium 210mg; Fibre 5.5g; Sodium 1845mg

TUNA AND CORN PASTA SALAD

THIS IS AN EXCELLENT MAIN COURSE SALAD FOR A SUMMER LUNCH OUTSIDE. IT TRAVELS VERY WELL, SO IT IS GOOD FOR PICNICS, TOO. FOR A SPECIAL TOUCH, BARBECUE A CORN ON THE COB AND SCRAPE THE KERNELS INTO THE SALAD RATHER THAN USING CANNED OR FROZEN CORN.

SERVES FOUR

INGREDIENTS
175g/6oz/1½ cups dried conchiglie
175g/6oz can tuna in olive oil,
  drained and flaked
175g/6oz can sweetcorn, drained
75g/3oz bottled roasted red pepper,
  rinsed, dried and finely chopped
1 handful of fresh basil leaves,
  chopped
salt and ground black pepper
For the dressing
60ml/4 tbsp extra virgin olive oil
15ml/1 tbsp balsamic vinegar
5ml/1 tsp red wine vinegar
5ml/1 tsp Dijon mustard
5–10ml/1–2 tsp honey, to taste

VARIATION
To save time, you could use canned corn with peppers.

1 Cook the pasta according to packet instructions. Drain it into a colander, and rinse under cold running water. Leave to drain until cold and dry, shaking the colander occasionally.

2 Make the dressing. Put the oil in a large bowl, add the two kinds of vinegar and whisk well together until emulsified. Add the mustard, honey and salt and pepper to taste and whisk again until thick.

3 Add the pasta to the dressing and toss well to mix, then add the tuna, corn and roasted pepper and toss again. Mix in about half the basil and taste for seasoning. Serve at room temperature or chilled, with the remaining basil sprinkled on top.

Energy 398kcal/1674kJ; Protein 18.6g; Carbohydrate 47.2g, of which sugars 8.7g; Fat 16.3g, of which saturates 2.4g; Cholesterol 22mg; Calcium 20mg; Fibre 2.2g; Sodium 247mg.

PINK AND GREEN PASTA SALAD

SPIKED WITH A LITTLE FRESH CHILLI, THIS PRETTY SALAD MAKES A DELICIOUS LIGHT LUNCH SERVED WITH HOT CIABATTA ROLLS AND A BOTTLE OF SPARKLING DRY ITALIAN WHITE WINE. PRAWNS AND AVOCADO ARE A WINNING COMBINATION, SO IT'S ALSO A POPULAR CHOICE FOR A BARBECUE BUFFET.

SERVES FOUR

INGREDIENTS

225g/8oz/2 cups dried farfalle
juice of ½ lemon
1 small fresh red chilli, seeded and
   very finely chopped
60ml/4 tbsp chopped fresh basil
30ml/2 tbsp chopped fresh coriander
   (cilantro)
60ml/4 tbsp extra virgin olive oil
15ml/1 tbsp mayonnaise
250g/9oz/1½ cups peeled
   cooked prawns (shrimp)
1 avocado
salt and ground black pepper

COOK'S TIP

This pasta salad can be made several hours ahead of time, without the avocado. Cover the bowl with clear film and chill in the fridge. Prepare the avocado and add it to the salad just before serving or it will discolour.

1 Cook the pasta in a large pan of salted boiling water according to the packet instructions.

2 Meanwhile, put the lemon juice and chilli in a bowl with half the basil and coriander and salt and pepper to taste. Whisk well to mix, then whisk in the oil and mayonnaise until thick. Add the prawns and gently stir to coat in the dressing.

3 Drain the pasta into a colander, and rinse under cold running water until cold. Leave to drain and dry, shaking the colander occasionally.

4 Halve, stone (pit) and peel the avocado, then cut the flesh into neat dice. Add to the prawns and dressing with the pasta, toss well to mix and taste for seasoning. Serve immediately, sprinkled with the remaining basil and coriander.

Energy 417kcal/1750kJ; Protein 18.7g; Carbohydrate 42.6g, of which sugars 2.4g; Fat 20.2g, of which saturates 3.2g; Cholesterol 125mg; Calcium 97mg; Fibre 3.2g; Sodium 144mg.

CLASSIC PASTA SALAD

PASTA SALAD IS A POPULAR AND SUSTAINING ACCOMPANIMENT TO ALL KINDS OF DISHES. THIS VERSION CONTAINS BRIGHT GREEN BEANS AND CHERRY TOMATOES ON THE VINE, WITH PARMESAN, OLIVES AND CAPERS TO GIVE IT PIQUANCY. COOK THE PASTA AL DENTE FOR THE BEST TEXTURE.

SERVES SIX

INGREDIENTS

300g/11oz/2¾ cups dried fusilli
150g/5oz green beans, topped and
    tailed and cut into 5cm/2in lengths
1 potato, about 150g/5oz, diced
200g/7oz cherry tomatoes on the
    vine, hulled and halved
2 spring onions (scallions),
    finely chopped
90g/3½oz Parmesan cheese, diced or
    coarsely shaved
6–8 pitted black olives, cut into rings
15–30ml/1–2 tbsp capers, to taste
For the dressing
90ml/6 tbsp extra virgin olive oil
15ml/1 tbsp balsamic vinegar
15ml/1 tbsp chopped fresh flat
    leaf parsley
salt and ground black pepper

1 Cook the pasta according to the instructions on the packet. Drain it into a colander, rinse under cold running water until cold, then shake the colander to remove as much water as possible. Leave to drain and dry, shaking the colander occasionally.

2 Cook the green beans and diced potato in a pan of salted boiling water for 5–6 minutes or until tender. Drain in a colander and leave to cool.

3 To make the dressing, put all the ingredients in a large bowl with salt and pepper to taste, and whisk well to mix.

4 Add the tomatoes, spring onions, Parmesan, olive rings and capers to the dressing, then add the cold pasta, beans and potato. Toss well to mix. Cover and leave to stand for about 30 minutes. Taste for seasoning before serving.

COOK'S TIP

To round off the soft textures of this superb salad, buy a piece of fresh Parmesan from the delicatessen to shave into wafer-thin slices. This version of the cheese is a mature, softer version of the harder cheese used for grating and sprinkling over hot dishes.

Energy 376kcal/1579kJ; Protein 13.2g; Carbohydrate 43g, of which sugars 3.7g; Fat 18g, of which saturates 5g; Cholesterol 15mg; Calcium 212mg; Fibre 2.9g; Sodium 359mg.

WILD RICE PILAFF

WILD RICE ISN'T A RICE AT ALL, BUT IS ACTUALLY A TYPE OF WILD GRASS. CALL IT WHAT YOU WILL, IT HAS A WONDERFUL NUTTY FLAVOUR AND COMBINES WELL WITH LONG GRAIN RICE IN THIS FRUITY MIXTURE. SERVE AS A SIDE DISH.

SERVES SIX

INGREDIENTS
   200g/7oz/1 cup wild rice
   40g/1½oz/3 tbsp butter
   ½ onion, finely chopped
   200g/7oz/1 cup long grain rice
   475ml/16fl oz/2 cups chicken stock
   75g/3oz/¾ cup sliced or
    flaked almonds
   115g/4oz/⅔ cup sultanas
   30ml/2 tbsp chopped fresh parsley
   salt and ground black pepper

1 Bring a large saucepan of water to the boil. Add the wild rice and 5ml/ 1 tsp salt. Lower the heat, cover and simmer gently for 45–60 minutes, until the rice is tender. Drain well.

4 Melt the remaining butter in a small pan. Add the almonds and cook until they are just golden. Set aside.

5 Put the rice mixture in a bowl and add the almonds, sultanas and half the parsley. Stir to mix. Taste and adjust the seasoning if necessary. Transfer to a warmed serving dish, sprinkle with the remaining parsley and serve.

2 Meanwhile, melt 15g/½oz/1 tbsp of the butter in another pan. Add the onion and cook over a medium heat for about 5 minutes until it is just softened. Stir in the long grain rice and cook for 1 minute more.

3 Stir in the stock and bring to the boil. Cover and simmer gently for 30–40 minutes, until the rice is tender and the liquid has been absorbed.

COOK'S TIP
Like all rice dishes, this one must be made with well-flavoured stock. If you haven't time to make your own, use a carton or can of good quality stock.

Energy 424kcal/1769kJ; Protein 8.4g; Carbohydrate 68.3g, of which sugars 14.5g; Fat 13g, of which saturates 4g; Cholesterol 14mg; Calcium 69mg; Fibre 1.7g; Sodium 48mg.

RICE SALAD

The sky's the limit with this recipe. Use whatever fruit, vegetables and even leftover meat that you might have, mix with cooked rice and pour over the fragrant dressing.

SERVES FOUR TO SIX

INGREDIENTS
350g/12oz/3 cups cooked rice
1 Asian pear, cored and diced
50g/2oz dried shrimp, chopped
1 avocado, peeled, stoned (pitted)
  and diced
½ medium cucumber, finely diced
2 lemon grass stalks, finely chopped
30ml/2 tbsp sweet chilli sauce
1 fresh green or red chilli, seeded
  and finely sliced
115g/4oz/1 cup flaked (sliced)
  almonds, toasted
small bunch fresh coriander
  (cilantro), chopped
fresh Thai sweet basil leaves,
  to garnish
For the dressing
  300ml/½ pint/1¼ cups water
  10ml/2 tsp shrimp paste
  15ml/1 tbsp palm sugar (jaggery) or
    light muscovado (brown) sugar
  2 kaffir lime leaves, torn into
    small pieces
  ½ lemon grass stalk, sliced

1 Make the dressing. Put the measured water in a small pan with the shrimp paste, sugar, kaffir lime leaves and lemon grass. Heat gently, stirring, until the sugar dissolves, then bring to boiling point and simmer for 5 minutes. Strain into a bowl and set aside until cold.

2 Put the cooked rice in a large salad bowl and fluff up the grains with a fork. Add the Asian pear, dried shrimp, avocado, cucumber, lemon grass and sweet chilli sauce. Mix well.

3 Add the diced chilli, almonds and coriander to the bowl and toss well. Garnish with Thai basil leaves and serve with the bowl of dressing to spoon over the top of individual portions.

COOK'S TIPS
• The Asian pear adds a fruit note and a crisp texture to the salad. A crisp, tart eating apple could be substituted.
• Basmati rice, carefully cooked so that the grains stay separate, has a wonderful flavour and is excellent in salads. You could also make the salad using whole-grain rice.

Energy 398kcal/1664kJ; Protein 16.2g; Carbohydrate 34.9g, of which sugars 6.7g; Fat 22.4g, of which saturates 2.6g; Cholesterol 63mg; Calcium 249mg; Fibre 4.1g; Sodium 550mg.

LEMON AND HERB RISOTTO CAKE

THIS UNUSUAL DISH CAN BE SERVED AS A MAIN COURSE WITH SALAD, OR AS A SATISFYING SIDE DISH. IT IS ALSO GOOD SERVED COLD, AND PACKS WELL FOR PICNICS.

SERVES FOUR

INGREDIENTS

1 small leek, finely sliced
600ml/1 pint/2½ cups chicken stock
225g/8oz/generous 1 cup risotto rice
finely grated rind of 1 lemon
30ml/2 tbsp snipped fresh chives
30ml/2 tbsp chopped fresh parsley
75g/3oz/¾ cup grated mozzarella
  cheese
salt and ground black pepper

COOK'S TIP
This risotto uses less liquid than normal
and therefore has a drier consistency.

1 Preheat the oven to 200°C/400°F/
Gas 6. Lightly oil a 21cm/8½ in round
loose-based cake tin (pan).

2 Put the leek in a large pan with
45ml/3 tbsp of the stock. Cook over a
medium heat, stirring occasionally, until
softened. Stir in the rice, then add the
remaining stock.

3 Bring to the boil. Lower the heat,
cover the pan and simmer gently,
stirring occasionally, for about
20 minutes, or until all the liquid has
been absorbed.

4 Stir in the lemon rind, herbs, cheese,
and seasoning. Spoon the mixture into
the tin, cover with foil and bake for
30–35 minutes or until lightly browned.
Leave to stand for 5 minutes, then turn
out. Serve hot or cold, in slices.

Energy 264kcal/1103kJ; Protein 8.7g; Carbohydrate 46.5g, of which sugars 1.3g; Fat 4.5g, of which saturates 2.6g; Cholesterol 11mg; Calcium 114mg; Fibre 1.6g; Sodium 79mg.

PILAU RICE WITH WHOLE SPICES

THIS FRAGRANT RICE DISH MAKES A PERFECT ACCOMPANIMENT TO MANY BARBECUE FAVOURITES, ESPECIALLY TANDOORI CHICKEN DRUMSTICKS OR MAIN DISHES COOKED WITH INDIAN SPICES.

SERVES FOUR

INGREDIENTS
    generous pinch of saffron
       strands
    600ml/1 pint/2½ cups hot
       chicken stock
    50g/2oz/¼ cup butter
    1 onion, chopped
    1 garlic clove, crushed
    ½ cinnamon stick
    6 green cardamom pods
    1 bay leaf
    250g/9oz/1⅓ cups basmati rice
    50g/2oz/⅓ cup sultanas (golden
       raisins)
    15ml/1 tbsp sunflower oil
    50g/2oz/½ cup cashew nuts
    naan bread and tomato and onion
       salad, to serve (optional)

1 Stir the saffron strands into a jug (pitcher) of hot stock and set aside.

2 Heat the butter in a pan and fry the onion and garlic for 5 minutes. Stir in the cinnamon stick, cardamoms and bay leaf and cook for 2 minutes.

3 Add the rice and cook, stirring, for 2 minutes more. Pour in the saffron-flavoured stock and add the sultanas. Bring to the boil, stir, then lower the heat, cover and cook gently for about 10 minutes or until the rice is tender and the liquid has all been absorbed.

4 Meanwhile, heat the oil in a frying pan and fry the cashew nuts until browned. Drain on kitchen paper. Scatter the cashew nuts over the rice. Serve with naan bread and a tomato and onion salad, if you like.

COOK'S TIP
Don't be tempted to use black cardamoms in this dish. They are coarser and more strongly flavoured than green cardamoms and are only used in highly spiced dishes that are cooked for a long time.

Energy 302kcal/1258kJ; Protein 5.8g; Carbohydrate 46.4g, of which sugars 1g; Fat 10.1g, of which saturates 1.1g; Cholesterol 0mg; Calcium 49mg; Fibre 0.8g; Sodium 2mg.

MUSHROOM PILAU

THIS DISH IS SIMPLICITY ITSELF. SERVE WITH ANY SPICY MEATS, ESPECIALLY WITH GRILLS THAT ARE COOKED WITH A PIQUANT SAUCE, WHICH CAN BE SPOONED OVER THE RICE.

SERVES FOUR

INGREDIENTS

30ml/2 tbsp vegetable oil
2 shallots, finely chopped
1 garlic clove, crushed
3 green cardamom pods
25g/1oz/2 tbsp ghee or butter
175g/6oz/2½ cups button (white)
  mushrooms, sliced
225g/8oz/generous 1 cup basmati
  rice, soaked
5ml/1 tsp grated fresh root ginger
good pinch of garam masala
450ml/¾ pint/scant 2 cups water
15ml/1 tbsp chopped fresh coriander
  (cilantro)
salt

1 Heat the oil in a flameproof casserole and fry the shallots, garlic and cardamom pods over a medium heat for 3–4 minutes until the shallots have softened and are beginning to brown.

2 Add the ghee or butter. When it has melted, add the mushrooms and fry for 2–3 minutes more.

3 Add the rice, ginger and garam masala. Stir-fry over a low heat for 2–3 minutes, then stir in the water and a little salt. Bring to the boil, then cover tightly and simmer over a very low heat for 10 minutes.

4 Remove the casserole from the heat. Leave to stand, covered, for 5 minutes. Add the chopped coriander and fork it through the rice. Spoon into a serving bowl and serve immediately.

Energy 309kcal/1286kJ; Protein 5.2g; Carbohydrate 46.3g, of which sugars 1g; Fat 11.2g, of which saturates 4g; Cholesterol 13mg; Calcium 18mg; Fibre 0.7g; Sodium 41mg.

RICE WITH DILL AND BROAD BEANS

THIS IS A FAVOURITE RICE DISH IN IRAN, WHERE IT IS CALLED BAGHALI POLO. *THE COMBINATION OF BROAD BEANS, DILL AND WARM SPICES WORKS VERY WELL, AND THE SAFFRON RICE ADDS COLOUR.*

SERVES FOUR

INGREDIENTS
275g/10oz/1½ cups basmati rice,
   soaked
750ml/1¼ pints/3 cups water
40g/1½oz/3 tbsp melted butter
175g/6oz/1½ cups frozen baby broad
   (fava) beans, thawed and peeled
90ml/6 tbsp finely chopped fresh
   dill, plus 1 fresh dill sprig, to
   garnish
5ml/1 tsp ground cinnamon
5ml/1 tsp ground cumin
2–3 saffron strands, soaked in
   15ml/1 tbsp boiling water
salt

1 Drain the rice, tip it into a pan and pour in the water. Add a little salt. Bring to the boil, then lower the heat and simmer very gently for 5 minutes. Drain, rinse well in warm water and drain once again.

2 Melt the butter in a non-stick pan. Pour two-thirds of the melted butter into a small jug and set aside. Spoon enough rice into the pan to cover the bottom. Add a quarter of the beans and a little dill. Spread over another layer of rice, then a layer of beans and dill. Repeat the layers until all the beans and dill have been used up, ending with a layer of rice. Cook over a gentle heat for 8 minutes until nearly tender.

3 Pour the reserved melted butter over the rice. Sprinkle with the ground cinnamon and cumin. Cover the pan with a clean dish towel and a tight-fitting lid, lifting the corners of the cloth back over the lid. Cook over a low heat for 25–30 minutes.

4 Spoon about 45ml/3 tbsp of the cooked rice into the bowl of saffron water; mix well. Mound the remaining rice mixture on a large serving plate and spoon the saffron rice on one side to decorate. Serve at once, decorated with the sprig of dill.

Energy 363kcal/1516kJ; Protein 9.2g; Carbohydrate 60.6g, of which sugars 1.1g; Fat 9.1g, of which saturates 5.3g; Cholesterol 21mg; Calcium 77mg; Fibre 3.8g; Sodium 70mg.

SWEET AND SOUR RICE

THIS POPULAR MIDDLE EASTERN RICE DISH IS FLAVOURED WITH FRUIT AND SPICES. IT IS OFTEN SERVED WITH LAMB OR CHICKEN, AND IS PERFECT WITH KEBABS AND A COOL YOGURT SAUCE.

SERVES FOUR

INGREDIENTS
 50g/2oz/½ cup zereshk (see
   Cook's Tip)
 45g/1½oz/3 tbsp butter
 50g/2oz/⅓ cup raisins
 50g/2oz/¼ cup granulated sugar
 5ml/1 tsp ground cinnamon
 5ml/1 tsp ground cumin
 350g/12oz/1¾ cups basmati rice,
   soaked
 2–3 saffron strands, soaked in
   15ml/1 tbsp boiling water
 pinch of salt

1 Thoroughly wash the zereshk in cold water at least four or five times to rinse off any bits of grit. Drain well.

2 Melt 15g/½oz/1 tbsp of the butter in a frying pan and fry the raisins for about 1–2 minutes.

3 Add the zereshk, fry for a few seconds, and then add the sugar, with half of the cinnamon and cumin. Cook briefly and then set aside.

4 Drain the rice, then put it in a pan with plenty of boiling, lightly salted water. Bring back to the boil, reduce the heat and simmer for 4 minutes. Drain and rinse once again, if you like.

COOK'S TIP
Zereshk are small dried berries. Look for them in Middle Eastern markets and shops. If you cannot locate them, use fresh cranberries instead.

5 Melt half the remaining butter in the clean pan, add 15ml/1 tbsp water and stir in half the cooked rice. Sprinkle with half the raisin and zereshk mixture and top with all but 45ml/3 tbsp of the rice. Sprinkle over the remaining raisin and zereshk mixture.

6 Mix the remaining cinnamon and cumin with the reserved rice, and scatter this mixture evenly over the layered mixture. Melt the remaining butter, drizzle it over the surface, then cover the pan with a clean dish towel. Cover with a tight-fitting lid, lifting the corners of the cloth back over the lid. Steam the rice over a very low heat for about 20–30 minutes.

7 Just before serving, mix 45ml/3 tbsp of the rice with the saffron water. Spoon the sweet and sour rice on to a large, flat serving dish and scatter the saffron rice over the top, to garnish.

Energy 465kcal/1943kJ; Protein 7g; Carbohydrate 87g, of which sugars 17.2g; Fat 9.8g, of which saturates 5.9g; Cholesterol 24mg; Calcium 32mg; Fibre 0.6g; Sodium 77mg.

HOT AND SOUR NOODLE SALAD

NOODLES MAKE THE PERFECT BASIS FOR A SALAD, ABSORBING THE DRESSING AND PROVIDING A CONTRAST IN TEXTURE TO THE CRISP VEGETABLES. THIS IS AN IDEAL DISH TO SERVE ALONGSIDE ANY MEAT, FISH OR TOFU THAT HAS BEEN PREPARED WITH A CHINESE-STYLE MARINADE.

SERVES TWO

INGREDIENTS
  200g/7oz thin rice noodles
  small bunch fresh coriander (cilantro)
  2 tomatoes, seeded and sliced
  130g/4½oz baby corn cobs, sliced
  4 spring onions (scallions),
    thinly sliced
  1 red (bell) pepper, seeded and
    finely chopped
  juice of 2 limes
  2 small fresh green chillies, seeded
    and finely chopped
  10ml/2 tsp sugar
  115g/4oz/1 cup peanuts, toasted
    and chopped
  30ml/2 tbsp soy sauce
  salt

1 Bring a large pan of lightly salted water to the boil. Snap the noodles into short lengths, add to the pan and cook for 3–4 minutes. Drain, then rinse under cold water and drain again.

2 Set aside a few coriander leaves for the garnish. Chop the remaining leaves and place them in a large serving bowl.

3 Add the noodles to the bowl, with the tomato slices, corn cobs, spring onions, red pepper, lime juice, chillies, sugar and toasted peanuts. Season with the soy sauce, then taste and add a little salt if you think the mixture needs it. Toss the salad lightly but thoroughly, then garnish with the reserved coriander leaves and serve immediately.

Energy 783kcal/3269kJ; Protein 24.7g; Carbohydrate 106.4g, of which sugars 20.4g; Fat 27.9g, of which saturates 5.2g; Cholesterol 0mg; Calcium 129mg; Fibre 8.5g; Sodium 1845mg.

LEMONY COUSCOUS SALAD

THIS IS A POPULAR SALAD OF OLIVES, ALMONDS AND COURGETTES MIXED WITH FLUFFY COUSCOUS AND DRESSED WITH HERBS, LEMON JUICE AND OLIVE OIL. IT HAS A DELICATE FLAVOUR AND MAKES AN EXCELLENT ACCOMPANIMENT TO GRILLED CHICKEN OR KEBABS.

SERVES FOUR

INGREDIENTS
275g/10oz/1⅔ cups couscous
550ml/18fl oz/2½ cups boiling
  vegetable stock
2 small courgettes (zucchini)
16–20 black olives
25g/1oz/¼ cup flaked (sliced)
  almonds, toasted
60ml/4 tbsp olive oil
15ml/1 tbsp lemon juice
15ml/1 tbsp chopped fresh
  coriander (cilantro)
15ml/1 tbsp chopped fresh parsley
good pinch of ground cumin
good pinch of cayenne pepper

1 Place the couscous in a bowl and pour over the boiling vegetable stock. Stir with a fork and then set aside for 10 minutes for the stock to be absorbed into the grains. Fluff up the couscous using a fork to separate the grains.

2 Trim the courgettes at both ends then cut into pieces about 2.5cm/1in long. Slice thinly and then cut into fine julienne strips with a sharp knife. Halve the black olives, discarding the stones (pits).

3 Carefully mix the courgettes, olives and almonds into the couscous so that they are well incorporated.

4 Blend together the olive oil, lemon juice, coriander, parsley, cumin and cayenne in a small bowl. Stir into the salad, tossing gently to mix the dressing thoroughly through the couscous and vegetables. Transfer to a large serving dish and serve immediately.

Energy 327kcal/1358kJ; Protein 6.9g; Carbohydrate 37.2g, of which sugars 1.6g; Fat 17.6g, of which saturates 2.3g; Cholesterol 0mg; Calcium 66mg; Fibre 1.9g; Sodium 425mg.

TABBOULEH

THIS IS A WONDERFULLY REFRESHING, TANGY SALAD OF SOAKED BULGUR WHEAT AND MASSES OF FRESH MINT, PARSLEY AND SPRING ONIONS. FEEL FREE TO INCREASE THE AMOUNT OF HERBS FOR A GREENER SALAD. IT CAN BE SERVED AS AN APPETIZER OR AS AN ACCOMPANIMENT TO A MAIN COURSE.

SERVES FOUR TO SIX

INGREDIENTS
250g/9oz/1½ cups bulgur wheat
1 large bunch spring onions
  (scallions), thinly sliced
1 cucumber, finely chopped or diced
3 tomatoes, chopped
1.5–2.5ml/¼–½ tsp ground cumin
1 large bunch fresh parsley, chopped
1 large bunch fresh mint, chopped
juice of 2 lemons, or to taste
60ml/4 tbsp extra virgin olive oil
salt
olives, lemon wedges, tomato wedges,
  cucumber slices and mint sprigs,
  to garnish (optional)
cos or romaine lettuce and natural
  (plain) yogurt, to serve (optional)

1 Pick over the bulgur wheat to remove any dirt. Place it in a bowl, cover with cold water and leave to soak for about 30 minutes.

2 Tip the wheat into a sieve (strainer) and drain well, shaking to remove any excess water, then return it to the bowl.

3 Add the spring onions to the bulgur wheat, then mix and squeeze together with your hands to combine.

4 Add the cucumber, tomatoes, cumin, parsley, mint, lemon juice, oil and salt to the bulgur wheat and toss to combine.

5 Heap the tabbouleh on to a bed of lettuce and garnish with olives, lemon and tomato wedges, cucumber and mint sprigs and serve with a bowl of natural yogurt, if you like.

VARIATIONS
Use couscous soaked in boiling water in place of the bulgur wheat and use chopped fresh coriander (cilantro) instead of parsley.

Energy 180kcal/748kJ; Protein 3.6g; Carbohydrate 24.3g, of which sugars 2.8g; Fat 8.1g, of which saturates 1.1g; Cholesterol 0mg; Calcium 42mg; Fibre 1.4g; Sodium 10mg.

TAGINE OF ARTICHOKE, POTATOES AND PEAS

THIS DISH IS IDEAL FOR A BARBECUE WHERE YOU PLAN TO SERVE FINE QUALITY GRILLED MEATS AND FISH. YOU CAN PREPARE IT IN ADVANCE, AND IT IS FULL OF THE WONDERFUL, NORTH AFRICAN FLAVOURS THAT TASTE SO GOOD WHEN EATEN OUTDOORS ON A SUNNY DAY.

SERVES FOUR TO SIX

INGREDIENTS

6 fresh globe artichoke hearts
juice of 1 lemon
30–45ml/2–3 tbsp olive oil
1 onion, chopped
675g/1½lb potatoes, peeled
  and quartered
small bunch of fresh flat leaf
  parsley, chopped
small bunch of fresh coriander
  (cilantro), chopped
small bunch of fresh mint, chopped
pinch of saffron threads
5ml/1 tsp ground turmeric
about 350ml/12fl oz/1½ cups
  vegetable stock
finely chopped rind of
  ½ preserved lemon
250g/9oz/2¼ cups shelled peas
salt and ground black pepper
couscous or bread, to serve

1 Poach the artichoke hearts very gently in plenty of simmering water with half the lemon juice, for 10–15 minutes, until tender. Drain and refresh under cold water, then drain again.

2 Heat the olive oil in a tagine or heavy pan. Add the onion and cook over a low heat for about 15 minutes, until softened but not browned. Add the potatoes, most of the chopped parsley, the chopped coriander and mint, the remaining lemon juice, and the saffron and turmeric to the pan.

3 Pour in the stock, bring to the boil, then reduce the heat. Cover the pan and cook for about 15 minutes, until the potatoes are almost tender.

4 Stir the preserved lemon, artichoke hearts and peas into the stew, and cook, uncovered, for a further 10 minutes. Season to taste, sprinkle with the remaining parsley, and serve with couscous or chunks of fresh bread.

COOK'S TIP
Once cut, the flesh of artichokes will blacken. To prevent this from happening, put the artichokes into acidulated water – use a good squeeze of lemon juice or white wine vinegar in a bowl of fresh, cold water.

Energy 260Kcal/1089kJ; Protein 8.6g; Carbohydrate 42g, of which sugars 10.6g; Fat 7.5g, of which saturates 1.2g; Cholesterol 0mg; Calcium 96mg; Fibre 7.9g; Sodium 47mg.

MARINADES AND ACCOMPANIMENTS

*You have decided on your barbecue meal, but there are all
kinds of accompaniments that will add to the satisfying
selection of food you are going to cook on the grill. Marinades,
of course, are essential for infusing your grilled dishes with
glorious flavour and colour. Nibbles make waiting for the
first course a pleasure so try some of the dips to serve with
crudités or pitta bread. This chapter also includes home-made
barbecue sauce, tomato ketchup and relishes that will really
make it an occasion. They work especially well alongside the
beautiful home-made breads — from ciabattas to burger buns
— sesame-topped perfection for your sumptuous burgers.
These accompaniments are what make outdoor eating such a
pleasure, with a choice of flavours to suit everyone.
Find marinating tips and more quick recipes on
pages 16–17.*

SPICY YOGURT MARINADE

THIS MARINADE WORKS EQUALLY WELL FOR CHICKEN, LAMB OR PORK. MARINATE THE MEAT, COVERED AND CHILLED, FOR 24–36 HOURS TO DEVELOP A MELLOW, SPICY FLAVOUR.

2 Leave the spices to cool, then grind coarsely with a pestle and mortar.

3 Finely chop the onion, garlic and ginger in a blender or food processor. Add the ground spices, chilli, turmeric, yogurt and lemon juice.

4 For large pieces of meat, make several deep slashes to allow the flavours to penetrate. Arrange the pieces in a single layer and pour over the marinade. Cover and leave in the fridge to marinate for at least 24 hours.

COOK'S TIP
Do not burn the spices when you fry them. You just need to release the aromas, so reduce the heat if necessary.

SERVES SIX

INGREDIENTS
5ml/1 tsp coriander seeds
10ml/2 tsp cumin seeds
6 cloves
2 bay leaves
1 onion, quartered
2 garlic cloves
5ml/2in piece fresh root ginger,
  roughly chopped
2.5ml/½ tsp chilli powder
5ml/1 tsp ground turmeric
150ml/¼ pint/⅔ cup natural
  (plain) yogurt
juice of 1 lemon

1 Spread the coriander and cumin seeds, cloves and bay leaves over the bottom of a large frying pan and dry-fry over a moderate heat until the bay leaves are crisp.

Energy 26kcal/110kJ; Protein 5.5g; Carbohydrate 0.4g, of which sugars 0.3g; Fat 0.3g, of which saturates 0.1g; Cholesterol 16mg; Calcium 7mg; Fibre 0.1g; Sodium 16mg.

ORANGE AND GREEN PEPPERCORN MARINADE

THIS IS AN EXCELLENT LIGHT MARINADE FOR DELICATELY FLAVOURED WHOLE FISH SUCH AS SEA TROUT, BASS OR BREAM. THE FISH IS PERFECTLY SET OFF BY THE SOFTLY COLOURED MARINADE.

FOR ONE MEDIUM-SIZE FISH

INGREDIENTS
1 red onion
2 small oranges
90ml/6 tbsp light olive oil
30ml/2 tbsp cider vinegar
30ml/2 tbsp green peppercorns in brine, drained
30ml/2 tbsp chopped fresh parsley
salt and sugar

1 Prepare the barbecue and position a grill rack over the coals. Slash the fish 3–4 times on each side.

2 Cut a piece of foil large enough to wrap the fish and use to line a large dish. Peel and slice the onion and oranges. Lay half the slices on the foil, place the fish on top and cover with the remaining onion and orange.

3 Mix the remaining marinade ingredients and pour over the fish. Cover and leave to marinate for 4 hours, occasionally spooning the marinade over the fish.

4 Fold the foil loosely over the fish and seal the edges securely. Bake on a medium barbecue for 15 minutes for 450g/1lb, plus 15 minutes over.

COOK'S TIP
You can cook this in a moderate oven instead if the weather suddenly changes!

Energy 777kcal/3218kJ; Protein 6.3g; Carbohydrate 39.8g, of which sugars 38.3g; Fat 67g, of which saturates 9.4g; Cholesterol 0mg; Calcium 283mg; Fibre 9.6g; Sodium 35mg.

GINGER AND LIME MARINADE

THIS FRAGRANT MARINADE WILL GUARANTEE A MOUTHWATERING AROMA FROM THE BARBECUE. SHOWN HERE ON PRAWN AND MONKFISH KEBABS, IT IS JUST AS DELICIOUS WITH CHICKEN OR PORK.

SERVES FOUR TO SIX

INGREDIENTS
3 limes
15ml/1 tbsp green cardamom pods
1 onion, finely chopped
2.5cm/1in piece fresh root
   ginger, grated
1 large garlic clove, peeled
   and crushed
45ml/3 tbsp olive oil
ground black pepper

1 Finely grate the rind from one lime and squeeze the juice from all of them.

2 Split the cardamom pods and remove the seeds. Crush the seeds with a pestle and mortar or the back of a heavy-bladed knife.

3 Mix all the marinade ingredients together and pour over the prepared meat or fish. Stir in gently, cover and leave in a cool place to marinate for 2–3 hours.

4 Drain the meat and fish when you are ready to cook it on the grill. Baste the meat occasionally with the marinade while cooking.

SUMMER HERB MARINADE

MAKE THE BEST USE OF SUMMER HERBS IN THIS MARINADE. TRY ANY COMBINATION OF HERBS, DEPENDING ON WHAT YOU HAVE TO HAND, AND USE WITH VEAL, CHICKEN, PORK, LAMB OR SALMON.

SERVES FOUR

INGREDIENTS

large handful of fresh herb sprigs,
e.g. chervil, thyme, parsley, sage,
chives, rosemary, oregano
90ml/6 tbsp olive oil
45ml/3 tbsp tarragon vinegar
1 garlic clove, crushed
2 spring onions (scallions), chopped
salt and ground black pepper

1 Discard any coarse stalks or damaged leaves from the herbs, then chop them very finely.

2 Add the chopped herbs to the remaining marinade ingredients in a large bowl. Stir to mix thoroughly.

COOK'S TIP
• Don't use dried or frozen herbs for this recipe – they need to be fresh for a good flavour and colour.

3 Place the meat or fish in a bowl and pour over the marinade. Cover and leave to marinate in a cool place for 4–6 hours.

4 Drain the meat or fish when you are ready to cook it on the barbecue. Use the marinade to baste the meat occasionally while cooking.

Energy 162kcal/668kJ; Protein 1.2g; Carbohydrate 1.6g, of which sugars 0.7g; Fat 16.9g, of which saturates 2.4g; Cholesterol 0mg; Calcium 52mg; Fibre 1.5g; Sodium 9mg.

SAMBAL BELACAN

IN MALAYSIA, A LITTLE DOLLOP OF THIS SAUCE SEEMS TO GO WITH EVERYTHING. FOR A BARBECUE IT IS IDEAL — MAKE UP A BATCH FOR DIPPING AND PAINT SOME ON TO CHICKEN, PORK OR FIRM FISH, INFUSING THE FLESH WITH A FIERY KICK BEFORE IT GOES ON TO THE BARBECUE.

SERVES FOUR

INGREDIENTS
15ml/1 tbsp shrimp paste
4 fresh red chillies, seeded (reserve
   the seeds)
2 kaffir lime leaves, spines removed,
   and chopped
2.5ml/$\frac{1}{2}$ tsp sugar
1.5ml/$\frac{1}{4}$ tsp salt
juice of 1 lime
1 lime, quartered, to serve

1 In a small, heavy pan, dry-roast the shrimp paste until it is aromatic and crumbly. Using a mortar and pestle or food processor, grind the roasted shrimp paste with the chillies to form a paste. Grind in half the chilli seeds and the lime leaves.

2 Add the sugar and salt, and stir in the rest of the chilli seeds. Moisten with the lime juice. Spoon the *sambal* into little dishes and serve with wedges of lime to squeeze over it.

COOK'S TIP
The fermented shrimp paste, *belacan*, is available in South-east Asian markets. If you cannot get hold of it, replace it with the readily available Thai shrimp paste.

Energy 17Kcal/69kJ; Protein 2.8g; Carbohydrate 0.8g, of which sugars 0.8g; Fat 0.3g, of which saturates 0g; Cholesterol 19mg; Calcium 53mg; Fibre 0g; Sodium 312mg.

SOY AND STAR ANISE MARINADE

CHICKEN COOKS QUICKLY AND BENEFITS FROM BEING MARINATED FIRST. AROMATIC STAR ANISE BRINGS CLEAR, PUNCHY FLAVOUR TO THIS UNCOMPLICATED MARINADE OF SOY SAUCE AND OLIVE OIL, WHICH WILL GIVE THE MEAT A DISTINCTLY 'CHINESE' FLAVOUR.

SERVES FOUR

INGREDIENTS
  4 skinless chicken breast fillets
  2 whole star anise
  45ml/3 tbsp olive oil
  30ml/2 tbsp soy sauce
  ground black pepper

1 Put the chicken breast fillets in a shallow, non-metallic dish and add the star anise.

2 In a small bowl, whisk together the oil and soy sauce and season with black pepper to make the marinade.

3 Pour the mixture over the chicken and turn the fillets to coat them all over. Cover the dish with clear film (plastic wrap) and leave in the refrigerator to marinate.

4 Prepare the barbecue. Position a lightly oiled grill rack over the hot coals. Cook the chicken on the rack for about 8 minutes on each side, until browned and cooked through. Serve immediately.

COOK'S TIPS
• If you are able to prepare ahead, leave the chicken in the marinade for 6–8 hours or overnight, as the flavour will be improved.
• If you prefer, cook the chicken under a preheated grill (broiler). Lift the chicken from the marinade and place on a rack in a grill pan. Cook for about 8 minutes each side, until cooked through.

Energy 206kcal/868kJ; Protein 36g; Carbohydrate 0g, of which sugars 0g; Fat 6.9g, of which saturates 1.2g; Cholesterol 105mg; Calcium 8mg; Fibre 0g; Sodium 90mg.

PARSLEY BUTTER

THIS FRESH-TASTING HERB BUTTER MAKES A CLASSIC AND SUBTLE ACCOMPANIMENT TO BARBECUED FOOD. ITS DELICATE FLAVOUR IS PARTICULARLY SUITED TO FISH. YOU CAN USE THE SAME METHOD TO PRODUCE FLAVOURED BUTTERS FOR MANY DIFFERENT DISHES.

<u>SERVES FOUR</u>

INGREDIENTS
115g/4oz/½ cup softened butter
30ml/2 tbsp fresh parsley, finely
   chopped
2.5ml/½ tsp lemon juice
cayenne pepper
salt and ground black pepper

1 Beat the butter until creamy, then beat in the parsley, lemon juice and cayenne pepper, and season lightly.

2 Spread the butter 5mm/¼in thick on to foil and chill, then cut into shapes with a knife or fancy cutter.

3 Alternatively, form the blended butter into a roll, wrap in clear film (plastic wrap) or foil and chill until needed. Cut off slices as required.

BASIL AND LEMON MAYONNAISE

THIS FRESH MAYONNAISE IS FLAVOURED WITH LEMON AND TWO TYPES OF BASIL. SERVE IT AS A DIP WITH POTATO CRISPS, BARBECUED WEDGES OR CRUDITÉS, OR WITH SALADS AND JACKET POTATOES. IT WOULD ALSO BE DELICIOUS WITH SALMON OR OTHER FISH.

SERVES FOUR

INGREDIENTS

2 very large egg yolks
15ml/1 tbsp lemon juice
150ml/¼ pint/⅔ cup olive oil
150ml/¼ pint/⅔ cup sunflower oil
handful of green basil leaves
handful of opal basil leaves
4 garlic cloves, crushed
salt and ground black pepper

1 Place the egg yolks and lemon juice in a blender or food processor and process them briefly together.

2 In a jug (pitcher), stir the two oils together. With the machine running, pour in the oil slowly, a drop at a time.

COOK'S TIP
For a less pungent mayonnaise, either use two garlic cloves instead of four, or roast the garlic in its papery skin first.

3 Once half the oil has been added the remainder can be incorporated more quickly. Continue processing to form a thick, creamy mayonnaise.

4 Tear both types of basil into small pieces and stir into the mayonnaise with the crushed garlic and seasoning. Transfer to a serving dish, cover and chill until ready to serve.

Energy 489kcal/2012kJ; Protein 2.2g; Carbohydrate 1.2g, of which sugars 0.4g; Fat 52.9g, of which saturates 7.4g; Cholesterol 101mg; Calcium 38mg; Fibre 0.8g; Sodium 9mg.

GARLIC MAYONNAISE

FRESH "WET" GARLIC IS AVAILABLE IN SPRING AND SUMMER, BUT FOR THIS MOUTHWATERING CREAMY MAYONNAISE IT'S BETTER TO USE DRIED, CURED BULBS AS THEY HAVE A MORE PUNGENT FLAVOUR.

4 When the mayonnaise is as thick as soft butter, stop adding oil. Season the mayonnaise to taste and add more lemon juice or vinegar as required.

5 Crush the garlic with the blade of a knife and stir it into the mayonnaise. For a slightly milder flavour, blanch the garlic twice in plenty of boiling water, then purée the cloves before beating them into the mayonnaise.

SERVES FOUR TO SIX

INGREDIENTS
2 large egg yolks
pinch of dried mustard
about 300ml/½ pint/1¼ cups mild olive oil
15–30ml/1–2 tbsp lemon juice, white wine vinegar or warm water
2–4 garlic cloves
sea salt and ground black pepper

COOK'S TIP
The very young, elderly, pregnant women and those with a compromised immune system are advised against consuming raw eggs or dishes containing them.

1 Make sure the egg yolks and the oil are both at room temperature before you start to make the mayonnaise. Place the egg yolks in a bowl with the mustard and a pinch of salt, and whisk together to mix.

2 Gradually add the oil, one drop at a time, whisking constantly. When almost half the oil has been fully incorporated and the mixture is starting to emulsify, you can add the rest in a slow, steady stream, still whisking all the time.

3 As the mayonnaise starts to thicken, thin it down with a few drops of lemon juice or vinegar, or a few teaspoons of warm water.

VARIATIONS
• To make Provençal aioli, crush 3–5 garlic cloves with a pinch of salt in a bowl, then whisk in the egg yolks. Omit the mustard but continue as above.
• For spicy garlic mayonnaise, omit the mustard and stir in 2.5ml/½ tsp harissa or red chilli paste and 5ml/1 tsp sun-dried tomato purée (paste) with the garlic.
• Use roasted garlic purée or puréed smoked garlic to create a different flavour.
• Beat in about 15g/½oz mixed fresh herbs such as tarragon, parsley, chervil and chives.

Energy 100kcal/420kJ; Protein 0g; Carbohydrate 0g, of which sugars 0g; Fat 11g, of which saturates 8g; Cholesterol 19mg; Calcium 38mg; Fibre 0.3g; Sodium 30mg.

WATERCRESS CREAM

THE DELICATE GREEN COLOUR OF THIS CREAM SAUCE LOOKS WONDERFUL AGAINST PINK-FLESHED FISH, SUCH AS SALMON OR SEA TROUT. THE FLAVOUR IS COMPLEMENTARY, TOO.

MAKES ABOUT 250ML/8FL OZ/1 CUP

INGREDIENTS

2 bunches watercress or
  rocket (arugula)
25g/1oz/2 tbsp butter
2 shallots, chopped
25g/1oz/¼ cup plain
  (all-purpose) flour
150ml/¼ pint/⅔ cup hot fish stock
150ml/¼ pint/⅔ cup dry white wine
5ml/1 tsp anchovy extract
150ml/¼ pint/⅔ cup single
  (light) cream
lemon juice
salt and cayenne pepper

1 Trim the watercress or rocket of any bruised leaves and coarse stalks. Blanch in boiling water for 3 minutes then drain and refresh under cold running water, and drain again in a sieve (strainer) or colander.

2 Press the watercress or rocket against the sides of the sieve or colander with a spoon to remove as much moisture as possible. Turn on to a board, chop finely and set aside.

3 Melt the butter in a pan and fry the shallots over a medium heat for 3–4 minutes, until soft. Stir in the flour and cook for 1–2 minutes.

4 Remove the pan from the heat and gradually stir in the fish stock and wine. Return the pan to the heat and bring the sauce to the boil, stirring constantly. Reduce the heat and simmer gently for 2–3 minutes, stirring occasionally.

5 Strain the sauce into a clean pan, then stir in the chopped watercress or rocket, and add the anchovy extract and cream.

6 Warm the sauce over a low heat without allowing it to boil. Season with salt and cayenne pepper and sharpen with lemon juice to taste. Serve immediately.

Energy 713kcal/2961kJ; Protein 12.6g; Carbohydrate 28.9g, of which sugars 8.5g; Fat 51.1g, of which saturates 31.7g; Cholesterol 139mg; Calcium 387mg; Fibre 3.1g; Sodium 449mg.

CREAMY AUBERGINE DIP

SERVE THIS VELVET-TEXTURED DIP WITH PITTA BREAD OR CRUDITÉS, OR SPREAD IT THICKLY ON TO SLICES OF FRENCH BREAD TOASTED ON THE BARBECUE, THEN TOP WITH SLIVERS OF SUN-DRIED TOMATO TO MAKE WONDERFUL ITALIAN-STYLE CROSTINI.

SERVES FOUR

INGREDIENTS
  1 large aubergine (eggplant)
  30ml/2 tbsp olive oil
  1 small onion, finely chopped
  2 garlic cloves, finely chopped
  60ml/4 tbsp chopped fresh parsley
  75ml/5 tbsp crème fraîche
  red Tabasco sauce, to taste
  juice of 1 lemon, to taste
  salt and ground black pepper

COOK'S TIP
The aubergine flesh can be whizzed to a pulp in a food processor if you want a very smooth purée.

1 Cook the whole aubergine on a medium barbecue or grill (broiler) for about 20 minutes, turning occasionally, until the skin is blackened and the aubergine soft. Cover the aubergine with an upturned bowl and set aside to cool for about 5–6 minutes.

2 Meanwhile, heat the olive oil in a frying pan and cook the chopped onion and garlic for 5 minutes, until soft but not browned.

3 Peel the aubergine and mash the flesh with a large fork or potato masher to make a pulpy purée.

4 Stir in the onion and garlic with their oil, and add the parsley and crème fraîche. Add Tabasco, lemon juice, and season to taste. Serve warm.

VARIATION
Beat in an extra 60ml/4 tbsp olive oil and omit the crème fraîche.

Energy 137kcal/566kJ; Protein 1.4g; Carbohydrate 3.1g, of which sugars 2.5g; Fat 13.4g, of which saturates 5.9g; Cholesterol 21mg; Calcium 42mg; Fibre 1.8g; Sodium 9mg.

FAT-FREE SAFFRON DIP

SERVE THIS MILD, FRESH-TASTING DIP WITH FRESH VEGETABLE CRUDITÉS — IT IS PARTICULARLY GOOD WITH FLORETS OF CAULIFLOWER, ASPARAGUS TIPS AND BABY CARROTS AND CORN. SAFFRON GIVES THE DIP A DELICATE YELLOW COLOUR AND A UNIQUE FLAVOUR.

SERVES FOUR

INGREDIENTS
    15ml/1 tbsp boiling water
    small pinch saffron strands
    200g/7oz/scant 1 cup fat-free
      fromage frais
    10 fresh chives
    10 fresh basil leaves
    salt and ground black pepper
    selection of trimmed fresh
      vegetables, to serve

1 Pour the boiling water into a small bowl and add the saffron strands. Leave to infuse for 3 minutes.

2 Turn the fromage frais into a large bowl and beat with a wooden spoon until smooth. Stir in the infused saffron liquid and the strands.

VARIATION
If you don't have any saffron, fromage frais and fresh herbs still make a delicious dip. Add a squeeze of lemon or lime juice and plenty of pepper.

3 Snip the chives into the dip. Tear the basil leaves into small pieces and stir them in. Mix thoroughly.

4 Add salt and ground black pepper to taste. Serve the dip with fresh vegetable crudités, if liked.

Energy 29kcal/124kJ; Protein 3.8g; Carbohydrate 3.1g, of which sugars 2.8g; Fat 0.3g, of which saturates 0.1g; Cholesterol 1mg; Calcium 69mg; Fibre 0.8g; Sodium 21mg.

HUMMUS

THIS CLASSIC MIDDLE EASTERN DISH IS MADE FROM COOKED CHICKPEAS GROUND TO A PASTE AND FLAVOURED WITH GARLIC, LEMON JUICE, TAHINI, OLIVE OIL AND CUMIN. IT IS DELICIOUS SERVED WITH WEDGES OF TOASTED PITTA BREAD OR CRUDITÉS.

SERVES FOUR TO SIX

INGREDIENTS
  400g/14oz can chickpeas
  60ml/4 tbsp tahini
  2–3 garlic cloves, chopped
  juice of ½–1 lemon
  cayenne pepper
  small pinch to 1.5ml/¼ tsp ground
    cumin, or more to taste
  salt and ground black pepper

VARIATION
Process 2 roasted red (bell) peppers with the chickpeas. Serve sprinkled with lightly toasted pine nuts and paprika mixed with olive oil.

1 Drain and rinse the chickpeas. Put them in a bowl and use a potato masher or food processor to mash them coarsely. If you prefer a smoother purée, process them in a food processor or blender.

2 Mix the tahini into the chickpeas, then stir in the remaining ingredients, with salt and pepper to taste. If the mixture seems too thick, add a little water. Serve at room temperature with grilled pittas.

Energy 144kcal/603kJ; Protein 7.2g; Carbohydrate 11.9g, of which sugars 0.4g; Fat 7.9g, of which saturates 1.1g; Cholesterol 0mg; Calcium 98mg; Fibre 3.8g; Sodium 149mg

GUACAMOLE

ONE OF THE BEST-LOVED MEXICAN SALSAS, THIS BLEND OF CREAMY AVOCADO, TOMATOES, CHILLIES, CORIANDER AND LIME NOW APPEARS ON TABLES THE WORLD OVER. SERVE WITH VEGETABLE CRUDITÉS, TORTILLA CHIPS OR BREADSTICKS. IT'S ALSO GREAT IN A BAP WITH A BURGER, RELISH AND CHEESE.

SERVES SIX TO EIGHT

INGREDIENTS
4 tomatoes
4 ripe avocados, preferably *fuerte*
freshly squeezed juice of 1 lime
½ small onion, finely chopped
2 garlic cloves, crushed
small bunch of fresh coriander
  (cilantro), chopped
3 fresh red fresno chillies
salt
tortilla chips or breadsticks, to serve

COOK'S TIP
Smooth-skinned *fuerte* avocados are native to Mexico, so would be authentic for this dip. If they are not available, use any avocados, but make sure that they are ripe. To test, gently press the top of the avocado; it should give a little but should not be too soft.

1 Cut a cross in the base of each tomato. Place the tomatoes in a heatproof bowl and pour over boiling water to cover.

2 Leave the tomatoes in the water for 30 seconds, then lift them out using a slotted spoon and plunge them into a bowl of cold water. Drain.

3 The tomato skins will have begun to peel back from the crosses. Remove the skins completely. Cut the tomatoes in half and cut out the cores. Scoop out the seeds with a teaspoon, then chop the flesh roughly and set it aside.

4 Cut the avocados in half then remove the stones (pits). Scoop the flesh out of the shells and place it in a food processor or blender. Process the pulp until almost smooth, then scrape into a bowl and stir in the lime juice. Alternatively, mash the flesh with a fork.

5 Add the onion and garlic to the avocado and mix well. Stir in the coriander until combined.

6 Remove the stalks from the chillies, slit them and scrape out the seeds with a small, sharp knife. Chop the chillies finely and add them to the avocado mixture, with the roughly chopped tomatoes. Mix well.

7 Taste the guacamole and add salt, if needed. Cover closely with clear film (plastic wrap) or a tight-fitting lid and chill for 1 hour before serving as a dip with tortilla chips or breadsticks. If it is well covered, guacamole will keep in the refrigerator for 2–3 days.

Energy 108kcal/449kJ; Protein 1.6g; Carbohydrate 3.3g, of which sugars 2.4g; Fat 9.9g, of which saturates 2.1g; Cholesterol 0mg; Calcium 23mg; Fibre 2.6g; Sodium 10mg.

BLUE CHEESE DIP

THIS DIP CAN BE MIXED UP IN NEXT TO NO TIME AND IS DELICIOUS SERVED WITH PEARS OR WITH FRESH VEGETABLE CRUDITÉS. THIS IS A VERY THICK DIP TO WHICH YOU CAN ADD A LITTLE MORE YOGURT FOR A SOFTER CONSISTENCY. ADD STILL MORE YOGURT TO MAKE A GREAT DRESSING.

SERVES FOUR

INGREDIENTS
   150g/5oz blue cheese, such as
      Stilton or Danish blue
   150g/5oz/⅔ cup soft cheese
   75ml/5 tbsp Greek (US strained
      plain) yogurt
   salt and ground black pepper,
      plus extra to garnish

1 Crumble the blue cheese and beat with a wooden spoon to soften it.

2 Add the soft cheese and beat well to blend the two cheeses together.

3 Gradually beat in the Greek yogurt, adding enough to give you the consistency you prefer.

4 Season with lots of black pepper and a little salt. Chill the dip until you are ready to serve it.

COOK'S TIP
If you like, add a handful of finely chopped walnuts to this dip, because they go very well with the cheese. Grind the nuts in a food processor to avoid the dip being too chunky in texture.

Energy 206kcal/855kJ; Protein 12.1g; Carbohydrate 2.6g, of which sugars 2.6g; Fat 16.5g, of which saturates 10.7g; Cholesterol 44mg; Calcium 219mg; Fibre 0g; Sodium 473mg.

GARLIC DIP

TWO WHOLE HEADS OF GARLIC MAY SEEM LIKE A LOT, BUT ROASTING TRANSFORMS THE FLESH TO A TENDER, SWEET AND MELLOW PULP. SERVE WITH CRUNCHY BREADSTICKS AND CRISPS. FOR A LOW-FAT VERSION OF THIS DIP, USE REDUCED-FAT MAYONNAISE AND LOW-FAT NATURAL YOGURT.

SERVES FOUR

INGREDIENTS
  2 whole garlic heads
  15ml/1 tbsp olive oil
  60ml/4 tbsp mayonnaise
  75ml/5 tbsp Greek (US strained
    plain) yogurt
  5ml/1 tsp wholegrain mustard
  salt and ground black pepper

1 Preheat the oven to 200°C/400°F/ Gas 6. Separate the garlic cloves and place them in a small roasting pan.

2 Pour the olive oil over the garlic cloves and turn them with a spoon to coat them evenly. Roast them for 20–30 minutes, or until tender and softened. Leave to cool for 5 minutes.

3 Trim off the root end of each roasted garlic clove. Peel the cloves and discard the skins. Place the roasted garlic on a chopping board and sprinkle with salt. Mash with a fork until puréed.

4 Combine the garlic, mayonnaise, yogurt and mustard in a small bowl.

5 Check and adjust the seasoning, then spoon the dip into a bowl. Cover and chill until ready to serve. Garnish with extra black pepper before serving.

COOK'S TIP
To cook on a barbecue, leave the garlic heads whole and cook until tender, turning occasionally. Peel and mash.

Energy 155kcal/640kJ; Protein 1.7g; Carbohydrate 0.8g, of which sugars 0.7g; Fat 16.4g, of which saturates 3.1g; Cholesterol 11mg; Calcium 34mg; Fibre 0.2g; Sodium 142mg.

THOUSAND ISLAND DIP

THIS VARIATION ON THE CLASSIC DRESSING IS QUICK AND EASY, AND IS IDEAL AS A DIP FOR GRILLED KING PRAWNS LACED ON TO BAMBOO SKEWERS, OR WITH A SIMPLE MIXED SEAFOOD SALAD.

SERVES FOUR

INGREDIENTS
4 tomatoes
150g/5oz/²/3 cup soft cheese
60ml/4 tbsp mayonnaise
30ml/2 tbsp tomato purée (paste)
30ml/2 tbsp chopped fresh parsley
4 sun-dried tomatoes in oil, drained
  and finely chopped
grated rind and juice of 1 lemon
red Tabasco sauce, to taste
5ml/1 tsp Worcestershire sauce
  or soy sauce
salt and ground black pepper

1 Skewer each tomato on a metal fork and hold in a gas flame for 1–2 minutes, or until the skin wrinkles and splits. Allow to cool, then slip off the skins. Alternatively, plunge the tomatoes into boiling water for 30 seconds, then refresh in cold water and peel. Halve the tomatoes and scoop out the seeds. Finely chop the flesh and set aside.

COOK'S TIP
Put together a colourful seafood medley – such as peeled prawns (shrimp), calamari rings and mussels – to accompany this vibrant party dip.

2 In a bowl, beat the soft cheese, then gradually beat in the mayonnaise and tomato purée until the mixture is smooth and a delicate pink.

3 Stir in the chopped parsley and sun-dried tomatoes, then add the chopped fresh tomatoes and mix well.

4 Add the lemon rind and juice, and Tabasco sauce to taste. Stir in the Worcestershire or soy sauce, and salt and pepper to taste.

5 Transfer the dip to a serving bowl, cover and chill until ready to serve.

Energy 194kcal/805kJ; Protein 4.7g; Carbohydrate 5.7g, of which sugars 5.6g; Fat 17.1g, of which saturates 5.2g; Cholesterol 27mg; Calcium 11mg; Fibre 1.2g; Sodium 184mg.

TZATZIKI

THIS CLASSIC GREEK DIP IS GREAT WITH STRIPS OF TOASTED PITTA BREAD OR AS AN ACCOMPANIMENT TO BARBECUED VEGETABLES. IT ALSO MAKES A TASTY ADDITION TO A SALAD SELECTION.

SERVES FOUR

INGREDIENTS

1 mini cucumber
4 spring onions (scallions)
1 garlic clove
200ml/7fl oz/scant 1 cup Greek
  (US strained plain) yogurt
45ml/3 tbsp chopped fresh mint
salt and ground black pepper
fresh mint sprig, to garnish
  (optional)

1 Trim the ends from the cucumber, then cut it into 5mm/¼in dice. Set aside.

2 Trim the spring onions and garlic, then chop both very finely.

COOK'S TIP
• Use Greek (US strained plain) yogurt for this dip if you have it – it has a higher fat content than most yogurts, but this gives it a deliciously rich, creamy texture.
• Mint or coriander (cilantro) leaves will make a suitable garnish for this recipe.

3 Beat the yogurt until smooth, if necessary, then gently stir in the cucumber, onions, garlic and mint.

4 Season to taste, then transfer the mixture to a serving bowl. Chill until ready to serve with pitta breads.

Energy 62kcal/258kJ; Protein 3.6g; Carbohydrate 1.7g, of which sugars 1.6g; Fat 5.2g, of which saturates 2.6g; Cholesterol 0mg; Calcium 84mg; Fibre 0.3g; Sodium 37mg.

FRIED BLACK CHILLI SAUCE

THIS SPICY, SALTY SAUCE FROM THAILAND IS A WONDERFUL DIPPING SAUCE FOR GRILLED AND ROASTED MEATS. IT GOES PARTICULARLY WELL WITH BEEF AND PORK, AND IS EQUALLY GOOD EATEN HOT OR COLD, SO CAN BE MADE IN ADVANCE.

MAKES ABOUT 200ML/7FL OZ/SCANT 1 CUP

INGREDIENTS

50g/2oz dried shrimp, soaked in
water for 20 minutes
12 dried red chillies, soaked in water
for 20 minutes
120ml/4fl oz/½ cup vegetable oil
8 garlic cloves, finely chopped
4 shallots or 1 onion, chopped
30ml/2 tbsp Thai shrimp paste
30ml/2 tbsp palm sugar (jaggery)

COOK'S TIP

Red chillies are used for this condiment
but, when they are fried, they turn a
deep red colour, almost black.

1 Drain the dried shrimp and, using a
mortar and pestle, pound them to a
paste. Drain the chillies, remove the
stalks and seeds and chop them finely.
Alternatively process the soaked shrimp
to a paste in a food processor then add
the chillies and pulse to chop.

2 Heat the oil in a wok or pan and stir-
fry the garlic and shallots or onion until
fragrant. Add the pounded shrimp,
chillies, Thai shrimp paste and palm
sugar. Stir-fry until the chillies are dark
in colour. Remove from the heat and
pour into a bowl. Serve hot or cold.

Energy 1059Kcal/4389kJ; Protein 30g; Carbohydrate 43g, of which sugars 40g; Fat 86g, of which saturates 10g; Cholesterol 253mg; Calcium 653mg; Fibre 2g; Sodium 2171mg

VIETNAMESE PEANUT DIPPING SAUCE

This hot dipping sauce is popular throughout Vietnam, where it is known as nuoc leo. Adjust the proportions of chilli, sugar or liquid, adding more or less according to taste. It is especially good served with chargrilled seafood or steamed vegetables.

MAKES ABOUT 300ML/10FL OZ/2¼ CUPS

INGREDIENTS

    15ml/1 tbsp vegetable oil
    2 garlic cloves, finely chopped
    2 red Thai chillies, seeded
    and chopped
    115g/4oz/⅔ cup unsalted roasted
    peanuts, finely chopped
    150ml/¼ pint/⅔ cup chicken stock
    60ml/4 tbsp coconut milk
    15ml/1 tbsp hoisin sauce
    15ml/1 tbsp Thai fish sauce
    15ml/1 tbsp sugar

1 Heat the oil in a wok and stir in the garlic and chillies. Stir-fry until they begin to colour, then add all but 15ml/1 tbsp of the peanuts. Stir-fry for a few minutes until the oil from the peanuts begins to weep. Add the remaining ingredients and bring the mixture to the boil.

2 Simmer until the sauce thickens and oil appears on the surface.

3 Transfer the sauce to a serving dish and garnish with the reserved peanuts.

Energy 848Kcal/3525kJ; Protein 31g; Carbohydrate 39g, of which sugars 31g; Fat 64g, of which saturates 11g; Cholesterol 0mg; Calcium 104mg; Fibre 8g; Sodium 2498mg

CHUNKY CHERRY TOMATO SALSA

SUCCULENT CHERRY TOMATOES AND REFRESHING CUCUMBER FORM THE BASE OF THIS DELICIOUS DILL-SEASONED SALSA WITH A FIERY CHILLI DRESSING. YOU CAN PREPARE IT UP TO ONE DAY IN ADVANCE AND STORE IN THE REFRIGERATOR UNTIL NEEDED.

SERVES FOUR

INGREDIENTS
1 ridge cucumber
5ml/1 tsp sea salt
500g/1¼lb cherry tomatoes
grated rind and juice of 1 lemon
45ml/3 tbsp chilli oil
2.5ml/½ tsp dried chilli flakes
30ml/2 tbsp chopped fresh dill
1 garlic clove, finely chopped
salt and ground black pepper

1 Trim the ends off the cucumber and cut it into 2.5cm/1in lengths, then cut each piece lengthways into thin slices.

2 Place the cucumber in a colander and sprinkle with sea salt. Leave for about 5 minutes, then rinse the slices under cold water and dry thoroughly with kitchen paper.

3 Quarter the cherry tomatoes and place in a bowl with the cucumber.

4 Whisk together the lemon rind and juice, chilli oil, chilli flakes, dill and garlic. Season, then pour over the tomato and cucumber and toss well. Marinate for 2 hours before serving.

COOK'S TIP
Try flavouring the salsa with other herbs: tarragon, coriander or mint.

Energy 45kcal/190kJ; Protein 2.2g; Carbohydrate 8.2g, of which sugars 7g; Fat 0.7g, of which saturates 0.1g; Cholesterol 0mg; Calcium 43mg; Fibre 2.3g; Sodium 16mg.

SALSA VERDE

THERE ARE MANY VERSIONS OF THE CLASSIC ITALIAN GREEN SAUCE. THIS ONE, INSTEAD OF BEING A SMOOTH, HERB-FLAVOURED PURÉE, HAS A THICK, CHUNKY TEXTURE. TRY IT SCATTERED OVER CHARGRILLED SQUID, OR WITH BAKED POTATOES.

SERVES FOUR

INGREDIENTS
   2–4 green chillies
   8 spring onions (scallions)
   2 garlic cloves
   50g/2oz salted capers
   sprig of fresh tarragon
   bunch of fresh parsley
   grated rind and juice of 1 lime
   juice of 1 lemon
   90ml/6 tbsp olive oil
   about 15ml/1 tbsp green Tabasco
     sauce, to taste
   ground black pepper

1 Halve the chillies and scrape out the seeds and membrane with the tip of a knife. Trim the spring onions and peel and halve the garlic cloves. Place all three ingredients in a food processor and pulse briefly until roughly chopped.

2 Use your fingers to rub the excess salt off the capers (what remains will season the salsa). Add them, with the tarragon and parsley, to the food processor and pulse again until the ingredients are quite finely chopped.

3 Transfer the mixture to a large bowl. Add the lime rind and juice, the lemon juice and the olive oil. Stir them in lightly so that the citrus juice and oil do not emulsify.

4 Add green Tabasco sauce, a little at a time, and black pepper to taste. Chill the salsa in the fridge until ready to serve, but do not prepare it more than 8 hours in advance.

Energy 158kcal/652kJ; Protein 0.9g; Carbohydrate 1.1g, of which sugars 1g; Fat 16.8g, of which saturates 2.4g; Cholesterol 0mg; Calcium 35mg; Fibre 1g; Sodium 6mg.

CLASSIC PESTO SAUCE WITH PASTA

BOTTLED PESTO IS USEFUL, BUT IT BEARS NO RESEMBLANCE TO THE HEADY AROMA AND FLAVOUR OF THE FRESH PASTE, WHICH IS EASY TO MAKE AND GLORIOUS AS A DRESSING FOR PASTA OR SALADS.

SERVES FOUR

INGREDIENTS
50g/2oz/1⅓ cups fresh basil leaves, plus fresh basil leaves, to garnish
2–4 garlic cloves
60ml/4 tbsp pine nuts
120ml/4fl oz/½ cup extra virgin olive oil
115g/4oz/1⅓ cups freshly grated Parmesan cheese, plus extra to serve
25g/1oz/⅓ cup freshly grated Pecorino cheese
400g/14oz dried pasta
salt and ground black pepper

COOK'S TIP
Pesto can be made 2–3 days in advance. Transfer it to a bowl and pour a thin film of olive oil over the surface. Cover tightly with clear film (plastic wrap) and keep it in the refrigerator. It can also be frozen, but do this at the end of step 2 and add the cheeses after defrosting.

1 Put the basil leaves, garlic and pine nuts in a blender or food processor. Add 60ml/4 tbsp of the olive oil. Process until the ingredients are finely chopped, then stop the machine, remove the lid and scrape down the mixture.

2 Turn the machine on again and slowly pour in the remaining oil in a thin, steady stream through the feeder tube. You may need to stop the machine and scrape down the mixture from the sides of the bowl once or twice to make sure everything is evenly mixed.

3 Scrape the mixture into a large bowl and beat in the cheeses with a wooden spoon. Taste and add salt and pepper if necessary.

4 Cook the pasta according to the instructions on the packet. Drain it well, then add it to the bowl of pesto and toss well. Serve immediately, garnished with the fresh basil leaves. Hand shaved Parmesan around separately.

Energy 713kcal/2969kJ; Protein 24.1g; Carbohydrate 43.2g, of which sugars 2.7g; Fat 50.5g, of which saturates 11.6g; Cholesterol 35mg; Calcium 468mg; Fibre 2.1g; Sodium 385mg.

FIERY CITRUS SALSA

THIS UNUSUAL, ZESTY SALSA MAKES A FANTASTIC MARINADE FOR PRAWNS AND OTHER SHELLFISH AND IT IS ALSO DELICIOUS SPOONED OVER BARBECUED KEBABS AND CHOPS.

SERVES FOUR

INGREDIENTS
- 1 orange
- 1 green apple
- 2 fresh red chillies
- 1 garlic clove
- 8 fresh mint leaves
- juice of 1 lemon
- salt and ground black pepper

1 Using a sharp knife, remove the peel and pith from the orange and, working over a bowl to catch the juices, cut out the segments. Squeeze any remaining juice into the bowl.

2 Use a sharp kitchen knife to peel the apple and slice it into wedges. Remove and discard the apple core.

3 Halve the chillies and remove the seeds, then place them in a blender or food processor with the orange segments and juice, apple wedges, garlic and mint.

4 Process until smooth. With the motor running, slowly pour in the lemon juice. Season to taste with salt and ground black pepper and serve immediately.

VARIATION
Finely chopped strawberries add a new dimension to this fresh, fruity salsa.

Energy 18kcal/75kJ; Protein 0.4g; Carbohydrate 4.1g, of which sugars 4.1g; Fat 0.1g, of which saturates 0g; Cholesterol 0mg; Calcium 18mg; Fibre 0.8g; Sodium 2mg.

BARBECUED CORN SALSA

*SERVE THIS SUCCULENT SALSA WITH GRILLED GAMMON OR PORK, OR WITH SMOKED MEATS. DON'T BE
TEMPTED TO USE CANNED OR FROZEN CORN FOR THIS RECIPE: THE SMOKY SWEET FLAVOUR OF THE
FRESH CHARGRILLED CORN COB MAKES THE SALSA PARTICULARLY FLAVOURSOME.*

2 To remove the kernels, stand each cob upright on a chopping board and use a large, heavy knife to slice down the length of the cob. Put the kernels in a mixing bowl.

3 Skewer the tomatoes and turn them over the coals for about 2 minutes, until the skin splits and wrinkles. Slip off the skins and dice the flesh. Add to the corn with the spring onions and chopped garlic.

SERVES FOUR

INGREDIENTS
  2 corn cobs
  30ml/2 tbsp melted butter
  4 tomatoes
  6 spring onions (scallions), finely
    chopped
  1 garlic clove, finely chopped
  30ml/2 tbsp lemon juice
  30ml/2 tbsp olive oil
  red Tabasco sauce, to taste
  salt and ground black pepper

1 Prepare the barbecue. Remove the husks and silks from the corn cobs and brush with the melted butter. Grill them gently for about 20 minutes, turning occasionally, until tender and charred.

4 Stir the lemon juice and olive oil together, adding Tabasco, salt and black pepper to taste. Stir into the salsa, cover and leave at room temperature for 1–2 hours before serving.

Energy 156kcal/650kJ; Protein 1.8g; Carbohydrate 10.3g, of which sugars 6g; Fat 12.3g, of which saturates 4.9g; Cholesterol 16mg; Calcium 15mg; Fibre 1.6g; Sodium 123mg.

TOFFEE ONION RELISH

SLOW, GENTLE COOKING REDUCES THE ONIONS TO A SOFT, CARAMELIZED RELISH, WHICH MAKES A TASTY ADDITION TO MANY BARBECUE MENUS. TRY IT WITH STEAKS, PORK CHOPS OR GAMMON, OR AS AN ACCOMPANIMENT TO GRILLED GOATS' CHEESE.

SERVES FOUR

INGREDIENTS
3 large onions
50g/2oz/4 tbsp butter
30ml/2 tbsp olive oil
30ml/2 tbsp light muscovado (brown) sugar
30ml/2 tbsp pickled capers
30ml/2 tbsp chopped fresh parsley
salt and ground black pepper

3 Roughly chop the capers and stir them into the toffee onions. Allow to cool completely.

4 Stir in the chopped parsley and add salt and ground black pepper to taste. Cover and chill until ready to serve.

1 Peel the onions and halve them vertically, through the core, using a sharp knife. Slice them thinly.

2 Heat the butter and oil together in a large pan. Add the onions and sugar and cook very gently for 30 minutes over a low heat, stirring occasionally, until reduced to a soft, rich brown caramelized mixture.

COOK'S TIP
Watch the mixture and keep stirring to ensure that the sugar caramelizes but does not burn too much. Use a heat diffuser under the pan if necessary.

Energy 151kcal/629kJ; Protein 5.8g; Carbohydrate 31.9g, of which sugars 22.7g; Fat 1g, of which saturates 0g; Cholesterol 0mg; Calcium 111mg; Fibre 5.6g; Sodium 15mg.

CONFIT <u>of</u> SLOW-COOKED ONIONS

THIS JAM OF SLOW-COOKED, CARAMELIZED ONIONS IN SWEET-SOUR BALSAMIC VINEGAR WILL KEEP FOR SEVERAL DAYS IN A SEALED JAR IN THE REFRIGERATOR. YOU CAN MAKE IT WITH RED, WHITE OR YELLOW ONIONS, BUT YELLOW ONIONS GIVE THE SWEETEST RESULT. IT'S WONDERFUL WITH STEAK.

MAKES ABOUT 500G/1¼LB

INGREDIENTS
30ml/2 tbsp olive oil
15g/½oz/1 tbsp butter
500g/1¼lb onions, sliced
3–5 fresh thyme sprigs
1 fresh bay leaf
30ml/2 tbsp light muscovado (brown)
   sugar, plus a little extra
50g/2oz/¼ cup ready-to-eat
   prunes, chopped
30ml/2 tbsp balsamic vinegar, plus a
   little extra
120ml/4fl oz/½ cup red wine
salt and ground black pepper

1 Reserve 5ml/1 tsp of the oil, then heat the remaining oil with the butter in a large pan. Add the onions, cover and cook gently over a low heat for about 15 minutes, stirring occasionally.

2 Season the onions with salt and ground black pepper, then add the thyme, bay leaf and sugar. Cook slowly, uncovered, for a further 15–20 minutes until the onions are very soft and dark. Stir the onions occasionally during cooking to prevent them sticking or burning.

3 Add the prunes, vinegar, wine and 60ml/4 tbsp water to the pan and cook over a low heat, stirring frequently, for 20 minutes, or until most of the liquid has evaporated. Add a little more water and reduce the heat if the mixture starts to look too dry.

4 Remove the pan from the heat. Adjust the seasoning if necessary, adding more sugar and/or vinegar to taste. Leave the confit to cool then stir in the remaining 5ml/1 tsp olive oil. Spoon into a serving bowl and serve at room temperature, or spoon into screw-top jars and chill.

VARIATION
Gently brown 500g/1¼lb peeled pickling (pearl) onions in 60ml/4 tbsp olive oil. Sprinkle in 45ml/3 tbsp brown sugar and caramelize a little, then add 7.5ml/1½ tsp crushed coriander seeds, 250ml/8fl oz/1 cup red wine, 2 bay leaves, a few thyme sprigs, 3 strips orange rind, 45ml/3 tbsp tomato purée (paste) and the juice of 1 orange. Cook gently, covered, for 1 hour, stirring occasionally. Uncover for the last 20 minutes. Sharpen with 15–30ml/ 1–2 tbsp sherry vinegar.

Energy 678kcal/2827kJ; Protein 7.5g; Carbohydrate 87.9g, of which sugars 76.4g; Fat 35.5g, of which saturates 11g; Cholesterol 32mg; Calcium 161mg; Fibre 9.8g; Sodium 113mg.

CHILLI RELISH

BURGERS OR BARBECUED SAUSAGES TASTE GREAT WITH A SPICY RELISH, AND A HOME-MADE ONE IS SO MUCH NICER THAN ONE FROM A JAR. THIS CHILLI RELISH WILL LAST FOR AT LEAST A WEEK STORED IN A REFRIGERATOR, SO YOU COULD MAKE IT A FEW DAYS IN ADVANCE OF YOUR BARBECUE.

SERVES EIGHT

INGREDIENTS

6 tomatoes
30ml/2 tbsp olive oil
1 onion, roughly chopped
1 red (bell) pepper, seeded
   and chopped
2 garlic cloves, chopped
5ml/1 tsp ground cinnamon
5ml/1 tsp chilli flakes
5ml/1 tsp ground ginger
5ml/1 tsp salt
2.5ml/½ tsp ground black pepper
75g/3oz/⅓ cup light muscovado
   (brown) sugar
75ml/5 tbsp cider vinegar
handful of fresh basil leaves,
   coarsely chopped

1 Skewer each tomato on a metal fork and hold in a gas flame for 1–2 minutes, turning, until the skin splits and wrinkles. Alternatively, plunge the tomatoes into boiling water for 30 seconds, then drain and refresh in cold water. Peel away the skins, scoop out the seeds and roughly chop the flesh.

2 Heat the olive oil in a large pan. Add the onion, red pepper and garlic to the pan. Cook the vegetables gently for 5–8 minutes, or until softened.

COOK'S TIP
This relish thickens slightly as it cools down so the mixture should be pulpy and thick but still a little wet at the end of step 5.

3 Add the chopped tomatoes to the pan, cover and cook for 5 minutes, until the tomatoes release their juices.

4 Stir in the remaining ingredients except for the basil. Bring the mixture gently to the boil, stirring, until the sugar dissolves.

5 Simmer, uncovered, for 20 minutes, or until the mixture is pulpy. Stir in the basil leaves and check the seasoning.

6 Allow to cool completely, then transfer to a glass jar or a plastic container with a tightly fitting lid. Store, covered, in the refrigerator.

Energy 84kcal/355kJ; Protein 0.9g; Carbohydrate 14.1g, of which sugars 13.9g; Fat 3.1g, of which saturates 0.5g; Cholesterol 0mg; Calcium 14mg; Fibre 1.2g; Sodium 8mg.

CORN RELISH

HERE IS A LOVELY INDIAN-INSPIRED RELISH TO PERK UP ALL KINDS OF BARBECUED DISHES. SERVE WITH BAKED OR ROASTED VEGETABLES, PLAIN GRILLED MEATS OR FISH, OR SCOOP UP WITH PITTA BREAD AS A NIBBLE WHILE THE FOOD COOKS ON THE GRILL.

<u>SERVES FOUR</u>

INGREDIENTS
   30ml/2 tbsp vegetable oil
   1 large onion, chopped
   1 red chilli, seeded and chopped
   2 garlic cloves, chopped
   5ml/1 tsp black mustard seeds
   10ml/2 tsp hot curry powder
   320g/11¼oz can corn, drained, or
      275g/10oz frozen corn
   grated rind and juice of 1 lime
   45ml/3 tbsp chopped fresh
      coriander (cilantro)
   salt and ground black pepper

1 Heat the oil in a large frying pan and cook the onion, chilli and garlic over a high heat for 5 minutes, or until the onions are just beginning to brown.

2 Stir in the mustard seeds and curry powder, then cook for 2 minutes more, stirring, until the seeds start to splutter and the onions are browned.

3 Remove the fried onion and spice mixture from the heat and allow to cool completely. Transfer the mixture to a glass bowl.

4 Add the drained corn to the bowl containing the onion mixture and stir to mix.

5 Add the lime rind and juice and the coriander. Mix well and season to taste with salt and pepper, then cover and serve at room temperature.

Energy 169kcal/708kJ; Protein 3.2g; Carbohydrate 25.5g, of which sugars 10.7g; Fat 6.7g, of which saturates 0.8g; Cholesterol 0mg; Calcium 36mg; Fibre 2.3g; Sodium 221mg.

QUICK SATAY SAUCE

THERE ARE MANY VERSIONS OF THIS TASTY PEANUT SAUCE. THIS ONE IS VERY SPEEDY AND IT TASTES DELICIOUS DRIZZLED OVER BARBECUED SKEWERS OF CHICKEN. FOR PARTIES, ARRANGE BARBECUED CHICKEN SKEWERS AROUND A BOWL OF WARM SAUCE TO MAKE A GREAT APPETIZER.

SERVES FOUR

INGREDIENTS

    200ml/7fl oz/scant 1 cup coconut
      cream
    60ml/4 tbsp crunchy peanut butter
    5ml/1 tsp Worcestershire sauce
    Tabasco sauce, to taste
    fresh coconut, to garnish (optional)

1 Pour the coconut cream into a small pan and heat it gently over a low heat for about 2 minutes.

2 Add the peanut butter and stir vigorously until it is blended into the coconut cream. Continue to heat until the mixture is warm but not boiling hot.

VARIATION

Replace the Worcestershire and Tabasco sauces with 5ml/1 tsp wine vinegar or lemon juice and 5ml/1 tsp chilli flakes.

COOK'S TIP

Thick coconut milk can be substituted for coconut cream, but take care to buy an unsweetened variety for this recipe.

3 Stir the Worcestershire sauce into the mixture and add a dash of Tabasco to taste. Pour into a serving bowl.

4 Use a potato peeler to shave thin curls from a piece of fresh coconut, if using. Scatter the coconut over the dish of your choice and serve immediately with the sauce.

Energy 108kcal/451kJ; Protein 3.6g; Carbohydrate 5.8g, of which sugars 4.9g; Fat 8g, of which saturates 2.1g; Cholesterol 0mg; Calcium 30mg; Fibre 0.8g; Sodium 150mg.

TOMATO KETCHUP

SWEET, TANGY, SPICY TOMATO KETCHUP IS PERFECT FOR SERVING WITH BARBECUED OR GRILLED BURGERS AND SAUSAGES. THIS HOME-MADE VARIETY IS SO MUCH BETTER THAN STORE-BOUGHT TOMATO KETCHUP, AND THE RECIPE WILL BE ENOUGH TO SERVE ABOUT 15 PEOPLE.

MAKES ABOUT 1.3KG/3LB

INGREDIENTS
    2.25kg/5lb very ripe tomatoes
    1 onion
    6 cloves
    4 allspice berries
    6 black peppercorns
    1 fresh rosemary sprig
    25g/1oz fresh root ginger,
      sliced
    1 celery heart and leaves,
      chopped
    30ml/2 tbsp soft light brown sugar
    65ml/4½ tbsp raspberry vinegar
    3 garlic cloves, peeled
    15ml/1 tbsp salt

1 Plunge the tomatoes into boiling water for 30 seconds, then refresh in cold water. Peel and remove the seeds then chop and place in a large pan. Peel the onion, leaving the tip and root intact, and stud it with the cloves.

2 Tie the onion in a double layer of muslin (cheesecloth) with the allspice, peppercorns, rosemary and ginger and add to the pan. Add the celery to the pan with the remaining ingredients.

3 Bring the mixture to the boil over a fairly high heat, stirring occasionally. Once it is beginning to bubble, reduce the heat and simmer for 1½–2 hours, stirring regularly, until the liquid has reduced by around half.

4 Purée the mixture in a food processor, then return to the pan, bring to the boil and simmer for 15 minutes. Bottle in clean, sterilized jars and store in the refrigerator. Use within 2 weeks.

Energy 586kcal/2509kJ; Protein 19.9g; Carbohydrate 116.3g, of which sugars 114.9g; Fat 8.2g, of which saturates 2.5g; Cholesterol 0mg; Calcium 329mg; Fibre 29.1g; Sodium 409mg.

ROASTED RED REPPER AND CHILLI KETCHUP

ROASTING THE PEPPERS FOR THIS KETCHUP GIVES IT A RICH, SMOKY FLAVOUR. YOU CAN ADD FEWER OR MORE CHILLIES ACCORDING TO TASTE. ONCE THE BOTTLE IS OPENED, STORE THE KETCHUP IN THE REFRIGERATOR AND USE WITHIN 3 MONTHS.

MAKES ABOUT 600ML/1 PINT/2½ CUPS

INGREDIENTS
900g/2lb red (bell) peppers
225g/8oz shallots
1 tart cooking apple, quartered,
  cored and roughly chopped
4 fresh red chillies, seeded
  and chopped
1 large sprig each thyme and parsley
1 bay leaf
5ml/1 tsp coriander seeds
5ml/1 tsp black peppercorns
600ml/1 pint/2½ cups water
350ml/12fl oz/1½ cups red
  wine vinegar
50g/2oz/scant ¼ cup granulated
  (white) sugar
5ml/1 tsp salt
7.5ml/1½ tsp arrowroot

1 Prepare the barbecue or preheat the grill (broiler). Grill the peppers for 10–12 minutes, turning regularly, until the skins have blackened. Put the peppers in a plastic bag and leave for 5 minutes.

2 When the peppers are cool enough to handle, peel away the skin, then quarter the peppers and remove the seeds. Roughly chop the flesh and place in a large pan.

3 Put the shallots in a bowl, pour over boiling water and leave to stand for 3 minutes. Drain, then rinse under cold running water and peel. Chop the shallots and add to the pan with the apple and chillies.

4 Tie the thyme, parsley, bay leaf, coriander and peppercorns together in a square of muslin (cheesecloth).

5 Add the bag of herbs and the water to the pan and bring to the boil. Reduce the heat, cover and simmer for 30 minutes. Leave to cool for 15 minutes, then remove and discard the muslin bag.

6 Purée the mixture in a food processor, then press through a sieve (strainer) and return the purée to the cleaned pan. Reserve 15ml/1 tbsp of the vinegar and add the rest to the pan with the sugar and salt.

7 Bring the mixture to the boil, stirring until the sugar has dissolved, then simmer for 45 minutes, or until the sauce is well reduced.

8 Blend the arrowroot with the reserved vinegar, stir into the sauce, then simmer for 2–3 minutes, or until slightly thickened and glossy.

9 Pour the sauce into hot sterilized bottles, then seal, heat process and store in a cool, dark place and use within 18 months.

Energy 553kcal/2341kJ; Protein 12.8g; Carbohydrate 123.2g, of which sugars 120.5g; Fat 4.1g, of which saturates 0.9g; Cholesterol 0mg; Calcium 155mg; Fibre 18.6g; Sodium 1045mg

BARBECUE SAUCE

THIS TRADITIONAL SAUCE CAN BE PREPARED IN ADVANCE, BOTTLED AND USED WHENEVER YOU FEEL LIKE HOLDING A BARBECUE, AS IT WILL LAST FOR SEVERAL MONTHS IN A REFRIGERATOR. SERVE IT WITH YOUR FAVOURITE BURGERS, SAUSAGES, GRILLED CHICKEN AND BARBECUED VEGETABLES.

MAKES ABOUT 900ML/1½ PINTS/3¾ CUPS

INGREDIENTS
  30ml/2 tbsp olive oil
  1 large onion, chopped
  1 garlic clove, crushed
  1 fresh red chilli, seeded and sliced
  2 celery sticks, sliced
  1 large carrot, sliced
  1 medium cooking apple, quartered,
    cored, peeled and chopped
  450g/1lb ripe tomatoes, quartered
  2.5ml/½ tsp ground ginger
  150ml/¼ pint/⅔ cup malt vinegar
  1 bay leaf
  4 cloves
  4 black peppercorns
  50g/2oz/¼ cup soft light brown sugar
  10ml/2 tsp English mustard
  2.5ml/½ tsp salt

1 Heat the oil in a large heavy pan. Add the onion and cook over a low heat for 5 minutes.

2 Stir the garlic, chilli, celery and carrot into the onions and cook for 5 minutes, stirring frequently, until the vegetables soften and the onion is just beginning to colour.

3 Add the apple, tomatoes, ground ginger and malt vinegar to the pan and stir to combine.

4 Put the bay leaf, cloves and peppercorns on a square of muslin (cheesecloth) and tie into a bag with fine string. Add to the pan and bring to the boil. Reduce the heat, cover and simmer for about 45 minutes, stirring the mixture occasionally.

5 Add the sugar, mustard and salt and stir until the sugar dissolves. Simmer for 5 minutes. Leave to cool for 10 minutes. Remove and discard the bag. Press the mixture through a sieve (strainer) and return to the cleaned pan. Simmer for 10 minutes, or until thickened. Adjust the seasoning.

6 Pour the sauce into hot sterilized bottles or jars, then seal. Store in a cool, dark place and use within 6 months. Once opened, store in the refrigerator and use within 2 months.

VARIATION
For Quick Barbecue Sauce, heat 20ml/2 tbsp oil in a pan and fry 1 finely chopped onion and 2 crushed garlic cloves until soft. Add a 200g/7oz can of chopped tomatoes, 30ml/2 tbsp tomato purée (paste), 15ml/1 tbsp soft light brown sugar, 15ml/1 tbsp Worcestershire sauce, a dash of Tabasco sauce, 30ml/2 tbsp vinegar and 15ml/1 tbsp English mustard. Simmer for 10 minutes and serve hot or cold.

Energy 723kcal/3036kJ; Protein 12.2g; Carbohydrate 114.3g, of which sugars 102.5g; Fat 29.1g, of which saturates 3.8g; Cholesterol 0mg; Calcium 243mg; Fibre 14.2g; Sodium 118mg.

CUMBERLAND SAUCE

THIS SAUCE IS THOUGHT TO HAVE BEEN NAMED AFTER THE DUKE OF CUMBERLAND, WHO BECAME RULER OF HANOVER AT A TIME WHEN FRUIT SAUCES WERE SERVED WITH MEAT AND GAME IN GERMANY. IT IS TRADITIONALLY SERVED WITH COLD CUTS, BUT GOES WELL WITH BARBECUED SAUSAGES.

MAKES ABOUT 750ML/1¼ PINTS/3 CUPS

INGREDIENTS
4 oranges
2 lemons
450g/1lb redcurrant or rowan jelly
150ml/¼ pint/⅔ cup port
20ml/4 tsp cornflour (cornstarch)
pinch of ground ginger

1 Scrub the oranges and lemons, then remove the rind thinly, paring away any white pith. Cut the orange and lemon rind into very thin matchstick strips. Put the strips in a heavy pan, cover them with cold water and bring the water to the boil.

2 Simmer the rind for 2 minutes, then drain, cover with cold water, bring to the boil and simmer for about 3 minutes. Drain well and return the rind to the pan.

3 Squeeze the juice from the fruits, then add it to the pan with the redcurrant or rowan jelly. Reserve 30ml/2 tbsp of the port and add the rest to the pan.

4 Slowly bring the mixture to the boil, stirring until the jelly has melted. Simmer for 10 minutes until slightly thickened. Blend the cornflour and ginger with the reserved port and stir into the sauce. Cook over a low heat, stirring until the sauce thickens and boils. Simmer for 2 minutes.

5 Leave the sauce to cool for about 5 minutes, then stir again briefly. Pour into warmed sterilized wide-necked bottles or jars, cover and seal. The sauce will keep for several weeks in the refrigerator or, if heat treated, for 6 months. Once opened, store in the refrigerator and use within 3 weeks.

Energy 1481kcal/6297kJ; Protein 3g; Carbohydrate 346.9g, of which sugars 328.5g; Fat 0.1g, of which saturates 0g; Cholesterol 0mg; Calcium 63mg; Fibre 0g; Sodium 147mg.

SHERRIED PLUM SAUCE

For this smooth sauce, sharp cooking plums, damsons or bullaces — globular, fleshy, black-skinned berry fruits — give the best flavour and help counteract the sweetness of the sauce. Wonderful served with grilled game, such as pheasant or venison.

2 Roughly chop the fruit and put in a large, heavy pan. If you're using damsons or bullaces, you may find it easier simply to chop them, leaving in the stones, which will be strained out later. Stir in the sherry and vinegar.

3 Slowly bring the mixture to the boil, then cover the pan and cook over a gentle heat for about 10 minutes, or until the plums are very soft. Push the fruit through a food mill or sieve (strainer) to remove the skins and any stones.

4 Return the plum purée to the pan and add the sugar, garlic, salt and ginger. Stir until the sugar has dissolved, then bring back to the boil and simmer uncovered for about 15 minutes, until thickened.

5 Remove the pan from the heat and stir in the Tabasco sauce. Ladle the sauce into hot sterilized jars. Add 5–10ml/1–2 tsp sherry to the top of each jar, then cover and seal. The sauce will keep for several weeks in the refrigerator or, if heat treated, for 6 months. Once opened, store in the refrigerator and use within 3 weeks.

COOK'S TIP
The sherry poured into the top of the jar will act as a preservative as well as adding zip to the sauce: stir it in when you open the bottle. A nutty dry amontillado or oloroso will add extra depth of flavour.

MAKES ABOUT 400ML/14FL OZ/1⅔ CUPS

INGREDIENTS
  450g/1lb dark plums or damsons
  120ml/4fl oz/½ cup dry sherry,
    plus extra
  30ml/2 tbsp sherry vinegar
  175g/6oz/scant 1 cup light
    muscovado (brown) sugar
  1 garlic clove, crushed
  1.5ml/¼ tsp salt
  2.5cm/1in piece fresh root ginger,
    finely chopped
  3–4 drops of Tabasco sauce

1 Cut each plum in half using a sharp knife, then twist the two halves apart and remove the stone (pit).

Energy 996kcal/4237kJ; Protein 4.2g; Carbohydrate 225g, of which sugars 224.2g; Fat 0.5g, of which saturates 0g; Cholesterol 0mg; Calcium 161mg; Fibre 7.4g; Sodium 1014mg.

APPLE AND TOMATO CHUTNEY

THIS MELLOW SPICY CHUTNEY IS A BRILLIANT ACCOMPANIMENT FOR GRILLED SAUSAGES AND PORK STEAKS, AND ALSO GOES WONDERFULLY WITH BREAD AND CHEESE. ANY TYPE OF TOMATOES CAN BE USED SUCCESSFULLY IN THIS RECIPE, AND IT'S A GREAT WAY TO USE UP A BUMPER HOME-GROWN CROP.

MAKES 1.8KG/4LB

INGREDIENTS
  1.3kg/3lb cooking apples
  1.3kg/3lb tomatoes
  2 large onions
  2 garlic cloves
  250g/9oz stoned (pitted) dates
  2 red (bell) peppers
  3 dried chillies
  15ml/1 tbsp black peppercorns
  4 cardamom pods
  15ml/1 tbsp coriander seeds
  10ml/2 tsp cumin seeds
  10ml/2 tsp ground turmeric
  15ml/1tbsp salt
  1kg/2¼lb/4½ cups sugar
  600ml/1 pint/2½ cups distilled
    malt vinegar

3 Add the sugar and vinegar and simmer for 30 minutes, stirring often. Add the red pepper. Cook for 30 minutes, stirring until thickened.

4 Spoon the chutney into warm, dry sterilized jars. Immediately top each one with a circle of waxed paper and cover tightly. Leave to cool.

1 Peel and chop the apples, tomatoes, onions and garlic. Quarter the dates. Core and seed the peppers, then cut into chunks. Put all the ingredients, except the peppers, into a large pan.

2 Slit the chillies. Put the peppercorns and remaining spices into a mortar and roughly crush with a pestle. Add the chillies, spices and salt to the pan.

COOK'S TIP
Sterilize preserving jars by washing them in hot, sudsy water, then boiling them in a kettle or pan for 15 minutes. You should always fill them while they are still hot. Be careful to handle them with a cloth or oven gloves.

Energy 5583kcal/23819kJ; Protein 35.8g; Carbohydrate 1432.9g, of which sugars 1420.3g; Fat 8.1g, of which saturates 1.9g; Cholesterol 0mg; Calcium 940mg; Fibre 56.4g; Sodium 6152mg.

MEDITERRANEAN CHUTNEY

REMINISCENT OF THE WARM MEDITERRANEAN CLIMATE, THIS MIXED VEGETABLE CHUTNEY IS COLOURFUL, MILD AND WARM IN FLAVOUR AND GOES PARTICULARLY WELL WITH GRILLED MEATS AND SAUSAGES. FOR A HOTTER, SPICIER FLAVOUR, ADD A LITTLE CAYENNE PEPPER WITH THE PAPRIKA.

MAKES ABOUT 1.8KG/4LB

INGREDIENTS
  450g/1lb Spanish (Bermuda) onions, chopped
  900g/2lb ripe tomatoes, skinned and chopped
  1 aubergine (eggplant), weighing about 350g/12oz, trimmed and cut into 1cm/½in cubes
  450g/1lb courgettes (zucchini), sliced
  1 yellow (bell) pepper, quartered, seeded and sliced
  1 red (bell) pepper, quartered, seeded and sliced
  3 garlic cloves, crushed
  1 small sprig of rosemary
  1 small sprig of thyme
  2 bay leaves
  15ml/1 tbsp salt
  15ml/1 tbsp paprika
  300ml/½ pint/1¼ cups malt vinegar
  400g/14oz/2 cups granulated (white) sugar

1 Put the chopped onions, tomatoes, aubergine, courgettes, peppers and garlic in a preserving pan. Cover the pan with a lid and cook gently over a very low heat, stirring occasionally, for about 15 minutes, or until the juices start to run.

COOK'S TIP
Use the chutney within 2 years. Once a jar is opened, store it in the refrigerator and use within 2 months.

2 Tie the rosemary, thyme and bay leaves in a piece of muslin (cheesecloth). Add to the pan with the salt, paprika and half the malt vinegar. Simmer, uncovered, for 25 minutes, or until the vegetables are tender and the juices reduced.

3 Add the remaining vinegar and sugar to the pan and stir over a low heat until the sugar has dissolved. Simmer for 30 minutes, stirring the chutney frequently towards the end of the cooking time.

4 When the chutney is reduced to a thick consistency and no excess liquid remains, remove the pan from the heat, discard the herbs, then spoon the chutney into warmed sterilized jars. Set aside until cool, then cover and seal with vinegar-proof lids.

5 Store the chutney in a cool, dark place and allow to mature for at least 2 months before eating.

COOK'S TIP
Organically grown peppers will give a superior depth of flavour to this chutney, as will substituting the white sugar for unrefined sugar, but the latter will make the colour slightly darker.

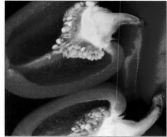

Energy 2114kcal/8986kJ; Protein 27.1g; Carbohydrate 516.4g, of which sugars 504.1g; Fat 7.6g, of which saturates 1.9g; Cholesterol 0mg; Calcium 550mg; Fibre 29g; Sodium 6036mg.

GREEN TOMATO CHUTNEY

THIS IS A CLASSIC CHUTNEY FOR USING THE LAST TOMATOES OF SUMMER THAT JUST NEVER SEEM TO RIPEN. APPLES AND ONIONS CONTRIBUTE ESSENTIAL FLAVOUR, WHICH IS ENHANCED BY THE ADDITION OF SPICE. TRY IT ON BURGERS TOPPED WITH MELTING BRIE — DELICIOUS.

MAKES ABOUT 2.5KG/5½LB

INGREDIENTS

1.8kg/4lb green (unripe) tomatoes, roughly chopped
450g/1lb cooking apples, peeled, cored and chopped
450g/1lb onions, chopped
2 large garlic cloves, crushed
15ml/1 tbsp salt
45ml/3 tbsp pickling spice
600ml/1 pint/2½ cups cider vinegar
450g/1lb/2¼ cups granulated (white) sugar

1 Place the tomatoes, apples, onions and garlic in a large pan and add the salt.

2 Tie the pickling spice in a piece of muslin (cheesecloth) and add to the ingredients in the pan.

3 Add half the vinegar to the pan and bring to the boil. Reduce the heat and simmer for 1 hour, or until the chutney is reduced and thick, stirring frequently.

COOK'S TIPS
• To avoid spillages and speed up the process of potting preserves, use a wide-necked jam funnel to transfer the chutney into the jars. Wipe the jars immediately, then label them when cold.
• Use a long-handled teaspoon to press and poke the chutney right down into the pots to exclude any trapped air pockets.
• Press wax discs on the surface of the chutney before sealing the jar.

4 Put the sugar and remaining vinegar in a pan and heat gently until the sugar has dissolved, then add to the chutney. Simmer for 1½ hours until the chutney is thick, stirring it occasionally.

5 Remove the muslin bag from the chutney, then spoon the hot chutney into warmed sterilized jars. Cover and seal immediately. Allow the chutney to mature for at least 1 month before eating it.

Energy 2399kcal/10233kJ; Protein 21.6g; Carbohydrate 601.6g, of which sugars 591.3g; Fat 6.8g, of which saturates 1.8g; Cholesterol 0mg; Calcium 496mg; Fibre 31.5g; Sodium 2177mg.

MINT SAUCE

THE FRESH, TART, ASTRINGENT FLAVOUR OF MINT SAUCE MAKES IT THE PERFECT FOIL FOR LAMB, SO HAVE IT READY TO SERVE WITH BARBECUED LAMB CHOPS AND STEAKS. IT IS VERY SIMPLE TO MAKE AND IS INFINITELY PREFERABLE TO READY-MADE VARIETIES.

MAKES ABOUT 250ML/8FL OZ/1 CUP

INGREDIENTS
1 large bunch fresh mint
105ml/7 tbsp boiling water
150ml/¼ pint/⅔ cup wine vinegar
30ml/2 tbsp granulated (white) sugar

1 Using a sharp knife, chop the mint very finely and place it in a 600ml/ 1 pint/2½ cup jug (pitcher). Pour the boiling water over the mint and leave to infuse for about 10 minutes.

2 When the mint infusion has cooled and is lukewarm, stir in the wine vinegar and sugar. Continue stirring (but do not mash up the mint leaves) until the sugar has dissolved completely.

3 Pour the mint sauce into a sterilized bottle or jar, seal and store in the refrigerator.

COOK'S TIP
This mint sauce will keep for up to 6 months stored in the refrigerator, but is best used within 3 weeks.

VARIATION
To make a quick Indian raita for serving with crispy poppadums, simply stir a little of this mint sauce into a small bowl of natural (US strained plain) yogurt. Serve the raita alongside a bowl of tangy mango chutney.

Energy 161kcal/685kJ; Protein 3.9g; Carbohydrate 36.6g, of which sugars 31.4g; Fat 0.7g, of which saturates 0g; Cholesterol 0mg; Calcium 226mg; Fibre 0g; Sodium 17mg.

TRADITIONAL HORSERADISH SAUCE

FIERY, PEPPERY HORSERADISH SAUCE IS WITHOUT DOUBT THE ESSENTIAL ACCOMPANIMENT TO ROAST OR CHARGRILLED BEEF AND IS ALSO DELICIOUS SERVED WITH SMOKED FISH OF ALL KINDS. HORSERADISH IS ALWAYS USED RAW — COOKING DESTROYS ITS FLAVOUR.

MAKES ABOUT 200ML/7FL OZ/¾ CUP

INGREDIENTS
  45ml/3 tbsp freshly grated
    horseradish root
  15ml/1 tbsp white wine vinegar
  5ml/1 tsp granulated (white)
    sugar
  pinch of salt
  150ml/¼ pint/⅔ cup thick double
    (heavy) cream, for serving

1 Place the grated horseradish in a bowl, then add the white wine vinegar, granulated sugar and just a pinch of salt.

2 Stir the ingredients together until thoroughly combined.

3 Pour the mixture into a sterilized jar. It will keep in the refrigerator for up to 6 months.

4 A few hours before serving, stir the double cream into the horseradish and leave to infuse (steep). Serve chilled or at room temperature.

COOK'S TIPS
• To counteract the potent fumes of the horseradish, keep the root submerged in water while you chop and peel it. Use a food processor to do the fine chopping or grating, and avert your head when removing the lid.

• Once grated, fresh horseradish must be used immediately as it loses its pungency very quickly.
• The root can be kept in the refrigerator for 1 week, and can also be frozen: cut it into chunks of a suitable size for a batch of the sauce and use as required.

Energy 774kcal/3190kJ; Protein 2.8g; Carbohydrate 9.9g, of which sugars 9.8g; Fat 80.7g, of which saturates 50.1g; Cholesterol 206mg; Calcium 98mg; Fibre 1.1g; Sodium 40mg.

MOUTARDE AUX FINES HERBES

THIS CLASSIC, FRAGRANT MUSTARD MAY BE USED EITHER AS A DELICIOUS CONDIMENT OR FOR COATING MEATS SUCH AS CHICKEN AND PORK, OR OILY FISH SUCH AS MACKEREL, BEFORE COOKING. STIR IT INTO CREAMY SAVOURY SAUCES AND SALAD DRESSINGS TO ENHANCE THEIR FLAVOUR.

MAKES ABOUT 300ML/½ PINT/1¼ CUPS

INGREDIENTS
   75g/3oz/scant ½ cup white
     mustard seeds
   50g/2oz/¼ cup soft light
     brown sugar
   5ml/1 tsp salt
   5ml/1 tsp whole peppercorns
   2.5ml/½ tsp ground turmeric
   200ml/7fl oz/scant 1 cup distilled
     malt vinegar
   60ml/4 tbsp chopped fresh mixed
     herbs, such as parsley, sage, thyme
     and rosemary

1 Put the mustard seeds, sugar, salt, whole peppercorns and ground turmeric into a food processor or blender and process for about 1 minute, or until the peppercorns are coarsely chopped.

2 Gradually add the vinegar to the mustard mixture, 15ml/1 tbsp at a time, processing well between each addition, then continue processing until a coarse paste forms.

3 Add the chopped fresh herbs to the mustard and mix well, then leave to stand for 10–15 minutes until the mustard thickens slightly.

4 Spoon the mustard into a 300ml/ ½ pint/1¼ cup sterilized jar. Cover the surface of the mustard with a waxed disc, then seal with a screw-top lid or a cork, and label.

COOK'S TIP
Store the mustard in a cool dark place to preserve its colour and flavour.

Energy 553kcal/2324kJ; Protein 23.4g; Carbohydrate 69.1g, of which sugars 53.4g; Fat 34.5g, of which saturates 1.1g; cholesterol 3mg; Calcium 374mg; Fibre 2.5g; Sodium 2mg.

HONEY MUSTARD

DELICIOUS HOME-MADE MUSTARDS MATURE TO MAKE THE MOST AROMATIC OF CONDIMENTS. THIS HONEY MUSTARD IS RICHLY FLAVOURED AND IS WONDERFUL SERVED WITH MEATS AND CHEESES OR STIRRED INTO SAUCES AND SALAD DRESSINGS TO GIVE AN EXTRA, PEPPERY BITE.

MAKES ABOUT 500G/1¼LB

INGREDIENTS
   225g/8oz/1 cup mustard seeds
   15ml/1 tbsp ground cinnamon
   2.5ml/½ tsp ground ginger
   300ml/½ pint/1¼ cups white
     wine vinegar
   90ml/6 tbsp dark clear honey

1 Put the mustard seeds in a bowl with the spices and pour over the vinegar. Stir well to mix, then leave the seeds to soak overnight.

2 The next day, put the spiced mustard mixture in a mortar and pound with a pestle to break up the seeds, adding the honey very gradually.

3 Continue pounding and mixing until the mustard resembles a stiff paste. If it is too stiff, add a little extra vinegar to achieve the desired consistency.

4 Spoon the mustard into four sterilized jars, seal and label, then store in the refrigerator and use within 4 weeks.

COOK'S TIP
This sweet, spicy mustard is perfect for adding extra flavour to cheese tarts or quiches. Spread a very thin layer of mustard across the base of the pastry case before adding the filling, then bake according to the recipe. The mustard will really complement the cheese, giving a mouthwatering result.

Energy 1276kcal/5345kJ; Protein 65.4g; Carbohydrate 115.3g, of which sugars 68.8g; Fat 101.5g, of which saturates 3.4g; Cholesterol 9mg; Calcium 747mg; Fibre 0g; Sodium 21mg.

SPICED TAMARIND MUSTARD

TAMARIND HAS A DISTINCTIVE SWEET AND SOUR FLAVOUR, A DARK BROWN COLOUR AND STICKY TEXTURE. COMBINED WITH SPICES AND GROUND MUSTARD SEEDS, IT MAKES A WONDERFUL CONDIMENT. SERVE WITH STEAKS AND GRILLED MEATS.

MAKES ABOUT 200G/7OZ

INGREDIENTS
    115g/4oz tamarind block
    150ml/¼ pint/⅔ cup warm water
    50g/2oz/¼ cup yellow mustard seeds
    25ml/1½ tbsp black or brown
      mustard seeds
    10ml/2 tsp clear honey
    pinch of ground cardamom
    pinch of salt

COOK'S TIP
The mustard will be ready to eat in
3–4 days. It should be stored in a cool,
dark place and used within 4 months.

1 Put the tamarind in a small bowl and pour over the water. Leave to soak for 30 minutes. Mash to a pulp with a fork, then strain through a fine sieve (strainer) into a bowl.

2 Grind the mustard seeds in a spice mill or coffee grinder and add to the tamarind with the remaining ingredients. Spoon into sterilized jars, cover and seal.

Energy 262kcal/1095kJ; Protein 15g; Carbohydrate 18.9g, of which sugars 8.5g; Fat 22.8g, of which saturates 0.8g; Cholesterol 2mg; Calcium 207mg; Fibre 1.1g; Sodium 64mg.

TARRAGON AND CHAMPAGNE MUSTARD

THIS MILD-TASTING MUSTARD GOES PARTICULARLY WELL WITH GRILLED OR ROASTED CHICKEN, WITH WHICH TARRAGON HAS A SPECIAL AFFINITY, AND IS ALSO LOVELY WITH FISH AND SHELLFISH. THIS WOULD MAKE A PERFECT GIFT TO TAKE TO A FRIEND'S BARBECUE, AS WELL AS SERVING AT YOUR OWN.

MAKES ABOUT 250G/9OZ

INGREDIENTS
    30ml/2 tbsp mustard seeds
    75ml/5 tbsp champagne vinegar
    115g/4oz/1 cup mustard powder
    115g/4oz/½ cup soft light
      brown sugar
    2.5ml/½ tsp salt
    50ml/3½2 tbsp virgin olive oil
    60ml/4 tbsp chopped fresh tarragon

COOK'S TIP
Champagne vinegar has a lovely flavour but can sometimes be hard to find. Look in specialist delicatessens and food stores, or large supermarkets.

1 Put the mustard seeds and vinegar in a bowl and leave to soak overnight.

2 The next day, tip the mixture of mustard seeds and vinegar into a food processor and add the mustard powder, sugar and salt.

3 Blend the mustard mixture until smooth, then slowly add the oil while continuing to blend.

4 Tip the mustard into a bowl, stir in the tarragon, then spoon into sterilized jars, seal and store in a cool, dark place.

Energy 1405kcal/5885kJ; Protein 42.5g; Carbohydrate 150.2g, of which sugars 120.2g; Fat 98.4g, of which saturates 6.9g; Cholesterol 6mg; Calcium 539mg; Fibre 0g; Sodium 14mg.

HORSERADISH MUSTARD

THIS TANGY MUSTARD HAS A WONDERFULLY CREAMY, PEPPERY TASTE AND IS THE IDEAL CONDIMENT FOR ALL CUTS OF BEEF, AS WELL AS HAM, SMOKED FISH AND CHEESE. IT ALSO MAKES A LOVELY SPREAD FOR COLD ROAST BEEF SANDWICHES.

MAKES ABOUT 400G/14OZ

INGREDIENTS
  25ml/1½ tbsp mustard seeds
  250ml/8fl oz/1 cup boiling water
  115g/4oz/1 cup mustard powder
  115g/4oz/scant ½ cup granulated
    (white) sugar
  120ml/4fl oz/½ cup white wine or
    cider vinegar
  50ml/2fl oz/¼ cup olive oil
  5ml/1 tsp lemon juice
  30ml/2 tbsp home-made or ready-
    made horseradish sauce

1 Put the mustard seeds in a bowl and pour over the boiling water. Set aside and leave the seeds to soak for at least 1 hour.

2 Drain the mustard seeds and discard the soaking liquid, then tip the seeds into a food processor.

3 Add the mustard powder, sugar, white wine or cider vinegar, olive oil, lemon juice and horseradish sauce to the mustard seeds in the food processor.

4 Process the ingredients into a smooth paste, then spoon the mustard into sterilized jars.

COOK'S TIP
Store horseradish mustard in the refrigerator and use it within 3 months.

Energy 1428kcal/5982kJ; Protein 41.8g; Carbohydrate 154.5g, of which sugars 124.7g; Fat 98.6g, of which saturates 7.1g; Cholesterol 10mg; Calcium 536mg; Fibre 0.8g; Sodium 287mg.

DILL PICKLES

REDOLENT OF GARLIC AND PIQUANT WITH FRESH CHILLI, SALTY DILL PICKLES CAN BE SUPPLE AND SUCCULENT OR CRISP AND CRUNCHY. EVERY PICKLE AFICIONADO HAS A FAVOURITE TYPE. IF YOU GROW YOUR OWN CUCUMBERS THIS RECIPE IS IDEAL FOR MAKING THE MOST OF A HIGH YIELD.

MAKES ABOUT 900G/2LB

INGREDIENTS
   20 small, ridged or knobbly pickling
      (small) cucumbers
   2 litres/3½ pints/8 cups water
   175g/6oz/¾ cup coarse sea salt
   15–20 garlic cloves, unpeeled
   2 bunches fresh dill
   15ml/1 tbsp dill seeds
   30ml/2 tbsp mixed pickling spice
   1 or 2 hot fresh chillies

1 Scrub the cucumbers and rinse well in cold water. Leave to dry.

2 Put the measured water and salt in a large pan and bring to the boil. Turn off the heat and leave to cool to room temperature.

3 Using the flat side of a knife blade or a wooden mallet, lightly crush each garlic clove, breaking the papery skin.

4 Pack the cucumbers tightly into one or two wide-necked, sterilized jars, layering them with the garlic, fresh dill, dill seeds and pickling spice.

5 Add one chilli to each jar. Pour over the cooled brine, making sure that the cucumbers are all completely covered. Tap the jars on the work surface to dispel any trapped air bubbles.

6 Cover the jars with lids and then leave to stand at room temperature for 4–7 days before serving. Store in the refrigerator.

COOK'S TIPS
• If you cannot find ridged or knobbly pickling (small) cucumbers, use any kind of small cucumbers instead.
• These pickles are delicious when sliced and used as a beef burger topping.
• Mix finely chopped dill pickles with mayonnaise for a delicious home-made tartare sauce – perfect with barbecued salmon or trout.

Energy 45kcal/180kJ; Protein 3.1g; Carbohydrate 6.8g, of which sugars 6.3g; Fat 0.5g, of which saturates 0g; Cholesterol 0mg; Calcium 83mg; Fibre 2.7g; Sodium 5909mg.

SHALLOTS IN BALSAMIC VINEGAR

THESE WHOLE SHALLOTS, COOKED IN BALSAMIC VINEGAR AND HERBS, ARE A MODERN VARIATION ON TRADITIONAL PICKLED ONIONS. THEY HAVE A MUCH MORE GENTLE, SMOOTH FLAVOUR AND ARE DELICIOUS SERVED WITH ALL KINDS OF MEAT OR ROBUSTLY FLAVOURED HARD CHEESES.

MAKES ONE LARGE JAR

INGREDIENTS
500g/1¼lb shallots
30ml/2 tbsp muscovado
 (soft brown) sugar
several bay leaves and/or fresh
 thyme sprigs
300ml/½ pint/1¼ cups balsamic
 vinegar

1 Put the unpeeled shallots in a bowl. Pour over boiling water and leave to stand for 2 minutes to loosen the skins. Drain and peel the shallots, leaving them whole.

2 Put the sugar, bay leaves and/or thyme and vinegar in a large heavy pan and bring to the boil.

3 Add the shallots to the pan, lower the heat, cover and simmer gently for about 40 minutes, or until the shallots are just tender.

4 Transfer the mixture to a warmed sterilized jar, packing the shallots down well.

5 Seal and label the jar, then store in a cool, dark place for about 1 month before eating.

VARIATIONS
• Use other robust herbs in place of the thyme sprigs. Rosemary, oregano or marjoram are all good choices.
• Add 5 fat cloves of garlic, peeled, to the shallots at the cooking stage. This will impart a good flavour. Remove them afterwards if you wish, although they are a pleasant addition to the final condiment.

Energy 298kcal/1254kJ; Protein 6.2g; Carbohydrate 70.8g, of which sugars 59.4g; Fat 1g, of which saturates 0g; Cholesterol 0mg; Calcium 141mg; Fibre 7g; Sodium 17mg.

HOT THAI PICKLED SHALLOTS

ALTHOUGH THEY MAY BE QUITE DIFFICULT TO FIND AND REQUIRE LENGTHY PREPARATION, THAI PINK SHALLOTS LOOK AND TASTE EXQUISITE IN THIS SPICED PICKLE. THE SHALLOTS TASTE GOOD FINELY SLICED, AND GO WELL WITH A WIDE RANGE OF SOUTH-EAST ASIAN AND OTHER DISHES.

3 To prepare the vinegar, put the cider vinegar, sugar, salt, ginger, coriander seeds, lemon grass and lime leaves or lime rind in a large pan and bring to the boil. Simmer over a low heat for 3–4 minutes, then remove from the heat and set aside to cool.

4 Using a slotted spoon, remove the sliced ginger from the pan and discard. Return the vinegar to the boil, then add the fresh coriander, garlic and chillies, and cook for about 1 minute.

5 Pack the shallots, spices and aromatics into warmed sterilized jars and pour over the hot vinegar. Cool, then seal. Leave in a dark place for 2 months before eating.

MAKES ABOUT THREE JARS

INGREDIENTS
  5–6 fresh red or green bird's eye
    chillies, halved and seeded if liked
  500g/1¼lb Thai pink shallots,
    peeled
  2 large garlic cloves, peeled, halved
    and green shoots removed
  600ml/1 pint/2½ cups cider vinegar
  45ml/3 tbsp granulated (white) sugar
  10ml/2 tsp salt
  5cm/2in piece fresh root ginger,
    sliced
  15ml/1 tbsp coriander seeds
  2 lemon grass stalks, cut in
    half lengthways
  4 kaffir lime leaves or strips of
    lime rind
  15ml/1 tbsp chopped fresh
    coriander (cilantro)

1 If you are leaving the bird's eye chillies whole (they will be hotter), prick each one several times with a cocktail stick (toothpick).

2 Bring a large pan of water to the boil. Blanch the chillies, shallots and garlic for 1–2 minutes, then drain. Rinse the vegetables under cold water and leave to drain.

VARIATION
Ordinary shallots and pickling (pearl) onions are widely available and can be preserved in the same way.

ENGLISH PICKLED ONIONS

THESE POWERFUL PICKLES ARE TRADITIONALLY SERVED WITH A PLATE OF COLD MEATS AND BREAD AND CHEESE, BUT ARE LOVELY WITH GRILLED SAUSAGES. THEY SHOULD BE MADE WITH MALT VINEGAR AND NEED TO BE STORED FOR AT LEAST 6 WEEKS BEFORE EATING.

MAKES ABOUT FOUR JARS

INGREDIENTS

1kg/2¼lb pickling (pearl) onions
115g/4oz/½ cup salt
750ml/1¼ pints/3 cups malt vinegar
15ml/1 tbsp granulated (white)
  sugar
2–3 dried red chillies
5ml/1 tsp brown mustard seeds
15ml/1 tbsp coriander seeds
5ml/1 tsp allspice berries
5ml/1 tsp black peppercorns
5cm/2in piece fresh root
  ginger, sliced
2–3 blades mace
2–3 fresh bay leaves

1 To peel the onions, trim off the root ends, but leave the onion layers attached. Cut a thin slice off the top (neck) end of the onion. Place the onions in a bowl, then cover with boiling water. Leave to stand for about 4 minutes, then drain. The skin should then be easy to peel using a small, sharp knife.

2 Place the peeled onions in a bowl and cover with cold water to check the amount needed. Drain the water into a large pan, keeping the onions in the bowl. Add the salt to the water and heat slightly to dissolve it, then cool before pouring the brine over the onions.

3 Place a plate inside the top of the bowl and weigh it down slightly so that it keeps all the onions submerged in the brine. Leave to stand for 24 hours.

4 Meanwhile, place the vinegar in a large pan. Wrap all the remaining ingredients, except the bay leaves, in a piece of muslin (cheesecloth). Bring to the boil, Simmer for about 5 minutes, then remove the pan from the heat. Set aside and leave to infuse overnight.

5 The next day, drain the onions, rinse them and pat them dry. Pack them into sterilized 450g/1lb jars.

6 Add some or all of the spice from the vinegar, except the ginger slices. The pickle will become hotter with keeping if you add the chillies. Pour the vinegar over to cover and add the bay leaves.

7 Seal the jars with non-metallic lids and store in a cool, dark place for at least 6 weeks before serving.

COOK'S TIP
Once the jars have been topped up, store any leftover vinegar in a bottle for making another batch of pickles. A bottle with a plastic screw top is ideal for this purpose.

Energy 105kcal/438kJ; Protein 3g; Carbohydrate 23.7g, of which sugars 17.9g; Fat 0.5g, of which saturates 0g; Cholesterol 0mg; Calcium 65mg; Fibre 3.5g; Sodium 8mg.

SAFFRON BREAD SKEWERS

THIS ANTIPODEAN'S FIRESIDE FAVOURITE, CALLED DAMPER, IS ALSO A BIT OF A GIRL GUIDE TRADITION. IT'S A FUN THING FOR A LONG, LAZY BEACH BARBECUE. IT IS USUAL TO COOK DAMPER IN THE EMBERS OF THE FIRE, BUT ROSEMARY SKEWERS ARE A STYLISH ALTERNATIVE.

SERVES EIGHT

INGREDIENTS
24 rosemary spikes or wooden
   skewers (or 12 of each)
500g/1¼lb/5 cups plain
   (all-purpose) flour
25ml/1½ tbsp baking powder
250g/9oz/generous 1 cup plus
   30ml/2 tbsp butter
30ml/2 tbsp chopped fresh rosemary,
   plus 1 sprig
1 large pinch of saffron threads
   mixed with 15ml/1 tbsp
   boiling water
175ml/6fl oz/¾ cup milk
salt

1 Soak the rosemary spikes or wooden skewers in cold water for 30 minutes to prevent them from burning.

2 Sift the flour, baking powder and salt into a large bowl. Rub in 200g/7oz/ scant 1 cup of the butter until the mixture looks like fine breadcrumbs, then add the chopped rosemary.

3 Strain the saffron water into the milk and add to the flour mixture all in one go. Mix to a paste with your hands and knead until the dough is smooth and elastic. Melt the remaining butter and stir it with the rosemary sprig to infuse it with the flavour.

4 Prepare the barbecue. Drain the skewers or rosemary spikes. Divide the dough into 24 equal pieces and twist one piece around each skewer or spike.

5 Position a lightly oiled grill rack over the hot coals. Grill the spiked dough over medium-high heat for 5 minutes, turning often, until cooked and golden. Brush occasionally with the rosemary dipped in butter and serve hot.

COOK'S TIP
If you're cooking a pan of soup *al fresco*, these breads taste terrific dipped in the soup.

Energy 456kcal/1905kJ; Protein 6.8g; Carbohydrate 49.8g, of which sugars 2.2g; Fat 26.9g, of which saturates 16.6g; Cholesterol 68mg; Calcium 119mg; Fibre 1.9g; Sodium 201mg.

SESAME BURGER BUNS

PUT YOUR HOME-MADE BURGERS INSIDE A TRADITIONAL SOFT BURGER BUN WITH A SESAME SEED TOPPING. SOFT BUNS WORK BEST WITH EITHER MEAT OR VEGETARIAN BURGERS AND ARE EASIER TO HOLD AND TO EAT THAN A CRUSTY ROLL. JUST ADD RELISH!

MAKES SIX

INGREDIENTS
  500g/1¼lb/5 cups strong white
    bread flour
  7.5ml/1½ tsp salt
  25g/1oz butter, softened
  5ml/1 tsp easy-blend (rapid-rise)
    dried yeast
  15ml/1 tbsp sugar
  150ml/¼ pint/⅔ cup lukewarm milk
  about 150ml/¼ pint/⅔ cup
    lukewarm water
  10ml/2 tsp sesame seeds

1 Sift the flour and salt into a bowl and rub in the butter with your fingertips. Add the yeast and sugar. Mix well. Make a well in the centre and pour in the milk and the water. Stir the liquid into the flour from the centre outwards to make a soft dough.

2 Knead the dough on a lightly floured surface for 10 minutes then return to the cleaned bowl and cover with lightly oiled clear film (plastic wrap). Leave in a warm place until doubled in size (about 1 hour).

3 Knock back (punch down) the dough then divide into six equal pieces. Form into rounds and place on a greased baking sheet. Cover with lightly oiled clear film and leave to rise for 1 hour or until doubled in size.

4 Meanwhile, preheat the oven to 220°C/425°F/Gas 7. Brush the buns with milk and sprinkle with sesame seeds. Cook for 15–20 minutes, or until golden brown. Cool on a wire rack.

VARIATION
To use a bread machine, substitute the milk and water quantities with 300ml/ ½ pint/1¼ cups water and include 30ml/2 tbsp milk powder to the above ingredients. Put the ingredients in the bread machine in the order specified in the manufacturer's instructions. Set to a basic dough setting and then shape into buns and proceed as above.

Energy 352kcal/1488kJ; Protein 9.2g; Carbohydrate 68.6g, of which sugars 5.1g; Fat 6.4g, of which saturates 2.8g; Cholesterol 10mg; Calcium 166mg; Fibre 2.8g; Sodium 39mg.

CORN TORTILLAS

THESE DELICIOUS AND VERSATILE MEXICAN SPECIALITIES COOK VERY QUICKLY. GRIDDLE THEM OVER THE BARBECUE AND HAVE A CLEAN DISH TOWEL ON HAND TO KEEP THE GROWING STACK WARM.

MAKES ABOUT FOURTEEN

INGREDIENTS
275g/10oz/2½ cups masa harina
250–350ml/8–12fl oz/
1–1½ cups water

COOK'S TIPS
• When making tortillas, it is important to get the dough texture right. If it is too dry and crumbly, add a little water; if it is too wet, add more masa harina. If you do not manage to flatten the ball of dough into a neat circle the first time, just re-roll it and try again.
• These tortillas can also be cooked in the oven at 150°C/300°F/Gas 2.

1 Prepare the barbecue. Put the masa harina into a bowl and stir in 250ml/8fl oz/1 cup of the measured water, mixing it to a soft dough that just holds together. If it is too dry, add a little more water. Cover the bowl with a cloth and set aside for 15 minutes.

2 Knead the dough lightly, divide into 14 pieces, and shape into balls.

3 Using a rolling pin, roll out each ball between sheets of clear plastic film until you have a thin round of dough measuring about 15cm/6in in diameter.

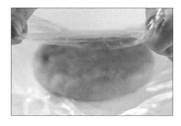

4 Put a griddle over the hot coals and griddle the first tortilla for 1 minute. Turn it over and cook for a minute more. Wrap in a clean dish towel and keep warm. Repeat to make the other tortillas, stacking them together in the dish towel to keep warm.

COOK'S TIP
An alternative to rolling out rounds of tortilla dough with a rolling pin is to use a tortilla press. Open the press and line both sides with sheets of clear plastic film. Shape the tortilla dough into balls, put one ball on the press and bring the top down firmly to flatten it into a neat round. Open the press, peel off the top layer of plastic and, using the bottom layer, lift the tortilla out of the press. Peel off this layer of plastic and repeat the process with the other dough balls.

Energy 72kcal/303kJ; Protein 1.9g; Carbohydrate 14.4g, of which sugars 0g; Fat 0.7g, of which saturates 0g; Cholesterol 0mg; Calcium 1mg; Fibre 0.4g; Sodium 0mg.

FLOUR TORTILLAS

HOME-MADE TORTILLAS TASTE SO GOOD WHEN FILLED WITH BARBECUED VEGETABLES AND THINLY SLICED CHICKEN OR MEAT. YOU CAN MAKE THEM IN ADVANCE AND THEN REHEAT THEM TO SERVE.

MAKES ABOUT FOURTEEN

INGREDIENTS
    225g/8oz/2 cups plain
      (all-purpose) flour
    5ml/1 tsp salt
    15ml/1 tbsp lard or white cooking fat
    120ml/4fl oz/½ cup water

1 Sift the flour and salt into a large mixing bowl. Gradually rub in the lard or white cooking fat using your fingertips until the mixture resembles coarse breadcrumbs.

2 Gradually add the water and mix lightly until the mixture forms a soft dough. Knead lightly, form into a ball, cover with a cloth and leave to rest for 15 minutes. Prepare the barbecue.

COOK'S TIPS
• Make flour tortillas whenever masa harina is difficult to find. To keep them soft and pliable, make sure they are kept warm until ready to serve, and eat as soon as possible.
• These flour tortillas can also be cooked in the oven at 150°C/300°F/Gas 2.

3 Carefully divide the dough into about 14 portions and form these portions into small balls. One by one, roll out each ball of dough on a lightly floured wooden board to a round measuring about 15cm/6in. Trim the rounds if necessary.

4 Heat an ungreased flat griddle or frying pan over a medium heat. Cook the tortillas for 1½–2 minutes on each side. Turn over with a palette knife or metal spatula when the bottom begins to brown. Wrap in a clean dish towel to keep warm until ready to serve.

Energy 64kcal/272kJ; Protein 1.5g; Carbohydrate 12.5g, of which sugars 0.2g; Fat 1.3g, of which saturates 0.5g; Cholesterol 1mg; Calcium 23mg; Fibre 0.5g; Sodium 141mg.

PITTA BREAD

IF YOU WANT A RELAXED BARBECUE WHERE FINGERS ARE KEPT FAIRLY CLEAN, YOU CAN'T BEAT SERVING TASTY SLICES OR CHUNKS OF FOOD IN PITTA BREAD POCKETS. YOU CAN MAKE THE DOUGH EARLIER AND THEN COOK IT IN A HEAVY FRYING PAN ON THE BARBECUE.

5 Prepare the barbecue. Heat a large, heavy frying pan over a medium-high heat. When it is smoking hot, gently lay one piece of flattened dough in the pan and cook for 15–20 seconds. Carefully turn it over and cook the second side for about 1 minute.

6 When large bubbles start to form on the bread, turn it over again. It should puff up. Using a clean dish towel, gently press on the bread where the bubbles have formed. Cook for a total of 3 minutes, then remove the pitta from the pan. Repeat with the remaining dough until all the breads have been cooked.

7 Wrap the pitta breads in a clean dish towel, stacking them together as each one is cooked to keep them warm. Serve the pitta breads hot, while they are soft and moist.

VARIATION
To cook the breads in the oven, preheat the oven to 220°C/425°F/Gas 7. Fill an unglazed or partially glazed dish with hot water and place in the bottom of the oven. Alternatively, arrange a handful of unglazed tiles in the bottom of the oven. Use either a non-stick baking sheet or a lightly oiled ordinary baking sheet and heat in the oven for a few minutes. Place two or three pieces of flattened dough on to the hot baking sheet and place in the hottest part of the oven. Bake for 2–3 minutes. They should puff up. Repeat with the remaining dough until all the pittas have been cooked.

MAKES TWELVE

INGREDIENTS
500g/1¼lb/4½ cups strong white
  bread flour, or half white and
  half wholemeal (whole-wheat)
7g/¼oz packet easy-blend
  (rapid-rise) dried yeast
15ml/1 tbsp salt
15ml/1 tbsp olive oil
250ml/8fl oz/1 cup water

1 Combine the flour, yeast and salt. In a large bowl, mix together the oil and water, then stir in half of the flour mixture, stirring in the same direction, until the dough is stiff. Knead in the remaining flour.

2 Place the dough in a clean bowl, cover with a clean dish towel and leave in a warm place for at least 30 minutes and up to 2 hours.

3 Knead the dough for 10 minutes, or until smooth. Lightly oil the bowl, place the dough in it, cover again and leave to rise in a warm place for about 1 hour, or until doubled in size.

4 Divide the dough into 12 equal-size pieces. With lightly floured hands, flatten each piece, then roll out into a round about 20cm/8in in diameter and 5mm–1cm/¼–½in thick. Keep the rolled breads covered with a clean dish towel while you make the remaining breads.

Energy 150kcal/638kJ; Protein 3.9g; Carbohydrate 32.4g, of which sugars 0.6g; Fat 1.5g, of which saturates 0.2g; Cholesterol 0mg; Calcium 59mg; Fibre 1.3g; Sodium 493mg.

THREE-HERB POTATO SCONES

THESE FLAVOURSOME SCONES ARE PERFECT SPLIT IN TWO WHILE STILL WARM AND FILLED WITH CHARGRILLED BACON AND SALAD OR GRILLED VEGETABLES WITH PARMESAN SHAVINGS. THEY ARE ALSO PERFECT FOR MOPPING UP GOOD OLIVE OIL AND BALSAMIC VINEGAR AS AN APPETIZER.

MAKES TWELVE

INGREDIENTS
225g/8oz/2 cups self-raising (self-rising) flour
5ml/1 tsp baking powder
pinch of salt
50g/2oz/4 tbsp butter, diced
25g/1oz potato flakes
15ml/1 tbsp chopped fresh parsley
15ml/1 tbsp chopped fresh basil
15ml/1 tbsp chopped fresh oregano
150ml/¼ pint/⅔ cup milk
oil, for greasing

1 Preheat the oven to 180°C/350°F/Gas 4. Sift the flour into a bowl with the baking powder. Add a pinch of salt. Rub in the butter with your fingertips to form crumbs. Place the potato flakes in bowl and pour over 200ml/7fl oz/scant 1 cup boiling water. Beat well and cool slightly.

2 Stir the potatoes into the dry ingredients with the herbs and milk.

3 Bring the mixture together to form a soft dough. Turn out on to a floured surface and knead the dough very gently for a few minutes, until soft and pliable.

COOK'S TIP
Don't be tempted to overseason the mixture, as once cooked the baking powder can also increase the salty flavour of the finished scone and this can overpower the taste of the herbs.

4 Roll the dough out on a floured surface to about 4cm/1½in thickness and stamp out rounds using a 7.5cm/3in cutter. Reshape any remaining dough and re-roll for more scones. Place the scones on a greased baking dish and brush the surfaces with a little more milk.

5 Cook for 15–20 minutes until risen and lightly browned, then turn out on to a rack. Serve warm. The scones can be eaten plain, or with a filling.

Energy 46kcal/193kJ; Protein 1g; Carbohydrate 8.1g, of which sugars 0.4g; Fat 1.3g, of which saturates 0.2g; Cholesterol 0mg; Calcium 12mg; Fibre 0.5g; Sodium 3mg.

CHEESE AND POTATO BREAD TWISTS

A COMPLETE "PLOUGHMAN'S LUNCH", WITH THE CHEESE COOKED RIGHT IN THE BREAD. THESE TWISTS ARE FANTASTIC TO NIBBLE WHILE THE BARBECUE GETS GOING. THEY ALSO MAKE AN EXCELLENT BASE FOR A FILLING OF SMOKED SALMON WITH LEMON JUICE.

MAKES EIGHT

INGREDIENTS
225g/8oz potatoes, diced
225g/8oz/2 cups strong white flour
5ml/1 tsp easy-blend dried yeast
150ml/¼ pint/⅔ cup lukewarm water
175g/6oz/1½ cups red Leicester
  cheese, finely grated
10ml/2 tsp olive oil, for greasing
salt

1 Cook the potatoes in a large pan with plenty of lightly salted boiling water for 20 minutes or until tender. Drain through a colander and return to the pan. Mash until smooth and set aside to cool.

VARIATION
Any hard, well-flavoured cheese can be used. Mature Cheddar is the traditional choice, or you could try a smoked cheese, or a variety with added herbs, such as sage Lancashire.

2 Meanwhile, sift the flour into a large bowl and add the yeast and a good pinch of salt. Stir in the potatoes and rub with your fingers to form a crumb consistency.

3 Make a well in the centre and pour in the lukewarm water. Start by bringing the mixture together with a round-bladed knife, then use your hands. Knead for 5 minutes on a well-floured surface. Return the dough to the bowl. Cover with a damp cloth and leave to rise in a warm place for 1 hour or until doubled in size.

4 Turn the dough out and knock back (punch down) the air bubbles. Knead again for a few seconds.

5 Divide the dough into 12 pieces and shape into rounds.

6 Scatter the grated cheese over a baking sheet. Take each ball of dough in turn and roll it in the cheese to cover it generously.

7 Roll each cheese-covered ball on a dry surface to a long sausage shape. Fold the two ends together and twist the bread. Lay the bread twists on an oiled baking sheet.

8 Cover with a damp cloth and leave the bread to rise in a warm place for 30 minutes. Preheat the oven to 220°C/425°F/Gas 7. Bake the bread for 10–15 minutes.

COOK'S TIP
These bread twists stay moist and fresh for up to 3 days if stored in airtight food bags.

Energy 231kcal/971kJ; Protein 8.7g; Carbohydrate 26.4g, of which sugars 0.8g; Fat 10.4g, of which saturates 5.2g; Cholesterol 21mg; Calcium 203mg; Fibre 1.2g; Sodium 162mg.

ITALIAN BREADSTICKS

THESE CRISP BREADSTICKS WILL KEEP FOR A COUPLE OF DAYS IF STORED IN AN AIRTIGHT CONTAINER. IF YOU LIKE, YOU CAN REFRESH THEM IN A HOT OVEN FOR A FEW MINUTES BEFORE SERVING. THE DOUGH CAN BE MADE IN ANY BREADMAKING MACHINE, REGARDLESS OF CAPACITY.

MAKES THIRTY

INGREDIENTS
200ml/7fl oz/⅞ cup water
45ml/3 tbsp olive oil, plus extra
  for brushing
350g/12oz/3 cups unbleached white
  bread flour
7.5ml/1½ tsp salt
7.5ml/1½ tsp easy-blend (rapid-rise)
  dried yeast
poppy seeds and coarse sea salt, for
  coating (optional)

1 Pour the water and olive oil into the bread machine pan. If the instructions for your machine specify that the yeast is to be placed in the pan first, reverse the order in which you add the liquid and dry ingredients.

2 Sprinkle over the flour, ensuring that it covers the water completely. Add the salt in one corner of the pan. Make a small indent in the centre of the flour (but not down as far as the liquid) and add the easy-blend dried yeast.

3 Set the bread machine to the dough setting: use basic dough setting (if available). Press Start.

4 Lightly oil two baking sheets. Preheat the oven to 200°C/400°F/Gas 6.

COOK'S TIP
If you are rolling the breadsticks in sea salt, don't use too much. Crush the sea salt slightly if the crystals are large.

5 When the dough cycle has finished, remove the dough from the machine, place it on a lightly floured surface and knock it back (punch it down).

6 Roll the dough out to a rectangle measuring 23 x 20cm/9 x 8in. Cut into three 20cm/8in long strips. Cut each strip widthways into ten. Roll and stretch each piece to 30cm/12in.

7 Roll the breadsticks in poppy seeds or sea salt if liked. Space well apart on the baking sheets. Brush with oil, cover with clear film (plastic wrap) and leave in a warm place for 10–15 minutes.

8 Bake for 15–20 minutes, or until golden, turning once. Transfer to a wire rack to cool.

Energy 128kcal/538kJ; Protein 3.4g; Carbohydrate 16.8g, of which sugars 0.6g; Fat 5.7g, of which saturates 0.8g; Cholesterol 0mg; Calcium 80mg; Fibre 1.3g; Sodium 199mg.

PARTYBROT

These traditional Swiss-German rolls are baked as one, in a round cake tin. They can be gently pulled apart when served, leaving soft "kissing crusts" round the sides. As the name suggests, partybrot is perfect for entertaining.

<u>MAKES NINETEEN ROLLS</u>

INGREDIENTS
For the milk rolls
  145ml/5fl oz/scant ⅔ cup milk
  225g/8oz/2 cups unbleached white
    bread flour
  7.5ml/1½ tsp sugar
  5ml/1 tsp salt
  15g/½oz/1 tbsp butter
  2.5ml/½ tsp easy-blend (rapid-rise)
    dried yeast
For the wholemeal rolls
  175ml/6fl oz/¾ cup water
  175g/6oz/1½ cups wholemeal (whole-
    wheat) bread flour
  75g/3oz/¾ cup unbleached white
    bread flour
  7.5ml/1½ tsp sugar
  5ml/1 tsp salt
  25g/1oz/2 tbsp butter
  2.5ml/½ tsp easy-blend dried yeast
For the topping
  1 egg yolk, mixed with 15ml/1 tbsp
    cold water
  15ml/1 tbsp rolled oats or
    cracked wheat
  15ml/1 tbsp poppy seeds

1 Pour the milk for the milk rolls into the bread machine pan. However, if the instructions for your bread machine specify that the yeast is to be placed in the pan first, reverse the order in which you add the liquid and dry ingredients.

2 Sprinkle over the white bread flour, making sure that it covers the milk completely. Add the sugar, salt and butter, placing them in separate corners of the bread pan.

3 Make a small indent in the centre of the flour (but not down as far as the liquid underneath) and add the easy-blend dried yeast.

4 Set the bread machine to the dough setting; use basic dough setting (if available). Press Start.

5 Lightly oil a 25cm/10in springform or loose-based cake tin (pan), and a large mixing bowl. When the dough cycle has finished, take out the dough and place it in the mixing bowl.

6 Cover the dough with oiled clear film (plastic wrap) and chill while you make the wholemeal dough. Follow the instructions for the milk roll dough, but use water instead of milk.

7 Remove the milk roll dough from the fridge 20 minutes before the end of the wholemeal dough cycle. When the wholemeal dough is ready, place it on a lightly floured surface. Knock it back (punch it down) gently. Do the same with the milk roll dough.

8 Divide the milk roll dough into nine pieces and the wholemeal dough into 10. Shape each into a small round ball.

9 Place 12 balls, equally spaced, round the edge of the prepared cake tin, alternating milk dough with wholemeal.

10 Add an inner circle of six more balls and place the remaining ball of wholemeal dough in the centre.

11 Cover the tin with lightly oiled clear film and leave the rolls to rise in a warm place for 30–45 minutes, or until they have doubled in size. Meanwhile, preheat the oven to 200°C/400°F/Gas 6.

12 Brush the wholemeal rolls with the egg yolk and water glaze. Sprinkle with rolled oats or cracked wheat. Glaze the white rolls and sprinkle with poppy seeds. Bake for 35–40 minutes, until the partybrot is golden. Leave for 5 minutes to cool in the tin, then turn out on to a wire rack to cool.

Energy 118kcal/496kJ; Protein 3.2g; Carbohydrate 19.6g, of which sugars 1.9g; Fat 3.4g, of which saturates 1.7g; Cholesterol 17mg; Calcium 42mg; Fibre 1.4g; Sodium 41mg.

RED ONION AND ROSEMARY FOCACCIA

MAKE THIS RICH AND TASTY ITALIAN BREAD WITH ITS TOPPING OF ROSEMARY AND RED ONION TO SERVE WITH YOUR BARBECUE FEAST. YOU COULD SERVE IT WITH A TOMATO, BASIL AND MOZZARELLA SALAD FOR A QUICK AND EASY FIRST COURSE WHILE YOU WAIT FOR THE COALS TO HEAT UP FOR BARBECUING.

MAKES ONE 30CM/12IN ROUND LOAF

INGREDIENTS
450g/1lb/4 cups strong white bread
  flour, plus extra for dusting
5ml/1 tsp salt
7g/¼oz fresh yeast or generous 5ml/
  1 tsp dried yeast
2.5ml/½ tsp light muscovado
  (brown) sugar
250ml/8fl oz/1 cup lukewarm water
60ml/4 tbsp extra virgin olive oil,
  plus extra for greasing
5ml/1 tsp very finely chopped fresh
  rosemary, plus 6–8 small sprigs
1 red onion, thinly sliced
coarse salt

1 Sift the flour and salt into a large mixing bowl. Set aside.

2 Cream the fresh yeast with the sugar, and gradually stir in half the water. If using dried yeast, stir the sugar into the water and sprinkle the dried yeast over the surface.

3 Set the yeast aside in a warm, but not hot, place for 10 minutes, until it has become frothy.

4 Add the yeast, the remaining water, 15ml/1 tbsp of the oil and the chopped rosemary to the flour. Mix all the ingredients together to form a dough, then gather the dough into a ball and knead on a floured work surface for about 5 minutes, until smooth and elastic. You may need to add a little extra flour if the dough is very sticky.

5 Place the dough in a lightly oiled bowl and slip it into a polythene bag or cover with oiled clear film (plastic wrap) and leave to rise. The temperature at which you leave the dough will govern the length of time it will take to rise: leave it all day in a cool place, overnight in the refrigerator, or for 1–2 hours in a warm, but not hot, place.

6 Lightly oil a baking sheet. Knead the dough to form a flat loaf that is about 30cm/12in round or square. Place on the baking sheet, cover with oiled polythene or clear film and leave to rise again in a warm place for a further 40–60 minutes.

7 Preheat the oven to 220°C/425°F/ Gas 7. Press indentations into the dough with your fingers Toss the onion in 15ml/1 tbsp of the oil and scatter over the loaf with the rosemary sprigs and some coarse salt. Bake for 15–20 minutes until golden brown. Serve the bread freshly baked or leave to cool on the baking sheet and serve warm.

Energy 496kcal/2094kJ; Protein 11g; Carbohydrate 90.4g, of which sugars 3.8g; Fat 12.5g, of which saturates 1.8g; Cholesterol 000mg; Calcium 167mg; Fibre 4g; Sodium 496mg.

FOCACCIA

THIS FLATTISH ITALIAN BREAD ORIGINATES FROM GENOA. THERE ARE MANY VARIATIONS FROM OTHER REGIONS BUT THIS IS THE TRADITIONAL TYPE, MADE SIMPLY WITH FLOUR, YEAST, OLIVE OIL AND SALT.

MAKES ONE 25CM/10IN ROUND LOAF

INGREDIENTS
25g/1oz fresh yeast
400g/14oz/3½ cups unbleached strong white bread flour
10ml/2 tsp sea salt
75ml/5 tbsp olive oil
10ml/2 tsp coarse sea salt

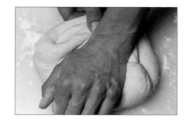

1 Dissolve the yeast in 120ml/4fl oz/ ½ cup warm water. Allow to stand for 10 minutes. Sift the strong white bread flour into a large bowl, make a well in the centre, and add the yeast, salt and 30ml/2 tbsp oil. Mix in the flour and add more water to make a dough.

2 Turn out on to a floured work surface and knead the dough until it is smooth and elastic. Return to the bowl, cover with a cloth, and leave the dough to rise in a warm place for 2–2½ hours until doubled in bulk.

3 Knock back (punch down) the dough and knead for a few minutes. Press into an oiled 25cm/10in tart tin (quiche pan) or form a round on an oiled baking tray, and cover with a damp cloth. Leave the dough to rise again for 30 minutes.

4 Preheat the oven to 200°C/400°F/ Gas 6. Poke the dough all over with your fingers, to make little dimples in the surface. Pour the remaining olive oil over the dough, using a pastry brush to spread it to the edges. Sprinkle with the coarse sea salt.

5 Bake for 20–25 minutes, until the bread is a pale gold. Carefully remove the loaf from the tin and leave to cool on a rack. The bread is best eaten on the same day it is made, but it also freezes very well.

VARIATIONS
Focaccia is often baked with a selection of different toppings. Before baking, lightly sprinkle over any or a combination of the following: chopped pitted olives, slices of red or yellow (bell) pepper or diced sun-dried tomatoes.

Energy 1661kcal/7020kJ; Protein 37.6g; Carbohydrate 310.8g, of which sugars 6g; Fat 38.2g, of which saturates 5.5g; Cholesterol 0mg; Calcium 561mg; Fibre 12.4g; Sodium 3942mg.

OLIVE BREAD

VARIATIONS OF THIS STRONGLY FLAVOURED BREAD ARE POPULAR ALL OVER THE MEDITERRANEAN.
FOR THIS GREEK RECIPE USE RICH, OILY OLIVES OR THOSE MARINATED WITH HERBS.

MAKES TWO 675G/1½LB LOAVES

INGREDIENTS
    2 red onions, thinly sliced
    30ml/2 tbsp olive oil
    225g/8oz/2 cups stoned (pitted)
        black or green olives
    50g/2oz fresh yeast
    800g/1¾lb/7 cups strong white
        bread flour
    7.5ml/1½ tsp salt
    45ml/3 tbsp each roughly chopped
        parsley, coriander (cilantro) or mint

1 Fry the onions in the oil until soft.
Roughly chop the olives.

2 Dissolve the yeast in 250ml/8fl oz/
1 cup warm water. Allow to stand for
10 minutes. Put the flour, salt and
herbs in a large bowl with the olives and
fried onions and add the yeast mixture.

3 Mix with a round-bladed knife, adding
enough warm water to make a soft
dough. Turn out on to a floured surface
and knead for about 10 minutes.

4 Put the dough in a clean bowl, cover
with clear film (plastic wrap) and leave
in a warm place until doubled in bulk.

5 Preheat the oven to 220°C/425°F/
Gas 7. Lightly grease two baking sheets.
Turn the dough on to a floured surface
and cut in half. Shape into two rounds
and place on the baking sheets. Cover
the dough loosely with lightly oiled clear
film and leave until doubled in size.

VARIATION
Shape the dough into 16 small rolls.
Slash the tops as in step 6 and reduce
the cooking time to 25 minutes.

6 Slash the tops of the loaves two or
three times with a sharp knife, then
bake in the preheated oven for about
40 minutes, or until the loaves sound
hollow when tapped on the bottom.
Transfer to a wire rack to cool.

Energy 1988kcal/8404kJ; Protein 47.4g; Carbohydrate 379g, of which sugars 7.3g; Fat 41.7g, of which saturates 6.3g; Cholesterol 0mg; Calcium 788mg; Fibre 20.1g; Sodium 5338mg.

PUMPKIN AND WALNUT BREAD

WALNUTS, NUTMEG AND PUMPKIN COMBINE TO YIELD A MOIST, TANGY AND SLIGHTLY SWEET BREAD WITH AN INDESCRIBABLY GOOD FLAVOUR. SERVE PARTNERED WITH MEATS OR CHEESE.

MAKES ONE LOAF

INGREDIENTS
    500g/1¼lb pumpkin, peeled, seeded
        and cut into chunks
    75g/3oz/6 tbsp caster
        (superfine) sugar
    5ml/1 tsp grated nutmeg
    50g/2oz/¼ cup butter, melted
    3 eggs, lightly beaten
    350g/12oz/3 cups unbleached strong
        white bread flour
    10ml/2 tsp baking powder
    2.5ml/½ tsp sea salt
    75g/3oz/¾ cup walnuts, chopped

1 Grease and neatly base-line a loaf tin (pan) measuring 21 x 12cm/8½ x 4½in. Preheat the oven to 180°C/350°F/Gas 4.

2 Place the pumpkin in a pan, add water to cover by about 5cm/2in, then bring to the boil. Cover, lower the heat and simmer for about 20 minutes, or until the pumpkin is very tender. Drain the pumpkin well, then turn into a food processor or blender and process to a purée. Leave to cool.

3 Place 275g/10oz/1¼ cups of the purée in a bowl. Mix in the sugar, nutmeg, melted butter and eggs. Sift the flour, baking powder and salt into a large bowl. Make a well in the centre.

4 Add the pumpkin mixture to the centre of the flour and stir until smooth. Mix in the walnuts.

5 Transfer to the prepared tin and bake for 1 hour, or until golden and starting to shrink from the sides of the tin. Turn out on to a wire rack to cool.

COOK'S TIP
If you have more pumpkin purée than you need, use the remainder in soup.

WHOLEMEAL SUNFLOWER BREAD

ORGANIC SUNFLOWER SEEDS GIVE A NUTTY CRUNCHINESS TO THIS HEARTY WHOLEMEAL LOAF, WHICH IS EXCELLENT AS PART OF A PARTY BUFFET, OR WHEN SIMPLY EATEN WITH A CHUNK OF CHEESE.

MAKES ONE LOAF

INGREDIENTS
25g/1oz fresh yeast
450g/1lb/4 cups strong wholemeal
  (whole-wheat) flour
2.5ml/½ tsp sea salt
50g/2oz/scant ½ cup sunflower
  seeds, plus extra for sprinkling

1 Dissolve the yeast in 120ml/4fl oz/ ½ cup warm water. Allow to stand for 10 minutes until the yeast becomes frothy. Grease and lightly flour a 450g/1lb loaf tin (pan).

2 Put the flour, salt and sunflower seeds in a large mixing bowl and stir to distribute the seeds evenly. Make a well in the centre of the flour and pour in the yeast mixture. Mix vigorously with a wooden spoon, gradually drawing the flour into the liquid and adding sufficient extra warm water to form a soft, sticky dough.

3 Cover the bowl with a damp dish towel and leave the dough to rise in a warm place for 45–50 minutes, or until doubled in size.

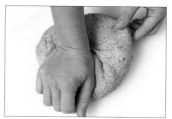

4 Preheat the oven to 200°C/400°F/ Gas 6. Turn out the dough on to a lightly floured work surface and knead for about 10 minutes until elastic – the dough will still be quite sticky, but resist the temptation to add more flour.

VARIATION
Other seeds would be good in this bread – try sesame seeds, pumpkin seeds or a mixture of your favourites.

5 Form the dough into a rectangle and place in the loaf tin. Sprinkle the top with sunflower seeds. Cover with a damp dishtowel and leave to rise again for a further 15 minutes.

6 Bake for 40–45 minutes until golden. When ready, the loaf should sound hollow when tapped underneath. Leave for 5 minutes, turn out of the tin and cool on a wire rack.

Energy 1686kcal/7136kJ; Protein 67g; Carbohydrate 296.9g, of which sugars 10.3g; Fat 33.7g, of which saturates 3.6g; Cholesterol 0mg; Calcium 226mg; Fibre 43.5g; Sodium 997mg.

CIABATTA

THE VERY WET DOUGH USED TO MAKE CIABATTA BREAD RESULTS IN A LIGHT AND AIRY CRUMB. CIABATTA IS ONE OF THE MOST POPULAR BREADS AND TASTES WONDERFUL WHEN HOME-MADE. IT CAN BE USED AS AN ACCOMPANIMENT TO BARBECUED FOOD OR SLICED, TOPPED WITH DELICIOUS MORSELS AND GRILLED.

MAKES THREE LOAVES

INGREDIENTS
For the starter
   7g/¼oz fresh yeast
   175–200ml/6–7fl oz/¾–scant 1 cup
     lukewarm water
   350g/12oz/3 cups unbleached strong
     white bread flour, plus extra
     for dusting
For the dough
   15g/½oz fresh yeast
   400ml/14fl oz/1⅔ cups warm water
   60ml/4 tbsp lukewarm milk
   500g/1¼lb/5 cups unbleached strong
     white bread flour
   10ml/2 tsp salt
   45ml/3 tbsp extra virgin olive oil

1 For the starter, cream the yeast with a little of the measured water. Sift the flour into a large bowl. Gradually mix in the yeast mixture and sufficient of the remaining water to form a firm dough.

2 Turn out the starter dough on to a lightly floured surface and knead for about 5 minutes until smooth and elastic. Return the dough to the bowl, cover with lightly oiled clear film (plastic wrap) and leave in a warm place for 12–15 hours, or until the dough has risen and is starting to collapse.

3 Sprinkle three baking sheets with flour. Mix the yeast for the dough with a little of the measured water until creamy, then mix in the remainder. Add the yeast mixture to the starter and gradually mix in.

4 Mix in the milk, beating thoroughly with a wooden spoon. Using your hand, gradually incorporate the flour, lifting the dough as you mix. Mixing the dough will take 15 minutes or more and it forms a very wet dough, which is impossible to knead on a work surface, so keep it in the bowl.

5 Beat in the salt and olive oil. Cover with lightly oiled clear film and leave to rise, in a warm place, for 1½–2 hours, or until doubled in bulk.

6 With a spoon, carefully tip one-third of the dough at a time on to the baking sheets without knocking back (punching down) the dough in the process.

7 Using floured hands, shape into rough oblong loaf shapes, about 2.5cm/1in thick. Flatten slightly with splayed fingers. Sprinkle with flour and leave to rise in a warm place for 30 minutes.

8 Meanwhile, preheat the oven to 220°C/425°F/Gas 7. Bake for 25–30 minutes, or until the loaves are golden brown and sounding hollow when tapped on the base. Transfer to a wire rack to cool.

VARIATIONS
Lightly knead a handful of chopped, stoned (pitted) black olives or sun-dried tomatoes into the dough.

Energy 1074kcal/4554kJ; Protein 27.3g; Carbohydrate 221.1g, of which sugars 5.2g; Fat 15g, of which saturates 2.4g; Cholesterol 1mg; Calcium 421mg; Fibre 8.8g; Sodium 1327mg.

GARLIC AND HERB BREAD

THIS IRRESISTIBLE GARLIC BREAD INCLUDES PLENTY OF FRESH MIXED HERBS. YOU CAN VARY THE OVERALL FLAVOUR BY USING DIFFERENT HERBS. PREPARE IT EARLIER AND HEAT IT IN THE OVEN WHEN YOU NEED IT, OR WARM IT UP ON THE GRILL RACK.

SERVES THREE TO FOUR

INGREDIENTS
1 baguette or bloomer loaf
For the garlic and herb butter
115g/4oz/½ cup unsalted (sweet) butter, softened
5–6 large garlic cloves, finely chopped or crushed
30–45ml/2–3 tbsp chopped fresh herbs (such as parsley, chervil and a little tarragon)
15ml/1 tbsp chopped fresh chives
coarse salt and ground black pepper

1 Preheat the oven to 200°C/400°F/ Gas 6. Make the garlic and herb butter by beating the butter with the garlic, herbs, chives and seasoning.

2 Cut the bread into 1cm/½in thick diagonal slices, leaving them attached at the base so that the loaf stays intact.

VARIATION
Flavour the butter with garlic, a little chopped fresh chilli, grated (shredded) lime rind and chopped fresh coriander (cilantro).

3 Spread the garlic and herb butter between the slices evenly, being careful not to detach them, and then spread any remaining butter over the top of the loaf.

4 Wrap the loaf in foil and bake in the preheated oven for 20–25 minutes, or until the butter is melted and the crust is golden and crisp. Cut the loaf into slices to serve.

COOK'S TIP
This loaf can also be cooked on the barbecue if space permits. Place the foil-wrapped loaf on the grill rack over medium-hot coals and cook for about the same length of time as for oven baking. Turn the foil parcel over several times to ensure it cooks evenly.

Energy 920kcal/3877kJ; Protein 22.1g; Carbohydrate 135.1g, of which sugars 7.2g; Fat 36.2g, of which saturates 20.8g; Cholesterol 82mg; Calcium 317mg; Fibre 6.3g; Sodium 1714mg.

DESSERTS AND DRINKS

The main course is cooked, the coals are still hot, so why not use the barbecue to grill or bake some mouthwatering desserts? Firm-fleshed fruits such as melons, pineapples and mangoes can easily be cooked on the grill rack or griddle and then served with a sauce or ice cream, but soft fruits can also be cooked on the barbecue. Try the recipe for strawberries cooked on cherry wood skewers with toasted marshmallows — a heavenly combination that adults as well as children will love. You can also wrap fruits in foil and bake them on the grill; to make them extra special, serve them with a sauce or stuff them with nuts or amaretti. If you want to prepare the dessert completely in advance, a simple salad of exotic fruits will make an excellent end to a satisfying barbecued meal. Also included in this chapter are some alcoholic and non-alcoholic drinks that are just right for a warm summer's day socializing with friends or enjoying a relaxing time outdoors with the family around the barbecue.

TOASTED BRIOCHE SLICES <u>WITH</u> ICE CREAM

WARM AND SYRUPY-SWEET BRIOCHE SLICES FLAVOURED WITH ORANGE AND CINNAMON MAKE A DELECTABLE CONTRAST TO VANILLA ICE CREAM IN THIS UNUSUAL VARIATION ON THE TOASTED BUN THEME. FINELY GRATED LEMON RIND AND JUICE INSTEAD WILL WORK JUST AS WELL THE ORANGE.

SERVES FOUR

INGREDIENTS
    butter, for greasing
    finely grated rind and juice of
      1 orange, such as navel or
      blood orange
    50g/2oz/¼ cup caster
      (superfine) sugar
    90ml/6 tbsp water
    1.5ml/¼ tsp ground cinnamon
    4 brioche buns
    15ml/1 tbsp icing
      (confectioners') sugar
    vanilla ice cream, to serve

1 Put the orange rind and juice, sugar, measured water and cinnamon in a heavy pan. Heat gently, stirring constantly, until the sugar has dissolved, then boil rapidly, without stirring, for 2 minutes, until thickened and syrupy.

2 Remove the orange syrup from the heat and pour into a shallow heatproof dish. Prepare the barbecue. Position a lightly oiled grill rack over the hot coals. Cut each brioche into three thick slices. Grill over high heat until lightly toasted on both sides. Remove with tongs.

3 Working quickly, lift each hot brioche slice from the grill and dip one side into the syrup. Turn it syrup-side up on to a tray while you dip the remainder.

4 Lightly dust the tops with icing sugar then transfer the brioche slices back to the barbecue grill rack. Grill for 1–2 minutes, or until the top of each slice is bubbling and the underneath is golden brown.

5 Transfer the hot brioches to serving plates and top with scoops of vanilla ice cream. Spoon the remaining syrup over them and serve immediately.

VARIATIONS
• For a subtle difference in spiciness, substitute the same amount of ground cardamom for the cinnamon.
• You could also use slices of a larger brioche, or madeleines, sliced horizontally in half. These are traditionally flavoured with lemon or orange flower water, making them especially tasty.

Energy 458kcal/1926kJ; Protein 9.1g; Carbohydrate 67.9g, of which sugars 45.8g; Fat 18.5g, of which saturates 10.2g; Cholesterol 1mg; Calcium 189mg; Fibre 1.8g; Sodium 253mg.

APPLE-STUFFED CRÊPES

WHILE THE COALS ARE STILL HOT AFTER THE BARBECUE YOU CAN HEAT UP TWO FRYING PANS AND COOK UP SOME LACE-THIN CRÊPES TO SERVE WITH GOLDEN FRIED APPLES. TOP THE CRÊPES WITH A DRIZZLE OF HONEY AND SOME CREAM AND THEY ARE SURE TO BE A POPULAR END TO THE MEAL.

SERVES FOUR

INGREDIENTS

115g/4oz/1 cup plain
  (all-purpose) flour
pinch of salt
2 large (US extra large) eggs
175ml/6fl oz/¾ cup milk
120ml/4fl oz/½ cup sweet cider
butter, for frying
4 eating apples
60ml/4 tbsp caster (superfine) sugar
120ml/4fl oz/½ cup clear honey, and
  150ml/¼ pint/⅔ cup double (heavy)
  cream, to serve

1 To make the batter, sift the flour and salt into a large bowl. Add the eggs and milk and beat until smooth. Stir in the cider. Leave to stand for 30 minutes. Prepare the barbecue. Position a grill rack over the hot coals.

2 Heat a small heavy frying pan or flat griddle on the rack. Add a knob (pat) of butter and enough batter to coat the pan thinly. Cook the crêpe for about 1 minute until it is golden underneath, then flip it over and cook the other side until golden. Slide the crêpe on to a plate, then repeat with the remaining batter to make seven more. Set the crêpes aside and keep warm under foil.

3 Core the apples and cut them into thick slices. Heat 15g/½oz butter in a large frying pan. Add the apples to the pan and cook until golden on both sides. Transfer the slices to a bowl and sprinkle with sugar.

4 Fold each crêpe in half, then in half again to form a cone and fill with fried apples. Place two filled crêpes on each plate. Drizzle with a little honey and serve immediately with cream.

COOK'S TIP
For the best results, use full-fat (whole) milk in the batter.

Energy 524kcal/2200kJ; Protein 8.3g; Carbohydrate 71.1g, of which sugars 49.2g; Fat 24.1g, of which saturates 13.8g; Cholesterol 149mg; Calcium 140mg; Fibre 2.1g; Sodium 71mg.

GRIDDLE CAKES WITH MULLED PLUMS

THESE DELECTABLY LIGHT LITTLE PANCAKES ARE FUN TO MAKE IN A GRIDDLE OR FRYING PAN ON THE BARBECUE. THEY ARE SERVED WITH A RICH, SPICY PLUM SAUCE.

4 Make a well in the centre of the ingredients and add the egg, then beat in the milk. Beat thoroughly to form a smooth batter. Beat in half the oil.

5 Heat a griddle or a heavy frying pan on a hot barbecue. Brush with the remaining oil, then drop tablespoons of batter on to it, allowing them to spread. Cook the griddle cakes for about a minute, until bubbles start to appear on the surface and the underside is golden brown.

6 Turn the cakes over and cook the other side for a further minute, or until golden. Serve the cakes hot from the griddle with a spoonful of mulled plums and cream or yogurt.

SERVES SIX

INGREDIENTS
500g/1¼lb red plums, stoned
   (pitted) and quartered
90ml/6 tbsp light muscovado
   (brown) sugar
1 cinnamon stick
2 whole cloves
1 piece star anise
90ml/6 tbsp apple juice
cream or Greek-style natural
   (US strained, plain) yogurt,
   to serve
For the griddle cakes
50g/2oz/½ cup plain
   (all-purpose) flour
10ml/2 tsp baking powder
pinch of salt
50g/2oz/½ cup fine cornmeal
30ml/2 tbsp light muscovado
   (brown) sugar
1 egg, beaten
300ml/½ pint/1¼ cups milk
30ml/2 tbsp corn oil

1 Place the plums in a flameproof pan, with the sugar, spices and apple juice.

2 Bring to the boil, then reduce the heat, cover the pan and simmer gently for 8–10 minutes, stirring occasionally, until the plums are soft. Remove the spices and keep the plums warm on the side of the barbecue.

3 For the griddle cakes, sift the plain flour, baking powder and salt into a large mixing bowl and stir in the cornmeal and muscovado sugar.

Energy 494kcal/2101kJ; Protein 3.7g; Carbohydrate 116.8g, of which sugars 84.5g; Fat 4.6g, of which saturates 0.8g; Cholesterol 1mg; Calcium 110mg; Fibre 2.2g; Sodium 28mg.

CHARGRILLED APPLES ON CINNAMON TOASTS

THIS SIMPLE, SCRUMPTIOUS DESSERT IS BEST MADE WITH AN ENRICHED BREAD SUCH AS BRIOCHE,
BUT ANY LIGHT SWEET BREAD WILL DO. ON A WARM, EARLY AUTUMN EVENING THIS IS PERFECT.

SERVES FOUR

INGREDIENTS
    4 sweet, dessert apples
    juice of ½ lemon
    4 individual brioches or muffins
    60ml/4 tbsp melted butter
    30ml/2 tbsp golden caster
      (superfine) sugar
    5ml/1 tsp ground cinnamon
    whipped cream or Greek-style (US
      strained, plain) yogurt, to serve

5 Sprinkle half the cinnamon sugar over the apple slices and brioche toasts and cook for a further minute on the barbecue, until the sugar is sizzling and the toasts are a rich golden brown.

6 To serve, arrange the apple slices over the toasts and sprinkle them with the remaining cinnamon sugar. Serve hot, with whipped cream or Greek-style yogurt, if liked.

1 Core the apples and cut into 3–4 thick slices. Sprinkle the apple slices with lemon juice and set them aside.

2 Cut the brioches or muffins into thick slices. Brush the slices with melted butter on both sides.

3 Mix together the caster sugar and ground cinnamon in a small bowl to make the cinnamon sugar. Set aside.

4 Place the apple and brioche slices on a medium-hot barbecue and cook them for about 3–4 minutes, turning once, until they are beginning to turn golden brown. Do not allow to burn.

Energy 218kcal/926kJ; Protein 5.6g; Carbohydrate 40.9g, of which sugars 17.4g; Fat 4.8g, of which saturates 0.4g; Cholesterol 0mg; Calcium 79mg; Fibre 2.5g; Sodium 92mg.

NECTARINES WITH MARZIPAN AND MASCARPONE

A LUSCIOUS DESSERT THAT NO ONE CAN RESIST — THE ALMONDS IN THE MARZIPAN AND CRUMBLED MACAROONS MAKE THEM NATURAL PARTNERS FOR THE FRUIT.

SERVES FOUR

INGREDIENTS
    4 firm, ripe nectarines or peaches
    75g/3oz marzipan
    75g/3oz/5 tbsp mascarpone cheese
    3 macaroon biscuits (cookies),
        crushed

COOK'S TIP
If the stone does not pull out easily when you halve the fruit, use a small, sharp knife to cut around it.

1 Cut the nectarines or peaches in half and remove the stones (pits).

2 Divide the marzipan into eight pieces, roll into balls, using your fingers, and press one piece of marzipan into the stone cavity of each nectarine half.

3 Spoon the mascarpone cheese on top of the fruit halves. Sprinkle the crushed macaroon biscuits over the mascarpone cheese.

4 Place the half-fruits on a hot barbecue for 3–5 minutes, until they are hot and the mascarpone starts to melt. Serve immediately.

VARIATION
Replace the mascarpone with ricotta or low-fat soft cheese.

Energy 206kcal/869kJ; Protein 5.2g; Carbohydrate 33.4g, of which sugars 30.2g; Fat 6.7g, of which saturates 2.4g; Cholesterol 8mg; Calcium 34mg; Fibre 2.1g; Sodium 31mg.

BARBECUED STRAWBERRY CROISSANTS

THE COMBINATION OF CRISP BARBECUED CROISSANTS, RICOTTA CHEESE AND SWEET STRAWBERRY CONSERVE MAKES FOR A DELICIOUSLY SIMPLE, SINFUL DESSERT, WHICH IS LIKE EATING WARM CREAM CAKES.

SERVES FOUR

INGREDIENTS
    4 croissants
    115g/4oz/½ cup ricotta cheese
    115g/4oz/½ cup strawberry conserve
        or jam

1 Use a sharp knife to split the croissants in half, cutting through them horizontally, and open them out.

2 Beat the ricotta cheese lightly with a fork to break it up. Spread the bottom half of each croissant with a generous layer of ricotta.

COOK'S TIP
As an alternative to croissants, try scones, brioches or muffins, toasted on the barbecue.

VARIATIONS
• Spread the croissants with good-quality apricot or blackcurrant conserve.
• Top the ricotta with sliced strawberries or peaches, or with a handful of blackcurrants or redcurrants.

3 Top the ricotta with a generous spoonful of strawberry conserve and replace the top half of the croissant.

4 Place the filled croissants on a hot barbecue and cook for 2–3 minutes, turning once. Serve immediately.

Energy 301kcal/1263kJ; Protein 7.4g; Carbohydrate 35.4g, of which sugars 12.6g; Fat 19.2g, of which saturates 8.1g; Cholesterol 42mg; Calcium 47mg; Fibre 1g; Sodium 255mg.

FRUIT KEBABS WITH CHOCOLATE FONDUE

FONDUES ARE ALWAYS LOTS OF FUN, AND THE DELICIOUS INGREDIENTS USED HERE — FRESH FRUIT, CHOCOLATE AND MARSHMALLOW — MAKE THIS RECIPE POPULAR WITH CHILDREN AND ADULTS ALIKE.

2 Mix together the melted butter, lemon juice and ground cinnamon and brush the mixture generously over the fruit skewers.

3 To make the fondue, place the chocolate, cream and marshmallows in a small pan and heat gently, without boiling, stirring continuously until the marshmallows and chocolate have melted and the mixture is smooth.

4 Cook the kebabs on a medium-hot barbecue for about 2–3 minutes, turning once, or until the fruit is golden.

SERVES FOUR

INGREDIENTS
    2 bananas
    2 kiwi fruit
    12 strawberries
    15ml/1 tbsp melted butter
    15ml/1 tbsp lemon juice
    5ml/1 tsp ground cinnamon
For the fondue
    225g/8oz plain (semi-sweet)
        chocolate
    120ml/4fl oz/½ cup single
        (light) cream
    8 marshmallows
    2.5ml/½ tsp vanilla extract

1 Soak four wooden skewers in water for 15 minutes to prevent them scorching on the barbecue. Peel the bananas and cut into thick chunks. Peel the kiwi fruit and quarter them. Thread the bananas, kiwi fruit and strawberries on to the skewers.

5 Stir the vanilla extract into the fondue. Empty the fondue into a small bowl and serve at once with the kebabs.

Energy 442kcal/1853kJ; Protein 5.1g; Carbohydrate 57.5g, of which sugars 53.7g; Fat 22.9g, of which saturates 13.9g; Cholesterol 27mg; Calcium 59mg; Fibre 2.7g; Sodium 42mg.

BAKED APPLES IN HONEY AND LEMON

TENDER BAKED APPLES WITH A CLASSIC FLAVOURING OF LEMON AND HONEY MAKE A SIMPLE DESSERT.
SERVE WITH CUSTARD OR A SPOONFUL OF WHIPPED CREAM, IF YOU WISH.

SERVES FOUR

INGREDIENTS
    4 medium cooking apples
    15ml/1 tbsp butter
    15ml/1 tbsp honey
    grated rind and juice of 1 lemon

3 Beat the butter in a small bowl until soft. Add the honey, lemon rind and juice and mix together.

4 Spoon the mixture into the apples and wrap in foil. Cook on a hot barbecue for 20 minutes, until the apples are tender.

1 Remove the cores from the apples, leaving them whole. Cut four squares of double-thickness baking foil, to wrap the apples, and brush with butter.

2 With a cannelle or sharp knife, cut lines through the apple skin at regular intervals.

Energy 70kcal/292kJ; Protein 0.5g; Carbohydrate 9.4g, of which sugars 9.4g; Fat 3.7g, of which saturates 1.7g; Cholesterol 6mg; Calcium 5mg; Fibre 1.2g; Sodium 42mg.

GRILLED STRAWBERRIES <u>AND</u> MARSHMALLOWS

IT IS ALWAYS A TREAT TO HAVE PERMISSION TO EAT MARSHMALLOWS. AFTER COOKING. DREDGE THESE LITTLE KEBABS WITH LOADS OF ICING SUGAR, SOME OF WHICH WILL MELT INTO THE STRAWBERRY JUICE. THE GRILL HAS TO BE VERY HOT TO SEAR THE MARSHMALLOWS QUICKLY BEFORE THEY MELT.

SERVES FOUR

INGREDIENTS
    16 mixed pink and white
    marshmallows, chilled
    16 strawberries
    icing (confectioners') sugar
    for dusting
    8 short lengths of cherry wood or
    metal skewers

COOK'S TIP
Chilling the marshmallows makes them firmer and easier to thread on skewers.

1 Prepare the barbecue. If you are using lengths of cherry wood, soak them in water for 30 minutes. Position a lightly oiled grill rack just above the hot coals to heat.

2 Spike two marshmallows and two strawberries on each drained length of wood or metal skewer and grill over the hot coals for 20 seconds on each side. If nice grill marks don't appear easily, don't persist for too long or the marshmallows may burn – cook until they are warm to the touch and only just beginning to melt.

3 Transfer the skewered strawberries and marshmallows to individual dessert plates or a large platter, dust generously with icing sugar and serve.

SPICED PEAR AND BLUEBERRY PARCELS

THIS FRUITY COMBINATION MAKES A DELICIOUS DESSERT FOR A HOT SUMMER'S EVENING, AND THE PARCELS CAN BE PREPARED BEFORE YOU START COOKING THE MEAL. YOU COULD SUBSTITUTE OTHER BERRY FRUITS FOR THE BLUEBERRIES IF YOU PREFER. CHOOSE PEARS THAT ARE RIPE BUT STILL FIRM.

SERVES FOUR

INGREDIENTS
    4 pears
    30ml/2 tbsp lemon juice
    15ml/1 tbsp melted butter
    150g/5oz/1¼ cups blueberries
    60ml/4 tbsp light muscovado
      (brown) sugar
    ground black pepper

1 Peel the pears thinly and cut them in half lengthways. Scoop out the core from each half, using a teaspoon and a sharp kitchen knife.

2 Brush the flesh of the pears inside and out with lemon juice, to prevent them discolouring before they are cooked.

COOK'S TIP
The parcels can be assembled in advance, but if you need to do this, line the foil with a layer of greaseproof (waxed) paper, otherwise the acid in the lemon juice may react with the foil and taint the flavour.

3 Cut four squares of double-thickness foil, large enough to wrap the pears, and brush them with melted butter. Place two pear halves on each, cut sides upwards. Gather the foil up around them, to hold them level.

4 Mix the blueberries with the sugar and spoon the mixture over the pears. Sprinkle with black pepper. Seal the edges of the foil over the pears and cook on a fairly hot barbecue for 20–25 minutes.

Energy 143kcal/605kJ; Protein 1.1g; Carbohydrate 32.6g, of which sugars 32.6g; Fat 1.8g, of which saturates 0.4g; Cholesterol 0mg; Calcium 41mg; Fibre 4.5g; Sodium 31mg.

CALVADOS-FLAMED BANANAS

SOFT AND CREAMY BAKED BANANAS, FLAMED WITH CALVADOS, ARE DELICIOUS SERVED WITH A RICH
BUTTERSCOTCH SAUCE. THE SAUCE CAN BE MADE IN ADVANCE AND THE BANANAS ARE QUICKLY
COOKED. THE FLAMING CALVADOS MAKES A SPECTACULAR END TO A MEAL.

SERVES SIX

INGREDIENTS
    115g/4oz/generous ½ cup sugar
    150ml/¼ pint/⅔ cup water
    25g/1oz/2 tbsp butter
    150ml/¼ pint/⅔ cup double
      (heavy) cream
    6 large, slightly underripe bananas
    90ml/6 tbsp Calvados

1 Place the sugar and measured water
in a large pan and heat gently until the
sugar has dissolved. Increase the heat
and boil until the mixture turns a rich
golden caramel colour. Remove from
the heat and carefully add the butter
and cream; the mixture will foam up in
the pan. Replace it over a gentle heat
and stir until smooth, then pour into a
bowl and leave to cool. Cover the sauce
and chill until needed.

2 Prepare the barbecue. Wrap the
bananas individually in foil. Position a
grill rack over the hot coals. Grill the
wrapped bananas over high heat for
10 minutes.

3 Transfer the bananas to a tray, open
up the parcels and slit the upper side of
each banana skin.

4 Meanwhile, gently warm the Calvados
in a small pan, then pour some into
each banana. Put them back on the
barbecue and wait for a few seconds
before carefully igniting the Calvados
with a long match. Serve with the sauce
as soon as the flames die down.

Energy 359kcal/1501kJ; Protein 1.7g; Carbohydrate 43.7g, of which sugars 41.4g; Fat 17.2g, of which saturates 10.6g; Cholesterol 43mg; Calcium 29mg; Fibre 1.1g; Sodium 33mg.

BAKED BANANAS WITH ICE CREAM

BANANAS, BAKED UNTIL SOFT, MAKE THE PERFECT PARTNER FOR DELICIOUS VANILLA ICE CREAM
TOPPED WITH A TOASTED HAZELNUT SAUCE. THIS IS A QUICK AND EASY DESSERT, WHICH IS SURE
TO BE ESPECIALLY POPULAR WITH CHILDREN.

SERVES FOUR

INGREDIENTS
    4 large bananas
    15ml/1 tbsp lemon juice
    4 large scoops of vanilla ice cream
For the sauce
    25g/1oz/2 tbsp unsalted
      (sweet) butter
    50g/2oz/½ cup hazelnuts
    45ml/3 tbsp golden (light corn) syrup
    30ml/2 tbsp lemon juice

1 Prepare the barbecue. Position a grill rack over the hot coals. Brush the bananas with the lemon juice and wrap each banana individually in a double thickness of foil. Grill the bananas for 20 minutes.

2 Meanwhile, make the sauce. Toast the hazelnuts lightly in a pan on the grill rack, then chop them roughly. Melt the butter in a small pan on the rack. Add the hazelnuts and cook gently for 1 minute. Add the golden syrup and lemon juice and heat, stirring, for 1 minute more.

3 To serve, slit each banana open with a knife along the upper side and open out the skins to reveal the tender flesh.

4 Transfer the bananas to serving plates and add scoops of ice cream. Pour the warm sauce over and serve immediately before the ice cream melts.

Energy 413kcal/1729kJ; Protein 6g; Carbohydrate 53.5g, of which sugars 49.6g; Fat 19.9g, of which saturates 8.6g; Cholesterol 32mg; Calcium 103mg; Fibre 2.2g; Sodium 115mg.

BAKED BANANAS <u>WITH</u> SPICY VANILLA FILLING

BANANAS ARE IDEAL FOR BARBECUE COOKING AS THEY BAKE TO A DELICIOUS SOFTNESS IN THEIR SKINS AND NEED NO PREPARATION AT ALL. THIS FLAVOURED BUTTER ADDS RICHNESS, THOUGH CHILDREN MAY PREFER MELTED CHOCOLATE, JAM OR HONEY WITH THEIR BANANAS.

2 Meanwhile, split the cardamom pods and remove the seeds. Crush lightly in a pestle and mortar.

3 Split the vanilla pod lengthways and scrape out the tiny seeds. Mix with the cardamom seeds, orange rind, brandy or juice, muscovado sugar and butter into a thick paste.

SERVES FOUR

INGREDIENTS

    4 bananas
    6 green cardamom pods
    1 vanilla pod (bean)
    finely grated rind of 1 small orange
    30ml/2 tbsp brandy or orange juice
    60ml/4 tbsp light muscovado
      (brown) sugar
    45ml/3 tbsp butter
    crème fraîche or Greek-style
      natural (US strained, plain) yogurt,
      to serve

1 Place the bananas, in their skins, on a hot barbecue and leave for 6–8 minutes, turning occasionally, until they are turning brownish-black.

4 As soon as the bananas are cooked and while they are still piping hot, use a sharp knife to slit the skin of each one along the upper side, then open out the skin and spoon in a little of the spice paste. Serve the bananas with a spoonful of crème fraîche or Greek-style yogurt, if liked.

Energy 184kcal/770kJ; Protein 2.9g; Carbohydrate 27g, of which sugars 25.1g; Fat 7.8g, of which saturates 4.6g; Cholesterol 0mg; Calcium 55mg; Fibre 0.9g; Sodium 31mg.

PINEAPPLE WEDGES WITH RUM BUTTER GLAZE

FRESH PINEAPPLE IS EVEN MORE FULL OF FLAVOUR WHEN COOKED, ESPECIALLY WHEN IT IS BARBECUED, AND A SPICED RUM GLAZE MAKES IT INTO A VERY SPECIAL DESSERT. COOKING THE WEDGES IN THE SKIN LOOKS SPECTACULAR AND HELPS TO RETAIN ALL THE LOVELY JUICE.

SERVES FOUR

INGREDIENTS
1 medium pineapple
30ml/2 tbsp dark muscovado
  (molasses) sugar
5ml/1 tsp ground ginger
60ml/4 tbsp melted butter
30ml/2 tbsp dark rum

3 Soak 4 bamboo skewers in water for 15 minutes to prevent them scorching on the barbecue. Push a skewer through each wedge, into the stalk, to hold the chunks in place.

4 Mix together the sugar, ginger, butter and rum and brush over the pineapple. Cook the wedges on the barbecue for 4 minutes; pour the remaining glaze over the top and serve.

1 With a large, sharp knife, cut the pineapple lengthways into four wedges, including the plume of leaves. Cut out and discard the central core.

2 Run the knife blade along between the flesh and the skin, to release the skin, but leave the flesh in place. Slice the flesh across and lengthways to make thick chunks.

COOK'S TIP
For a less elaborate version of this dessert, simply remove the skin and then cut the whole pineapple into thick slices and cook as above. Alternatively, cut the pineapple into thick chunks and thread them on to wooden skewers.

Energy 203kcal/853kJ; Protein 3.7g; Carbohydrate 23g, of which sugars 23g; Fat 9.6g, of which saturates 4.4g; Cholesterol 162mg; Calcium 51mg; Fibre 1.8g; Sodium 63mg.

CHARGRILLED PINEAPPLE

THIS IS A BOLD DESSERT — ATTRACTIVE TOO, IF YOU LEAVE THE GREEN TOPS ON THE PINEAPPLE.
HEATING PINEAPPLE REALLY BRINGS THE FLAVOUR TO THE FORE AND, WITH THE ICE-COLD GRANITA,
IT'S THE IDEAL FINISH TO A GLAMOROUS BARBECUE.

SERVES EIGHT

INGREDIENTS
  2 medium pineapples
  15ml/1 tbsp caster (superfine) sugar
    mixed with 15ml/1 tbsp water
For the granita
  15ml/1 tbsp sugar
  1 fresh long mild red chilli, seeded
    and finely chopped
  900ml/1½ pints/3¾ cups pineapple
    juice or fresh purée

COOK'S TIP
Chilli is a regular ingredient in fruit
granitas, as it counters the sharp taste.

1 To make the granita, place the sugar
and chilli in a small heavy pan with
30ml/2 tbsp of the pineapple juice.
Heat gently until the sugar has
dissolved, then bring to a fast boil for
30 seconds. Pour the remaining
pineapple juice into a large, shallow
freezerproof container. The ideal size is
about 25 x 14cm/10 x 5½in. Stir in the
chilli mixture and freeze for 2 hours.

2 Fork the frozen edges of the sorbet
mixture into the centre of the container
and freeze for a further 1½ hours until
crunchy. Give it another fork over.
Return it to the freezer, where it can
stay for up to 1 week.

3 Prepare the barbecue. Thaw the
granita for about 10 minutes in the
refrigerator before serving, and fork it
over to break up the ice crystals.

4 Cut each pineapple lengthways into
four equal wedges, slicing right through
the leafy crown. Remove the core from
each wedge.

5 Heat a griddle on the grill rack over
hot coals. Lower the heat slightly. Brush
the cut sides of the pineapple wedges
with the sugar and water mixture and
grill for about 1 minute on each side, or
until branded by the griddle. Serve
warm with the granita.

Energy 112kcal/482kJ; Protein 0.9g; Carbohydrate 28.4g, of which sugars 28.4g; Fat 0.4g, of which saturates 0g; Cholesterol 0mg; Calcium 34mg; Fibre 1.5g; Sodium 12mg.

NECTARINES WITH PEACH SYLLABUB

THIS ITALIAN DESSERT IS HIGHLY ADDICTIVE, WITH ITS IRRESISTIBLE SYLLABUB FLAVOURED WITH PEACH SCHNAPPS. DELECTABLE FLAVOURS RESULT FROM MARRYING FRUIT WITH ALMONDS AND HERE, RIPE NECTARINES LOOK STUNNING CARAMELIZED ON TOP AND DECORATED WITH GRILL MARKS.

SERVES EIGHT

INGREDIENTS

120ml/4fl oz/½ cup peach
  schnapps
juice of ½ lemon
25g/1oz/¼ cup icing
  (confectioners') sugar
300ml/½ pint/1¼ cups double
  (heavy) cream
4 large ripe nectarines, halved
  and stoned
5ml/1 tsp clear honey
24 amaretti morbidi
  (soft almond macaroons)

1 Mix the peach schnapps, lemon juice and icing sugar in a large, deep bowl. Cover and chill.

2 Prepare the barbecue. Whisking constantly with a hand-held electric whisk, gradually add the cream to the chilled schnapps mixture, until the syllabub just holds its shape. Don't over-whip. Chill the syllabub while you cook the fruit.

COOK'S TIP
The nectarines can be cooked on a griddle or on the stovetop.

3 Brush each of the nectarine halves with a little clear honey. Once the flames of the barbecue have died down, position a lightly oiled grill rack over the coals to heat. When the coals are medium-hot, or with a moderate coating of ash, place the nectarine halves cut-side down on the grill rack and leave them to cook for about 1 minute, until caramelized.

4 Grill the amaretti morbidi for about 45 seconds on each side, to warm them through and let the surface caramelize a little. Serve the nectarines and amaretti with the syllabub.

Energy 318kcal/1324kJ; Protein 2.4g; Carbohydrate 24.4g, of which sugars 24.4g; Fat 20.3g, of which saturates 12.5g; Cholesterol 51mg; Calcium 29mg; Fibre 1.6g; Sodium 13mg.

FRUIT SKEWERS <u>WITH</u> LIME CHEESE

GRILLED FRUITS MAKE A FINE FINALE TO A BARBECUE, AND ARE ESPECIALLY GOOD COOKED ON LEMON GRASS SKEWERS, WHICH GIVE THE FRUIT A SUBTLE LEMON TANG. THE FRUITS USED HERE MAKE AN IDEAL EXOTIC MIX, BUT ALMOST ANY SOFT FRUIT CAN BE SUBSTITUTED.

SERVES FOUR

INGREDIENTS

  4 long fresh lemon grass stalks
  1 mango, peeled, stoned (pitted) and
    cut into chunks
  1 papaya, peeled, seeded and cut
    into chunks
  1 star fruit (carambola), cut into
    thick slices and halved
  8 fresh bay leaves
  freshly grated nutmeg
  60ml/4 tbsp maple syrup
  50g/2oz/¼ cup demerara (raw) sugar
For the lime cheese
  150g/5oz/⅔ cup curd cheese or
    low-fat soft cheese
  120ml/4fl oz/½ cup double
    (heavy) cream
  grated rind and juice of ½ lime
  30ml/2 tbsp icing (confectioner's) sugar

1 Prepare the barbecue. Position a lightly oiled grill rack over the hot coals. Cut the top of each lemon grass stalk into a point with a sharp knife. Discard the outer leaves, then use the back of the knife to bruise the length of each stalk to release the aromatic oils. Thread each stalk, skewer-style, with the fruit pieces, alternating one or two chunks with the bay leaves.

2 To make the lime cheese, mix all the ingredients together in a bowl and chill until ready to serve.

3 Place a piece of foil on a baking sheet. Lay the kebabs on top and sprinkle a little nutmeg over each. Drizzle the maple syrup over and dust liberally with the demerara sugar. Grill for 5 minutes, until lightly charred, basting with the maple syrup from the foil, if necessary. Serve the lightly charred fruit kebabs with the lime cheese.

COOK'S TIP
Only fresh lemon grass will work as skewers for this recipe. It is now possible to buy lemon grass stalks in jars. These are handy for curries and similar dishes, but are too soft to use as skewers.

Energy 360kcal/1508kJ; Protein 7.1g; Carbohydrate 43.4g, of which sugars 43.3g; Fat 19.3g, of which saturates 12g; Cholesterol 50mg; Calcium 98mg; Fibre 3.7g; Sodium 219mg.

GRILLED MANGO SLICES ^{WITH} LIME SORBET

IF YOU CAN LOCATE THEM, USE ALPHONSO MANGOES FOR THIS DISH. MAINLY CULTIVATED IN INDIA, THEY HAVE A HEADY SCENT AND GLORIOUSLY SENSUAL, SILKY TEXTURE. THE SCORED FLESH AND DIAMOND BRANDING MAKE A VISUALLY APPEALING DESSERT.

SERVES SIX

INGREDIENTS
250g/9oz/1¼ cups sugar
juice of 6 limes
3 star anise
6 small or 3 medium to large
  mangoes
groundnut (peanut) oil, for brushing

1 Place the sugar in a heavy pan and add 250ml/8fl oz/1 cup water. Heat gently until the sugar has dissolved. Increase the heat and boil for 5 minutes. Cool completely.

2 Add the lime juice to the syrup, together with any pulp that has collected in the squeezer. Strain the mixture and reserve 200ml/7fl oz/scant 1 cup in a bowl. Add the star anise and leave to infuse.

3 Pour the remaining liquid into a measuring jug or cup and make up to 600ml/1 pint/2½ cups with cold water. Mix well and pour into a freezerproof container. Freeze for 1½ hours, stir well to bring the frozen crystals to the centre, then return the mixture to the freezer until set.

4 Transfer the sorbet mixture to a processor and pulse to a smooth icy purée. Freeze for another hour. Alternatively, make the sorbet in an ice cream maker; it will take about 20 minutes, and should then be frozen for at least 30 minutes before serving.

5 Prepare the barbecue. Pour the reserved syrup into a pan and boil for 2–3 minutes, or until thickened a little. Leave to cool. Cut the cheeks from either side of the stone (pit) on each unpeeled mango, and score the flesh on each in a diamond pattern. Brush with a little oil. Heat a griddle on the grill rack over hot coals. Lower the heat a little and grill the mango halves, cut-side down, for 30–60 seconds until branded with golden grill marks.

6 Invert the mango cheeks on individual plates and serve hot or cold with the syrup drizzled over and a scoop or two of the sorbet. Decorate with star anise.

COOK'S TIP
If this dessert is part of a larger barbecue meal, cook the mangoes in advance using a griddle set over the first red hot coals. Set aside until ready, and serve cold.

Energy 250kcal/1068kJ; Protein 1.3g; Carbohydrate 64.7g, of which sugars 64.2g; Fat 0.3g, of which saturates 0.2g; Cholesterol 0mg; Calcium 40mg; Fibre 3.9g; Sodium 6mg.

GRILLED PAPAYA WITH GINGER

AMARETTI AND STEM GINGER MAKE A TASTY FILLING FOR PAPAYA, AND THE WARM FLAVOUR OF GINGER ENHANCES THE SWEETNESS OF THE FRUIT. THE DISH TAKES NO MORE THAN TEN MINUTES TO PREPARE. DON'T OVERCOOK PAPAYA OR THE FLESH WILL BECOME VERY WATERY.

SERVES FOUR

INGREDIENTS

2 ripe papayas
2 pieces of stem ginger in syrup,
    drained, plus 15ml/1 tbsp syrup
    from the jar
8 amaretti or other dessert biscuits,
    coarsely crushed
45ml/3 tbsp raisins
shredded, finely pared rind and juice
    of 1 lime
25g/1oz/¼ cup pistachio
    nuts, chopped
15ml/1 tbsp light muscovado
    (brown) sugar
60ml/4 tbsp crème fraîche, plus
    extra to serve

VARIATION

Use Greek yogurt and almonds instead of crème fraîche and pistachio nuts.

1 Prepare the barbecue. Position a grill rack over the hot coals. Cut the papayas in half, scoop out their seeds and discard. Using a sharp knife, slice the stem ginger into fine pieces the size of matchsticks.

2 Tip the crushed amaretti biscuits into a bowl, add the stem ginger matchsticks and the raisins, and use your fingers to rub the contents together into a rough, dry crumble.

3 Stir in the lime rind and juice, and two-thirds of the nuts, then add the sugar and the crème fraîche. Mix well.

4 Place each papaya half on a piece of double-thickness foil. Fill the halves with the amaretti mixture and drizzle with the ginger syrup. Sprinkle with the remaining nuts and close up the foil. Place on the grill rack over hot coals and cook for about 25 minutes, or until tender. Serve with extra crème fraîche.

Energy 292kcal/1228kJ; Protein 3.6g; Carbohydrate 44.6g, of which sugars 35.7g; Fat 12.3g, of which saturates 5.7g; Cholesterol 17mg; Calcium 84mg; Fibre 4.2g; Sodium 127mg.

FRUIT WEDGES WITH GRANITAS

THESE WATERMELON AND ORANGE GRANITAS ARE PERFECT FOR A HOT SUMMER'S DAY AND IDEAL TO FINISH A MEAL. PREPARE THEM IN ADVANCE BUT MAKE SURE THEY ARE NICE AND SLUSHY WHEN READY TO SERVE. FRESH PINEAPPLE, MANGO AND BANANA GRILL QUICKLY AND MAKE A GREAT CONTRAST.

SERVES SIX TO EIGHT

INGREDIENTS
  1 pineapple
  1 mango
  2 bananas
  45–60ml/3–4 tbsp icing
    (confectioner's) sugar
For the watermelon granita
  1kg/2¼lb watermelon, seeds removed
  250g/9oz/1¼ cups caster
    (superfine) sugar
  150ml/¼ pint/⅔ cup water
  juice of ½ lemon
  15ml/1 tbsp orange flower water
  2.5ml/½ tsp ground cinnamon
For the spiced orange granita
  900ml/1½ pints/3¾ cups water
  350g/12oz/1¾ cups sugar
  5–6 cloves
  5ml/1 tsp ground ginger
  2.5ml/½ tsp ground cinnamon
  600ml/1 pint/2½ cups fresh
    orange juice
  15ml/1 tbsp orange flower water

1 To make the watermelon granita, purée the watermelon flesh in a blender. Put the sugar and water in a pan and stir until dissolved. Bring to the boil, simmer for 5 minutes, then cool.

2 Stir in the lemon juice, orange flower water and cinnamon, then beat in the watermelon purée. Pour the mixture into a bowl and place in the freezer. Stir every 15 minutes for 2 hours and then at one-hour intervals so that the mixture freezes but remains slushy.

3 To make the spiced orange granita, heat the water and sugar together in a pan with the cloves, stirring until the sugar has dissolved, then bring to the boil and boil for about 5 minutes. Leave to cool and stir in the ginger, cinnamon, orange juice and orange flower water.

4 Remove the cloves, then pour the mixture into a bowl and cover. Freeze in the same way as the granita, above.

5 Prepare the barbecue. Position a lightly oiled grill rack over the hot coals. Peel, core and slice the pineapple. Peel the mango and cut the flesh off the stone (pit) in thick slices. Peel and halve the bananas. Sprinkle the fruit with icing sugar and grill for 3–4 minutes over high heat until slightly softened and lightly browned. Arrange the fruit on a serving platter and scoop the granitas into dishes. Serve immediately.

Energy 433kcal/1848kJ; Protein 2g; Carbohydrate 111.8g, of which sugars 111.2g; Fat 0.7g, of which saturates 0.2g; Cholesterol 0mg; Calcium 71mg; Fibre 1.6g; Sodium 16mg.

HONEY-SEARED MELON

THIS FABULOUSLY SIMPLE DESSERT CAN BE MADE WITH MELON THAT IS SLIGHTLY UNDERRIPE, BECAUSE THE HONEYCOMB WILL SWEETEN IT UP BEAUTIFULLY. IT'S IDEAL TO MAKE DURING THE SUMMER WHEN RASPBERRIES ARE IN SEASON AND LAVENDER IS IN FLOWER.

SERVES SIX

INGREDIENTS
  1.3kg/3lb melon, preferably
    canteloupe
  200g/7oz honeycomb
  5ml/1 tsp water
  a bunch of lavender, plus extra
    flowers for decoration
  300g/11oz/2 cups raspberries

COOK'S TIP
Make sure that the lavender you use in this recipe is fresh.

1 Prepare the barbecue. Cut the melon in half, scoop out the seeds then cut each half into three slices. Put a third of the honeycomb in a bowl and dilute by stirring in the water. Make a brush with the bunch of lavender and dip the flowers into the honey.

2 Heat a griddle on the grill rack over hot coals. Lightly brush the melon with the honey mixture. Grill for 30 seconds on each side. Serve hot, sprinkled with the raspberries and remaining lavender flowers, and topped with the remaining honeycomb.

Energy 113kcal/480kJ; Protein 1.9g; Carbohydrate 27.2g, of which sugars 27.2g; Fat 0.4g, of which saturates 0.1g; Cholesterol 0mg; Calcium 42mg; Fibre 2.1g; Sodium 71mg.

MELON <u>WITH</u> GRILLED STRAWBERRIES

SPRINKLING THE STRAWBERRIES WITH A LITTLE SUGAR, THEN GRILLING THEM, HELPS BRING OUT THEIR FLAVOUR. SERVE THIS DELICIOUS FAT-FREE DESSERT ON ITS OWN OR WITH A SCOOP OF THE TANGY LEMON SORBET FEATURED A LITTLE LATER IN THIS CHAPTER.

SERVES FOUR

INGREDIENTS
115g/4oz/1 cup strawberries
15ml/1 tbsp icing (confectioner's) sugar, plus extra for dusting
½ cantaloupe melon

1 Soak four wooden skewers for 40 minutes to prevent them burning on the barbecue. Meanwhile, scoop out the seeds from the half melon using a spoon, and discard them. Using a sharp knife, remove and discard the skin, then cut the flesh into wedges and arrange on a serving plate.

2 Prepare the barbecue. Hull the strawberries and cut them in half. Arrange the fruit in a single layer, cut-side up, on a baking sheet and dust with the icing sugar.

3 Thread the strawberry halves onto skewers and place on a grill rack over hot coals. Grill for 3–4 minutes or until the sugar starts to bubble and turn golden. Remove from the skewers and scatter over the melon slices, dusting with the remaining icing sugar.

COOK'S TIPS
• If possible, place the skewered strawberry halves in a wire basket over the grill rack.
• Remove the strawberries from the heat as soon as the sugar starts to bubble. If left to burn, it will ruin their flavour.

Energy 46kcal/197kJ; Protein 1g; Carbohydrate 10.9g, of which sugars 10.9g; Fat 0.2g, of which saturates 0g; Cholesterol 0mg; Calcium 32mg; Fibre 1.6g; Sodium 12mg.

NECTARINES <u>WITH</u> PISTACHIO NUTS

FRESH, RIPE NECTARINES STUFFED WITH A GROUND ALMOND AND PISTACHIO NUT FILLING ARE SIMPLE TO COOK IN FOIL PARCELS ON THE BARBECUE. MAKE THE PARCELS AHEAD AND GRILL THEM WHILE YOU EAT YOUR MAIN COURSE. WHEN OPENED, THE NECTARINES ARE IMMERSED IN A FRUITY LIQUEUR SAUCE.

SERVES FOUR

INGREDIENTS
  50g/2oz/½ cup ground almonds
  15ml/1 tbsp caster (superfine) sugar
  1 egg yolk
  50g/2oz/½ cup shelled pistachio
    nuts, chopped
  4 nectarines
  200ml/7fl oz/scant 1 cup orange juice
  2 ripe passion fruit
  45ml/3 tbsp Cointreau or other
    orange liqueur

1 Prepare the barbecue. Position a grill rack over the hot coals. Mix the ground almonds, sugar and egg yolk to a paste, then stir in the pistachio nuts.

2 Cut the nectarines in half and carefully remove the stones (pits). Pile the ground almond and pistachio filling into the nectarine halves, packing in plenty of filling, and then place them in pairs on pieces of double-thickness foil. Wrap them up, leaving a space at the top.

3 Pour the orange juice around the nectarines, then close the tops. Place on the grill rack over medium-high heat and cook for 25 minutes.

4 Cut the passion fruit in half and scoop out the seeds. Open the foil tops and add a little of the passion fruit to each parcel. Sprinkle over the liqueur. Cook for a further 5 minutes. Place the nectarines on serving plates and spoon the sauce over and around them.

COOK'S TIP
The sugar in the nutty stuffing should caramelize in the heat, creating a lovely golden-brown crumble effect.

Energy 272kcal/1135kJ; Protein 7.6g; Carbohydrate 20.7g, of which sugars 20g; Fat 15.4g, of which saturates 1.9g; Cholesterol 50mg; Calcium 62mg; Fibre 3.5g; Sodium 74mg.

HONEY-BAKED FIGS

*IN THIS DELECTABLE DESSERT, FRESH FIGS ARE BAKED IN FOIL PARCELS WITH A LIGHTLY SPICED LEMON
AND HONEY SYRUP. THEY ARE SERVED WITH HOME-MADE HAZELNUT ICE CREAM: ROASTING THE NUTS
BEFORE GRINDING THEM GIVES A WONDERFUL DEPTH OF FLAVOUR.*

SERVES FOUR

INGREDIENTS
finely pared rind of 1 lemon
1 cinnamon stick, roughly broken
60ml/4 tbsp clear honey
8 large figs
For the hazelnut ice cream
450ml/¾ pint/scant 2 cups double
(heavy) cream
50g/2oz/¼ cup caster
(superfine) sugar
3 large (US extra large) egg yolks
1.5ml/¼ tsp vanilla extract
75g/3oz/¾ cup hazelnuts

1 To make the ice cream, gently heat
the cream in a pan until almost boiling.
Meanwhile, beat the sugar and egg
yolks in a bowl until creamy.

2 Pour a little hot cream into the egg
yolk mixture and stir with a wooden
spoon. Pour the whole lot back into the
pan and mix well.

3 Cook over a low heat, stirring
constantly, until the mixture thickens
slightly and lightly coats the back of the
spoon – do not allow it to boil or the
eggs will start to set. Pour the custard
into a bowl, stir in the vanilla extract
and leave to cool.

4 Preheat the oven to 180°C/350°F/
Gas 4. Place the hazelnuts on a baking
sheet and roast for 10–12 minutes, or
until golden. Leave the nuts to cool,
then grind them in a food processor.

5 If you have an ice cream maker, pour
in the cold custard and churn until half-
set. Add the ground hazelnuts and
continue to churn until the ice cream is
thick. Freeze until firm.

6 To make by hand, pour the custard
into a freezerproof container and freeze
for 2 hours. Turn into a bowl and beat
with an electric whisk or turn into a food
processor and beat until smooth. Stir in
the hazelnuts and freeze until half-set.
Beat once more, then freeze until firm.

7 Prepare the barbecue. Position a grill
rack over the hot coals. Remove the ice
cream from the freezer and allow to
soften slightly.

VARIATION
Use pecans instead of hazelnuts.

8 Put the lemon rind, cinnamon stick,
honey and 200ml/7fl oz/scant 1 cup
water in a small pan and heat slowly
until boiling. Simmer the mixture for
5 minutes, then leave to stand for
15 minutes.

9 Using a sharp knife, cut the figs
almost into quarters but leaving them
attached at the base. Place them in
pairs on pieces of double-thickness foil.
Wrap them up, leaving a space at the
top. Pour the honey syrup around and
over the figs, then close the tops. Place
on the grill rack over medium-high heat
and cook for 15 minutes.

10 Arrange the figs on small serving
plates, with the cooking syrup poured
around them. Serve accompanied by a
scoop or two of ice cream.

Energy 909kcal/3770kJ; Protein 8.2g; Carbohydrate 48.7g, of which sugars 48.4g; Fat 77.1g, of which saturates 39.6g; Cholesterol 305mg; Calcium 206mg; Fibre 4.2g; Sodium 60mg.

ORANGES IN MAPLE AND COINTREAU SYRUP

THIS IS ONE OF THE MOST DELICIOUS WAYS TO EAT AN ORANGE, AND A LUXURIOUS WAY TO ROUND OFF A BARBECUED MEAL. THE HEAT INTENSIFIES THE FLAVOUR OF THE ORANGE WONDERFULLY. FOR A CHILDREN'S OR ALCOHOL-FREE VERSION, OMIT THE LIQUEUR.

SERVES FOUR

INGREDIENTS
20ml/4 tsp butter, plus extra, melted, for brushing
4 medium oranges
30 ml/2 tbsp maple syrup
30ml/2 tbsp Cointreau or Grand Marnier liqueur
crème fraîche or fromage frais, to serve

2 Remove the rind from one of the oranges thinly using a vegetable peeler and cut into fine shreds to decorate the dish. To blanch the shreds, put them in a small pan of water and bring to the boil. Boil for 1 minute, then drain. Dry the shreds and set them aside.

3 Peel all the oranges, removing all the white pith and working over a bowl to catch the juice.

5 Tuck the baking foil up securely around the oranges to keep the stacks of slices in shape, leaving the foil open at the top.

1 Cut four squares of double baking foil, large enough to wrap an orange. Brush the centre of each square with plenty of melted butter.

4 Using a sharp knife, slice the oranges crossways into thick slices. Reassemble them and place each orange on a square of baking foil.

6 Mix together the reserved orange juice, maple syrup and orange liqueur and spoon the mixture over the oranges in the foil.

7 Add a knob of butter to each parcel and close the foil securely at the top to seal in the juices.

8 Place the parcels on a hot barbecue for 10–12 minutes, until hot. Top with the reserved shreds of rind and serve with crème fraîche or fromage frais.

Energy 93kcal/395kJ; Protein 1.7g; Carbohydrate 17.4g, of which sugars 17.2g; Fat 0.5g, of which saturates 0g; Cholesterol 0mg; Calcium 67mg; Fibre 2.2g; Sodium 34mg.

FRESH FRUIT SALAD

AFTER A RICH MEAL, NOTHING QUITE HITS THE SPOT LIKE A CLEAR-TASTING SALAD OF FRESH FRUIT.
THIS SALAD HAS A PASSION FRUIT AND HONEY DRESSING THAT REALLY ACCENTUATES THE FLAVOUR OF
THE EXOTIC FRUIT USED. SERVE IT WITH SCOOPS OF COCONUT OR VANILLA ICE CREAM, IF YOU LIKE.

SERVES SIX

INGREDIENTS
 1 mango
 1 papaya
 2 kiwi fruit
 coconut or vanilla ice cream, to serve
For the dressing
 3 passion fruit
 thinly pared rind and juice of 1 lime
 5ml/1 tsp hazelnut or walnut oil
 15ml/1 tbsp clear honey

COOK'S TIP
Honey scented with orange or acacia
blossom is perfect for the dressing.

1 Peel the mango, cut it into three
slices, then cut the flesh into chunks
and place it in a large bowl. Peel the
papaya and cut it in half. Scoop out the
seeds and discard, then chop the flesh
and put in the bowl with the mango.

2 Cut both ends off each kiwi fruit, then
stand them on a board. Using a small
sharp knife, cut off the skin from top to
bottom. Cut each kiwi fruit in half
lengthways, then cut into thick slices.
Combine all the fruit in a large bowl.

3 Make the dressing. Cut each passion
fruit in half and scoop the seeds out
into a sieve set over a small bowl. Press
the seeds well to extract all their juices.
Lightly whisk the remaining dressing
ingredients into the passion fruit juice,
then pour the dressing over the fruit.
Mix gently to combine. Leave to chill
for 1 hour before serving with scoops
of coconut or vanilla ice cream.

Energy 57kcal/240kJ; Protein 0.9g; Carbohydrate 12.4g, of which sugars 12.3g; Fat 0.7g, of which saturates 0.1g; Cholesterol 0mg; Calcium 21mg; Fibre 2.4g; Sodium 6mg.

LEMON SORBET

THIS SMOOTH, TANGY SORBET CREATES A LIGHT AND REFRESHING DESSERT THAT CAN BE SERVED AS IT IS OR TO ACCOMPANY FRESH FRUIT. IF YOU HAVE COOKED A RICH BARBECUE, THIS CLEAN-TASTING DESSERT MIGHT BE JUST THE RIGHT CHOICE TO END THE MEAL.

SERVES SIX

INGREDIENTS
  200g/7oz/1 cup caster
    (superfine) sugar
  300ml/½ pint/1¼ cups water
  4 lemons
  1 large (US extra large) egg white
  a little sugar, for sprinkling

VARIATIONS
Sorbet can be made from any citrus fruit. As a guide, you will need 300ml/½ pint/ 1¼ cups of fresh fruit juice and the pared rind of half the squeezed fruits. For example, use four oranges or two oranges and two lemons, or, to make a grapefruit sorbet, use the rind of one ruby grapefruit and the juice of two.

1 Put the sugar and water into a heavy pan and bring slowly to the boil, stirring occasionally, until the sugar dissolves.

2 Pare the rind thinly from two of the lemons directly into the pan. Simmer for about 2 minutes without stirring, then remove the pan from the heat. Leave the syrup to cool, then chill.

3 Squeeze the juice from the lemons and strain it into the syrup. Take out the lemon rind and set it aside.

4 If you have an ice cream maker, strain the syrup into the bowl and churn for 10 minutes, or until it is thickening.

5 Lightly whisk the egg white with a fork, then pour it into the ice cream maker. Churn for 10–15 minutes, or until the sorbet is firm enough to scoop.

6 If working by hand, strain the syrup into a shallow freezerproof container and freeze for 4 hours, or until mushy. Scoop into a blender or food processor and process until smooth.

7 Whisk the egg white with a fork until it is just frothy. Spoon the sorbet back into its container; beat in the egg white. Freeze for 1 hour.

8 To make the decoration, use the blanched rind from step 2. Cut into very thin strips and sprinkle with sugar. Scoop the sorbet into bowls and decorate with the sugared lemon rind.

Energy 133kcal/569kJ; Protein 0.7g; Carbohydrate 34.8g, of which sugars 34.8g; Fat 0g, of which saturates 0g; Cholesterol 0mg; Calcium 18mg; Fibre 0g; Sodium 12mg.

LYCHEE AND ELDERFLOWER SORBET

THE FLAVOUR OF ELDERFLOWERS IS WELL KNOWN FOR BRINGING OUT THE ESSENCE OF GOOSEBERRIES, BUT WHAT IS LESS WELL KNOWN IS HOW WONDERFULLY ELDERFLOWERS COMPLEMENT LYCHEES. THIS IS A DELICIOUSLY FRAGRANT AND REFRESHING SORBET.

SERVES FOUR

INGREDIENTS

    175g/6oz/¾ cup caster
      (superfine) sugar
    400ml/14fl oz/1⅔ cups water
    500g/1¼lb fresh lychees, peeled
      and stoned (pitted)
    15ml/1 tbsp elderflower cordial
    dessert biscuits (cookies), to serve

COOK'S TIP

Switch the freezer to the coldest setting before making the sorbet – the faster the mixture freezes, the better the final texture will be. To ensure rapid freezing, use a metal freezerproof container and place it directly on the freezer shelf.

1 Place the sugar and water in a pan and heat gently until the sugar has dissolved. Increase the heat and boil for 5 minutes, then add the lychees. Lower the heat and simmer for 7 minutes. Remove from the heat and allow to cool.

2 Purée the fruit and syrup in a blender or food processor. Place a sieve (strainer) over a bowl and pour the purée into it. Press through as much of the purée as possible with a spoon.

3 Stir the elderflower cordial into the strained purée, then pour the mixture into a freezerproof container. Freeze for 2 hours, until ice crystals start to form around the edges.

4 Remove the sorbet from the freezer and process briefly in a food processor or blender to break up the crystals. Repeat this process twice more, then freeze until firm. Transfer to the refrigerator for 10 minutes to soften before serving in scoops with biscuits.

Energy 249kcal/1064kJ; Protein 1.4g; Carbohydrate 64.7g, of which sugars 64.7g; Fat 0.1g, of which saturates 0g; Cholesterol 0mg; Calcium 31mg; Fibre 0.9g; Sodium 4mg.

RED BERRY SORBET

THIS VIBRANT RED SORBET SEEMS TO CAPTURE THE TRUE FLAVOUR OF SUMMER. PICK YOUR OWN BERRIES, IF YOU CAN, AND USE THEM AS SOON AS POSSIBLE.

SERVES SIX

INGREDIENTS

150g/5oz/¾ cup caster
(superfine) sugar
200ml/7fl oz/scant 1 cup water
500g/1¼lb/5 cups mixed berries,
hulled, including two or more of the
following: strawberries, raspberries,
tayberries or loganberries
juice of ½ lemon
1 egg white
small whole and halved strawberries
and strawberry leaves and flowers,
to decorate

VARIATION

For a hidden kick, add 45ml/3 tbsp
vodka or cassis to the fruit purée.

1 Put the sugar and water into a pan
and bring to the boil, stirring until the
sugar has dissolved. Pour the syrup into
a bowl, leave to cool, then chill.

2 Purée the fruits in a food processor
or blender, then press through a sieve
into a large bowl. Stir in the syrup and
lemon juice.

3 Churn in an ice cream maker until
thick, then add the whisked egg white.
Continue to churn until firm enough to
scoop. Scoop on to plates and decorate
with strawberries, leaves and flowers.

Energy 123kcal/523kJ; Protein 1.3g; Carbohydrate 31.1g, of which sugars 31.1g; Fat 0.1g, of which saturates 0g; Cholesterol 0mg; Calcium 27mg; Fibre 0.9g; Sodium 17mg.

BLACKCURRANT SORBET

WONDERFULLY SHARP AND BURSTING WITH FLAVOUR, THIS IS A VERY POPULAR SORBET. IF YOU FIND IT A BIT TART, ADD A LITTLE MORE SUGAR BEFORE FREEZING.

SERVES SIX

INGREDIENTS
500g/1¼lb/5 cups blackcurrants, trimmed
350ml/12fl oz/1½ cups water
150g/5oz/¾ cup caster (superfine) sugar
1 egg white
sprigs of blackcurrants, to decorate

1 Put the blackcurrants in a pan and add 150ml/¼ pint/⅔ cup of the measured water.

2 Cover the pan and simmer for 5 minutes or until the fruit is soft. Cool slightly, then purée in a food processor or blender.

3 Set a large sieve (strainer) over a bowl, pour the purée into the sieve then press it through the mesh with the back of a wooden spoon into the bowl below.

4 Pour the remaining measured water into the clean pan. Add the sugar and bring to the boil, stirring until the sugar has dissolved.

5 Pour the syrup into a bowl. Cool, then chill. Mix in the blackcurrant purée.

6 Churn in an ice cream maker until thick. Add the egg white and continue churning until it is firm enough to scoop. Serve decorated with the blackcurrant sprigs.

Energy 84kcal/361kJ; Protein 1.3g; Carbohydrate 21.2g, of which sugars 21.2g; Fat 0g, of which saturates 0g; Cholesterol 0mg; Calcium 58mg; Fibre 3g; Sodium 14mg.

STRAWBERRY AND LAVENDER SORBET

DELICATELY PERFUMED WITH JUST A HINT OF LAVENDER, THIS DELIGHTFUL, COLOURFUL SORBET IS PERFECT FOR MAKING THE MOST OF THE SUMMER STRAWBERRY CROP.

SERVES SIX

INGREDIENTS

150g/5oz/¾ cup caster
(superfine) sugar
300ml/½ pint/1¼ cups water
6 fresh lavender flowers, plus extra
to decorate
500g/1¼lb/5 cups strawberries,
hulled
1 egg white

1 Bring the sugar and water slowly to the boil in a pan, stirring until the sugar has dissolved.

2 Take the pan off the heat, add the lavender flowers, stir the mixture and leave to infuse for 1 hour. Chill the syrup before using.

3 Purée the strawberries in a food processor or in batches in a blender, then press the purée through a large sieve (strainer) into a bowl.

4 Pour the strawberry purée into the bowl of an ice cream maker and strain in the lavender syrup. Churn until thick. Add the whisked egg white and continue to churn until the sorbet is firm enough to scoop.

5 Serve piled into tall glasses, and decorate with sprigs of lavender flowers.

COOK'S TIP
The size of lavender flowers can vary; if they are very small you may need to use more than six. To double check, taste a little of the cooled lavender syrup. If you think the flavour is too mild, add 2–3 more flowers, reheat and cool again before using.

Energy 123kcal/523kJ; Protein 1.3g; Carbohydrate 31.1g, of which sugars 31.1g; Fat 0.1g, of which saturates 0g; Cholesterol 0mg; Calcium 27mg; Fibre 0.9g; Sodium 17mg.

MINTED EARL GREY SORBET

ORIGINALLY FAVOURED BY THE GEORGIANS AT GRAND SUMMER BALLS, THIS REFRESHING, SLIGHTLY TART SORBET IS IDEAL FOR A LAZY AFTERNOON IN THE GARDEN.

SERVES SIX

INGREDIENTS
200g/7oz/1 cup caster
  (superfine) sugar
300ml/½ pint/1¼ cups water
1 lemon, well scrubbed
45ml/3 tbsp Earl Grey tea leaves
450ml/¾ pint/2 cups boiling water
1 egg white
30ml/2 tbsp chopped fresh
  mint leaves
fresh mint sprigs or frosted mint,
  to decorate

1 Put the sugar and water into a pan and bring the mixture slowly to the boil, stirring until the sugar has completely dissolved.

2 Thinly pare the rind from the lemon so that it falls straight into the pan of syrup. Simmer for 2 minutes then pour into a bowl. Cool, then chill.

3 Put the tea into a pan and pour on the boiling water. Cover and leave to stand for 5 minutes, then strain into a bowl. Cool, then chill.

COOK'S TIPS
• If you only have Earl Grey tea bags these can be used instead, but add enough to make 450ml/¾ pint/ scant 2 cups strong tea.
• To make frosted mint leaves, select some of the best leaves, dip them in egg white and sprinkle them with caster (superfine) sugar. Leave them on a plate to dry.

4 Remove the strips of lemon rind from the syrup and add the cold tea. Pour the mixture into the bowl of an ice cream maker and churn until thick.

5 Add the mint to the mixture. Lightly whisk the egg white until just frothy, then tip it into the ice cream maker and churn until firm. Serve decorated with fresh or frosted mint leaves.

Energy 135kcal/578kJ; Protein 0.8g; Carbohydrate 35.1g, of which sugars 34.8g; Fat 0g, of which saturates 0g; Cholesterol 0mg; Calcium 29mg; Fibre 0g; Sodium 13mg.

COCONUT ICE

DESPITE ITS CREAMY TASTE AND RICH SOFT TEXTURE, THIS DESSERT CONTAINS NEITHER CREAM NOR EGG AND IS VERY REFRESHING. TRY IT ACCOMPANIED BY SLICES OF FRESH MANGO.

SERVES FOUR TO SIX

INGREDIENTS
150ml/¼ pint/⅔ cup water
115g/4oz/½ cup caster
(superfine) sugar
2 limes
400ml/14fl oz can coconut milk
toasted coconut shavings, to decorate
(see Cook's Tip)

COOK'S TIP
Use the flesh from a coconut to make a pretty decoration. Cut off thin slices using a swivel-blade vegetable peeler. Toast the slices under a moderate grill (broiler) until the coconut has curled and the edges are golden. Cool slightly, then sprinkle the shavings over the coconut ice.

1 Put the water in a small pan. Tip in the caster sugar and bring to the boil over a low heat, stirring constantly until the sugar has all dissolved.

2 Remove the pan from the heat and leave the syrup to cool, then chill well.

3 Grate the rind of the limes finely, taking care to avoid the bitter pith. Squeeze them and pour the juice and rind into the pan of syrup. Add the coconut milk.

4 Churn the mixture in an ice cream maker until firm enough to scoop. Serve in dishes, decorated with the toasted coconut shavings.

Energy 90kcal/386kJ; Protein 0.3g; Carbohydrate 23.3g, of which sugars 23.3g; Fat 0.2g, of which saturates 0.1g; Cholesterol 0mg; Calcium 30mg; Fibre 0g; Sodium 75mg.

CRÈME FRAÎCHE AND HONEY ICE CREAM

THIS DELICATELY FLAVOURED VANILLA ICE CREAM IS NATURALLY SWEETENED WITH FRAGRANT FLOWER HONEY AND IS ABSOLUTELY DELICIOUS EITHER ON ITS OWN OR WITH HOT APPLE OR CHERRY PIE.

SERVES FOUR

INGREDIENTS
  4 egg yolks
  60ml/4 tbsp clear flower honey
  5ml/1 tsp cornflour (cornstarch)
  300ml/½ pint/1¼ cups
    semi-skimmed (low-fat) milk
  7.5ml/1½ tsp natural vanilla extract
  250g/9oz/generous 1 cup
    crème fraîche
  nasturtium, pansy or herb flowers,
    to decorate

1 Whisk the egg yolks, honey and cornflour until thick and foamy. Bring the milk just to the boil in a heavy pan, then gradually pour on to the yolk mixture, whisking constantly.

2 Return the mixture to the pan and cook over a gentle heat, stirring all the time until it thickens enough to coat the back of the spoon. Do not overheat or the custard will curdle.

3 Pour the honey custard into a jug (pitcher) and then chill until it is completely cold.

4 Stir the vanilla extract and crème fraîche into the custard, then pour the mixture into the bowl of an ice cream maker and churn until thick and firm enough to scoop.

5 Serve the ice cream in glass dishes, decorated with nasturtiums, pansies or edible herb flowers.

Energy 386kcal/1602kJ; Protein 6.9g; Carbohydrate 16.5g, of which sugars 16.3g; Fat 33g, of which saturates 19.5g; Cholesterol 277mg; Calcium 151mg; Fibre 0g; Sodium 57mg.

RHUBARB AND GINGER ICE CREAM

THE CLASSIC COMBINATION OF GENTLY POACHED RHUBARB AND CHOPPED GINGER IS BROUGHT UP TO DATE BY BLENDING IT WITH MASCARPONE, TO MAKE THIS PRETTY BLUSH-PINK ICE CREAM.

SERVES FOUR TO SIX

INGREDIENTS
    5 pieces of preserved stem ginger
    450g/1lb trimmed rhubarb, sliced
    115g/4oz/½ cup caster
      (superfine) sugar
    30ml/2 tbsp water
    150g/5oz/⅔ cup mascarpone
    150ml/¼ pint/⅔ cup
      whipping cream
    wafer baskets, to serve (optional)

COOK'S TIP
Use delicate pink forced rhubarb, available in spring and early summer, to make this ice cream. It has the best flavour and colour. If the rhubarb purée is rather pale, add a few drops of pink food colouring when you put the mixture in the blender.

1 Using a sharp knife, roughly chop the stem ginger and set it aside. Put the rhubarb slices into a pan and add the sugar and water. Cover and simmer for 5 minutes until the rhubarb is just tender and still bright pink.

2 Tip the mixture into a food processor or blender and process until smooth, then leave to cool. Chill the purée if time permits.

3 Churn the rhubarb purée in an ice cream maker for 15–20 minutes until it is thick.

4 Put the mascarpone into a bowl, soften it with a wooden spoon, then gradually beat in the cream. Add the chopped ginger and rhubarb puree, then pour into the ice cream maker and churn until firm. Serve as scoops in bowls or wafer baskets.

Energy 221kcal/924kJ; Protein 3.6g; Carbohydrate 22.1g, of which sugars 22.1g; Fat 13.8g, of which saturates 8.6g; Cholesterol 37mg; Calcium 94mg; Fibre 1.1g; Sodium 10mg.

GOOSEBERRY AND CLOTTED CREAM ICE CREAM

GOOSEBERRIES MAKE SOME LOVELY TRADITIONAL DESSERTS, BUT THIS INDULGENT ICE CREAM SHOWS THEM IN A NEW LIGHT. IT GOES PARTICULARLY WELL WITH TINY, MELT-IN-THE-MOUTH MERINGUES.

SERVES FOUR TO SIX

INGREDIENTS
500g/1¼lb/4 cups gooseberries, trimmed
60ml/4 tbsp water
75g/3oz/6 tbsp caster (superfine) sugar
150ml/¼ pint/⅔ cup whipping cream
a few drops of green food colouring (optional)
120ml/4fl oz/½ cup clotted cream
fresh mint sprigs, to decorate
meringues, to serve

COOK'S TIP
Just a small amount of clotted cream adds a surprising richness to this simple ice cream. If the gooseberry purée is very tart, you can add extra sugar when mixing in the whipping cream.

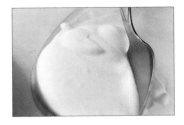

1 Whip the cream to a very soft spooning consistency and refrigerate.

2 Put the gooseberries in a pan and add the water and sugar. Cover and simmer for 10 minutes or until soft. Tip into a food processor or blender and process to a smooth purée. Press through a sieve (strainer) placed over a bowl. Cool, then chill thoroughly.

2 Mix the chilled purée with the whipping cream, add a few drops of green food colouring if using and churn in an ice cream maker until thickened and semi-frozen. Add the clotted cream and continue to churn until thick enough to scoop.

3 To serve, scoop the ice cream into dishes or small plates, decorate with fresh mint sprigs and add a few small meringues to each serving.

Energy 278kcal/1152kJ; Protein 1.8g; Carbohydrate 16.7g, of which sugars 16.7g; Fat 23.1g, of which saturates 14.3g; Cholesterol 60mg; Calcium 52mg; Fibre 2g; Sodium 12mg.

COOKIES <u>AND</u> CREAM ICE CREAM

THIS WICKEDLY INDULGENT ICE CREAM IS A FAVOURITE IN THE USA. TO MAKE THE RESULT EVEN MORE LUXURIOUS, USE FRESHLY BAKED HOME-MADE COOKIES THAT INCLUDE LARGE CHUNKS OF PREMIUM-QUALITY CHOCOLATE AND NUTS.

SERVES FOUR TO SIX

INGREDIENTS
    4 egg yolks
    75g/3oz/6 tbsp caster (superfine)
      sugar
    5ml/1 tsp cornflour (cornstarch)
    300ml/½ pint/1¼ cups
      semi-skimmed (low-fat) milk
    5ml/1 tsp natural vanilla extract
    300ml/½ pint/1¼ cups
      whipping cream
    150g/5oz chunky chocolate and
      hazelnut cookies, crumbled into
      chunky pieces

1 Whisk the egg yolks, sugar and cornflour in a bowl until the mixture is thick and foamy. Pour the milk into a heavy pan, bring it just to the boil, then pour it on to the yolk mixture in the bowl, whisking constantly.

2 Return the mixture to the pan and cook over a gentle heat, stirring constantly, until the custard thickens and is smooth. Pour it back into the bowl and cover closely. Leave to cool, then chill.

3 Stir the vanilla extract into the custard. Stir in the whipping cream and churn in an ice cream maker until thick. Scrape the mixture into a freezer-proof container.

4 Fold in the cookie chunks and freeze for 2–3 hours until firm.

Energy 428kcal/1782kJ; Protein 6.2g; Carbohydrate 36.3g, of which sugars 27.1g; Fat 29.7g, of which saturates 16.4g; Cholesterol 189mg; Calcium 135mg; Fibre 0.5g; Sodium 129mg.

CLASSIC DARK CHOCOLATE ICE CREAM

RICH, DARK AND WONDERFULLY LUXURIOUS, THIS ICE CREAM CAN BE SERVED SOLO OR DRIZZLED WITH WARM CHOCOLATE SAUCE. IF YOU ARE MAKING IT IN ADVANCE, DON'T FORGET TO SOFTEN THE ICE CREAM BEFORE SERVING SO THAT THE FULL FLAVOUR OF THE CHOCOLATE COMES THROUGH.

SERVES FOUR TO SIX

INGREDIENTS

4 egg yolks
75g/3oz/6 tbsp caster
  (superfine) sugar
5ml/1 tsp cornflour (cornstarch)
300ml/½ pint/1¼ cups
  semi-skimmed (low-fat) milk
200g/7oz dark (bittersweet)
  chocolate
300ml/½ pint/1¼ cups
  whipping cream
shaved chocolate, to decorate

1 Whisk the egg yolks, sugar and cornflour in a bowl until thick and foamy. Pour the milk into a pan, bring it just to the boil, then gradually whisk it into the yolk mixture.

2 Return the mixture to the pan and cook over a gentle heat, stirring constantly until the custard thickens. Take the pan off the heat.

COOK'S TIP
For the best flavour use a good quality chocolate with at least 75 per cent cocoa solids, such as top-of-the-range Belgian dark (bittersweet) chocolate or Continental-style dark (bittersweet) cooking chocolate.

3 Break the chocolate into small pieces and add it to the custard in the pan. Stir constantly until the heat of the custard has melted the chocolate and the mixture is smooth. Leave to cool, then chill.

4 Whip the cream, and mix with the cool chocolate custard.

5 Place in an ice cream maker and churn until firm enough to scoop. Serve the ice cream in scoops, decorated with chocolate shavings.

Energy 349kcal/1461kJ; Protein 4.8g; Carbohydrate 36.8g, of which sugars 35.8g; Fat 21.4g, of which saturates 11.9g; Cholesterol 162mg; Calcium 78mg; Fibre 0.7g; Sodium 29mg.

CHOCOLATE DOUBLE MINT ICE CREAM

FULL OF BODY AND FLAVOUR, THIS CREAMY ICE CREAM COMBINES THE SOPHISTICATION OF DARK CHOCOLATE WITH THE SATISFYING COOLNESS OF FRESH CHOPPED MINT. CRUSHED PEPPERMINTS PROVIDE EXTRA CRUNCH, AND THE COMBINATION WILL BE LOVED BY CHILDREN AND ADULTS ALIKE.

2 Scrape the mixture back into the pan and cook over a gentle heat, stirring constantly until the custard thickens and is smooth. Scrape it back into the bowl, add the chocolate, a little at a time, and stir until melted. Cool, then chill.

3 Put the peppermints in a strong plastic bag and crush them with a rolling pin. Stir them into the custard with the chopped mint.

4 Mix the custard and cream together and churn the mixture in an ice cream maker until firm enough to scoop.

5 Serve the ice cream in scoops and decorate with mint sprigs dusted with sifted icing sugar.

SERVES FOUR

INGREDIENTS
4 egg yolks
75g/3oz/6 tbsp caster
  (superfine) sugar
5ml/1 tsp cornflour (cornstarch)
300ml/½ pint/1¼ cups
  semi-skimmed (low-fat) milk
200g/7oz dark (bittersweet)
  chocolate, broken into squares
40g/1½ oz/¼ cup peppermints
60ml/4 tbsp chopped fresh mint
300ml/½ pint/1¼ cups
  whipping cream
sprigs of fresh mint dusted with icing
  (confectioners') sugar, to decorate

1 Put the egg yolks, sugar and cornflour in a bowl and whisk until thick and foamy. Pour the milk into a heavy pan, bring to the boil, then gradually whisk into the yolk mixture.

COOK'S TIP
If you freeze the ice cream in a tub rather than using an ice cream maker, don't beat it in a food processor when breaking up the ice crystals, or the crunchy texture of the crushed peppermints will be lost.

Energy 757kcal/3159kJ; Protein 9.8g; Carbohydrate 68.3g, of which sugars 66.7g; Fat 51.4g, of which saturates 29.8g; Cholesterol 299mg; Calcium 186mg; Fibre 1.3g; Sodium 66mg.

COFFEE TOFFEE SWIRL ICE CREAM

A WONDERFUL COMBINATION OF CREAMY VANILLA ICE CREAM, MARBLED WITH COFFEE-FLAVOURED TOFFEE. SERVE ON ITS OWN AS AN IMPRESSIVE GRAND FINALE TO A BARBECUE, OR ON A HOT DAY AS AN ICE CREAM SUNDAE WITH CLASSIC COFFEE AND CHOCOLATE ICE CREAM.

SERVES FOUR TO SIX

INGREDIENTS

For the toffee sauce
    10ml/2 tsp cornflour (cornstarch)
    170g/5¾oz can evaporated milk
    75g/3oz/6 tbsp light muscovado
    (brown) sugar
    20ml/4 tsp instant coffee granules
    15ml/1 tbsp boiling water

For the ice cream
    4 egg yolks
    75g/3oz/6 tbsp caster
    (superfine) sugar
    5ml/1 tsp cornflour (cornstarch)
    300ml/½ pint/1¼ cups
    semi-skimmed (low-fat) milk
    5ml/1 tsp vanilla extract
    300ml/½ pint/1¼ cups
    whipping cream

1 To make the coffee toffee sauce, put the cornflour and a little evaporated milk in a small, heavy pan and mix to a smooth paste. Add the sugar and the remaining evaporated milk.

2 Cook the mixture over a gentle heat, stirring, until the sugar has dissolved, then increase the heat and cook, stirring continuously, until it has thickened slightly and is just beginning to darken in colour.

3 Take the pan off the heat. Mix the instant coffee granules with the boiling water and stir into the sauce until well blended. Cool the sauce quickly by plunging the base of the pan into cold water.

4 To make the ice cream, whisk the egg yolks, sugar and cornflour together until thick and foaming. Bring the milk just to the boil in a heavy pan then gradually whisk into the yolk mixture.

5 Return the mixture to the pan and cook over a gentle heat, stirring until thick and smooth. Pour back into the bowl, stir in the vanilla and leave to cool.

6 Mix the custard and cream together and pour into the bowl of an ice cream maker. Churn until thick but not completely firm. Transfer the semi-frozen churned ice cream to a plastic container.

COOK'S TIP
If the sauce is too thick to drizzle, gently warm the base of the pan for a few seconds, stirring well.

7 Beat the toffee sauce well and drizzle it thickly over the ice cream. Marble the two together by roughly running a knife through the mixture.

8 Cover and freeze the ice cream for 4–5 hours until it is firm enough to scoop. Serve in scoops.

VARIATION
The sauce is also delicious drizzled over plain vanilla ice cream.

Energy 580kcal/2432kJ; Protein 24.5g; Carbohydrate 46.3g, of which sugars 44g; Fat 34.6g, of which saturates 20.4g; Cholesterol 225mg; Calcium 805mg; Fibre 0g, Sodium 297mg.

SIMPLE STRAWBERRY ICE CREAM

CAPTURE THE ESSENCE OF CHILDHOOD SUMMERS WITH THIS EASY-TO-MAKE ICE CREAM. IT IS BETTER TO USE WHIPPING CREAM THAN DOUBLE CREAM FOR THIS RECIPE AS IT IS LIGHTER AND DOESN'T OVERWHELM THE TASTE OF THE FRESH FRUIT. SERVE WITH EXTRA STRAWBERRIES OR OTHER SUMMER FRUITS SUCH AS RASPBERRIES OR REDCURRANTS.

SERVES FOUR TO SIX

INGREDIENTS
   500g/1¼lb/4 cups
      strawberries, hulled
   50g/2oz/½ cup icing
      (confectioners') sugar
   juice of ½ lemon
   300ml/½ pint/1¼ cups
      whipping cream
   extra strawberries, to decorate

VARIATION

Raspberry or any other berry fruit can be used to make this ice cream, in the same way as strawberry.

1 Purée the strawberries in a food processor or blender until smooth, then add the icing sugar and lemon juice and process again to mix. Press the purée through a sieve (strainer) into a bowl. Chill until very cold.

2 Pour the purée into an ice cream maker and churn until it is mushy, then pour in the cream and churn again until thick enough to scoop. Scoop into dishes and decorate with a few extra strawberries, halved or sliced.

Energy 2026kcal/8391kJ; Protein 19.9g; Carbohydrate 101.4g, of which sugars 86.5g; Fat 169.2g, of which saturates 100.2g; Cholesterol 420mg; Calcium 606mg; Fibre 5.4g; Sodium 267mg.

RUM AND RAISIN ICE CREAM

A PERENNIAL FAVOURITE, THIS ICE CREAM HAS A BEAUTIFUL SILKY TEXTURE WITH SWEET, CHEWY RAISINS. ADULTS MAY APPRECIATE AN EXTRA TOT OF RUM POURED OVER THEIR HELPING. THE LONGER YOU CAN LEAVE THE RAISINS TO SOAK IN THE RUM, THE STRONGER THE FLAVOUR WILL BE. AMARETTI BISCUITS MAKE A GOOD ACCOMPANIMENT, BUT PLAIN OR CHOCOLATE WAFER STRAWS ARE BEST.

SERVES FOUR TO SIX

INGREDIENTS
150g/5oz/scant 1 cup large raisins
60ml/4 tbsp dark rum
4 egg yolks
75g/3oz/6 tbsp light muscovado
   (molasses) sugar
5ml/1 tsp cornflour (cornstarch)
300ml/½ pint/1¼ cups
   semi-skimmed (low-fat) milk
300ml/½ pint/1¼ cups
   whipping cream
dessert biscuits (cookies)

1 Put the raisins in a bowl, add the rum and mix together well. Cover the bowl and leave the raisins to soak for 3–4 hours or overnight.

2 Whisk the egg yolks, muscovado sugar and the cornflour together in a large bowl until the mixture is thick and foamy.

3 Pour the milk into a heavy pan, and bring it to just below boiling point. Gradually whisk the milk into the egg mixture, then pour the custard back into the pan.

4 Cook over a gentle heat, stirring constantly until the custard thickens and is smooth. Take the pan off the heat and leave to cool.

5 Pour the cream into the custard, then churn until thick. Transfer to a plastic container.

6 Fold the soaked raisins into the ice cream, cover and freeze for 2–3 hours or until firm enough to scoop. Pile scoops into tall glasses and serve with dessert biscuits.

COOK'S TIP
Instead of dark rum, white rum, brandy or even whisky can be used instead.

Energy 397kcal/1654kJ; Protein 5.2g; Carbohydrate 34.9g, of which sugars 34.1g; Fat 24.8g, of which saturates 14.2g; Cholesterol 190mg; Calcium 123mg; Fibre 0.5g; Sodium 56mg.

HOT FUDGE SAUCE

If you're looking for a quick and easy barbecue dessert, make up some of this wicked sauce to accompany ice cream or barbecued fruit, and simply reheat it in a small pan on the grill rack. It also makes a luscious sundae with bananas, cream, ice cream and almonds.

SERVES FOUR

INGREDIENTS
  60ml/4 tbsp light muscovado
    (brown) sugar
  115g/4oz/⅓ cup golden (light
    corn) syrup
  45ml/3 tbsp strong black coffee
  5ml/1 tsp ground cinnamon
  150g/5oz dark (bittersweet)
    chocolate, broken up
  75ml/5 tbsp whipping cream
  45ml/3 tbsp coffee liqueur (optional)
To serve
  600ml/1 pint/2½ cups vanilla
    ice cream
  600ml/1 pint/2½ cups coffee
    ice cream
  2 large ripe bananas
  whipped cream and toasted sliced
    almonds, to top

1 Combine the sugar, golden syrup, coffee and cinnamon in a heavy pan. Bring to the boil. Boil the mixture, stirring constantly, for about 5 minutes.

COOK'S TIP
Use a good quality dark (bittersweet) chocolate with at least 70 per cent cocoa solids for a richer sauce.

2 Remove from the heat and stir in the chocolate. When melted and smooth, stir in the cream and liqueur, if using. Let the sauce cool just to lukewarm, or, if made ahead, reheat gently while assembling the sundaes.

3 To serve as an ice cream sundae, using an ice-cream scoop, fill four sundae dishes with 1 scoop each of vanilla and coffee ice cream.

4 Slice the bananas on top of each dish. Pour the warm sauce over the bananas.

5 Add a generous rosette of whipped cream over the bananas, and top with the toasted almonds.

Energy 986kcal/4137kJ; Protein 13.8g; Carbohydrate 133.7g, of which sugars 128.9g; Fat 44g, of which saturates 29.4g; Cholesterol 95mg; Calcium 339mg; Fibre 1.5g; Sodium 266mg.

SABAYON SAUCE

THIS FROTHY SAUCE IS VERY VERSATILE AND CAN BE SERVED ALONE WITH DESSERT BISCUITS OR HOT OVER CAKE, FRUIT OR ICE CREAM. IT IS ALSO GOOD SERVED COLD WITH BARBECUED FRUIT, BUT YOU MAY NEED TO ENLIST HELP TO WHISK IT: NEVER LET IT STAND BEFORE SERVING AS IT WILL COLLAPSE.

SERVES FOUR TO SIX

INGREDIENTS
1 egg
2 egg yolks
75g/3oz/scant ½ cup caster
  (superfine) sugar
150ml/¼ pint/⅔ cup Marsala or
  other sweet white wine
finely grated rind and juice of
  1 lemon
dessert biscuits, to serve

1 Put the egg, yolks and sugar into a medium bowl and whisk until they are pale and thick.

2 Stand the bowl over a pan of hot, but not boiling, water. Gradually add the Marsala or sweet white wine and lemon juice, a little at a time, whisking vigorously all the time.

COOK'S TIP
A generous pinch of powdered arrowroot whisked together with the egg yolks and sugar will prevent the sauce collapsing too quickly.

3 Continue whisking the mixture until it is thick enough to leave a trail across the surface when you lift the whisk. If you are serving the sabayon hot, pour it into dessert cups or glasses and serve immediately.

4 To serve the sabayon cold, place it over a bowl of iced water and continue whisking until chilled. Add the finely grated lemon rind and stir in. Pour into small glasses and serve at once, with the dessert biscuits.

Energy 105kcal/444kJ; Protein 2.1g; Carbohydrate 14.5g, of which sugars 14.5g; Fat 2.8g, of which saturates 0.8g; Cholesterol 99mg; Calcium 23mg; Fibre 0g; Sodium 19mg.

HAZELNUT DIP FOR SWEET SUMMER FRUITS

FRESH FRUIT IS ALWAYS A GOOD CHOICE FOR A COLOURFUL, SIMPLE DESSERT, AND THIS RECIPE MAKES IT COMPLETE, WITH A DELICIOUS SAUCE FOR DIPPING. CHOOSE ANY FRUIT THAT CAN BE SERVED RAW.

SERVES TWO

INGREDIENTS
    selection of fresh fruits, such as
    satsumas, kiwi fruit, grapes,
    physalis and whole strawberries and
    raspberries
For the hazelnut dip
    50g/2oz/¼ cup soft cheese
    150ml/¼ pint/⅔ cup hazelnut yogurt
    5ml/1 tsp vanilla extract
    5ml/1 tsp caster (superfine) sugar
    50g/2oz/⅓ cup shelled hazelnuts,
    chopped

COOK'S TIP
You can use any soft cheese, but Italian ricotta is to be recommended. It is a very perishable cheese, so make sure it is perfectly fresh when you buy it.

1 First prepare the fruits: peel and segment the satsumas. Peel the kiwi fruit and cut into wedges. Wash the grapes and peel the physalis by piercing the papery casing and pulling back.

2 To make the dip, beat the soft cheese with the hazelnut yogurt, vanilla extract and sugar. Stir in three-quarters of the chopped hazelnuts.

3 Spoon the hazelnut dip into a glass serving dish and place this on a serving platter. Alternatively, serve the dip in small dishes on individual plates. Scatter the remaining hazelnuts over the dip.

4 Arrange the prepared fruits around the bowl – or bowls – of dip and serve immediately.

Energy 365kcal/1521kJ; Protein 10.9g; Carbohydrate 32.7g, of which sugars 31.3g; Fat 22g, of which saturates 5g; Cholesterol 13mg; Calcium 168mg; Fibre 4.4g; Sodium 60mg.

MALTED CHOCOLATE AND BANANA DIP

CHOCOLATE AND BANANA COMBINE IRRESISTIBLY IN THIS RICH DIP, SERVED WITH FRESH FRUIT IN SEASON. FOR A CREAMIER DIP, STIR IN SOME LIGHTLY WHIPPED CREAM JUST BEFORE SERVING.

SERVES FOUR

INGREDIENTS
  50g/2oz plain (semisweet) chocolate
  2 large ripe bananas
  15ml/1 tbsp malt extract
  mixed fresh fruit, such as
    strawberries, peaches and kiwi fruit,
    halved or sliced, to serve

1 Break the chocolate into pieces and place in a small, heatproof bowl. Stand the bowl over a pan of gently simmering water and stir the chocolate occasionally until it melts. Allow to cool slightly.

2 Break the bananas into pieces and place in a food processor or blender. Pulse the power until the bananas are finely chopped.

COOK'S TIPS
• The last-minute addition of a few drops of melted butter to the dip gives it a lovely sheen.
• Loosen the mixture with a little cream if your dipping fruits are fairly soft.

3 With the motor running, pour the malt extract into the bananas, and continue processing the mixture until it is thick and frothy.

4 Drizzle in the chocolate in a steady stream and process until well blended. Serve immediately, with the prepared fruit alongside.

Energy 144kcal/607kJ; Protein 2.1g; Carbohydrate 27.1g, of which sugars 26.1g; Fat 3.7g, of which saturates 2.2g; Cholesterol 1mg; Calcium 27mg; Fibre 2.1g; Sodium 19mg.

STRAWBERRY AND APPLE SLUSH

SWEET, JUICY STRAWBERRIES MAKE WONDERFULLY FRAGRANT JUICES, ESPECIALLY WHEN THEY ARE GROWN OUTSIDE IN THE SUMMER. THE JUICE HAS A LOVELY CONSISTENCY THAT'S NOT TOO THICK. THE ADDITION OF APPLE JUICE AND JUST A HINT OF VANILLA CREATES A TANTALIZING, FRUITY TREAT THAT'S IDEAL FOR CHILDREN AND ADULTS ALIKE ON A LAZY SUMMER AFTERNOON IN THE GARDEN.

1 Pick out a couple of the prettiest strawberries and reserve for the decoration. Hull the remaining strawberries and roughly chop the apples into large chunks.

2 Push the fruits through a juicer and add to the jug with the syrup.

3 Half-fill two tall glasses with ice. Add straws or stirrers and pour over the juice. Decorate with the reserved strawberries (slicing them, if you like) and serve immediately.

MAKES 2 TALL GLASSES

INGREDIENTS
300g/11oz/2½ cups ripe strawberries
2 small, crisp eating apples
10ml/2 tsp vanilla syrup
crushed ice

COOK'S TIP
Vanilla syrup can be bought in jars from supermarkets and delicatessens. As an alternative, you could add a few drops of vanilla essence (extract) and a sprinkling of sugar, if necessary.

Energy 78kcal/331kJ; Protein 1.4g; Carbohydrate 18.8g, of which sugars 18.8g; Fat 0.2g, of which saturates 0g; Cholesterol 0mg; Calcium 28mg; Fibre 2.7g; Sodium 24mg.

LEMON FLOAT

OLD-FASHIONED LEMONADE MADE WITH FRESHLY SQUEEZED LEMONS IS A FAR CRY FROM THE CARBONATED, SYNTHETIC COMMERCIAL VARIETIES. SERVED WITH GENEROUS SCOOPS OF ICE CREAM AND SODA WATER, IT MAKES THE ULTIMATE REFRESHING DESSERT DRINK. THE LEMONADE CAN BE STORED IN THE REFRIGERATOR FOR UP TO TWO WEEKS, SO IT IS WELL WORTH MAKING A DOUBLE BATCH.

MAKES 4 LARGE GLASSES

INGREDIENTS
6 lemons, plus wafer-thin lemon
    slices,
    to decorate
200g/7oz/1 cup caster (superfine)
    sugar
8 scoops vanilla ice cream
soda water (club soda)

1 Finely grate the rind from the lemons, then squeeze out the juice using a citrus juicer or by hand.

2 Put the rind in a bowl with the sugar and pour over 600ml/1 pint/2½ cups boiling water. Stir until the sugar dissolves, then leave to cool.

3 Stir in the lemon juice. Strain into a jug (pitcher) and chill for several hours.

4 Put a scoop of the vanilla ice cream in each of the glasses, then half-fill with the lemonade and add plenty of lemon slices to decorate. Top up each glass with soda water, add another scoop of ice cream to each one and serve immediately with long-handled spoons.

Energy 412kcal/1742kJ; Protein 4.5g; Carbohydrate 81.9g, of which sugars 80.7g; Fat 9.6g, of which saturates 6.3g; Cholesterol 31mg; Calcium 159mg; Fibre 0g; Sodium 76mg.

CRANBERRY AND APPLE SPRITZER

DON'T FORGET TO LOOK AFTER THE NON-DRINKERS AT YOUR PARTY — ALL TOO OFTEN THEY'RE LEFT WITH JUST THE MIXERS, FIZZY DRINKS OR TAP WATER. THIS COLOURFUL, ZINGY COOLER COMBINES TANGY CRANBERRIES WITH FRESH JUICY APPLES AND A SUBTLE, FRAGRANT HINT OF VANILLA.

MAKES SIX TO EIGHT GLASSSES

INGREDIENTS
    6 red eating apples
    375g/13oz/3½ cups fresh or frozen
      cranberries, plus extra to decorate
    45ml/3 tbsp vanilla syrup
    ice cubes
    sparkling mineral water

COOK'S TIP
To make vanilla syrup, heat a vanilla pod (bean) with 50g/2oz/¼ cup sugar and 30ml/2fl oz water in a pan until the sugar dissolves. Simmer for 5 minutes then leave to cool.

1 Quarter and core the apples then cut the flesh into pieces small enough to fit through a juicer. Push the cranberries and apple chunks through the juicer. Add the vanilla syrup to the juice and chill until ready to serve.

2 Pour the juice into glasses and add one or two ice cubes to each. Top up with sparkling mineral water and decorate with extra cranberries, threaded on to cocktail sticks (toothpicks). Serve immediately.

Energy 51kcal/218kJ; Protein 0.3g; Carbohydrate 13.1g, of which sugars 13.1g; Fat 0.1g, of which saturates 0g; Cholesterol 0mg; Calcium 5mg; Fibre 1.6g; Sodium 17mg.

GRAPEFRUIT AND RASPBERRY COOLER

MAKE PLENTY OF FRESHLY JUICED BLENDS LIKE THIS GORGEOUS COMBINATION AND YOUR GUESTS WILL KEEP COMING BACK FOR MORE. GRAPEFRUIT AND RASPBERRY JUICE MAKE A GREAT PARTNERSHIP, PARTICULARLY IF YOU ADD A LITTLE CINNAMON SYRUP TO COUNTERACT ANY TARTNESS IN THE FRUIT.

MAKES EIGHT TALL GLASSES

INGREDIENTS
    1 cinnamon stick
    50g/2oz/¼ cup caster
      (superfine) sugar
    4 pink grapefruits
    250g/9oz/1½ cups fresh or
      frozen raspberries
    wedge of watermelon
    crushed ice
    borage flowers, to decorate (optional)

COOK'S TIP
Make non-alcoholic drinks more interesting by dressing them up with extra fruits and decorations.

VARIATION
Provide sugar stirrers so guests can sweeten their drinks to suit their own personal preference.

1 Put the cinnamon stick in a small pan with the sugar and 200ml/7fl oz/scant 1 cup water. Heat gently until the sugar has dissolved, then bring to the boil and boil for 1 minute. Reserve to cool.

2 Cut away the skins from the pink grapefruits. Cut the flesh into pieces small enough to fit through a juicer funnel. Juice the grapefruits and raspberries, and pour into a small glass jug (pitcher).

3 Remove the cinnamon from the syrup and add the syrup to the grapefruit and raspberry juice in the jug.

4 Carefully slice the watermelon into long thin wedges and place in eight tall glasses. Half-fill the glasses with the crushed ice and sprinkle with borage flowers, if you like. Pour over the pink fruit juice and serve immediately with plenty of napkins to allow your guests to eat the watermelon wedges.

Energy 57kcal/240kJ; Protein 1.1g; Carbohydrate 13.4g, of which sugars 13.4g; Fat 0.2g, of which saturates 0g; Cholesterol 0mg; Calcium 30mg; Fibre 1.8g; Sodium 4mg.

ALCOHOLIC FRUITY PUNCH

THE TERM "PUNCH" COMES FROM THE HINDU WORD PANCH (FIVE), *RELATING TO THE FIVE*
INGREDIENTS TRADITIONALLY CONTAINED IN THE DRINK: ALCOHOL, CITRUS, TEA, SUGAR AND WATER.
PUNCHES STILL COMBINE A MIXTURE OF SPIRITS, FLAVOURINGS AND A TOP-UP OF FIZZ OR JUICE.

MAKES ABOUT FIFTEEN GLASSES

INGREDIENTS
    2 large papayas
    4 passion fruit
    300g/11oz lychees, peeled and
        stoned (pitted)
    300ml/½ pint/1¼ cups freshly
        squeezed orange juice
    200ml/7fl oz/scant 1 cup Grand
        Marnier or other orange liqueur
    8 whole star anise
    2 small oranges
    ice cubes
    1.5 litres/2½ pints/6¼ cups soda
        water (club soda)

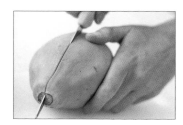

1 Halve the papayas using a sharp
knife and discard the seeds. Halve the
passion fruit and press the pulp through
a sieve (strainer) into a small punch
bowl or a pretty serving bowl.

2 Push the papayas through a juicer,
adding 105ml/7 tbsp water to help
the pulp through. Juice the lychees.
Add the juices to the bowl with the
orange juice, liqueur and star anise.

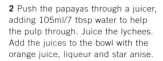

3 Thinly slice the oranges and add to
the bowl. Chill for at least 1 hour, or
until ready to serve.

4 Add plenty of ice cubes to the bowl
and top up with soda water. Ladle into
punch cups or small glasses to serve.

COOK'S TIP
This punch also makes a fabulous fruit
syrup with papaya halves stuffed with
frozen yogurt, or poured over a sorbet.

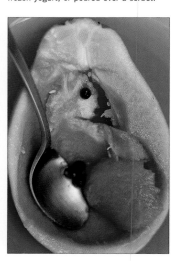

Energy 65kcal/274kJ; Protein 0.5g; Carbohydrate 11.6g, of which sugars 11.6g; Fat 0.1g, of which saturates 0g; Cholesterol 0mg; Calcium 10mg; Fibre 0.9g; Sodium 6mg.

APPLE-SPICED BEER

LIGHT BEER TAKES ON A WHOLE NEW DIMENSION IN THIS FUN AND FRUITY COOLER. DILUTED WITH FRESHLY JUICED APPLE AND FLAVOURED WITH GINGER AND STAR ANISE, IT'S A GREAT DRINK THAT IS REFRESHING AND LESS ALCOHOLIC THAN STRAIGHT BEER.

MAKES EIGHT TO TEN TALL GLASSES

INGREDIENTS
    8 eating apples
    25g/1oz fresh root ginger
    6 whole star anise
    800ml/1⅓ pints/3½ cups light beer
    crushed ice

1 Quarter and core the apples and, using a small, sharp knife, cut the flesh into pieces small enough to fit through a juicer. Roughly chop the ginger. Push half the apples through the juicer, then juice the ginger and the remaining apples.

2 Put 105ml/7 tbsp of the juice in a small pan with the star anise and heat gently until almost boiling. Add to the remaining juice in a large jug (pitcher) and chill for at least 1 hour.

3 Add the light beer to the juice and stir gently until the froth has dispersed a little. Pour the spiced beer over crushed ice in tall glasses, allow to settle again and serve immediately.

Energy 42kcal/178kJ; Protein 0.4g; Carbohydrate 4.8g, of which sugars 4.8g; Fat 0.1g, of which saturates 0g; Cholesterol 0mg; Calcium 6mg; Fibre 0.9g; Sodium 7mg.

HERBAL PUNCH

THIS REFRESHING PARTY DRINK WILL HAVE PEOPLE COMING BACK FOR MORE, AND IT IS AN ORIGINAL NON-ALCOHOLIC CHOICE FOR DRIVERS AND CHILDREN.

SERVES THIRTY PLUS

INGREDIENTS
    450ml/¾ pint/2 cups clear
      honey
    4 litres/7 pints water
    450ml/¾ pint/2 cups freshly
      squeezed lemon juice
    45ml/3 tbsp fresh rosemary leaves,
      plus extra to decorate
    1.5kg/3½lb/8 cups sliced
      strawberries
    450ml/¾ pint/2 cups freshly
      squeezed lime juice
    1.75 litres/3 pints/7½ cups
      sparkling mineral water
    ice cubes
    3–4 scented geranium leaves,
      to decorate

1 Combine the honey, 1 litre/1¾ pints/ 4 cups water, one-eighth of the lemon juice and the fresh rosemary leaves in a saucepan. Bring to the boil, stirring, until the honey is dissolved. Remove from the heat and allow to stand for about 5 minutes. Strain into a large punch bowl and set aside to cool.

2 Press the strawberries through a fine sieve (strainer) into the punch bowl, add the rest of the water, the lemon juice, lime juice and sparkling mineral water. Stir gently to combine. Add the ice cubes just 5 minutes before serving, and float the geranium and rosemary leaves on the surface.

Energy 58kcal/246kJ; Protein 0.5g; Carbohydrate 14.7g, of which sugars 14.7g; Fat 0.1g, of which saturates 0g; Cholesterol 0mg; Calcium 10mg; Fibre 0.6g; Sodium 5mg.

MINT CUP

MINT IS A PERENNIALLY POPULAR FLAVOURING AND THIS DELICATE CUP IS A WONDERFUL MIXTURE WITH AN INTRIGUING TASTE. IT IS THE PERFECT SUMMER DRINK TO SERVE WITH MEALS OUTDOORS.

SERVES FOUR TO SIX

INGREDIENTS
    handful fresh mint leaves
    15ml/1 tbsp caster (superfine)
      sugar
    crushed ice
    15ml/1 tbsp lemon juice
    175ml/6fl oz/¾ cup yellow
      grapefruit juice
    600ml/1 pint/2½ cups tonic water,
      chilled
    mint sprigs and lemon slices,
      to decorate

1 Crush the mint leaves with the sugar and put into a jug (pitcher). Fill the jug to the top with crushed ice.

2 Add the lemon juice, grapefruit juice and tonic water. Stir gently and decorate with mint sprigs and slices of lemon.

Energy 53kcal/224kJ; Protein 0.1g; Carbohydrate 13.8g, of which sugars 5g; Fat 0g, of which saturates 0g; Cholesterol 0mg; Calcium 6mg; Fibre 0g; Sodium 6mg.

STRAWBERRY AND MINT CHAMPAGNE

THIS IS A SIMPLE CONCOCTION THAT MAKES A BOTTLE OF CHAMPAGNE OR SPARKLING WHITE WINE GO MUCH FURTHER. IT TASTES VERY SPECIAL ON A HOT SUMMER'S EVENING.

SERVES FOUR TO SIX

INGREDIENTS
500g/1¼lb strawberries
6–8 fresh mint leaves
1 bottle champagne or sparkling
  white wine
fresh mint sprigs, to decorate

1 Purée the strawberries and fresh mint leaves in a food processor.

2 Strain through a fine sieve (strainer) into a large bowl. Half fill a glass with the mixture and top up with champagne or sparkling wine. Decorate with a sprig of fresh mint.

Energy 105kcal/438kJ; Protein 0.8g; Carbohydrate 5.8g, of which sugars 5.8g; Fat 0.1g, of which saturates 0g; Cholesterol 0mg; Calcium 25mg; Fibre 0.9g; Sodium 10mg.

MELON, GINGER AND BORAGE CUP

MELON AND GINGER COMPLEMENT EACH OTHER MAGNIFICENTLY. IF YOU PREFER, YOU CAN LEAVE OUT THE POWDERED GINGER — THE RESULT IS MILDER BUT EQUALLY DELICIOUS.

SERVES SIX TO EIGHT

INGREDIENTS
½ large honeydew melon
1 litre/1¾ pints/4 cups ginger beer
powdered ginger, to taste
borage sprigs with flowers,
   to decorate

1 Discard the seeds from the half melon and scoop the flesh into a food processor. Blend the melon to a purée.

2 Pour the purée into a large jug (pitcher) and chill. When ready to serve, top up with ginger beer. Add powdered ginger to taste and stir well.

3 Pour into glasses and decorate with borage flowers.

COOKS TIPS
• Galia melon can be used in this drink, and will give it a richer, more orange colour.
• Borage is easy to grow and makes a delicious addition to many cold drinks, tea infusions and salads.

Energy 34kcal/141kJ; Protein 0.3g; Carbohydrate 8.4g, of which sugars 8.4g; Fat 0.1g, of which saturates 0g; Cholesterol 0mg; Calcium 8mg; Fibre 0.3g; Sodium 19mg.

CUCUMBER PIMM'S PUNCH

THIS TANGY BLEND OF FRESHLY JUICED CUCUMBER, GINGER AND APPLES ISN'T AS INNOCENT AS IT LOOKS — OR TASTES. IT'S LAVISHLY LACED WITH ALCOHOL, SO IS DEFINITELY A DRINK TO ENJOY ON A LAZY SUMMER AFTERNOON. TO TAKE IT ON A PICNIC, JUST CHILL THE JUICE REALLY WELL, POUR INTO A VACUUM FLASK AND TOP UP WITH CHILLED GINGER ALE WHEN YOU REACH YOUR DESTINATION.

2 Peel the remaining cucumber and cut it into large chunks. Roughly chop the ginger and apples. Push the apples, then the ginger and cucumber through a juicer and pour the juice into a large jug (pitcher) or bowl.

3 Stir the Pimm's into the juice, add the cucumber, lemon slices and mint and borage sprigs, then chill.

4 Just before serving, add the ice cubes and borage flowers to the punch and top up with ginger ale. Ladle into glasses or glass cups.

MAKES TWELVE SMALL GLASSES

INGREDIENTS
  1 cucumber
  1 lemon
  50g/2oz fresh root ginger
  4 eating apples
  600ml/1 pint/2½ cups Pimm's
  sprigs of mint and borage
  ice cubes
  borage flowers
  1.5 litres/2½ pints/6¼ cups
    ginger ale

1 Cut off a 5cm/2in length from the cucumber and cut into thin slices. Slice the lemon and set both aside.

Energy 140kcal/586kJ; Protein 0.1g; Carbohydrate 21.5g, of which sugars 21.5g; Fat 0g, of which saturates 0g; Cholesterol 0mg; Calcium 3mg; Fibre 0.5g; Sodium 6mg.

TOP POPS

CHUNKY ICE-LOLLY STIRRERS GIVE THIS FRUIT-PACKED SMOOTHIE PLENTY OF CHILD-APPEAL, AND IT'S ALSO MUCH BETTER FOR CHILDREN THAN FIZZY DRINKS. IT'S GREAT FOR A PARTY OR AS AN AFTER-SCHOOL TREAT ON A HOT DAY. THE LOLLIES CAN BE FROZEN AHEAD AND STORED SO THEY'RE READY ON DEMAND, AND THE JUICE TAKES JUST MOMENTS TO PREPARE.

MAKES TWO GLASSES

INGREDIENTS
    1 apple
    300ml/½ pint/1¼ cups apple juice
    2 kiwi fruit
    90g/3½oz/generous ½ cup
      raspberries
    10ml/2 tsp caster (superfine) sugar
    150g/5oz/1 cup red grapes
    150g/5oz/1¼ cups blackcurrants or
      blackberries
    1 large banana

1 Peel, core and roughly chop the apple. Place in a food processor or blender with 100ml/3½fl oz/scant ½ cup of the apple juice and blend to a smooth purée. Pour into a third of the sections of an ice-cube tray.

4 To make the smoothie, put the grapes, blackcurrants or blackberries, and banana into the blender or food processor and blend until smooth. If the children won't tolerate "bits", push the mixture through a coarse sieve (strainer) after blending to remove the seeds and skins.

5 Push several of the fruit lollies out of the tray and place on separate plates for each child. Pour the fruit juice into two glasses and place on plates with the lollies. Serve immediately as the lollies will start to melt very quickly – and don't forget to supply the children with plenty of napkins.

2 Peel and roughly chop the kiwi fruit and blend until smooth with 100ml of the apple juice. Pour into another third of the ice-cube tray sections.

3 Blend the raspberries with the sugar and the remaining apple juice and spoon into the final sections. Freeze the tray for about 30 minutes then push a wooden ice-lolly (popsicle) stick into each. Freeze until solid.

COOK'S TIP
These little lollies are a great way to get children to eat plenty of fresh fruit: keep a supply of different flavours in the freezer for everyday treats.

Energy 233kcal/999kJ; Protein 3g; Carbohydrate 57.3g, of which sugars 56.2g; Fat 0.8g, of which saturates 0.1g; Cholesterol 0mg; Calcium 98mg; Fibre 6.5g; Sodium 12mg.

INDEX

A
aïoli 24
almonds 50
apple and tomato chutney 419
apple-spiced beer 501
apricot duck with beansprouts
196
apricot sauce 188
artichoke halves, stuffed 301
artichoke hearts, potatoes, peas
and saffron tagine 381
artichoke, radicchio and walnut
salad 325
artichokes, grilled baby 55
asparagus, tomato and orange
salad 344
asparagus with prosciutto 77
aubergines
aubergine and butternut salad
297
aubergine ratatouille 284
aubergine rolls in tomato sauce
298
baby aubergines with raisins
and pine nuts 324
chargrilled aubergine and
lemon salad 326
creamy aubergine dip 394
grilled aubergine parcels 299
smoked aubergine and yogurt
purée 28
smoked aubergine with chilli
dressing 313
smoky aubergine on ciabatta
42
spiced aubergine salad 327
stuffed aubergines with lamb
224
walnut bread with mashed
aubergine 43
avocado guacamole 397
avocado, hot 56
avocado, tomato and orange
salad 345

B
bacon 227, 336
bacon koftas 226

nutty bacon stuffing 111
oyster and bacon brochettes
228
trout with bacon 124
banana 88, 497
barbecues 10–11
cooking techniques 18–20
cooking times 19–20
lighting 12–13
low-fat 20–1
basil 130, 230, 347
basil and lemon mayonnaise
391
basil salsa 145
beans 304, 376
apricot duck with beansprouts
196
broad bean and feta salad
333
broad bean, mushroom and
chorizo salad 332
cannellini bean salad 334
halloumi and bean salad
294
red bean and mushroom
burgers 266
beef 17
barbecue roast beef 256
barbecued marinated beef 251
beef rib with onion sauce 247
gaucho barbecue 252
home-made burgers with relish
241
Indonesian beef burgers 250
kneaded sirloin steak 85
mini burgers with mozzarella
84
New Orleans steak salad 257
peppered steaks in beer and
garlic 243
sirloin steaks with Bloody Mary
sauce 246
spiced beef satay 254
spicy beef koftas with chickpea
purée 249
spicy meatballs 82
steak ciabatta 244
Stilton burgers 242
Thai beef salad 256
vegetable-stuffed beef rolls 255
beer 243, 501
beetroot with fresh mint 320
beetroot with garlic sauce 319
Bloody Mary sauce 246
blueberries with smoked
mackerel 114
bread
aubergine on ciabatta 42
cheese and potato bread twists
438
ciabatta 446

ciabatta with mozzarella and
onions 36
crostini 33
crostini with tomato and
anchovy 37
focaccia 441
garlic and herb bread 447
Italian breadsticks 439
olive bread 443
partybrot 440
pitta bread 436
pumpkin and walnut 444
red onion and rosemary
focaccia 441
sesame burger buns 433
steak ciabatta 244
walnut bread with mashed
aubergine 43
wholemeal sunflower bread
445
butters 17, 288
anchovy 17
basil 240
garlic 17
herb 17
horseradish 17
lemon 17
lime 104
mustard 17
olive 17
parsley 390

C
Caesar salad 331
carrot and orange salad 337
cassava and vegetable kebabs
268
cheese 44, 53, 64, 178, 230
blue cheese dip 398
Brie parcels with almonds 50

broad bean and feta salad 333
Caesar salad 331
cheese and potato bread 438
ciabatta with mozzarella 36
classic pesto sauce 406
classic quesadillas 45
couscous with halloumi 329
feta-stuffed squid 59
griddled cheese bites 46
grilled goat's cheese pizza 278
halloumi and bean salad 294
halloumi and grape salad 335
leek and grilled pepper salad
with goats cheese 318
mini burgers with mozzarella
84
onions stuffed with goat's
cheese 302
potato and cheese polpettes
279
potato and feta salad 359
squash stuffed with goat's
cheese 286
squash with Parmesan 286
Stilton burgers 242
summer salad 367
tomato and feta salad 348
tomato and mozzarella 347
vegetables with paneer 269
watermelon and feta salad 349
chicken 15, 17
baked poussins with yogurt
and saffron 201
barbecued chicken salad
180
barbecued chicken tikka 173
Cajun drummers 172
Caribbean chicken kebabs 164
chicken cooked in spices and
coconut 162

chicken fajitas 186
chicken salad with coriander
  dressing 184
chicken salad with lavender
  and herbs 183
chicken satay sticks 73
chicken wings teriyaki style 75
chicken wings with blood
  oranges 157
chicken with fresh herbs and
  garlic 179
chicken with herb and ricotta
  stuffing 178
chicken with lemon grass and
  ginger 167
chicken with peppers 170
chicken with pineapple 159
citrus kebabs 160
griddled chicken with salsa
  169
grilled cashew nut chicken 163
grilled chicken balls 70
hot and sour chicken salad
  182
jerk chicken 166
Maryland salad 185
mini chicken fillets 71
skewered poussins with lime
  and chilli 202
smoked chicken with butternut
  pesto 174
spicy chicken wings 74
spicy coated barbecued
  chicken 168
spicy Indonesian chicken satay
  156
spicy masala chicken 165
stuffed corn-fed chicken 176
sweet and sour kebabs 161
tandoori chicken sticks 72
tandoori drumsticks 175
Thai grilled chicken 158
chickpea purée 249
chilli 138, 202
chilli and herb polenta 47
chilli relish 411
chilli rub 15
chilli sambal 141
fried black chilli sauce 396
garlic and chilli sauce 57, 265
pepper and chilli ketchup 415
salsa verde 405
spring onion and chilli dressing
  313
sweet and sour chilli dipping
  sauce 148
tamarind chilli sauce 261
chocolate
chocolate double mint ice
  cream 488
dark chocolate ice cream 487

malted chocolate and banana
  dip 495
chorizo 332
ciabatta 36
citrus
citrus kebabs 160
citrus salsa 401
Cumberland sauce 417
monkfish with peppered citrus
  marinade 142
red mullet with basil and citrus
  130
sea bass with citrus fruit 134
clams and mussels in banana
  leaves 88
coconut
coconut ice 482
salmon kebabs with coconut
  122
coffee toffee swirl ice cream 489
coleslaw 356
cookies and cream ice cream 486
coriander 213
chicken salad with coriander
  dressing 184
duck with pineapple and
  coriander 199
corn griddle cakes 34
corn on the cob 322
corn relish 412
corn salsa 408
corn tostaditas with salsa 32
courgette wraps 54
courgettes, stuffed 285
couscous 206, 281
lemony couscous salad 379
spiced couscous with halloumi
  329
cranberry and apple spritzer 498
cream and cookies ice cream 486
cream and gooseberry ice cream
  485
crème fraîche and honey ice
  cream 483
cucumber and dill salad 338
cucumber and shallot salad 339
cucumber Pimm's punch 506
cucumber tzatziki 401
cumin 352

D
dill 338, 376
dill pickles 428
duck
apricot duck with beansprouts
  196
duck breasts with red plums
  200
duck sausages with spicy plum
  sauce 194
duck with pineapple and

coriander 199
glazed duck breasts 197
rare gingered duck 195
spiced duck with pears 198

E
endive salad with bacon 336
equipment 11

F
falafel 30
fattoush 342
fennel and grapefruit salad 109
fennel and leek salad 355
fennel salad 295
fennel with sea bass 133
fennel, orange and rocket 341
fish 15, 16, 17, 18, 87
barbecued red snapper 136
chargrilled fish with sambal
  belacan 138
cod fillet with fresh mixed-herb
  crust 144
crostini with tomato and
  anchovy 37
fish brochettes with peperonata
  149
fish parcels 152
griddled halibut 146
grilled fish in vine leaves with
  sweet and sour chilli dipping
  sauce 148
grilled salted sardines 105
grilled stingray wings with chilli
  sambal 141
grilled swordfish skewers 128
halibut with tomato and
  basil salsa 146
ham-wrapped trout 126
herby wrapped salmon 123

hot smoked salmon 115
Indonesian chargrilled fish 138
mackerel kebabs with sweet
  pepper salad 112
mackerel with nutty bacon
  stuffing 111
mackerel with tomatoes, pesto
  and onion 110
marinated monkfish and
  mussel kebabs 101
marinated sea trout 125
Mexican barbecue salmon 116
monkfish with peppered citrus
  marinade 142
paprika-crusted monkfish 147
peppers with tomatoes and
  anchovies 315
red mullet with basil and citrus
  130
red mullet with lavender 131
salmon kebabs with coconut
  122
salmon steaks with oregano
  salsa 117
salmon with red onion
  marmalade 121
salmon with spicy pesto 69
salmon with fruit salsa 120
sardines in vine leaves 66
sardines with herb salsa 106
sardines with plum paste 108
sea bass in vine leaves 132
sea bass with citrus fruit 134
sea bass with fennel 133
sea bream with orange butter
  sauce 151
seared tuna with ginger 140
seared tuna with ginger, chilli
  and watercress salad 138
smoked mackerel with

blueberries 114
snapper with mango salsa 135
spiced fish Thai style 150
spiced sardines with grapefruit
  and fennel salad 109
stuffed sardines 107
swordfish with roasted
  tomatoes 127
swordish kebabs 129
tangy grilled salmon with
  pineapple 118
trout with bacon 124
trout with red vegetables 68
tuna and corn salad 368
tuna chargrilled slices 67
tuna with pepper purée 139
foie gras, grilled 76
foil parcels 19
fruit salsa 120
fruit top pops 507
fruity punch 500
fudge sauce 492

G
garlic 179, 243, 364, 447
  garlic dip 399
  garlic mayonnaise 392
  garlic sauce 319
  mushrooms with garlic and
    chilli sauce 57
gazpacho sauce 191
ginger 17, 139, 140, 167, 312
  ginger and honey glaze 15
  melon, ginger and borage cup
    505
  pork ribs with ginger relish 231
  rare gingered duck 195
  rhubarb and ginger ice cream
    484
  skewered wild boar with ginger

dipping sauce 79
goat's cheese 278
gooseberry and clotted cream
  ice cream 485
grape and halloumi salad 335
grapefruit and fennel salad 109
grapefruit and raspberry cooler
  498

H
ham pizzettas with mango 40
ham-wrapped trout 126
hazelnut dip 494
herbs 179, 183, 373, 437, 447
  chicken with herb and ricotta
    stuffing 178
  chilli and herb polenta 47
  cod fillet with fresh mixed-herb
    crust 144
  herb aïoli 24
  herb polenta 48
  herb-flavoured lamb 220
  herb-stuffed mini-vegetables 52
  herbal punch 502
  herby wrapped salmon 123
  marinades 16, 429
  sardines with herb salsa 106
honey 15, 17, 418
  honey ice cream 483
horseradish mustard 427
horseradish sauce 422
hummus 396

I
ice creams 482–491
iced oysters with Merguez
  sausages 60
Indonesian burgers 250
Indonesian chargrilled fish 138
ingredients 14–15

J K
jerk chicken 166
juniper 259
kangaroo with tamarind chilli
  sauce 261
king prawns 58, 62, 369, 89, 92,
  100

L
lamb 17
  barbecued lamb steaks with
    red pepper salsa 221
  barbecued lamb with potato
    slices 222
  grilled skewered lamb 214
  herb-flavoured lamb 220
  Iranian kebabs 212
  lamb burgers with redcurrant
    sauce 219
  lamb cutlets with lavender 218
  lamb kebabs with mint chutney
    210
  lamb steaks marinated in mint
    and sherry 216
  mixed grill skewers 225
  Moroccan spiced lamb 215
  rosemary-scented lamb 217
  shish kebabs 211
  skewered lamb with coriander
    yogurt 213
  skewered lamb with red onion
    salsa 82
  stuffed aubergines with lamb
    224
  stuffed kibbeh 81
lavender 131, 183, 218
leek and fennel salad with spicy
  tomato dressing 355
leek and grilled pepper salad with
  goats cheese 318
lemon 192, 304, 326, 378, 385
  lemon and herb risotto cake
    373
lemon float 497
lemon grass 17, 167
  lemon grass pork chops with
    mushrooms 234
  pork on lemon grass 78

lime 16, 17, 89, 202, 428
lobster, grilled 102
loofah ratatouille 284

M
mango
  ham pizzettas with mango 40
  mango, tomato and red onion
    salad 343
  snapper with mango salsa 135
marinades 16–17. 384–389
  ginger and lime 386
  herb 16
  honey citrus 17
  lavender balsamic 17
  lemon grass and ginger 17
  lemon grass and lime 17
  orange and green peppercorn
    385
  red wine 16
  sambal belacan 388
  soy and star anise 389
  summer herb 387
meat 15, 16, 17, 209
melon, ginger and borage cup
  505
mint 216, 320, 488, 504
  mint chutney 210
  mint cup 503
  mint sauce 422
  minted Earl Grey sorbet 481
mixed grill skewers 225
mushrooms
  bean and lemon-stuffed
    mushrooms 304
  Belmont sausage with
    mushroom relish 239
  broad bean, mushroom and
    chorizo salad 331
  ceps with parsley and walnut
    dressing 354
  farmhouse pizza 236
  mushrooms with garlic and
    chilli sauce 57
  pork chops with field
    mushrooms 234
  red bean and mushroom
    burgers 266
mussels
  clams and mussels in banana
    leaves 88
  grilled parsley and Parmesan
    mussels 64
  marinated monkfish and
    mussel kebabs 101
mustard
  honey mustard 424
  moutarde aux fines herbes 424
  mustard dip 366
  mustard glaze 15
  spiced tamarind mustard 425

tarragon and champagne
    mustard 426

N
nuoc leo 397
nuts 43, 325, 444
    grilled cashew nut chicken 163
    hazelnut dip for sweet summer
        fruits 494
    nutty bacon stuffing 111
    peanut and tofu cutlets 273
    quick satay sauce 413
    walnut dressing 354

O
octopus marinated on sticks 96
olive and potato salad 362
olive bread 443
onions 441
    beef rib with onion sauce 247
    ciabatta with mozzarella and
        onions 36
    English pickled onions 431
    mackerel with tomatoes, pesto
        and onion 110
    mango, tomato and red onion
        salad 343
    onion confit 410
    onions stuffed with goat's
        cheese 302
    orange and red onion salad
        with cumin 352
    roasted onions with sun-dried
        tomatoes 317
    salmon with red onion
        marmalade 121
    seafood and spring onion
        skewers 97
    seared mixed onion salad 316
    skewered lamb with red onion
        salsa 80
    stuffed parsleyed onions 303
    sweet and sour onion salad
        330
    toffee onion relish 409
orange
    asparagus, tomato and orange
        salad 344
    avocado, tomato and orange
        salad 345
    carrot and orange salad 337
    chicken wings with blood
        oranges 157
    fennel, orange and rocket salad
        341
    orange and onion salad 352
    oranges in maple and
        cointreau syrup 474
    sea bream with orange butter
        sauce 151
oregano salsa 117

oyster and bacon brochettes 228
oysters with sausages 60

P
paprika-crusted monkfish 147
parsley 64, 302, 354, 390
pasta salad 370
pasta salad with chargrilled
    peppers 296
pears with spiced duck 198
peas 381
peppercorns 142, 243
    peppercorn sauce 267
peppers
    barbecued lamb steaks with
        red pepper salsa 221
    chicken with peppers 170
    fish brochettes with peperonata
        149
    leek and grilled pepper salad
        with goats cheese 318
    mackerel kebabs with sweet
        pepper salad 112
    pasta salad with chargrilled
        peppers 296
    pepper and chilli ketchup 415
    pepper and tomato salad 346
    pepper salad with pesto 328
    peppers with tomatoes and
        anchovies 315
    roasted pepper antipasto 26
    stuffed tomatoes and peppers
        282
    sweet romanos stuffed with two
        cheeses and peppers 51
    tofu and pepper kebabs 271
    tuna with pepper purée 139
pesto 69, 114, 174, 289
    classic pesto sauce with pasta
        406

pheasants with sage and lemon
    192
pine nuts 324
pineapple
    chicken with pineapple 159
    duck with pineapple and
        coriander 199
    pork and pineapple satay 229
    tangy grilled salmon with
        pineapple 118
plums
    duck breasts with red plums
        200
    duck sausages with spicy plum
        sauce 194
    sardines with plum paste 108
    sherried plum sauce 418
polenta 47, 48
pork 15, 17
    basil and Pecorino stuffed pork
        230
    five-spice rib-stickers 80
    pork and pineapple satay 229
    pork chops with field
        mushrooms 234
    pork on lemon grass sticks 78
    pork ribs with ginger relish 231
    pork satay kebabs 232
    pork schnitzel 237
    skewered wild boar with ginger
        dipping sauce 79
potatoes 381, 438
    deli-style salad 357
    ensaladilla 353
    grilled potatoes with chive
        flowers 363
    lamb with potato slices 222
    potato and cheese polpettes
        279
    potato and feta salad 359

potato and olive salad 362
potato and radish salad 361
potato skewers with mustard
    dip 366
potato skins with Cajun dip 27
potato wedges with garlic and
    rosemary 364
warm potato and bacon salad
    360
Spanish potatoes 365
tangy potato salad 358
three herb potato scones 437
poultry 15, 17, 155
prawns 16
    butterfly prawns 58
    grilled prawns with romesco
        sauce 62
    pink and green salad 369
    prawns in lime leaves 89
    spiced prawns with vegetables
        92
    tiger prawn skewers 100
prosciutto with asparagus 77
prunes and bacon with sausages
    227
pumpkin and walnut bread 444
pumpkin roasted with spices 306
purslane 348

Q
quail spatchcocked with
    couscous 206
quail with a five-spice marinade
    204

R
radicchio, artichoke and walnut
    salad 325
radish and potato salad 361
raisins 324
    rum and raisin ice cream 491
raspberry and grapefruit cooler
    498
redcurrant sauce 219
rhubarb and ginger ice cream
    484
rice 373
    mushroom pilau 375
    Peruvian salad 293
    pilau rice with whole spices
        374
    rice salad 372
    rice with dill and broad beans
        376
    sweet and sour rice 377
    wild rice pilaff 371
    wild rice with grilled vegetables
        300
rocket
    fennel, orange and rocket salad
        341

griddled cheese with rocket
   salad 39
   wild green salad 340
romesco sauce 62, 258
rosemary 221, 364, 441
rum and raisin ice cream 491

S
sabayon sauce 493
safety 13
saffron 201, 381
   saffron bread skewers 432
   saffron dip 290, 395
sage 192
sausage with mushroom relish
   239
sausages with oysters 60
sausages with prunes and bacon
   227
scallops with chilli 61
scallops with lime butter 104
seafood
   quick seafood pizza 65
   seafood and spring onion
      skewers 97
   seafood bake 94
   seafood on sugar cane 90
shallots
   cucumber and shallot salad
339
   hot Thai pickled shallots 430
   shallots in balsamic vinegar 429
shellfish 15, 16, 87
sherry 216, 412
soy 431
spices 162, 306, 374
   Cajun spice rub 15
squash
   aubergine and butternut salad
      297

baked squash with Parmesan
   287
smoked chicken with butternut
   pesto 174
squash à la grecque 321
squash stuffed with goat's
   cheese 286
squid
   calamari with two tomato
      stuffing 93
   feta-stuffed squid 59
   whole stuffed squid 98
star anise 489
strawberry and apple slush 496
strawberry and lavender sorbet
   480
strawberry and mint champagne
   504
strawberry ice cream 490
sweet potato salad 314

T
tabbouleh 380
tamarind chilli sauce 261
tapenade 24
toffee coffee swirl ice cream 489
tofu
   peanut and tofu cutlets 273
   stuffed and grilled thin tofu 38
   tofu and pepper kebabs 271
   tofu satay 272
   tofu steaks 53
   vegetable tofu burgers 274
tomatoes
   apple and tomato chutney 418
   asparagus, tomato and orange
      salad 344
   aubergine in tomato sauce 298
   avocado, tomato and orange
      salad 345

barbecue sauce 416
calamari with two tomato
   stuffing 93
cherry tomato salsa 404
crostini with tomato and
   anchovy 37
Greek salad 350
green tomato chutney 420
grilled tomato and mozzarella
   salad with basil dressing 347
halibut with fresh tomato and
   basil salsa 146
mackerel with tomatoes, pesto
   and onion 110
mango, tomato and red onion
   salad 343
Mediterranean chutney 414
pepper and tomato salad 346
peppers with tomatoes and
   anchovies 315
roasted onions with sun-dried
   tomatoes 317
smoked tomato salsa 310
spiced tomato salad 351
spicy tomato dressing 355
stuffed tomatoes and peppers
   282
swordfish with roasted
   tomatoes 127
Thousand Island dip 400
tomato and feta salad 348
tomato ketchup 414
tortillas 434, 435
turkey patties 189
turkey rolls with gazpacho sauce
   191
turkey skewers 190
turkey sosaties with apricot sauce
   188

V
veal chops with basil butter 240
vegetables 17, 263
   barbecued vegetables with
      smoked tomato salsa 310
   cassava and vegetable kebabs
      268
   chargrilled vegetables with
      Pecorino 44
   grilled vegetable sticks 31
   grilled vegetables with saffron
      dip 290
   grilled vegetables with salsa
      verde 305
   vegetables with yogurt pesto 289
   herb-stuffed mini-vegetables 52
   Marrakesh pizza 275
   Moroccan-style vegetables 275
   vegetable quesadillas 276
   spiced prawns with vegetables
      92

stuffed vegetable cups 292
summer vegetable kebabs 270
sweet and sour vegetables 269
Thai vegetable cakes 264
trout with red vegetables 68
vegetable kebabs with
   peppercorn sauce 267
vegetable parcels with flowery
   butter 288
vegetable tofu burgers 274
vegetable-stuffed beef rolls 255
vegetables in coconut and
   ginger paste 312
vegetables with tapenade and
   herb aïoli 24
wild rice with grilled vegetables
   300
venison chops with juniper 259
venison chops with romesco
   sauce 258
venison sausages 260
vine leaves
   chargrilled sardines in vine
      leaves 66
   grilled fish in vine leaves with
      sweet and sour chilli dipping
      sauce 148
   sea bass in vine leaves 132

W
watercress 138
   watercress cream 393
watermelon and feta cheese salad
   349
wine 16

Y
yogurt 201
   skewered lamb with coriander
      yogurt 213
   smoked aubergine and yogurt
      purée 28
   spicy yogurt marinade 384
   yogurt pesto 289